DEFINING DOCUMENTS
IN AMERICAN HISTORY

Postwar 1940s
(1945-1950)

WHEREAS it is essential that there be maintained in the armed services of the United States the highest standards of democracy, with equality of treatment and opportunity for all those who serve in our country's defense:

NOW, THEREFORE, by virtue of the authority vested in me as President of the United States, by the Constitution and the statutes of the United States, and as Commander in Chief of the armed services, it is hereby ordered as follows:

1. It is hereby declared to be the policy of the President that there shall be equality of treatment and opportunity for all persons in the armed services without regard to race, color, religion or national origin. This policy shall be put into effect as rapidly as possible, having due regard to the time required to effectuate any necessary changes without impairing efficiency or morale.

2. There shall be created in the National Military Establishment an advisory committee to be known as the President's Committee on Equality of Treatment and Opportunity in the Armed Services, which shall be composed of seven members to be designated by the President.

3. The Committee is authorized on behalf of the President to examine into the rules, procedures and practices of the armed services in order to determine in what respect such rules, procedures and practices may be altered or improved with a view to carrying out the policy of this order. The Committee shall confer and advise with the Secretary of Defense, the Secretary of the Army, the Secretary of the Navy, and the Secretary of the Air Force, and shall make such recommendations to the President and to said Secretaries as in the judgment of the Committee will effectuate the policy hereof.

4. All executive departments and agencies of the Federal Government are authorized and directed to cooperate with the Committee in its work, and to furnish the Committee such information or the services of such persons as the Committee may require in the performance of its duties.

5. When requested by the Committee to do so, persons in the armed services or in any of the executive departments

DEFINING DOCUMENTS
IN AMERICAN HISTORY

Postwar 1940s
(1945-1950)

Editor

Michael Shally-Jensen, PhD

SALEM PRESS
A Division of EBSCO Information Services
Ipswich, Massachusetts

GREY HOUSE PUBLISHING

Library of Congress Cataloging-in-Publication Data

Publisher's Cataloging-In-Publication Data
(Prepared by The Donohue Group, Inc.)

Postwar 1940s (1945-1950) / editor, Michael Shally-Jensen, PhD. -- [First
edition].

  pages : illustrations, maps ; cm. -- (Defining documents in American history)

Edition statement supplied by publisher.
Includes bibliographical references and index.
ISBN: 978-1-61925-739-9 (hardcover)

  1. United States--History--1945-1953--Sources. 2. United States--Politics and government--1945-1953--Sources. 3. United States--Foreign relations--1945-1953--Sources. 4. United States--Social conditions--1945---Sources. 5. Reconstruction (1939-1951)--United States--Sources. 6. Cold War--Sources. I. Shally-Jensen, Michael. II. Series: Defining documents in American history (Salem Press)

E813 .P67 2015
973.918

FIRST PRINTING
PRINTED IN THE UNITED STATES OF AMERICA

Table of Contents

Publisher's Note ix

Editor's Introduction xi

Contributors xv

WAR CRIMES AND TRIBUNALS

Executive Order 9547 1

Nuremberg Code 4

Establishment and Proceedings of the Tribunal 7

Convention on the Prevention and Punishment of the Crime of Genocide 15

THE NEW WORLD ORDER

Preamble of the UN Charter 23

Potsdam Agreement 26

Statement by General MacArthur on the Occupation of Japan 40

No Sacrificing of Basic Principles for Expediency 43

Complete Integration of Military Operations 48

The World Needs the Tonic of Universal Truth 52

No Country Fears a Strong America 61

"The Sources of Soviet Conduct" 67

Truman Statement on Immigration into Palestine 79

Truman Doctrine Speech 83

Speech on the Marshall Plan 89

Vyshinsky's Speech to the UN General Assembly 94

NATO Treaty 98

Memorandum on Lifting the Soviet Blockade 102

AMERICAN ALLIANCES

Act of Chapultepec 107

Inter-American Treaty of Reciprocal Assistance 112

Pact of Bogota 120

Address by Secretary Acheson, September 19, 1949 132

Atomic Policy

Atomic Energy and International Trade 143
Atomic Explosion in the USSR 149
International Control of Atomic Energy 152

The Red Scare

Executive Order 9835 163
Testimony of J. Edgar Hoover before the House Un-American Activities Committee. 171
Ronald Reagan's Testimony before the House Un-American Activities Committee 176
Testimony Regarding Communist Investigations 181

Domestic Affairs

A Reason Must Be Substituted for Force 189
Twenty-Second Amendment. 195
Taft-Hartley Act 198
Practical Peacetime Applications 211
Truman's State of the Union Speech 220

The Rise of Civil Rights

Mendez et al. v. Westminister School District of Orange County et al.. 231
Morgan v. Virginia (1946) 241
Report of the President's Committee on Civil Rights 250
Shelley v. Kraemer (1948) 263
Executive Order 9981 274
Southern Legislators Protest Proposed Anti-lynching Legislation 278

APPENDIXES

Chronological List 289

Web Resources 291

Bibliography 293

Index. 299

Publisher's Note

Defining Documents in American History series, produced by Salem Press, consists of a collection of essays on important historical documents by a diverse range of writers on a broad range of subjects in American history. *Defining Documents in American History: Postwar 1940s* surveys key documents produced from 1945-1950, organized under seven broad categories:

War Crimes and Tribunals
The New World Order
American Alliances
Atomic Policy
The Red Scare
Domestic Affairs
The Rise of Civil Rights

Historical documents provide a compelling view of this unique period of American history. Designed for high school and college students, the aim of the series is to advance historical document studies as an important activity in learning about history.

Essay Format

Postwar 1940s contains 40 primary source documents – many in their entirety. Each document is supported by a critical essay, written by historians and teachers, that includes a Summary Overview, Defining Moment, Author Biography, Document Analysis, and Essential Themes. Readers will appreciate the diversity of the collected texts, including journals, letters, speeches, political sermons, laws, government reports, and court cases, among other genres. An important feature of each essays is a close reading of the primary source that develops evidence of broader themes, such as the author's rhetorical purpose, social or class position, point of view, and other relevant issues. In addition, essays are organized by section themes, listed above, highlighting major issues of the period, many of which extend across eras and continue to shape American life. Each section begins with a brief introduction that defines questions and problems underlying the subjects in the historical documents. A brief glossary included at the end of each document highlights keywords important in the study of the primary source. Each essay also includes a Bibliography and Additional Reading section for further research.

Appendixes

- **Chronological List** arranges all documents by year.
- **Web Resources** is an annotated list of web sites that offer valuable supplemental resources.
- **Bibliography** lists helpful articles and books for further study.

Contributors

Salem Press would like to extend its appreciation to all involved in the development and production of this work. The essays have been written and signed by scholars of history, humanities, and other disciplines related to the essay's topics. Without these expert contributions, a project of this nature would not be possible. A full list of contributor's names and affiliations appears in the front matter of this volume.

Editor's Introduction

The years after World War II marked a unique era in American history, one characterized by increased economic prosperity and a great expansion of the role played by the United States in world affairs. But all that glittered was not gold. Shortly after the end of the war, relations between the United States and its former ally the Soviet Union took a dramatic turn for the worse. The Cold War, as it came to be known, pitted the capitalist, democratic Western powers against the communist regime of the Soviet Union and its eastern European client states. Although the United States and the Soviet Union never directly engaged in hostilities, they did come near to blows on several occasions and participated in various proxy wars in later decades. The Cold War, as threatening as it was, was made all the more dangerous by the presence of nuclear weapons on both sides.

Postwar International Involvement

The establishment of the United Nations in 1945 brought hope that a new and better world would emerge from the ashes of World War II. A charter member of the new international body, which was headquartered in New York, the United States was expected to play a leading role in the institution. Unlike the situation after World War I, when the US Congress refused to join the League of Nations, this time, a bipartisan Senate majority backed the idea. The tradition of isolationism seemed to have been broken. It was thought that the permanent members of the UN's all-important Security Council, consisting of the great powers from the postwar period (the Soviet Union, the United Kingdom, France, China, and the United States), would work in concert to serve as a police enforcer in the world, maintaining the peace among the smaller nations.

There were internal divisions within the United States government, of course. Some in the administration of President Harry S. Truman wished immediately to expand US power, intending to make use of the nuclear diplomacy at the 1945 Potsdam Conference (involving the United States, Britain, and the Soviet Union) to do so. At that point, only the Americans had the atom bomb. But other forces in Washington countermanded this prospect. Secretary of State James F. Byrnes, for one, let it be known at foreign ministers conferences in London and Moscow that the United States would silently accept Soviet-sponsored governments in eastern Europe. Thus, through much of 1946 US policy officials continued to treat the Soviet Union with kid gloves rather than assert US nuclear superiority.

And the Soviet Union took advantage of the situation. It pursued expansionist aims in Iran, made inroads into the Mediterranean, and solidified its grip on eastern Europe. US reactions to such advances started to become more oppositional. Though he did not coin the phrase, Winston Churchill spoke in Fulton, Missouri, about an "Iron Curtain" descending in Europe, dividing East from West, and by late 1946 many US lawmakers agreed. Central to the turnaround was the work of George F. Kennan, an American embassy official in Moscow, who, in a detailed policy memorandum from 1946 and subsequent writings, prescribed the strategy of "containment" with respect to the Soviets. Kennan argued for a firm hand in controlling the spread of communism, primarily by reacting immediately to Soviet forays abroad.

It was on this basis that President Truman announced his Truman Doctrine in March 1947, which drew on the concept of containment. The doctrine stated that the United States was compelled to assist, both economically and militarily, "free peoples" who were working to resist subjugation by totalitarian regimes. The cases-in-point at the time were the Greeks and the Turks, both of whom faced struggles that could, Truman noted, result in communist advances. In each case, therefore, support should be given to anticommunist elements in these countries, both to bolster democracy and to limit Soviet influence.

In Europe the postwar reconstruction plan known as the Marshall Plan (after its chief proponent, George Marshall) became another reflection of the Truman Doctrine. Announced in mid-1947 and launched in earnest a year later, the plan called for assistance on a grand scale ($13 billion) to war-torn areas of western Europe, which otherwise stood to become breeding grounds for communism. Soviet leaders fought the plan's implementation tooth-and-nail, but to no avail. In Germany, by 1948 the three Western occupying powers (France, Britain, and the United States) had consolidated their separate control zones, causing the Soviets to respond with a blockade of Berlin. The Americans and British responded, in turn, by establishing an airlift to supply the city with food and other goods and to bring out its exports. After 11 months the Russians, facing the reality of the situation, removed the blockade. In the end, the Marshall Plan showed itself to be a significant intervention that both helped western European economies and spread American ideas, influence, and culture throughout the region.

In Japan, too, a large-scale occupation and rebuilding effort got under way behind American leadership. A new democratic constitution, which barred the development of a permanent military, went into effect in 1947. American culture and ideas took hold in various areas of society, above all in industrial production. New technologies and production methods yielded significant economic benefits, eventually turning Japan into an Asian powerhouse. In China, on the other hand, American efforts to support General Chiang Kai-shek and his Nationalists against Chinese communist forces failed, and in 1949 Chiang was relegated to the island of Formosa (Taiwan). Hard-line anticommunists in the United States began searching for State Department officials to blame for the "loss" of China.

In April 1949 the United States, along with 11 other powers, entered into the North Atlantic Treaty Organization (NATO). This treaty capped the move away from isolationism, as it represented the first time in nearly 150 years that the United States was in a peacetime military alliance with a European power. Additional broad-based treaties linked nations in the Americas together in a mutual assistance pact—an extension of the Monroe Doctrine, as far as the United States was concerned. This solidifying of Cold War camps, communist versus capitalist, was viewed as the inevitable outcome under the circumstances. It provided a context when, in August 1949, the Soviet Union conducted its first atomic bomb test. Leaders around the globe began to concern themselves with the control of nuclear weapons. Meanwhile, the United States ramped up its own production of such weapons (and developed more deadly versions of them), as did military leaders in Moscow. The arms race was under way.

Domestic Developments

The Cold War influenced domestic affairs profoundly, as political opponents of the Truman administration sought to attach blame for the rise of the communist threat. As a result, Truman achieved fewer of his goals in areas such as civil rights than he had hoped to. The end of the war was followed by a rapid demobilization of the armed forces, but it also brought shortages in housing, an inflationary trend in the economy, conflicts between labor and management, and the emergence of a new "red scare" wherein innocent citizens and government officials alike were persecuted for their alleged ties to communist organizations. Those who actually professed left-leaning politics were essentially forced underground.

Truman himself, no friend of communism, gave impetus to the red scare—partly to forestall his critics. In March 1947 he established a Federal Employees Loyalty and Security Program in order to examine the backgrounds of the 4 million-plus workers in the federal government and dismiss those deemed to be "disloyal" (a vaguely defined concept). Those accused of disloyalty, or of belonging to any one of a list of supposedly subversive organizations, had no legal recourse. With the cooperation of the House Un-American Activities Committee (HUAC), thousands were investigated, nearly 400 were discharged, and close to 2,500 resigned—despite the fact that hard evidence of espionage was largely absent. (In one notable case, that of Alger Hiss, a perjury charge was later proved.) The effort helped Truman get reelected in 1948. HUAC continued its pursuits into the early 1950s, gaining notoriety when it attacked Hollywood screenwriters and directors for their alleged radical sympathies. Eventually, the committee was overshadowed by the even more hysteric efforts of Senator Joseph McCarthy.

On the labor front, the picture was mixed in the postwar years. By the end of the war, the labor movement had made major gains, having organized nearly 35 percent of the industrial work force. After the war, a strike wave swept through the nation's industrial base. Instead of seeking to break the unions, as in earlier eras, employers worked with them to establish collective bargaining rights and improved wages and benefits in exchange for concessions to management. In 1947, a Republican-controlled Congress passed the Taft-Hartley Act, which President Truman attempted to veto. The act banned labor practices that were regarded as unfair, bolstered employers' ability to resist unions, gave greater power to the government to intervene in disputes, and outlawed the closed shop (i.e., union-only shop), jurisdictional strikes (strikes stemming from internal union disagreements), and secondary boycotts (boycotts against firms doing business with the main target of a boycott). It also required union leaders to sign loyalty oaths stating that they were not communists. Union critics of Taft-Hartley called it a "slave labor law." Yet, through it all, unions continued to grow and the industrial economy continued to expand.

Civil rights activity intensified but did not achieve great success in the late 1940s. President Truman desegregated the armed forces and created a presidential commission on civil rights. The Congress of Racial Equality (CORE) sponsored a "Freedom Ride" through the upper South to challenge segregation. The National Association for the Advancement of Colored People (NAACP) likewise continued its legal assault on Jim Crow laws. And the US Supreme Court issued a series of favorable rulings on civil rights. Even major league sports yielded to the trend when Jackie Robinson joined a Brooklyn Dodgers farm team in 1945 and advanced to the majors two years later. Nevertheless, at the end of the 1940s segregation was still in place in the South, and racial discrimination was still practiced in much of the rest of the country. It was not until the 1950s and 60s that the Civil Rights Movement really took off.

-Michael Shally-Jensen, PhD

Bibliography and Additional Reading

Bundy, McGeorge. *Danger and Survival: Choices about the Bomb in the First Fifty Years.* New York: Random House, 1988.

Byrnes, Mark S. *The Truman Years, 1945-1953.* New York: Longman, 2000.

Lingeman, Richard B. *The Noir Forties: The American People from Victory to Cold War.* New York: Nation Books, 2012.

May, Lary, ed. *Recasting America: Culture and Politics in the Age of the Cold War.* Chicago: University of Chicago Press, 1989.

Rose, Lisle A. *The Cold War Comes to Main Street: America in 1950.* Lawrence, KS: University Press of Kansas, 1999.

Contributors

Michael P. Auerbach, MA
Marblehead, Massachusetts

Steven L. Danver, PhD
Mesa Verda Publishing

Christina Dendy
Dayton, Ohio

Tracey DiLascio, JD
Framingham, MA

Bethany Groff, MA
Historic New England

Laurence W. Mazzeno, PhD
Norfolk, Virginia

Vanessa E. Vaughan, MA
Chicago, Illinois

DEFINING DOCUMENTS
IN AMERICAN HISTORY

Postwar 1940s
(1945-1950)

WAR CRIMES AND TRIBUNALS

At the end of World War II, international courts were established in Nuremberg, Germany, and Tokyo, Japan, to prosecute Nazi leaders and high Japanese officials for war crimes committed during the global conflict. The crimes of which the defendants were accused ranged from conventional war crimes (violations of the laws of war, including murder and ill treatment of civilians) to crimes against peace (conducting war in violation of treaties) and crimes against humanity (political, religious, or racial persecution). By agreement among the major prosecuting powers (the United States, Britain, France, and the Soviet Union), the court was permitted to indict even a head of state if the evidence warranted it. In this case, however, Hitler was already dead and Emperor Hirohito was seen to have played only an indirect role in supporting the Japanese military machine. Plus, the Emperor was deemed useful in sustaining the Japanese people during the ensuing US military occupation and therefore was retained.

In Germany, twenty-two defendants were brought before the court; all but three were found guilty and were hanged or sent to prison. The principal judge for the United States at Nuremberg was US Attorney General Francis Biddle, while the chief US prosecutor was Supreme Court Justice Robert H. Jackson. In Japan, twenty-eight military and political leaders were accused of high crimes (and several hundred more were charged with lesser crimes). An assistant US attorney general and two US justices served on the prosecution team and the judicial panel. Twenty-five defendants were found guilty and the remaining three either died during the trial or were found incompetent.

■ Executive Order 9547

Date: May 2, 1945
Author: Harry S. Truman
Genre: law

Summary Overview

On May 2, 1945, President Harry S. Truman issued Executive Order 9547. At the time, World War II was ending in Europe, and representatives from dozens of nations were meeting in San Francisco to draft the United Nations Charter. President Truman himself had just taken office, following the death of his predecessor, Franklin D. Roosevelt, a few weeks before. He had inherited a world war to finish and an international peace to negotiate. He had also inherited the new mantle of American world leadership. With this executive order, President Truman appointed a US official to prosecute international war crimes and dedicated the United States to a prolonged engagement in international affairs.

Defining Moment

On May 8, 1945, Germany signed an unconditional surrender at Reims, France, thus ending the war in Europe. World War II had begun, officially, with the invasion of Poland in 1939 and raged across multiple continents and oceans. However, the aggression of Nazi Germany under Adolf Hitler and the Axis allies had begun much earlier. In Europe alone, millions of men and women had died in combat as well as in bombings and air raids. However, beyond the casualties of the fighting, more than six million Jewish people and other Europeans had perished under Nazi persecution. They had died from mass shootings; from forced marches; from violence in ghettoes; from starvation, disease, and exhaustive labor in concentration camps; and from extermination policies carried out in gas chambers in Nazi death camps.

The systematic murder of so many civilians led to an unprecedented international response. As early as December 17, 1942, the leaders of the Allied Powers condemned Nazi extermination policies and promised retribution. As the war progressed, the Allies began planning for the conclusion of the war and its after-math. In October 1943, the governments of the United States, the United Kingdom, the Soviet Union, and China issued a joint declaration known as the Moscow Declaration, in which they stated that all persons guilty of "atrocities, massacres and cold-blooded mass executions" would be sent back to the countries of their crimes for trial or would be tried by joint decision of the Allied Powers at the end of the war.

In 1945, with the surrender of the Axis powers in Europe, the Allies followed through on the promises of the Moscow Declaration. Even before peace was declared, the United States had begun to plan for the postwar trial of designated war criminals. Some debate had occurred among leaders of the Moscow Conference nations, as some Soviet officials preferred to forego trials and immediately execute members of the Nazi leadership. Others, including President Roosevelt, insisted on public trials to establish a new international precedent for the illegality of atrocities such as those committed by the Nazis. Truman inherited this charge.

To that end, on May 2, 1945, the newly sworn-in President Truman issued Executive Order 9547, by which he appointed US Supreme Court Associate Justice Robert H. Jackson the chief prosecutor for the United States in the war crimes trials that would follow an armistice in Europe. By this order, Truman committed the United States to the conduct of an international tribunal.

A few months later, on August 8, 1945, the United States, the United Kingdom, France, and the Soviet Union signed the London Agreement to establish the International Military Tribunal "for the trial of war criminals whose offenses have no particular geographical location whether they be accused individually or in their capacity as members of the organizations or groups or in both capacities" and to begin the Nuremberg Trial Proceedings of those identified as war criminals. Under the charter of the tribunal, each signatory nation had to appoint a member and an alternate to serve on the tribunal, to hear the evidence, and to render a decision.

Truman's Executive Order 9547 had already designated the official for the United States.

HISTORICAL DOCUMENT

By virtue of the authority vested in me as President and as Commander in Chief of the Army and Navy, under the Constitution and statutes of the United States, it is ordered as follows:

1. Associate Justice Robert H. Jackson is hereby designated to act as the Representative of the United States and as its Chief of Counsel in preparing and prosecuting charges of atrocities and war crimes against such of the leaders of the European Axis powers and their principal agents and accessories as the United States may agree with any of the United Nations to bring to trial before an international military tribunal. He shall serve without additional compensation but shall receive such allowance for expenses as may be authorized by the President.

2. The Representative named herein is authorized to select and recommend to the President or to the head of any executive department, independent establishment, or other federal agency necessary personnel to assist in the performance of his duties hereunder. The head of each executive department, independent establishment, and other federal agency is hereby authorized to assist the Representative named herein in the performance of his duties hereunder and to employ such personnel and make such expenditures, within the limits of appropriations now or hereafter available for the purpose, as the Representative named herein may deem necessary to accomplish the purposes of this order, and may make available, assign, or detail for duty with the Representative named herein such members of the armed forces and other personnel as may be requested for such purposes.

3. The Representative named herein is authorized to cooperate with, and receive the assistance of, any foreign Government to the extent deemed necessary by him to accomplish the purposes of this order.

HARRY S. TRUMAN
THE WHITE HOUSE,
May 2, 1945.

GLOSSARY

hereunder: subsequent to this; below this

Document Analysis

Executive Order 9547 is a fairly direct document. It signifies the executive power of the US president in appointing federal officials and in navigating international affairs and treaties. The document's first line cites this executive authority—"the authority vested in me as President and as Commander in Chief of the Army and Navy, under the Constitution and statutes of the United States"—to give credence to the terms of the order that followed. Although not a treaty approved by Congress, the document obligates the United States to an international standard of justice and sets a precedent that remains a source of debate today.

The primary provision confirms the appointment of Robert H. Jackson as the US representative and chief counsel "in preparing and prosecuting charges of atroci-ties and war crimes against such of the leaders of the European Axis powers and their principal agents and accessories." Provision 1 goes on to state that the US counsel will serve on an international military tribunal to hear the charges against those brought to trial. With this provision, Truman formalizes American support not only for prosecution of war crimes but also for the conduct of trials by a joint body, an international military tribunal.

The second and third provisions of the document give added substance to Jackson's appointment. Truman is not just appointing an official representative, he is putting the full force of the executive branch of the US government behind that representative and his work for the tribunal. With Provision 2, Truman commands all executive agencies as well as the armed forces—which fall under his authority—to make available any personnel and resources needed by the representative to fulfill his duties to the tribunal. In a similar vein, Provision 3 vests the representative with the power "to cooperate with, and receive the assistance of" foreign governments in order to "accomplish the purposes of this order." By this provision, President Truman gives Jackson the authority to treat with representatives of other nations to accomplish an international charge.

However, the document is not merely an order intended to authorize a new appointment and to command executive agencies and armed forces to support that appointment. It is not just a structural and legal tenet. The order is also an ideological statement. On August 24, 1941, British prime minister Winston Churchill referred to Nazi atrocities in Europe as "a crime without a name." This document, and the trials that followed, signaled the effort made by the international community to name and respond to those crimes.

Essential Themes

The underlying theme of Executive Order 9547 is a new move toward international collaboration and standards. As President Truman took office and issued this order, officials from fifty nations were meeting to form an international body, the United Nations, to promote and protect global peace. Although separate from the United Nations, the International Military Tribunal served a similar purpose. The tribunal and the Nuremberg trials of Nazi officials that followed set a new precedent for international affairs. Just as the United Nations signaled a collective will to pursue international security and cooperation, the war crimes trials indicated that nations and their citizens could be called to account for what became known as "crimes against humanity." Executive Order 9547 signified US support for a standard of international justice and a system of international collaboration. The United States was poised to emerge from World War II as a world power, and Truman's order served as yet another mark of the rise of American world leadership.

Bibliography and Additional Reading

Donovan, Robert J. *Conflict and Crisis: The Presidency of Harry S. Truman, 1945–1948*. New York: Norton, 1977. Print.

Ferrell, Robert H., ed. *Off the Record: The Private Papers of Harry S. Truman*. New York: Harper, 1980. Print.

Kochavi, Arieh J. *Prelude to Nuremberg: Allied War Crimes Policy and the Question of Punishment*. Chapel Hill: U of North Carolina P, 1998. Print.

Rice, Earl, Jr. The Nuremberg Trials. San Diego: Lucent, 1997. Print.

Tusa, Ann, & John Tusa. *The Nuremberg Trial.* New York: Skyhorse, 2010. Print

■ Nuremberg Code

Date: August 20, 1947
Author: Leo Alexander
Genre: court opinion

Summary Overview

Between 1945 and 1949, thirteen trials were held in Nuremberg, Germany. Their purpose was to bring Nazi war criminals to justice, and the defendants included Nazi officials and military officers, as well as doctors, businessmen, and lawyers, who were indicted on such charges as crimes against peace and crimes against humanity. In December 1946, twenty-three German physicians were charged with participating in war crimes and crimes against humanity for their part in euthanasia programs and for performing medical experiments on concentration camp inmates, most of whom either died or were permanently injured as a result. In the so-called Doctors Trial, judges confronted the complex ethical questions that surrounded medical experiments. Many of the defendants argued that there was not a specific international law preventing such experiments and that they were unaware of the difference between legal and illegal experimentation. American doctor Leo Alexander, who along with Dr. Andrew Ivy was assisting the prosecution, developed a framework for ethical medical experiments on human subjects that formed the basis of the Nuremberg Code.

Defining Moment

The United States, the United Kingdom, France, and the Soviet Union established the International Military Tribunal (IMT) in Nuremberg, Germany, to prosecute "the major war criminals of the European Axis," mostly senior Nazi political and military leaders. The trial before the IMT began in 1945. Twenty-four Nazi officials were indicted, and on October 16, 1946, ten of them were executed by hanging. Twelve more trials took place between 1946 and 1949 and are collectively known as the "subsequent Nuremberg trials." These cases were tried not before the IMT, but before a US military tribunal, as growing disagreements among the Allies, particularly between the Soviet Union and the United States, had made further joint international trials impossible.

The first of these subsequent trials began on December 9, 1946, when twenty-three prominent German physicians and medical administrators were brought to trial before an American military tribunal. The defendants in the "Doctors Trial" were accused of war crimes and crimes against humanity for the murder and mutilation of hundreds of thousands of people—mostly Jews, Poles, Russians, and Romani (Gypsies). The accused fell into two broad categories. Some doctors had participated in euthanasia programs, which systematically murdered those considered undesirable by the Nazis, including those with physical and mental disabilities. The other principal accusation was against doctors who had performed medical experiments on concentration camp inmates without their consent. These experiments usually resulted in the death of the subject, or left them with lifelong physical impairments, and so were also a form of systematic murder.

The Doctors Trial lasted for 140 days, as the court considered nearly 1,500 documents and heard the testimony of eighty-five witnesses. On August 19, 1947, the tribunal paused before announcing its verdicts to consider the matter of ethical medical experimentation. Many of the accused doctors had claimed that there was no international law preventing human experiments and that their methods did not differ substantially from those of previous German and American experiments. Two American doctors, Andrew Ivy and Leo Alexander, who were working with the prosecution, had considered the ethical implications of human experiments, and Alexander had presented a draft of guidelines for legitimate research to the court in April. Alexander's memo included six guidelines for ethical experiments. The court opinion, rendered on August 19, enlarged these guidelines to ten points, under the heading "Permissible Medical Experiments," and it became known subsequently as the Nuremberg Code. This continues to be a cornerstone of medical ethics and has informed regulations governing experiments with human subjects ever since. Sixteen of the men accused in the Doctors Trials were found guilty, and seven were executed on June 2, 1948.

Author Biography

Leo Alexander was born in 1905 in Vienna, then part of the Austro-Hungarian Empire. He was the son of a Jewish physician and studied medicine at the University of Vienna and the University of Frankfurt. Alexander immigrated to the United States in 1933 and held positions at Worcester State Hospital, Boston City Hospital, Harvard Medical School, and Boston State Hospital before joining the faculty at Duke Medical School in 1941. Alexander worked as an Army medical investigator during World War II and was appointed chief medical officer to the US Council for War Crimes. He was a key advisor during the Nuremberg trials and helped to craft the Nuremberg Code, which established a widely accepted ethical framework for experimentation with human subjects. After the war, Alexander joined the faculty at Tufts University Medical School in Boston, where he taught for nearly thirty years. He worked with hospitals across the country to treat forty former concentration camp inmates who had been victims of Josef Mengele, the infamous Nazi physician at Auschwitz (who eluded capture and was thus not tried at Nuremberg). Alexander died in 1985 in Weston, Massachusetts.

HISTORICAL DOCUMENT

1. The voluntary consent of the human subject is absolutely essential. This means that the person involved should have legal capacity to give consent; should be so situated as to be able to exercise free power of choice, without the intervention of any element of force, fraud, deceit, duress, over-reaching, or other ulterior form of constraint or coercion; and should have sufficient knowledge and comprehension of the elements of the subject matter involved as to enable him to make an understanding and enlightened decision. This latter element requires that before the acceptance of an affirmative decision by the experimental subject there should be made known to him the nature, duration, and purpose of the experiment; the method and means by which it is to be conducted; all inconveniences and hazards reasonable to be expected; and the effects upon his health or person which may possibly come from his participation in the experiment.

The duty and responsibility for ascertaining the quality of the consent rests upon each individual who initiates, directs or engages in the experiment. It is a personal duty and responsibility which may not be delegated to another with impunity.

2. The experiment should be such as to yield fruitful results for the good of society, unprocurable by other methods or means of study, and not random and unnecessary in nature.

3. The experiment should be so designed and based on the results of animal experimentation and a knowledge of the natural history of the disease or other problem under study that the anticipated results will justify the performance of the experiment.

4. The experiment should be so conducted as to avoid all unnecessary physical and mental suffering and injury.

5. No experiment should be conducted where there is an *a priori* reason to believe that death or disabling injury will occur; except, perhaps, in those experiments where the experimental physicians also serve as subjects.

6. The degree of risk to be taken should never exceed that determined by the humanitarian importance of the problem to be solved by the experiment.

7. Proper preparations should be made and adequate facilities provided to protect the experimental subject against even remote possibilities of injury, disability, or death.

8. The experiment should be conducted only by scientifically qualified persons. The highest degree of skill and care should be required through all stages of the experiment of those who conduct or engage in the experiment.

9. During the course of the experiment the human

subject should be at liberty to bring the experiment to an end if he has reached the physical or mental state where continuation of the experiment seems to him to be impossible.

10. During the course of the experiment the scientist in charge must be prepared to terminate the experiment at any stage, if he has probable cause to believe, in the exercise of the good faith, superior skill and careful judgment required of him that a continuation of the experiment is likely to result in injury, disability, or death to the experimental subject.

Document Analysis

The Nuremberg Code begins with the single most crucial element in ethical medical experimentation, and the thing that was most egregiously missing from the experiments performed in concentration camps: consent. Point one defines consent as voluntary permission without any coercion, from a person who is legally able to provide this consent. The person who is performing the experiment is responsible for making sure that the subject understands exactly the potential consequences of the experiment and cannot delegate this to another person. This voluntary consent is the most important of these points and the basis for all of the other points. In addition to voluntary consent, the experiment must be useful and necessary and conducted in such a way that there is a reasonable expectation that the results will be useful. Humans should only be used for experiments after preliminary animal experiments and other study, so the outcome can generally be predicted. Many of the experiments performed by the doctors on trial were not useful in the end because they were not conducted under appropriate conditions and could not be replicated. The betterment of humanity through science is paramount—only experiments whose risks are outweighed by the potential benefit to humanity should be conducted, and then only if the known risks do not include death or permanent damage.

Even with skilled practitioners, safeguards, and best intentions, experiments do sometimes go wrong, and the subject should be protected from harm, but also made aware of any potential consequences. The subject has the right to withdraw from an experiment at any time, and the scientist is obliged to end an experiment if it seems that injury will result. None of the points in the Nuremberg Code were followed by the doctors on trial, who caused permanent harm and even death, and did not have the permission of their subjects. This document lays out a framework within which future experiments can be conducted in an ethical manner.

Essential Themes

In the aftermath of the unimaginable brutality of the Holocaust, the victorious powers in World War II worked diligently to ensure that war criminals were brought to justice. Those accused of war crimes often argued that they were just following orders, or that they had not violated any specific international laws that they could be tried under. Forced medical experiments on concentration camp prisoners fell into the second category, argued the defendants. The court decision in the Doctors Trial included the ten points that became known as the Nuremberg Code, which outlined ethical behavior for medical experiments. The essential theme in this document is the necessity of fully informed consent, and the steps that must taken for the reduction of harm to the subject of the experiment. None of the prisoners in concentration camps were given the chance to consent, and the experiments on them caused great harm, suffering, and often death. The Nuremberg Code established the ethical framework for all medical experiments involving human beings and has been used as a standard ever since.

—*Bethany Groff, MA*

Bibliography and Additional Reading

Annas, George J., & Michael A. Grodin. *The Nazi Doctors and the Nuremberg Code: Human Rights in Human Experimentation*. New York: Oxford UP, 1992. Print.

"The Doctors Trial: The Medical Case of the Subsequent Nuremberg Proceedings." *Holocaust Encyclopedia*. United States Holocaust Memorial Museum, 20 June 2014. Web. 27 Feb. 2015.

Spitz, Vivien. *Doctors from Hell: The Horrific Account of Nazi Experiments on Humans*. Boulder: Sentient, 2005. Print.

■ Establishment and Proceedings of the Tribunal

Date: November 1948
Author: International Military Tribunal for the Far East
Genre: government document

Summary Overview

By the end of World War II, the world had experienced brutality and human rights violations on a massive scale, and the international community demanded that the leaders of Germany and Japan be held responsible. In addition, the 1928 Kellogg-Briand Pact that prohibited war against peaceful countries provided a framework within which war itself could be declared a war crime. The first international war crimes tribunals were established to seek some measure of justice through the prosecution of high-ranking military and political officials. The United States, Great Britain, France, and the Soviet Union established the International Military Tribunal in Nuremberg, Germany, to prosecute "the major war criminals of the European Axis," mostly senior Nazi political and business leaders. The International Military Tribunal for the Far East (IMTFE) was created in Tokyo, Japan, to prosecute senior Japanese officials. The IMTFE was established in January 1946, with a charter approved by US general Douglas MacArthur, who was the Allied leader in occupied Japan. It convened in late April 1946 and adjourned on November 12, 1948.

Defining Moment

In the Cairo Declaration of 1943, the United States, Great Britain, and China promised to "punish the aggression of Japan." The Allies used the term "war criminals" in the July 1945 Potsdam Declaration, which also demanded Japan's "unconditional surrender." In December, at the Moscow Conference of 1945, the United States, Great Britain, China, and the Soviet Union (which by then was at war with Japan as well) named General MacArthur as the ultimate authority in occupied Japan and authorized to carry out the "occupation and control" of Japan as he saw fit. In his role as Supreme Commander for the Allied Powers, MacArthur first arrested many top Japanese military leaders and, in

January 1946, issued the proclamation and charter that established the IMTFE.

The charter laid out the selection of judges and prosecution teams from countries that had signed the Japanese surrender document. It laid out the categories for prosecution, which mirrored the Nuremburg trials. Defendants were charged with "crimes against peace," or the planning and waging of war; "war crimes," or violations of the laws of war; and "crimes against humanity," violations of human rights. Charges reached back as far as 1928 to the first Japanese invasions. There was no specific defense in the charter, though the accused were allowed to have a lawyer. When Japanese counsel had difficulty following Western-style legal proceedings, an American lawyer was also assigned to each defendant.

During the two-and-a-half years that the IMTFE was in session, twenty-eight Japanese officials were indicted, and nine political leaders and eighteen military were prosecuted. One was deemed mentally unfit to stand trial and thus not prosecuted. All were accused of crimes against peace, with additional charges brought if appropriate. MacArthur selected Joseph B. Keenan as chief prosecutor. The Japanese emperor Hirohito was not indicted and was allowed to retain his title. The IMTFE trials ran from May 1946 to November 1948. The language and cultural barriers between the prosecution and the defendants and between the judges proved very difficult and simultaneous translation nearly impossible. The verdicts were announced on November 4, 1948, and the court passed sentence between November 4 and 12. Two of the accused, foreign-affairs minister Matsuoka Yosuke and naval minister Nagano Osami, had died during the trial, and another seven were sentenced to death by hanging, which was carried out on December 23, 1948. Sixteen other defendants were sentenced to life imprisonment. Two others received shorter prison sentences. Four died in prison, and the rest were paroled in the 1950s.

Other trials were held after the IMTFE to try lower-level war criminals, but these were not international tribunals dealing with the larger issue of waging war as a crime. Both the Nuremberg and the Tokyo trials were the first tests of international criminal law and served as models for the prosecution of later war crimes.

Author Biography

Each country among the Allied Powers was represented by a justice in the tribunal. American major-general Myron Cady Cramer replaced John Patrick Higgins early in the proceedings. India and the Philippines also lobbied to have justices on the tribunal, raising the initial number allotted from nine to eleven. Thus, comprising the panel of IMTFE judges were Cramer, Delfin Jaranilla of the Philippines, Henri Bernard of France, Mei Ju-ao of China, Edward Stuart McDougall of Canada, Erima Harvey Northcroft of New Zealand, Radha Binod Pal of British India, William Donald Patrick of Great Britain, Bernard Victor Röling of the Netherlands, William Flood Webb of Australia, and Ivan Michyevich Zaryanov of the Soviet Union. Most were members of their respective justice systems, and Cramer, Jaranilla, Mei, and Zaryanov were military officers. Webb was appointed tribunal president.

HISTORICAL DOCUMENT

The several military missions have agreed upon future military operations against Japan. The Three Great Allies expressed their resolve to bring unrelenting pressure against their brutal enemies by sea, land, and air. This pressure is already mounting.

The Three Great Allies are fighting this war to restrain and punish the aggression of Japan. They covet no gain for themselves and have no thought of territorial expansion. It is their purpose that Japan shall be stripped of all the islands in the Pacific which she has seized or occupied since the beginning of the first World War in 1914, and that all the territories Japan has stolen from the Chinese, such as Manchuria, Formosa, and the Pescadores, shall be restored to the Republic of China. Japan will also be expelled from all other territories which she has taken by violence and greed. The aforesaid three great powers, mindful of the enslavement of the people of Korea, are determined that in due course Korea shall become free and independent.

With these objects in view the three Allies, in harmony with those of the United Nations at war with Japan, will continue to persevere in the serious and prolonged operations necessary to procure the unconditional surrender of Japan.

The Declaration of Potsdam was made by the President of the United States of America, the President of the National Government of the Republic of China, and the Prime Minister of Great Britain and later adhered to by the Union of Soviet Socialist Republics. Its principal relevant provisions are:

Japan shall be given an opportunity to end this war.

There must be eliminated for all time the authority and influence of those who have deceived and misled the people of Japan into embarking on world conquest, for we insist that a new order of peace, security, and justice will be impossible until irresponsible militarism is driven from the world.

The terms of the Cairo Declaration shall be carried out, and Japanese sovereignty shall be limited to the islands of Honshu, Hokkaido, Kyushu, Shikoku, and such minor islands as we determine.

We do not intend that the Japanese shall be enslaved as a race nor destroyed as a nation, but stern justice well be meted out to all war criminals, including those who have visited cruelties upon our prisoners.

The Instrument of Surrender was signed on behalf of the Emperor and Government of Japan and on behalf of the nine Allied Powers. It contains inter alia the following proclamation, undertaking, and order:

We hereby proclaim the unconditional surrender to the Allied Powers of the Japanese Imperial General Headquarters and of all Japanese armed forces and all armed forces under the Japanese control wherever situated.

We hereby undertake for the Emperor, the Japanese Government and their successors to carry out the provisions of the Potsdam Declaration in good faith, and to issue whatever orders and take whatever actions may be required by the Supreme Commander for the Allied Powers or by any other designated representative of the Allied Powers for the purpose of giving effect to that Declaration.

The authority of the Emperor and the Japanese Government to rule the state shall be subject to the Supreme Commander for the Allied Powers who will take such steps as he deems proper to effectuate these terms of surrender. We hereby command all civil, military, and naval officials to obey and enforce all proclamations, orders, and directives deemed by the Supreme Commander for the Allied Powers to be proper to effectuate this surrender and issued by him or under his authority.

By the Moscow Conference it was agreed by and between the Governments of the United States of America, Great Britain, and the Union of Soviet Socialist Republics with the concurrence of China that:

The Supreme Commander shall issue all orders for the implementation of the Terms of Surrender, the occupation and control of Japan and directives supplementary thereto.

Acting on this authority on the 19th day of January, 1946, General MacArthur, the Supreme Commander for the Allied Powers, by Special Proclamation established the Tribunal for "the trial of those persons charged individually or as members of organizations or in both capacities with offences which include crimes against peace." The constitution, jurisdiction, and functions of the Tribunal were by the Proclamation declared to be those set forth in the Charter of the Tribunal approved by the Supreme Commander on the same day. Before the opening of the Trial the Charter was amended in several respects.

On the 15th day of February, 1946, the Supreme Commander issued an Order appointing the nine members of the Tribunal nominated respectively by each of the Allied Powers. This Order also provides that "the responsibilities, powers, and duties of the Members of the Tribunal are set forth in the Charter thereof. . . ."

By one of the amendments to the Charter the maximum number of members was increased from nine to eleven to permit the appointment of members nominated by India and the Commonwealth of the Philippines. By subsequent Orders the present members from the United States and France were appointed to succeed the original appointees who resigned and the members from India and the Philippines were appointed.

Pursuant to the provisions of Article 9(c) of the Charter, each of the accused before the opening of the Trial appointed counsel of his own choice to represent him; each accused being represented by American and Japanese counsel.

On the 29th of April, 1946, an indictment, which had previously been served on the accused in conformity with the rules of procedure adopted by the Tribunal, was lodged with the Tribunal.

The Indictment is long, containing fifty-five counts charging twenty-eight accused with Crimes against Peace, Conventional War Crimes, and Crimes against Humanity during the period from the 1st of January, 1928, to the 2nd of September, 1945.

It may be summarized as follows:

In Count 1 all accused are charged with conspiring as leaders, organisers, instigators or accomplices between 1st January 1928 and 2nd September 1945 to have Japan, either alone or with other countries, wage wars of aggression against any country or countries which might oppose her purpose of securing the military, naval, political and economic domination of East Asia and of the Pacific and Indian oceans and their adjoining countries and neighbouring islands.

Count 2 charges all accused with conspiring throughout the same period to have Japan wage aggressive war against China to secure complete domination of the Chinese provinces of Liaoning, Kirin, Heilungkiang, and Jehol (Manchuria).

Count 3 charges all accused with conspiracy over the same period to have Japan wage aggressive war against China to secure complete domination of China.

Count 4 charges all accused with conspiring to have Japan, alone or with other countries, wage aggressive war against the United States, the British Commonwealth, France, the Netherlands, China, Portugal, Thailand, the Philippines and the Union of Soviet Socialist Republics to secure the complete domination of East Asia and the Pacific and Indian Oceans and their adjoining countries and neighboring islands.

Count 5 charges all accused with conspiring with Germany and Italy to have Japan, Germany and Italy mutually assist each other in aggressive warfare against any country which might oppose them for the purpose of having these three nations acquire complete domination of the entire world, each having special domination in its own sphere, Japan's sphere to cover East Asia and the Pacific and Indian Oceans.

Counts 6 to 17 charge all accused except SHIRA-TORI with having planned and prepared aggressive war against named countries.

Counts 18 to 26 charge all accused with initiating aggressive war against named countries.

Counts 27 to 36 charge all accused with waging aggressive war against named countries.

Count 37 charges certain accused with conspiring to murder members of the armed forces and civilians of the United States, the Philippines, the British Commonwealth, the Netherlands and Thailand by initiating unlawful hostilities against those countries in breach of the Hague Convention No. III of 18th October 1907.

Count 38 charges the same accused with conspiring to murder soldiers and civilians by initiating hostilities in violation of the agreement between the United States and Japan of 30th November, 1908, the Treaty between Britain, France, Japan and the United States of 13th December 1921, the Pact of Paris of 27th August 1928, and the Treaty of Unity between Thailand and Japan of 12th June 1940.

Counts 30 to 43 charge the same accused with the commission on 7th and 8th December 1941 of murder at Pearl Harbour (Count 39), Kohta Baru (Count 40), Hong Kong (Count 41), on board H.M.S. *Petrel* at Shanghai (Count 42), and at Davao (Count 43).

Count 44 charges all accused with conspiring emporeto murder on a wholesale scale prisoners of war and civilians in Japan's power.

Counts 45 to 50 charge certain accused with the murder of disarmed soldiers and civilians at Nanking (Count 45), Canton (Count 46), Hankow (Count 47), Changsha (Count 48), Hengyang (Count 49), and Kwei-lin and Luchow (Count 50).

Count 51 charges certain accused with the murder of members of the armed forces of Mongolia and the Soviet Union in the Khalkin-Gol River area in 1939.

Count 52 charges certain accused with the murder of members of the armed forces of the Soviet Union in the Lake Khasan area in July and August 1938.

Counts 53 and 54 charge all the accused except OKAWA and SHIRATORI with having conspired to order, authorize or permit the various Japanese Theatre Commanders, the officials of the War Ministry and local camp and labour unit officials to frequently and habitually commit breaches of the laws and customs of war against the armed forces, prisoners of war, and civilian internees of complaining powers and to have the Government of Japan abstain from taking adequate steps to secure the observance and prevent breaches of the laws and customs of war.

Count 55 charges the same accused with having recklessly disregarded their legal duty by virtue of their offices to take adequate steps to secure the observance and prevent breaches of the laws and customs of war.

There are five appendices to the Indictment:

Appendix A summarises the principal matters and events upon which the counts are based.

Appendix B is a list of Treaty Articles.

Appendix C specifies the assurances Japan is alleged to have broken.

Appendix D contains the laws and customs of war alleged to have been infringed.

Appendix E is a partial statement of the facts with respect to the alleged individual responsibility of the accused.

These appendices are included in Annex 6.

During the course of the Trial, two of the accused, MATSUOKA and NAGANO, died, and the accused OKAWA was declared unfit to stand his trial and unable to defend himself. MATSUOKA and NAGANO were therefore discharged from the indictment. Further proceedings upon the Indictment against OKAWA at this Trial were suspended.

On the 3rd and 4th of May the Indictment was read in open court in the presence of all the accused, the Tribunal then adjourning till the 6th to receive the pleas of the accused. On the latter date pleas of "not guilty" were entered by all the accused now before the Tribunal.

The Tribunal then fixed the 3rd of June following as the date for the commencement of the presentation of evidence by the Prosecution.

In the interval the Defence presented motions challenging the jurisdiction of the Tribunal to hear and decide the charges contained in the Indictment. On the 17th of May, 1946, after argument, judgment was delivered dismissing all the said motions "for reasons to be given later". These reasons will be given in dealing with the law of the case in Chapter II of this part of the judgment.

The Prosecution opened its case on the 3rd of June, 1946, and closed its case on the 24th of January 1947.

The presentation of evidence for the Defence opened on the 24th of February, 1947, and closed on the 12th of January, 1948, an adjournment having been granted form the 19th of June to the 4th of August, 1947, to permit Defence Counsel to coordinate their work in the presentation of evidence common to all the accused.

Prosecution evidence in rebuttal and Defence evidence in reply were permitted; the reception of evidence terminating on the 10th of February, 1948. In all 4336 exhibits were admitted as evidence, 419 witnesses testified, in court, 779 witnesses gave evidence in depositions and affidavits, and the transcript of the proceedings covers 48,412 pages.

Closing arguments and summations of Prosecution and Defence opened on the 11th of February and closed on the 16th of April, 1948.

Having regard to Article 12 of the Charter which requires "an expeditious hearing of the issues" and the taking of "strict measures to prevent any action which would cause any unreasonable delay", the length of the present trial requires some explanation and comment.

In order to avoid unnecessary delay which would have been incurred by adopting the ordinary method of translation by interrupting from time to time evidence, addresses and other matters which could be prepared in advance of delivery, an elaborate public address system was installed. Through this system whenever possible a simultaneous translation into English or Japanese was given and in addition when circumstances required form or into Chines, Russian, and French. Without such aids the trial might well have occupied a very much longer period. Cross-examination and *extempore* argument on objections and other incidental proceedings had, however, to be translated in the ordinary way as they proceeded.

Article 13(a) of the Charter provides that "the Tribunal shall not be bound by technical rules of evidence. It shall . . . admit any evidence which it deems to have probative value. . . . The application of this rule to the mass of documents and oral evidence offered inevitably resulted in a great expenditure of time. moreover, the charges in the Indictment directly involved an inquiry into the history of Japan during seventeen years, the years between 1928 and 1945. In addition our inquiry has extended to a less detailed study of the earlier history of Japan, for without that the subsequent actions of Japan and her leaders could not be understood and assessed.

The period covered by the charges was one of intense activity in Japanese internal and external affairs.

Internally, the Constitution promulgated during the Meiji Restoration was the subject of a major struggle between the military and the civilian persons who operated it. The military elements ultimately gained a predominance which enabled them to dictate, not only in matters of peace or war, but also in the conduct of foreign and domestic affairs. In the struggle between the civilian and the military elements in the Government the Diet, the elected representatives of the people, early cased to be of account. The battle between the civilians and the military was fought on the civilian side by the professional civil servants, who almost exclusively filled the civilian ministerial posts in the Cabinet and the advisory posts around the Emperor. The struggle between the military and the civil servants was [a] protracted one. Many incidents marked the ebb and flow of the battle, and there was seldom agreement between the Prosecution and the Defence as to any incident. Both the facts and the meaning of each incident were the subject of controversy and the topic towards which a wealth of evidence was directed.

Internally, also, the period covered by the Indictment saw the completion of the conversion of Japan into a modern industrialized state, and the growth of the demand for the territory of other nations as an outlet for her rapidly increasing population, a source form which she might draw raw materials for her manufacturing plants, and a market for her manufactured goods. Externally the period saw the efforts of Japan to satisfy that demand. In this sphere also the occurrence and meaning of events was contested by the Defence, often to the extent of contesting the seemingly incontestable.

The parts played by twenty-five accused in these events had to be investigated, and again every foot of the way was fought.

The extensive field of time and place involved in the issues placed before the Tribunal and the controversy waged over every event, important or unimportant, have prevented the trial from being "expeditious," as required by the Charter. In addition, the need to have every word spoken in Court translated form English into Japanese, or vice versa, has at least doubled the length of the proceedings. Translations cannot be made from the one language into the other with the speed and certainty which can be attained in translating one Western speech into another. Literal translation from Japanese into English or the reverse is often impossible. To a large extend nothing but a paraphrase can be achieved, and experts in both languages will often differ as to the correct paraphrase. In the result the interpreters in Court often had difficulty as to the rendering they should announce, and the Tribunal was compelled to set up a Language Arbitration Board to settle matters of disputed interpretation.

To these delays was added a tendency for counsel and witnesses to be prolix and irrelevant. This last tendency at first was controlled only with difficulty as on many occasions the over-elaborate or irrelevant question or answer was in Japanese and the mischief done, the needless time taken, before the Tribunal was given the translation in English and objection could be taken to it. At length it became necessary to impose special rules to prevent this waste of time.

The principle rules to this end were the prior filing of a written deposition of the intended witness and a limitation of cross-examination to matters within the scope of the evidence in chief.

Neither these nor any other of the rules imposed by the Tribunal were applied with rigidity. Indulgences were granted form time to time, having regard to the paramount need for the Tribunal to do justice to the accused and to possess itself of all facts relevant and material to the issues.

Much of the evidence tendered, especially by the Defence, was rejected, principally because it had too little or no probative value or because it was not helpful as being not at all or only very remotely relevant or because it was needlessly cumulative of similar evidence already received.

Much time was taken up in argument upon the admissibility of evidence but even so the proceedings would have been enormously prolonged had the Tribunal received all evidence prepared for tendering. Still long would have been the trial without these controls, as without them much more irrelevant or immaterial evidence than was in fact tendered would have been prepared for presentation. Much of the evidence was given viva voce or at least by the witness being sworn and acknowledging his deposition which, to the extent that it was ruled upon as admissible, was then read by Counsel. The witnesses were cross-examined, often by a member of Counsel representing different interests, and then re-examined.

When it was not desired to cross-examine the witness, in most cases his sworn deposition was tendered and read without the attendance of the witness.

A large part of the evidence which was presented has been a source of disappointment to the Tribunal. An explanation of events is unconvincing unless the witness will squarely meet his difficulties and persuade the Court that the inference, which would normally arise from the undoubted occurrence of these events, should on this occasion be rejected. In the experience of this Tribunal most of the witnesses for the Defence have not attempted to face up to their difficulties. They have met them with prolix equivocations and evasions, which only arouse distrust.

Most of the final submissions of Counsel for the Defence have been based on the hypothesis that the Tribunal would accept the evidence tendered in defence as reliable. It could not have been otherwise, for counsel could not anticipate which witnesses the Tribunal was prepared to accept as witnesses of credit, and which witnesses it would reject. In large part these submissions have failed because the argument was based on evidence of witnesses whom the Tribunal was not prepared to accept as reliable because of their lack of candour.

Apart from this testimony of witnesses a great many documents were tendered and received in evidence. These were diverse in nature and from many sources including the German Foreign Office. The Tribunal was handicapped by the absence of many originals of important Japanese official records of the Army and Navy, Foreign Office, Cabinet and other policy-making organs of the Japanese Government. In some case what purported to be copies were tendered and received for what value they might be found to have. The absence of official records was attributed to burning during bombing raids on Japan and to deliberate destruction by the Fighting Services of their records after the surrender. It seems strange that documents of such importance as those of the Foreign Office, the Cabinet secretariat and other important departments should not have been removed to places of safety when bombings commenced or were imminent. If it should prove that they were not thus destroyed but were withheld from this Tribunal then a marked disservice will have been done to the cause of international justice.

We have perforce to rely upon that which was made available to us, relating it by way of check to such other evidence as was received by us. Although handicapped in our search for facts by the absence of these documents we have been able to obtain a good deal of relevant information from other sources. Included in this other evidence of a non-official or at least of only a semi-official nature were the diary of the accused KIDO and the Saionji-Harada Memoirs.

KIDO's voluminous diary is a contemporary record covering the period from 1930 to 1945 of the transactions of KIDO with important personages in his position as secretary to the Lord Keeper of the Privy Seal, State Minister and later as confidential adviser of the Emperor while holding the Office of Lord Keeper of the Privy Seal. Having regard to these circumstances we regard it as a document of importance.

Another document or series of documents of importance are the Saionji-Harada Memoirs. These have been the subject of severe criticism by the Defence, not unnaturally, as they contain passages the Defence consider embarrassing. We are of opinion the criticisms are not well founded and have attached more importance to these records than the Defence desired us to do. The special position of Prince Saionji as the last of the Genro provided full and candid disclosure to him through his secretary Harada. Harada's long period of service to the Genro in this special task of obtaining information from the very highest functionaries of the Government and the Army and Navy is a test of his reliability and discretion. Had he been unreliable and irresponsible, as the Defence suggest, this would soon have been discovered by Prince Saionji, having regard to his own frequent associations with the important personages from whom Harada received his information, and Harada would not have continued in that office. As to the authenticity of the Saionji-Harada documents presented to the Tribunal, the Tribunal is satisfied that these are the original memoranda as dictated by Harada and edited by Saionji. To the extent to which they are relevant the tribunal considers them helpful and reliable contemporary evidence of the matters recorded.

GLOSSARY

covet: want or desire wrongfully, inordinately, or without due regard for the rights of others

effectuate: to bring about; effect

extempore: spoken or done without preparation

indictment: a formal accusation initiating a criminal case

probative: serving or designed for testing or trial; affording proof or evidence

prolix: extended to great, unnecessary, or tedious length; long and wordy

promulgated: to make known by open declaration; proclaim formally

rebuttal: an act of rebutting or refuting by evidence or argument

tender: to present formally for acceptance

viva voce: by word of mouth; orally

Document Analysis

This excerpt from the IMTFE judgment begins with the background of the tribunal. The Japanese had been repeatedly warned that their aggression would be punished, and three specific incidents are mentioned. The tribunal was set up to "implement the Cairo Declaration of the 1st of December 1943, the Declaration of Potsdam of the 26th of July, 1945, the Instrument of Surrender of the 2nd of September, 1945, and the Moscow Conference of the 26th of December 1945." These are all crucial dates in the Allies' handling of Japan, and each text is reproduced in part within the introduction to this document. The Cairo Declaration informed Japan that its aggression would be punished. The Declaration of Potsdam warned that Japan would be held accountable for "war crimes." The Japanese surrender included language that allowed the Allies to carry out the Potsdam Declaration and instructed the Japanese to give General MacArthur the authority to carry out whatever he deemed necessary "to effectuate this surrender." The Moscow Conference gave MacArthur the authority to occupy Japan in order to ensure its compliance. This section of the report details the process of appointing judges and the charges brought against the defendants—"fifty-five counts charging twenty-eight accused with Crimes against Peace, Conventional War Crimes, and Crimes against Humanity during the period from the 1st of January, 1928, to the 2nd of September, 1945." A summary of all the charges is listed, with the crimes against peace listed first, and by the country or group of countries against which Japan waged war. The charges range from the very general, as in count 1, which charged the accused with waging a war of aggression, to the very specific, as in count 51, which "charges certain accused with the murder of members of the armed forces of Mongolia and the Soviet Union in the Khalkin-Gol River area in 1939."

Significant detail is presented pertaining to the difficulties in conducting the trials in a timely manner. Not only were there significant language barriers, they went in every direction, making communication between judges, prosecutors, defendants and their counsel very difficult. Perhaps anticipating procedural challenges, steps were taken to ensure that a timely trial could be held while allowing appropriate evidence and testimony to be presented. The report concedes that the "length of the present trial requires some explanation and comment" and goes on to explain that there were not only language delays, but also that the amount of evidence, much of it deemed irrelevant, presented was overwhelming. In addition, the trials covered a period of seventeen years and needed to take into account Japanese military and political history. Finally, a vigorous defense was mounted, and "every foot of the way was fought." The admissibility of evidence, particularly a pair of key diaries/memoirs, is hotly debated, with the report going so far as to accuse lawyers of defending the indefensible. The background given in this section of the report is useful to understand the length of the trial and the complexities experienced by the participants.

Essential Themes

Though it would seem that the primary theme of this document would be the war crimes of which the defendants are accused, this section is actually more focused on the structure and procedures of the IMTFE trials and on the multiple obstacles the tribunal encountered. In addition to determining what evidence is needed to prove responsibility for waging war and the troublesome nature of a reverse defense (many of the defendants were accused of failing to prevent war crimes, rather than committing them in person), translation between the accused and their judges and lawyers, and between the judges themselves, proved very difficult and time consuming. Several witnesses were rejected as unreliable and lacking candor. Moreover, key documents purportedly had been destroyed in the US bombing raids or burned by military personnel following surrender, or else were being hidden somewhere and not presented to the tribunal. In order to fulfill the requirement of their charter to carry out the trials without unnecessary delay, the tribunal had to make some difficult choices about what evidence and witness testimony to review. The document thus also serves to impart lessons learned about conducting international war crimes trial proceedings.

—*Bethany Groff, MA*

Bibliography and Additional Reading

Madoka Futamura. *War Crimes Tribunals and Transitional Justice: The Tokyo Trial and the Nuremberg Legacy.* New York: Routledge, 2008. Digital file.

Maga, Timothy P. *Judgment at Tokyo: The Japanese War Crimes Trials.* Lexington: UP of Kentucky, 2001. Print.

The Tokyo War Crimes Trial: A Digital Exhibition." University of Virginia School of Law, n.d. Web. 12 Jan. 2015.

■ Convention on the Prevention and Punishment of the Crime of Genocide

Date: December 9, 1948
Author: United Nations
Genre: treaty

Summary Overview

During World War II, the Nazi regime of Germany systematically killed a total of some fifteen to twenty million European Jews, Romani, and other ethnic and social minorities. The killing began before the official outbreak of war in 1939, as the Nazis prosecuted a relentless campaign against Jewish and other populations deemed undesirable. In the ensuing years, these peoples died from forced marches and forced labor, mass shootings, euthanasia, abortion, starvation, and disease in ghettos and concentration camps, as well as extermination plans carried out in six death camps. On December 9, 1948, the United Nations General Assembly adopted Resolution 260 (III), the Convention on the Prevention and Punishment of the Crime of Genocide, to prevent such crimes from ever happening again and to ensure punishment of those who violated its provisions.

Defining Moment

In August 1941, British prime minister Winston Churchill referred to Nazi atrocities against Jews and other peoples in Europe as "a crime without a name." In 1944, Polish Jewish lawyer Raphael Lemkin coined the word "genocide" to describe the murderous campaign waged by the Nazis.

As early as December 1942, the Allied powers had condemned and promised retribution for Nazi atrocities committed against the peoples of Europe. Before the war ended in 1945, Allied leaders had begun making plans for postwar trials of "crimes against peace," "war crimes," and "crimes against humanity." The Nuremberg trials lasted from October 1945 to October 1946, and nineteen leading Nazi officials were convicted and sentenced, with ten executed, three imprisoned for life, and four serving prison terms of more than a decade. However, although the term "genocide" occurred in trial records and indictments, it did not appear in the charter of the International Military Tribunal (IMT) or in the final verdicts. Also, the IMT confined its verdicts to crimes committed during wartime. This caused Lemkin and others great concern as Nazi policies of persecution began well before official declarations of war in 1939. Millions had already died.

Many world leaders wanted to provide safeguards against genocide during peacetime and wartime. So, following the conclusion of the Nuremberg trials, several nations introduced a draft resolution to declare genocide an international crime (during times of war and peace) and to make crimes of genocide "subject to universal jurisdiction." This would have enabled crimes of genocide to be tried by any state as well as by international courts established by relevant parties. On December 11, 1946, Resolution 96 (I), "The Crime of Genocide," entered an official definition of genocide into the General Assembly: "Genocide is a denial of the right of existence of entire human groups . . . and is contrary to the spirit and aims of the United Nations." The resolution further called on the UN General Assembly to legislate against genocide.

That legislation took the form of the Convention on the Prevention and Punishment of the Crime of Genocide. Drafting and passage of the convention took time. Lemkin, along with Vespasian Pella and Henri Donnedieu de Vabres, contributed to the writing of the first draft, which then went through committee revisions before being submitted to the General Assembly for adoption in December 1948. At the time, forty-one member nations signed the convention, and its provisions went into effect on January 12, 1951; since then, a total of 146 member nations have ratified the convention.

Author Biography

The United Nations (UN) was formally established on October 24, 1945. President Franklin D. Roosevelt had first used the term to refer to an alliance of nations against the Axis powers in 1942. Following the end of World War II, representatives from fifty nations gathered to form an official international body charged with securing international peace, security, and cooperation. The UN came into being with the signature of the UN Charter. The General Assembly was one of the principal bodies within the UN. Every member nation was to be represented and have one vote. The primary purpose of the General Assembly is to discuss international matters relating to charges under the charter and to make recommendations for international action. The General Assembly has no law-making or enforcement power. The first General Assembly, with representatives from fifty-one nations, met in London on January 10, 1946. Since that time, the body has passed thousands of resolutions. As of 2014, the General Assembly comprised representatives from all 193 UN member nations; only two independent countries in the world were not members.

HISTORICAL DOCUMENT

The Contracting Parties,

Having considered the declaration made by the General Assembly of the United Nations in its resolution 96 (I) dated 11 December 1946 that genocide is a crime under international law, contrary to the spirit and aims of the United Nations and condemned by the civilized world;

Recognizing that at all periods of history genocide has inflicted great losses on humanity; and

Being convinced that, in order to liberate mankind from such an odious scourge, international co-operation is required;

Hereby agree as hereinafter provided.

Article 1.

The Contracting Parties confirm that genocide, whether committed in time of peace or in time of war, is a crime under international law which they undertake to prevent and to punish.

Art. 2.

In the present Convention, genocide means any of the following acts committed with intent to destroy, in whole or in part, a national, ethnical, racial or religious group, as such:

(a) Killing members of the group; (b) Causing serious bodily or mental harm to members of the group; (c) Deliberately inflicting on the group conditions of life calculated to bring about its physical destruction in whole or in part; (d) Imposing measures intended to prevent births within the group; (e) Forcibly transferring children of the group to another group.

Art. 3.

The following acts shall be punishable:

(a) Genocide; (b) Conspiracy to commit genocide; (c) Direct and public incitement to commit genocide; (d) Attempt to commit genocide; (e) Complicity in genocide.

Art. 4.

Persons committing genocide or any of the other acts enumerated in Article 3 shall be punished, whether they are constitutionally responsible rulers, public officials or private individuals.

Art. 5.

The Contracting Parties undertake to enact, in accordance with their respective Constitutions, the necessary legislation to give effect to the provisions of the present Convention and, in particular, to provide effective penalties for persons guilty of genocide or any of the other acts enumerated in Article 3.

Art. 6.

Persons charged with genocide or any of the other acts enumerated in Article 3 shall be tried by a competent tribunal of the State in the territory of which the act was committed, or by such international penal tribunal as may have jurisdiction with respect to those Contracting Parties which shall have accepted its jurisdiction.

Art. 7.

Genocide and the other acts enumerated in Article 3 shall not be considered as political crimes for the purpose of extradition.

The Contracting Parties pledge themselves in such

cases to grant extradition in accordance with their laws and treaties in force.

Art. 8.

Any Contracting Party may call upon the competent organs of the United Nations to take such action under the Charter of the United Nations as they consider appropriate for the prevention and suppression of acts of genocide or any of the other acts enumerated in Article 3.

Art. 9.

Disputes between the Contracting Parties relating to the interpretation, application or fulfilment of the present Convention, including those relating to the responsibility of a State for genocide or any of the other acts enumerated in Article 3, shall be submitted to the International Court of Justice at the request of any of the parties to the dispute.

Art. 10.

The present Convention, of which the Chinese, English, French, Russian and Spanish texts are equally authentic, shall bear the date of 9 December 1948.

Art. 11.

The present Convention shall be open until 31 December 1949 for signature on behalf of any Member of the United Nations and of any non-member State to which an invitation to sign has been addressed by the General Assembly.

The present Convention shall be ratified, and the instruments of ratification shall be deposited with the Secretary-General of the United Nations.

After 1 January 1950, the present Convention may be acceded to on behalf of any Member of the United Nations and of any non-member State which has received an invitation as aforesaid.

Instruments of accession shall be deposited with the Secretary-General of the United Nations.

Art. 12.

Any Contracting Party may at any time, by notification addressed to the Secretary-General of the United Nations, extend the application of the present Convention to all or any of the territories for the conduct of whose foreign relations that Contracting Party is responsible.

Art. 13.

On the day when the first twenty instruments of ratification or accession have been deposited, the Secretary-General shall draw up a procès-verbal and transmit a copy of it to each Member of the United Nations and to each of the non-member States contemplated in Article 11.

The present Convention shall come into force on the ninetieth day following the date of deposit of the twentieth instrument of ratification or accession.

Any ratification or accession effected subsequent to the latter date shall become effective on the ninetieth day following the deposit of the instrument of ratification or accession.

Art. 14.

The present Convention shall remain in effect for a period of ten years as from the date of its coming into force.

It shall thereafter remain in force for successive periods of five years for such Contracting Parties as have not denounced it at least six months before the expiration of the current period.

Denunciation shall be effected by a written notification addressed to the Secretary-General of the United Nations.

Art. 15.

If, as a result of denunciations, the number of Parties to the present Convention should become less than sixteen, the Convention shall cease to be in force as from the date on which the last of these denunciations shall become effective.

Art. 16.

A request for the revision of the present Convention may be made at any time by any Contracting Party by means of a notification in writing addressed to the Secretary-General.

The General Assembly shall decide upon the steps, if any, to be taken in respect of such request.

Art. 17.

The Secretary-General of the United Nations shall notify all Members of the United Nations and the non-member States contemplated in Article 11 of the following:

(a) Signatures, ratifications and accessions received in accordance with Article 11; (b) Notifications received in accordance with Article 12; (c) The date upon which the present Convention comes into force in accordance with Article 13; (d) Denunciations received in accordance with Article 14; (e) The abrogation of the Convention in accordance with Article 15; (f) Notifications received in accordance with Article 16.

Art. 18.

The original of the present Convention shall be deposited in the archives of the United Nations.

A certified copy of the Convention shall be transmitted to all Members of the United Nations and to the non-member States contemplated in Article 11.

Art. 19.

The present Convention shall be registered by the Secretary-General of the United Nations on the date of its coming into force.

GLOSSARY

abrogation: the act or instance of repealing

denounce: to condemn or censure openly or publicly; to make a formal accusation against, as in court

extradition: the procedure by which a state or nation, upon receipt of a formal request by another state or nation, turns over to that second jurisdiction an individual charged with or convicted of a crime

odious: hateful; highly offensive; deserving or causing hatred

scourge: a cause of affliction or calamity

Document Analysis

The opening lines of the convention introduce its purpose in protecting the world from the "odious scourge" of genocide and articulate its origin as a response to UN General Assembly Resolution 96 (I). This is noteworthy in that it cites the need for an international, collaborative response to the threat of genocide and specifically names genocide as a crime. The provisions of the convention are enumerated in nineteen articles, the first nine of which deal with the definition of genocide, the trial and punishment of crimes of genocide, and the roles of contracting parties and the United Nations. The subsequent ten articles deal largely with procedural matters, including the convention's ratification, its duration of effect, and processes of revision and cancellation.

The convention's punch lies in the first batch of articles. Article 1 gives the document its power, by declaring that "genocide, whether committed in time of peace or in time of war, is a crime under international law which [the contracting parties] undertake to prevent and to punish." This article elaborates on the purpose of the convention as both preventing and punishing genocide and, significantly, indicates that genocide may occur during peacetime. Article 2 then extends the precedents of the International Military Tribunal

Charter by defining specific acts of genocide. Notable in this article is that it defines genocide not only as killing members of national, ethnic, racial, and religious groups "with intent to destroy" but also as committing other acts, including imposing conditions meant to bring about "physical destruction in whole or in part," attempts to prevent births and to remove children, and other methods inflicting "serious bodily or mental harm."

Article 3 builds on the preceding article by defining crimes of genocide in addition to its perpetration that the UN considers punishable. Item (a) names genocide itself, which would include the terms of the definition in the preceding provision. Items (b) through (e) extend punishable crimes to corollary actions including conspiracy and complicity, attempted genocide, and incitement. This article is perhaps most significant, as it holds accountable not only individuals who actually deal in death, but also those who orchestrate, support, collaborate, and encourage genocide. Article 4 elaborates this principle by clarifying that all persons, from the highest to the lowest ranks of a society, may be prosecuted and punished under the convention.

Articles 5 through 9 address the processes of trial, prosecution, and punishment and outline the obligations of contracting parties. In article 5, states commit to pass their own national laws to enforce the terms of the convention. Article 6 defines two methods of prosecution: either by trial in states where the genocide has been committed or by international tribunal. Article 7 also obligates states to uphold the convention by granting extradition. Article 8 offers contracting parties a means of invoking the UN to take action to prevent or stop genocide. Finally, article 9 allows for mediation of disputes regarding the convention by the International Court of Justice.

Among the procedural articles, article 14 may be the most significant, as it defines the duration of the convention's effectiveness. After its initial ten years in force, the convention renews itself automatically for five-year periods and continues to do so until states denounce it in writing. Even then, per article 15, the convention remains in effect until the number of contracting parties becomes fewer than sixteen. Only if the number of contracting parties drops below sixteen does the convention become void. Similarly, article 16 states that any party may submit a request to revise the convention, which the General Assembly will then review.

Essential Themes

At its heart, the Genocide Convention (as it is commonly known) is an international call to action regarding the crime of genocide. The provisions combine to ensure prevention and prosecution. Indeed, the key to the document is in that dual purpose "to prevent and to punish." The comprehensive scope of the first nine articles serves as a deterrent to those who would undertake to commit genocide. Its terms also guide the international community in how to respond to crimes of genocide.

This convention set an important precedent for international justice—and defense of human rights—that has been revisited again and again in the decades since its ratification. Its terms, and subsequent documents and events, have remained a source of much debate within the international community. However, that is perhaps the convention's most lasting legacy: it put a spotlight on the need for debate. Though many might argue that the convention has not prevented or even adequately punished acts of genocide since its inception, it has ensured that such crimes draw an increasing degree of international attention and debate. In that sense, it might be considered an important early step toward the achievement of its goals.

—Christina Dendy

Bibliography and Additional Reading

Cooper, John. *Raphael Lemkin and the Struggle for the Genocide Convention.* New York: Palgrave Macmillan, 2008. Print.

Jones, Adam. *Genocide: A Comprehensive Introduction.* New York: Routledge, 2006. Print.

Lemkin, Raphael. *Axis Rule in Occupied Europe: Laws of Occupation, Analysis of Government, Proposals for Redress.* Clark: Lawbook Exchange, 2005. Print.

Meisler, Stanley. *United Nations: A History.* New York: Grove, 2011. Print.

Schabas, William A. "Convention on the Prevention and Punishment of the Crime of Genocide." *United Nations Audiovisual Library of International Law.* Codification Division, Office of Legal Affairs, United Nations, 2013. Web. 6 Jan. 2015.

_____. *Genocide in International Law: The Crime of Crimes.* Cambridge: Cambridge UP, 2009. Print.

United Nations. "Resolutions Adopted by the General Assembly during Its First Session." *UN.org.* United Nations General Assembly, n.d. Web. 6 Jan. 2015.

The New World Order

As with World War I, so too with World War II did the political geography of Europe change dramatically following the end of hostilities. In this case, there were adjustments in the Far East as well. And in both Germany and Japan, occupying forces held sway after the war. Germany was sectioned into various "zones" that were controlled by different Allied powers. Japan was put under the control of the United States, principally, with support from the British Commonwealth. Throughout Western Europe and parts of East Asia, the US-sponsored Marshall Plan for economic recovery went into effect, providing billions of dollars in aid. Meanwhile, the Soviet Union, having expelled Hitler's forces from the east in Germany, played a major role in the German occupation and ultimately incorporated East Germany into the so-called Iron Curtain of communist Eastern Europe. In Japan, however, the Soviets were left out of the postwar occupation and rebuilding plan. A situation thus developed whereby political tensions increased between the Soviet Union and the West, producing the so-called Cold War. During the Cold War, Soviet and Eastern Bloc leaders continually challenged American and other Western leaders on the world political stage, only to be counter-challenged by the West in return. Adding fuel to the fire were growing caches of nuclear weapons on both sides. As the Cold War continued, positions hardened, ideologies (communism versus capitalism) took root, and proxy wars eventually erupted across the globe. The American strategy of "containment," or limiting the spread of communism, became the order of the day in US politics and all US spheres of influence.

■ Preamble of the UN Charter

Date: June 26, 1945
Author: Government of the United States, et al.
Genre: charter

Summary Overview

As it became increasingly apparent that Nazi Germany would be defeated at the end of World War II, one of the main topics of discussion among the Big Three leaders of the Allied nations—the United States, Great Britain, and the Soviet Union—was how the peace would be kept after the war. Created in the aftermath of World War I, the League of Nations had been ineffective in its goal to create an international organization through which countries could resolve their differences peacefully. The Big Three, eager to learn from the failure of the League of Nations, held discussions in Tehran, Iran, in 1943 that set the general framework. Over the following year, conferences were held at Bretton Woods, New Hampshire, and at the Dumbarton Oaks estate in Washington, DC, focusing on the specifics of the new peacekeeping organization. Finally, from April through June of 1945, delegates from fifty nations met in San Francisco to conclude the charter for the United Nations.

Defining Moment

Early in World War II, before the United States even became involved, Allied leaders like US president Franklin D. Roosevelt and British prime minister Winston Churchill saw both the weaknesses and the still-unrealized potential of an international group devoted to peace. One of the main weaknesses of the League of Nations had been the unwillingness of the United States to participate in the organization, which US president Woodrow Wilson had himself proposed at the end of World War I. Given the role of the United States as an emerging superpower at the end of World War II, it was more important than ever that it play a key role in another such organization.

The 1941 Atlantic Charter articulated the first vision of what would become the United Nations (UN), and twenty-six nations together issued the Declaration of the United Nations on January 1, 1942—less than a month after the United States entered the war—agreeing to fight the Axis powers and then establish the United Nations once the Axis was defeated. Roosevelt, a Democrat, involved Republicans in the process of creating the UN in order to avoid a repeat of Wilson's failure. Roosevelt's secretary of state, Cordell Hull, worked directly with Congress to build bipartisan consensus around the idea and draft a potential charter for the UN, while Congress passed a number of resolutions stating support for the UN after the war was over. The foreign ministers of the United States, Great Britain, and the Soviet Union, and the Chinese ambassador to the Soviet Union issued the Moscow Declaration in October 1943, officially committing all of the Allies to the idea of the UN.

Throughout late 1944, as the American and British armies executed the D-Day invasion and drove through Europe into the heart of Germany, representatives of the four signatories to the Moscow Declaration met at the Dumbarton Oaks estate in Washington, DC, in order to have the plans for the UN prepared for the eventual Axis defeat. The US government even staged a public relations effort, taking the argument for the UN directly to the American people.

At the Yalta Conference in February 1945, the Big Three leaders invited representatives of the world's nations to convene next in San Francisco, California, in April 1945 in order to draft the charter that would officially establish the UN. Though Roosevelt died only days before the San Francisco Conference convened, President Harry S. Truman, newly sworn-in, stated that the conference would take place as planned. After two months of work rewriting the proposed charter produced at Dumbarton Oaks, the fifty countries in attendance passed the United Nations Charter.

Author Biography

The "Peoples of the United Nations," in whose name

the United Nations Charter was written, were represented at the San Francisco Conference by 850 delegates from the original member nations. The delegation from the United States was made up of two secretaries of state, Edward R. Stettinius, Jr. and his predecessor, Cordell Hull, as well as representatives from both houses of Congress. Not all of the nations, however, could agree on who would be included. Many of the delegates opposed the Soviet insistence upon—and United States acquiescence to—the inclusion of two

of its member republics, the Ukraine and Byelorussia (now Belarus), giving it essentially three votes. Further, the Soviets opposed Argentina's inclusion, as it had supported the Axis during the war, and the Polish government was not seated, as the formation of a new Polish government was a source of discord between the Soviets on one hand and the Americans and British on the other. However, in the end, fifty nations were able to pass the charter and create the UN.

HISTORICAL DOCUMENT

WE THE PEOPLES OF THE UNITED NATIONS DETERMINED
  • to save succeeding generations from the scourge of war, which twice in our lifetime has brought untold sorrow to mankind, and
  • to reaffirm faith in fundamental human rights, in the dignity and worth of the human person, in the equal rights of men and women and of nations large and small, and
  • to establish conditions under which justice and respect for the obligations arising from treaties and other sources of international law can be maintained, and
  • to promote social progress and better standards of life in larger freedom,
AND FOR THESE ENDS
  • to practice tolerance and live together in peace with one another as good neighbours, and

  • to unite our strength to maintain international peace and security, and
  • to ensure, by the acceptance of principles and the institution of methods, that armed force shall not be used, save in the common interest, and
  • to employ international machinery for the promotion of the economic and social advancement of all peoples,
HAVE RESOLVED TO COMBINE OUR EFFORTS TO ACCOMPLISH THESE AIMS
  Accordingly, our respective Governments, through representatives assembled in the city of San Francisco, who have exhibited their full powers found to be in good and due form, have agreed to the present Charter of the United Nations and do hereby establish an international organization to be known as the United Nations.

Document Analysis

The Preamble to the United Nations Charter is a brief visionary statement that specified the goals of the fifty nations that met at the San Francisco Conference. In total, it consists of eight statements of principle and a single concluding sentence that officially established the UN. The fact that it is a simple document does not detract from its profundity, as each of the statements was very timely to the delegates at San Francisco. The world was just emerging from its second cataclysmic conflict in thirty years. The failure of the earlier League of Nations, the world's descent into a second world war, and the realization of the horrendous atrocities committed by the Axis powers during the war formed the

context for a statement of ideology and commitment to a peaceful future.

The first four statements begin with the words, "We the peoples of the United Nations determined," before stating the shared resolve to create a peaceful future. The two world wars had brought horrors unlike anything seen in human history, with the widespread use of chemical weapons in World War I and the development and use of atomic weapons in World War II. To eliminate the possibility of a third such war, the delegates committed themselves to saving "succeeding generations from the scourge of war." The other three statements commit the group to affirming and protecting human rights; ensuring justice and honoring treaties and international law; and promoting "social progress and better standards of life in larger freedom." This is followed by a set of four ideals to which the nations would commit themselves to further the aims enumerated in the first four statements. Tolerance and peace with other nations is enshrined. The role of the UN as a united body to protect peace and security is recognized. The use of armed force by nations as a tool of policy is discouraged. Finally, the UN's role in "the economic and social advancement of all peoples" is established. The document concludes with a brief statement that the nations "have agreed to the present Charter of the United Nations and do hereby establish an international organization to be known as the United Nations." The lessons of the two world wars were learned well, and the hope was that the UN would be able to prevent the horrors that had characterized so much of the first half of the twentieth century.

Essential Themes

President Harry S. Truman attended the final session at the San Francisco Conference and then went about the work of gaining the ratification of the US Senate. US ratification was quick, taking a little over a month, and overwhelmingly supported, with a vote of eighty-nine in favor, two opposed, and five abstentions. Once the Allies, as well the vast majority of other signatory nations, had all approved the charter, the United Nations became a reality on October 24, 1945. Opening its first session less than four months later, the UN General Assembly agreed to establish its headquarters in New York City.

Over the ensuing years, the UN continued to produce visionary statements, such as the Universal Declaration of Human Rights in 1948. However, its role in mitigating international conflict saw its first major test with the onset of the Korean War in 1950. The Soviets, whose permanent seat on the Security Council gave them veto power, were protesting the UN's refusal to allow delegates from Communist China. Seeking to act against the invasion of South Korea by North Ko-rea—a vote that the Soviets would have opposed—the Security Council voted in the Soviets' absence, thus enabling the UN to provide aid to South Korea in its self-defense.

Just as the League of Nations was frequently hindered by its rule that certain votes needed to be unanimous, decisions on military issues in the UN Security Council have often been obstructed by the veto power that each member holds. As the United States and the Soviet Union seldom saw eye to eye, the UN's military role became increasingly difficult. However, votes in the General Assembly are easier, as no nation has a veto, allowing the UN to create offices and assist in matters of human rights, famine and disaster relief, economic development, and the environment.

The military and humanitarian roles played by the UN have become increasingly intertwined as the end of the Cold War made Security Council votes somewhat easier. Sending peacekeepers into situations where the human rights of ordinary people are threatened has become a hallmark of the modern UN.

—*Steven L. Danver, PhD*

Bibliography and Additional Reading

Alger, Chadwick F. *The United Nations System: A Reference Handbook*. Santa Barbara: ABC-CLIO, 2006. Print.

Hearden, Patrick J. *Architects of Globalism: Building a New World Order during World War II*. Fayetteville: U of Arkansas P, 2002. Print.

Hoopes, Townsend, & Douglas Brinkley. *FDR and the Creation of the UN*. New Haven: Yale UP, 1997. Print.

Krasno, Jean E., ed. *The United Nations: Confronting the Challenges of a Global Society*. Boulder: Rienner, 2004. Print.

Schlesinger, Stephen C. *Act of Creation: The Founding of the United Nations*. Boulder: Westview, 2003. Print.

■ Potsdam Agreement

Date: August 1, 1945
Authors: Governments of the United States, Soviet Union, China, and United Kingdom
Genre: government document

Summary Overview

Shortly after Germany surrendered to the Allies on May 8, 1945, US president Harry S. Truman, British prime minister Winston Churchill, and Soviet premier Joseph Stalin met at the Potsdam Conference to complete an agreement on the treatment of postwar Germany. The leaders agreed to completely dismantle the Nazi Party (the National Socialist Party) and Germany's military in order to prevent that country's potential for remilitarization. Furthermore, the Potsdam participants established an agreement, in principle, for the division of Germany and the reestablishment of previously conquered European, Middle Eastern, and North African nations, as well as a plan of action for dealing with Japan once it was defeated.

Defining Moment

By the spring of 1945, fighting in the European theater (which included portions of North Africa and the Middle East) came to an end with the unconditional surrender of Nazi Germany. Approximately thirty-nine million soldiers and civilians died in this theater alone, while fighting, destruction, and casualties continued in the Pacific theater. The conflict left the entire region in a state of near chaos. Toppled governments left leadership vacuums, and long-standing borders had been erased. National economies had collapsed. Millions of displaced civilians, escaping the battlefield as well as Nazi persecution, sought new places in which to reside when hostilities came to an end.

Having gained an advantage against the Axis in Europe by early 1945, the "Big Three"—US president Franklin D. Roosevelt, Stalin, and Churchill—had met in February at the Crimean resort town of Yalta to discuss how to rebuild after the war and how to treat the vanquished enemy. To be sure, war continued in Japan, but the three leaders anticipated that that war would soon come to a close now that the Allies were gaining momentum. On May 7, with Adolf Hitler dead and his Nazi regime disintegrated, German officials signed the instrument of surrender at Reims in northwestern France, and the terms of the surrender came into effect on the following day. The groundwork laid at the Yalta Conference now required rapid and comprehensive development.

At this point, however, the complexion of the Big Three had changed as well as the political conditions in which they met. In March, Soviet troops finally expelled German forces from Poland, leaving the Soviet Union with a sizable spoil before the war was officially over. On April 12, Roosevelt suffered stroke and died, and his vice president, Harry S. Truman, assumed the presidency. Meanwhile, Churchill, who was an integral leader in the wartime coalition, had been replaced in the 1945 election by Labour Party leader Clement Attlee. Finally, Truman was preparing to end the war in the Pacific theater by dropping the first atomic bomb on Japan.

When Truman, Attlee, Churchill (who attended the conference for a week before being replaced by Attlee), and Stalin convened at Potsdam, theirs was a monumental and highly complex task. The principal item on their agenda was a discussion of how to treat the defeated Germans, including the complete dismantlement of the Nazi regime and military in such a way that prevented future incarnations of Nazi-style nationalism. Also pressing was the resettlement of millions of refugees, who had scattered across the globe in search of refuge from war and persecution. Furthermore, after the Axis forces invaded and annexed sovereign nations, there remained a question of how to redraw the borders of Europe's nations.

HISTORICAL DOCUMENT

Protocol of the Proceedings, August l, 1945

The Berlin Conference of the Three Heads of Government of the U.S.S.R., U.S.A., and U.K., which took place from July 17 to August 2, 1945, came to the following conclusions:

I. ESTABLISHMENT OF A COUNCIL OF FOREIGN MINISTERS.

A. The Conference reached the following agreement for the establishment of a Council of Foreign Ministers to do the necessary preparatory work for the peace settlements:

"(1) There shall be established a Council composed of the Foreign Ministers of the United Kingdom, the Union of Soviet Socialist Republics, China, France, and the United States.

"(2) (i) The Council shall normally meet in London which shall be the permanent seat of the joint Secretariat which the Council will form. Each of the Foreign Ministers will be accompanied by a high-ranking Deputy, duly authorized to carry on the work of the Council in the absence of his Foreign Ministers, and by a small staff of technical advisers.

" (ii) The first meeting of the Council shall be held in London not later than September 1st 1945. Meetings may be held by common agreement in other capitals as may be agreed from time to time.

" (3) (i) As its immediate important task, the Council shall be authorized to draw up, with a view to their submission to the United Nations, treaties of peace with Italy, Rumania, Bulgaria, Hungary and Finland, and to propose settlements of territorial questions outstanding on the termination of the war in Europe. The Council shall be utilized for the preparation of a peace settlement for Germany to be accepted by the Government of Germany when a government adequate for the purpose is established.

"(ii) For the discharge of each of these tasks the Council will be composed of the Members representing those States which were signatory to the terms of surrender imposed upon the enemy State concerned. For the purposes of the peace settlement for Italy, France shall be regarded as a signatory to the terms of surrender for Italy. Other Members will be invited to participate when matters directly concerning them are under discussion.

"(iii) Other matters may from time to time be referred to the Council by agreement between the Member Governments.

"(4) (i) Whenever the Council is considering a question of direct interest to a State not represented thereon, such State should be invited to send representatives to participate in the discussion and study of that question.

"(ii) The Council may adapt its procedure to the particular problems under consideration. In some cases it may hold its own preliminary discussions prior to the participation of other interested States. In other cases, the Council may convoke a formal conference of the State chiefly interested in seeking a solution of the particular problem."

B. It was agreed that the three Governments should each address an identical invitation to the Governments of China and France to adopt this text and to join in establishing the Council. The text of the approved invitation was as follows:

Council of Foreign Ministers Draft for identical invitation to be sent separately by each of the Three Governments to the Governments of China and France.

"The Governments of the United Kingdom, the United States and the U.S.S.R. consider it necessary to begin without delay the essential preparatory work upon the peace settlements in Europe. To this end they are agreed that there should be established a Council of the Foreign Ministers of the Five Great Powers to prepare treaties of peace with the European enemy States, for submission to the United Nations. The Council would also be empowered to propose settlements of outstanding territorial questions in Europe and to consider such other matters as member Governments might agree to refer to it.

"The text adopted by the Three Governments is as follows:

"In agreement with the Governments of the United States and U.S.S.R., His Majesty's Government in the United Kingdom and U.S.S.R., the United States Government, the United Kingdom and the Soviet Government extend a cordial invitation to the Government of

China (France) to adopt the text quoted above and to join in setting up the Council. His Majesty's Government, The United States Government, The Soviet Government attach much importance to the participation of the Chinese Government (French Government) in the proposed arrangements and they hope to receive an early and favorable reply to this invitation."

C. It was understood that the establishment of the Council of Foreign Ministers for the specific purposes named in the text would be without prejudice to the agreement of the Crimea Conference that there should be periodical consultation between the Foreign Secretaries of the United States, the Union of Soviet Socialist Republics and the United Kingdom.

D. The Conference also considered the position of the European Advisory Commission in the light of the Agreement to establish the Council of Foreign Ministers. It was noted with satisfaction that the Commission had ably discharged its principal tasks by the recommendations that it had furnished for the terms of surrender for Germany, for the zones of occupation in Germany and Austria and for the inter-Allied control machinery in those countries. It was felt that further work of a detailed character for the coordination of Allied policy for the control of Germany and Austria would in future fall within the competence of the Control Council at Berlin and the Allied Commission at Vienna. Accordingly it was agreed to recommend that the European Advisory Commission be dissolved.

II. THE PRINCIPLES TO GOVERN THE TREATMENT OF GERMANY IN THE INITIAL CONTROL PERIOD

A. POLITICAL PRINCIPLES.

1. In accordance with the Agreement on Control Machinery in Germany, supreme authority in Germany is exercised, on instructions from their respective Governments, by the Commanders-in-Chief of the armed forces of the United States of America, the United Kingdom, the Union of Soviet Socialist Republics, and the French Republic, each in his own zone of occupation, and also jointly, in matters affecting Germany as a whole, in their capacity as members of the Control Council.

2. So far as is practicable, there shall be uniformity of treatment of the German population throughout Germany.

3. The purposes of the occupation of Germany by which the Control Council shall be guided are:

(i) The complete disarmament and demilitarization of Germany and the elimination or control of all German industry that could be used for military production. To these ends:—

(a) All German land, naval and air forces, the SS., SA., SD., and Gestapo, with all their organizations, staffs and institutions, including the General Staff, the Officers' Corps, Reserve Corps, military schools, war veterans' organizations and all other military and semi-military organizations, together with all clubs and associations which serve to keep alive the military tradition in Germany, shall be completely and finally abolished in such manner as permanently to prevent the revival or reorganization of German militarism and Nazism;

(b) All arms, ammunition and implements of war and all specialized facilities for their production shall be held at the disposal of the Allies or destroyed. The maintenance and production of all aircraft and all arms. ammunition and implements of war shall be prevented.

(ii) To convince the German people that they have suffered a total military defeat and that they cannot escape responsibility for what they have brought upon themselves, since their own ruthless warfare and the fanatical Nazi resistance have destroyed German economy and made chaos and suffering inevitable.

(iii) To destroy the National Socialist Party and its affiliated and supervised organizations, to dissolve all Nazi institutions, to ensure that they are not revived in any form, and to prevent all Nazi and militarist activity or propaganda.

(iv) To prepare for the eventual reconstruction of German political life on a democratic basis and for eventual peaceful cooperation in international life by Germany.

4. All Nazi laws which provided the basis of the Hitler regime or established discriminations on grounds of race, creed, or political opinion shall be abolished. No such discriminations, whether legal, administrative or otherwise, shall be tolerated.

5. War criminals and those who have participated in planning or carrying out Nazi enterprises involving or

resulting in atrocities or war crimes shall be arrested and brought to judgment. Nazi leaders, influential Nazi supporters and high officials of Nazi organizations and institutions and any other persons dangerous to the occupation or its objectives shall be arrested and interned.

6. All members of the Nazi Party who have been more than nominal participants in its activities and all other persons hostile to Allied purposes shall be removed from public and semi-public office, and from positions of responsibility in important private undertakings. Such persons shall be replaced by persons who, by their political and moral qualities, are deemed capable of assisting in developing genuine democratic institutions in Germany.

7. German education shall be so controlled as completely to eliminate Nazi and militarist doctrines and to make possible the successful development of democratic ideas.

8. The judicial system will be reorganized in accordance with the principles of democracy, of justice under law, and of equal rights for all citizens without distinction of race, nationality or religion.

9. The administration in Germany should be directed towards the decentralization of the political structure and the development of local responsibility. To this end:

(i) local self-government shall be restored throughout Germany on democratic principles and in particular through elective councils as rapidly as is consistent with military security and the purposes of military occupation;

(ii) all democratic political parties with rights of assembly and of public discussion shall be allowed and encouraged throughout Germany;

(iii) representative and elective principles shall be introduced into regional, provincial and state (Land) administration as rapidly as may be justified by the successful application of these principles in local self-government;

(iv) for the time being, no central German Government shall be established. Notwithstanding this, however, certain essential central German administrative departments, headed by State Secretaries, shall be established, particularly in the fields of finance, transport, communications, foreign trade and industry. Such departments will act under the direction of the Control Council.

10. Subject to the necessity for maintaining military security, freedom of speech, press and religion shall be permitted, and religious institutions shall be respected. Subject likewise to the maintenance of military security, the formation of free trade unions shall be permitted.

B. ECONOMIC PRINCIPLES.

11. In order to eliminate Germany's war potential, the production of arms, ammunition and implements of war as well as all types of aircraft and sea-going ships shall be prohibited and prevented. Production of metals, chemicals, machinery and other items that are directly necessary to a war economy shall be rigidly controlled and restricted to Germany's approved post-war peacetime needs to meet the objectives stated in Paragraph 15. Productive capacity not needed for permitted production shall be removed in accordance with the reparations plan recommended by the Allied Commission on Reparations and approved by the Governments concerned or if not removed shall be destroyed.

12. At the earliest practicable date, the German economy shall be decentralized for the purpose of eliminating the present excessive concentration of economic power as exemplified in particular by cartels, syndicates, trusts and other monopolistic arrangements.

13. In organizing the German Economy, primary emphasis shall be given to the development of agriculture and peaceful domestic industries.

14. During the period of occupation Germany shall be treated as a single economic unit. To this end common policies shall be established in regard to:

(a) mining and industrial production and its allocation;

(b) agriculture, forestry and fishing;

(c) wages, prices and rationing;

(d) import and export programs for Germany as a whole;

(e) currency and banking, central taxation and customs;

(f) reparation and removal of industrial war potential;

(g) transportation and communications.

In applying these policies account shall be taken, where appropriate, of varying local conditions.

15. Allied controls shall be imposed upon the German economy but only to the extent necessary:

(a) to carry out programs of industrial disarmament,

demilitarization, of reparations, and of approved exports and imports.

(b) to assure the production and maintenance of goods and services required to meet the needs of the occupying forces and displaced persons in Germany and essential to maintain in Germany average living standards not exceeding the average of the standards of living of European countries. (European countries means all European countries excluding the United Kingdom and the U.S.S.R.).

(c) to ensure in the manner determined by the Control Council the equitable distribution of essential commodities between the several zones so as to produce a balanced economy throughout Germany and reduce the need for imports.

(d) to control German industry and all economic and financial international transactions including exports and imports, with the aim of preventing Germany from developing a war potential and of achieving the other objectives named herein.

(e) to control all German public or private scientific bodies research and experimental institutions, laboratories, et cetera connected with economic activities.

16. In the imposition and maintenance of economic controls established by the Control Council, German administrative machinery shall be created and the German authorities shall be required to the fullest extent practicable to proclaim and assume administration of such controls. Thus it should be brought home to the German people that the responsibility for the administration of such controls and any break-down in these controls will rest with themselves. Any German controls which may run counter to the objectives of occupation will be prohibited.

17. Measures shall be promptly taken:

(a) to effect essential repair of transport;

(b) to enlarge coal production;

(c) to maximize agricultural output; and

(d) to erect emergency repair of housing and essential utilities.

18. Appropriate steps shall be taken by the Control Council to exercise control and the power of disposition over German-owned external assets not already under the control of United Nations which have taken part in the war against Germany.

19. Payment of Reparations should leave enough resources to enable the German people to subsist without external assistance. In working out the economic balance of Germany the necessary means must be provided to pay for imports approved by the Control Council in Germany. The proceeds of exports from current production and stocks shall be available in the first place for payment for such imports.

The above clause will not apply to the equipment and products referred to in paragraphs 4 (a) and 4 (b) of the Reparations Agreement.

III. REPARATIONS FROM GERMANY.

1. Reparation claims of the U.S.S.R. shall be met by removals from the zone of Germany occupied by the U.S.S.R., and from appropriate German external assets.

2. The U.S.S.R. undertakes to settle the reparation claims of Poland from its own share of reparations.

3. The reparation claims of the United States, the United Kingdom and other countries entitled to reparations shall be met from the Western Zones and from appropriate German external assets.

4. In addition to the reparations to be taken by the U.S.S.R. from its own zone of occupation, the U.S.S.R. shall receive additionally from the Western Zones:

(a) 15 per cent of such usable and complete industrial capital equipment, in the first place from the metallurgical, chemical and machine manufacturing industries as is unnecessary for the German peace economy and should be removed from the Western Zones of Germany, in exchange for an equivalent value of food, coal, potash, zinc, timber, clay products, petroleum products, and such other commodities as may be agreed upon.

(b) 10 per cent of such industrial capital equipment as is unnecessary for the German peace economy and should be removed from the Western Zones, to be transferred to the Soviet Government on reparations account without payment or exchange of any kind in return.

Removals of equipment as provided in (a) and (b) above shall be made simultaneously.

5. The amount of equipment to be removed from the Western Zones on account of reparations must be determined within six months from now at the latest.

6. Removals of industrial capital equipment shall begin as soon as possible and shall be completed within

two years from the determination specified in paragraph 5. The delivery of products covered by 4 (a) above shall begin as soon as possible and shall be made by the U.S.S.R. in agreed installments within five years of the date hereof. The determination of the amount and character of the industrial capital equipment unnecessary for the German peace economy and therefore available for reparation shall be made by the Control Council under policies fixed by the Allied Commission on Reparations, with the participation of France, subject to the final approval of the Zone Commander in the Zone from which the equipment is to be removed.

7. Prior to the fixing of the total amount of equipment subject to removal, advance deliveries shall be made in respect to such equipment as will be determined to be eligible for delivery in accordance with the procedure set forth in the last sentence of paragraph 6.

8. The Soviet Government renounces all claims in respect of reparations to shares of German enterprises which are located in the Western Zones of Germany as well as to German foreign assets in all countries except those specified in paragraph 9 below.

9. The Governments of the U.K. and U.S.A. renounce all claims in respect of reparations to shares of German enterprises which are located in the Eastern Zone of occupation in Germany, as well as to German foreign assets in Bulgaria, Finland, Hungary, Rumania and Eastern Austria.

10. The Soviet Government makes no claims to gold captured by the Allied troops in Germany.

IV. DISPOSAL OF THE GERMAN NAVY AND MERCHANT MARINE

A. The following principles for the distribution of the German Navy were agreed:

(1) The total strength of the German surface navy, excluding ships sunk and those taken over from Allied Nations, but including ships under construction or repair, shall be divided equally among the U.S.S.R., U. K., and U.S.A.

(2) Ships under construction or repair mean those ships whose construction or repair may be completed within three to six months, according to the type of ship. Whether such ships under construction or repair shall be completed or repaired shall be determined by the tech-

nical commission appointed by the Three Powers and referred to below, subject to the principle that their completion or repair must be achieved within the time limits above provided, without any increase of skilled employment in the German shipyards and without permitting the reopening of any German ship building or connected industries. Completion date means the date when a ship is able to go out on its first trip, or, under peacetime standards, would refer to the customary date of delivery by shipyard to the Government.

(3) The larger part of the German submarine fleet shall be sunk. Not more than thirty submarines shall be preserved and divided equally between the U.S.S.R., U. K., and U.S. A. for experimental and technical purposes.

(4) All stocks of armament, ammunition and supplies of the German Navy appertaining to the vessels transferred pursuant to paragraphs (1) and (3) hereof shall be handed over to the respective powers receiving such ships.

(5) The Three Governments agree to constitute a tripartite naval commission comprising two representatives for each government, accompanied by the requisite staff, to submit agreed recommendations to the Three Governments for the allocation of specific German warships and to handle other detailed matters arising out of the agreement between the Three Governments regarding the German fleet. The Commission will hold its first meeting not later than 15th August, 1945, in Berlin, which shall be its headquarters. Each Delegation on the Commission will have the right on the basis of reciprocity to inspect German warships wherever they may be located.

(6) The Three Governments agreed that transfers, including those of ships under construction and repair, shall be completed as soon as possible, but not later than 15th February, 1946. The Commission will submit fortnightly reports, including proposals for the progressive allocation of the vessels when agreed by the Commission.

B. The following principles for the distribution of the German Merchant Marine were agreed:—

(1) The German Merchant Marine, surrendered to the Three Powers and wherever located, shall be divided equally among the U.S.S.R., the U. K., and the U.S. A. The actual transfers of the ships to the respective coun-

tries shall take place as soon as practicable after the end of the war against Japan. The United Kingdom and the United States will provide out of their shares of the surrendered German merchant ships appropriate amounts for other Allied States whose merchant marines have suffered heavy losses in the common cause against Germany, except that the Soviet Union shall provide out of its share for Poland.

(2) The allocation, manning, and operation of these ships during the Japanese War period shall fall under the cognizance and authority of the Combined Shipping Adjustment Board and the United Maritime Authority.

(3) While actual transfer of the ships shall be delayed until after the end of the war with Japan, a Tripartite Shipping Commission shall inventory and value all available ships and recommend a specific distribution in accordance with paragraph (1).

(4) German inland and coastal ships determined to be necessary to the maintenance of the basic German peace economy by the Allied Control Council of Germany shall not be included in the shipping pool thus divided among the Three Powers.

(5) The Three Governments agree to constitute a tripartite merchant marine commission comprising two representatives for each Government, accompanied by the requisite staff, to submit agreed recommendations to the Three Governments for the allocation of specific German merchant ships and to handle other detailed matters arising out of the agreement between the Three Governments regarding the German merchant ships. The Commission will hold its first meeting not later than September 1st, 1945, in Berlin, which shall be its headquarters. Each delegation on the Commission will have the right on the basis of reciprocity to inspect the German merchant ships wherever they may be located.

V. CITY OF KOENIGSBERG AND THE ADJACENT AREA.

The Conference examined a proposal by the Soviet Government to the effect that pending the final determination of territorial questions at the peace settlement, the section of the western frontier of the Union of Soviet Socialist Republics which is adjacent to the Baltic Sea should pass from a point on the eastern shore of the Bay of Danzig to the east, north of Braunsberg-Goldap, to the meeting point of the frontiers of Lithuania, the Polish Republic and East Prussia.

The Conference has agreed in principle to the proposal of the Soviet Government concerning the ultimate transfer to the Soviet Union of the City of Koenigsberg and the area adjacent to it as described above subject to expert examination of the actual frontier.

The President of the United States and the British Prime Minister have declared that they will support the proposal of the Conference at the forthcoming peace settlement.

VI. WAR CRIMINALS.

The Three Governments have taken note of the discussions which have been proceeding in recent weeks in London between British, United States, Soviet and French representatives with a view to reaching agreement on the methods of trial of those major war criminals whose crimes under the Moscow Declaration of October, 1943 have no particular geographical localization. The Three Governments reaffirm their intention to bring these criminals to swift and sure justice. They hope that the negotiations in London will result in speedy agreement being reached for this purpose, and they regard it as a matter of great importance that the trial of these major criminals should begin at the earliest possible date. The first list of defendants will be published before 1st September.

VII. AUSTRIA.

The Conference examined a proposal by the Soviet Government on the extension of the authority of the Austrian Provisional Government to all of Austria.

The three governments agreed that they were prepared to examine this question after the entry of the British and American forces into the city of Vienna.

It was agreed that reparations should not be exacted from Austria.

VIII. POLAND.
A. DECLARATION.

We have taken note with pleasure of the agreement reached among representative Poles from Poland and abroad which has made possible the formation, in accordance with the decisions reached at the Crimea Conference, of a Polish Provisional Government of National Unity recognized by the Three Powers. The establishment by the British and United States Governments of diplomatic relations with the Polish Provisional Government of National Unity has resulted in the withdrawal of their recognition from the former Polish Government in London, which no longer exists.

The British and United States Governments have taken measures to protect the interest of the Polish Provisional Government of National Unity as the recognized government of the Polish State in the property belonging to the Polish State located in their territories and under their control, whatever the form of this property may be. They have further taken measures to prevent alienation to third parties of such property. All proper facilities will be given to the Polish Provisional Government of National Unity for the exercise of the ordinary legal remedies for the recovery of any property belonging to the Polish State which may have been wrongfully alienated.

The Three Powers are anxious to assist the Polish Provisional Government of National Unity in facilitating the return to Poland as soon as practicable of all Poles abroad who wish to go, including members of the Polish Armed Forces and the Merchant Marine. They expect that those Poles who return home shall be accorded personal and property rights on the same basis as all Polish citizens

The Three Powers note that the Polish Provisional Government of National Unity, in accordance with the decisions of the Crimea Conference, has agreed to the holding of free and unfettered elections as soon as possible on the basis of universal suffrage and secret ballot in which all democratic and anti-Nazi parties shall have the right to take part and to put forward candidates, and that representatives of the Allied press shall enjoy full freedom to report to the world upon developments in Poland before and during the elections.

B. WESTERN FRONTIER OF POLAND.

In conformity with the agreement on Poland reached at the Crimea Conference the three Heads of Government have sought the opinion of the Polish Provisional Government of National Unity in regard to the accession of territory in the north 'end west which Poland should receive. The President of the National Council of Poland and members of the Polish Provisional Government of National Unity have been received at the Conference and have fully presented their views. The three Heads of Government reaffirm their opinion that the final delimitation of the western frontier of Poland should await the peace settlement.

The three Heads of Government agree that, pending the final determination of Poland's western frontier, the former German territories east of a line running from the Baltic Sea immediately west of Swinamunde, and thence along the Oder River to the confluence of the western Neisse River and along the Western Neisse to the Czechoslovak frontier, including that portion of East Prussia not placed under the administration of the Union of Soviet Socialist Republics in accordance with the understanding reached at this conference and including the area of the former free city of Danzig, shall be under the administration of the Polish State and for such purposes should not be considered as part of the Soviet zone of occupation in Germany.

IX. CONCLUSION on PEACE TREATIES AND ADMISSION TO THE UNITED NATIONS ORGANIZATION.

The three Governments consider it desirable that the present anomalous position of Italy, Bulgaria, Finland, Hungary and Rumania should be terminated by the conclusion of Peace Treaties. They trust that the other interested Allied Governments will share these views.

For their part the three Governments have included the preparation of a Peace Treaty for Italy as the first among the immediate important tasks to be undertaken by the new Council of Foreign Ministers. Italy was the first of the Axis Powers to break with Germany, to whose defeat she has made a material contribution, and has now joined with the Allies in the struggle against Japan. Italy has freed herself from the Fascist regime and is making good progress towards reestablishment of a democratic government and institutions. The conclusion of such a Peace Treaty with a recognized and democratic Italian Government will make it possible for the three Governments to fulfill their desire to support an application from Italy for membership of the United Nations.

The three Governments have also charged the Council of Foreign Ministers with the task of preparing Peace Treaties for Bulgaria, Finland, Hungary and Rumania.

The conclusion of Peace Treaties with recognized democratic governments in these States will also enable the three Governments to support applications from them for membership of the United Nations. The three Governments agree to examine each separately in the near future in the light of the conditions then prevailing, the establishment of diplomatic relations with Finland, Rumania, Bulgaria, and Hungary to the extent possible prior to the conclusion of peace treaties with those countries.

The three Governments have no doubt that in view of the changed conditions resulting from the termination of the war in Europe, representatives of the Allied press will enjoy full freedom to report to the world upon developments in Rumania, Bulgaria, Hungary and Finland.

As regards the admission of other States into the United Nations Organization, Article 4 of the Charter of the United Nations declares that:

1. Membership in the United Nations is open to all other peace-loving States who accept the obligations contained in the present Charter and, in the judgment of the organization, are able and willing to carry out these obligations;

2. The admission of any such State to membership in the United Nations will be effected by a decision of the General Assembly upon the recommendation of the Security Council.

The three Governments, so far as they are concerned, will support applications for membership from those States which have remained neutral during the war and which fulfill the qualifications set out above.

The three Governments feel bound however to make it clear that they for their part would not favour any application for membership put forward by the present Spanish Government, which, having been founded with the support of the Axis Powers, does not, in view of its origins, its nature, its record and its close association with the aggressor States, possess the qualifications necessary to justify such membership.

X. TERRITORIAL TRUSTEESHIP.

The Conference examined a proposal by the Soviet Government on the question of trusteeship territories as defined in the decision of the Crimea Conference and in the Charter of the United Nations Organization.

After an exchange of views on this question it was decided that the disposition of any former Italian colonial territories was one to be decided in connection with the preparation of a peace treaty for Italy and that the question of Italian colonial territory would be considered by the September Council of Ministers of Foreign Affairs.

XI. REVISED ALLIED CONTROL COMMISSION PROCEDURE IN RUMANIA, BULGARIA, AND HUNGARY.

The three Governments took note that the Soviet Representatives on the Allied Control Commissions in Rumania, Bulgaria, and Hungary, have communicated to their United Kingdom and United States colleagues proposals for improving the work of the Control Commissions, now that hostilities in Europe have ceased.

The three Governments agreed that the revision of the procedures of the Allied Control Commissions in these countries would now be undertaken, taking into account the interests and responsibilities of the three Governments which together presented the terms of armistice to the respective countries, and accepting as a basis, in respect of all three countries, the Soviet Government's proposals for Hungary as annexed hereto. (Annex I)

XII. ORDERLY TRANSFER OF GERMAN POPULATIONS.

The Three Governments, having considered the question in all its aspects, recognize that the transfer to Germany of German populations, or elements thereof, remaining in Poland, Czechoslovakia and Hungary, will have to be undertaken. They agree that any transfers that take place should be effected in an orderly and humane manner.

Since the influx of a large number of Germans into Germany would increase the burden already resting on the occupying authorities, they consider that the Control Council in Germany should in the first instance examine the problem, with special regard to the question of the equitable distribution of these Germans among the several zones of occupation. They are accordingly instructing their respective representatives on the Control Council to report to their Governments as soon as possible the extent to which such persons have already entered Germany from Poland, Czechoslovakia and Hungary, to submit an estimate of the time and rate at which further transfers could be carried out having regard to the present situation in Germany.

The Czechoslovak Government, the Polish Provisional Government and the Control Council in Hungary are at the same time being informed of the above and are being requested meanwhile to suspend further expulsions pending an examination by the Governments concerned of the report from their representatives on the Control Council.

XIII. OIL EQUIPMENT IN RUMANIA.

The Conference agreed to set up two bilateral commissions of experts, one to be composed of United Kingdom and Soviet Members and one to be composed of United States and Soviet Members, to investigate the facts and examine the documents, as a basis for the settlement of questions arising from the removal of oil equipment in Rumania. It was further agreed that these experts shall begin their work within ten days, on the spot.

XIV. IRAN.

It was agreed that Allied troops should be withdrawn immediately from Tehran, and that further stages of the withdrawal of troops from Iran should be considered at the meeting of the Council of Foreign Ministers to be held in London in September, 1945.

XV. THE INTERNATIONAL ZONE OF TANGIER.

A proposal by the Soviet Government was examined and the following decisions were reached:

Having examined the question of the Zone of Tangier, the three Governments have agreed that this Zone, which includes the City of Tangier and the area adjacent to it, in view of its special strategic importance, shall remain international.

The question of Tangier will be discussed in the near future at a meeting in Paris of representatives of the Governments of the Union of Soviet Socialist Republics, the United States of America, the United Kingdom and France.

XVI. THE BLACK SEA STRAITS.

The Three Governments recognized that the Convention concluded at Montreux should be revised as failing to meet present-day conditions.

It was agreed that as the next step the matter should be the subject of direct conversations between each of the three Governments and the Turkish Government.

XVII. INTERNATIONAL INLAND WATERWAYS.

The Conference considered a proposal of the U.S. Delegation on this subject and agreed to refer it for consideration to the forthcoming meeting of the Council of Foreign Ministers in London.

XVIII. EUROPEAN INLAND TRANSPORT CONFERENCE.

The British and U.S. Delegations to the Conference informed the Soviet Delegation of the desire of the British and U.S. Governments to reconvene the European Inland Transport Conference and stated that they would welcome assurance that the Soviet Government would participate in the work of the reconvened conference. The Soviet Government agreed that it would participate in this conference.

XIX. DIRECTIVES TO MILITARY COMMANDERS ON ALLIED CONTROL COUNCIL FOR GERMANY.

The Three Governments agreed that each would send a directive to its representative on the Control Council for Germany informing him of all decisions of the Conference affecting matters within the scope of his duties.

XX. USE OF ALLIED PROPERTY FOR SATELLITE REPARATIONS OR WAR TROPHIES.

The proposal (Annex II) presented by the United States Delegation was accepted in principle by the Conference, but the drafting of an agreement on the matter was left to be worked out through diplomatic channels.

XXI. MILITARY TALKS.

During the Conference there were meetings between the Chiefs of Staff of the Three Governments on military matters of common interest.

ANNEX I

TEXT OF A LETTER TRANSMITTED ON JULY 12 TO THE REPRESENTATIVES OF THE U.S. AND

U. K. GOVERNMENTS ON THE ALLIED CONTROL COMMISSION IN HUNGARY.

In view of the changed situation in connection with the termination of the war against Germany, the Soviet Government finds it necessary to establish the following order of work for the Allied Control Commission [ACC] in Hungary.

1. During the period up to the conclusion of peace with Hungary the President (or Vice-President) of the ACC will regularly call conferences with the British and American representatives for the purpose of discussing the most important questions relating to the work of the ACC. The conferences will be called once in 10 days, or more frequently in case of need.

Directives of the ACC on questions or principle will be issued to the Hungarian authorities by the President of the Allied Control Commission after agreement on these directives with the English and American representatives.

2. The British and American representatives in the ACC will take part in general conferences of heads of divisions and delegates of the ACC, convoked by the President of the ACC, which meetings will be regular in nature. The British and American representatives will also participate personally or through their representatives in appropriate instances in mixed commissions created by the President of the ACC for questions connected with the execution by the ACC of its functions

3. Free movement by the American and British representatives in the country will be permitted provided that the ACC is previously informed of the time and route of the journeys.

4. All questions connected with permission for the entrance and exit of members of the staff of the British and American representatives in Hungary will be decided on the spot by the President of the ACC within a time limit of not more than one week.

5. The bringing in and sending out by plane of mail, cargoes and diplomatic couriers will be carried out by the British and American representatives on the ACC under arrangements and within time limits established by the ACC, or in special cases by previous coordination with the President of the ACC.

I consider it necessary to add to the above that in all other points the existing Statutes regarding the ACC in Hungary, which was confirmed on January 20, 1945, shall remain in force in the future.

ANNEX II
USE OF ALLIED PROPERTY FOR SATELITE REPARATIONS OR WAR TROPHIES

1. The burden of reparation and "war trophies" should not fall on Allied nationals.

2. Capital Equipment—We object to the removal of such Allied property as reparations, "war trophies," or under any other guise. Loss would accrue to Allied nationals as a result of destruction of plants and the consequent loss of markets and trading connections. Seizure of Allied property makes impossible the fulfillment by the satellite of its obligation under the armistice to restore intact the rights and interests of the Allied Nations and their nationals.

The United States looks to the other occupying powers for the return of any equipment already removed and the cessation of removals. Where such equipment will not or cannot be returned, the U.S. will demand of the satellite adequate, effective and prompt compensation to American nationals, and that such compensation have priority equal to that of the reparations payment.

These principles apply to all property wholly or substantially owned by Allied nationals. In the event of removals of property in which the American as well as the entire Allied interest is less than substantial, the U.S. expects adequate, effective, and prompt compensation.

3. Current Production—While the U.S. does not oppose reparation out of current production of Allied investments, the satellite must provide immediate and adequate compensation to the Allied nationals including sufficient foreign exchange or products so that they can recover reasonable foreign currency expenditures and transfer a reasonable return on their investment. Such compensation must also have equal priority with reparations.

We deem it essential that the satellites not conclude treaties, agreements or arrangements which deny to Allied nationals access, on equal terms, to their trade, raw materials and industry; and appropriately- modify any existing arrangements which may have that effect.

(b) Proclamation Defining Terms for Japanese Surrender, July 26, 1945

(1) We—The President of the United States, the

President of the National Government of the Republic of China, and the Prime Minister of Great Britain, representing the hundreds of millions of our countrymen, have conferred and agree that Japan shall be given an opportunity to end this war.

(2) The prodigious land, sea and air forces of the United States, the British Empire and of China, many times reinforced by their armies and air fleets from the west, are poised to strike the final blows upon Japan. This military power is sustained and inspired by the determination of all the Allied Nations to prosecute the war against Japan until she ceases to resist.

(3) The result of the futile and senseless German resistance to the might of the aroused free peoples of the world stands forth in awful clarity as an example to the people of Japan. The might that now converges on Japan is immeasurably greater than that which, when applied to the resisting Nazis, necessarily laid waste to the lands, the industry and the method of life of the whole German people. The full application of our military power, backed by our resolve, All mean the inevitable and complete destruction of the Japanese armed forces and just as inevitably the utter devastation of the Japanese homeland.

(4) The time has come for Japan to decide whether she will continue to be controlled by those self-willed militaristic advisers whose unintelligent calculations have brought the Empire of Japan to the threshold of annihilation, or whether she will follow the path of reason.

(5) Following are our terms. We will not deviate from them. There are no alternatives. We shall brook no delay.

(6) There must be eliminated for all time the authority and influence of those who have deceived and misled the people of Japan into embarking on world conquest, for we insist that a new order of peace security and justice will be impossible until irresponsible militarism is driven from the world.

(7) Until such a new order is established and until there is convincing proof that Japan's war-making power is destroyed, points in Japanese territory to be designated by the Allies shall be occupied to secure the achievement of the basic objectives we are here setting forth.

(8) The terms of the Cairo Declaration shall be carried out and Japanese sovereignty shall be limited to the islands of Honshu, Hokkaido, Kyushu, Shikoku and such minor islands as we determine.

(9) The Japanese military forces, after being completely disarmed, shall be permitted to return to their homes with the opportunity to lead peaceful and productive lives.

(10) We do not intend that the Japanese shall be enslaved as a race or destroyed as a nation, but stern justice shall be meted out to all war criminals, including those who have visited cruelties upon our prisoners. The Japanese Government shall remove all obstacles to the revival and strengthening of democratic tendencies among the Japanese people. Freedom of speech, of religion, and of thought, as well as respect for the fundamental human rights shall be established.

(11) Japan shall be permitted to maintain such industries as will sustain her economy and permit the exaction of just reparations in kind, but not those [industries] which would enable her to re-arm for war. To this end, access to, as distinguished from control of, raw materials shall be permitted. Eventual Japanese participation in world trade relations shall be permitted.

(12) The occupying forces of the Allies shall be withdrawn from Japan as soon as these objectives have been accomplished and there has been established in accordance with the freely expressed will of the Japanese people a peacefully inclined and responsible government.

(13) We call upon the government of Japan to proclaim now the unconditional surrender of all Japanese armed forces, and to provide proper and adequate assurances of their good faith in such action. The alternative for Japan is prompt and utter destruction.

GLOSSARY

potash: potassium carbonate

tripartite: divided into or consisting of three parts

Document Analysis

After Germany formally surrendered in May 1945, President Truman, Premier Stalin, and Prime Ministers Churchill and Attlee were able to build on the groundwork that had been laid at Yalta when they convened at the Potsdam Conference in July. The main areas of focus of the Potsdam Agreement are the establishment of a council that would resolve latent territorial and security issues from the war, addressing postwar Germany and redrawing national borders (including establishing areas of influence) that had been erased during the war.

The first focal point the Potsdam Agreement addresses is the establishment of a Council of Foreign Ministers. This council is to be comprised of representatives from the United States, the Soviet Union, and the United Kingdom, as well as China and France (neither of which were represented at Potsdam and, therefore, required an invitation to join). This organization is to meet periodically to address unresolved territorial disputes and formalize treaties with Italy, Bulgaria, Hungary, Romania, and Finland. The council will also serve as the successor to the European Advisory Commission, which had already divided Germany into zones occupied by the Allies; the Potsdam Agreement concludes that the European Advisory Commission is to be summarily dissolved. The agreement also addresses territories gained or liberated by the Allies during the war, including Soviet-acquired territories extending westward to (and including) the easternmost German city of Königsberg in the Baltic region.

One of the most pressing issues facing the Potsdam Conference was the question of Germany. The Potsdam Agreement supports the Agreement on Control of Machinery in Germany, which had been signed at the European Advisory Commission in July 1945, and divides Germany into four separate zones of occupation, overseen by United States, the United Kingdom, the Soviet Union, and France. The agreement states that Germany's military, economic, and political infrastructures be either fully dismantled or redirected in such a way that they prevented any future resurgence of Nazi groups or other nationalistic, militaristic trends in that country. The document lays plans for Germany's military (including the navy and merchant marine, in particular) to be completely dissolved, with weaponry destroyed, and for the Nazi Party to be fully abolished, with its members purged from government and replaced with democratically-elected leaders. Furthermore, the agreement calls for German war criminals to be captured and placed on trial for their actions. On the economic side, the Potsdam Agreement outlines plans for Germany's main industries to be strictly regulated, with an emphasis placed on traditional, nonviolent areas such as agriculture, fishing, and forestry. Finally, the agreement establishes a system by which German reparations should be paid to the Allies.

In addition to the aforementioned issues surrounding Germany and territories gained by the Allies, the Potsdam Agreement addresses the establishment of a Polish provisional government as well as the extension of Poland's borders to the Oder and Neisse Rivers, known as the Oder-Neisse line. The Potsdam Agreement attempts to compensate for Polish territorial losses in the east to the Soviet Union, which had been agreed upon at the Yalta Conference, by extending the Polish borders westward into Germany. Poland had been invaded in September 1939 by Germany from the west and the Soviet Union from the east and remained a major postwar issue in terms of rebuilding that nation's government. Questions also remained about Soviet-occupied territory and resettling the millions of Poles who had either fled or were deported from their homeland after these invasions. The Potsdam Agreement asserts that Poles returning to their home country "shall be accorded personal and property rights on the same basis as all Polish citizens."

The agreement also establishes rules for the conduct of the occupying powers. Those forces that destroyed property or natural resources, as well as those who took "war trophies," while serving in occupied territories would be expected to account for and compensate the governments of those territories. Similarly, any war trophies regained by the Allies from defeated Axis forces should be returned.

Finally, the Allies used Potsdam as a platform to offer Japan terms for its unconditional surrender. The European victory, the leaders said, should send a message to the Japanese emperor that his own country's defeat was imminent. The Potsdam Agreement calls upon Japan to immediately disarm and return any illegally conquered lands. Such a step would be toward international peace, the leaders advised; refusal to agree to the Allied terms of surrender, on the other hand, would result in Japan's "prompt and utter destruction."

Essential Themes

The Potsdam Conference convened in the wake of the surrender of Germany in the spring of 1945. The conference's main three participants—US president Truman, Soviet premier Stalin, and British prime ministers Churchill and then Attlee—used the opportunity to build on the foundation laid at the Yalta Conference earlier in the year. With what the participants saw as an inevitable victory over Japan, the conferees set out to create a framework to dissolve German military forces and Nazi organizations, to address latent security and territorial issues, and to establish a plan to repatriate millions of wartime refugees.

Central to addressing a wide range of wartime and postwar security and territorial issues was the Council of Foreign Ministers, which this agreement established would be comprised of the United States, Soviet Union, and United Kingdom, as well as France and China. Other issues—such as the Baltic territories acquired by the Soviet Union during the war and the Polish question—were given significant exposure at this conference, although the Soviet Union's established presence and clout in these regions largely rendered such issues moot. Many historians point to the Yalta and Potsdam Conferences as the groundwork for the subsequent Cold War, particularly for the decision to divide Germany into separate zones of occupation and for granting British and American recognition of Soviet control in Eastern Europe. For example, although the Potsdam Agreement asserted that the Polish Provisional Government of National Unity would hold "free and unfettered elections as soon as possible," these elections were postponed and manipulated by Soviet and Polish Communists.

—*Michael P. Auerbach, MA*

Bibliography and Additional Reading

Dobbs, Michael. *Six Months in 1945: FDR, Stalin, Churchill, and Truman—From World War to Cold War.* New York: Vintage, 2013. Print.

Piotrowski, Tadeusz, ed. *The Polish Deportees of World War II: Recollections of Removal to the Soviet Union and Dispersal throughout the World.* Jefferson: McFarland, 2004. Print.

Plokhy, S. M. *Yalta: The Price of Peace.* New York: Viking, 2010. Print.

"The Potsdam Conference, 1945." *Office of the Historian.* United States Dept. of State, n.d. Web. 7 Jan. 2014.

■ Statement by General MacArthur on the Occupation of Japan

Date: September 14, 1945
Author: Douglas MacArthur
Genre: letter

Summary Overview

Shortly after the official surrender of Japan in September 1945, General Douglas MacArthur issued a statement in response to press reports that the American occupation of Japan was not proceeding in optimal or timely fashion. MacArthur argued that Japan was on the brink of total military, political, and economic collapse thanks to the American victory. He added that the occupation should not proceed hastily, however, as the total demobilization of the Japanese military, as well as the reconstruction of the postwar Japanese government, would take time, patience, and precision.

Defining Moment

In 1941, the United States was embroiled in military conflicts in both Europe and the Pacific. US engagement in the Pacific was brutal and exhaustive. As US forces advanced toward Japan, the casualties grew. At Guadalcanal, sixteen hundred American servicemen were killed in action. At Iwo Jima in 1944, more than twenty-five thousand US and Japanese troops lost their lives. At the Battle of Okinawa, more than ninety thousand Americans and Japanese were killed. The Japanese fiercely defended their homeland, while US forces pushed closer toward the invasion and occupation of Japan.

Because of both the mounting casualties and the Japanese refusal to surrender, US president Harry S. Truman decided to use the atomic bomb on two Japanese cities (Hiroshima and Nagasaki) in August 1945 in an attempt to end the war. In light of the cataclysmic casualties and destruction the atomic bombs caused, Japanese emperor Hirohito and his advisors agreed to surrender on August 14, announcing the decision to the Japanese people via radio the following day. Three days later, a US delegation landed on an island near Okinawa to meet with a Japanese delegation. General MacAr-

thur, the supreme commander for the Allied Powers, did not participate in the negotiations, which included Japanese acceptance of the terms of surrender set forth by the Potsdam Conference in early August.

MacArthur later flew to Tokyo to finalize the agreement reached at Okinawa. MacArthur proclaimed that Japan's military power was to be destroyed, its war criminals prosecuted, and the government in Tokyo replaced with a democratic system, and Japanese society was to be liberated from the oppressive environment Hirohito had imposed. MacArthur's attitude toward the postwar Japanese was to assume a "paternal" role, attempting to remake Japan into a peaceful country by reshaping Japanese society through democracy. Meanwhile, US forces took over virtually every aspect of Japan's government, economy, and society as the occupation of that nation began.

Author Biography

Douglas MacArthur was born on an Army base in Little Rock, Arkansas, on January 26, 1880. His father, General Arthur MacArthur, Jr., was a celebrated military leader during the Spanish-American War, but he was ousted in 1901 for insubordination. MacArthur graduated from West Point at the top of his class in 1903. Although he was reprimanded occasionally for insubordination, MacArthur rose quickly through the ranks in light of his heroics during World War I. After serving as superintendent at West Point, MacArthur was recalled to active duty by President Franklin D. Roosevelt in 1941. A general by this point, MacArthur led the US Far East campaign. In 1945, President Harry S. Truman appointed him supreme commander for the Allied Powers, overseeing the US occupation of Japan until war broke out on the Korean Peninsula in 1950. He was relieved of his command in 1951, after repeatedly criticizing Truman's strategy in Korea. MacArthur would advise later presidents on military strategy. He died on April 5, 1964, in Washington, DC.

HISTORICAL DOCUMENT

I have noticed some impatience in the press, based upon the assumption of a so-called soft policy in Japan. This can only arise from an erroneous concept of what is occurring.

The first phase of the occupation must of necessity be based on military considerations which involved the deployment forward of our troops and the disarming and demobilization of the enemy. This is coupled with the paramount consideration of withdrawing our former prisoners of war and war internees from internment camps and evacuating them to their homes.

Safety and security require that all of the steps shall proceed with precision and completeness, lest calamity may be precipitated.

The military phase is proceeding in an entirely satisfactory way.

Over half of the enemy's force in Japan proper is now demobilized and the entire program will be practically complete by the middle of October. During this interval of time, safety and complete security must be assured.

When the first phase is completed, other phases as provided in the surrender terms will infallibly follow. No one need have any doubt about the prompt, complete, entire fulfillment of the terms of surrender. The process, however, takes time. It is well understandable that in the face of atrocities committed by the enemy there should be impatience. This natural impulse, however, should be tempered by the fact that security and military expediency still require an exercise of some restraint. The surrender terms aren't soft and they won't be applied in kid-glove fashion.

Economically and industrially as well as militarily, Japan is completely exhausted and depleted. She is in a condition of utter collapse. Her governmental structure is controlled completely by occupation forces and is operating only to the extent necessary to insure such an orderly and controlled procedure as will prevent social chaos, disease and starvation.

The over-all objectives for Japan have been clearly outlined in the surrender terms and will be accomplished in an orderly, concise and comprehensive way without delays beyond those imposed by the magnitude of the physical problems involved.

It is extraordinarily difficult for me at times to exercise that degree of patience which is unquestionably demanded if the long-time policies which have been decreed are to be successfully accomplished without repercussions which would be detrimental to the well-being of the world, but I am restraining myself to the best of my ability and am generally satisfied with the progress being made.

Document Analysis

General MacArthur issued this statement in the wake of what he believed to be an "erroneous" public perception that the occupation of Japan was proceeding neither at an agreeable pace nor in a successful manner. MacArthur reaffirms the immediate goals of the occupation—namely the dismantlement of the Japanese military and imperial government as well as the pacification of the Japanese people. In pursuit of each goal, he says, the occupying US force was achieving great success despite what he sees as great challenges (in both Japan and around the world) to their satisfactory accomplishment.

MacArthur describes the pursuit of each goal as a delicate and deliberate process. MacArthur says that each phase of the demilitarization program—the most pressing element of the postwar occupation—for example, is proceeding positively and at a reasonable pace. The total dismantlement of the sizable Japanese military would take time, he says, but any actions taken to hasten the process could result in a backlash with calamitous results. An approach that underscores the need for an emphasis on security and safety overrides the need for any effort to speed up the process, he says.

MacArthur says that providing an update on the state of Japan within the context of the occupation is important to do. He notes that every element of Japan's infrastructure has been "exhausted," and the military is being deconstructed after having been defeated on the Pacific. The country's industrial sector is depleted, he adds, as is the Japanese economy as a whole. Even the government, with its imperial underpinnings removed as a result of the surrender, is on the verge of total collapse. The US occupying forces are the only factor keeping the nation from imploding completely, MacArthur says. Still, he argues, the US has sufficiently kept these sectors upright to keep the country out of utter chaos until the Japanese can rebuild in a peaceful manner consistent with the terms of surrender.

MacArthur reiterates the complexity of the operation, which entails not only completely deconstructing the Japanese military and imperial infrastructures, but also replacing them. This work is delicate, he advises. After all, the effort is burdened with the stress of impatience from the United States and other nations, all of which witnessed and/or suffered from war atrocities committed by the Japanese military. With Japan finally defeated, these foreign nations have pushed for immediate results—the total demilitarization and pacification of Japan—from the occupying forces. MacArthur, who admits to wishing for a similar result, nonetheless advises that the pursuit of the goals outlined in the terms of surrender must proceed at a reasonable pace. He argues that expediting the process might create a backlash that could undermine the occupation's ability to steer postwar Japan toward a lasting peaceful mentality.

Essential Themes

The 1945 surrender and subsequent occupation of Japan represented a major shift in the power structure of East Asia and the Pacific. Japan had been defeated on battlefields within its own territory, seen its civilian population bombed heavily, and was devastated by the awesome destruction of two atomic bombs. After years of ruthless war, Japan teetered on the edge of total collapse politically, economically, and socially. Helmed by General Douglas MacArthur, the US-led occupation

was charged with replacing Japan's militaristic infrastructure with a more democratic and stable framework.

MacArthur understood the enormous pressure exerted by China, Korea, the United States, and other nations to swiftly dismantle and pacify Japan. In this statement, he admitted to sharing such sentiment. However, he argued, the process of deconstruction and reconstruction in Japan was not one that could be hastened. Japan was in a delicate and precarious state; any effort to speed up this process could result in a backlash that could destabilize and undo the occupation's efforts.

MacArthur reminded his audience that he was fully versed in the terms of Japanese surrender. He stated that the Japanese military was being dismantled at as fast a pace as possible. The more precarious phase—namely the replacement of the imperial government with a democratic system, management of nonmilitary industries, and the pacification of the Japanese people—would take more time than the simple collection of arms. Nonetheless, he concluded, the occupation was proceeding in a manner consistent with the goals set forth in the terms of surrender.

—*Michael P. Auerbach, MA*

Bibliography and Additional Reading

Buckley, Roger, ed. *The Post-War Occupation of Japan, 1945–1952: Surrender, 1945*. 10 Vols. Leiden: Global Oriental, 2011. Print.

Dower, John. *War without Mercy*. New York: Pantheon, 1993. Print.

Manchester, William. *American Caesar: Douglas MacArthur 1880–1964*. 1978. New York: Little, 2008. Print.

Takemae, Eiji. *Allied Occupation of Japan*. London: A&C Black, 2003. Print.

"World War II Timeline." *National Geographic*. National Geographic Soc., 2001. Web. 6 Jan. 2015.

■ No Sacrificing of Basic Principles for Expediency

Date: October 6, 1945
Author: John Foster Dulles
Genre: speech

Summary Overview

After World War II ended with the defeat of Nazi Germany and Japan, key countries of the victorious Allied Powers, including the United States, Great Britain, and the Soviet Union, began constructing plans for the postwar world. John Foster Dulles, at the time the chief adviser to the secretary of state, acknowledged that this was no easy task, as the experience of the peace talks at the end of World War I had taught him. Rather than making the world "safe for democracy," as American president Woodrow Wilson had put it, the Treaty of Versailles became a pretext and prelude to another war. It was much easier for allies to agree upon war strategy to defeat their common enemies than it was to determine the best course of action for the future of mankind in a time of hopeful peace. However, that is exactly what the Council of Foreign Ministers—the representatives of five major Allied countries—set out to do in their talks during October 1945.

Defining Moment

With the conclusion of World War II came a determination not to repeat the mistakes that had characterized the peace negotiations at the end of World War I. Although US president Woodrow Wilson had outlined an idealistic vision of the future and emphasized the role of the League of Nations in peacefully resolving differences between nations, the other allies that had borne the brunt of the fighting for the majority of the war— Great Britain, France, and Italy—were more concerned about punishing Germany for what they saw as its key role in starting the war. Emphasizing large reparations that would keep Germany impoverished, land concessions to each of the European nations to keep Germany small, and disarmament to keep Germany weak, the penalties imposed had the opposite effect, as Germany rearmed and became aggressive again after the rise of Adolf Hitler during the late 1920s and 1930s. Further, the League of Nations was less effective than it might

have been because the United States did not participate.

During World War II, John Foster Dulles, a Republican, worked to create a new international organization that would take the place of the League of Nations once the war was over. He insisted that rather than shrinking from the world stage after the war, the United States must be prominently involved in what would become the United Nations. Only with the active leadership of the United States could the United Nations become the international advocate for peace. Dulles participated in the Dumbarton Oaks Conference—which outlined the future United Nations—that took place as Allied forces drove into Nazi Germany in late 1944. As the war drew to a conclusion, the Allied leaders, meeting at Potsdam in mid-1945, created the Council of Foreign Ministers, which met shortly after the conclusion of the Potsdam Conference to draw up the peace treaties with the Axis nations.

The Council of Foreign Ministers consisted of representatives from the United States, Great Britain, the Soviet Union, France, and China. Meeting first in London in September 1945, the council sought to begin the work of creating peace treaties between the Allies and Bulgaria, Finland, Hungary, Italy, and Romania, as well as laying the groundwork for a treaty with Germany by negotiating the territorial claims that the victorious nations might have against Germany. However, the council was not able to come to an agreement at the end of the London conference, largely because of the lack of cooperation on the part of the Soviet Union, which did not want peace treaties concluded until its dominant position in Eastern Europe was made permanent by the installation of Communist governments.

Author Biography

Grandson of Secretary of State John W. Foster and nephew of Secretary of State Robert Lansing, John

Foster Dulles seemed destined for a career in international relations. At the Paris Peace Conference at the end of World War I, he was appointed by President Wilson to serve as legal counsel for Lansing. He opposed the reparations that the other Allies demanded from Germany, which played a large role in setting the stage for a second war. After serving as foreign policy advisor for Democratic presidential candidate Thomas E. Dewey in 1944, Dulles was appointed as an advisor to the Council of Foreign Ministers by President Harry S. Truman. Dulles became secretary of state in 1953, serving until April 1959, at which time he resigned because of his failing health. He died a month later.

HISTORICAL DOCUMENT

At London the Council of Foreign Ministers began the task of peace making. This is no easy task. It is not a matter of victors imposing their will upon defeated enemies. When we get to that, it will be easy. Before we get to that, the victors must try to agree on what their joint will shall be. So, we are not now negotiating peace with Italy or Rumania or Germany. We are negotiating peace with the Soviet Union, Great Britain, France and other United Nations. These nations have different interests and different ideals. To reconcile them is not a process of coercion but of reason.

I am under no illusion that that will be an easy task. I was at the peace conference which followed the First World War and there learned, at first hand, how difficult it is for a war coalition to maintain unity after victory has been won. It is possible that, this time also, we shall not agree on the post-war settlement. If that happens, it would lead to different nations' carrying out their will in particular areas. That is not necessarily a permanent disaster, but it would be most unfortunate. It would tend to divide the world into blocs and spheres of influence. That would be a bad heritage for the victors to bequeath the United Nations Organization.

Final Agreement Seen

So far as the United States delegation to London is concerned, we are determined to preserve in peace the unity we had in war and to apply the lesson we have so painfully learned, that peace is indivisible. There will be no bloc of Western powers if the United States can avoid it. Also, I may say, nothing that has happened so far makes me feel that we may not all come to agree.

I realize that it came as a shock to the American people that the Council of Foreign Ministers ended their first session without producing a public statement of unity and accomplishment. That is because for over four years every meeting of representatives of the great powers was followed by a pronouncement which gave the impression that complete harmony had been achieved. That was a war diet of soothing syrup. The reality was that there was unity in so far as it related to joint effort against common enemies. But behind that there have always been the differences which are now coming to light.

It is not healthy, and I am glad that it is no longer necessary, to try to cover up the fact that we have differences. Only if our people realize the magnitude of the task we face will we put forward the effort and achieve the unity needed for success.

I said that in the task upon which we have embarked the permissible tool is reason, not coercion. The American delegation was alive to that. We presented only propositions which seemed to us to be reasonable.

Basic Principles Espoused

The basic principles which we espoused were these:

1. Territorial settlements should, as far as possible, conform to the wishes of the peoples concerned. Strategic and economic considerations ought to be subordinated to human considerations. This principle would call for some territorial readjustments. But it would not give to Yugoslavia the large Italian population of Trieste.

2. The treaties should realize the conception of an international bill of rights. At Moscow in 1943 the Big Three had agreed that they sought for Italy a regime which would assure the Italian people freedom of speech, religious worship, political belief and public meeting. We were determined that the treaties of peace should give reality to that goal and make a practical beginning in the

great project of assuring to all the enjoyment of human rights and fundamental freedoms.

3. Colonies should be dealt with primarily from the standpoint of the welfare of the colonial peoples and, as in the case of territorial adjustments, human considerations should prevail over strategic and commercial considerations. We called for independence within a fixed term and we proposed trusteeship by the United Nations Organization, rather than by any single power. That was the only solution which would avoid a disastrous struggle between the great powers for colonial prizes. Without it, there was no way to decide the rival claims for the Italian colonies of North Africa.

Supervision of Armaments

4. Armament of our ex-enemies should be limited and subjected to a system of supervision which would prevent secret rearmament as occurred after the last war in the case of Germany. This supervision is particularly important in view of the development of modern weapons of vast destructive power. This, we felt, compelled the inauguration of a system, which might later on be extended, whereby the human race would have facilities to protect itself against its own total destruction.

5. Finally we made it clear that we could not negotiate and conclude treaties of peace with governments which, as in Rumania, failed to provide those freedoms which, in conjunction with the Soviet Union and Great Britain, we had promised to seek for the liberated peoples of Europe.

The first ten days of the conference were devoted to considering the application of such principles to Italy, Finland, Rumania and Bulgaria. During the course of these discussions it became increasingly evident that the Soviet Union was dissatisfied with the trend of the conference. The American proposals, which in the main were supported by Great Britain, France and China, cut across certain political ends which the Soviet Union sought. For example, the Soviet Union was disposed to support the claim of Yugoslavia to Trieste. It wanted for itself trusteeship of Italy's most valuable colonial area in North Africa in order that it might develop for itself a great warm-water port in the Mediterranean comparable to what it had obtained in the Far East at Port Arthur and Dairen. Above all, the Soviet delegation objected to the refusal of the United States, under existing conditions, to conclude peace treaties with Rumania and Bulgaria.

Soviet Seeks a Test

It was discussion about Rumania on Sept. 21 which led the Soviet Union on Sept. 22 to move to test out the determination of the United States. The means chosen was to insist on a change of procedure. The underlying and understood purpose was to make it appear that the Soviet Union could and would interrupt any procedure which did not lead to results more satisfactory to it.

A great deal has been said, and much more doubtless will be said, as to whether the procedure under which the Conference was operating was in strict conformity with the Berlin agreement, which established the Council. I do not intend tonight to discuss that highly technical matter. It is not really very important. It is enough to say that the procedure which permitted France and China to be present at all Council meetings, though with no power of vote in certain cases, was agreed to by the Soviet Union on Sept. 11 and had been followed for ten days without question. Certainly the Soviet Union would not have accepted and followed a procedure which it believed to be violative of the Berlin agreement. Only when the procedure failed to produce results satisfactory to the Soviet Union did it demand a change which would have eliminated France and China. That change was demanded as a means of indicating Soviet displeasure with the course the negotiations were taking and as a means of finding out whether or not the United States was really determined to hold the basic principles I have described.

U. S. Unwilling to Sacrifice

The Soviet delegation believed, and rightly believed, that the United States attached great importance to preserving the appearance of unity among the Big Three. They also knew that we were anxious quickly to conclude peace with Italy. They wanted to find out how much of our principle we would sacrifice to attain these goals. They did find out. They found out that the United States was not willing to sacrifice its principles or its historic friendship with China and France.

That American decision vitally concerned the future of our nation. As Secretary Byrnes said last night, I participated with him in the making of that decision. I unqualifiedly concurred in it. However, he, as the Secretary of State, had to assume the primary responsibility, and he is entitled to the support of the American people, without regard to party, in standing for principle rather than expediency, in keeping with the best American tradition.

Let me hasten to say that I have no feeling that the Soviet delegation, in forcing that decision upon us, did anything that was not within their rights. In every important negotiation, public or private, there comes a moment when the negotiators test each other out. It was inevitable that a time should come when the Soviet Union would want to test us out. It is a good thing that that has happened and that it is now behind us.

The American people should see what has happened in its true proportions. We are at the beginning of a long and difficult negotiation which will involve the structure of the post-war world. The Soviet Union wants to know what our political attitude will be toward the states which border them, particularly in the Balkans. They want to know what our attitude is toward sharing with them the control of defeated Japan. They want to know what our attitude will be toward giving them economic aid. These and other matters must, in due course, be explored, and it may be that until that whole area has been explored, progress will be slow.

Good Beginning Made

Let us be calm and be mature. We have made not a bad, but a good, beginning. That beginning has not created difficulties. It has merely revealed difficulties of long standing, which war has obscured. It is healthy that we now know the facts. Furthermore, we have at the beginning shown that we stand firm for basic principles. That is of transcendent importance.

We are emerging from six years of war, during which morality and principle have increasingly been put aside in favor of military expediency. The war has now ended and with that ending principle and morality must be re-established in the world. The United States ought to take a lead in that. We are the only great nation whose people have not been drained, physically and spiritually. It devolves upon us to give leadership in restoring principle as a guide to conduct. If we do not do that, the world will not be worth living in. Indeed, it probably will be a world in which human beings cannot live. For we now know that this planet will, like others, become uninhabitable unless men subject their physical power to the restraints of moral law.

GLOSSARY

violative: involving violation

Document Analysis

Speaking after the conclusion of the London meeting of the Council of Foreign Ministers, Dulles looks both backward and forward. At the end of a four-year alliance between the United States and the Soviet Union, the Soviet actions at the London conference represent a distinct change in orientation. Given that the common enemy has been vanquished, Dulles speaks to the issues emerging in the Allies' attempts to create a peaceful postwar world at a difficult time. The conclusion of a conference demonstrates that negotiations between the victorious nations might be more difficult in peacetime than they had been during the war.

Dulles begins by stating that the negotiations that took place at London were less about peace with the Axis powers than they were about the victorious nations learning how to work together. His experience at Versailles in 1919 taught him "how difficult it is for a war coalition to maintain unity after victory has been won," and the negotiations at London had reinforced the point, as the council had ended the meeting without any agreements, or even a public statement of unity between the powers. Rather, the conference exposed the differences between the powers that Dulles argued had always been there, but had been ignored by all sides during the war.

He then moves on to discuss the "reasonable" proposals shared, for the most part, by the United States,

Great Britain, China, and France, beginning with the idea that people of the conquered regions—whether other nations or former colonies—should have the right of self-determination after the war. Also, he summarizes the point that the defeated powers should be armed for self-defense, but only under the supervision of the Allies. Finally, he emphasizes the belief that peace treaties should only be negotiated with governments that guarantee human rights and freedoms to their citizens. The problem, he concludes, lies in the divergence of opinion on these matters by the Soviet Union.

The Allies had refused to craft a peace treaty with Romania because of its refusal to guarantee human rights. The Soviets wanted a peace treaty that guaranteed that they would play a dominant role in Romania, as well as in the rest of Eastern Europe, and to that end sought to eliminate France and China from the conference. As the Soviet Union had allowed those two nations to take part in the conference earlier in the proceedings, Dulles explains this turn of events as a hypocritical method for the Soviets to undermine the unsatisfactory trajectory of the discussions. However, Dulles paints this first disagreement between the Allies in a positive way, expressing hopes that the US refusal to acquiesce to Soviet demands would set an example and pay dividends by conveying the unswerving resolve of the United States to "give leadership in restoring principle as a guide to conduct."

Essential Themes

At the conclusion of the London conference, Dulles was well aware of the potential problems that characterized the postwar relations between the victorious powers; however, he thought that compromises made between the Americans and Soviets could create a peaceful postwar world. Over the course of the following few years, Dulles would realize that the Soviet Union's geopolitical aims were such that compromise was not an effective paradigm for foreign relations. The realities of what would quickly become the Cold War

revealed that the Soviet intransigence demonstrated for the first time at the London conference was but a harbinger of prolonged political hostility. The Soviet desire to dominate Eastern Europe was not negotiable and would create, more than anything else, the shape of postwar Europe.

Dulles was a staunch opponent of any policies that appeased Soviet demands. As early as 1946, Dulles published an article called "Thoughts on Soviet Foreign Policy and What to Do about It," which argued that the basic ideological differences between the United States and the Soviet Union were likely to lead to conflict between the nations for the foreseeable future. Later meetings of the Council of Foreign Ministers in 1947 strengthened that belief in Dulles.

After Dwight D. Eisenhower became president in January 1953, he appointed Dulles secretary of state; views derived from his encounters with the Soviets at the end of World War II directly shaped American policy. During his term, the basic stance of the United States was that peace with the Soviets could only be forged through the policy of containment of Communism—which stood in direct opposition to the Soviet desire to expand Communism throughout Europe. To ensure the success of the Cold War order, Dulles was instrumental in the creation of the North Atlantic Treaty Organization, which would unite the nations of Western Europe and North America against Communism.

—*Steven L. Danver, PhD*

Bibliography and Additional Reading

Immerman, Richard H. *John Foster Dulles: Piety, Pragmatism, and Power in US Foreign Policy.* Wilmington: Scholarly Resources, 1999. Print.

Mastny, Vojtech. *The Cold War and Soviet Insecurity: The Stalin Years.* New York: Oxford UP, 1996. Print.

Toulouse, Mark G. *The Transformation of John Foster Dulles: From Prophet of Realism to Priest of Nationalism.* Macon: Mercer UP, 1985. Print.

■ Complete Integration of Military Operations

Date: October 16, 1945
Author: Douglas MacArthur
Genre: speech

Summary Overview

Speaking shortly after the Japanese surrender that ended hostilities in World War II and the ensuing demilitarization of Japan, US General Douglas MacArthur congratulated US military forces on their achievements in the Pacific theater and applauded military leadership for executing a well-integrated strategy that used ground, naval, and air forces to the best of their abilities. MacArthur also spoke highly of the rapid and thorough demilitarization of the surrendered Japanese, noting that it signaled the completeness of the Allied victory—a victory that he saw as certain and inevitable due to the differences in the strategies applied by the two competing forces in the Pacific. MacArthur pointed out the flawed nature of Japan's independently operating military branches and argued that the complete integration of US services assured victory and set a precedent for success in all future military conflicts.

Defining Moment

During World War II, the conflict in the Pacific theater was intense and often brutal. Tensions between the United States and imperial Japan had begun to rise before the start of the war, as the United States opposed the militaristic territorial expansion of Japan into mainland East Asia. Those tensions exploded into open conflict with the Japanese bombing of the US naval base at Pearl Harbor, Hawaii, in December of 1941. Within hours, the United States declared war on Japan, activating a series of alliances that brought it into the global conflict with Germany and other Axis powers as well. Although the United States and the Allies agreed to follow an overall Eurocentric strategy, American sentiment against Japan was high, and the Pacific campaign was launched immediately. At first, Japan's forces seemed superior, winning victories in the Philippines and elsewhere. Japan also earned a reputation for harsh treatment of conquered territory and abuse of prisoners, such as leading captives on the infamous

Bataan Death March. As the war progressed, however, General MacArthur's leadership, the island-hopping strategy used to win back territory, and intense waves of US air attacks on Japanese cities helped turn the tide.

With the Axis powers defeated in Europe by mid-1945, Allied leaders met in Potsdam, Germany, to discuss plans for the reorganization of the continent and the conclusion of the war in the Pacific. Armed with the knowledge of the successful testing of an atomic weapon by US scientists, US president Harry S. Truman pushed for a hard line against the Japanese. The resulting Potsdam Declaration demanded that the Japanese agree to an immediate and unconditional surrender or face immense destruction. No surrender followed, however, and Truman agreed to the use of atomic bombs on the Japanese cities of Hiroshima and Nagasaki. The resulting devastation, combined with the Soviet Union's declaration of war on Japan, finally forced Japanese emperor Hirohito to agree to surrender.

As the supreme commander of the Allied forces in the Pacific, MacArthur was among those who accepted the formal Japanese surrender in early September 1945, and he became the head of the Allied occupation of the Japanese islands. Over the next several weeks, he led efforts to ensure that Japan's military was completely demobilized and that it lacked the ability to muster offensive forces again. Military leaders were removed from political leadership, and further reforms over the next several years addressed Japan's economic, social, and governmental systems.

Author Biography

Douglas MacArthur was born on January 26, 1880, in Little Rock, Arkansas. A lifelong military man, he served in Europe during World War I and spent time overseeing operations in the Philippines, then a US holding, during the 1920s. He gained the rank of general in 1930 when he was appointed the US Army's chief of staff. MacArthur spent much of the 1930s working with the Philippine Army. After the United States entered World War II in 1941, he oversaw the ultimately unsuccessful Allied effort to prevent the Philippines from falling to Japan before rising to become a top Allied military officer in the southwest Pacific region in early 1942. Over the next few years, MacArthur led Allied forces in regaining territory lost to the Japanese, and his successes led to his appointment as head of US Army and Army Air Force operations in the Pacific in 1945. After the war's end, MacArthur oversaw the occupation, demilitarization, and rebuilding of Japan. He also served for a time as head of the United Nations coalition forces in the Korean War. MacArthur died on April 5, 1964.

HISTORICAL DOCUMENT

Today the Japanese armed forces throughout Japan completed their demobilization and ceased to exist as such. These forces are now completely abolished. I know of no demobilization in history either in war or peace by our own or by any other country that has been accomplished so rapidly or so frictionlessly. Everything military, naval or air is forbidden to Japan. This ends its military might and its military influence in international affairs. It no longer reckons as a world power either large or small. Its path in the future, if it is to survive must be confined to the ways of peace. Approximately 7,000,000 armed men, including those in the outlying theatres, have laid down their weapons.

In the accomplishment of the extraordinarily difficult and dangerous surrender in Japan, unique in the annals of history, not a shot was necessary, not a drop of Allied blood was shed.

The vindication of the great decision of Potsdam is complete. Nothing could exceed the abjectness, the humiliation and the finality of this surrender. It is not only physically thorough, but has been equally destructive on Japanese spirit. From swaggering arrogance, the former Japanese military have passed to servility and fear. They are thoroughly beaten and cowed, and tremble before the terrible retribution the surrender terms impose upon their country in punishment for its great sins.

Again I wish to pay tribute to the magnificent conduct of our troops. With a few exceptions, they could well be taken as a model for all time, as a conquering army. No historian in later years when passions cool can arraign their conduct. They could so easily and understandably have emulated the ruthlessness which their enemy freely practiced when conditions were reversed. But their perfect balance between implacable firmness of duty on the one hand and resolute restraint from cruelness and brutalities on the other has' taught a lesson to the Japanese civil population that is startling in its impact.

Nothing has so tended to impress Japanese thought, not even the catastrophic fact of military defeat itself. They have for the first time seen the free man's way of life in actual action and it has stunned them into new thought and new ideas. A revolution—or more properly speaking, the evolution—which will restore the dignity and freedom of the common man, has begun. It will take much time, and require great patience, but if world public opinion will permit of these two essential factors, mankind will be repaid. Herein lies the way to true and final peace.

The Japanese Army, contrary to some concepts that have been advanced, was thoroughly defeated before the surrender. The strategic maneuvering of the Allies so scattered and divided them; their thrusts had so immobilized, disintegrated and split its units; its supply and transportation lines were so utterly destroyed; its equipment was so exhausted, its morale so shattered, that its early surrender became inevitable.

Bastion after bastion, considered by it as impregnable in barring our way, had been by-passed and rendered impotent and useless, while our tactical penetrations and envelopments resulted in piecemeal destruction of many isolated fragments. It was weak everywhere, forced to fight where it stood, unable to render mutual support between its parts and presented a picture of collapse that was complete and absolute.

The basic cause of the surrender is not to be attributed to an arbitrary decision of authority. It was inevitable because of the strategic and tactical circumstances forced upon it. The situation had become hopeless. It was merely a question of when, with our troops poised for final invasion. This invasion would have been annihilating, but might well have cost hundreds of thousands of American lives.

The victory was a triumph for the concept of the complete integration of the three dimensions of war—ground, sea and air. By a thorough use of each arm in conjunction with the corresponding utilization of the other two, the enemy was reduced to a condition of helplessness. By largely avoiding methods involving the separate use of the services and by avoiding methods of frontal assault as far as possible, our combined power forced the surrender with relative life loss probably unparalleled in any campaigns in history.

This latter fact indeed was the most inspiring and significant feature: the unprecedented saving in American life. It is for this we have to say truly, "Thank God." Never was there a more intensive application of the principle of the strategic and tactical employment of limited forces as compared with the accumulation of overwhelming forces.

Illustrating this concept, General Yamashita recently stated in an interview in Manila, explaining reasons for his defeat, that the diversity of Japanese command resulted in the complete lack of cooperation and coordination between the services. He complained that he was not in supreme command, that the air forces were run by Field Marshal Teraushi at Saigon and the fleet run directly from Tokyo, that he only knew of the intended naval strike at Leyte Gulf five days before it got under way and professed ignorance of its details.

The great lesson for the future is that success in the art of war depends upon a complete integration of the services. In unity will lie military strength. We cannot win with only backs and ends. And no line, however strong can go alone. Victory will rest with the team.

GLOSSARY

abjectness: the state of utter hopelessness, misery, or humiliation; shamelessly servile

annals: records of events, especially in a yearly record, usually in chronological order; historical records

bastion: a fortification; a fortified place

cowed: to frighten with threats or violence; intimidate

demobilization: to disband (as with troops or an army); to discharge someone from military service

frictionlessly: done without dissension or conflict between persons owing to differing ideas, etc.

theatres: major areas of military action

Document Analysis

In his speech, MacArthur focuses on two main points: the causes and processes of the Japanese surrender and the success of the Allied military branches in achieving "complete integration of the services," or the strong and effective coordination of efforts among ground, air, and naval operations. According to MacArthur, this coordination allowed for the Allied forces to triumph decisively over the Japanese, which suffered from a lack of this kind of interservice planning and communication. The general thus asserts that the victories celebrated in the first portion of his speech are due to the connectivity emphasized in the second half and further proposes that future military successes will rest on a similarly integrated approach: "Victory will rest with the team."

The general first hails the Allies for overseeing a complete demobilization of the Japanese military in only about two months in what he calls a "vindication of the great decision of Potsdam," a reference to the Potsdam Declaration's call for the strict demilitarization of Japan. Indeed, the surrender that followed the pair of atomic bombings and Soviet attack on Japan was a full and nearly unconditional one that demanded the Japanese completely disband its military. MacArthur asserts that millions of Japanese soldiers have been discharged from their posts and the US occupiers have acted firmly, but fairly and humanely. The imperial military that attacked the United States in 1941 and wreaked havoc in the Pacific from China to the Philippines is no more, and MacArthur sees this outcome as a strongly positive one for Japan and the world.

MacArthur uses the rest of the speech to explain what he sees as the "strategic and tactical circumstances" leading to this inevitable Japanese surrender, focusing on the implementation of a three-pronged strategy incorporating ground, naval, and air forces. The military functions most effectively by relying on a balance of all three branches rather than emphasizing one at the expense of the others, he suggests, protecting its members from needless loss of life and wielding a combined power that can overwhelm any defense. To illustrate the efficacy of this three-pronged approach, MacArthur points to the contrast between the winning Allied strategy and the ultimately losing Japanese strategy. He notes that even the Japanese general Tomoyuki Yamashika attributed the Japanese defeat to the lack of coordination among the leaders of its armed forces, which were managed by different men and even from different command points. MacArthur thus supports the usage of a single integrated strategy in future military conflicts to maintain US superiority.

Essential Themes

At the heart of MacArthur's speech is the argument that cooperative strategies among different types of military forces were central to Allied success against Japan, and that such cooperation would be central to US successes in the future. Although earlier wars had been conducted mostly by one branch of the military—World War I, for example, had been fought mostly on land with a lesser reliance on air and water power—conflict in World War II drew on a blend of tactics to achieve its aims, and MacArthur saw this as the way of the future. Integration of leadership, planning, and resources would allow the nation to wield the combined efforts of each military branch against any challenge. Physical geography may limit the implementation of naval forces, but modern warfare typically blends focused air attacks with strategic advances by ground troops.

Indeed, coordination among military branches and even among forces operated by separate nations has increased exponentially in the time since MacArthur's speech. Improved communications and military technology continue to support this goal. Instant electronic communications allow for easier coordination of efforts among soldiers and officers regardless of their relative locations. Technology also eases efforts to conduct simultaneous or strategically linked air, land, and sea attacks, and permits for the oversight of key missions from secure locations thousands of miles away.

The rise of the United Nations (UN) after World War II has allowed troops from different member nations to work together on certain missions, beginning with the campaign led by MacArthur himself in the Korean War during the early 1950s. Such operations take integration beyond individual military branches to coordination on a global level. Other international defense organizations, such as the North Atlantic Treaty Organization (NATO) established in 1949, increased military cooperation among allied nations during the Cold War era and beyond. During the twenty-first century, the concept of "coalition forces" formed by international consensus is seen by many as necessary to undertake any military action with potential global consequences. With this strategy a threat can be faced with broad support, while unilateral acts of war may be discouraged.

—Vanessa E. Vaughn, MA

Bibliography and Additional Reading

James, Dorris Clayton. *The Years of MacArthur*. 3 vols. Boston: Houghton, 1985. Print.

MacArthur, Douglas. *Reminiscences*. Annapolis: Naval Inst. P, 1964. Print.

"Milestones: 1945–1952: Occupation and Reconstruction of Japan, 1945–52." *Office of the Historian*. Office of the Historian, Bureau of Public Affairs, US Dept. of State, n.d. Web. 21 Jan. 2015.

■ The World Needs the Tonic of Universal Truth

Date: November 15, 1945
Author: Arthur H. Vandenberg
Genre: speech

Summary Overview

Less than three months after the official end of the World War II, the United States, its allies, and the United Nations began the work of reconstruction. During a Senate debate over an appropriation to the UN Relief and Rehabilitation Administration (UNRRA), Michigan senator Arthur H. Vandenberg expressed his concerns over the "iron curtain" that repressed democracy and the free flow of information in the Soviet-occupied nations of central and Eastern Europe. Vandenberg also cautioned against the sharing of information about the American atomic energy program in light of the secretive behavior of the Soviets.

Defining Moment

During the 1930s, war raged in two separate theaters, causing the deaths of millions and seemingly incalculable amounts of destruction. In Europe, the rapid and seemingly unstoppable force of Adolf Hitler's Nazi military spread like wildfire, northward into Scandinavia, eastward into Poland, southward toward the Mediterranean, and westward toward Great Britain. In East Asia and the Pacific, Japanese emperor Hirohito sent his forces across the Korean Peninsula and into China, into the South China Sea and eastward toward US territory.

With virtually every corner of the world living under the specter of war, the people and leaders of the United States—geographically separated from either theater by thousands of miles—largely embraced the philosophies of neutrality and isolationism. Although President Franklin D. Roosevelt advocated for a larger American role in the conflicts—mainly through diplomatic channels and in financial support of US allies in both regions—such ideals were rebuffed by many in Congress, including the opposition Republican Party. This trend changed dramatically, however, when the Japanese launched its infamous attack on the US naval fleet on December 7, 1941. Suddenly, war had thrust itself into the American way of life—isolationism quickly became extinct.

The Allied effort—headed in Europe by the United States, Great Britain, and the Soviet Union—ultimately turned Hitler's forces backward and into oblivion as Hitler committed suicide and his regime disintegrated. In the Pacific, the American-led campaign of "island-hopping" pushed the Japanese back toward their homeland before the atomic bombings at Hiroshima and Nagasaki brought about an unconditional Japanese surrender. The war was over, but there existed another daunting challenge: pacification and reconstruction.

At the end of the European conflict, the "Big Three"— US president Harry S. Truman, British prime minister Clement Attlee (who replaced Winston Churchill at the end of the war), and Soviet premier Joseph Stalin—met at Potsdam, Germany, to address this challenge as well as how to reestablish national borders. Germany was divided into two general zones—one occupied by the US, British and other Western powers, the other by the Soviet Union. The Soviet Union had also taken hold of Poland at the end of the war and had also occupied portions of Eastern Europe during its efforts against Germany. During the Potsdam Conference, these territorial gains were ceded to the Soviet Union with the expectation that Moscow would promote freedom and democracy during their reconstruction.

The use of the atomic bomb, coupled with a distrust of Soviet tactics in Europe, helped give rise to what would soon be known as the Cold War. The previously isolationist United States was now positioning itself as a world leader, hosting the United Nations General Assembly and continuing to build coalitions with like-minded nations in Western Europe and around the world in the face of the Soviet Union, which seemed to be pursuing a similar course of action in its postwar occupied territories. Shortly after the war came to an end, Churchill cautioned, in a letter to Truman, that an iron curtain had been drawn down in front of the Soviet-occupied territories, with any information about the goings-on behind that curtain carefully controlled by Moscow.

Author Biography

Arthur Hendrick Vandenberg was born on March 22, 1884, in Grand Rapids, Michigan. After a public school education, he studied law for one year at the University of Michigan. In 1901, he pursued a career as a journalist and, starting in 1906, as the editor of the Grand Rapids Herald. In March of 1928, Vandenberg, a Republican, was appointed to the US Senate seat vacated with the death of Woodbridge Ferris (Vandenberg would formally win election to the seat in November of that year). An isolationist prior to the war, Vandenberg became more of an internationalist after the attack on Pearl Harbor. He held several leadership positions during his twenty-three-year tenure as senator and served as a delegate to the UN General Assembly. He also helped garner bipartisan support of the Truman Doctrine and the formation of NATO. He died of cancer on April 18, 1951.

HISTORICAL DOCUMENT

Mr. President, I was very glad to yield a moment ago to the able Senator from New Mexico [Mr. Hatch] to present for the Record the address made last evening by Under Secretary of State Acheson on the subject of international friendship. I was particularly interested in the comments of the Senator from New Mexico in assigning a particular significance to the importance of friendship between the United States and the Soviets of Russia. It is that subject, Mr. President, which I wish to discuss quite frankly today. By way of approach, there are one or two related matters to which I wish to refer.

Mr. President, the pending bill now in the Appropriations Committee carrying the balance of our committed appropriation to the United Nations Relief and Rehabilitation Administration, confronts the Senate with the decision of the House of Representatives that our American participation in serving basic international humanities this winter shall be limited to those countries which permit our free press to have free access to free news regarding UNRRA. This heavily underscores a major and a ramifying problem in our international relationships. It has been a smoldering menace for some time. It now breaks out into open conflagration; and it is not calculated to be a mere passing blaze in view of the fact that similar restrictions are prophesied in respect to all subsequent relief and rehabilitation and loan legislation. Therefore I think it would be wise for us and our allies to face the facts in friendly candor and see if something cannot be done about it for their sakes quite as much as for ours.

I shall presently indicate that I think the hope of world peace and fraternity—the achievement of stable and happy relationships between the nations of this earth—are dependent to an amazing degree upon full freedom of international communications. The mutual disclosure of free information and the liberty of a worldwide free press are becoming increasingly indispensable to the successful operation of an interdependent world society. This is no longer just an altruistic theory. It has come to be a matter of grim reality. "Black-outs" make international confidence impossible. When the iron curtain of secrecy falls around an area suspicion is unavoidable, restless conjecture substitutes for knowledge, and dependable trust is out of the question. These are not the implements of peace and progress. Understanding and good will cannot flourish in a vacuum.

I quote from a recent address by Secretary of State Byrnes: Understanding brings tolerance and a willingness to cooperate in the adjustment of differences. Censorship and black-outs breed suspicion and distrust. And all too often this suspicion and distrust are justified. For censorship and black-outs are the hand maidens of oppression.

This is also my view, Mr. President. I believe it to be an unassailable axiom that all of the victors of this war must be prepared at all times freely and frankly to submit their actions and their aspirations to untrammeled audit by the conscience of the world. I believe that every departure from this rule is a threat to the peace of which men dream and for which other men have fought and died.

Since these are my convictions, it will be readily

understood why I think the House has rendered a real service by bringing this desperately important subject squarely into the open. At the same time, I hope it may be just as readily understood why I am unable to agree that we should suddenly choose UNRRA, on the threshold of winter, as the vehicle for the initial application of an ironclad rule to implement this doctrine. I am unable, Mr. President, to make mercy an arbitrary hostage to the lifting of the iron curtain, at this tragic moment in human misery.

It is unnecessary, Mr. President, to the achievement of our point. The point is amply emphasized when the whole world has seen that one great branch of the American Congress feels so keenly upon this subject that is has decided that not even the Good Samaritan can proceed upon these errands of mercy behind the iron curtain where, quoting from the House bill:

The controlling government interferes with or refuses full and free access to the news of any and all activities of the United Nations Relief and Rehabilitation Administration * * * or censors, or attempts to censor, in time of peace, news of any and all activities of UNRRA which may be prepared or dispatched from such country by representatives of the press and radio of the United States.

At the risk of being charged with inconsistency—which I deny—I unequivocally support this principle, and I shall presently argue for it with all the earnestness at my command. But I cannot and do not support its present summary application to the fulfillment of a humanitarian obligation to which we are already solemnly committed. I think the principle is too important to the welfare of the world to be used against the welfare of starving millions in the war-scorched cockpits of this recent conflict. I am unable, Mr. President, to tie these two unrelated things together. Furthermore, Mr. President, I cannot escape the impact of a headline which I read the other day: "Starving people ripe for revolts in Europe; general discontent in occupied areas calls for quick cooperation by big nations."

I agree with the House that not even the holy business of relieving human suffering can be properly understood or adequately handled in the absence of the authenticated truth. I agree that we are entitled to know the needs we are asked to serve. I agree that we are entitled to know that our service reaches those for whom it is intended. I agree that we are entitled to know from the lips and pens of our own seasoned observers. This would not be a matter of espionage. It would be a matter of mutual understanding. Indeed, it is of greatest concern to our suffering neighbors themselves, because I venture the assertion that if America knew from her own trusted news correspondents, from day to day, the whole running story of human suffering in the war-wasted places of the earth, there would be not an instant's delay in the prodigal American response. We cannot see through the iron curtain. I agree that every rational effort, even in connection with UNRRA, must be made to lift it. We should strive for the full information to which we are entitled, and I endorse an urgent mandate to UNRRA that it make every possible effort to this end.

But, Mr. President, the iron curtain is in the control of governments. It is the people in these areas who die for want of bread. They do not control the curtain. It is the people-pitiful, suffering, starving millions of them facing what probably will be the blackest, crudest winter since the age of plagues; it is the people from whom our aid would be withheld by an unequivocal order of this nature. You may say the blame would rest upon the government which denied our requirement. But the dead, Mr. President, would not know the difference.

So I do not support this particular amendment in the form approved by the House. But, nonetheless, I support the principle to which it is addressed, and I say again that the House has done a service to the cause by illustrating the extent to which the iron curtain can jeopardize the welfare of people everywhere—and, most of all, those who are "blacked out" themselves.

And now, Mr. President, I want to talk about that principle and the magnitude of its importance. I hope it will be no wrench to our international contacts to deal with it in specific terms. It seems to me that candor holds the greatest hope for correction.

Another current and extraordinarily ominous example will readily come to mind to prove how the iron curtain interferes with the international confidence which is prerequisite to peace. This example can become a crisis in human existence itself. Desperately important discussions are already at fever heat respecting the future of atomic energy. In every chancellery and at every hearthstone the question is being anxiously asked as to what shall become of the atomic bomb. We are frightened by our responsibilities. There is wide divergence of opinion as to what shall be done. I want to make it distinctly plain that I do riot enter upon this field of decision in this discussion. I simply point out that there is one phase of the problem upon which there is practically no divergence of opinion at all. Even those who most vehemently advocate I the internationalization of this deadly secret never fail to assert the corollary necessity that there must be unlimited, wide-open, world-wide facilities for mutual inspection and the total exchange of unlimited information upon this score. There can be no dark corners in an atomic age.

President Truman said in his Navy Day speech upon this point that only "frank cooperation among the peace-loving nations can save the world from unprecedented disaster. "Frank" cooperation. I quote the adjective.

The Russian radio last week broadcast an atomic analysis which one newspaper headlined as follows: "Red radio sees world disaster in atom secrecy." It, of course, was speaking about secrecy in the first instance. I repeat that I do not here discuss that phase. I am speaking about secrecy in the last instance; and I am saying that we cannot deal with the former until we have successfully answered the latter, I assert that it would be utterly unthinkable that we, and our British and Canadian associates, would voluntarily or consciously permit any nation to take this so-called secret behind an iron curtain which blacks out all information as to what is being done with it. Then, indeed, would the Red headline be bitterly justified—"sees world disaster in atom secrecy."

The point is, Mr. President, that here again we find a vital international situation wherein any lack of the full, free exchange of peacetime information inevitably intrudes upon international contacts and renders what the President calls frank cooperation impossible. Here, again, those who may deny this free exchange are calculated chiefly to victimize themselves. Indeed, the more this subject is explored the more obvious it becomes that uncensored truth is elemental and prerequisite in seeking peace and friendship in a better world. No amount of expedient appeasement can escape this net result.

Mr. President, bearing upon this particular phase of my discussion, I call attention to the joint statement issued a few moments ago by the President of the United States, the Prime Minister of the United Kingdom, and the Prime Minister of Canada, regarding their preliminary conclusions in respect to the control of this tremendously challenging problem. I call attention to the fact that what to me is the key paragraph in the entire statement issued by these three distinguished spokesmen, the prime paragraph, the controlling paragraph, the sine qua non paragraph, reads as follows:

We are not convinced that the spreading of the specialized information regarding the practical application of atomic energy, before it is possible to devise effective, reciprocal, and enforceable safeguards acceptable to all nations, would contribute to a constructive solution of the problem of the atomic bomb. On the contrary, we think it might have the opposite effect. We are, however, prepared to share, on a reciprocal basis with others of the United Nations, detailed information concerning the practical industrial application of atomic energy—

When?—

just as soon as effective enforceable safeguards against its use for destructive purposes can be devised.

In other words, Mr. President, this paper, issued a few moments ago, says—put very bluntly—that the iron curtain must be lifted in this world if there is to be any safe existence for humankind hereafter.

The President, joining with the chief spokesmen for our partners in the possession of this secret, has made public a very interesting, significant, and very helpful series of recommendations. I do not comment on their substance except to say that I approve the emphasis that was put upon the United Nations Organization as the world's best, continuing hope for organized peace and security, that I agree I would rather attempt to control the international outlawry of atomic bombs than the international use of atomic weapons, and that I agree that these things, cannot be done behind an iron curtain. I am confident that the President's statement will receive the most serious and sympathetic consideration of the Congress—of the Congress, Mr. President—where a basic and unavoidable share of the responsibility for these fateful decisions inevitably resides under our constitutional form of government, and where it is going to stay.

Wherever you probe this problem you learn the same lesson, Mr. President. Many of our past and present frictions are traceable to the iron curtain. In some instances let us frankly admit that it was our own iron curtain—as, for example, at that famous initial international conference in the United States where the press was virtually held at bay with bayonets. Again, we certainly shared responsibility for the iron curtain at epochal Yalta where global decisions were made which will affect destiny for centuries to come and which were never fully and frankly exposed to bur people. I doubt if we yet know the whole truth. Too often our own diplomacy—too often right here in Washington our own diplomacy—has practiced the reverse of Woodrow Wilson's admonition that peace and justice require "open covenants openly arrived at." In a practical sense, we understand that international negotiation—particularly in time of war—cannot always proceed in a goldfish bowl. But as rational students of past and present history, we also understand that the less often the iron curtain blacks out such negotiation, the less likely is it that liberty and justice will be throttled in the process.

Mr. President, the best evidence of good faith on the part of major powers in executing the trust which they have insisted upon assuming in the peacetime liquidation of this war will be to lift the iron curtain and let in the light upon the evolution of events which will prove or disprove the bona fides of their programs. Let me illustrate.

At Yalta, it was solemnly agreed among other Polish decisions to which I shall never get the consent of my conscience, as follows:

The Polish Provisional Government of National Unity shall be pledged to the holding of free and unfettered elections as soon as possible on the basis of universal suffrage and secret ballot.

Those were fair and reassuring words. But by the time the great powers subsequently reached Potsdam, the potential shadow of the iron curtain had fallen athwart this comfortable prospectus. It had been the assumption of this Government that "free and unfettered elections" included freedom of reporting on these elections. But inasmuch as events in other countries showed the necessity of making specific provision for such freedom of reporting, the great powers—all three of them—wrote the following postscript at Potsdam:

The three powers note that the Polish Provisional Government in accordance with the decisions of the Crimea Conference has agreed to the holding of free and unfettered elections as soon as possible on the basis of universal suffrage and secret ballot in which all democratic and anti-Nazi parties shall have the right to take part and to put forward candidates, and that representatives of the allied press shall enjoy full freedom to report to the world upon developments in Poland before and during the elections.

At the same time they looked at Bulgaria, Hungary, and Rumania, and said:

The three [great powers] governments have no doubt that in view of the changed conditions resulting from the termination of the war in Europe, representatives of the allied press will enjoy full freedom to report to the world upon developments in Rumania, Bulgaria, Hungary, and Finland.

During the last week in August, a very limited number of American newspaper men were admitted to these countries. The iron curtain lifted—just a few inches. But at least it lifted, and I want to give full credit to the great powers for this omen of better days to come. It still remains to be demonstrated to what extent this boon is a reality. It remains to be seen whether this limited corps of correspondents will generally enjoy full freedom to report. But again let me report encouragement. There appears to have been a reasonably free press, reporting upon a reasonably free election, in Hungary within the past fortnight. Also it is important to observe that the three major powers have just extended tentative recognition to Albania. The British and American notes—the only ones available—contain this proviso:

Foreign press correspondents shall be permitted to enter Albania to observe and report freely on the elections and the work of the constituent assembly. The point I make, Mr. President, is that only in this fashion can we establish international faith and confidence.

The world is grimly skeptical. Too many promises in the Atlantic Charter have been scuttled. Suppression of news—suppression of authenticated facts—inevitably invites the suspicion that behind the iron curtain there is a suppression of promised human rights.

Hard-hitting Ernest Bevin, British Foreign Secretary, made a public statement a few weeks ago, in which he referred to some of the temporary governments that have been set up in the controlled areas of Europe. Among other things, he said:

The governments set up in those countries do not, in our view, represent the majority of the people and the impression we get is that one kind of totalitarianism is being replaced by another. This is not what we understand by the much-overworked word, "democracy," which appears to me to need definition.

There is only one antidote for such suspicions, if they are groundless, Mr. President. That antidote is the authenticated truth reported in the free press of America and the world. If the suspicions are not groundless, I submit that our own Government has no greater responsibility than to seek, with every emphasis at its command, a true disclosure of the facts.

Mr. President, I do not know why we cannot be as candid in a friendly discussion of our Soviet-American relations as is the Russian press and the Russian spokesmanship, both at home and abroad, particularly since I embrace no such latitudes as they often give themselves. The truth is that the iron curtain has been one of the greatest obstacles to the Soviet-American liaison upon which so much of the world's hope for peace and progress depends. I respectfully suggest that this is not good for either them or us.

When the distinguished senior Senator from Florida stopped recently in Moscow in the course of his global odyssey, it is reported that he asked Marshal Stalin whether the Generalissimo wanted to give him any special message to us. The great Russian leader is reported to have hesitated and then said:

Just judge the Soviet Union objectively. Do not either praise us or scold us. Just know us and judge us as we are and base your estimate of us upon facts and not on rumors.

Mr. President that is a fair request. It is for a chance to honor that request that I am pleading this afternoon. It seems to me, in this instance, that Marshal Stalin and I are asking for precisely the same thing. But how can we judge the Soviets objectively—how can we separate "facts" from "rumors"—if the Soviets themselves discourage us from doing so? Only a week ago last Wednesday when the few Anglo-American correspondents in Moscow addressed a plea to the distinguished People's Commissar of Foreign Affairs to relax the stern censorship

which rests upon them, Mr. Molotov replied, through a Foreign Office spokesman, that he "did not find it necessary to give the protest his attention." Yet the appeal of these correspondents was only for a chance to apply the Stalin prescription. It pointed out that the Soviet Union was the only great allied power that retained wartime censorship, and said:

Censorship in peacetime of all dispatches relating not only to military affairs but to politics, economic, cultural affairs and every aspect of life in the Soviet Union destroys the value of foreign correspondence in a free world and has created general distrust abroad of all news emanating from the Soviet Union.

Under such circumstances, I repeat, how can we view Russia "objectively" and discard the rumors from the facts? The iron curtain intervenes. It prevents us from knowing them, and—an equal tragedy—it prevents them from knowing us. I quote a recent metropolitan editorial at this point:

Probably nothing else in the world is so important at this moment as good relations between Russia and the United States. Probably nothing would do so much to promote and cement those good relations as an end of Russian black-outs, foreign and domestic.

I am glad to note a Reuters dispatch from Moscow on November 11, which states that "during the last 2 weeks the rigid application of wartime restrictions appears to have been somewhat relaxed." I am glad to note still further and subsequent statements out of Moscow which indicate a feeling that the "black-out" is being relieved, very recently, to a degree. I cannot overemphasize my conviction that such news is of paramount importance. The more progress we can make in this direction, the less thorny will be the paths of international comity. The better it will be for both of us and for the world. I agree with the editorial comment which said: It might be a mistake to assume too much, but if this gesture betokens that Russia is willing to drop her traditional suspicions * * * if it means that she is willing to meet the world half way, then the world will not fail to meet her. And if that is the case, then the present proposals can, indeed, mark the beginning of a new era of peace and plenty which in time may even lift the specter of an atomic cataclysm now hanging over the world.

Secretary Byrnes stated, in a recent New York speech,

that we are fully aware of Russia's special security interests in her central and eastern European neighbors and that we can appreciate her desire for insulations. He drew a rather startling parallel with our own good-neighbor policy under the Monroe Doctrine and our inter-American relationships. I shall have to say frankly that I think this was a sadly strained analogy. We Americans do have special security interests in our neighbors; but the world can come and see to its heart's content that we glory in treating them all as sovereign equals. They are our partners; not our satellites. We shall never complain of any kindred special security interests when similarly exercised by others. But this phrase-special security interests—often has another, a different and an ominous connotation in diplomacy. It could be reminiscent, for example, of the notorious Lansing-Ishii agreement of 1917 which Japan used to bedevil China for many years, although I make no such application now. But I shall have to say that I, for one, do not "appreciate"—the Secretary's word—what has happened, for example, in so-called liberated Poland—our faithful ally—where few, if any, of the literal guarantees of the Atlantic Charter, pleasantly reiterated in the recent speeches of both the President and the Secretary, have been fulfilled.

If the Secretary was speaking of special security interests in the true pattern of an inter-American analogy, then I agree. Certainly we can fully understand the Soviet insistence, for example, upon her special security interests against any resurgence of her erstwhile Axis neighbors. With that objective I am in total sympathy. It is part and parcel of the San Francisco Charter. If the iron curtain is one of the devices upon which Moscow feels it must rely for these special security interests, then here is another vital reason to revert to the theme of my speech of last January 10 that, for the sake of all concerned, we had best completely clear the track of all such Russian fears of her erstwhile Axis enemies by signing with all the major Allies a long-time treaty, agreeing to stand together—one for all and all for one—in the event of any Axis resurgence, and thus bulwark the United Nations Organization with another and a final steel beam. If that would relieve the pressure on the Balkan and the Baltic States and the related areas, if it would recall the Red army from so-called liberated areas, if it would renew forgotten parts of the Atlantic Charter, and if it would roll up the iron curtain, it would be the greatest bargain ever written into history,

I do not too often agree with Mr. Harold J. Laski, chairman of the British Labor Party; but I do emphatically agree when he wrote last week: "We and the Americans alike must convince the Russians that we have no thought or sentiment which jeopardizes their security." Mutual assurances—both ways—upon this score will do more for peace than any other possible supplement to the San Francisco Charter.

Secretary Byrnes has said: "America will not join any groups in those countries in hostile intrigue against the Soviet Union." Mr. President, in return for the reciprocal realities to which I have referred—and they are essential to peace with justice in this world—I would go even further than the Secretary has gone, and agree affirmatively to join in permanently resisting any such axis threats as those defined.

Mr. President, I conclude as I began. Not in a challenge but in an appeal. I beg of all nations, wherever they may be, to consider their own self-interest in lifting the iron curtains of secrecy, censorship, and blacked-out truth. Otherwise, is it not perfectly obvious that they will increasingly plague us and our allies in matters of relief, in matters of rehabilitation, in the matter of loans, in the matter of atomic bombs, in the entire evolution of the United Nations Organization—indeed, in all future international relationships? Is there anything to which men of good will need more earnestly to address their efforts and their prayers?

This shattered world is in need of new sources of dependable confidence, new well-springs of hope. It cries out for mutual understandings. It needs the tonic of universal truth. It needs the inspiration which San Francisco has sought to breathe into the General Assembly of the United Nations as the free and untrammeled "town meeting of the world." We can only stumble if the dark persists. In the words of the Psalmist: "Light is sown for the righteous."

GLOSSARY

axiom: a self-evident truth that requires no proof

boon: something to be thankful for; blessing; benefit; a favor sought

chancellery: the position of a chancellor; the office attached to an embassy or consulate

corollary: an immediate consequence or easily drawn conclusion; a natural consequence or result

prodigal: wastefully or recklessly extravagant; lavish; profuse

scuttled: abandoned; withdrawn from or caused to be abandoned or destroyed

unfettered: free from restraint; liberated

untrammeled: unhindered; opposite of trammels, which means a hindrance or impediment to free action

Document Analysis

Churchill's famous iron curtain reference (made shortly after the war's end but repeated in his iconic speech in Fulton, Missouri, in 1946) strongly influenced the growing number of American leaders who were concerned about the Soviet Union's growing power. Michigan Republican Arthur H. Vandenberg, during a speech on the US Senate floor in November 1945, echoes this term as he cautions fellow members of Congress on appropriating funds to support the reconstruction of postwar Europe. Vandenberg argues that the nobility of the proposed financial support to UNRRA is being undermined by the Soviet Union. Moscow, Vandenberg says, should openly communicate with the rest of the world and promote the freedom and liberties espoused by the UN.

Vandenberg embraces his newly found internationalism during this speech, emphasizing the significance of the international fraternity of nations in the postwar era. He adds that this fraternity depends on the open and free exchange of information among these nations. This point is particularly important in light of the enormous task of providing humanitarian support to war-torn Europe. Indeed, he argues, there exists a major crisis in this region—countless people are sick, homeless, starving and facing the coming winter. UNRRA, he says, has been created to deal with this moral imperative. It is designed to facilitate an integrated multinational response to this crisis, Vandenberg says.

However, Vandenberg adds, the Soviet Union stands in the way of UNRRA's potential efficacy. The Soviet Union is carefully controlling and withholding any information that comes from behind the aforementioned iron curtain. Western journalists, Vandenberg says, have even been refused access to Soviet-occupied areas. As a result, he argues, the extent of the crisis remains unknown. Such "black-outs," Vandenberg suggests, only worsen the situation and run counter to the international community's efforts to relieve suffering.

Vandenberg addresses a Soviet argument that the idea of "international communication" should include the United States sharing information about its atomic energy program. Vandenberg cites the testimony of non-US world leaders and experts, all of whom argue that the atomic energy arena is still nascent. There are to date no uniform, international protocols or standards regarding safety and health, Vandenberg says. In the absence of such regulations and in light of the still-developing field, it is necessary to keep the American atomic energy program out of international communications discussions.

Meanwhile, he continues, the onus is on the Soviet Union to lift the iron curtain and promote openness, cooperation and democratic ideals in every nation under Moscow's control. Although reports show that the Soviet Union is relaxing some of its militaristic policies in the Balkan and Baltic states, he says, it is clear that the Soviet Union needs to do more to promote democracy in its occupied territories. Vandenberg reminds his colleagues that the Soviet Union pledged to do so at Yalta and again at Potsdam, but evidence shows that Moscow is not yet true to its word. The Soviet Union has security interests in the region, Vandenberg acknowledges, but those interests do not supersede the broader need for international cooperation, "universal truth," and humanitarianism.

Essential Themes

Senator Vandenberg's speech to Congress showed both a commitment to maintaining peaceful ties with the United States' wartime allies and an understanding of the growing rift between forces in Eastern and Western Europe. Vandenberg acknowledged a philosophy that dated to the early years of the war: that the United States and its allies should remain on amicable terms with the Soviet Union if international peace and cooperation were to continue. However, he also indicated that what Churchill had earlier dubbed the iron curtain of Soviet occupation endangered the spirit of this "Grand Alliance" and must be addressed as an international issue.

Vandenberg took the floor acknowledging the comments of his colleagues and many other world leaders on the need for international cooperation during the postwar reconstruction. Without a multinational campaign, headed by the United Nations, countless people around the world were threatened with starvation and death during the upcoming winter months. As long as each participating nation—particularly those who maintained occupations of nations whose governments were felled during the war—was willing to communicate openly with the others, Vandenberg advised, the humanitarian goals of the UNRRA could be met.

However, Vandenberg argued, the Soviet Union was not embracing the spirit of international cooperation that fostered UNRRA. The Soviet Union, he said, was consistently blocking Western journalists from entry into its occupied territories, thereby preventing the world from knowing the true severity of those nations' poverty and starvation issues. Furthermore, instead of promoting freedom and democracy in these occupied territories, he charged, Moscow was establishing Soviet-style totalitarian regimes only months after the German-borne Fascist regimes had been removed.

Vandenberg dismissed Soviet calls for transparency on the US atomic energy program. The dangers associated with the atomic "problem" (as he called it) required that the United States' burgeoning nuclear capability remain secret, he said. Such an argument from Moscow was irrelevant to the humanitarian crisis at hand, he added. Only when the iron curtain was lifted from Soviet-occupied territories and truly cooperative and communicative policies were put into action by Moscow, Vandenberg said, could the international community successfully address the issues of postwar Europe.

—*Michael P. Auerbach, MA*

Bibliography and Additional Reading

Applebaum, Anne. *Iron Curtain: The Crushing of Eastern Europe*, 1944–1956. Toronto: McClelland, 2012. Print.

Brager, Bruce L. *The Iron Curtain: The Cold War in Europe.* New York: Infobase, 2004. Print.

"Finding Aid for Arthur H. Vandenberg Papers, 1884–1971." *Bentley Historical Lib.* Bentley Hist. Lib, U of Michigan Digital Lib., n.d. Web. 16 Jan. 2015.

Giangreco, D. M., and Robert E. Griffin. "Background on Conflict with USSR." *Harry S. Truman Lib. and Museum.* Natl. Archives and Records Admin., 13 Jan. 2015. Web. 16 Jan. 2015.

"Vandenberg, Arthur Hendrick, (1884–1951)." *Biographical Directory of the United States Congress.* US Congress, n.d. Web. 16 Jan. 2015.

■ No Country Fears a Strong America

Date: November 20, 1945
Author: Dwight D. Eisenhower
Genre: speech

Summary Overview

Less than a month after President Harry S. Truman declared the end of World War II, General Dwight D. Eisenhower addressed a dinner convocation attended by members of the American Legion. Eisenhower told the audience of military veterans that the United States should maintain the strength of its armed forces. A nation that promotes peace and international law can only be respected when it possesses a strong military, Eisenhower said. The general argued that such a policy would not create a militaristic philosophy among Americans, but would instead continue to promote the traditional and peaceful cultural philosophies the nation has demonstrated since its beginning. Eisenhower reminded the audience of how long it took for the United States to become involved in World War II after the attack on Pearl Harbor and suggested that the nation should be prepared to defend itself at all times.

Defining Moment

The latter years of World War II were marked by a number of high-profile events—most notably the invasion of France known as "D-Day." However, a fact often overlooked is that the United States' entry into the war—prompted by the Japanese attack on Pearl Harbor on December 7, 1941—took place two years after Germany invaded Poland, prompting England and France to declare war. Even after the United States' official declaration of war, it took several months for US troops to have significant involvement in combat. Among the issues preventing a more timely response were geography (the thousands of miles of ocean between the United States and battlefields in both Europe and the Pacific) and logistics (sending American troops to the optimal locations to engage Axis forces).

When the United States did reach the battlefield, however, the strength of the American armed forces was essential to an Allied victory. Working in partnership largely with English and French forces, US troops contributed heavily to the invasion at Normandy on June 6, 1944, and the Battle of the Bulge in December 1944–January 1945. In the Pacific, after sustaining heavy casualties during the year after Pearl Harbor, the US Navy began securing major victories at Midway and Guadalcanal (in June and August, respectively, of 1942) before dropping two atomic bombs on Japan in August 1945, bringing the international conflict to a close.

The United States' participation in World War II was also marked by the personalities and leadership of the US armed forces. General George S. Patton, for example, was a charismatic and yet intense officer who almost lost his command after famously slapping two US servicemen who suffered from combat fatigue. Lt. Gen. Eisenhower, viewed by many early in his command as a reluctant leader, privately clashed with President Roosevelt in 1942. Eisenhower, the new commander of the US force in northern Africa, pushed for the United States to cross the English Channel and invade France in concert with the English forces instead of engaging Germany's weaker forces across the Mediterranean.

The overwhelming destruction caused by the two American atomic bombs in Japan, coupled with the performance of the US military in Europe, vaulted the United States to the status of international leader. Following the war's end, the nation's leaders began an assessment of the next step for the United States in light of this new position in the international community. Less than one month after President Truman declared an official end to the war, General Eisenhower was invited to a dinner hosted in Chicago by the National Commanders of the American Legion, where he offered his thoughts on the future of the country's armed forces.

Author Biography

Dwight David Eisenhower was born in Denison, Texas, on October 14, 1890. He was raised in Abilene, Kansas.

Inspired by a childhood friend, who attended the US Naval Academy, Eisenhower gained admittance to the US Military Academy at West Point in 1911, graduating in 1915. In 1926, he graduated from the US Army's Command and General Staff School, leaving as an aide to General John Pershing. Two years later, he graduated from the Army War College and, shortly thereafter, accompanied General Douglas MacArthur to the Philippines. In 1942, he served as the commanding officer of the Army's European theater of operations, eventually leading Operation Torch in North Africa. A year later, he commanded the D-Day invasion of France. In 1952, he entered politics as a moderate Republican, winning the presidential election. He was reelected in 1956, earning his legacy as a prominent face of the Cold War. He retired from public service in 1961 and moved to a farm in Gettysburg, Pennsylvania. He died on March 28, 1969.

HISTORICAL DOCUMENT

For any soldier there is always a feeling of special satisfaction in receiving a summons to appear as an honored guest before a convocation of his own country's fighting men. Among all those that have worn their country's uniform in past wars there unfailingly exists a bond, a union, that can scarcely be felt by any one that is not of that band. Moreover, that feeling of brotherhood makes no particular note of the element in which the service of the individual was rendered, land, sea or air. It appears that the warrior who has returned to ways of peace automatically responds to the truism that a country's defenders are—and should be—one. Consequently I have a special pride and high sense of distinction in the honors accorded me today by this great Legion. Those honors I accept as a tribute to the services of 3,000,000 American fighting men that contributed so decisively to the defeat of Hitler and his hordes.

Associated with those Americans in a single Allied command were soldiers of other nations—the majority from the British Empire and large numbers from France. It is therefore particularly gratifying to me that there have appeared before this convention military representatives of those two great peoples, two men who served intimately with me in the Allied Expeditionary Force. This happy circumstance gives me opportunity to pay tribute to Sir Arthur Tedder, Marshal of the Royal Air Force and my deputy during all the operations in northwest Europe. A gallant leader and one of the finest airmen of the world, he was in every sense a true ally and a worthy representative of his country and of the more than 1,000,000 British Empire fighting men of all arms that marched shoulder to shoulder with the Americans through eleven months of bitter campaigning from the Normandy beachhead to final junction with the great Red Army in the heart of Germany.

Every American that served with me in Europe is proud to pay tribute to Sir Arthur Tedder and General Koenig, and to the fighting forces of their two countries. In equal measure we are proud of the magnificent work done by the Red Army and by the Allied forces that battled the long and tortuous way up the Italian peninsula to be present in the last few weeks in the final roundup of the once invincible Wehrmacht and Luftwaffe

Some members of that American Expeditionary Force of World War II are undoubtedly here today. Others of you are the fathers and older friends of the men who so courageously, loyally and successfully carried out the tasks that it was my responsibility to place before them in Europe. But whether of this war or of the one waged with equally brilliant results by the former generation, all of you here have special knowledge of things that our country must clearly understand and cannot afford to forget.

You have seen battle and you have experienced the tests it places upon man's moral and physical endurance, upon his skill and upon his ability to follow and to lead.

You understand, more than others, the indispensable requirement of teamwork upon the battlefield and you have seen the costs of disintegration, when the power derived from complete confidence in the union of the team disappears in the disorganization of purely individual action. In short, you understand and can bear witness to the priceless battlefield value of training. This value has persisted during all wars of history.

A question is: Does it still prevail?

We have just entered upon a scientific age which, in its most fearsome aspects, contains unimaginable threats for civilization. It may be possible that the time will come when the age-old virtues of physical and moral stamina, of courage, of patriotism, and of readiness for self-sacrifice will be meaningless to the nation's preservation. Conceivably—we are told—the day may come when any nation, no matter how small, if guided by perverted thinking, may suddenly unleash upon us or any other, destructive forces against which we would be powerless to defend ourselves. There is implied no limit to the capacity of science to reach the maximum in destructive effect unless that limit be found in the destruction of man himself. When the day of that capability comes, if it does, the only hope for the world as we know it will be complete spiritual regeneration, a strengthening of moral fiber that will place upon all men self-imposed determination to respect the rights of others.

To struggle toward the development of that world spirit is one of the noblest and most necessary efforts to which a man can devote himself. But to participate in that struggle does not, of itself, meet the requirements of today.

Three thousand years of recorded history lie behind us to prove that neither will the day of international order, nor that of complete spiritual regeneration, come suddenly and instantly. A thousand practical considerations always assure that the old gives way only gradually to the new! Although man has recoiled in fear from the introduction of gun powder and, later, explosives of multiplied power, although he has trembled at the advent of the big bomber, of the submarine, the tank, and pilotless missiles capable of reaching across hundreds of miles of distance, he has not yet been able to resolve his deep political and economic issues without recourse to violence. Neither has he sufficiently progressed in the development of moral and spiritual values as to compel him to adhere consistently to the principles inherent in his great historic religions.

We come then to this: We dwell in a world in which the possibilities of destruction are so great as to terrify peoples everywhere. Yet we must still acknowledge human weaknesses within ourselves and others. It is with this world that we must now concern ourselves, even as we reach toward and strive for a better one. I see no incompatibility between enlisting ourselves under the banner of peace based upon international co-operation and common appreciation of human value on the one hand and, on the other, the effort to make certain that our beloved country shall not become, the victim of predatory force. It is idle to say that our nation can never be endangered. Pearl Harbor should have effectively dispelled that delusion. It is equally idle to say that reasonable preparation to care for ourselves constitutes unwarranted suspicion of those who have been and whom we are glad to class as friends. We call war an emergency, and it is just that. Like all emergencies, it usually comes, at least to us, unexpectedly, and from quarters that are not revealed until too late.

From the time that Japan invaded Manchuria in 1931 up until the moment when we were attacked in 1941, we had a few far-seeing statesmen that constantly pointed out to us the danger building up in Asia and Europe to ourselves and to our way of living.

Because we entertained no thought of aggressive war it was difficult, indeed, for us to ascribe to any other such a motive. And though, eventually we became sufficiently alarmed to undertake increased measures of preparation, Pearl Harbor Day found us with a pitifully small air force, an inadequate fleet, and a poorly equipped and badly trained Army.

To be strong nationally is not a sin, it is a necessity! We must be strong first to defend ourselves, secondly, to give the necessary dignity and influence to the words of our leaders as they labor to perfect machinery by which the world may settle its difficulties legally and peaceably, rather than illegally and by force. A weakling, particularly a rich and opulent weakling, seeking peaceable solution of a difficulty, is likely to invite contempt; but the same plea from the strong is listened to most respectfully.

We, as soldiers and veterans, bear the conviction that, given the latest and plentiful equipment, strength still springs from unity, from stamina, from teamwork and from perfected technique. These result from training! And training requires time! The minimum is a year!

With your knowledge of the difference between trained and untrained men in battle, what greater boon, what greater privilege could be given to all our young men than a degree of training which in emergency will allow them quickly to be integrated into the forces that may have to stand between our country and a thousand Buchenwalds? Even though we should become the victims of sudden and devastating raids, does anyone imagine that America would abjectly sue for peace at the price of surrendering the traditions of free life that have made her great?

Moreover, does anyone imagine that, even under these conditions, trained and disciplined men, ready to fight the conflagrations, to rescue the wounded and to rally instantly behind their leaders, would not be more valuable than an equal number of equally brave and courageous men that had no modicum of training?

A reasonable period of peacetime experience in teamwork, in the development of mutual confidence, in perfected technique of weapons, and in coming to comprehend the leadership and organization that are inherent in intelligent military instruction, would provide for our young men an opportunity they deserve, and would do much to give our nation justified confidence in the matter of national security.

We are still congratulating ourselves and giving thanks to the Almighty for the great victories that this year have crowned our efforts in both hemispheres. Yet let us not forget the circumstances of the early months of that war. From Dec. 7, 1941, it was eight months before we made our first relatively small counter-move, in the bitter Guadalcanal campaign of the western Pacific. It was eleven months before we attacked with our first few divisions in North Africa, and these, because of the circumstances of that year, were only sketchily trained. It was almost exactly two and one-half years from the day the Japs treacherously attacked us before we made our decisive move in Europe to cross the Channel. And it was several months more before we became strong enough in the Pacific to move definitely against the Philippines. The time we needed was gained for us by the courage of the British Empire, the sacrifices of Russia, and the vastness of the Pacific Ocean and the selfless devotion of the initially few American soldiers, sailors, marines and airmen in the Pacific theater. Thus, in two world wars, we have been dependent upon friends to protect us while we, over a period of many months, devoted feverish attention to repairing the woeful states of unpreparedness in which the outbreak of hostilities found us.

Let us now resolve to be reasonably forehanded in this matter, so far as it is possible for a peaceful citizenry to be.

There is another aspect to this question that deserves attention. Based upon numberless contacts with many people of other nations, I hold the conviction that no other country fears a strong America, no decent preparations of our own will be regarded suspiciously by others, because we are trusted. Indeed, I am convinced that others would interpret any return of ours to our former levels of unpreparedness as an intention to return to what we thought was isolation. They view with concern what they regard as our unseemly haste in disintegration of the mighty forces that did so much to bring Hitler, Mussolini and Hirohito to their deaths or to their knees, A respectably strong America means to others a willingness on our part to bear our full share of the burdens of preserving peace—not an intention to resort to force for our own enrichment or advantage.

I know of no more sincere pacifists than American soldiers and veterans. No one could wish more passionately than they for the assurance that no longer need we devote any of our time and treasure to the maintenance of organizations whose very purpose is, and should be, negative rather than to constructive development of our country. No consideration of rank, renown, regard or personal advancement has the slightest weight with any officer of my acquaintance, as compared to his concern for peace and his country's welfare. Moreover, this problem does not primarily belong to the active soldier, except in an advisory capacity. The fighting forces of this country belong to you, our nation's citizens and voters. Your responsibilities are great—and the broader and deeper your knowledge on the requirements of security the more it devolves upon you to give to others that same understanding of the issue here involved.

I am told that the purpose of training all our youth, for their own good and for that of the country, is opposed by many of those to whom we have a right to look for spiritual and educational leadership. If this is true, I feel that it must arise from a reluctance to face realities, to study our own history, a history that amply provides the futility of chronic weakness and lack of training in preserving the peace. There appears to be a failure to understand that if we trust our own motives then our strength can never be that of the bully, but of the peacemaker. If we sincerely believe, as I believe, that the America of the future will be true to our traditions of the past; that we will respect the rights of others and be considerate of the weak; that we will work to increase the fruitfulness of the earth but will not steal from others to satisfy a desire of our own; that so far as it is given for mortals to do, we will act in the international field in the spirit of the golden rule—if we have faith in these things, then we and the world will be advantaged by our strength.

This country can never be militaristic in its thinking—and to pretend that a year of training will develop such a national philosophy can but be answered by yourselves. You—all of you—have military training—do you feel militaristic? Do you feel inclined to urge one country to adhere to a policy of aggressive war? I am perfectly satisfied—I leave that answer to you.

So, why should not we give our sons opportunity in time of peace so to prepare themselves that in the event of war they may, at a minimum risk to themselves, serve their nation as brilliantly, effectively and successfully, but with less delay, than you of World Wars I and II have already done. For in the event of another war it could well be that we would be the first rather than the last to be attacked.

With this great arsenal of democracy destroyed or defeated, while it was still unready and therefore weak, the aggressive assaults on other peace-loving nations would be less hazardous. But if we are strong—there will be given this hypothetical Hitler of the future no advantage in singling us out first for attack, and so he may be deterred by the lessons of two world wars from attempting any resort to force.

A strong America is a trained and an integrated America. Nowhere is that integration more necessary than in our armed forces. We must not think, primarily, in terms of ground forces, naval forces, air forces. We must think in terms of coordinated action. Every consideration of efficiency, economy and progress in research demands the closest possible unity among all our fighting forces, all the way from bottom to top. This great and necessary purpose, I believe, can be best achieved by unified control at the top.

And now, once more, may I say that the American and Allied forces that I had the high privilege to lead in Europe, join with you and with me in the devout hope that never again will the children of America be summoned from their peaceful pursuits to face the purgatory of battle.

You, here, can be an effective force in assuring realization of that hope.

Document Analysis

Eisenhower uses the platform provided to him by the American Legion to praise not only the Allied victory in World War II, but also the spirit and camaraderie of American military veterans. These men, Eisenhower says, are part of an organization that was dedicated both to defending the United States and to promoting international peace. Eisenhower tells his audience that the United States must continue to be prepared to protect itself—through war, if necessary—while promoting the traditional American values of freedom, democracy, and peace. Such a policy is not inherently militaristic, he argues. Instead, a strong, well-trained, and organized military lends a high degree of legitimacy to the United States as it seeks to become a world leader in the postwar era.

Eisenhower begins his speech by paying homage to the veterans before him as well as to the entire Allied Expeditionary Force (AEF) that, in concert, defeated Germany, Italy, and Japan in Europe and the South Pacific. Every serviceman who took part in the war, he says, has seen battle and the benefits of his training to surviving on the battlefield. Despite the fact that the atomic bomb and pilotless missiles signal a new era in military technology, he says, it is the experience and knowledge of every survivor of World War II that will help the rest of the world appreciate the moral value of peace. However, Eisenhower cautions, not every nation or society will share this perspective. Indeed, the world saw such belligerence in the form of the unprovoked attack on Pearl Harbor, he suggests. War is an emergency, and "like all emergencies, it usually comes, at least to us, unexpectedly."

It is, therefore, imperative that the US military continue to recruit, train, and enhance its armed forces, Eisenhower says. He reminds the audience that the United States was not only caught by surprise by the Japanese attack on the Pacific Fleet, but it was also slow to react in both the European and Pacific theaters even after the declaration of war had been issued. The United States was only successful because of the assistance of Britain, France, and the other Allies, he argues.

When the emergency of war occurs in the future, the United States should learn from this experience and ensure that its armed forces are well-trained, organized, and prepared to respond with great vigor and strength. Eisenhower says that, in addition to giving security to the nation, a strong military—which is "not a sin, . . . [but] a necessity"—lends credibility to a country that looks to confront would-be aggressors on the international diplomatic stage, effectively deterring them from considering attacking it. The United States' strength "can never be that of the bully." The United States has a reputation in the world as a defender of the weak and a promoter of peace and democracy. Strengthening the armed forces, he argues, will not generate a culture of militarism; throughout American history, the reasonable actions of US soldiers and sailors prove that investment in enhanced military training does not lead to militarism. Rather, he assures, it is a prudent and sensible policy that protects the interests of the United States, both at home and abroad.

Essential Themes

Eisenhower arrived at the 1945 American Legion dinner with a celebratory eye on the American victory in World War II a month earlier and a cautionary eye toward the future. Eisenhower lauded his audience as well as the entire military (and the Allies), honoring their dedication and unity to preserving the United States and international peace. He also stressed the importance of the United States maintaining its military might, not only to avoid being caught unprepared again, but also to better keep the peace and to back up its authority as a major world power. The speech implied that no country that was truly a US ally would feel threatened by the country continuing to build the strength of its armed forces and emphasized that this would not encourage aggressive or militaristic behavior on the part of the United States.

The idea of the United States as international peacekeeper has remained a part of the country's self-image and building and maintaining a strong military has remained a major concern. Though Eisenhower eventually came to be critical of the military-industrial complex, devoting his final speech from the White House to warning of what he considered the dangers of its growing influence, the United States continues to devote significant resources to its armed forces.

In his farewell speech, President Eisenhower notes the end of World War II marked a turning point in the American conception of the military establishment and its role in peacetime. At the time, there was no permanent armaments industry, and there had generally been less focus on building national defense outside of wartime. However, as many in the government and armed forces felt that they had been caught unprepared by World War II, they began to believe that this model was no longer viable and that the nation should maintain a constant state of readiness for war. Thus, Eisenhower's 1945 speech illustrates a change in thought that would continue to affect US government policy for decades to come.

—*Michael P. Auerbach, MA*

Bibliography and Additional Reading

Atkinson, Rick. "Ike's Dark Days." *US News and World Report* 133.16 (2002): 42. Print.

Darby, Jean. *Dwight D. Eisenhower*. Minneapolis: Twenty-First Century, 2004. Print.

"The Eisenhower Presidency, 1953–1961." *Eisenhower Presidential Library, Museum, and Boyhood Home*. Natl. Archives and Records Administration, n.d. Web. 5 Nov. 2014.

Freidel, Frank, & Hugh Sidey. "Dwight D. Eisenhower." *White House*. United States Govt., 2006. Web. 5 Nov. 2014.

"A Life in Brief: Dwight David Eisenhower." *Miller Center*. U of Virginia, n.d. Web. 5 Nov. 2014.

Norton, Richard. "Rivals, Victors: Eisenhower, Patton, Bradley, and the Partnership that Drove the Allied Conquest in Europe." *Naval War College Review*, 65.2 (2012): 178–80. Print.

"World War II Time Line." *National Geographic*. National Geographic Soc., 2001. Web. 5 Nov. 2014.

■ "The Sources of Soviet Conduct"

Date: July 1947
Author: George F. Kennan
Genre: article; editorial

Summary Overview

Within two years after the end of World War II, it was becoming increasingly clear in the United States that the nation's wartime alliance with the Soviet Union under Joseph Stalin was turning sour. Many in the United States wondered how this could have happened so quickly. One man who not only gave an answer, but also a prescription for what to do about it was America's chargé d'affaires in Moscow, George F. Kennan. Writing in the July 1947 issue of the journal *Foreign Affairs*, under the pseudonym "X," Kennan wrote from his first-hand knowledge of the Soviet government. He wrote of the history of Russia's desire to expand and the ideological backing now given to it by Stalinism, advising a policy that came to be known as "containment"—the long-term limitation of the Soviets to their own sphere of influence and swift attention whenever they tried to exceed that.

Defining Moment

As World War II came to an end, Americans became increasingly concerned with the geopolitical aspirations of the Soviet Union. With the Soviet Army still occupying large swaths of Eastern Europe and the nations of that region quickly setting up Communist governments, foreign policy experts in the United States and Western Europe scrambled to figure out the best course of action. Some urged cooperation with the Soviet Union, since the United States and most of Europe had just concluded its second cataclysmic war in less than thirty years. Others, such as US senator James O. Eastland, cited the example of the appeasement of Nazi Germany during the 1930s, which only emboldened Hitler to continue German militarization and expansion.

During 1945 and 1946, Communism spread across Eastern Europe at an alarming rate, with East Germany, Poland, Hungary, Bulgaria, Czechoslovakia, Romania, Albania, and Yugoslavia establishing Communist governments. Under Stalin, the Soviet Union worked to foster Communist uprisings in other nations as well. The very first complaint dealt with by the new United Nations had to do with the Soviet refusal to withdraw its troops from Iran after the war. Communists, supported by Yugoslavia, fought nationalists in Greece. In Turkey, the Soviet Union demanded that it be given free access from the Black Sea to the Mediterranean through the two Turkish straits known as the Dardanelles and the Bosporus; the Soviets staged naval exercises in the Black Sea and sent troops to the Balkans—both actions aimed at intimidating Turkey.

As early as February 1946, many in the federal government sought to formulate a coherent policy toward the Soviets. It was at this point that George F. Kennan began to articulate his opinions in what became known as the "Long Telegram." In it, he made observations about the factors that contributed to the Soviet desire to expand, stating that Soviet actions were shaped both by Marxist ideology and the long tradition of Russian expansionism and imperialism. As such, he argued that the United States could expect Soviet behavior to continue to seek expansion and that the combination of this with the paranoia he asserted to be inherent in Communist ideology was going to pose an ongoing threat to the United States and Western Europe.

By mid-1947, Secretary of State George C. Marshall had proposed what became known as the Marshall Plan, which gave massive US economic aid to the nations of Europe under the premise that economically-secure nations would be much less likely to succumb to Communist agitation. But although the Marshall Plan was seen as a part of the American policy to make Soviet expansion more difficult, it still did not deal with how to respond to Stalin's aggressive plans to foster Communist revolutions around the world when they came to bear in particular nations. It was at this point that Kennan wrote an opinion for Defense Secretary James V. Forrestal, which was published in the journal *Foreign*

Affairs under the pseudonym "X" and became the basis for the policy of containment.

Author Biography

George F. Kennan was one of the few American diplomats with significant experience in Soviet policy when he wrote "The Sources of Soviet Conduct" in Foreign Affairs. After graduating from Princeton University, Kennan entered the diplomatic corps, being assigned to Moscow in 1933. He spent a number of years in Berlin before the outbreak of World War II and was briefly interred by Nazi Germany after the United States entered the war in late 1941. He returned to Moscow in 1944 as chargé d'affaires, a key advisory position to the US ambassador. After writing the "Long Telegram," Kennan was recalled to Washington, DC, where he was appointed chairman of the Policy Planning Staff at the State Department, and it was in this position that he wrote "The Sources of Soviet Conduct," as an opinion piece at the behest of Defense Secretary James V. Forrestal.

HISTORICAL DOCUMENT

The political personality of Soviet power as we know it today is the product of ideology and circumstances: ideology inherited by the present Soviet leaders from the movement in which they had their political origin, and circumstances of the power which they now have exercised for nearly three decades in Russia. There can be few tasks of psychological analysis more difficult than to try to trace the interaction of these two forces and the relative role of each in the determination of official Soviet conduct. yet the attempt must be made if that conduct is to be understood and effectively countered.

It is difficult to summarize the set of ideological concepts with which the Soviet leaders came into power. Marxian ideology, in its Russian-Communist projection, has always been in process of subtle evolution. The materials on which it bases itself are extensive and complex. But the outstanding features of Communist thought as it existed in 1916 may perhaps be summarized as follows: (a) that the central factor in the life of man, the factor which determines the character of public life and the "physiognomy of society," is the system by which material goods are produced and exchanged; (b) that the capitalist system of production is a nefarious one which inevitable leads to the exploitation of the working class by the capital-owning class and is incapable of developing adequately the economic resources of society or of distributing fairly the material good produced by human labor; (c) that capitalism contains the seeds of its own destruction and must, in view of the inability of the capital-owning class to adjust itself to economic change, result eventually and inescapably in a revolutionary transfer of power to the working class; and (d) that imperialism, the final phase of capitalism, leads directly to war and revolution.

The rest may be outlined in Lenin's own words: "Unevenness of economic and political development is the inflexible law of capitalism. It follows from this that the victory of Socialism may come originally in a few capitalist countries or even in a single capitalist country. The victorious proletariat of that country, having expropriated the capitalists and having organized Socialist production at home, would rise against the remaining capitalist world, drawing to itself in the process the oppressed classes of other countries." [Footnote: "Concerning the Slogans of the United States of Europe," August 1915, Official Soviet edition of Lenin's works.] It must be noted that there was no assumption that capitalism would perish without proletarian revolution. A final push was needed from a revolutionary proletariat movement in order to tip over the tottering structure. But it was regarded as inevitable that sooner or later that push be given.

For 50 years prior to the outbreak of the Revolution, this pattern of thought had exercised great fascination for the members of the Russian revolutionary movement. Frustrated, discontented, hopeless of finding self-expression—or too impatient to seek it—in the confining limits of the Tsarist political system, yet lacking wide popular support or their choice of bloody revolution as a means of social betterment, these revolutionists found in Marxist theory a highly convenient rationalization for their own instinctive desires. It afforded pseudo-scientific justification for their impatience, for their categoric denial of all value in the Tsarist system, for their yearning for power and revenge and for their inclination to cut corners in the pursuit of it. It is therefore no wonder that they had come to believe implicitly in the truth and soundness of the Marxist-Leninist teachings, so congenial to their own impulses and emotions. Their sincerity need not be impugned. This is a phenomenon as old as human nature itself. It has never been more aptly described than by Edward Gibbon, who wrote in *The Decline and Fall of the Roman Empire*: "From enthusiasm to imposture the step is perilous and slippery; the demon of Socrates affords a memorable instance of how a wise man may deceive himself, how a good man may deceive others, how the conscience may slumber in a mixed and middle state between self-illusion and voluntary fraud." And it was with this set of conceptions that the members of the Bolshevik Party entered into power.

Now it must be noted that through all the years of preparation for revolution, the attention of these men, as indeed of Marx himself, had been centered less on the future form which socialism would take than on the necessary overthrow of rival power which, in their view, had to precede the introduction of socialism. [Footnote: Here and elsewhere in this paper "socialism refers to Marxist or Leninist communism, not to liberal socialism of the Second International variety.] Their views, therefore, on the positive program to be put into effect, once power was attained, were for the most part nebulous, visionary and impractical. Beyond the nationalization of industry and the expropriation of large private capital holdings there was no agreed program. The treatment of the peasantry, which, according to the Marxist formulation was not of the proletariat, had always been a vague spot in the pattern of Communist thought: and it remained an object of controversy and vacillation for the first ten years of Communist power.

The circumstances of the immediate post-revolution period—the existence in Russia of civil war and foreign intervention, together with the obvious fact that the Communists represented only a tiny minority of the Russian people—made the establishment of dictatorial power a necessity. The experiment with war Communism" and the abrupt attempt to eliminate private production and trade had unfortunate economic consequences and caused further bitterness against the new revolutionary regime. While the temporary relaxation of the effort to communize Russia, represented by the New Economic Policy, alleviated some of this economic distress and thereby served its purpose, it also made it evident that the "capitalistic sector of society" was still prepared to profit at once from any relaxation of governmental pressure, and would, if permitted to continue to exist, always constitute a powerful opposing element to the Soviet regime and a serious rival for influence in the country. Somewhat the same situation prevailed with respect to the individual peasant who, in his own small way, was also a private producer.

Lenin, had he lived, might have proved a great enough man to reconcile these conflicting forces to the ultimate benefit of Russian society, thought this is questionable. But be that as it may, Stalin, and those whom he led in the struggle for succession to Lenin's position of leadership, were not the men to tolerate rival political forces in the sphere of power which they coveted. Their sense of insecurity was too great. Their particular brand of fanaticism, unmodified by any of the Anglo-Saxon traditions of compromise, was too fierce and too jealous to envisage any permanent sharing of power. From the Russian-Asiatic world out of which they had emerged they carried with them a skepticism as to the possibilities of permanent and peaceful coexistence of rival forces. Easily persuaded of their own doctrinaire "rightness," they insisted on the submission or destruction of all competing power. Outside the Communist Party, Russian society was to have no rigidity. There were to be no forms of collective human activity or association which would not be dominated by the Party. No other force in Russian society was to be permitted to achieve vitality or integrity. Only the Party was to have structure. All else was to be an amorphous mass.

And within the Party the same principle was to apply. The mass of Party members might go through the motions of election, deliberation, decision and action; but in these motions they were to be animated not by their own individual wills but by the awesome breath of the Party leadership and the overbrooding presence of "the word."

Let it be stressed again that subjectively these men probably did not seek absolutism for its own sake. They doubtless believed—and found it easy to believe—that they alone knew what was good for society and that they would accomplish that good once their power was secure and unchallengeable. But in seeking that security of their own rule they were prepared to recognize no restrictions, either of God or man, on the character of their methods. And until such time as that security might be achieved, they placed far down on their scale of operational priorities the comforts and happiness of the peoples entrusted to their care.

Now the outstanding circumstance concerning the Soviet regime is that down to the present day this process of political consolidation has never been completed and the men in the Kremlin have continued to be predominantly absorbed with the struggle to secure and make absolute the power which they seized in November 1917. They have endeavored to secure it primarily against forces at home, within Soviet society itself. But they have also endeavored to secure it against the outside world. For ideology, as we have seen, taught them that the outside world was hostile and that it was their duty eventually to overthrow the political forces beyond their borders. Then powerful hands of Russian history and tradition reached up to sustain them in this feeling. Finally, their own aggressive intransigence with respect to the outside world began to find its own reaction; and they were soon forced, to use another Gibbonesque phrase, "to chastise the contumacy" which they themselves had provoked. It is an undeniable privilege of every man to prove himself right in the thesis that the world is his enemy; for if he reiterates it frequently enough and makes it the background of his conduct he is bound eventually to be right.

Now it lies in the nature of the mental world of the Soviet leaders, as well as in the character of their ideology, that no opposition to them can be officially recognized as having any merit or justification whatsoever. Such opposition can flow, in theory, only from the hostile and incorrigible forces of dying capitalism. As long as remnants of capitalism were officially recognized as existing in Russia, it was possible to place on them, as an internal element, part of the blame for the maintenance of a dictatorial form of society. But as these remnants were liquidated, little by little, this justification fell away, and when it was indicated officially that they had been finally destroyed, it disappeared altogether. And this fact created one of the most basic of the compulsions which came to act upon the Soviet regime: since capitalism no longer existed in Russia and since it could not be admitted that there could be serious or widespread opposition to the Kremlin springing spontaneously from the liberated masses under its authority, it became necessary to justify the retention of the dictatorship by stressing the menace of capitalism abroad.

This began at an early date. In 1924 Stalin specifically defended the retention of the "organs of suppression," meaning, among others, the army and the secret police, on the ground that "as long as there is a capitalistic encirclement there will be danger of intervention with all the consequences that flow from that danger." In accordance with that theory, and from that time on, all internal opposition forces in Russia have consistently been portrayed as the agents of foreign forces of reaction antagonistic to Soviet power.

By the same token, tremendous emphasis has been placed on the original Communist thesis of a basic antagonism between the capitalist and Socialist worlds. It is clear, from many indications, that this emphasis is not founded in reality. The real facts concerning it have been confused by the existence abroad of genuine resentment provoked by Soviet philosophy and tactics and occasionally by the existence of great centers of military power, notably the Nazi regime in Germany and the Japanese Government of the late 1930s, which indeed have aggressive designs against the Soviet Union. But there is ample evidence that the stress laid in Moscow on the menace confronting Soviet society from the world outside its borders is founded not in the realities of foreign antagonism but in the necessity of explaining away the maintenance of dictatorial authority at home.

Now the maintenance of this pattern of Soviet power, namely, the pursuit of unlimited authority domestically, accompanied by the cultivation of the semi-myth of implacable foreign hostility, has gone far to shape the actual machinery of Soviet power as we know it today. Internal organs of administration which did not serve this purpose withered on the vine. Organs which did serve this purpose became vastly swollen. The security of Soviet power came to rest on the iron discipline of the Party, on the severity and ubiquity of the secret police, and on the uncompromising economic monopolism of the state. The "organs of suppression," in which the Soviet leaders had sought security from rival forces, became in large measures the masters of those whom they were designed to serve. Today the major part of the structure of Soviet power is committed to the perfection of the dictatorship and to the maintenance of the concept of Russia as in a state of siege, with the enemy lowering beyond the walls. And the millions of human beings who form that part of the structure of power must defend at all costs this concept of Russia's position, for without it they are themselves superfluous.

As things stand today, the rulers can no longer dream of parting with these organs of suppression. The quest for absolute power, pursued now for nearly three decades with a ruthlessness unparalleled (in scope at least) in modern times, has again produced internally, as it did externally, its own reaction. The excesses of the police apparatus have fanned the potential opposition to the regime into something far greater and more dangerous than it could have been before those excesses began.

But least of all can the rulers dispense with the fiction by which the maintenance of dictatorial power has been defended. For this fiction has been canonized in Soviet philosophy by the excesses already committed in its name; and it is now anchored in the Soviet structure of thought by bonds far greater than those of mere ideology.

II

So much for the historical background. What does it spell in terms of the political personality of Soviet power as we know it today?

Of the original ideology, nothing has been officially junked. Belief is maintained in the basic badness of capitalism, in the inevitability of its destruction, in the obligation of the proletariat to assist in that destruction and to take power into its own hands. But stress has come to be laid primarily on those concepts which relate most specifically to the Soviet regime itself: to its position as the sole truly Socialist regime in a dark and misguided world, and to the relationships of power within it.

The first of these concepts is that of the innate antagonism between capitalism and Socialism. We have seen how deeply that concept has become imbedded in foundations of Soviet power. It has profound implications for Russia's conduct as a member of international society. It means that there can never be on Moscow's side a sincere assumption of a community of aims between the Soviet Union and powers which are regarded as capitalist. It must inevitably be assumed in Moscow that the aims of the capitalist world are antagonistic to the Soviet regime, and therefore to the interests of the peoples it controls. If the Soviet government occasionally sets it signature to documents which would indicate the contrary, this is to regarded as a tactical maneuver permissible in dealing with the enemy (who is without honor) and should be taken in the spirit of caveat emptor. Basically, the antagonism remains. It is postulated. And from it flow many of the phenomena which we find disturbing in the Kremlin's conduct of foreign policy: the secretiveness, the lack of frankness, the duplicity, the wary suspiciousness, and the basic unfriendliness of purpose. These phenomena are there to stay, for the foreseeable future. There can be variations of degree and of emphasis. When there is something the Russians want from us, one or the other of these features of their policy may be thrust temporarily into the background; and when that happens there will always be Americans who will leap forward with gleeful announcements that "the Russians have changed," and some who will even try to take credit for having brought about such "changes." But we should not be misled by tactical maneuvers. These characteristics of Soviet policy, like the postulate from which they flow, are basic to the internal nature of Soviet power, and will be with us, whether in the foreground or the background, until the internal nature of Soviet power is changed.

This means we are going to continue for long time to find the Russians difficult to deal with. It does not mean that they should be considered as embarked upon a do-or-die program to overthrow our society by a given date. The theory of the inevitability of the eventual fall of capitalism has the fortunate connotation that there is no hurry about it. The forces of progress can take their time in preparing the final coup de grâce. meanwhile, what is vital is that the "Socialist fatherland"—that oasis of power which has already been won for Socialism in the person of the Soviet Union—should be cherished and defended by all good Communists at home and abroad, its fortunes promoted, its enemies badgered and confounded. The promotion of premature, "adventuristic" revolutionary projects abroad which might embarrass Soviet power in any way would be an inexcusable, even a counter-revolutionary act. The cause of Socialism is the support and promotion of Soviet power, as defined in Moscow.

This brings us to the second of the concepts important to contemporary Soviet outlook. That is the infallibility of the Kremlin. The Soviet concept of power, which permits no focal points of organization outside the Party itself, requires that the Party leadership remain in theory the sole repository of truth. For if truth were to be found elsewhere, there would be justification for its expression in organized activity. But it is precisely that which the Kremlin cannot and will not permit.

The leadership of the Communist Party is therefore always right, and has been always right ever since in 1929 Stalin formalized his personal power by announcing that decisions of the Politburo were being taken unanimously.

On the principle of infallibility there rests the iron discipline of the Communist Party. In fact, the two concepts are mutually self-supporting. Perfect discipline requires recognition of infallibility. Infallibility requires the observance of discipline. And the two go far to determine the behaviorism of the entire Soviet apparatus of power. But their effect cannot be understood unless a third factor be taken into account: namely, the fact that the leadership is at liberty to put forward for tactical purposes any particular thesis which it finds useful to the cause at any particular moment and to require the faithful and unquestioning acceptance of that thesis by the members of the movement as a whole. This means that truth is not a constant but is actually created, for all intents and purposes, by the Soviet leaders themselves. It may vary from week to week, from month to month. It is nothing absolute and immutable—nothing which flows from objective reality. It is only the most recent manifestation of the wisdom of those in whom the ultimate wisdom is supposed to reside, because they represent the logic of history. The accumulative effect of these factors is to give to the whole subordinate apparatus of Soviet power an unshakable stubbornness and steadfastness in its orientation. This orientation can be changed at will by the Kremlin but by no other power. Once a given party line has been laid down on a given issue of current policy, the whole Soviet governmental machine, including the mechanism of diplomacy, moves inexorably along the prescribed path, like a persistent toy automobile wound up and headed in a given direction, stopping only when it meets with some unanswerable force. The individuals who are the components of this machine are unamenable to argument or reason, which comes to them from outside sources. Their whole training has taught them to mistrust and discount the glib persuasiveness of the outside world. Like the white dog before the phonograph, they hear only the "master's voice." And if they are to be called off from the purposes last dictated to them, it is the master who must call them off. Thus the foreign representative cannot hope that his words will make any impression on them. The most that he can hope is that they will be transmitted to those at the top, who are capable of changing the party line. But even those are not likely to be swayed by any normal logic in the words of the bourgeois representative. Since there can be no appeal to common purposes, there can be no appeal to common mental approaches. For this reason, facts speak louder than words to the ears of the Kremlin; and words carry the greatest weight when they have the ring of reflecting, or being backed up by, facts of unchallengeable validity.

But we have seen that the Kremlin is under no ideological compulsion to accomplish its purposes in a hurry. Like the Church, it is dealing in ideological concepts which are of long-term validity, and it can afford to be patient. It has no right to risk the existing achievements of the revolution for the sake of vain baubles of the future. The very teachings of Lenin himself require great caution and flexibility in the pursuit of Communist purposes. Again, these precepts are fortified by the lessons of Russian history: of centuries of obscure battles between nomadic forces over the stretches of a vast unfortified plain. Here caution, circumspection, flexibility and deception are the valuable qualities; and their value finds a natural appreciation in the Russian or the oriental mind. Thus the Kremlin has no compunction about retreating in the face of superior forces. And being under the compulsion of no timetable, it does not get panicky under the necessity for such retreat. Its political action is a fluid stream which moves constantly, wherever it is permitted to move, toward a given goal. Its main concern is to make sure that it has filled every nook and cranny available to it in the basin of world power. But if it finds unassailable barriers in its path, it accepts these philosophically and accommodates itself to them. The main thing is that there should always be pressure, unceasing constant pressure, toward the desired goal. There is no trace of any feeling in Soviet psychology that that goal must be reached at any given time.

These considerations make Soviet diplomacy at once easier and more difficult to deal with than the diplomacy of individual aggressive leaders like Napoleon and Hitler. On the one hand it is more sensitive to contrary force, more ready to yield on individual sectors of the diplomatic front when that force is felt to be too strong, and thus more rational in the logic and rhetoric of power. On the other hand it cannot be easily defeated or discouraged by a single victory on the part of its opponents. And the patient persistence by which it is animated means that it can be effectively countered not by sporadic acts which represent the momentary whims of democratic opinion but only be intelligent long-range policies on the part of Russia's adversaries—policies no less steady in their purpose, and no less variegated and resourceful in their application, than those of the Soviet Union itself.

In these circumstances it is clear that the main element of any United States policy toward the Soviet Union must be that of long-term, patient but firm and vigilant containment of Russian expansive tendencies. It is important to note, however, that such a policy has nothing to do with outward histrionics: with threats or blustering or superfluous gestures of outward "toughness." While the Kremlin is basically flexible in its reaction to political realities, it is by no means unamenable to considerations of prestige. Like almost any other government, it can be placed by tactless and threatening gestures in a position where it cannot afford to yield even though this might be dictated by its sense of realism. The Russian leaders are keen judges of human psychology, and as such they are highly conscious that loss of temper and of self-control is never a source of strength in political affairs. They are quick to exploit such evidences of weakness. For these reasons it is a sine qua non of successful dealing with Russia that the foreign government in question should remain at all times cool and collected and that its demands on Russian policy should be put forward in such a manner as to leave the way open for a compliance not too detrimental to Russian prestige.

III

In the light of the above, it will be clearly seen that the Soviet pressure against the free institutions of the western world is something that can be contained by the adroit and vigilant application of counter-force at a series of constantly shifting geographical and political points, corresponding to the shifts and maneuvers of Soviet policy, but which cannot be charmed or talked out of existence. The Russians look forward to a duel of infinite duration, and they see that already they have scored great successes. It must be borne in mind that there was a time when the Communist Party represented far more of a minority in the sphere of Russian national life than Soviet power today represents in the world community.

But if the ideology convinces the rulers of Russia that truth is on their side and they can therefore afford to wait, those of us on whom that ideology has no claim are free to examine objectively the validity of that premise. The Soviet thesis not only implies complete lack of control by the west over its own economic destiny, it likewise assumes Russian unity, discipline and patience over an infinite period. Let us bring this apocalyptic vision down to earth, and suppose that the western world finds the strength and resourcefulness to contain Soviet power over a period of ten to fifteen years. What does that spell for Russia itself?

The Soviet leaders, taking advantage of the contributions of modern techniques to the arts of despotism, have solved the question of obedience within the confines of their power. Few challenge their authority; and even those who do are unable to make that challenge valid as against the organs of suppression of the state.

The Kremlin has also proved able to accomplish its purpose of building up Russia, regardless of the interests of the inhabitants, and industrial foundation of heavy metallurgy, which is, to be sure, not yet complete but which is nevertheless continuing to grow and is approaching those of the other major industrial countries. All of this, however, both the maintenance of internal political security and the building of heavy industry, has been carried out at a terrible cost in human life and in human hopes and energies. It has necessitated the use of forced labor on a scale unprecedented in modern times under conditions of peace. It has involved the neglect or abuse of other phases of Soviet economic life, particularly agriculture, consumers' goods production, housing and transportation.

To all that, the war has added its tremendous toll of destruction, death and human exhaustion. In consequence of this, we have in Russia today a population which is physically and spiritually tired. The mass of the people are disillusioned, skeptical and no longer as accessible as they once were to the magical attraction which Soviet power still radiates to its followers abroad. The avidity with which people seized upon the slight respite accorded to the Church for tactical reasons during the war was eloquent testimony to the fact that their capacity for faith and devotion found little expression in the purposes of the regime.

In these circumstances, there are limits to the physical and nervous strength of people themselves. These limits are absolute ones, and are binding even for the cruelest dictatorship, because beyond them people cannot be driven. The forced labor camps and the other agencies of constraint provide temporary means of compelling people to work longer hours than their own volition or mere economic pressure would dictate; but if people survive them at all they become old before their time and must be considered as human casualties to the demands of dictatorship. In either case their best powers are no longer available to society and can no longer be enlisted in the service of the state.

Here only the younger generations can help. The younger generation, despite all vicissitudes and sufferings, is numerous and vigorous; and the Russians are a talented people. But it still remains to be seen what will be the effects on mature performance of the abnormal emotional strains of childhood which Soviet dictatorship created and which were enormously increased by the war. Such things as normal security and placidity of home environment have practically ceased to exist in the Soviet Union outside of the most remote farms and villages. And observers are not yet sure whether that is not going to leave its mark on the over-all capacity of the generation now coming into maturity.

In addition to this, we have the fact that Soviet economic development, while it can list certain formidable achievements, has been precariously spotty and uneven. Russian Communists who speak of the "uneven development of capitalism" should blush at the contemplation of their own national economy. Here certain branches of economic life, such as the metallurgical and machine industries, have been pushed out of all proportion to other sectors of economy. Here is a nation striving to become in a short period one of the great industrial nations of the world while it still has no highway network worthy of the name and only a relatively primitive network of railways. Much has been done to increase efficiency of labor and to teach primitive peasants something about the operation of machines. But maintenance is still a crying deficiency of all Soviet economy. Construction is hasty and poor in quality. Depreciation must be enormous. And in vast sectors of economic life it has not yet been possible to instill into labor anything like that general culture of production and technical self-respect which characterizes the skilled worker of the west.

It is difficult to see how these deficiencies can be corrected at an early date by a tired and dispirited population working largely under the shadow of fear and compulsion. And as long as they are not overcome, Russia will remain economically as vulnerable, and in a certain sense an impotent, nation, capable of exporting its enthusiasms and of radiating the strange charm of its primitive political vitality but unable to back up those articles of export by the real evidences of material power and prosperity.

Meanwhile, a great uncertainty hangs over the political life of the Soviet Union. That is the uncertainty involved in the transfer of power from one individual or group of individuals to others.

This is, of course, outstandingly the problem of the personal position of Stalin. We must remember that his succession to Lenin's pinnacle of pre-eminence in the Communist movement was the only such transfer of individual authority which the Soviet Union has experienced. That transfer took 12 years to consolidate. It cost the lives of millions of people and shook the state to its foundations. The attendant tremors were felt all through the international revolutionary movement, to the disadvantage of the Kremlin itself.

It is always possible that another transfer of pre-eminent power may take place quietly and inconspicuously, with no repercussions anywhere. But again, it is possible that the questions involved may unleash, to use some of Lenin's words, one of those "incredibly swift transitions" from "delicate deceit" to "wild violence" which characterize Russian history, and may shake Soviet power to its foundations.

But this is not only a question of Stalin himself. There has been, since 1938, a dangerous congealment of political life in the higher circles of Soviet power. The All-Union Congress of Soviets, in theory the supreme body of the Party, is supposed to meet not less often than once in three years. It will soon be eight full years since its last meeting. During this period membership in the Party has numerically doubled. Party mortality during the war was enormous; and today well over half of the Party members are persons who have entered since the last Party congress was held. Meanwhile, the same small group of men has carried on at the top through an amazing series of national vicissitudes. Surely there is some reason why the experiences of the war brought basic political changes to every one of the great governments of the west. Surely the causes of that phenomenon are basic enough to be present somewhere in the obscurity of Soviet political life, as well. And yet no recognition has been given to these causes in Russia.

It must be surmised from this that even within so highly disciplined an organization as the Communist Party there must be a growing divergence in age, outlook and interest between the great mass of Party members, only so recently recruited into the movement, and the little self-perpetuating clique of men at the top, whom most of these Party members have never met, with whom they have never conversed, and with whom they can have no political intimacy.

Who can say whether, in these circumstances, the eventual rejuvenation of the higher spheres of authority (which can only be a matter of time) can take place smoothly and peacefully, or whether rivals in the quest for higher power will not eventually reach down into these politically immature and inexperienced masses in order to find support for their respective claims? If this were ever to happen, strange consequences could flow for the Communist Party: for the membership at large has been exercised only in the practices of iron discipline

and obedience and not in the arts of compromise and accommodation. And if disunity were ever to seize and paralyze the Party, the chaos and weakness of Russian society would be revealed in forms beyond description. For we have seen that Soviet power is only concealing an amorphous mass of human beings among whom no independent organizational structure is tolerated. In Russia there is not even such a thing as local government. The present generation of Russians have never known spontaneity of collective action. If, consequently, anything were ever to occur to disrupt the unity and efficacy of the Party as a political instrument, Soviet Russia might be changed overnight from one of the strongest to one of the weakest and most pitiable of national societies.

Thus the future of Soviet power may not be by any means as secure as Russian capacity for self-delusion would make it appear to the men of the Kremlin. That they can quietly and easily turn it over to others remains to be proved. Meanwhile, the hardships of their rule and the vicissitudes of international life have taken a heavy toll of the strength and hopes of the great people on whom their power rests. It is curious to note that the ideological power of Soviet authority is strongest today in areas beyond the frontiers of Russia, beyond the reach of its police power. This phenomenon brings to mind a comparison used by Thomas Mann in his great novel Buddenbrooks. Observing that human institutions often show the greatest outward brilliance at a moment when inner decay is in reality farthest advanced, he compared one of those stars whose light shines most brightly on this world when in reality it has long since ceased to exist. And who can say with assurance that the strong light still cast by the Kremlin on the dissatisfied peoples of the western world is not the powerful afterglow of a constellation which is in actuality on the wane? This cannot be proved. And it cannot be disproved. But the possibility remains (and in the opinion of this writer it is a strong one) that Soviet power, like the capitalist world of its conception, bears within it the seeds of its own decay, and that the sprouting of these seeds is well advanced.

IV

It is clear that the United States cannot expect in the foreseeable future to enjoy political intimacy with the Soviet regime. It must continue to regard the Soviet Union as a rival, not a partner, in the political arena. It must continue to expect that Soviet policies will reflect no abstract love of peace and stability, no real faith in the possibility of a permanent happy coexistence of the Socialist and capitalist worlds, but rather a cautious, persistent pressure toward the disruption and, weakening of all rival influence and rival power.

Balanced against this are the facts that Russia, as opposed to the western world in general, is still by far the weaker party, that Soviet policy is highly flexible, and that Soviet society may well contain deficiencies which will eventually weaken its own total potential. This would of itself warrant the United States entering with reasonable confidence upon a policy of firm containment, designed to confront the Russians with unalterable counter-force at every point where they show signs of encroaching upon he interests of a peaceful and stable world.

But in actuality the possibilities for American policy are by no means limited to holding the line and hoping for the best. It is entirely possible for the United States to influence by its actions the internal developments, both within Russia and throughout the international Communist movement, by which Russian policy is largely determined. This is not only a question of the modest measure of informational activity which this government can conduct in the Soviet Union and elsewhere, although that, too, is important. It is rather a question of the degree to which the United States can create among the peoples of the world generally the impression of a country which knows what it wants, which is coping successfully with the problem of its internal life and with the responsibilities of a World Power, and which has a spiritual vitality capable of holding its own among the major ideological currents of the time. To the extent that such an impression can be created and maintained, the aims of Russian Communism must appear sterile and quixotic, the hopes and enthusiasm of Moscow's supporters must wane, and added strain must be imposed on the Kremlin's foreign policies. For the palsied decrepitude of the capitalist world is the keystone of Communist philosophy. Even the failure of the United States to experience the early economic depression which the ravens of the Red Square have been predicting with such complacent confidence since hostilities ceased would have deep and important repercussions throughout the Communist world.

By the same token, exhibitions of indecision, disunity and internal disintegration within this country have an exhilarating effect on the whole Communist movement. At each evidence of these tendencies, a thrill of hope and excitement goes through the Communist world; a new jauntiness can be noted in the Moscow tread; new groups of foreign supporters climb on to what they can only view as the band wagon of international politics; and Russian pressure increases all along the line in international affairs.

It would be an exaggeration to say that American behavior unassisted and alone could exercise a power of life and death over the Communist movement and bring about the early fall of Soviet power in Russia. But the United States has it in its power to increase enormously the strains under which Soviet policy must operate, to force upon the Kremlin a far greater degree of moderation and circumspection than it has had to observe in recent years, and in this way to promote tendencies which must eventually find their outlet in either the breakup or the gradual mellowing of Soviet power. For no mystical, Messianic movement—and particularly not that of the Kremlin—can face frustration indefinitely without eventually adjusting itself in one way or another to the logic of that state of affairs.

Thus the decision will really fall in large measure in this country itself. The issue of Soviet-American relations is in essence a test of the overall worth of the United States as a nation among nations. To avoid destruction the United States need only measure up to its own best traditions and prove itself worthy of preservation as a great nation.

Surely, there was never a fairer test of national quality than this. In the light of these circumstances, the thoughtful observer of Russian-American relations will find no cause for complaint in the Kremlin's challenge to American society. He will rather experience a certain gratitude to a Providence which, by providing the American people with this implacable challenge, has made their entire security as a nation dependent on their pulling themselves together and accepting the responsibilities of moral and political leadership that history plainly intended them to bear.

GLOSSARY

adroit: expert or nimble in the use of the hands or body; resourceful

amorphous: lacking definite form; having no specific shape

caveat emptor: "let the buyer beware"; the principle that the seller of a product cannot be held responsible for its quality unless it is guaranteed in a warranty

expropriated/expropriation: to take possession of by taking away the title of the private owner

glib: readily fluent, often thoughtlessly, superficially, or insincerely

intransigence: the state or quality of being intransigent; refusing to compromise or agree; inflexibility

physiognomy: the outward appearance of anything, taken as offering some insight into its character

proletariat/proletarian: the class of workers, especially industrial wage workers, who do not possess capital or property and who are dependent on their own labor to survive

quixotic: extravagantly chivalrous or romantic; impractical; impulsive; resembling or befitting Don Quixote

Document Analysis

In July 1947, former American chargé d'affaires in Moscow George F. Kennan, writing under a pseudonym so as to avoid the appearance of articulating the official policy of the United States, published an article entitled "The Sources of Soviet Conduct," which put forward a convincing explanation of why the Soviet Union pursued the courses of action that it did and what the United States must do in response, so as to avoid a continuation of the Soviet takeover of Eastern Europe during 1945 and 1946. Kennan argues that the main approach of the United States toward its new Cold War foe should not be one of placating the Soviets or trying to work with them to create the new postwar world, but rather that American policy must be one of containment, stating, "The main element of any United States policy toward the Soviet Union must be that of a long-term, patient but firm and vigilant containment of Russian expansive tendencies."

Kennan begins the lengthy article by outlining the seeds of the Soviet drive to expand, in much the same way as he had in the "Long Telegram." The Soviet Union, and especially Joseph Stalin, had combined the long-term expansionism and imperialism of the Russian past with the ideology of Marxism to form a potent type of Communism that saw itself as the catalyst for successive Communist revolutions in other nations.

To Kennan, only this could explain Stalin's refusal to honor the agreements made with the other Allies at the Yalta Conference, where the leaders of the World War II Allies outlined what they envisioned happening after the end of the war. Despite their wartime alliance, the Soviet Union and the other Western powers were destined to have a difficult relationship, based simply on the Marxist formulation that socialism (the ideology of the Soviet Union) was destined to do away with capitalism (the ideology of the Western powers). However, Kennan did not see this as an immediate issue, as the basic idea of Marxian socialism was that capitalism would collapse on its own and that the Soviets saw no reason to press the matter. Individual setbacks meant little when the victory of socialism was seen as inevitable.

What this meant to Kennan was that the United States needed to apply policies containing Soviet expansionism for the long haul. The Soviets might give up a particular Cold War battle when counterforce was applied by the United States, but they would certainly pursue the same strategies in other locations at other times, and the United States needed to be ready there as well. According to Kennan, following his advice would "promote tendencies which must eventually find their outlet in either the break-up or the gradual mellowing of Soviet power."

Essential Themes

Although Kennan wrote the article under a pseudonym, it did not take those in Washington and in the press long to realize he was the author. He was already the foremost expert on Soviet policy, and his views on the roots of Soviet expansionism were well known. Though he wrote as "X" in order to avoid the appearance of articulating official American policy, what he wrote basically constituted the Truman administration's early Cold War strategy. The strategy of containment formed the context for the implementation of the Marshall Plan, the formation of the North Atlantic Treaty Organization, and the commencement of covert espionage in order to counter Soviet threats wherever they cropped up.

Though many cited Kennan's containment policy as the justification for military responses to Soviet aggression, Kennan himself saw containment as more political and psychological than military. Economic aid, propaganda, and covert operations to change public opinion in countries under threat from Communism were much more in line with Kennan's philosophies. However, as influential as Kennan was during the first three years of the Cold War, his star fell precipitously at the end of the 1940s. In 1950, the Truman administration produced a new policy document, National Security Council Report 68 (NSC 68), which advocated dramatic increases in the military budget. It also expanded the idea of containment from individual instances responding to Soviet aggressiveness to a worldwide military strategy.

Upon his election to the presidency in 1952, Dwight D. Eisenhower appointed John Foster Dulles secretary of state. Dulles viewed containment and Kennan himself as insufficiently vigilant against Communism and its expansion both abroad and at home. Dulles called for a rolling back of Soviet influence, hoping that the United States' taking a more aggressive position would eventually lead to the liberation of Eastern Europe from Communist rule. However, Kennan remained influential, as the basic idea of containment remained the basis of American strategy throughout the Cold War, with each successive administration determining its own interpretation of its mandates.

—*Steven L. Danver, PhD*

Bibliography and Additional Reading

Gaddis, John Lewis. *George F. Kennan: An American Life*. New York: Penguin, 2011. Print.

Kennan, George F. "Containment: 40 Years Later." *Foreign Affairs*. Council on Foreign Relations, Spring 1987. Web. 25 Feb. 2015.

Mastny, Vojtech. *The Cold War and Soviet Insecurity: The Stalin Years*. New York: Oxford UP, 1996. Print.

Mayers, David. *George Kennan and the Dilemmas of US Foreign Policy*. New York: Oxford UP, 1990. Print.

Miscamble, Wilson D. *George F. Kennan and the Making of American Foreign Policy, 1947–1950*. Princeton: Princeton UP, 1992. Print.

Pechatnov, Vladimir O. "The Soviet Union and the World, 1944–1953." *The Cambridge History of the Cold War*, Volume I: Origins. Ed. Melvyn P. Leffler & Odd Arne Westad. New York: Cambridge UP, 2010. 90–111. Print.

■ Truman Statement on Immigration into Palestine

Date: October 4, 1946
Author: Harry S. Truman
Genre: government document

Summary Overview

In 1946, as the debate over whether Jews should be allowed to establish a homeland in Palestine raged, President Harry S. Truman advocated strongly in favor of the Jews' position. However, when a London conference on the issue abruptly ended without a clear series of recommendations for resolution, Truman issued a statement on the eve of Yom Kippur (the Day of Atonement in Judaism) expressing his disappointment about that conference's outcome. Truman reiterated his position that 100,000 displaced Jews should be allowed to immigrate to Palestine. He urged world leaders to endorse a peaceable solution to the Palestine issue and to create liberal immigration policies that would welcome Jews and other displaced groups to take up residence in their respective nations.

Defining Moment

When Adolf Hitler published his book *Mein Kampf* (1925, 1927), he outlined a personal philosophy that the Jews and other racial minorities were to be eradicated. Upon assuming power as chancellor (or Führer) of Germany in 1933, Hitler quickly moved to make this idea a reality. By 1945, about six million of Europe's nine-and-a-half million Jews (a 1933 estimate) had died as a result of the Holocaust, with hundreds of thousands more displaced before and during World War II. Most of the survivors moved to the Western Hemisphere, but a sizable population still sought refuge in Europe.

One option for them had been under consideration for decades. In 1917, Russian-born Zionist Chaim Weizmann convinced the British government to honor the Jews, who had supported Britain against the Turks during World War I, by calling for a Jewish state in Palestine. However, by the 1930s, Jews escaping Hitler's genocide began entering Palestine, inciting a political backlash from the Arabs living there. Because Arabs already enjoyed a strong relationship with Britain (which,

after World War I, controlled the region), Great Britain withdrew its support of the Jewish state. Zionist coalitions, feeling betrayed by the British change of course, turned to the United States for support.

President Franklin D. Roosevelt was supportive of the idea, particularly as the Holocaust showed the world the horrors to which the Jews were subjected. Near the end of World War II, Roosevelt's successor, Harry Truman, also showed great sympathy for the Zionist cause. He was, however, cognizant of the political risks of dividing Palestine into two distinct, autonomous states. In 1946, Truman worked with the Anglo-American Committee of Inquiry to address the issue in two areas: first, the Palestine issue, and second, the travel arrangements for 100,000 Jews who would be taken there.

In the United States, Congress was increasingly in favor of the idea of a Jewish state in Palestine. However, the manner by which the state would be established—whether a singular, all-inclusive state or a divided nation (one for Jews, the other for Arabs)—could not be settled. Truman, himself an advocate of a single state, believed that the partitioned model invited conflict and war. In an election year, Truman made the difficult decision of turning down the partition plan in Congress. Nevertheless, he continued to call for a Jewish state, which would be essential to harboring the 100,000 Jewish refugees whose fate had yet to be decided.

In September 1946, a conference was held in London to bring a resolution to the Palestinian issue. However, the conference only lasted three weeks, as a large number of its participants looked to attend the meeting of the United Nations General Assembly on October 23. The conference was adjourned abruptly, with its organizers planning to reconvene after the middle of December, though they did not ultimately meet again until February. Truman, in response, issued a statement in which he presented his thoughts on the adjournment and the issue as a whole.

Author Biography

Harry S. Truman was born on May 8, 1884, in Lamar, Missouri. He spent most of his childhood living in Independence, Missouri, outside of Kansas City. He enlisted in the National Guard and served from 1905 to 1911, rising to the rank of captain by World War I. In 1922, he won election as judge in Jackson County, Missouri. In 1934, Truman was elected to the US Senate and won reelection in 1940. In 1944, he was nominated Franklin D. Roosevelt's running mate in the presidential election. In 1945, after Roosevelt's sudden death, Truman assumed the role of president, overseeing the end of World War II and introducing the Fair Deal domestic economic reform package. He won reelection in 1948, faced with the Cold War, and during this term helped form the North Atlantic Treaty Organization (NATO). After his second term, Truman retired to Independence. He died on December 26, 1972.

HISTORICAL DOCUMENT

I have learned with deep regret that the meetings of the Palestine Conference in London have been adjourned and are not to be resumed until December 16, 1946. In the light of this situation it is appropriate to examine the record of the administration's efforts in this field, efforts which have been supported in and not of Congress by members of both political parties, and to state my views on the situation as it now exists.

It will be recalled that, when Mr. Earl Harrison reported on September 29, 1945, concerning the condition of displaced persons in Europe, I immediately urged that steps be taken to relieve the situation of these persons to the extent at least of admitting 100,000 Jews into Palestine. In response to this suggestion the British Government invited the Government of the United States to cooperate in setting up a joint Anglo-American Committee of Inquiry, an invitation which this Government was happy to accept in the hope that its participation would help to alleviate the situation of the displaced Jews in Europe and would assist in finding a solution for the difficult and complex problem of Palestine itself. The urgency with which this Government regarded the matter is reflected in the fact that a 120-day limit was set for the completion of the Committee's task.

The unanimous report of the Anglo-American Committee of Inquiry was made on April 20, 1946, and I was gratified to note that among the recommendations contained in the Report was an endorsement of my previous suggestion that 100,000 Jews be admitted into Palestine. The administration immediately concerned itself with devising ways and means for transporting the 100,000 and caring for them upon their arrival. With this in mind, experts were sent to London in June 1946 to work out provisionally the actual travel arrangements. The British Government cooperated with this group but made it clear that in its view the Report must be considered as a whole and that the issue of the 100,000 could not be considered separately.

On June 11, I announced the establishment of a Cabinet Committee on Palestine and Related Problems, composed of the Secretaries of State, War, and Treasury, to assist me in considering the recommendations of the Anglo-American Committee of Inquiry. The alternates of this Cabinet Committee, headed by Ambassador Henry F. Grady, departed for London on July 10, 1946, to discuss with British Government representatives how the Report might best be implemented. The alternates submitted on July 24, 1946 a report, commonly referred to as the "Morrison plan," advocating a scheme of provincial autonomy which might lead ultimately to a binational state or to partition. However, opposition to this plan developed among members of the major political parties in the United States—both in the Congress and throughout the country. In accordance with the principle which I have consistently tried to follow, of having a maximum degree of unity within the country and between the parties on major elements of American foreign policy, I could not give my support to this plan.

I have, nevertheless, maintained my deep interest in the matter and have repeatedly made known and have urged that steps be taken at the earliest possible moment to admit 100,000 Jewish refugees to Palestine.

In the meantime, this Government was informed of the efforts of the British Government to bring to London representatives of the Arabs and Jews, with a view to finding a solution to this distressing problem. I expressed the hope that as a result of these conversations a fair solution of the Palestine problem could be found. While all the parties invited had not found themselves able to attend, I had hoped that there was still a possibility that representatives of the Jewish Agency might take part. If so, the prospect for an agreed and constructive settlement would have been enhanced.

The British Government presented to the Conference the so-called "Morrison plan" for provincial autonomy and stated that the Conference was open to other proposals. Meanwhile, the Jewish Agency proposed a solution of the Palestine problem by means of the creation of a viable Jewish state in control of its own immigration and economic policies in an adequate area of Palestine instead of in the whole of Palestine. It proposed furthermore the immediate issuance of certificates for 100,000 Jewish immigrants. This proposal received wide-spread attention in the United States, both in the press and in public forums. From the discussion which has ensued it is my belief that a solution along these lines would command the support of public opinion in the United States. I cannot believe that the gap between the proposals which have been put forward is too great to be bridged by men of reason and good-will. To such a solution our Government could give its support.

In the light of the situation which has now developed

I wish to state my views as succinctly as possible:

1. In view of the fact that winter will come on before the Conference can be resumed I believe and urge that substantial immigration into Palestine cannot await a solution to the Palestine problem and that it should begin at once. Preparations for this movement have already been made by this Government and it is ready to lend its immediate assistance.

2. I state again, as I have on previous occasions, that the immigration laws of other countries, including the United States, should be liberalized with a view to the admission of displaced persons. I am prepared to make such a recommendation to the Congress and to continue as energetically as possible collaboration with other countries on the whole problem of displaced persons.

3. Furthermore, should a workable solution for Palestine be devised, I would be willing to recommend to the Congress a plan for economic assistance for the development of that country.

In the light of the terrible ordeal which the Jewish people of Europe endured during the recent war and the crisis now existing, I cannot believe that a program of immediate action along the lines suggested above could not be worked out with the cooperation of all people concerned. The administration will continue to do everything it can to this end.

Document Analysis

Even prior to his first term as president, Harry Truman had a reputation as a Zionist advocate. Truman and the rest of the international community had an opportunity to reach this goal at the end of World War II, as millions of refugees (a large number of whom were Jewish) sought safe havens after years of Nazi persecution. However, Truman was surprised and disappointed to learn that the international community could not come to an agreement on whether to allow 100,000 Jewish refugees to immigrate to Palestine. On the eve of Yom Kippur, Truman issued this statement, underscoring his commitment to peaceably enabling Jewish refugees to settle in the predominantly Arab region.

Truman begins his statement by expressing regret that the September Palestine Conference in London adjourned with no resolution and would not reconvene until the winter. Truman suggests that such an impasse undid the groundwork that he and other leaders laid over the course of decades. The preceding year, he says, Earl Harrison (the US representative of the Intergovernmental Committee on Refugees and dean of the University Pennsylvania Law School) issued a moving report depicting the plight of the Jews immediately after the Holocaust. Given the treatment the Jews had received by the Nazis and their continuing misery, Truman and the British government looked to relieve at least some of this suffering by giving 100,000 Jews entry into Palestine. As part of a bilateral commission, the US and British governments worked to generate attention about the Jews; Truman says that that commission's report suggested that these 100,000 refugees and their potential entry into Palestine could not be made a separate issue from the larger issue of postwar refugees.

Truman acknowledges, however, that the notion of moving a large number of Jews into the predominantly Arab area of Palestine was politically charged. The initial plan, dubbed the Morrison plan, entailed the division of Palestine into either two federated parts or two autonomous states. Truman says that although he supports the Morrison plan in theory, neither the Republican nor the Democratic Party in Congress would agree to such a plan. He, therefore, begrudgingly abstains from supporting it. Nevertheless, he says, he will continue to advocate for the Palestine option. Other versions of the Morrison plan still existed, each of which calling for a Jewish state in Palestine and for the immigration of Jewish refugees to that state. Such proposals received a great deal of attention from the media and political leaders, he adds, ensuring that the issue itself remained highly relevant.

He argues that the US and other governments should liberalize their immigration policies to give safe haven to Jews and other wartime refugees. Second, according to him, the Palestine proposal should be immediately revisited and settled. Given the experiences of the Jews before and during the war, Truman says, it was only right that they be given prompt attention.

Essential Themes

President Harry Truman's statement served as a reiteration of his position on the plight of Europe's Jews. Truman expressed disappointment that the London conference adjourned without resolution. Keenly aware of the reports that came out of German-occupied territories before and during the war, Truman reiterated his call for to allow 100,000 Jewish refugees to enter and live in Palestine as well as the liberalization of international immigration policy to address the broader refugee crisis.

Truman used the opportunity to summarize the work that he, the US government, and their counterparts in Great Britain had performed to date in order to resolve this issue. He stated that there appeared to be forward momentum on the matter, particularly as the world was becoming increasingly aware of and sympathetic toward the plight of the Jews. However, he acknowledged, there were political forces at work that impeded the process. At home, during an election year, there was congressional partisanship with which to contend; Truman knew that were his effort to succeed, he needed not only congressional support, but the support of the voters as well. Internationally, the landscape was also challenging: the Arabs had successfully lobbied against the effort before, and the pressure was on the president to encourage a peaceful, diplomatic solution that would ensure that both Arabs and the increasing Jewish population would live in peace. Regardless how the Palestine concept would take shape—whether as a single state or as a binational state—it was imperative to address the refugees' welfare promptly.

The decisions made at that time continue to have resonance in the twenty-first century. The Palestinians were ultimately promised a state of their own, alongside that established for the Jewish people, Israel. However, wars soon ensued between the Palestinians and the Israelis, and the contentious debate over the "one-state solution" and the "two-state solution" remains.

—*Michael P. Auerbach, MA*

Bibliography and Additional Reading

Benson, Michael T. *Harry S. Truman and the Founding of Israel*. Westport: Greenwood, 1997. Print.

"Jewish Population of Europe in 1945." *Holocaust Encyclopedia*. United States Holocaust Memorial Museum, 20 Jun. 2014. Web. 2 Jan. 2015.

Judis, John B. "Seeds of Doubt: Harry Truman's Concerns about Israel and Palestine Were Prescient—and Forgotten." *New Republic*. The New Republic, 15 Jan. 2014. Web. 2 Jan. 2015.

"London Conference on Palestine Suddenly Adjourns until after U.N. General Assembly." *JTA*. Jewish Telegraphic Agency, 2015. Web. 2 Jan. 2015.

McCullough, David. *Truman*. New York: Simon, 2003. Print.

"The Recognition of the State of Israel." *Harry S. Truman Library and Museum*. Harry S. Truman Library and Museum, 2014. Web. 2 Jan. 2015.

■ Truman Doctrine Speech

Date: March 12, 1947
Author: Harry S. Truman
Genre: speech

Summary Overview

Less than two years after the end of World War II, President Harry S. Truman gave a speech in which he articulated a new American foreign policy that would become known as the Truman Doctrine, intended to address the postwar geopolitical climate. Since the end of World War II, the Soviet Union had expanded its reach throughout Eastern Europe and was threatening to spur Communist revolutions in the Middle East. The focus of Truman's speech was the situation in Greece and Turkey, two nations that were threatened in different ways by the spread of Communism. Though the threats were different, the response, Truman argued, needed to be the same—financial aid to help contain the tide of Communist expansion. The United States was only just becoming accustomed to its new role as a world superpower; in the postwar order, Truman asserted, the United States was the only nation able to provide such aid, and the country had an ongoing responsibility to safeguard the world from the spread of Communism.

Defining Moment

In the two years following the defeat of Nazi Germany, US relations with its wartime ally the Soviet Union had changed dramatically. At the Yalta Conference in February 1945, the leaders of the United States, Great Britain, and the Soviet Union had agreed that the nations Germany had conquered during the war should be able to freely choose their governments through democratic elections. Very quickly after the conclusion of the war, however, it became clear that the Soviet Union was doing everything it could to ensure that all of the nations along its borders came under Communist rule. This direct disregard for the Yalta Agreement meant that the United States now had a new foe in a "cold war," which pitted democracy against totalitarianism.

American foreign policy experts struggled to determine the best course of action; George F. Kennan, who had perhaps the most familiarity with the Soviet government, having served as a US diplomat in Moscow for seven years, articulated what he saw as the reasons for Soviet aggressiveness in his "long telegram" in February 1946. To Kennan, Soviet expansionism was shaped by Russia's history of imperialistic conquest as well as by Marxist ideology, which saw Communism in an ongoing war against capitalism. He believed the only policy that could stop the Soviets' expansionist influence was one of containment, which required a commitment by the United States to the long-term limitation of the Soviets to their own sphere of influence. This had dramatic implications for American policy, as Kennan had no doubt that the Soviets would continue their drive to expand for the foreseeable future.

The need to articulate a new policy came to a head in February 1947, when the British government, which had suffered far greater economic hardship than the United States during World War II, informed American officials that it would no longer be able to provide economic and military aid to Greece and Turkey, both of which were facing important threats related to Communist expansionism. In Greece, leftist rebels, supported by Yugoslavia and the Soviet Union, had waged an insurgency against the Greek royal government. In Turkey, the Soviet Union was aggressively seeking to share control over the Dardanelles and the Bosporus straits, which connect the Mediterranean to the Black Sea, where the Soviets had large naval bases. Truman administration officials believed that if Greece and Turkey were overtaken by Communists, the appeasement of Soviet demands would only embolden the Soviets to go further, and country after country would fall to Communism—an idea that became popularly known as the "domino theory." The only way to stop the dominos from falling—or to contain the Soviet threat to Greece, Turkey, and the rest of the free world—was for the United States to take an active role in international affairs by meeting Soviet aggression with countervailing political, economic, and military force whenever necessary. With this policy in mind, Truman spoke to a joint session of Congress on March 12, 1947.

Author Biography

Following the death of President Franklin D. Roosevelt in April 1945, in the last days of World War II, Harry S. Truman became president of the United States. The peace that followed the war was short-lived, however, as almost immediately, Truman was faced with a new kind of war, a "cold war," pitting the United States against its wartime ally the Soviet Union. Relations began to break down even before World War II had ended, due to the ideological differences between the two nations, with the United States supporting capitalism and democracy, while the Soviet Union championed socialism and an authoritarian form of government. Though these differences had existed since the Russian Revolution in 1917, they took on geopolitical overtones after World War II and became a much more pressing concern for Truman. Much of Truman's presidency was defined by the nascent Cold War, and in 1947, Truman sought to define what the US government's response to the Soviet threat would be.

HISTORICAL DOCUMENT

The gravity of the situation which confronts the world today necessitates my appearance before a joint session of the Congress. The foreign policy and the national security of this country are involved.

One aspect of the present situation, which I wish to present to you at this time for your consideration and decision, concerns Greece and Turkey.

The United States has received from the Greek Government an urgent appeal for financial and economic assistance. Preliminary reports from the American Economic Mission now in Greece and reports from the American Ambassador in Greece corroborate the statement of the Greek Government that assistance is imperative if Greece is to survive as a free nation.

I do not believe that the American people and the Congress wish to turn a deaf ear to the appeal of the Greek Government.

Greece is not a rich country. Lack of sufficient natural resources has always forced the Greek people to work hard to make both ends meet. Since 1940, this industrious and peace loving country has suffered invasion, four years of cruel enemy occupation, and bitter internal strife.

When forces of liberation entered Greece they found that the retreating Germans had destroyed virtually all the railways, roads, port facilities, communications, and merchant marine. More than a thousand villages had been burned. Eighty-five per cent of the children were tubercular. Livestock, poultry, and draft animals had almost disappeared. Inflation had wiped out practically all savings.

As a result of these tragic conditions, a militant minority, exploiting human want and misery, was able to create political chaos which, until now, has made economic recovery impossible.

Greece is today without funds to finance the importation of those goods which are essential to bare subsistence. Under these circumstances the people of Greece cannot make progress in solving their problems of reconstruction. Greece is in desperate need of financial and economic assistance to enable it to resume purchases of food, clothing, fuel and seeds. These are indispensable for the subsistence of its people and are obtainable only from abroad. Greece must have help to import the goods necessary to restore internal order and security, so essential for economic and political recovery.

The Greek Government has also asked for the assistance of experienced American administrators, economists and technicians to insure that the financial and other aid given to Greece shall be used effectively in creating a stable and self-sustaining economy and in improving its public administration.

The very existence of the Greek state is today threatened by the terrorist activities of several thousand armed men, led by Communists, who defy the government's authority at a number of points, particularly along the northern boundaries. A Commission appointed by the United Nations Security Council is at present investigating disturbed conditions in northern Greece and alleged border violations along the frontier between Greece on the one hand and Albania, Bulgaria, and Yugoslavia on the other.

Meanwhile, the Greek Government is unable to cope with the situation. The Greek army is small and poorly equipped. It needs supplies and equipment if it is to restore the authority of the government throughout Greek territory. Greece must have assistance if it is to become a self-supporting and self-respecting democracy.

The United States must supply that assistance. We have already extended to Greece certain types of relief and economic aid but these are inadequate.

There is no other country to which democratic Greece can turn.

No other nation is willing and able to provide the necessary support for a democratic Greek government.

The British Government, which has been helping Greece, can give no further financial or economic aid after March 31. Great Britain finds itself under the necessity of reducing or liquidating its commitments in several parts of the world, including Greece.

We have considered how the United Nations might assist in this crisis. But the situation is an urgent one requiring immediate action and the United Nations and its related organizations are not in a position to extend help of the kind that is required.

It is important to note that the Greek Government has asked for our aid in utilizing effectively the financial and other assistance we may give to Greece, and in improving its public administration. It is of the utmost importance that we supervise the use of any funds made available to Greece; in such a manner that each dollar spent will count toward making Greece self-supporting, and will help to build an economy in which a healthy democracy can flourish.

No government is perfect. One of the chief virtues of a democracy, however, is that its defects are always visible and under democratic processes can be pointed out and corrected. The Government of Greece is not perfect. Nevertheless it represents eighty-five per cent of the members of the Greek Parliament who were chosen in an election last year. Foreign observers, including 692 Americans, considered this election to be a fair expression of the views of the Greek people.

The Greek Government has been operating in an atmosphere of chaos and extremism. It has made mistakes. The extension of aid by this country does not mean that the United States condones everything that the Greek Government has done or will do. We have condemned in the past, and we condemn now, extremist measures of the right or the left. We have in the past advised tolerance, and we advise tolerance now.

Greece's neighbor, Turkey, also deserves our attention.

The future of Turkey as an independent and economically sound state is clearly no less important to the freedom-loving peoples of the world than the future of Greece. The circumstances in which Turkey finds itself today are considerably different from those of Greece. Turkey has been spared the disasters that have beset Greece. And during the war, the United States and Great Britain furnished Turkey with material aid.

Nevertheless, Turkey now needs our support.

Since the war Turkey has sought financial assistance from Great Britain and the United States for the purpose of effecting that modernization necessary for the maintenance of its national integrity.

That integrity is essential to the preservation of order in the Middle East.

The British government has informed us that, owing to its own difficulties can no longer extend financial or economic aid to Turkey.

As in the case of Greece, if Turkey is to have the assistance it needs, the United States must supply it. We are the only country able to provide that help.

I am fully aware of the broad implications involved if the United States extends assistance to Greece and Turkey, and I shall discuss these implications with you at this time.

One of the primary objectives of the foreign policy of the United States is the creation of conditions in which we and other nations will be able to work out a way of life free from coercion. This was a fundamental issue in the war with Germany and Japan. Our victory was won over countries which sought to impose their will, and their way of life, upon other nations.

To ensure the peaceful development of nations, free from coercion, the United States has taken a leading part in establishing the United Nations. The United Nations is designed to make possible lasting freedom and independence for all its members. We shall not realize our objectives, however, unless we are willing to help free peoples to maintain their free institutions and their national integrity against aggressive movements that seek to impose upon them totalitarian regimes. This is no more than a frank recognition that totalitarian regimes imposed on free peoples, by direct or indirect aggression, undermine the foundations of international peace and hence the security of the United States.

The peoples of a number of countries of the world have recently had totalitarian regimes forced upon them against their will. The Government of the United States has made frequent protests against coercion and intimidation, in violation of the Yalta agreement, in Poland, Rumania, and Bulgaria. I must also state that in a number of other countries there have been similar developments.

At the present moment in world history nearly every nation must choose between alternative ways of life. The choice is too often not a free one.

One way of life is based upon the will of the majority, and is distinguished by free institutions, representative government, free elections, guarantees of individual liberty, freedom of speech and religion, and freedom from political oppression.

The second way of life is based upon the will of a minority forcibly imposed upon the majority. It relies upon terror and oppression, a controlled press and radio; fixed elections, and the suppression of personal freedoms.

I believe that it must be the policy of the United States to support free peoples who are resisting attempted subjugation by armed minorities or by outside pressures.

I believe that we must assist free peoples to work out their own destinies in their own way.

I believe that our help should be primarily through economic and financial aid which is essential to economic stability and orderly political processes.

The world is not static, and the status quo is not sacred. But we cannot allow changes in the status quo in violation of the Charter of the United Nations by such methods as coercion, or by such subterfuges as political infiltration. In helping free and independent nations to maintain their freedom, the United States will be giving effect to the principles of the Charter of the United Nations.

It is necessary only to glance at a map to realize that the survival and integrity of the Greek nation are of grave importance in a much wider situation. If Greece should fall under the control of an armed minority, the effect upon its neighbor, Turkey, would be immediate and serious. Confusion and disorder might well spread throughout the entire Middle East.

Moreover, the disappearance of Greece as an independent state would have a profound effect upon those countries in Europe whose peoples are struggling against great difficulties to maintain their freedoms and their independence while they repair the damages of war.

It would be an unspeakable tragedy if these countries, which have struggled so long against overwhelming odds, should lose that victory for which they sacrificed so much. Collapse of free institutions and loss of independence would be disastrous not only for them but for the world. Discouragement and possibly failure would quickly be the lot of neighboring peoples striving to maintain their freedom and independence.

Should we fail to aid Greece and Turkey in this fateful hour, the effect will be far reaching to the West as well as to the East.

We must take immediate and resolute action.

I therefore ask the Congress to provide authority for assistance to Greece and Turkey in the amount of $400,000,000 for the period ending June 30, 1948. In requesting these funds, I have taken into consideration the maximum amount of relief assistance which would be furnished to Greece out of the $350,000,000 which I recently requested that the Congress authorize for the prevention of starvation and suffering in countries devastated by the war.

In addition to funds, I ask the Congress to authorize the detail of American civilian and military personnel to Greece and Turkey, at the request of those countries, to assist in the tasks of reconstruction, and for the purpose of supervising the use of such financial and material assistance as may be furnished. I recommend that authority also be provided for the instruction and training of selected Greek and Turkish personnel.

Finally, I ask that the Congress provide authority which will permit the speediest and most effective use, in terms of needed commodities, supplies, and equipment, of such funds as may be authorized.

If further funds, or further authority, should be needed for purposes indicated in this message, I shall not hesitate to bring the situation before the Congress. On this subject the Executive and Legislative branches of the Government must work together.

This is a serious course upon which we embark.

I would not recommend it except that the alternative is much more serious. The United States contributed $341,000,000,000 toward winning World War II. This is an investment in world freedom and world peace.

The assistance that I am recommending for Greece and Turkey amounts to little more than 1 tenth of 1 per cent of this investment. It is only common sense that we should safeguard this investment and make sure that it was not in vain.

The seeds of totalitarian regimes are nurtured by misery and want. They spread and grow in the evil soil of poverty and strife. They reach their full growth when the hope of a people for a better life has died. We must keep that hope alive.

The free peoples of the world look to us for support in maintaining their freedoms.

If we falter in our leadership, we may endanger the peace of the world—and we shall surely endanger the welfare of our own nation.

Great responsibilities have been placed upon us by the swift movement of events.

I am confident that the Congress will face these responsibilities squarely.

Document Analysis

The Truman Doctrine represents a dramatic turning point in the history of American foreign policy. President Harry S. Truman spoke to a joint session of Congress and announced a new direction in US foreign policy, marking what many consider to be the beginning of the Cold War. In his speech, he speaks directly about the situation faced by Greece and Turkey as they sought to avoid Communist domination. In a larger sense, however, Truman used the speech to articulate a new vision of the United States' role in the world. According to Truman, the United States could no longer shrink back to an isolated existence as it had at the conclusion of previous wars. A new geopolitical landscape, a new position as a world superpower, and the spread of Communism created the need for a new strategy to deal with the situation.

Truman begins by explaining the two crises in Greece and Turkey. The Communist-led insurgency in Greece, funded by the Communist government of Yugoslavia, threatened to overthrow the pro-Western monarchy. Great Britain had been providing financial assistance to the Greek government but, due to their own economic crisis, were unable to continue. Truman asserts that, without American aid, Greece could very well fall to the Communists. In Turkey, the Soviet Union was pressuring the small, weak nation to share control over the Dardanelles and the Bosporus. Without assistance from the United States, the Soviet Union could dominate the eastern Mediterranean Sea and the Middle East. Truman speaks briefly about how he had considered asking the United Nations (UN) to assist Greece and Turkey, as the settlement of international disputes was the very reason for its existence, but he came to the conclusion that the situation needed immediate assistance of a greater extent than the UN could provide.

The larger issue, however, was the choice the nations of the world faced between a way of life "based upon the will of the majority" that had free elections and institutions as well as guaranteed protection of individual freedoms, and a way of life "based upon the will of a minority forcibly imposed upon the majority," where the state is coercive and totalitarian, suppressing individual and social freedoms. The role of the United States in this new world was to contain Soviet expansion by helping nations such as Greece to "become a self-supporting and self-respecting democracy." Truman sums up his intentions by stating that "it must be the policy of the United States to support free peoples who are resisting attempted subjugation by armed minorities or by outside pressures." According to Truman, the United States must meet any challenge put forward by the Soviet Union and its desire to expand Communist control, arguing that "there is no other country to which democratic Greece can turn. No other nation is willing and able to provide the necessary support."

Essential Themes

The Truman Doctrine outlined the ideas that shaped America's foreign policy during the early years of the Cold War, particularly the idea that the Soviet Union needed to be contained and that the United States was the only nation in the world capable of doing so. The United States relied primarily on political and economic means, though the fact that the American military was kept on a permanent war-footing demonstrated that armed conflict was always a possibility. Though Congress approved the aid package that Truman requested for Greece and Turkey, not everyone was convinced by Truman's long-term strategy. Former vice president Henry A. Wallace, who had been the secretary of commerce until he gave a speech in 1946 critical of the Truman administration's foreign policy toward the Soviet Union, thought that cooperation with the Soviets would be far more effective. Others thought the Truman Doctrine too soft and argued that the Soviets would only respect military power in equal measure to its own.

In retrospect, the results of the aid package to Greece and Turkey were ambiguous. Both countries were able to stand firm in the face of the Communist threats they faced, but the aid did not guarantee a more democratic government in either country, as both saw the rise of authoritarian right-wing governments. However, the die was cast, and the Truman Doctrine inspired the Marshall Plan that, beginning in 1948, provided large amounts of financial aid to friendly governments in Europe, with the idea being that when the people of a nation are not economically threatened, they would be far less likely to succumb to Communist propaganda or support an overthrow of their government. The military component of the Truman Doctrine began to take shape with the administration's approval of NSC-68 in 1950, a document that set in motion plans to strengthen the US military as a counterweight to the massive Soviet military.

Though later presidents recast the conflict in ways that suited their own style, the basic ideas contained in the Truman Doctrine formed the basis of the United States' Cold War strategy from the beginning to the end, and the second half of the twentieth century was to be dominated by the global showdown between the two superpowers.

—*Steven L. Danver, PhD*

Bibliography and Additional Reading

Bostdorff, Denise M. *Proclaiming the Truman Doctrine: The Cold War Call to Arms*. College Station: Texas A&M UP, 2008. Print.

Jones, Howard. "A New Kind of War": *America's Global Strategy and the Truman Doctrine in Greece*. New York: Oxford UP, 1989. Print.

Mastny, Vojtech. *The Cold War and Soviet Insecurity: The Stalin Years*. New York: Oxford UP, 1996. Print.

Offner, Arnold A. *Another Such Victory: President Truman and the Cold War, 1945–1953*. Stanford: Stanford UP, 2002. Print.

Pechatnov, Vladimir O. "The Soviet Union and the World, 1944–1953." *The Cambridge History of the Cold War: Origins*. Vol. 1. Ed. Melvyn P. Leffler and Odd Arne Westad. New York: Cambridge UP, 2010. 90–111. Print.

■ Speech on the Marshall Plan

Date: June 5, 1947
Author: George C. Marshall
Genre: speech

Summary Overview

Growing increasingly worried about the slow pace of economic recovery in Europe after World War II, and concerned that the Soviet Union might take advantage of unrest caused by the continuing impoverishment of many people in Western Europe, US secretary of state George C. Marshall spearheaded an effort to deliver aid to countries in the region. Marshall publicly announced his initiative in a speech delivered at Harvard University in June 1947. During the next nine months, members of the administration of President Harry S. Truman shepherded through Congress legislation that Truman signed into law on April 3, 1948. Though officially designated the European Recovery Program, the initiative quickly became known as the Marshall Plan.

Defining Moment

When armed conflict ceased in 1945, the countries of Europe struggled to overcome the devastation caused by World War II. Many teetered on the verge of bankruptcy; food supplies were short and infrastructure severely damaged. The Soviet Union demanded $10 billion in reparations from Germany—a country in no position to send any money outside its borders, given its dire economic conditions. On the other hand, France, Germany's enemy in three wars over less than a century, was skeptical about any efforts to speed up German recovery. Some leaders in the United States recognized that help from the United States might be needed, but most citizens had little interest in foreign affairs once the war ended.

The situation remained unresolved when President Truman appointed George C. Marshall secretary of state in January 1947. The former Army chief of staff, dubbed the "organizer of victory" by British prime minister Winston Churchill, considered it a matter of national security to address problems in Europe. In March, Marshall went to Moscow for a meeting of the Council of Foreign Ministers, a group established in

1945 by the Treaty of Potsdam to hammer out postwar issues. At the conference he discovered that the Soviet Union had no wish to see Western European nations recover quickly because economic unrest would make conditions more favorable for the rise of Communism in those countries. Marshall's fears about Soviet intentions were confirmed by George Kennan, the newly appointed head of the State Department's Policy Planning Staff and a Soviet specialist. A report from Undersecretary of State for Economic Affairs Will Clayton assured Marshall that his worries about precarious economic conditions in Europe were well founded.

Marshall was convinced that long-term economic recovery, not temporary relief, was essential, and that European nations would have to take the lead in developing their own recovery plan; the United States must be seen as assisting, not directing, these efforts. Although Marshall professed no party allegiance, he had been appointed by a Democrat. Knowing that any plan he proposed must get through a Republican-controlled Congress, he was also concerned about how Americans' apathy toward conditions in Europe might sway legislators.

Late in May 1947, Marshall agreed to accept an honorary degree from Harvard University, deciding to use this occasion to make public his ideas about the need for the United States to support European recovery. He had staff members Kennan and Charles Bohlen prepare separate drafts of remarks he might make; from these he composed a brief speech. During commencement ceremonies on June 5 he spoke to a group of Harvard alumni, outlining the principles on which the Marshall Plan would be built.

Author Biography

The descendant of an old Virginia family, George Catlett Marshall, Jr. was born in Uniontown, Pennsylvania, in 1880. He graduated from Virginia Military

Institute and was commissioned a lieutenant in the US Army in 1902. Marshall served with the American Expeditionary Force in World War I. Rising steadily through the ranks, he became a brigadier general in 1936 and in 1939 was named the Army's chief of staff. Almost immediately, he began preparing the army for war. Throughout World War II he was one of President Franklin D. Roosevelt's closest advisors. He retired in 1945, but was immediately asked by President Truman to head a delegation to China to try (unsuccessfully) to broker peace between the Communists and Nationalists in that country's civil war. In January 1947, Truman named Marshall secretary of state. He stepped down in January 1949, but in September 1950, Truman appointed him secretary of defense, a position he held for a year. In 1953, he was awarded the Nobel Peace Prize for his work on postwar reconstruction in Europe. He died in 1959.

HISTORICAL DOCUMENT

I need not tell you gentlemen that the world situation is very serious. That must be apparent to all intelligent people. I think one difficulty is that the problem is one of such enormous complexity that the very mass of facts presented to the public by press and radio make it exceedingly difficult for the man in the street to reach a clear appraisement of the situation. Furthermore, the people of this country are distant from the troubled areas of the earth and it is hard for them to comprehend the plight and consequent reaction of the long-suffering peoples, and the effect of those reactions on their governments in connection with our efforts to promote peace in the world.

In considering the requirements for the rehabilitation of Europe the physical loss of life, the visible destruction of cities, factories, mines, and railroads was correctly estimated, but it has become obvious during recent months that this visible destruction was probably less serious than the dislocation of the entire fabric of European economy. For the past 10 years conditions have been highly abnormal. The feverish maintenance of the war effort engulfed all aspects of national economics. Machinery has fallen into disrepair or is entirely obsolete. Under the arbitrary and destructive Nazi rule, virtually every possible enterprise was geared into the German war machine. Long-standing commercial ties, private institutions, banks, insurance companies and shipping companies disappeared, through the loss of capital, absorption through nationalization or by simple destruction. In many countries, confidence in the local currency has been severely shaken. The breakdown of the business structure of Europe during the war was complete. Recovery has been seriously retarded by the fact that 2 years after the close of hostilities a peace settlement with Germany and Austria has not been agreed upon. But even given a more prompt solution of these difficult problems, the rehabilitation of the economic structure of Europe quite evidently will require a much longer time and greater effort than had been foreseen.

There is a phase of this matter which is both interesting and serious. The farmer has always produced the foodstuffs to exchange with the city dweller for the other necessities of life. This division of labor is the basis of modern civilization. At the present time it is threatened with breakdown. The town and city industries are not producing adequate goods to exchange with the food-producing farmer. Raw materials and fuel are in short supply. Machinery is lacking or worn out. The farmer or the peasant cannot find the goods for sale which he desires to purchase. So the sale of his farm produce for money which he cannot use seems to him an unprofitable transaction. He, therefore, has withdrawn many fields from crop cultivation and is using them for grazing. He feeds more grain to stock and finds for himself and his family an ample supply of food, however short he may be on clothing and the other ordinary gadgets of civilization. Meanwhile people in the cities are short of food and fuel. So the governments are forced to use their foreign money and credits to procure these necessities abroad. This process exhausts funds which are urgently needed for reconstruction. Thus a very serious situation is rapidly developing which bodes no good for the world. The modern system of the division of labor upon which the exchange of products is based is in danger of breaking down.

The truth of the matter is that Europe's requirements

for the next 3 or 4 years of foreign food and other essential products—principally from America—are so much greater than her present ability to pay that she must have substantial additional help, or face economic, social, and political deterioration of a very grave character.

The remedy lies in breaking the vicious circle and restoring the confidence of the European people in the economic future of their own countries and of Europe as a whole. The manufacturer and the farmer throughout wide areas must be able and willing to exchange their products for currencies the continuing value of which is not open to question.

Aside from the demoralizing effect on the world at large and the possibilities of disturbances arising as a result of the desperation of the people concerned, the consequences to the economy of the United States should be apparent to all. It is logical that the United States should do whatever it is able to do to assist in the return of normal economic health in the world, without which there can be no political stability and no assured peace. Our policy is directed not against any country or doctrine but against hunger, poverty, desperation, and chaos. Its purpose should be the revival of working economy in the world so as to permit the emergence of political and social conditions in which free institutions can exist. Such assistance, I am convinced, must not be on a piecemeal basis as various crises develop. Any assistance that this Government may render in the future should provide a cure rather than a mere palliative. Any government that is willing to assist in the task of recovery will find full cooperation, I am sure, on the part of the United States Government. Any government which maneuvers to block the recovery of other countries cannot expect help from us. Furthermore, governments, political parties, or groups which seek to perpetuate human misery in order to profit therefrom politically or otherwise will encounter the opposition of the United States.

It is already evident that, before the United States Government can proceed much further in its efforts to alleviate the situation and help start the European world on its way to recovery, there must be some agreement among the countries of Europe as to the requirements of the situation and the part those countries themselves will take in order to give proper effect to whatever action might be undertaken by this Government. It would be neither fitting nor efficacious for this Government to undertake to draw up unilaterally a program designed to place Europe on its feet economically. This is the business of the Europeans. The initiative, I think, must come from Europe. The role of this country should consist of friendly aid in the drafting of a European program so far as it may be practical for us to do so. The program should be a joint one, agreed to by a number, if not all European nations.

An essential part of any successful action on the part of the United States is an understanding on the part of the people of America of the character of the problem and the remedies to be applied. Political passion and prejudice should have no part. With foresight, and a willingness on the part of our people to face up to the vast responsibilities which history has clearly placed upon our country, the difficulties I have outlined can and will be overcome.

GLOSSARY

efficacious: capable of having the desired result or effect; effective as a means, measure, or remedy

palliative: serving to palliate which is to relieve or lessen without curing; mitigate; alleviate

Document Analysis

Marshall's speech is directed at multiple audiences: opinion leaders (including the group to whom he speaks at Harvard), the American public at large, leaders of other nations (including the Soviet Union), and members of Congress. As a consequence, although his speech focuses on economic issues, it contains few statistics. Instead, Marshall relies on broad descriptions of economic conditions and stories that personalize problems so his many audiences can appreciate the gravity of the situation in Europe.

Marshall recites a litany of catastrophes to show how "the entire fabric of [the] European economy" has been upended by a decade of "highly abnormal" conditions:

first the Nazis' efforts to transform Germany into a war economy, which prompted other countries to do the same, followed by the war itself, which wreaked havoc on infrastructure and destroyed "many long-standing commercial ties" that permitted businesses to function efficiently. The Allies' inability to agree on a final peace settlement for Germany and Austria has exacerbated problems. This remark is one of several veiled references to the Soviet Union's intransigence in postwar negotiations.

At the heart of his speech, Marshall describes the breakdown of the most basic form of economic exchange: the trade of food produced in rural areas for manufactured goods produced in urban areas. In a long paragraph, he details the changed situation in Europe, dispassionately describing the logical progression of events for both farmer and city dweller to demonstrate that "the modern system of the division of labor" is "in danger of breaking down." Though expressed in measured language, the message is alarmist—almost apocalyptic. Marshall identifies the crux of the problem in a single sentence: Europe's needs over the next three or four years exceed "her present ability to pay."

Arguing that problems of this nature are not simply regional but global, Marshall insists the United States should act to alleviate Europe's plight. In another veiled allusion to the Soviet Union, he insists that US aid is not intended to undermine other nations' efforts; in fact, the United States would welcome their assistance. He follows immediately with a warning: countries that block recovery efforts may find the United States actively opposing them. Additionally, throughout the speech, Marshall insists that the success of any recovery depends on European nations taking the lead in planning and implementing recovery efforts. This tactic is intended to blunt objections from some in Washington and in the Soviet Union that the United States is attempting to impose its will on Western Europe.

Having laid out the problems and potential solutions, Marshall ends on a note of confidence, assuring his audience(s) that Europe can overcome its present difficulties—as long as Americans display the "foresight" and "willingness" to live up to "the vast responsibilities which history has clearly placed upon our country." This unmistakable call to action signals to the world that the United States is ready to do what is can—and must—to aid both its allies and former enemies in returning to economic health.

Essential Themes

Marshall's speech has been compared to Abraham Lincoln's Gettysburg Address and is cited as the first visible sign of America's willingness to assume its role as a superpower in world affairs. Unquestionably, passage of the Marshall Plan had significant impact in the United States and abroad.

Between June and December 1947, State Department officials drafted legislation to implement the principles set out by Marshall in his Harvard speech. The plan called for $17 billion in aid over four years for countries that agreed to work jointly to restore industrial production. With the support of Republican senator Arthur Vandenberg, chair of the Foreign Relations Committee, the European Recovery Program (the official name of the legislation commonly called the Marshall Plan) was approved by both houses of Congress and signed into law by President Truman on April 3, 1948. During this period of negotiation and debate, a coordinated campaign to convince the American people that aid to Europe was important for US national security turned public opinion in favor of the Marshall Plan.

The implementation of the Marshall Plan also exposed Soviet intentions in Europe. Offered a chance to assist in the recovery, Soviet leader Joseph Stalin declined and directed countries in the Soviet sphere of influence to refuse to participate. These actions gave American politicians eager to combat the spread of Communism further cause to champion efforts aimed at curbing Soviet aggression.

Western European nations were euphoric over the prospect of American aid. British foreign secretary Ernest Bevin called the Marshall Plan a "life-line." By the time aid delivered under the Marshall Plan ended in December 1951, infrastructure across Western Europe was being rebuilt and production of important commodities, such as steel and food, had increased substantially. While grants and loans from the United States provided only a small portion of the funds spent on recovery, the psychological impact was significant. Britain, France, those portions of Germany not under Soviet control, and many smaller nations that had suffered from the war knew that the United States was not abandoning them to their fate, as had happened at the end of World War I. The Marshall Plan's most lasting impact may be in preserving Western-style democracy in a number of nations that might have otherwise become socialist states.

—*Laurence W. Mazzeno, PhD*

Bibliography and Additional Reading

Behrman, Greg. *The Most Noble Adventure: The Marshall Plan and the Time When America Saved Europe.* New York: Free, 2007. Print.

Clesse, Armand, & Archie C. Epps, eds. *Present at the Creation: The Fortieth Anniversary of the Marshall Plan.* New York: Harper, 1990. Print.

Killick, John. *The United States and European Reconstruction, 1945–1960.* Chicago: Fitzroy Dearborn, 1997. Print.

Mills, Nicolaus. *Winning the Peace: The Marshall Plan and America's Coming of Age as a Superpower.* Hoboken: Wiley, 2008. Print.

Pogue, Forrest C. George C. Marshall: *Statesman.* New York: Viking, 1987. Print.

■ Vyshinsky's Speech to the UN General Assembly

Date: September 18, 1947
Author: Andrey Vyshinsky
Genre: speech

Summary Overview

Europe suffered from the aftermath of World War II throughout the 1940s. Many nations faced poverty, unemployment, and housing shortages, but lacked the financial solvency and administrative support necessary to address these issues. Europe was also divided along political lines. Led by the United States, the United Kingdom, and France, Western European governments were mostly democratic. Led by the Soviet Union, the governments of Eastern Europe were mostly Communist.

In 1947, the United States established the Truman Doctrine and began formulating the Marshall Plan to provide economic assistance to help European countries rebuild after the war. However, the Soviet Union objected to these plans. In a September 1947 speech to the United Nations (UN) General Assembly, Soviet Deputy Minister of Foreign Affairs Andrey Vyshinsky argued that these policies directly contradicted the UN requirement that foreign aid not be "used as a political weapon." He believed the United States violated this requirement by financing European struggles against Communism under the guise of humanitarian aid.

Defining Moment

World War II wrought considerable destruction throughout most of Europe. Although the war officially ended in 1945, Europe continued to feel its destructive effects throughout the 1940s. Nations struggled with a multitude of problems due to poverty, unemployment, housing shortages, and lack of infrastructure. The threat of instability loomed, as governments lacked the resources needed to rebuild economies and infrastructure.

On May 22, 1947, President Harry S. Truman signed the Agreements on Aid to Greece and Turkey, which marked a major shift in US foreign policy that became known as the Truman Doctrine. The United Kingdom had been providing economic and military support to

help the Greek government block a takeover by the Communist Party, but eventually needed to redirect these funds toward its own postwar economic concerns. The United States stepped in to provide $400 million in aid to Greece and Turkey, hoping to prevent a Communist takeover of Greece and to prevent the conflict from spilling over into neighboring Turkey. In his speech to Congress to advocate for the agreement in March 1947, President Truman emphasized that the "foreign policy and national security" of the United States was at stake any time democratic systems of government were threatened and thus argued that intervention was critical.

Although some debate exists, many scholars and historians view the Marshall Plan as following directly from the Truman Doctrine. Officially known as the European Recovery Program, the Marshall Plan was developed by Secretary of State George C. Marshall after visiting postwar Europe. Marshall saw the widespread poverty, hunger, and unemployment facing Europeans and felt the United States should provide assistance. He also feared that, without immediate economic assistance to rebuild, all of Europe could quickly and easily fall to Communism as the Soviet Union sought to expand its reach across the continent. In a speech made at Harvard University on June 5, 1947, Marshall outlined his plan for the United States to assist Europe with the organizational and economic resources to rebuild.

Approved by Congress in March 1948, the Marshall Plan was authorized to provide $17 billion (about $90 billion in 2015 dollars) in grants to European countries in order to purchase food, equipment, medicine, and transportation system upgrades. However, the Soviet Union believed the Truman Doctrine and the Marshall Plan were thinly veiled attempts by the United States to exert political influence in postwar Europe, in violation of a United Nations resolution stating that relief should "at no time be used as a political weapon." In September 1947, shortly after the announcement of these two policies, Soviet Deputy Minister of Foreign Affairs Andrey Vyshinsky gave a speech to the United Nations General Assembly, in which he described his government's interpretation and disapproval of the Truman Doctrine and the Marshall Plan.

Author Biography

Andrey Vyshinsky was born on December 10, 1883, in Odessa, Russia. He graduated from Kiev University in 1913 and became a lawyer. He relocated to Moscow to work as an attorney and participate in national politics, joining the Communist Party in 1920. He became the prosecutor general of the Soviet Union in 1935 and oversaw many trials that were part of the Great Purge to remove dissenters from the Communist Party.

In 1940, Vyshinsky was appointed deputy minister of foreign affairs. In this role, he made numerous speeches to the United Nations and became known for his long, flourishing, and often aggressive rhetoric. He was promoted to minister of foreign affairs in 1949 and served in this position until 1953, when he was demoted to first deputy foreign minister. Vyshinsky died on November 22, 1954.

HISTORICAL DOCUMENT

The so-called Truman Doctrine and the Marshall Plan are particularly glaring examples of the manner in which the principles of the United Nation are violated, of the way in which the organization is ignored.

As the experience of the past few months has shown, the proclamation of this doctrine meant that the United States government has moved towards a direct renunciation of the principles of international collaboration and concerted action by the great powers and towards attempts to impose its will on other independent states, while at the same time obviously using the economic resources distributed as relief to individual needy nations as an instrument of political pressure. This is clearly proved by the measures taken by the United States government with regard to Greece and Turkey which ignore and bypass the United Nations as well as by the measures proposed under the so-called Marshall Plan in Europe. This policy conflicts sharply with the principle expressed by the General Assembly in its resolution of 11 December 1946, which declares that relief supplies to other countries "should ... at no time be used as a political weapon."

As is now clear, the Marshall Plan constitutes in essence merely a variant of the Truman Doctrine adapted to the conditions of postwar Europe. In bringing forward this plan, the United States government apparently counted on the cooperation of governments of the United Kingdom and France to confront the European countries in need of relief with the necessity of renouncing their inalienable right to dispose of their economic resources and to plan their national economy in their own way. The United States also counted on making all these countries directly dependent on the interests of American monopolies, which are striving to avert the approaching depression by an accelerated export of commodities and capital to Europe....

It is becoming more and more evident to everyone that the implementation of the Marshall Plan will mean placing European countries under the economic and political control of the United States and direct interference by the latter in the internal affairs of those countries.

Moreover, this plan is an attempt to split Europe into two camps and, with the help of the United Kingdom and France, to complete the formation of a bloc of several European countries hostile to the interests of the democratic countries of Eastern Europe and most particularly to the interests of the Soviet Union.

An important feature of this plan is the attempt to confront the countries of Eastern Europe with a bloc of Western European states including Western Germany. The intention is to make use of Western Germany and German heavy industry (the Ruhr) as one of the most important economic bases for American expansion in Europe, in disregard of the national interests of the countries which suffered from German aggression.

I need only recall these facts to show the utter incompatibility of this policy of United States, and of the British and French governments which support it, with the fundamental principles of the United Nations.

GLOSSARY

bloc: a group of persons, businesses, or nations united for a particular purpose or acting in concert from common interests

Document Analysis

Andrey Vyshinsky opens his speech to the United Nations General Assembly by stating that the Truman Doctrine and the Marshall Plan are "particularly glaring examples of the manner in which the principles of the United Nations are violated." He says these two policies demonstrate the US government's "direct renunciation of the principles of international collaboration" by using economic aid to impose its political will on independent nations. Vyshinsky believes this directly violates UN principles and cites a resolution from a session on December 11, 1946, which states that relief to other countries should not be used as a "political weapon." He also notes that both of these plans effectively bypass the United Nations' oversight by providing aid and advisement directly to nations such as Greece and Turkey. He asserts the US government is "using the economic resources distributed as relief to individual needy nations as an instrument of political pressure."

Vyshinsky argues that the Marshall Plan is simply a more widely applicable variation of the Truman Doctrine. He believes that the United States is relying on the United Kingdom and France to persuade other European nations to give in to political pressure and accept the aid, even though it means "renouncing their inalienable right to dispose of their economic resources and to plan their national economy in their own way." He also accuses the United States of creating these policies to further its own self-interest in averting an economic depression by exporting goods and money to Europe. Vyshinsky states that "it is becoming more and more evident to everyone that the implementation of the Marshall Plan will mean placing European countries under the economic and political control of the United States," which will lead to the US government directly interfering with those countries' internal affairs.

Finally, Vyshinsky accuses the United States of using the Marshall Plan to establish its influence over heavy industrial manufacturing in Western Europe, particularly in West Germany. He believes the United States intends to use the region as "one of the most important economic bases for American expansion into Europe" in disregard of the needs of nations that had been only recently freed from German occupation. Vyshinsky concludes that both policies conflict with the fundamental principles of the United Nations and notes the complicity of the United Kingdom and France in the Marshall Plan.

Essential Themes

Disputes over postwar revitalization caused a significant rift between the Soviet-influenced countries of Eastern Europe and the American-influenced countries of Western Europe. The United States intervened in Europe's recovery partly for humanitarian reasons and partly in hopes of quelling the growing Communist influences across the continent. Also at issue was concern that Soviet control over Greece and Turkey would block access to Middle Eastern oil for the United States and the countries of Western Europe.

The Truman Doctrine and the Marshall Plan marked a significant change in the US government's historic policy of nonintervention in foreign affairs during times of peace. The $17 billion authorized under the Marshall Plan was an unprecedented sum for the United States to spend on foreign interests during peacetime. The Soviet Union accused the United States of taking advantage of war-torn countries' desperate need for funding to influence them to choose democracy over Communism and align politically with the United States.

In contrast to President Franklin D. Roosevelt's more tolerant approach to diplomacy with the Soviet Union, President Truman took a much firmer stance in the face of perceived insolence and lack of cooperation. This change in policy, and particularly the way it was reflected in the Truman Doctrine and the Marshall Plan, is thought to be a factor that led to the decades-long Cold War.

The idea behind the Marshall Plan was that the European countries themselves would draft and direct their own plan for recovery and the United States would advise and assist, as well as provide the necessary administration and funding. Of the twenty-two nations invited to the Paris conference to draw up recovery plans, sixteen accepted; the Soviet Union did not participate and forbade the countries under its control from participating or accepting aid.

US funding for the Marshall Plan ended in 1951. Scholars and policy analysts continue to debate the program's significance in Europe's postwar recovery, and some believe its enactment contributed to the tensions that spawned the Cold War. Despite its conflicting place in American history, George C. Marshall won the Nobel Peace Prize in 1953 for his plan.

—*Tracey M. DiLascio, JD*

Bibliography and Additional Reading

Bandow, Doug. "A Look behind the Marshall Plan Mythology." *Investor's Business Daily.* Cato Inst., 3 June 1997. Web. 2 Feb. 2015.

Behrman, Greg. *The Most Noble Adventure: The Marshall Plan and How America Helped Rebuild Europe.* New York: Free, 2007. Print.

Folly, Martin H. "Truman, Harry S." *Oxford Reference Online.* Oxford UP, 2014. Web. 2 Feb. 2015.

"For European Recovery: The Fiftieth Anniversary of the Marshall Plan." *Library of Congress Online Exhibition.* LoC, 2015. Web. 2 Feb. 2015.

"History of the Marshall Plan." *George C. Marshall Research Library.* George C. Marshall Foundation, 2015. Web. 2 Feb. 2015.

Israelyan, Victor. *On the Battlefields of the Cold War: A Soviet Ambassador's Confession.* University Park: Pennsylvania State UP, 2003. Print.

■ NATO Treaty

Date: April 4, 1949
Author: John D. Hickerson
Genre: government document

Summary Overview

On April 4, 1949, the North Atlantic Treaty was signed in Washington, DC, by foreign ministers from Canada, the United States, and ten European nations—Belgium, Denmark, France, Great Britain, Iceland, Italy, Luxembourg, the Netherlands, Norway, and Portugal. Secretary of State Dean Acheson signed the treaty for the United States. The North Atlantic Treaty was a key agreement for the United States, and its fifth article was a mutual defense pact against aggression toward any of the signers, in support of which the North Atlantic Treaty Organization (NATO) was established. In the context of a rising Soviet threat, the treaty served to establish a bulwark against any Soviet maneuvers in Europe.

Defining Moment

The North Atlantic Treaty was preceded by European agreements that sought to counter a perceived growing threat from the Soviet Union. In the years following the end of World War II, the Soviet Union set up Communist governments in many central and Eastern European states, and tensions were high between the Soviet Union and its erstwhile World War II allies in Western Europe. Though the Soviet Union was a member of the United Nations, the rest of Europe had reason to fear its expansionist goals. In March 1948, France, the United Kingdom, Belgium, the Netherlands, and Luxembourg signed the Treaty of Brussels. Under this treaty, the Western Union Defence Organization was created in September 1948. The United States and Canada were not included in either of these, however, and a broader alliance between Western Europe and North America was soon underway. The North Atlantic Treaty drew on the Treaty of Brussels and the Inter-American Treaty of Reciprocal Assistance, known as the Rio Treaty, for much of its language. (Signed in 1947, the Rio Treaty was an example of a regional agreement among the nations of the Americas.)

Members of the North Atlantic Treaty agreed to mutual defense—an armed attack against any of them would be considered an attack against all. The United Nations allowed for self-defense, and if an attack were to happen, each member nation would be obligated to assist, though there was discretion as to what type of assistance could be offered. The United Nations remained the primary means of dealing with an international crisis; however, the North Atlantic Treaty allowed for self-defense in light of an attack. Article 5 of the North Atlantic Treaty, which established mutual defense, has been invoked only once, by the United States, following the September 11, 2001, terrorist attacks.

The treaty also allows its members to consult on military affairs without invoking an armed response. This provision, stated in article 4, has been invoked several times in NATO history to seek a resolution to a dispute or to determine a response to a military act. Turkey has invoked the article in conflicts with Syria, and Poland did so in 2014 to determine how to respond to Russian aggression in Crimea. NATO is headquartered in Brussels, Belgium, and its membership has grown from twelve to twenty-eight countries. In addition to military security and cooperation, NATO promotes democratic values and international cooperation.

Author Biography

John Dewey Hickerson was the US diplomat responsible for much of the North Atlantic Treaty's language. He was born in Crawford, Texas, in 1898, graduated from the University of Texas, and joined the Foreign Service soon after. Hickerson served in a variety of posts in Latin American and Canada until 1928, when he became the assistant chief of the US State Department's Division of West European Affairs in Washington, DC. He held this position for twelve years, also serving on the State Department's Board of Appeals and Review from 1934 until 1941. Hickerson became the secretary of the American section of the Permanent Joint Board on Defense in 1940 and held this position through the war. He was chief of the State Department's Division of British Commonwealth Affairs and deputy director of the Office of European Affairs from 1944 to 1947, and he was deeply involved in the establishment of the United Nations. He was promoted to director of the Office of European Affairs in 1947, and in this capacity, he led the team that drafted the North Atlantic Treaty. Hickerson was the assistant secretary of state from 1949 to 1953 and then served as US ambassador to Finland and the Philippines. Hickerson retired to Washington, DC, and died in Bethesda, Maryland, in 1989.

HISTORICAL DOCUMENT

The Parties to this Treaty reaffirm their faith in the purposes and principles of the Charter of the United Nations and their desire to live in peace with all peoples and all governments.

They are determined to safeguard the freedom, common heritage and civilisation of their peoples, founded on the principles of democracy, individual liberty and the rule of law.

They seek to promote stability and well-being in the North Atlantic area.

They are resolved to unite their efforts for collective defence and for the preservation of peace and security.

They therefore agree to this North Atlantic Treaty:

ARTICLE 1

The Parties undertake, as set forth in the Charter of the United Nations, to settle any international dispute in which they may be involved by peaceful means in such a manner that international peace and security and justice are not endangered, and to refrain in their international relations from the threat or use of force in any manner inconsistent with the purposes of the United Nations.

ARTICLE 2

The Parties will contribute toward the further development of peaceful and friendly international relations by strengthening their free institutions, by bringing about a better understanding of the principles upon which these institutions are founded, and by promoting conditions of stability and well-being. They will seek to eliminate conflict in their international economic policies and will encourage economic collaboration between any or all of them.

ARTICLE 3

In order more effectively to achieve the objectives of this Treaty, the Parties, separately and jointly, by means of continuous and effective self-help and mutual aid, will maintain and develop their individual and collective capacity to resist armed attack.

ARTICLE 4

The Parties will consult together whenever, in the opinion of any of them, the territorial integrity, political independence or security of any of the Parties is threatened.

ARTICLE 5

The Parties agree that an armed attack against one or more of them in Europe or North America shall be considered an attack against them all, and consequently they agree that, if such an armed attack occurs, each of them, in exercise of the right of individual or collective self-defence recognised by Article 51 of the Charter of the United Nations, will assist the Party or Parties so attacked by taking forthwith, individually, and in concert with the other Parties, such action as it deems necessary, including the use of armed force, to restore and maintain the security of the North Atlantic area.

Any such armed attack and all measures taken as a result thereof shall immediately be reported to the Security Council. Such measures shall be terminated when the Security Council has taken the measures necessary to restore and maintain international peace and security.

ARTICLE 6

For the purpose of Article 5, an armed attack on one or more of the Parties is deemed to include an armed attack:

• on the territory of any of the Parties in Europe or North America, on the Algerian Departments of France, on the territory of Turkey or on the islands under the jurisdiction of any of the Parties in the North Atlantic area north of the Tropic of Cancer;

• on the forces, vessels, or aircraft of any of the Parties, when in or over these territories or any area in Europe in which occupation forces of any of the Parties were stationed on the date when the Treaty entered into force or the Mediterranean Sea or the North Atlantic area north of the Tropic of Cancer.

ARTICLE 7

The Treaty does not effect, and shall not be interpreted as affecting, in any way the rights and obligations under the Charter of the Parties which are members of the United Nations, or the primary responsibility of the Security Council for the maintenance of international peace and security.

ARTICLE 8

Each Party declares that none of the international engagements now in force between it and any other of the Parties or any third State is in conflict with the provisions of this Treaty, and undertakes not to enter into any international engagement in conflict with this Treaty.

ARTICLE 9

The Parties hereby establish a Council, on which each of them shall be represented to consider matters concerning the implementation of this Treaty. The Council shall be so organised as to be able to meet promptly at any time. The Council shall set up such subsidiary bodies as may be necessary; in particular it shall establish immediately a defence committee which shall recommend measures for the implementation of Articles 3 and 5.

ARTICLE 10

The Parties may, by unanimous agreement, invite any other European State in a position to further the principles of this Treaty and to contribute to the security of the North Atlantic area to accede to this Treaty. Any State so invited may become a party to the Treaty by depositing its instrument of accession with the Government of the United States of America. The Government of the United States of America will inform each of the Parties of the deposit of each such instrument of accession.

ARTICLE 11

This Treaty shall be ratified and its provisions carried out by the Parties in accordance with their respective constitutional processes. The instruments of ratification shall be deposited as soon as possible with the Government of the United States of America, which will notify all the other signatories of each deposit. The Treaty shall enter into force between the States which have ratified it as soon as the ratification of the majority of the signatories, including the ratifications of Belgium, Canada, France, Luxembourg, the Netherlands, the United Kingdom and the United States, have been deposited and shall come into effect with respect to other States on the date of the deposit of their ratifications.

ARTICLE 12

After the Treaty has been in force for ten years, or at any time thereafter, the Parties shall, if any of them so requests, consult together for the purpose of reviewing the Treaty, having regard for the factors then affecting peace and security in the North Atlantic area including the development of universal as well as regional arrangements under the Charter of the United Nations for the maintenance of international peace and security.

ARTICLE 13

After the Treaty has been in force for twenty years, any Party may cease to be a Party one year after its notice of denunciation has been given to the Government of the United States of America, which will inform the Governments of the other Parties of the deposit of each notice of denunciation.

ARTICLE 14
This Treaty, of which the English and French texts are equally authentic, shall be deposited in the archives of the Government of the United States of America. Duly certified copies will be transmitted by that government to the governments of the other signatories.

Document Analysis

The North Atlantic Treaty begins with both a reaffirmation of the principals of the Charter of the United Nations and confirmation that this agreement is not a replacement for it. The introduction makes plain that the treaty's role is as an anti-Communist political alliance. The nations who signed it are protecting "democracy, individual liberty and the rule of law." The treaty protects the "peace and security" of its adherents, who also resolve to settle disputes peacefully, in agreement with the founding principles of the United Nations. Signers pledge to refrain "from the threat or use of force" in their dealings with other nations. In addition, the signers will promote democracy around the world by "strengthening their free institutions" and encouraging economic cooperation. These countries will be prepared to meet an attack through vigorous self-defense and pledge to consult when "territorial integrity, political independence or security of any of the Parties is threatened."

Article 5 of the North Atlantic Treaty goes to the heart of the alliance. The treaty is one of mutual defense, and, as such, an attack against any one country in the alliance will be considered an attack against all of them. The treaty stops short of requiring that assistance be rendered through armed force and leaves it to the determination of the nations involved to decide how they will respond. If the right of self-defense is invoked, the United Nations Security Council will be immediately informed and will devise a proper response. An armed NATO response is designed to provide temporary defense, while the United Nations remains the ultimate governing body. Article 6 expands the range of the territory covered under this treaty to include areas not in the North Atlantic, but under the control of member states.

Article 9 establishes the organization that is to administer the treaty and provides for a way for nations to easily consult with one another. It also calls for the immediate establishment of a "defense committee," and invites "any other European State in a position to further the principles of this Treaty" to join NATO. The treaty can be reviewed after ten years, signers can leave after twenty, and the signed treaty is to be deposited in Washington, DC.

Essential Themes

The North Atlantic Treaty went into effect on August 24, 1949, when President Harry S. Truman accepted the ratification of the other nations. The primary goal of the treaty was to provide for the defense of Western Europe and North America against the mounting threat from the Soviet Union. Though the United Nations held ultimate responsibility for international peacekeeping, the Soviet Union and other Communist countries were members; therefore, the United Nations could not be relied upon to deter potential Soviet aggression. After World War II, Western European nations sought a strong alliance that would discourage Soviet expansion. With the addition of the United States and Canada, the North Atlantic Treaty became a powerful bulwark against Communism and a political organization for the promotion of democracy.

—*Bethany Groff, MA*

Bibliography and Additional Reading

Gaddis, John Lewis. *The Cold War: A New History.* New York: Penguin, 2005. Print.

Kaplan, Lawrence S. *NATO 1948: The Birth of the Transatlantic Alliance.* Lanham, MD: Rowman & Littlefield, 2007. Print.

"The North Atlantic Treaty." *National Archives Featured Documents.* US National Archives and Records Administration, n.d. Web. 12 Jan. 2015.

■ Memorandum on Lifting the Soviet Blockade

Date: April 11, 1949
Author: Harry S. Truman
Genre: government document

Summary Overview

Since the Potsdam Agreement at the end of World War II in August 1945, both the German nation as a whole and its capital city of Berlin had been divided into four zones, each occupied by one of the four victorious Allied Powers. In what became one of the first crises of the Cold War, on June 24, 1948, the Soviet Union began a blockade of the American, British, and French sectors of Berlin, which lay entirely within the Soviet sector of Germany. This resulted in the Berlin Airlift—an unprecedented effort to sustain the food and fuel needs of an entire city. After the blockade had been in effect for nearly ten months, the Soviets showed no signs of weakening resolve, and the Americans showed no signs of ending their flights of supplies. The situation had devolved into a stalemate. At that point, US ambassador-at-large Philip Caryl Jessup contacted Jacob Malik, the Soviet representative to the United Nations Security Council, in an attempt to begin back-channel negotiations that would allow the blockade to come to an end.

Defining Moment

Ever since the 1945 Potsdam Agreement, the United States, the Soviet Union, Great Britain, and France had jointly occupied Germany. Each of the four Allies governed one sector of the country as a whole and one sector of the German capital, Berlin. However, between 1945 and 1948, relations between the Soviet Union and the other three Allies became increasingly strained, as the Soviets showed no inclination to withdraw from the Eastern European nations they had occupied while fighting Nazi Germany. Many of the Soviet leaders were waiting for the other three Allies to end their occupation of Germany, after which time they expected Germany to become a Communist nation. With postwar economic chaos and strong Communist parties in many other Western European nations, the Soviets hoped to foment Communist uprisings throughout Europe.

However, in 1947, US secretary of state George C. Marshall proposed a plan for massive US investment in European economic recovery, while at the same time, the Americans, British, and French tried futilely to convince the Soviet Union that the time had come for German reunification and the establishment of a democratic postwar German government. With the Soviets opposing the end of its occupation of the eastern sector of Germany, the other three Allies began the process of unifying their sectors by reforming Germany's currency, in essence creating an economic separation from the Soviet sectors of both Germany and Berlin.

In response, on June 24, 1948, the Soviet Union had established a blockade in an attempt to force the United States, Great Britain, and France to abandon their sectors of Berlin, which lay entirely within the Soviet sector of Germany. The other Allies immediately responded by beginning a massive airlift that would help keep West Berlin alive. As the months wore on, it became clear to the Soviet leadership that the political and economic gains they hoped would come from the blockade were not going to happen, and that the counterblockade of Western goods needed by East Germany was proving increasingly costly.

On January 31, 1949, Soviet premier Joseph Stalin stated that the blockade could be ended if the three Allies ended the counterblockade—making no mention of West German unification or the currency issue. In order to determine if this was, indeed, a softening of the Soviet position, US secretary of state Dean Acheson asked Ambassador-at-Large Philip Jessup to continue discussions with Soviet UN representative Jacob Malik as to whether talks could commence to end the blockade. Once Jessup was sufficiently sure of the Soviet desire to negotiate an end to the crisis, he informed Acheson, who then briefed President Harry S. Truman, who wrote this memorandum to inform the necessary diplomatic personnel of the talks and the US position regarding the future of West Germany and West Berlin after the blockade.

Author Biography

When Harry S. Truman (1884–1972) became president of the United States on April 12, 1945, after Franklin D. Roosevelt died in the waning days of World War II, he had been vice president for less than three months. However, he quickly put his own stamp on American policy in the face of increasing tension between the United States and its World War II ally the Soviet Union. In 1947, he had responded with military aid to subdue Soviet-supported Communist uprisings in Greece and Turkey. However, a more direct crisis loomed when the Soviets began the blockade of Berlin in 1948. Truman responded by ordering the massive airlift that helped to supply the city throughout the blockade. While seeking to negotiate an end to the blockade, Truman did not relent in his effort to unify the American, British, and French sectors of Germany, as well as in his determination to create a military alliance between the Western European nations to withstand Soviet aggression.

HISTORICAL DOCUMENT

MEMORANDUM

Mr. Malik, Soviet representative on the Security Council of the United Nations, recently approached Mr. Jessup in a private conversation with suggestions which intimated that the Soviet Government might be prepared to lift the Berlin blockade if the Western Powers would lift the counter-blockade and would agree to a meeting of the Council of Foreign Ministers. Mr. Malik indicated that the Soviet Government might agree that the lifting of the blockade could precede the convening of the Council of Foreign Ministers, provided a date was fixed for the latter.

In light of the extreme delicacy and importance of this matter, I instructed the Secretary of State to have this approach followed up in further private discussions between Mr. Jessup and Mr. Malik, with a view to ascertaining whether it had any real substance. Mr. Jessup was instructed in particular to obtain confirmation of Soviet readiness to lift the blockade prior to the meeting of the Ministers.

Pending such clarification I instructed the Secretary of State not to disclose information about this discussion without my authorization. The British and French Foreign Ministers were naturally kept personally informed of the progress of these talks.

The discussion to date have now indicated that there is a sufficient degree of seriousness on the Russian side to warrant our proceeding further and entering, if the Russians are willing, on the negotiation of the actual arrangements; and we are now consulting further with the British and French Foreign Ministers on this point.

In these circumstances I think it important that Secretary Royall, Mr. Voorhees, General Bradley and General Clay be acquainted with the above, for their strictly personal information, and suggest that you make the appropriate arrangements. Until further notice, I would appreciate it if you would see to it that no other persons are apprised of the matter.

I am similarly authorizing the Secretary of State to inform the political representatives of the United States at Berlin and Moscow.

Document Analysis

When President Harry S. Truman was notified by Secretary of State Dean Acheson (Marshall's successor) that the talks between US ambassador at large Philip Jessup and Soviet UN representative Jacob Malik had proven promising and had revealed that the Soviets were willing to end their blockade of West Berlin, he issued a memorandum that first instructed US diplomatic personnel on the matter and then restated the American determination to create a non-Communist German state in the aftermath.

At the start, Truman acknowledges the terms that Jessup and Malik have agreed upon: ending the Soviet blockade of West Berlin in return for the end of the Allies' counterblockade of East Germany, and a meeting of the Conference of Foreign Ministers, the group consisting of the foreign ministers from all four of the victorious World War II allies, that would presumably give the Soviets a voice in the ongoing plans for postwar Germany. Given that the Soviets were not insisting upon the cessation of Allied plans to unite the currency of their three sectors, Truman felt that there was sufficient ground to ask for the beginning of official talks to end the crisis. Though he had kept the British and French updated on these developments, he now thought it time to inform others in the American government, including Secretary of the Army Kenneth Royall, Assistant Secretary of the Army Tracy Voorhees, Army Chief of Staff Omar Bradley, and US Zone military governor Lucius Clay, as well as members of the US diplomatic corps in Berlin and Moscow. However, he does stress the importance to restricting the information to select individuals only.

Truman then discusses the need for the talks between Jessup and Malik to clarify the specific Soviet and Western blockade restrictions that will be lifted—that is, the Soviet restrictions on "communications, transportation and trade between Berlin and the Western zones of Germany, and on the other hand by the three powers on communications, transportation and trade to and from the Eastern zone of Germany." Truman concludes by outlining what the Allies would not compromise, specifically "the continuation of the preparations for the establishment of a Western German Government," essentially stating that the United States was not willing to compromise its position regarding the protection of non-Communist nations in Western Europe, while basically acknowledging that Soviet occupation of Eastern Europe, including East Germany, was a fait accompli.

Essential Themes

At the same time that the Berlin crisis was coming to an end, other events were taking place on both sides of what British prime minister Winston Churchill had, in 1946, dubbed the Iron Curtain that would shape much of the emerging Cold War. Most importantly, as Jessup and Malik were negotiating an end to the blockade, the three Allies and the other nations of Western Europe were in negotiations that would result in the creation of the North Atlantic Treaty Organization (NATO) on April 4, 1949.

On May 12, about a month after this memo, the blockade and counterblockade were lifted. By the end of 1949, the occupation of Germany and Berlin had officially ended, with the establishment of two German governments: the pro-Western German Federal Republic (or West Germany, established on May 23, 1949), with its capital in Bonn, and the pro-Soviet German Democratic Republic (or East Germany, established on October 7, 1949), of which East Berlin was the capital. In the early Cold War years that followed the Berlin blockade, hundreds of thousands of East German residents fled the Soviet-controlled country for the West. In response, in May 1952, the border between East and West Germany was closed and barbed wire fencing erected by the East Germans. However, the border within Berlin remained open until 1961, when the East Germans commenced construction of the Berlin Wall, which served to close off almost all immigration between the east and the west, and also became one of the most recognizable symbols of the Cold War.

The status of West Berlin, as it was not technically within the borders of West Germany, was ambiguous until the Berlin Constitution was adopted in August 1950. That document officially added West Berlin to West Germany, though it remained under the protection and jurisdiction of the United States, Great Britain, and France until the reunification of Germany at the end of the Cold War on October 3, 1990.

—*Steven L. Danver, PhD*

Bibliography and Additional Reading

Harrington, Daniel F. *Berlin on the Brink: The Blockade, the Airlift, and the Early Cold War.* Lexington: UP of Kentucky, 2012. Print.

Mastny, Vojtech. *The Cold War and Soviet Insecurity: The Stalin Years.* New York: Oxford UP, 1996. Print.

Shlaim, Avi. *The United States and the Berlin Blockade, 1948–1949: A Study in Crisis Decision-Making.* Berkeley: U of California P, 1983. Print.

Stivers, William. "The Incomplete Blockade: Soviet Zone Supply of West Berlin, 1948–49." *Diplomatic History* 21.4 (1997): 569–602. Print.

AMERICAN ALLIANCES

In the years following World War II, the United States and other countries of the Western Hemisphere recognized their common interest in preserving their boundaries and providing, to a degree at least, a common defense against foreign incursions. Particularly with the emergence of the United Nations after the war, there was a growing awareness of the need to maintain alliances within the world community and especially within one's own sphere of influence. To that end, a series of alliances were formalized across the Americas, in part as an anticommunist measure. These included the Act of Chapultepec (a preliminary "framework" agreement, really), the Inter-American Treaty of Reciprocal Assistance, and the Pact of Bogota (designed to settle disputes within the alliance). As useful as these measures were, not every nation in the Americas sought to participate in them, of course, and even those that did sometimes harbored reservations or ended up taking contrary courses of action in the years to come. Nevertheless, these treaties served to represent the workings of postwar diplomatic efforts on behalf of hemispheric neighbors.

■ Act of Chapultepec

Date: March 8, 1945
Genre: government document

Summary Overview

As World War II drew to a close, nations in the Americas were eager to reaffirm their relationships with each other and with the United States. All Central and South American nations had supported the Allies throughout the war, except Uruguay and Argentina, which both remained neutral for much of the war before finally siding with the Allies. An inter-American conference met at the Chapultepec Castle in Mexico City between February 21 and March 8, 1945, with delegations attending from Argentina, Bolivia, Brazil, Chile, Colombia, Costa Rica, Cuba, the Dominican Republic, Ecuador, El Salvador, Guatemala, Haiti, Honduras, Mexico, Nicaragua, Panama, Paraguay, Peru, the United States, Uruguay, and Venezuela. The conference, formally named the Inter-American Conference on War and Peace, produced the Act of Chapultepec, a framework for security in the Americas. Nations who signed the act agreed that an act of aggression against any American state would be seen as an act against all and promised to consult with one another and, if necessary, to act to repel the aggression. They promised to use collective measures, including diplomatic pressure, the interruption of commerce and communication, even armed force if needed, to bring aggressive states into line. At the United Nations Conference on International Organization, held a month later in San Francisco, Latin American countries confirmed their Chapultepec agreements, and in 1948, the Organization of American States (OAS) was founded in order to settle disputes between American states and provide a structure for mutual defense and economic cooperation.

Defining Moment

The United States had been concerned with the defense of Americas against further European conquest or influence since the founding of the nation, and in 1823, the Monroe Doctrine stated clearly that European attempts to further colonize or interfere with American nations would be considered acts of aggression to which the United States would respond. Though defense was critical, economic and political cooperation was pursued as well. In the First International Conference of American States, held in Washington, DC, in 1890, American nations discussed how to encourage greater communication among themselves and also promoted economic cooperation and an arbitration system to settle disputes. From this meeting sprang the International Union of American Republics, followed by the Pan American Union, and eventually the Organization of American States. It is this First International Conference of American States that the Act of Chapultepec refers to when it states, "The American states have been incorporating in their international law, since 1890, by means of conventions, resolutions and declarations" certain shared principals.

With the coming of the world wars of the twentieth century, however, American countries grew increasingly concerned with their common defense. In the years before the outbreak of World War II, Adolf Hitler made overtures toward South and Central American states, asking for military cooperation and negotiating trade agreements. Of particular concern to the United States was the security of the Panama Canal, the ability of spies to enter the United States through Latin America, and the capacity of these spies to set up communications networks to relay information abroad. In 1936, the Inter-American Conference for the Maintenance of Peace agreed to mutual defense in case of a European war. During the war, all American states supported the Allies, with the exception of Uruguay and Argentina, and nine Central American states signed the 1942 Declaration by the United Nations (an international statement of intention to create a world body, the United Nations), joined by others in subsequent years.

By March 1945, Germany was on the verge of collapse, and Japan was in retreat in the Pacific. American states were eager to reaffirm their relationships with and obligations to each other and with the United States and to play a role in shaping the postwar world. The Inter-American Conference on War and Peace convened in Mexico City in late February and early March 1945, with high-ranking delegates from twenty-one countries. The conference was a turning point in Pan-American relationships, with the attendees agreeing to mutual defense and arbitration and reaffirming shared statements of belief in principals of international law that had been agreed on at other American conferences throughout the previous decades. These agreements came at a time when international relations were in flux and the structure of the new postwar world was being vigorously debated. The United Nations had been formed, but was yet to be established internationally. The 1944 Dumbarton Oaks Conference had seen delegations from China, the Soviet Union, the United Kingdom, and the United States debating the form and structure of the organization that would be responsible for world security in the future. American states also wanted to play a role in this shaping of the postwar world.

HISTORICAL DOCUMENT

60 Stat. 1831; Treaties and Other International Acts Series 1543

RECIPROCAL ASSISTANCE AND AMERICAN SOLIDARITY

WHEREAS:

The peoples of the Americas, animated by a profound love of justice, remain sincerely devoted to the principles of international law;

It is their desire that such principles, notwithstanding the present difficult circumstances, prevail with even greater force in future international relations;

The inter-American conferences have repeatedly proclaimed certain fundamental principles, but these must be reaffirmed at a time when the juridical bases of the community of nations are being re-established;

The new situation in the world makes more imperative than ever the union and solidarity of the American peoples, for the defense of their rights and the maintenance of international peace;

The American states have been incorporating in their international law, since 1890, by means of conventions, resolutions and declarations, the following principles:

a) The proscription of territorial conquest and the non-recognition of all acquisitions made by force (First International Conference of American States, 1890);

b) The condemnation of intervention by one State in the internal or external affairs of another (Seventh International Conference of American States, 1933, and Inter-American Conference for the Maintenance of Peace 1936);

c) The recognition that every war or threat of war affects directly or indirectly all civilized peoples, and endangers the great principles of liberty and justice which constitute the American ideal and the standard of American international policy Inter-American Conference for the Maintenance of Peace, 1936);

d) The system of mutual consultation in order to find means of peaceful cooperation in the event of war or threat of war between American countries (Inter-American Conference for the Maintenance of Peace, 1936);

e) The recognition that every act susceptible of disturbing the peace of America affects each and every one of the American nations and justifies the initiation of the procedure of consultation (Inter-American Conference for the Maintenance of Peace, 1936);

f) The adoption of conciliation, unrestricted arbitration, or the application of international justice, in the solution of any difference or dispute between American nations, whatever its nature or origin (Inter-American Conference for the Maintenance of Peace, 1936);

g) The recognition that respect for the personality, sovereignty and independence of each American State constitutes the essence of international order sustained by continental solidarity, which historically has been expressed and sustained by declarations and treaties in force (Eighth International Conference of American States, 1938);

h) The affirmation that respect for and the faithful observance of treaties constitute the indispensable rule for the development of peaceful relations between States, and that treaties can only be revised by agreement of the contracting parties (Declaration of American

Principles, Eighth International Conference of American States, 1938);

i) The proclamation that, in case the peace, security or territorial integrity of any American republic is threatened by acts of any nature that may impair them, they proclaim their common concern and their determination to make effective their solidarity, coordinating their respective sovereign wills by means of the procedure of consultation, using the measures which in each case the circumstances may make advisable (Declaration of Lima, Eighth International Conference of American States, 1938);

j) The declaration that any attempt on the part of a non-American state against the integrity or inviolability of the territory, the sovereignty or the political independence of an American State shall be considered as an act of aggression against all the American States (Declaration XV of the Second Meeting of the Ministers of Foreign Affairs, Habana, 1940);

The furtherance of these principles, which the American States have constantly practiced in order to assure peace and solidarity among the nations of the Continent, constitutes an effective means of contributing to the general system of world security and of facilitating its establishment;

The security and solidarity of the Continent are affected to the same extent by an act of aggression against any of the American States by a non-American State, as by an act of aggression of an American State against one or more American States;

PART I
The Governments Represented at the Inter-American Conference on Problems of War and Peace
DECLARE:

1. That all sovereign States are juridically equal among themselves.

2. That every State has the right to the respect of its individuality and independence, on the part of the other members of the international community.

3. That every attack of a State against the integrity or the inviolability of the territory, or against the sovereignty or political independence of an American State, shall, conformably to Part III hereof, be considered as an act of aggression against the other States which sign this Act.

In any case invasion by armed forces of one State into the territory of another trespassing boundaries established by treaty and demarcated in accordance therewith shall constitute an act of aggression.

4. That in case acts of aggression occur or there are reasons to believe that an aggression is being prepared by any other State against the integrity or inviolability of the territory, or against the sovereignty or political independence of an American State, the States signatory to this Act will consult among themselves in order to agree upon the measures it may be advisable to take.

5. That during the war, and until the treaty recommended in Part II hereof is concluded, the signatories of this Act recognize that such threats and acts of aggression, as indicated in paragraphs 3 and 4 above, constitute an interference with the war effort of the United Nations, calling for such procedures, within the scope of their constitutional powers of a general nature and for war, as may be found necessary, including: recall of chiefs of diplomatic missions; breaking of diplomatic relations; breaking of consular relations; breaking of postal, telegraphic, telephonic, radio-telephonic relations; interruption of economic, commercial and financial relations; use of armed force to prevent or repel aggression.

6. That the principles and procedure contained in this Declaration shall become effective immediately, inasmuch as any act of aggression or threat of aggression during the present state of war interferes with the war effort of the United Nations to obtain victory. Henceforth, and to the end that the principles and procedures herein stipulated shall conform with the constitutional processes of each Republic, the respective Governments shall take the necessary steps to perfect this instrument in order that it shall be in force at all times.

PART II
The Inter-American Conference on Problems of War and Peace

RECOMMENDS:

That for the purpose of meeting threats or acts of aggression against any American Republic following the establishment of peace, the Governments of the American Republics consider the conclusion, in accordance with their constitutional processes, of a treaty establishing procedures whereby such threats or acts may be met by the use, by all or some of the signatories of said treaty, of any one or more of the following measures: recall of chiefs of diplomatic missions; breaking of diplomatic relations; breaking of consular relations; breaking of postal, telegraphic, telephonic, radio-telephonic relations; interruption of economic, commercial and financial relations; use of armed force to prevent or repel aggression.

PART III

The above Declaration and Recommendation constitute a regional arrangement for dealing with such matters relating to the maintenance of international peace and security as are appropriate for regional action in this Hemisphere. The said arrangement, and the pertinent activities and procedures, shall be consistent with the purposes and principles of the general international organization, when established.

This agreement shall be known as the "Act of Chapultepec."

[The final act of the Inter-American Conference on Problems of War and Peace was signed on March 8, 1945, by delegates representing Argentina, Bolivia, Brazil, Chile, Colombia, Costa Rica, Cuba, the Dominican Republic, Ecuador, El Salvador, Guatemala Haiti, Honduras, Mexico, Nicaragua, Panama, Paraguay, Peru, the United States, Uruguay, and Venezuela.]

GLOSSARY

conciliation: to overcome the distrust or hostility of; placate; win over

demarcated: to determine or mark off the boundaries or limits of; to separate distinctly

juridical: of or relating to the administration of justice; legal

proscription: the act or state of proscribing; outlawry, interdiction or prohibition

Document Analysis

The Act of Chapultepec is divided roughly into sections representing the past, present, and future. The first section begins by reaffirming the long-standing relationship held among American states. The "peoples of the Americas" had been meeting since 1890 and are committed to common principals of international law. Although all the nations of the Americas were in agreement about basic principles, the signers are also in agreement that there is an opportunity for significant shifts in international relations in the postwar world, and these principals, therefore, "must be reaffirmed at a time when the juridical bases of the community of nations are being re-established." Ten principals, established at other meetings and summits, are reaffirmed by the signers of the act. As additional confirmation of the unity of purpose of these nations, the dates and names of these previous meetings are given along with the agreement. The American states have agreed not to recognize territory taken by force and to condemn the intervention of states in each other's affairs. The countries have agreed that they are against war, and that disputes between any of them will impact all of them. Because of this, they have also agreed that a system of arbitration is the most appropriate way to settle disputes, and "continental solidarity" should be upheld and treaties respected. If outside nations invade or threaten any American state, it will be viewed as "an act of aggression against all the American States." These common principals will ensure that the American states are part of the "general system of world security and of facilitating its establishment"—a reference to the pending establishment of the United Nations.

After the previous agreements have been confirmed, the act turns to how these principals should be applied immediately, while global war is still being waged, and what penalties would be appropriate to respond to aggression. It is agreed that any violation of national sovereignty in the Americas constitutes "interference with the war effort of the United Nations" ("United Nations" being another term for the Allies before the establishment of the formal world body). The nations signing the treaty agree to deal with aggression with escalating consequences as necessary, laid out in detail: "recall of chiefs of diplomatic missions; breaking of diplomatic relations; breaking of consular relations; breaking of postal, telegraphic, telephonic, radio-telephonic relations; interruption of economic, commercial and financial relations; use of armed force to prevent or repel aggression."

The final section deals with the future. Once the war is over, the nations of the Americas will need to consider a treaty that will lay out consequences for aggression in a permanent form. This treaty will need to be "consistent with the purposes and principles of the general international organization, when established"—another reference to the United Nations.

Essential Themes

The primary theme of this agreement is the need for the states of the Americas to band together for mutual support and to repel any attack anywhere in the Americas. An attack on any member state would be considered an attack on all. At the same time, conflicts among American states needed to be settled by arbitration rather than war. Pan-American conferences had addressed these issues before, but it was necessary, in light of the international upheaval caused by World War II, to revisit previous agreements. The form of this agreement—a reaffirmation of the common principals established over the previous decades, as well as a declaration of how the nations of the Americas would use these principals to discourage aggression and provide for mutual defense, and finally a desire to conclude a treaty in keeping with the aims of the nascent United Nations—demonstrates the uncertainty of international relations in March 1945, when the war was ending, but not over, and the postwar world was imagined, with its outlines laid out by the presumed victors. The Act of Chapultepec was a step in this process, a regional agreement that upheld the principles of the United Nations.

—*Bethany Groff, MA*

Bibliography and Additional Reading

Canyes, Manuel S. "The Inter-American System and the Conference of Chapultepec." *American Journal of International Law* 39.3 (1945): 504–17. Print.

Green, David. *The Containment of Latin America: A History of the Myths and Realities of the Good Neighbor Policy.* Chicago: Quadrangle, 1971. Print.

Luard, Evan. A *History of the United Nations: The Years of Western Domination, 1945–1955.* New York: Macmillan, 1982. Print.

Schlesinger, Stephen C. *Act of Creation: The Founding of the United Nations.* Cambridge: Perseus, 2004. Print.

■ Inter-American Treaty of Reciprocal Assistance

Date: September 2, 1947
Genre: charter

Summary Overview

In February and March of 1945, delegations from Argentina, Bolivia, Brazil, Chile, Colombia, Costa Rica, Cuba, the Dominican Republic, Ecuador, El Salvador, Guatemala, Haiti, Honduras, Mexico, Nicaragua, Panama, Paraguay, Peru, the United States, Uruguay, and Venezuela met at the Chapultepec Castle in Mexico City to discuss the regional defense and cooperation of American states. The conference, formally named the Inter-American Conference on Problems of War and Peace, produced the Act of Chapultepec, a framework for security in the Americas. That act laid out many of the principals for pan-American military cooperation, but since it was created during World War II and it was clear to the participating nations that the international situation was in flux, the signing of a formal treaty was left to be concluded in the future.

When these nations met again after the war, in Rio de Janeiro, Brazil, at the Inter-American Conference for the Maintenance of Continental Peace and Security in 1947, they finalized the defense policy that had been born in Chapultepec. The Inter-American Treaty of Reciprocal Assistance would plan for the long-term mutual defense of the American states against any outside aggressor and mediate any internal conflict between treaty members. This regional agreement also conformed to the global security framework established by the United Nations (UN), which had come into existence on October 24, 1945.

Defining Moment

The Inter-American Treaty of Reciprocal Assistance, also known as the Rio Treaty, was the culmination of many years of discussion and negotiation. The United States had long been concerned with the defense of American states against European interference; in 1823, the Monroe Doctrine stated that any European attempts to further colonize or interfere with American nations would be considered acts of aggression to which the United States would respond. At the First International Conference of American States, held in Washington, DC, from October 1889 to April 1890, eighteen American nations discussed how to encourage greater regional communication, promote economic cooperation, and adopt an arbitration system to settle disputes. From this initiative, the International Union of American Republics was founded, which later developed into the Pan American Union and then the Organization of American States.

American states grew increasingly concerned with their common defense as the two world wars demonstrated the global scope of conflicts in the twentieth century. In the years before the outbreak of World War II, German leader Adolf Hitler made overtures toward South and Central American states, asking for military cooperation and negotiating trade agreements. The United States feared that such alliances would make it vulnerable to spies who could more easily transmit information to Germany through Latin America. Also of concern to the United States was the security of the Panama Canal, a key transportation link.

In 1936, the participating nations at the Inter-American Conference for the Maintenance of Peace agreed to mutual defense in case of a European war. During World War II, all American states with the exception of Uruguay and Argentina supported the Allies, and nine Central American and Caribbean states joined the United States in signing the 1942 Declaration by the United Nations, the document that established the precursor to the UN. In February and March 1945, with the Axis powers of Germany and Japan close to collapse, the Inter-American Conference on Problems of War and Peace convened in Mexico City, with high ranking delegates present from twenty-one countries. The resulting Act of Chapultepec laid out a framework for mutual defense and conflict arbitration, with the understanding that these agreements would need to be formalized after the war was over. In 1947, the Rio Treaty did just that, turning the agreements of Chapultepec into a long-term formalized treaty that went into effect on December 3, 1948. The first cracks in Pan-American unity were already beginning to show, however, as American states attempted to reaffirm their claims on disputed territory. These claims, particularly that of Argentina in the Falkland Islands, would be later points of conflict that would ultimately weaken the treaty.

HISTORICAL DOCUMENT

Inter-American Treaty of Reciprocal Assistance

In the name of their Peoples, the Governments represented at the Inter-American Conference for the Maintenance of Continental Peace and Security, desirous of consolidating and strengthening their relations of friendship and good neighborliness, and

Considering:

That Resolution VIII of the Inter-American Conference on Problems of War and Peace, which met in Mexico City, recommended the conclusion of a treaty to prevent and repeal threats and acts of aggression against any of the countries of America;

That the High Contracting Parties reiterate their will to remain united in an inter-American system consistent with the purposes and principles of the United Nations, and reaffirm the existence of the agreement which they have concluded concerning those matters relating to the maintenance of international peace and security which are appropriate for regional action;

That the High Contracting Parties reaffirm their adherence to the principles of inter-American solidarity and cooperation, and especially to those set forth in the preamble and declarations of the Act of Chapultepec, all of which should be understood to be accepted as standards of their mutual relations and as the juridical basis of the Inter-American System;

That the American States propose, in order to improve the procedures for the pacific settlement of their controversies, to conclude the treaty concerning the "Inter-American Peace System" envisaged in Resolutions IX and XXXIX of the Inter-American Conference on Problems of War and Peace,

That the obligation of mutual assistance and common defense of the American Republics is essentially related to their democratic ideals and to their will to cooperate permanently in the fulfillment of the principles and purposes of a policy of peace;

That the American regional community affirms as a manifest truth that juridical organization is a necessary prerequisite of security and peace, and that peace is founded on justice and moral order and, consequently, on the international recognition and protection of human rights and freedoms, on the indispensable well-being of the people, and on the effectiveness of democracy for the international realization of justice and security,

Have resolved, in conformity with the objectives stated above, to conclude the following Treaty, in order to assure peace, through adequate means, to provide for effective reciprocal assistance to meet armed attacks against any American State, and in order to deal with threats of aggression against any of them:

Article 1.

The High Contracting Parties formally condemn war and undertake in their international relations not to resort to the threat or the use of force in any manner inconsistent with the provisions of the Charter of the United Nations or of this Treaty.

Article 2.

As a consequence of the principle set forth in the preceding Article, the High Contracting Parties undertake to submit every controversy which may arise between them to methods of peaceful settlement and to endeavor to settle any such controversies among themselves by means of the procedures in force in the Inter-American System before referring it to the General Assembly or the Security Council of the United Nations.

Article 3.

1. The High Contracting Parties agree that an armed attack by any State against an American State shall be considered as an attack against all the American States and, consequently, each one of the said Contracting Parties undertakes to assist in meeting the attack in the exercise of the inherent right of individual or collective

self-defense recognized by Article 51 of the Charter of the United Nations.

2. On the request of the State or States directly attacked and until the decision of the Organ of Consultation of the Inter-American System, each one of the Contracting Parties may determine the immediate measures which it may individually take in fulfillment of the obligation contained in the preceding paragraph and in accordance with the principle of continental solidarity. The Organ of Consultation shall meet without delay for the purpose of examining those measures and agreeing upon the measures of a collective character that should be taken.

3. The provisions of this Article shall be applied in case of any armed attack which takes place within the region described in Article 4 or within the territory of an American State. When the attack takes place outside of the said areas, the provisions of Article 6 shall be applied.

4. Measures of self-defense provided for under this Article may be taken until the Security Council of the United Nations has taken the measures necessary to maintain international peace and security.

Article 4.

The region to which this Treaty refers is bounded as follows: beginning at the North Pole; thence due south to a point 74 degrees north latitude, 10 degrees west longitude; thence by a rhumb line to a point 47 degrees 30 minutes north latitude, 50 degrees west longitude; thence by a rhumb line to a point 35 degrees north latitude, 60 degrees west longitude; thence due south to a point in 20 degrees north latitude; thence by a rhumb line to a point 5 degrees north latitude, 24 degrees west longitude; thence due south to the South Pole; thence due north to a point 30 degrees south latitude, 90 degrees west longitude; thence by a rhumb line to a point on the Equator at 97 degrees west longitude; thence by a rhumb line to a point 15 degrees north latitude, 120 degrees west longitude; thence by a rhumb line to a point 50 degrees north latitude, 170 degrees east longitude; thence due north to a point in 54 degrees north latitude; thence by a rhumb line to a point 65 degrees 30 minutes north latitude, 168 degrees 58 minutes 5 seconds west longitude: thence due north to the North Pole.

Article 5.

The High Contracting Parties shall immediately send to the Security Council of the United Nations, in conformity with Articles 51 and 54 of the Charter of the United Nations, complete information concerning the activities undertaken or in contemplation in the exercise of the right of self-defense or for the purpose of maintaining inter-American peace and security.

Article 6.

If the inviolability or the integrity of the territory or the sovereignty or political independence of any American State should be affected by an aggression which is not an armed attack or by an extracontinental or intracontinental conflict, or by any other fact or situation that might endanger the peace of America, the Organ of Consultation shall meet immediately in order to agree on the measures which must be taken in case of aggression to assist the victim of the aggression or, in any case, the measures which should be taken for the common defense and for the maintenance of the peace and security of the Continent.

Article 7.

In the case of a conflict between two or more American States, without prejudice to the right of self-defense in conformity with Article 51 of the Charter of the United Nations, the High Contracting Parties, meeting in consultation shall call upon the contending States to suspend hostilities and restore matters to the status quo ante bellum, and shall take in addition all other necessary measures to reestablish or maintain inter-American peace and security and for the solution of the conflict by peaceful means. The rejection of the pacifying action will be considered in the determination of the aggressor and in the application of the measures which the consultative meeting may agree upon.

Article 8.

For the purposes of this Treaty, the measures on which the Organ of Consultation may agree will comprise one or more of the following: recall of chiefs of diplomatic missions; breaking of diplomatic relations; breaking of consular relations; partial or complete interruption of economic relations or of rail, sea, air, postal, telegraphic, telephonic, and radiotelephonic or radio-telegraphic communications; and use of armed force.

Article 9.

In addition to other acts which the Organ of Consultation may characterize as aggression, the following shall be considered as such:

a. Unprovoked armed attack by a State against the territory, the people, or the land, sea or air forces of another State;

b. Invasion, by the armed forces of a State, of the territory of an American State, through the trespassing of boundaries demarcated in accordance with a treaty, judicial decision, or, arbitral award, or, in the absence of frontiers thus demarcated, invasion affecting a region which is under the effective jurisdiction of another State.

Article 10.

None of the provisions of this Treaty shall be construed as impairing the rights and obligations of the High Contracting Parties under the Charter of the United Nations.

Article 11.

The consultations to which this Treaty refers shall be carried out by means of the Meetings of Ministers of Foreign Affairs of the American Republics which have ratified the Treaty, or in the manner or by the organ which in the future may be agreed upon.

Article 12.

The Governing Board of the Pan American Union may act provisionally as an organ of consultation until the meeting of the Organ of Consultation referred to in the preceding Article takes place.

Article 13.

The consultations shall be initiated at the, request addressed to the Governing Board of the Pan American Union by any of the Signatory States which has ratified the Treaty.

Article 14.

In the voting referred to in this Treaty only the representatives of the Signatory States which have ratified the Treaty may take part.

Article 15.

The Governing Board of the Pan American Union, shall act in all matters concerning this Treaty as an organ of liaison among the Signatory States which have ratified this Treaty and between these States and the United Nations.

Article 16.

The decisions of the Governing Board of the Pan American Union referred to in Articles 13 and 15 above shall be taken, by an absolute majority of the Members entitled to vote.

Article 17.

The Organ of Consultation shall take its decisions by a vote of two-thirds of the Signatory States which have ratified the Treaty.

Article 18.

In the case of a situation or dispute between American States, the parties directly interested shall be excluded from the voting referred to in the two preceding Articles.

Article 19.

To constitute a quorum in all the meetings referred to in the previous Articles, it shall be necessary that the number of States represented shall be at least equal to the number of votes necessary for the taking of the decision.

Article 20.

Decisions which require the application of the measures specified in Article 8 shall be binding upon all the Signatory States which have ratified this Treaty, with the sole exception that no State shall be required to use armed force without its consent.

Article 21.

The measures agreed upon by the Organ of Consultation shall be executed through the procedures and agencies now existing or those which may in the future be established.

Article 22.

This Treaty shall come into effect between the States which ratify it as soon as the ratifications of two-thirds of the Signatory States have been deposited.

Article 23.

This Treaty is open for signature by the American States at the city of Rio de Janeiro, and shall be ratified by the Signatory States as soon as possible in accordance with their respective constitutional processes. The ratifications shall be deposited with the Pan American Union, which shall notify the Signatory States of each deposit. Such notification shall be considered as an exchange of ratifications.

Article 24.

The present Treaty shall be registered with the Secretariat of the United Nations through the Pan American Union, when two-thirds of the Signatory States have deposited their ratification.

Article 25.

This Treaty shall remain in force indefinitely, but may be denounced by any High Contracting Party by a notification in writing to the Pan American Union, which shall inform all the other High Contracting Parties of each notification of denunciation received. After the expiration of two years from the date of the receipt by the Pan American Union of a notification of denunciation by any High Contracting Party, the present Treaty shall cease to be in force with respect to such State, but shall remain in full force and effect with respect to all the other High Contracting Parties.

Article 26.

The principles and fundamental provisions of this Treaty shall be incorporated in the Organic Pact of the Inter-American System.

In witness whereof, the, undersigned Plenipotentiaries, having deposited their full powers found to be in due and proper form, sign this Treaty on behalf of their respective Governments, on the dates appearing opposite their signatures.

Done in the City of Rio de Janeiro, in four texts in the English, French, Portuguese and Spanish languages, on the second of September, nineteen hundred forty-seven.

Reservation of Honduras:

The Delegation of Honduras, in signing the present Treaty and in connection with Article 9, section (b), does so with the reservation that the boundary between Honduras and Nicaragua is definitively demarcated by the Joint Boundary Commission of nineteen hundred and nineteen hundred and one, starting from a point in the Gulf of Fonseca, in the Pacific Ocean, to Portillo de Teotecacinte and, from this point to the Atlantic, by the line that His Majesty the King of Spain's arbitral award established on the twenty-third of December of nineteen hundred and six.

STATEMENTS

Argentina:

The Argentine Delegation declares that within the waters adjacent to the South American Continent, along the coasts belonging to the Argentine Republic in the Security Zone, it does not recognize the existence of colonies or possessions of European countries and it adds that it especially reserves and maintains intact the legitimate titles and rights of the Argentine Republic to the Falkland (Malvinas) Islands, the South Georgia Islands, the South Sandwich Islands, and the lands included in the Argentine Antarctic sector, over which the Republic exercises the corresponding sovereignty.

Guatemala:

Guatemala wishes to place on record that it does not recognize any right of legal sovereignty of Great Britain over the territory of Belice, called British Honduras, included in the Security Zone, and that once again, it expressly reserves its rights, which are derived from the Constitution of the Republic, historical documents, juridical arguments and principles of equity which have on appropriate occasions been laid before the universal conscience.

Mexico:

Only because the Delegation of Guatemala has seen fit to make the preceding declaration, the Delegation of Mexico finds it necessary to reiterate that, in case there should occur a change in the status of Belice, there cannot fail to be taken into account the rights of Mexico to a part of the said territory, in accordance with historical and juridical precedents.

Chile:

The Delegation of Chile declares that, within the waters adjacent to the South American Continent, in the extension of coast belonging to the Republic of Chile, comprised within the Security Zone, it does not recognize the existence of colonies or possessions of European countries and it adds that it specially reserves and maintains intact the legitimate title and rights of the Republic of Chile to the lands included in the Chilean Antarctic zone, over which the Republic exercises the corresponding sovereignty.

United States of America:

With reference to the reservations made by other Delegations concerning territories located within the region defined in the Treaty, their boundaries, and questions of sovereignty over them, the Delegation of the United States of America wishes to record its position that the Treaty of Rio de Janeiro has no effect upon the sovereignty, national or international status of any of the territories included in the region defined in Article 4 of the Treaty. (1) Department of State Bulletin of September 21, 1917, pp. 565–567, 572. Senate document, Executive II, 80th Cong., 1st sess. The treaty was ratified by the President on behalf of the United States on December 19, 1947, and the instrument of ratification was deposited with the Pan American Union in Washington on December 30, 1947.

GLOSSARY

arbitral: of or pertaining to arbitration, which is the hearing and determining of a dispute or the settling of differences between parties by a person or persons chosen or agreed to by them

juridical: of or relating to the administration of justice or law; legal

pacific: tending to make or preserve peace; conciliatory

Plenipotentiaries: a person, especially a diplomat, who has the full power or authority to transact business for someone else.

quorum: the number of members of a group or organization required to be present to transact business legally, usually a majority

reiterate: to say or do again or repeatedly; repeat

rhumb line: the curve on the surface of a sphere that cuts all meridians (perpendicular lines) at the same angle

Document Analysis

The Inter-American Treaty of Reciprocal Assistance begins with an affirmation that its principals had been previously agreed upon in the Act of Chapultepec. In the spirit of "friendship and good neighborliness," the nations of the Americas agree to "mutual assistance and common defense of the American Republics," and agree that there needs to be a "juridical organization" to provide "security and peace." The preamble to the treaty's twenty-six articles states that principles of "inter-American solidarity and cooperation" had been established in the Act of Chapultepec and that nations agreed to these principals by signing the treaty. The articles themselves range from general (renouncing war) to specific (terms for adopting or rejecting the treaty). The treaty establishes a defensive zone around the continents of North and South America, including Greenland and Antarctica.

The first article of the Rio Treaty reiterates the founding principal of the United Nations: the denunciation of war and the threat of force. The second articles states that, in order to prevent such conflict, the American states agree that they will seek to settle disputes between themselves using the procedures of the "Inter-American System" before referring the matter to the UN's General Assembly or Security Council. These important inclusions make it clear that regional conflict mediation and cooperation is part of, rather than in place of, the United Nations. Article 10 further establishes that nothing in the treaty will interfere with any nation's obligations and rights under the UN charter.

The other main point of the treaty is that all participating nations will unite to respond to an attack from an outside power. An attack on one state would be considered an attack on all. Indeed, anything that threatened the "peace of America" would be dealt with by the united forces of each country. States are allowed to respond to an attack in self-defense until the UN is able to intervene, but the UN will be fully informed of any action taken in self-defense. Signing nations agree to confront aggression with escalating consequences, laid out in detail: "Recall of chiefs of diplomatic missions; breaking of diplomatic relations; breaking of consular relations; partial or complete interruption of economic relations or of rail, sea, air, postal, telegraphic, telephonic, and radiotelephonic or radiotelegraphic communications; and use of armed force." Use of force is a last resort.

Other articles deal with the details of how the treaty's administrative body, the Organ of Consultation, will function. Any signer of the treaty can call a meeting, with the help of the Pan American Union, and all signers can vote. No member can be made to use force without its consent, and members engaged in a conflict cannot vote on matters pertaining to that conflict. When two thirds of the participating nations deposit their ratification of the treaty with the Pan American Union and the United Nations, it will be in force indefinitely. There is an escape clause, however. Any state wishing to leave the treaty can announce their intention, and they will be released two years later.

Several countries include specific statements and reservations to the treaty. These additions identify simmering tensions in the region, generally about contested territories and colonial legacy. Notably, Argentina claims the Falkland Islands and Guatemala announces that it does not recognize British sovereignty over Belize, or British Honduras.

Essential Themes

The primary theme of this agreement is the need for the states of the Americas to cooperate for mutual defense and to resolve disputes between member states. The treaty attempted to reduce the prospect of war by taking steps to both promote "friendship and good neighborliness" and discourage conflict. By considering attacks from outside forces attacks on all, the American states bound themselves together in a global-scale defense system intended to deter other countries from intervening in the Americas. This so-called hemispheric defense became a key strategy for avoiding further world wars and served as the foundation for Pan-American cooperation on all levels. Coming out of World War II, the need for alliances was clear, and the geographic basis of the Inter-American Conference held distinct strategic and economic advantages for partnership.

The treaty's resolution that regional conflicts between American states would to be settled by arbitration rather than war promoted the idea of international governance and directly supported the efforts of the UN. It acknowledged the UN's power as the highest level of international cooperation by deferring to it on all matters and relying on it for military support beyond basic self-defense. Many of the principals of cooperation and mutual defense that were agreed to in the Rio Treaty had been discussed for decades and built on earlier ideas such as the Act of Chapultepec, but this agreement clearly established rules for arbitration and the rights and obligations of its signers.

The treaty was invoked nineteen times between 1948 and 2001, including during the 1962 Cuban Missile Crisis, but it has also been ignored in some cases, such as in the war over the Falkland Islands in 1982, in which the United States refused to support Argentina against Great Britain. It was also activated following the terrorist attacks of September 11, 2001. A number of signatories have also invoked their right to release themselves from the treaty, including Mexico, Bolivia, Ecuador, Nicaragua, and Venezuela.

—*Bethany Groff, MA*

Bibliography and Additional Reading

Green, David. *The Containment of Latin America: A History of the Myths and Realities of the Good Neighbor Policy*. Quadrangle, Chicago, 1971. Print.

"Inter-American Treaty of Reciprocal Assistance (Rio Treaty)." *Council on Foreign Relations*. CFR, 2014. Web. 16 Jan. 2015.

Luard, Evan. *A History of the United Nations: The Years of Western Domination, 1945–55*. London: Macmillan, 1982. Print.

Schlesinger, Stephen C. *Act of Creation: The Founding of the United Nations*. Boulder: Westview, 2005. Print.

Rabe, Stephen G. "Inter-American Treaty of Reciprocal Assistance." *The Oxford Companion to American Military History*. Ed. John Whiteclay Chambers II. Oxford: Oxford UP, 2004. 337. Print.

■ Pact of Bogota

Date: April 30, 1948
Author: Organization of American States
Genre: government document

Summary Overview

During the nineteenth and early twentieth centuries, the independent nations of North, Central, and South America held conferences and established committees to address pressing issues related to human rights, economics, public health, and general security in the region. But as the world recovered from World War II, the Americas recognized the importance of having a comprehensive procedure for conflict resolution and a permanent governing body to enforce those procedures.

In 1948, these nations established the Organization of American States (OAS) by signing the Charter of the OAS in Bogota, Colombia. That same year, the OAS member states entered into the Pact of Bogota. This pact outlined procedures for resolving international conflict, ranging from nonbinding mediation to binding arbitration. It also established guidelines for involvement of the International Court of Justice or the United Nations Security Council in any dispute.

Defining Moment

As early as the nineteenth century, the independent nations in North, Central, and South America sought to organize their efforts to address common issues and promote regional peace and prosperity. In 1826, Simón Bolívar, the president of Gran Colombia (which included what would later become the nations of Colombia, Venezuela, Ecuador, and Panama, as well as northern Peru, western Guyana, and northwest Brazil), invited representatives from Central and South America to join the Congress of Panama. This congress drafted and signed the Treaty of Perpetual Union, League, and Confederation, hoping it would foster greater international cooperation. However, only Gran Colombia ratified the treaty.

During the early twentieth century, the nations of the Americas periodically met to address specific issues. Held under the auspices of the Pan American Union, these piecemeal conferences addressed matters related to human rights, economics, public health, and general security. Examples included the Sanitary Conference, which established the Pan American Sanitary Code to address issues of public health, hygiene, and sanitation; the Fourth Pan American Child Congress in 1924, responsible for the International American Institute for the Protection of Childhood; and the 1940 First Inter-American Conference on Indian Life that created the Inter-American Indian Institute. While these conferences helped address some of the region's issues, there was a limit to what the nations could accomplish without a formal and permanent approach.

World War II provided additional motivation to establish an official protocol for cooperation. Nations of the Americas sought to avoid the destruction wrought across Europe and Asia. Throughout the 1930s and early 1940s, many German immigrants settled in South America, especially in Brazil and Argentina. The United States was concerned about Central and South America's role as both a staging ground for Nazi spies to enter the United States and a hub for relaying strategic information to Germany. In response, President Franklin D. Roosevelt established the Special Intelligence Service in 1940 to monitor for such activities. The efforts uncovered numerous potential threats, and by 1946, the United States had identified nearly nine hundred Axis spies, as well as hundreds of propaganda agents, smugglers, and saboteurs. They also located twenty-four Axis-controlled radio stations and either confiscated their broadcasting equipment or used the network to pass false information back to Germany.

By the end of the 1940s, the Americas needed a formal protocol to safeguard their collective national security, peace, and prosperity. The Organization of American States officially formed in 1948 with the signing of the Charter of the OAS in Bogota, Colombia. That same year, the states entered into the Pact of Bogota, which defined procedures for conflict resolution. The states hoped that the OAS and the Pact of Bogota would provide the infrastructure and encouragement to resolve conflicts regionally.

Author Biography

The Organization of American States was officially established by the Charter of the OAS signed in 1948, in Bogota, Colombia. Article 1 of the charter states that the goal of the OAS is to establish "an order of peace and justice, to promote their solidarity, to strengthen their collaboration, and to defend their sovereignty, their territorial integrity, and their independence." The charter took effect in December 1951 and has been modified four times between its original signing and 2015.

As of 2015, all thirty-five independent states of the Americas had ratified the OAS Charter and were members of the organization. This includes the United States, Canada, and Mexico in North America; Brazil, Chile, Argentina, and others in South America; and several island nations, including Barbados, Haiti, and Jamaica.

HISTORICAL DOCUMENT

In the name of their peoples, the Governments represented at the Ninth International Conference of American States have resolved, in fulfillment of Article XXIII of the Charter of the Organization of American States, to conclude the following Treaty:

CHAPTER 1. GENERAL OBLIGATION TO SETTLE DISPUTES BY PACIFIC MEANS

ARTICLE I

The High Contracting Parties, solemnly reaffirming their commitments made in earlier international conventions and declarations, as well as in the Charter of the United Nations, agree to refrain from the threat or the use of force, or from any other means of coercion for the settlement of their controversies, and to have recourse at all times to pacific procedures.

ARTICLE II

The High Contracting Parties recognize the obligation to settle international controversies by regional pacific procedures before referring them to the Security Council of the United Nations.

Consequently, in the event that a controversy arises between two or more signatory states which, in the opinion of the parties, cannot be settled by direct negotiations through the usual diplomatic channels, the parties bind themselves to use the procedures established in the present Treaty, in the manner and under the conditions provided for in the following articles, or, alternatively, such special procedures as, in their opinion, will permit them to arrive at a solution.

ARTICLE III

The order of the pacific procedures established in the present Treaty does not signify that the parties may not have recourse to the procedure which they consider most appropriate in each case, or that they should use all these procedures, or that any of them have preference over others except as expressly provided.

ARTICLE IV

Once any pacific procedure has been initiated, whether by agreement between the parties or in fulfillment of the present Treaty or a previous pact, no other procedure may be commenced until that procedure s concluded.

ARTICLE V

The aforesaid procedures may not be applied to matters which, by their nature, are within the domestic jurisdiction of the state. If the parties are not in agreement as to whether the controversy concerns a matter of domestic jurisdiction, this preliminary question shall be submitted to decision by the International Court of Justice, at the request of any of the parties.

ARTICLE VI

The aforesaid procedures, furthermore, may not be applied to matters already settled by arrangements between the parties, or by arbitral award or by decision of an international court, or which are governed by agreements or treaties in force on the date of the conclusion of the present Treaty.

ARTICLE VII

The High Contracting Parties bind themselves not to make diplomatic representations in order to protect their nationals, or to refer a controversy to a court of international jurisdiction for that purpose, when the said nationals have had available the means to place their case before competent domestic courts of the respective state.

ARTICLE VIII

Neither recourse to pacific means for the solution of controversies, nor the recommendations of their use, shall, in the case of an armed attack, be ground for delaying the exercise of the right of individual or collective self-defense, as provided for in the Charter of the United Nations.

CHAPTER 2. PROCEDURES OF GOOD OFFICES AND MEDIATION

ARTICLE IX

The procedure of good offices consists in the attempt by one or more American Governments not parties to the controversy, or by one or more eminent citizens of any American State which is not a party to the controversy, to bring the parties together, so as to make it possible for them to reach an adequate solution between themselves.

ARTICLE X

Once the parties have been brought together and have resumed direct negotiations, no further action is to be taken by the states or citizens that have offered their good offices or have accepted an invitation to offer them; they may, however, by agreement between the parties be present at the negotiations.

ARTICLE XI

The procedure of mediation consists in the submission of the controversy to one or more American Governments not parties to the controversy, or to one or more eminent citizens of any American State not a party to

the controversy. In either case the mediator or mediators shall be chosen by mutual agreement between the parties.

ARTICLE XII

The functions of the mediator or mediators shall be to assist the parties in the settlement of controversies in the simplest and most direct manner, avoiding formalities and seeking an acceptable solution. No report shall be made by the mediator and, so far as he is concerned, the proceedings shall be wholly confidential.

ARTICLE XIII

In the event that the High Contracting Parties have agreed to the procedure of mediation but are unable to reach an agreement within two months on the selection of the mediator or mediators, or no solution to the controversy has been reached within five months after mediation has begun, the parties shall have recourse without delay to any one of the other procedures of peaceful settlement established in the present Treaty.

ARTICLE XIV

The High Contracting Parties may offer their mediation, either individually or jointly, but they agree not to do so while the controversy is in process of settlement by any of the other procedures established in the present Treaty.

CHAPTER 3. PROCEDURE OF INVESTIGATION AND CONCILIATION

ARTICLE XV

The procedure of investigation and conciliation consists in the submission of the controversy to a Commission of Investigation and Conciliation, which shall be established in accordance with the provisions established in subsequent articles of the present Treaty, and which shall function within the limitations prescribed therein.

ARTICLE XVI

The party initiating the procedure of investigation and conciliation shall request the Council of the Organization of American States to convoke the Commission of

Investigation and Conciliation. The Council for its part shall take immediate steps to convoke it.

Once the request to convoke the Commission has been received, the controversy between the parties shall immediately be suspended, and the parties shall refrain from any act that might make conciliation more difficult. To that end, at the request of one of the parties, the Council of the Organization of American States may, pending the convocation of the Commission, make appropriate recommendations to the parties.

ARTICLE XVII

Each of the High Contracting Parties may appoint, by means of a bilateral agreement consisting of a simple exchange of notes with each of the other signatories, two members of the Commission of Investigation and Conciliation, only one of whom may be of its own nationality. The fifth member who shall perform the functions of chairman, shall be selected immediately by common agreement of the members thus appointed.

Any one of the contracting parties may remove members whom it has appointed, whether nationals or aliens; at the same time it shall appoint the successor. If this is not done, the removal shall be considered as not having been made. The appointments and substitutions shall be registered with the Pan American Union, which shall endeavor to ensure that the commissions maintain their full complement of five members.

ARTICLE XVIII

Without prejudice to the provisions of the foregoing article, the Pan American Union shall draw up a permanent panel of American conciliators, to be made up as follows:

(a) Each of the High Contracting Parties shall appoint, for three-year periods, two of their nationals who enjoy the highest reputation for fairness, competence and integrity;

(b) The Pan American Union shall request of the candidates notice of their formal acceptance, and it shall place on the panel of conciliators the names of the persons who so notify it;

(c) The governments may, at any time, fill vacancies occurring among their appointees; and they may reappoint their members.

ARTICLE XIX

In the event that a controversy should arise between two or more American States that have not appointed the Commission referred to in Article XVII, the following procedure shall be observed:

(a) Each party shall designate two members from the permanent panel of American conciliators, who are not of the same nationality as the appointing party.

(b) These four members shall in turn choose a fifth member, from the permanent panel, not of the nationality of either party.

(c) If, within a period of thirty days following the notification of their selection, the four members are unable to agree upon a fifth member, they shall each separately list the conciliators composing the permanent panel, in order of their preference, and upon comparison of the lists so prepared the one who first receives a majority of votes shall be declared elected. The person so elected shall perform the duties of chairman of the Commission.

ARTICLE XX

In convening the Commission of Investigation and Conciliation, the Council of the Organization of American States shall determine the place where the Commission shall meet. Thereafter the Commission may determine the place or places in which it is to function, taking into account the best facilities for the performance of its work.

ARTICLE XXI

When more than two states are involved in the same controversy, the states that hold similar points of view shall be considered as a single party. If they have different interests they shall be entitled to increase the number of conciliators in order that all parties may have equal representation. The chairman shall be elected in the manner set forth in Article XIX.

ARTICLE XXII

It shall be the duty of the Commission of Investigation and Conciliation to clarify the points in dispute between the parties and to endeavor to bring about an agreement between them upon mutually acceptable terms. The Commission shall institute such investigations of the facts involved in the controversy as it may deem necessary for the purpose of proposing acceptable bases of settlement.

ARTICLE XXIII

It shall be the duty of the parties to facilitate the work of the Commission and to supply it, to the fullest extent possible, with all useful documents and information, and also to use the means at their disposal to enable the Commission to summon and hear witnesses or experts and perform other tasks in the territories of the parties, in conformity with their laws.

ARTICLE XXIV

During the proceedings before the Commission, the parties shall be represented by plenipotentiary delegates or by agents, who shall serve as intermediaries between them and the Commission. The parties and the Commission may use the services of technical advisers and experts.

ARTICLE XXV

The Commission shall conclude its work within a period of six months from the date of its installation; but the parties may, by mutual agreement, extend the period.

ARTICLE XXVI

If, in the opinion of the parties, the controversy relates exclusively to questions of fact, the Commission shall limit itself to investigating such questions, and shall conclude its activities with an appropriate report.

ARTICLE XXVII

If an agreement is reached by conciliation. The final report of the Commission shall be limited to the text of the agreement and shall be published after its transmittal to the parties, unless the parties decide otherwise. If no agreement is reached, the final report shall contain a summary of the work of the Commission; it shall be delivered to the parties, and shall be published after the expiration of six months unless the parties decide otherwise. In both cases, the final report shall be adopted by a majority vote.

ARTICLE XXVIII

The reports and conclusions of the Commission of Investigation and Conciliation shall not be binding upon the parties, either with respect to the statement of facts or in regard to questions of law, and they shall have no other character than that of recommendations submitted for the consideration of the parties in order to facilitate a friendly settlement of the controversy.

ARTICLE XXIX

The Commission of Investigation and Conciliation shall transmit to each of the parties, as well as to the Pan American Union, certified copies of the minutes of its proceedings. These minutes shall not be published unless the parties so decide.

ARTICLE XXX

Each member of the Commission shall receive financial remuneration, the amount of which shall be fixed by agreement between the parties. If the parties do not agree thereon, the Council of the Organization shall determine the remuneration. Each government shall pay its own expenses and an equal share of the common expenses of the Commission, including the aforementioned remunerations.

CHAPTER 4. JUDICIAL PROCEDURE

ARTICLE XXXI

In conformity with Article 36, paragraph 2, of the Statute of the International Court of Justice, the High Contracting Parties declare that they recognize, in relation to any other American State, the jurisdiction of the Court as compulsory *ipso facto*. without the necessity of any special agreement so long as the present Treaty is in force, in all disputes of a juridicial nature that arise among them concerning:

(a)   The interpretation of a treaty;

(b)   Any question of international law

(c) The existence of any fact which, if established, would constitute the breach of an international obligation;

(d) The nature or extent of the reparation to be made for the breach of an international obligation.

ARTICLE XXXII

When the conciliation procedure previously established in the present Treaty or by agreement of the parties does not lead to a solution, and the said parties have not agreed upon an arbitral procedure, either of them shall be entitled to have recourse to the International Court of Justice in the manner prescribed in Article 40 of the Statute thereof. The Court shall have compulsory jurisdiction in accordance with Article 36, paragraph 1, of the said Statute.

ARTICLE XXXIII

If the parties fail to agree as to whether the Court has jurisdiction over the controversy, the Court itself shall first decide that question.

ARTICLE XXXIV

If the Court, for the reasons set forth in Articles V, VI and VII of this Treaty, declares itself to be without jurisdiction to hear the controversy, such controversy shall be declared ended.

ARTICLE XXXV

If the Court for any other reason declares itself to be without jurisdiction to hear and adjudge the controversy, the High Contracting Parties obligate themselves to submit it to arbitration, in accordance with the provisions of Chapter Five of this Treaty.

ARTICLE XXXVI

In the case of controversies submitted to the judicial procedure to which this Treaty refers, the decision shall devolve upon the full Court, or, if the parties so request, upon a special chamber in conformity with Article 26 of the Statute of the Court. The parties may agree, moreover, to have the controversy decided *ex aequo et bono*.

ARTICLE XXXVII

The procedure to be followed by the Court shall be that established in the Statute thereof.

CHAPTER 5. PROCEDURE OF ARBITRATION

ARTICLE XXXVIII

Notwithstanding the provisions of Chapter 4 of this Treaty, the High Contracting Parties may, if they so agree, submit to arbitration differences of any kind, whether Juridical or not, that have arisen or may arise in the future between them.

ARTICLE XXXIX

The Arbitral Tribunal to which a controversy is to be submitted shall, in the cases contemplated in Articles XXXV and XXXVIII of the present Treaty, be constituted in the following manner, unless there exists an agreement to the contrary.

ARTICLE XL

(1) Within a period of two months after notification of the decision of the Court in the case provided for in Article XXXV, each party shall name one arbiter of recognized competence in questions of international law and of the highest integrity, and shall transmit the designation to the Council of the Organization. At the same time, each party shall present to the Council a list of ten jurists chosen from among those on the general panel of members of the Permanent Court of Arbitration of The Hague who do not belong to its national group and who are willing to be members of the Arbitral Tribunal.

(2) The Council of the Organization shall, within the month following the presentation of the lists, proceed to establish the Arbitral Tribunal in the following manner:

(a) If the lists presented by the parties contain three names in common, such persons, together with the two directly named by the parties, shall constitute the Arbitral Tribunal;

(b) In case these lists contain more than three names in common, the three arbiters needed to complete the Tribunal shall be selected by lot;

(c) In the circumstances envisaged in the two preceding clauses, the five arbiters designated shall choose one of their number as presiding officer;

(d) If the lists contain only two names in common, such candidates and the two arbiters directly selected by the parties shall by common agreement choose the fifth arbiter, who shall preside over the Tribunal. The choice shall devolve upon a jurist on the aforesaid general panel of the Permanent Court of Arbitration of The Hague who has not been included in the lists drawn up by the parties;

(e) If the lists contain only one name in common, that person shall be a member of the Tribunal, and another name shall be chosen by lot from among the eighteen jurists remaining on the above-mentioned lists. The presiding officer shall be elected in accordance with the procedure established in the preceding clause;

(f) If the lists contain no names in common, one arbiter shall be chosen by lot from each of the lists; and the fifth arbiter, who shall act as presiding officer, shall be chosen in the manner previously indicated;

(g) If the four arbiters cannot agree upon a fifth arbiter within one month after the Council of the Organization has notified them of their appointment each of them shall separately arrange the list of jurists in the order of their preference and, after comparison of the lists so formed the person who first obtains a majority vote shall be declared elected.

ARTICLE XLI

The parties may be mutual agreement establish the Tribunal in the manner they deem most appropriate; they may even select a single arbiter, designating in such case a chief of state, an eminent jurist, or any court of justice in which the parties have mutual confidence.

ARTICLE XLII

When more than two states are involved in the same controversy, the states defending the same interests shall be considered as a single party. If they have opposing interests they shall have the right to increase the number of arbiters so that all parties may have equal representation. The presiding officer shall be selected by the method established in Article XL.

ARTICLE XLIII

The parties shall in each case draw up a special agreement clearly defining the specific matter that is the subject of the controversy, the seat of the Tribunal, the rules of procedure to be observed, the period within the award is to be handed down, and such other conditions as they may agree upon among themselves.

If the special agreement cannot be drawn up within three months after the date of the installation of the Tribunal, it shall be drawn up by the International Court of Justice through summary procedure, and shall be binding upon the parties.

ARTICLE XLIV

The parties may be represented before the Arbitral Tribunal by such persons as they may designate.

ARTICLE XLV

If one of the parties fails to designate its arbiter and present its list of candidates within the period provided for in Article XL, the other party shall have the right to request the Council of the Organization to establish the Arbitral Tribunal. The Council shall immediately urge the delinquent party to fulfill its obligations within an additional period of fifteen days, after which time the Council itself shall establish the Tribunal in the following manner:

(a) It shall select a name by lot from the list presented by the petitioning party.

(b) It shall choose, by absolute majority vote, two jurists from the general panel of the Permanent Court of Arbitration of The Hague who do not belong to the national group of any of the parties.

(c) The three persons so designated, together with the one directly chosen by the petitioning party, shall select the fifth arbiter, who shall act as presiding officer, in the manner provided for in Article XL.

(d) Once the Tribunal is installed, the procedure established in Article XLIII shall be followed.

ARTICLE XLVI

The award shall be accompanied by a supporting opinion, shall be adopted by a majority vote, and shall be published after notification thereof has been given to the parties. The dissenting arbiter or arbiters shall have the right to state the grounds for their dissent.

The award, once it is duly handed down and made known to the parties shall settle the controversy definitively, shall not be subject to appeal, and shall be carried out immediately.

ARTICLE XLVII

Any differences that arise in regard to the interpretation or execution of the award shall be submitted to the decision of the Arbitral Tribunal that rendered the award.

ARTICLE XLVIII

Within a year after notification thereof, the award shall be subject to review by the same Tribunal at the request of one of the parties, provided a previously existing fact is discovered unknown to the Tribunal and to the party requesting the review, and provided the Tribunal is of the opinion that such fact might have a decisive influence on the award.

ARTICLE XLIX

Every member of the Tribunal shall receive financial remuneration, the amount of which shall be fixed by agreement between the parties. If the parties do not agree on the amount, the Council of the Organization shall determine the remuneration. Each Government shall pay its own expenses and an equal share of the common expenses of the Tribunal, including the aforementioned remunerations.

CHAPTER 6. FULFILLMENT OF DECISIONS

ARTICLE L

If one of the High Contracting Parties should fail to carry out the obligations imposed upon it by a decision of the International Court of Justice or by an arbitral award, the other party or parties concerned shall, before resorting to the Security Council of the United Nations, propose a Meeting of Consultation of Ministers of Foreign Affairs to agree upon appropriate measures to ensure the fulfillment of the judicial decision or arbitral award.

CHAPTER 7. ADVISORY OPINIONS

ARTICLE LI

The parties concerned in the solution of a controversy may, by agreement petition the General Assembly or the Security Council of the United Nations to request an advisory opinion of the International Court of Justice on any juridical question.

The petition shall be made through the Council of the Organization of American States.

CHAPTER 8. FINAL PROVISIONS

ARTICLE LII

The present Treaty shall be ratified by the High Contracting Parties in accordance with their constitutional procedures. The original instrument shall he deposited in the Pan American Union, which shall transmit an authentic certified copy to each Government for the purpose of ratification. The instruments of ratification shall be deposited in the archives of the Pan American Union' which shall notify the signatory governments of the deposit. Such notification shall be considered as an exchange of ratifications.

ARTICLE LIII

This Treaty shall come into effect between the High Contracting Parties in the order in which they deposit their respective ratifications.

ARTICLE LIV

Any American State which is not a signatory to the present Treaty, or which has made reservations thereto, may adhere to it, or may withdraw its reservations in whole or in part, by transmitting an official instrument to the Pan American Union, which shall notify the other High Contracting Parties in the manner herein established.

ARTICLE LV

Should any of the High Contracting Parties make reservations concerning the present Treaty, such reservations shall, with respect to the state that makes them, apply to all signatory states on the basis of reciprocity.

ARTICLE LVI

The present Treaty shall remain in force indefinitely, but may be denounced upon one year's notice, at the end of which period it shall cease to be in force with respect to the state denouncing it, but shall continue in force for the remaining signatories. The denunciation shall be addressed to the Pan American Union, which shall transmit it to the other Contracting Parties.

The denunciation shall have no effect with respect to pending procedures initiated prior to the transmission of the particular notification.

ARTICLE LVII

The present Treaty shall be registered with the Secretariat of the United Nations through the Pan American Union.

ARTICLE LVIII

As this Treaty comes into effect through the successive ratifications of the High Contracting Parties, the following treaties, conventions and protocols shall cease to be in force with respect to such parties:

Treaty to Avoid or Prevent Conflicts between the American States, of May 3, 1923

General Convention of Inter-American Conciliation, of January 5, 1929;

General Treaty of Inter-American Arbitration and Additional Protocol of Progressive Arbitration, of January 5,1929;

Additional Protocol to the General Convention of Inter-American Conciliation, of December 26,1933;

Anti-War Treaty of Non-Aggression and Conciliation, of October 10, 1933;

Convention to Coordinate, Extend and Assure the Fulfillment of the Existing Treaties between the American States, of December 23, 1936;

Inter-American Treaty on Good Offices and Mediation, of December 23, 1936;

Treaty on the Prevention of Controversies, of December 23, 1936.

ARTICLE LIX

The provisions of the foregoing Article shall not apply to procedures already initiated or agreed upon in accordance with any of the above-mentioned international instruments.

ARTICLE LX

The present Treaty shall be called the "PACT OF BOGOTA".

In WITNESS WHEREOF, the undersigned Plenipotentiaries, having deposited their full powers, found to be in good and due form, sign the present Treaty, in the name of their respective Governments, on the dates appearing below their signatures.

Done at the City of Bogota, in four texts, in the English, French, Portuguese and Spanish languages respectively, on the thirtieth day of April, nineteen hundred forty-eight.

RESERVATIONS

Argentina

"The Delegation of the Argentine Republic, on signing the American Treaty on Pacific Settlement (Pact of Bogota), makes reservations in regard to the following articles, to which it does not adhere:

(1) VII, concerning the protection of aliens

(2) Chapter 4 (Articles XXXI to XXXVII), Judicial Procedure;

(3) Chapter 5 (Articles XXXVIII to XLIX), Procedure of Arbitration;

(4) (chapter 6 (Article L), Fulfillment of Decisions.

Arbitration and judicial procedure have as institutions, the firm adherence of the Argentine Republic, but the Delegation cannot accept the form in which the Procedures for their application have been regulated, since, in its opinion, they should have been established only for controversies arising in the future and not originating in or having any relation to causes, situations or facts existing before the signing of this instrument. The compulsory execution of arbitral or judicial decisions and the limitation which prevents the states from judging for themselves in regard to matters that pertain to their domestic jurisdiction in accordance with Article V are contrary to Argentine tradition. The protection of aliens, who in the Argentine Republic are protected by its Supreme Law to the same extent as the nationals, is also contrary to that tradition."

Bolivia

"The Delegation of Bolivia makes a reservation with regard to Article VI, inasmuch as it considers that pacific procedures may also be applied to controversies arising from matters settled by arrangement between the Parties' when the said arrangement affects the vital interests of a state."

Ecuador

"The Delegation of Ecuador, upon signing this Pact, makes an express reservation with regard to Article VI and also every provision that contradicts or is not in harmony with the principles proclaimed by or the stipulations contained in the Charter of the United Nations, the Charter of the Organization of American States, or the Constitution of the Republic of Ecuador."

United States of America

"1. The United States does not undertake as the complainant State to submit to the International Court of Justice any controversy which is not considered to be properly within the jurisdiction of the Court.

2. The submission on the part of the United States of any controversy to arbitration, as distinguished from judicial settlement, shall be dependent upon the conclusion of a special agreement between the parties to the case.

3. The acceptance by the United States of the jurisdiction of the International Court of Justice as compulsory *ipso facto* and without special agreement, as provided in this Treaty, is limited by any jurisdictional or other limitations contained in any Declaration deposited by the United States under Article 36, paragraph 4, of the Statute of the Court, and in force at the time of the submission of any case.

4. The Government of the United States cannot accept Article VII relating to diplomatic protection and the exhaustion of remedies. For its part, the Government of the United States maintains the rules of diplomatic protection, including the rule of exhaustion of local remedies by aliens, as provided by international law."

Paraguay

"The Delegation of Paraguay makes the following reservation:

Paraguay stipulates the prior agreement of the parties as a prerequisite to the arbitration procedure established in this Treaty for every question of a nonjudicial nature affecting national sovereignty and not specifically agreed upon in treaties now in force."

Peru

"The Delegation of Peru makes the following reservations:

1. Reservation with regard to the second part of Article V, because it considers that domestic jurisdiction should be defined by the state itself.

2. Reservation with regard to Article XXXIII and the pertinent part of Article XXXIV, inasmuch as it considers that the exceptions of *res judicata*, resolved by settlement between the parties or governed by agreements and treaties in force, determine, in virtue of their objective and peremptory nature, the exclusion of these cases from the application of every procedure.

3. Reservation with regard to Article XXXV, in the sense that, before arbitration is resorted to, there may be, at the request of one of the parties, a meeting of the Organ of Consultation, as established in the Charter of the Organization of American States.

4. Reservation with regard to Article LXV http://avalon.law.yale.edu/20th_century/intam09.asp - 1[i.e., Article XLV] because it believes that arbitration set up without the participation of one of the parties is in contradiction with its constitutional provisions."

Nicaragua

"The Nicaraguan Delegation, on giving its approval to the American Treaty on Pacific Settlement (Pact of Bogota) wishes to record expressly that no provisions contained in the said Treaty may prejudice any position assumed by the Government of Nicaragua with respect to arbitral decisions the validity of which it has contested on the basis of the principles of international law, which clearly permit arbitral decisions to be attacked when they are adjudged to be null or invalidated. Consequently, the signature of the Nicaraguan Delegation to the Treaty in question cannot be alleged as an acceptance of any arbitral decisions that Nicaragua has contested and the validity of which is not certain.

Hence the Nicaraguan Delegation reiterates the statement made on the 28th of the current month on approving the text of the above-mentioned Treaty in Committee III."

GLOSSARY

arbitral: pertaining to an arbiter or arbitration which is the hearing and determining of a dispute or the settles of differences between parties by a person or persons chosen or agreed to by them

convoke: to call together; summon to meet or assemble

ex aequo et bono: according to the right and good; from equity and conscience

ipso facto: by the fact itself; by the very nature of the deed

pacific: tending to make or preserve peace; conciliatory

peremptory: leaving no opportunity for denial or refusal; imperious or dictatorial

plenipotentiary: a person, especially a diplomat, invested with full power or authority to transact business on behalf of another

remuneration: the act of remunerating which to pay, recompense, or reward for work or trouble

res judicata: the thing adjudicated; a case that has been decided

Document Analysis

Chapter one establishes that the signatory countries agree to use peaceful means to settle disputes and to address conflicts regionally before contacting the United Nations. However, if direct negotiation fails, the parties agree to use the procedures outlined in the treaty. Nations must use their domestic court systems when appropriate. If there is disagreement about the appropriateness of domestic jurisdiction, the International Court of Justice will make that determination. The pact does not prevent, or require the delay of, exercising self-defense in the event of an armed attack.

Chapter two defines the procedures of "good office" and mediation, whereby disinterested countries help the parties to a conflict find their own amicable solution. Chapter three discusses the procedure of "investigation and conciliation." In this process, a specially established Commission of Investigation and Conciliation assists in conflict resolution. This commission clarifies the points of dispute, investigates any necessary facts, and finds a solution that is agreeable to both parties. The parties in the dispute must provide any information requested by the commission, including documents, witnesses, and experts. The reports and conclusions of the commission are not binding with respect to either statements of fact or questions of law.

Chapter four addresses judicial procedure. The sig-natory countries acknowledge the authority of the International Court of Justice in matters related to interpretation of the pact, any question of international law, the existence of facts that would constitute a breach of international law, and the nature or extent of reparations for any such breach. If the conciliation procedure does not lead to a solution, then the parties have recourse to the International Court of Justice. If there is a dispute about the court's jurisdiction, the International Court of Justice will decide that question first. If it determines that it lacks jurisdiction, the parties must submit to arbitration.

Chapter five describes the arbitration procedures, including how members are to be selected for the Arbitral Tribunal. The parties to the dispute draw up an agreement defining the matter of controversy, the location of the tribunal, the rules of procedure, the duration of the arbitration period, and any other necessary condition. The tribunal makes a ruling, which settles the controversy definitively and must be carried out immediately; it cannot be appealed.

Chapters six, seven, and eight establish additional procedures applicable to the pact. These include provisions whereby countries agree to propose a Meeting of Consultation of Ministers of Foreign Affairs to settle any noncompliance before contacting the Security Council of the United Nations. Additionally, the parties to a controversy may petition the United Nations to request an advisory opinion from the International Court of Justice on questions of law.

Essential Themes

The Pact of Bogota and the Charter of the OAS were established while the world was recovering from World War II. The global crisis reinforced the importance of settling conflicts regionally before they escalated. The nations of the Americas had made many piecemeal attempts at cooperation over the years, but World War II renewed their determination to define comprehensive, mutually-agreeable procedures for resolving conflicts without resorting to the United Nations or the International Court of Justice.

The OAS also came at a pivotal time for many nations in Central and South America. Throughout the 1940s, many governments in the region shifted from authoritarian to democratic regimes, and the influence and membership levels of labor unions expanded. Many countries' economies also shifted significantly as they severed ties with Axis nations and came to rely more heavily on trade with the United States. But as the 1940s ended, the movement toward democracy struggled. Concerned about the potential impact on the stability of the region, the American states made a final—and finally successful—push to formalize their cooperation efforts.

The Pact of Bogota provided increasingly stricter approaches to conflict resolution. At the lightest end, "good office" simply provided a neutral meeting ground, while mediation allowed a disinterested party to facilitate the discussion. Investigation and conciliation, administered by the OAS, allowed disinterested parties to suggest a specific resolution, but all these approaches were nonbinding: the disputing parties could choose to

follow the recommendations, but were not obligated to do so. The hope was that these procedures would foster good communication and cooperation among the American states, as well as encourage independent, regional conflict resolution. However, the pact allowed the OAS to administer binding arbitration if these efforts failed.

If the OAS could not resolve the conflict regionally, the parties could petition the International Court of Justice or the United Nations Security Council. Depending on the nature of the inquiry, these decisions could also be binding. However, many American nations wanted to avoid the involvement of these international bodies. Despite the global reach of their authority, both the International Court of Justice and the United Nations were European-based organizations. Countries in the Americas worried that the organizations lacked the nuanced understanding of their history, economy, social structures, and geography necessary to render a decision best suited to the region's goals. The Pact of Bogota provided a framework for the OAS member states to resolve their own conflicts on a regional level, where they felt their needs would be better understood.

—*Tracey M. DiLascio, JD*

Bibliography and Additional Reading

"About the OAS." *Organization of American States*. OAS, 2015. Web. 21 Jan. 2015.

Ball, M. Margaret. *The Problem of Inter-American Organization*. Stanford: Stanford UP, 1944. Print.

Rock, David, ed. *Latin America in the 1940s: War and Postwar Transitions*. Berkeley: U of California P, 1994. Print.

"World War, Cold War, 1939–1953." *FBI. US Dept. of Justice*, 2015. Web. 27 Jan. 2015.

■ Address by Secretary Acheson, September 19, 1949

Date: September 19, 1949
Author: Dean Acheson
Genre: speech

Summary Overview

In 1949, Secretary of State Dean Acheson addressed the Pan American Society, an organization founded in 1910 to foster fellowship between the United States and Central and South America, headquartered in New York City. It was a critical time in Pan-American relations, with unrest in Panama, Columbia, Cuba, and throughout the Caribbean. At the end of August, the Soviet Union tested an atomic weapon, and though this news was not made public until September 23, it was certainly foremost on Acheson's mind as he gave this speech, and American foreign policy over the following decades would focus on preventing Communist expansion, particularly critical in neighboring countries that could provide bases for nuclear weapons aimed at the United States. Acheson reminded his audience of the values and agreements that the nations of the Americas shared, the challenges to "hemisphere security," and opportunities for economic expansion and the growth of democracy.

Defining Moment

The 1947 Inter-American Treaty of Reciprocal Assistance, known as the Rio Treaty, was the governing document for American relations when Secretary Acheson gave this speech in 1949. The United States had long been concerned with the defense of the Americas; per the Monroe Doctrine of 1823, European attempts to further colonize or interfere with any nation in the hemisphere would be considered an act of aggression to which the United States would respond. At the First International Conference of American States, held in Washington, DC, from October 1889 to April 1890, American nations discussed how to encourage greater communication with one another and also promoted economic cooperation and an arbitration system to settle disputes. From this body sprang the International Union of American Republics, followed by the Pan American Union, and then, in 1948, the Organization of American States.

In 1936, the Inter-American Conference for the Maintenance of Peace agreed to mutual defense in case of a European war. During World War II, all American nations supported the Allies, with the exception of Uruguay and Argentina, who stayed neutral for most of the war before finally siding with the Allies; six Central American states signed the 1942 United Nations Declaration, joined by other American states in subsequent years. In March 1945, with Germany and Japan close to collapse, the Inter-American Conference on War and Peace convened in Mexico City, with high-ranking delegates from twenty-one countries. The Act of Chapultepec (1945) that resulted from this conference laid out a framework for mutual defense and arbitration, with the understanding that these agreements would need to be formalized after the war was over. In 1947, the Rio Treaty did just that—making the agreements of Chapultepec into a long-term formalized treaty that went into effect in 1948. The Rio Treaty established the principles that an attack against any American nation would be an attack against all, and that conflicts between American nations would to be settled by arbitration rather than war. The first cracks in Pan-American unity were already present at the signing of the treaty, however, and it included clauses by the signers reaffirming their claims on disputed territory. In addition, former colonial territories in the Caribbean agitated for independence, and there were violent uprisings in Columbia, Cuba, and Panama.

Author Biography

Dean Gooderham Acheson was born on April 11, 1893, in Middletown, Connecticut, the son of Canadian immigrants. His mother, Eleanor Gooderham Acheson, came from a well-to-do family in Toronto; his father, Edward Campion Acheson, was an Episcopal minister who later became bishop of Connecticut. Acheson attended the Groton School and, later, Yale University and Harvard Law School, where he was appointed to the *Harvard Law Review.* Acheson, a Navy Auxiliary Reserve enlistee, served as an ensign at the Brooklyn Navy Yard toward the end of World War I. Acheson was a clerk for Supreme Court Justice Louis Brandeis from 1919 until 1921 and then entered a law firm, Covington and Burling, leaving briefly in 1933 when appointed undersecretary of the United States Treasury. In 1941, Acheson joined the Department of State as assistant secretary of state for economic affairs, where he oversaw the oil embargo of Japan. During and after the war, Acheson assumed increasing leadership roles in the State Department, and in 1949, he was appointed secretary of state by President Truman. Acheson's was one of the strongest voices in the formation of United States foreign policy during the Cold War. He was influential in the formation of the North Atlantic Treaty Organization (NATO) and worked with George Kennan to develop the policy of containment, intended to stop the spread of Communism. Acheson retired at the end of the Truman administration in 1953 and returned to private law practice. He acted as an unofficial advisor to subsequent administrations, and in 1964, he received the Presidential Medal of Freedom. Acheson died in Maryland on October 12, 1971, and is buried in Washington, DC.

HISTORICAL DOCUMENT

Waging Peace in the Americas

I am grateful to the Pan American Society for this welcome opportunity to meet with its distinguished membership and with so many friends from throughout the Western Hemisphere. It is a most appropriate setting in which to discuss the relations within our community of American Republics. There are two reasons in particular why I am glad to be able to discuss this subject tonight. The first is so obvious that we tend to take it for granted. It is that our countries are close neighbors, bound together by a common heritage of struggles for liberty and freedom.

The second reason is that the community between our countries presents us with a unique opportunity to press forward toward the positive objectives of our foreign policy. Much of our effort in other parts of the world has had to be devoted to repairing the destruction caused by war and to strengthening the free nations against aggression. We in this hemisphere have fortunately been spared the terrible destruction of war, and we are relatively remote from any direct threat against our independence. The prospects are, therefore, bright that we can continue to work together in an atmosphere of relative peace and stability. We are in a real sense waging peace, in the Americas.

BASIC PRINCIPLES

Before discussing specific policies, it seems well to restate once more the basic principles on which our policy in this hemisphere must rest. They are:

Our essential faith in the worth of the individual;

the preservation of our way of life without trying to impose it on others;

the observance by all governments of ethical standards based on justice and respect for freely accepted international obligations;

protection of the legitimate interests of our people and government, together with respect for the legitimate interests of all other peoples and governments;

the juridical equality of all the American Republics;

nonintervention in the internal or external affairs of any American Republic;

the stimulation of private effort as the most important factor in political, economic, and social purposes;

freedom of information and the development of free exchanges, in all fields;

the perfection, with the other American countries, of regional and universal arrangements for maintaining international peace;

and the promotion of the economic, social, and political welfare of the people of the American Republics.

These men are our guiding principles. A statement of the specific, policies which rest on these principles can best be made in conjunction with a review of our long-term objective.

NATIONAL AND HEMISPHERE SECURITY

The primary objective of any government is necessarily the security of its territory and people. The Monroe Doctrine is an acknowledgement that the security of this hemisphere is indivisible. With the development of the inter-American system, our countries have jointly created an effective security organization consistent with the Charter of the United Nations.

The Rio de Janeiro treaty of 1947 provides that in case of armed attack on an American Republic, each party pledges itself to assist in meeting the attack. One of the foremost policies of our country in foreign affairs is to fulfill its obligations under the Rio treaty and to seek the maximum cooperation among the American nations in achieving the objective of a secure and peaceful continent.

I stress this point because the security system which has culminated in the Rio treaty is now facing a crucial test.

For more than 2 years the Caribbean area has been disturbed by plots and counterplots. These plots have in themselves been inconsistent with our common commitments not to intervene in each other's affairs. Increasingly, however, denunciations have been succeeded by overt attempts at military adventure. Since 1945 few nations in the Caribbean area have escaped involvement, and at times the entire area has approached a state of political turmoil.

This situation is repugnant to the entire fabric of the inter-American System. The United States could not be faithful to its international obligations if it did not condemn it in the strongest terms. The energies spent in these adventures could much better have been put to use for peaceful purposes and improving the lot of the ordinary citizen. Aggression or plotting against any nation of this hemisphere is of concern to us. Wherever it occurs, or may be threatened, we shall use our strongest efforts, in keeping with our international commitments, to oppose it and to defend the peace of the hemisphere.

Only last Wednesday the Inter-American Peace Committee, meeting at the Pan American Union, set forth the principles and standards that bear on this situation. It is my hope that rigorous adherence to these principles and standards by all American governments will assure peace, not only in the Caribbean area, but also throughout the hemisphere.

We, the nations of this hemisphere, have a responsibility not only to ourselves but also to the rest of the world to live together in peace and harmony. Together we have played an important part in creating the United Nations. We must live up to the responsibilities which we have thus assumed toward the other member nations. This means, among other things, that we must abide by our regional commitments and maintain peace in our own midst, if all of the countries of the hemisphere proceed along these lines, as we in this country intend to do, there is no reason why any nation in the hemisphere should fear aggression.

DEVELOPMENT OF REPRESENTATIVE DEMOCRACY

What I have said, however, should not be construed as blind adherence to the status quo. We oppose aggression; we do not oppose change. Indeed, we welcome and encourage change where it is in the direction of liberty and democracy. We have worked long and persistently in common with our neighbors toward this end.

We would like to see a world in which each citizen participates freely in determining periodically the identity of the members of his government. This is an objective for which we will continue to work, subject always to our common policy of nonintervention.

In the Americas we have had periods of high hope and periods of bitter discouragement as we have seen democratic institutions flourish in some countries, only to see them subverted in others. We always deplore the action of any group in substituting its judgment for that of the electorate. We especially deplore the overthrow by force of a freely elected government. In such situations we do not cease to hope that the people will regain the right to choose their leaders.

We realize, however, that the attainment of the democratic ideal in any country depends fundamentally upon the desires and efforts of the people of that country. The nature of democracy is such that it can be achieved only from within.

Democracy as we endeavor to practice it is a continuing development toward political maturity—not a formula to be imposed upon a nation by a self-appointed ruling class, as is the case with certain other forms of government. Its attainment is essentially a spiritual and personal problem to be solved by the people of each country for themselves.

We are encouraged in our purpose by the realization that the strength of democratic institutions throughout the hemisphere today is measurably greater than a generation ago. In spite of occasional disappointments, we note a steady forward progress. The spirit of democracy is alive and bearing fruit.

RECOGNITION

Our policy with respect to recognizing new governments in the hemisphere is not inconsistent with our encouragement of democracy. We maintain diplomatic relations with other countries primarily because we are all on the same planet and must do business with each other. We do not establish an embassy or legation in a foreign country to show approval of its government. We do so to have a channel through which to conduct essential governmental relations and to protect legitimate United States interests.

When a freely elected government is overthrown and a new and perhaps militaristic government takes over, we do not need to recognize the new government automatically and immediately. We can wait to see if it really controls its territory and intends to live up to its international commitments. We can consult with other governments, as we have often done.

But if and when we do recognize a government under these circumstances, our act of recognition need not be taken to imply approval of it or its policies. It is recognition of a set of facts, nothing more. We may have the gravest reservations as to the manner in which it has come into power. We may deplore its attitude toward civil liberties. Yet our long-range objectives in the promotion of democratic institutions may, in fact, be best served by recognizing it and thus maintaining a channel of communication with the country involved. In this way we are also able to discharge our basic function of protecting the interests of our government and our citizens there. Since recognition is not synonymous with approval, however, our act of recognition need not necessarily be understood as the forerunner of a policy of intimate cooperation with the government concerned.

ECONOMIC POLICY

The economic field offers the greatest opportunity for constructive action. Two sets of problems arise. The first are derived largely from the disruptions of the war, and we hope may be described as short-run problems. The second results from the fact that in wide areas the standard of living is still miserably low. This is a long-run problem, although no less urgent.

It was apparent that the war would be followed by a period of economic stress. In some areas the effectiveness of the economic machine had been destroyed. The effect of the war on various relationships which previously had been the basis of world trade—for example, the reduction in earnings on overseas investment by European countries—raised new issues with respect to achieving equilibrium. Although the heaviest initial impact of this problem fell on Europe, the fundamental disequilibrium has now extended around the world so that for every country the maintenance of trade and the balance of payments has become a major problem of foreign relations. It was obvious in its initial stage that there could be no real recovery in trade without the revival of production in Europe. Therefore, the European Recovery Program must be regarded not merely as a program to meet the individual problems of the European countries but also to revive the flow of goods to and from Europe. We are all aware of the serious character of the present balance-of-payments problems, and it is one to which we must direct our thoughts in the most constructive way possible.

While material well-being is no guaranty that democracy will flourish, a healthy and prosperous people is a far more fertile field for the development of democracy than one which is undernourished and unproductive. That is why we are and must be preoccupied with the long-term problem of economic development.

The record of our economic cooperation in this hemisphere is substantial. It is one of such proved soundness that it forms the precedent and the basis for the more constructive labor ahead.

For 10 years past a large work of technical cooperation has been under way throughout our countries. Our government participates in this work through many of its agencies, such as the Department of Agriculture and the Public Health Service. Our Institute of Inter-American Affairs is cooperating with agencies of the other governments in outstandingly successful programs to improve basic living conditions. Technicians and administrators from the United States and from the host countries work side by side in partnership with each other. They work among the peoples in the remote countryside as well as in the cities. The Institute of Inter-American Affairs has now been authorized by Congress to continue and to expand this work. These programs have furnished the inspiration and the proving ground for the world-wide program of technical cooperation envisaged in Point 4 of President Truman's inaugural address.

In 1935, we created the Export-Import Bank which has become a uniquely successful institution in the field of economic development. The steel mill at Volta Redonda in Brazil is in full operation and a lifelong desire of many Brazilian statesmen and businessmen has become a reality with a plentiful supply of steel products to complement the vigorous growth of industry in that country. At Concepcion in Chile we shall soon see the realization of another project which has been brought about by the combination of energy on the part of Chil-

ean leaders and cooperation by the Export-Import Bank in supplying the material needs to bring the idea into fruit. There are constructive evidences throughout the Americas of the good use to which Export-Import credits have been put—in the Artibonite Valley in Haiti, in meat packing plants in Mexico—in highways in many countries, in ships, power systems, public works, agricultural projects, large and small industrial undertakings. The total amount of loans advanced by the Bank to the other American Republics is over 700 million dollars. Defaults on these loans are insignificant.

The International Bank and the International Monetary Fund created at Bretton Woods in 1944 largely on the initiative of the United States, today are actively contributing to economic development and fiscal stability in this hemisphere. The Bank already has made loans to several American nations for basic development, and the Fund has assisted in the solution of currency problems. Through our representation in both institutions, we shall continue our vigorous support of these constructive policies.

These specific programs represent actual deeds—not merely words. Nor are they isolated examples, but rather parts of a broad program of economic cooperation which, while reflecting our national self-interest, can leave no doubt as to our deep and lasting concern with the economic welfare of the other American Republics.

PRIVATE CAPITAL AND PUBLIC FUNDS

Loans of public funds, however, can only be supplementary to the efforts of private capital, both local and foreign. This country has been built by private initiative, and it remains a land of private initiative. The preponderance of our economic strength depends today as in the past upon the technical and financial resources and, even more, upon the abilities and morale of private citizens. I venture to say that the same thing is true of the other American nations.

In providing assistance for economic development, it would be contrary to our traditions to place our government's public funds in direct and wasteful competition with private funds. Therefore, it will be our policy, in general, not to extend loans of public funds for projects for which private capital is available. It is our purpose, also, to emphasize the desirability of loans which increase productivity.

Nor do we necessarily believe that rapid industrialization is good per se. Industrial development is an important factor in raising living standards, and therefore we have cooperated actively to this end. However, we feel that a balance should be achieved between industry, agriculture, and other elements of economic life. In many countries, large and small, the greatest immediate progress toward material well-being may be made through modern and diversified cultivation of the land. Irrigation projects, the use of agricultural machinery, the restoration of old land through fertilizers—these simple measures may do more to raise the standard of living than a dozen new industries.

We have had these principles in mind in elaborating the Point 4 program. Because we believe that the job ahead should be done primarily through private initiative, we have requested Congress to authorize the Export-Import Bank to offer certain guaranties against risks peculiar to foreign private investment.

We hope that the flow of private capital can be stimulated also by the negotiation of treaties to create an atmosphere favorable to increased private investment abroad. We are concerned with two types of treaties: first, treaties to avoid double taxation; second, treaties to define our economic relations and give reasonable assurances to our investors while safeguarding the interests and integrity of the other country.

SPECIAL NEEDS OF COUNTRIES

We believe that this general program can best be developed in full consideration of the special needs of individual countries. The conditions of the various nations of the hemisphere differ widely. Nor can all of our international problems be dealt with in the same way. In the field of economic development we have a common goal of high living standards and increased trade—just as in the political field we have a common goal of security and individual freedom. However, the process of economic development depends upon the efforts and resources of each individual country. There is no com-

mon formula. To be sure, the process can be facilitated in various ways by international organizations, such as the United Nations and its specialized agencies and the Organization of American States. But, in the last analysis, it depends upon the energy and resources of the individual countries themselves. The United States is prepared to lend its assistance, both directly and through international bodies, to working out specific programs with individual countries. Possibly this principle might be expanded to the working out of regional programs if two or more countries should seek to plan jointly for economic development.

I cannot stress too strongly that progress will come most rapidly in countries that help themselves vigorously. Economic development, like democracy, cannot be imposed from outside. Positive self-help is also essential to establishing conditions of economic stability and of fair treatment for private investment and the rights of labor. In countries where such conditions are provided, it will follow that we can collaborate more effectively in working out development programs. Public and private capital will be attracted more readily to such countries. While this is dictated by logic rather than emotion, it has been our experience that these conditions are generally founded in countries where constitutional and political democracy exists.

CONCLUSION

These then are our three major objectives—the security of our nation and of the hemisphere; the encouragement of democratic representative institutions; and positive cooperation in the economic field to help in the attainment of our first two objectives. If I have said nothing new tonight, it may well be because, in a family of nations as in families of individuals we should expect nothing more sensational than growth.

We can take satisfaction in the stability of our policy in the hemisphere. The good-neighbor policy as we practice it today is, for us, an historic, bipartisan, national policy. It has been wrought by Democrats at both ends of Pennsylvania Avenue—President Roosevelt, Secretary Hull, and Senator Connally, and also by Republicans at both ends of the Avenue—President Hoover, Secretary

Stimson, and Senator Vandenberg. And this by no means exhausts the distinguished list who have contributed to this great policy.

It is the firm intention of President Truman, as it is of myself as Secretary of State—of the entire personnel of my Department and, I believe, of the people of my country—to work for ever closer relations between the nations of this hemisphere. We seek by positive good will and effort to strengthen the Organization of American States, within the more extensive design of the United Nations, as the most effective expression of law and order in this hemisphere.

We and the other American Republics have determined and pledged ourselves to carry on our common policy of the Good Neighbor as a living and constantly growing reality.

GLOSSARY

denunciations: public censure or condemnation; an act or instance of denouncing

equilibrium: a state of rest of balance due to the equal action of opposing forces; an equal balance between any powers or influences

fiscal: of or relating to the public treasury or revenues; of or relating to financial matters in general

preponderance: superiority in weight, power and/or numbers

Document Analysis

Secretary Acheson begins his address to the Pan American Society by reaffirming the reasons for the importance of Central and South American relations to United States foreign policy. First, the nations are neighbors and should be friends. Second, US foreign policy across the rest of the world is necessarily focused on repairing the damage done by the war, while the Americas are relatively unscathed. The nations of the Americas can, therefore, "work together in an atmosphere of relative peace and stability."

In the face of growing ideological threats, particularly that of Communism, Acheson is eager to reassert that the hemisphere's shared values included free enterprise and individual rights. The Rio Treaty is front and center in this speech—reminding the other nations of the Americas that they have pledged to treat an attack on any of them as an attack on them all, and to submit their conflicts to arbitration rather than resorting to the use of force. This agreement is "facing a crucial test" as conflicts throughout the Caribbean multiply. In fact, "at times the entire area has approached a state of political turmoil." However, if the nations of the Americas honor their commitments to each other and abide by the terms of the Rio Treaty, Acheson asserts, they will have no reason to worry about security in the Western Hemisphere.

This is not to say, however, that the United States would not embrace positive, democratic change, according to Acheson: "Indeed, we welcome and encourage change where it is in the direction of liberty and democracy." The United States will always welcome the strengthening of democratic institutions in the Americas. Having said that, Acheson tackles the problem of the recognition of undemocratic governments. Recognition of a government should not be confused with approval or support of it, he says. "We maintain diplomatic relations with other countries primarily because we are all on the same planet and must do business with each other." If a government is willing to adhere to its international obligations, and is in control of a country, it is often necessary to recognize it, though this does not "imply approval of it or its policies."

A key element of relations between the American nations is economic support and cooperation. Acheson lays out the steps that the United States has taken to encourage economic growth in the rest of the Americas, but also champions the role of private investment. Loans and aid can only be "supplementary to the efforts of private capital, both local and foreign," and because the needs of countries vary, they require slightly different forms and amounts of assistance. The common message, however, is that countries that help themselves will succeed.

Acheson encourages steady growth based on three key foreign policy goals: "the security of our nation and of the hemisphere; the encouragement of democratic representative institutions; and positive cooperation in the economic field," and he expresses confidence that the American nations will continue to work together.

Essential Themes

The security of the Americas, and the cooperation needed for positive growth, is the primary theme of this speech. Adherence to the Rio Treaty and its mutual assistance agreement would ensure the safety of American nations. Economic ties between nations, with the judicious use of private investment as well as loans and other aid, would help to further this growth.

A second, more subtle theme is the need to bolster democratic institutions in these nations as a bulwark against a looming Communist threat. Instability in the area threatened the security of the United States, while stable, democratic governments in the Americas would provide for greater economic investment, cooperation, and security.

—*Bethany Groff, MA*

Bibliography and Additional Reading

Acheson, Dean. *Present at the Creation: My Years in the State Department*. 1960. New York: Norton, 1987. Print.

Beisner, Robert. *Dean Acheson: A Life in the Cold War*. New York: Oxford UP, 2006. Print.

Green, David. *The Containment of Latin America: A History of the Myths and Realities of the Good Neighbor Policy*. Chicago: Quadrangle, 1971. Print.

ATOMIC POLICY

The first atomic bomb, developed by the Manhattan Project during World War II, was tested on July 16, 1945, at the so-called Trinity site in the New Mexico desert. As with all such weapons, the bomb's destructive effects included not only the actual blast—the most powerful known at the time—but also blinding light, intense heat, and deadly radioactive fallout. An atomic bomb was first used in warfare on August 6, 1945, when the United States dropped one on Hiroshima, Japan; a second bomb was dropped on Nagasaki three days later. After the war, the United States conducted additional atomic tests in the Pacific and in Nevada. In 1949 the Soviet Union conducted its first atomic bomb test, causing leaders in the United States and elsewhere to begin to think about the international control of atomic weapons. At the same time, the Soviet explosion led to a nuclear arms race between the United States and the Soviet Union—a race that would last for several decades, despite eventual test bans and additional restrictions.

■ Atomic Energy and International Trade

Date: November 16, 1945
Author: James F. Byrnes
Genre: speech

Summary Overview

James Francis Byrnes was the secretary of state under President Harry S. Truman when he delivered a speech summarizing the positions of the United States, the United Kingdom, and Canada on the issues of nuclear technology and international trade. It was broadcast over the radio in November 1945, shortly after the end of World War II. The three nations that met were the ones that had shared technology to help create the first atomic weapon, used by the United States against Japan to devastating effect. Since the United States was the only nation to have this capability in 1945, it took steps to ensure that other countries, particularly the Soviet Union, would not be able to develop an atomic weapon, while assuring the world that it was interested in sharing information on the promise of nuclear power generation. Byrnes assured his listeners that information about atomic energy would be released only when it was certain that it could be controlled, and there was an international body set up to regulate its use. Byrnes also presented the argument for free and unrestricted international trade, supported by loans from the United States, as the United States and its allies saw atomic regulation and economic freedom as key factors for peace in the postwar world.

Defining Moment

In 1942, afraid that Germany would develop an atomic weapon, the United States, with the support of Great Britain and Canada, began a secret research-and-development project called the Manhattan Project. The project was headed by physicist J. Robert Oppenheimer and engaged top scientists, many expatriates from Europe, in the race to develop an atomic weapon. On July 16, 1945, the first successful test of this weapon was held in the desert in New Mexico. On August 6 and 9, two atomic bombs were dropped on the Japanese cities of Hiroshima and Nagasaki, killing over a hundred thousand people instantly, and dooming many more to die of aftereffects, such as burns, radiation poisoning, and cancer. The bombs were dropped by executive order of President Truman, at the recommendation of top advisers, including Secretary of State Byrnes. The atomic bombing of Japan was seen by many as the only alternative to an invasion that would potentially cost hundreds of thousands of lives, and it was, therefore, justified as a necessary evil. It also sent a strong message to the rest of the world, particularly the Soviet Union, that the United States held a serious military advantage. Having demonstrated the power of atomic weapons to the world, the United States rushed to ensure that the technology needed to make these weapons was protected, while arguing that atomic energy could be used for peacetime purposes, once it was properly regulated.

In addition to Japan, most of the major industrial centers of the world had been devastated by the bombing campaigns of World War II. Long-standing trade relationships were also destroyed. Millions of civilians were displaced and relied on food aid from the United Nations. Transportation networks lay in ruins, and the economic structures of European nations were in shambles—most had exhausted all of their resources and amassed crippling debt. The United States and Canada had avoided damage to their infrastructure, and despite billions of dollars spent on the war, the United States economy was booming. As nations around the world considered how best to rebuild their shattered economies, the United States reminded them that many had signed agreements during the war pledging to reduce trade barriers (which would clearly be advantageous to the United States). The United States believed that economic aid in the form of loans to other nations would open up markets for American goods, while providing financing to rebuild shattered infrastructure and industry.

Author Biography

James Francis Byrnes was born in 1882 in Charleston, South Carolina. His father died when he was young, and Byrnes left school to work in a law office. Byrnes apprenticed with a lawyer and passed the bar in 1903 without attending law school. He served as a circuit court solicitor in South Carolina until 1910, when he was elected a US congressman as a Democrat. Byrnes resigned this position to run for the US Senate in 1924; when he lost, he returned to private law practice. In 1930, he ran for the Senate again and won. Byrnes was a close political ally and personal friend of Franklin D. Roosevelt, and he was influential in the passing of Roosevelt's New Deal legislation. In 1941, Roosevelt appointed Byrnes a Supreme Court justice. He resigned from the court in October 1942 to head the wartime Office of Economic Stabilization and then the Office of War Mobilization. After Roosevelt's death, President Truman appointed Byrnes secretary of state, and he served until 1947. He then returned again to private law practice before being elected governor of South Carolina in 1951. He retired in 1955 and died in his home state on April 9, 1972.

HISTORICAL DOCUMENT

....From the day the first bomb fell on Hiroshima, one thing has been clear to all of us. The civilized world cannot survive an atomic war.

This is the challenge to our generation. To meet it we must let our minds be bold. At the same time we must not imagine wishfully that overnight there can arise full-grown a world government wise and strong enough to protect all of us and tolerant and democratic enough to command our willing loyalty.

If we are to preserve the continuity of civilized life, we must work with the materials at hand, improving and adding to existing institutions until they can meet the stern test of our time.

Accordingly, the President of the United States and the Prime Ministers of Great Britain and Canada—the partners in the historic scientific and engineering undertaking that resulted in the release of atomic energy—have taken the first step in an effort to rescue the world from a desperate armament race.

In their statement, they declared their willingness to make immediate arrangements for the exchange of basic scientific information for peaceful purposes. Much of this kind of basic information essential to the development of atomic energy has already been disseminated. We shall continue to make such information available.

In addition to these immediate proposals the conference recommended that at the earliest practicable date a Commission should be established under the United Nations Organization. This can be done within sixty days.

It would be the duty of this Commission to draft recommendations for extending the international exchange of basic scientific information for peaceful purposes, for the control of atomic energy to the extent necessary to insure its use only for peaceful purposes, and for the elimination from national armaments of atomic weapons and of all other weapons adaptable to mass destruction.

The Commission would recommend effective safeguards by way of inspection or other means to protect complying states against the hazards of violations and evasions.

Such protection would be afforded by having the work proceed by stages.

As a starting point the Commission might recommend the wide exchange of scientists and scientific information. The next step might be the sharing of knowledge about the raw materials necessary to the release of atomic energy.

The successful completion of each stage would develop the confidence to proceed to the next stage.

A very serious question arises, however, when we reach the stage of exchanging detailed information about the practical industrial application of atomic energy. The thought to be borne in mind here is that up to a certain rather advanced point, the so-called know-how of production is the same whether atomic energy is to be stored in bombs or harnessed as power for a peaceful industrial purpose.

And so it was necessary for the conferees to determine in the light of this fact, how soon information concerning the practical application of atomic energy should be disseminated.

Only one answer was possible. Until effective safeguards can be developed, in the form of international inspection or otherwise, the secrets of production know-how must be held, in the words of the President, as a sacred trust—a trust in the exercise of which we are already under definite international obligation.

Under the charter of the United Nations we have pledged ourselves not to use force except in support of the purposes and principles of the charter. The suggestion that we are using the atomic bomb as a diplomatic or military threat against any nation is not only untrue in fact but is a wholly unwarranted reflection upon the American Government and people.

It is one of the inherent characteristics of our democracy that we can fight a war only with the genuine consent of our people. No President in the absence of a declaration of war by the Congress could authorize an atomic bombing without running the risk of impeachment.

No one who knows the peace-loving temper of our people can believe that our Congress would adopt a declaration of war contrary to our solemnly undertaken obligations under the United Nations Charter.

The history of 1914 to 1917 and of 1939 to 1941 is convincing proof of the slowness of Congress to declare war. There is surely no reason to believe that it would be more eager to engage in a future war more terrible than any we have known.

While we consider it proper and necessary, therefore, to continue for a time to hold these production secrets in trust, this period need not be unnecessarily prolonged.

As experience demonstrates that the sharing of information is full and unreserved, it is to be hoped that the exchange for peaceful purposes, can be extended to some and eventually to all the practical applications of atomic energy and of other scientific discoveries. This is the objective we seek.

It is our purpose and grave duty to act in our relations with other nations with the boldness and generosity that the atomic age demands of us. No officials of government have ever been called upon to make a decision fraught with more serious consequences. We must act. But we will act in a manner that will not undermine our safety or the safety of the world.

Our declaration of willingness to exchange immediately the basic scientific information and our plans for the setting up of a Commission under United Nations sponsorship have been sent by me to members of the United Nations Organization. We look forward to their cooperation.

No one appreciates more keenly than those who have advanced these proposals that they represent a very modest first step in what is certain to prove a long and difficult journey. I wish to emphasize our conviction that the creation and development of safeguards to protect us all from unspeakable destruction is not the exclusive responsibility of the United States or Great Britain or Canada. It is the responsibility of all governments.

Without the united effort and unremitting cooperation of all the nations of the world, there will be no enduring and effective protection against the atomic bomb. There will be no protection against bacteriological warfare, an even more frightful method of human destruction.

Atomic energy is a new instrument that has been given to man. He may use it to destroy himself and a civilization which centuries of sweat and toil and blood have built. Or he may use it to win for himself new dignity and a better and more abundant life.

If we can move gradually but surely toward free and unlimited exchange of scientific and industrial information, to control and perhaps eventually to eliminate the manufacture of atomic weapons and other weapons capable of mass destruction, we will have progressed toward achieving freedom from fear.

But it is not enough to banish atomic or bacteriological warfare. We must banish war. To that great goal of humanity we must ever rededicate our hearts and strength.

To help us move toward that goal we must guard not only against military threats to world security but economic threats to world well-being.

Political peace and economic warfare cannot long exist together. If we are going to have peace in this world, we must learn to live together and work together. We must be able to do business together.

Nations that will not do business with one another or try to exclude one another from doing business with other countries are not likely in the long run to be good neighbors.

Trade blackouts, just as much as other types of blackouts, breed distrust and disunity. Business relations bring nations and their peoples closer together and, perhaps more than anything else, promote good will and determination for peace.

Many of the existing restrictions on world trade result from present day conditions and practices, largely growing out of the war.

Many countries, and not least Great Britain, had to sacrifice their foreign earning power to win the war. They have sold most of their foreign stocks and bonds, borrowed heavily abroad, let their foreign commerce go, and lost ships and factories to enemy attack.

Their needs for foreign goods are great and pressing but they lack foreign exchange, that is, purchasing power to buy abroad. Without aid they cannot see their way to buy as they used to abroad, not to speak of the additional things they need from abroad to rehabilitate their shattered and devastated economies.

In a situation of this kind what can a country do? It can seek to borrow currencies it needs, which will enable it to apply the liberal principles of trade which must be the basis of any permanent prosperity.

Or it can draw in its belt. It can reduce the standard of living of its people, conserve in every way the foreign currencies that it finds hard to get, and transfer its foreign trade by Government decree to countries whose currencies are easier to obtain.

In the latter way lies increased discrimination and the division of the commerce of the world into exclusive blocs. We cannot oppose exclusive blocs if we do not help remove the conditions which impel other nations, often against their will, to create them.

We must not only oppose these exclusive trading blocs but we must also cooperate with other nations in removing conditions which breed discrimination in world trade.

Whatever foreign loans we make will of course increase the markets for American products, for in the long run the dollars we lend can be spent only in this country.

The countries devastated by the war want to get back to work. They want to get back to production which will enable them to support themselves. When they can do this, they will buy goods from us. America, in helping them, will be helping herself.

We cannot play Santa Claus to the world but we can make loans to governments whose credit is good, provided such governments will make changes in commercial policies which will make it possible for us to increase our trade with them.

In addition to loans, lend-lease settlements, and the disposal of our surplus war materials, we have been discussing with Great Britain the principle of commercial relations—principles we want to see applied by all nations in the postwar world.

These are the same liberal principles which my friend and predecessor, Cordell Hull, urged for so many years.

They are based on the conviction that what matters most in trade is not the buttressing of particular competitive positions, but the increase of productive employment, the increase of production, and the increase of general prosperity.

The reasons for poverty and hunger are no longer the stinginess of nature. Modern knowledge makes it technically possible for mankind to produce enough good things to go around. The world's present capacity to produce gives it the greatest opportunity in history to increase the standards of living for all peoples of the world.

Trade between countries is one of the greatest forces leading to the fuller use of these tremendously expanded productive powers. But the world will lose this opportunity to improve the lot of her peoples if their countries do not learn to trade as neighbors and friends. If we are going to have a real people's peace, world trade cannot be throttled by burdensome restrictions.

Some of these restrictions are imposed by Government decree; others by private combination. They must be removed if we are to have full employment.

To do this it will be necessary to agree upon some general rules, and to apply them in detail. We shall shortly submit to the peoples of the world our views about these matters.

We intend to propose that commercial quotas and embargoes be restricted to a few really necessary cases, and that discrimination in their application be avoided.

We intend to propose that tariffs be reduced and tariff preferences be eliminated. The Trade Agreements Act is our standing offer to negotiate to that end.

We intend to propose that subsidies, in general, should be the subject of international discussion, and that subsidies on exports should be confined to exceptional cases, under general rules, as soon as the period of emergency adjustment is over.

We intend to propose that governments conducting public enterprises in foreign trade should agree to give fair treatment to the commerce of all friendly states, that they should make their purchases and sales on purely economic grounds, and that they should avoid using a monopoly of imports to give excessive protection to their own producers.

We intend to propose that international cartels and monopolies should be prevented by international action from restricting the commerce of the world.

We intend to propose that the special problems of the great primary commodities should be studied internationally, and that consuming countries should have an equal voice with producing countries in whatever decisions may be made.

We intend to propose that the efforts of all countries to maintain full and regular employment should be guided by the rule that no country should solve its domestic problems by measures that would prevent the expansion of world trade, and no country is at liberty to export its unemployment to its neighbors.

We intend to propose that an International Trade Organization be created, under the Economic and Social Council, as an integral part of the structure of the United Nations.

We intend to propose that the United Nations call an International Conference on Trade and Employment to deal with all these problems.

In preparation for that Conference we intend to go forward with actual negotiations with several countries for the reduction of trade barriers, under the Reciprocal Trade Agreements Act.

Just when these negotiations will commence has not been determined. They will be announced in the usual way, as required by the Act, and due notice will be given in order that all interested persons may be heard before the detailed offers to be made by the United States are settled.

Success in those negotiations will be the soundest preparation for the general Conference we hope will be called by the United Nations Organization.

By proposing that the United Nations Organization appoint a commission to consider the subject of atomic energy and by proposing that the Organization likewise call a conference to enable nations to consider the problems of international trade, we demonstrate our confidence in that Organization as an effective instrumentality for world cooperation and world peace.

After the First World War we rejected the plea of Woodrow Wilson and refused to join the League of Nations. Our action contributed to the ineffectiveness of the League.

Now the situation is different. We have sponsored the United Nations Organization. We are giving it our wholehearted and enthusiastic support. We recognize our responsibility in the affairs of the world. We shall not evade that responsibility.

With other nations of the world we shall walk hand in hand in the paths of peace in the hope that all peoples can find freedom from fear and freedom from want.

GLOSSARY

buttressing: the use of any external prop or support to steady a structure; to prop up; to encourage or support

cartels: an international syndicate, combine or trust formed especially to regulate prices and output in some field of business

disseminated: scattered or spread widely; broadcast

Document Analysis

Byrnes's radio address follows a meeting of President Truman, Prime Minister Clement Attlee of the United Kingdom, and Prime Minister William Lyon Mackenzie King of Canada to address what they saw as the key issues of the day for global security: nuclear technology and international trade. Byrnes asserts that the recent atomic bombing of Japan had proven that the world could not survive an atomic war. To try to avoid the specter of a global nuclear arms race, he says the three nations are calling for a United Nations commission to be set up to ensure that atomic energy will only be used for peaceful purposes. Until there are sufficient regulations in place, "secrets of production know-how must be held" by the United States. In the meantime, the world would have to trust that the United States would not use atomic weapons "as a diplomatic or military threat against any nation." Ultimately, responsibility for keeping the world safe is to be shared by all: "Without the united effort and unremitting cooperation of all the nations of the world, there will be no enduring and effective protection against the atomic bomb."

Equally critical to the pursuit of world peace is economic cooperation because "political peace and economic warfare cannot long exist together." Barriers to trade lead to mistrust and disunity, says Byrnes, while trade between nations is a strong incentive to maintain peace. However, he warns that the devastation of World War II has created the risk that the world will break apart into competitive trading blocs as countries strive to rebuild. The United States should, therefore, make loans to nations that would then rebuild their commercial infrastructure and, in turn, spend money on American goods; thus, says Byrnes, "America, in helping them, will be helping herself." Liberal trade relations will lead to general prosperity, which, in turn, will keep the world at peace. Byrnes outlines specific steps that need to be taken to relieve world trade of "burdensome restrictions," including the removal of tariffs and quotas, and tight regulation of the use of subsidies. International cartels and monopolies should be prevented, and trade relations overseen by a governing body under the United Nations—the proposed International Trade Organization.

By referring both atomic energy regulation and trade relations to the United Nations, the United States demonstrated its confidence and full commitment to the organization—knowing that the League of Nations had failed, in part, because the United States had declined to become a member. After this latest world war, however, the United Nations would have the "wholehearted and enthusiastic support" of the United States.

Essential Themes

This speech reflects two major concerns of the Western democracies in the postwar world: the threat of the proliferation of nuclear weapons and a doctrinaire faith in the ability of free trade to solve most of the world's problems over the long term.

Regarding the first issue, and the call for a UN body to regulate nuclear technology on a global scale, the following month, in December 1945, the United Nations Atomic Energy Commission was created. Amid ongoing disagreement between the Soviet Union and the Western nations, however, the commission was unable to develop a framework for eliminating nuclear weapons and restricting nuclear technology to use for power generation; in 1948, the commission disbanded. In 1949, the Soviet Union tested its first nuclear weapon; the United Kingdom followed in 1952. In 1957, a permanent international body, the International Atomic Energy Agency, was finally created, but it did not prevent France, China, India, and Pakistan, among others, from acquiring nuclear weapons in the ensuing decades.

Though trade relationships and infrastructure had been destroyed in World War II, the United States and other countries saw an opportunity to establish new liberal international relationships that were not based on restrictive tariffs and controls. The United States also saw the United Nations as the appropriate governing body for the oversight of trade relations. Although the proposed International Trade Organization never came into being, something similar, the General Agreement on Tariffs and Trade, was signed by eight countries in 1947 and grew in membership until being replaced in 1995 by the World Trade Organization.

—*Bethany Groff, MA*

Bibliography and Additional Reading

Luard, Evan. *A History of the United Nations: The Years of Western Domination, 1945–1955.* New York: Macmillian, 1982. Print.

Robertson, David. *Sly and Able: A Political Biography of James F. Byrnes.* New York: Norton, 1994. Print.

Schlesinger, Stephen C. *Act of Creation: The Founding of the United Nations.* Cambridge: Perseus, 2004. Print.

■ Atomic Explosion in the USSR

Date: September 23, 1949
Author: Harry S. Truman
Genre: speech

Summary Overview

On August 29, 1949, the Soviet Union (officially, the Union of Soviet Socialist Republics, or USSR) exploded an atomic bomb at a remote site in Kazakhstan, making it the second world power to have atomic weapons. The United States had used two atomic bombs at the end of World War II against Japan, and the Soviet Union had been in pursuit of this technology for a decade. The bomb, code-named First Lightning, produced an eighty-kiloton explosion. On September 3, a specially equipped US plane picked up radiation readings off the coast of Siberia, telegraphing the event. On September 23, US president Harry Truman revealed to the world that the Soviet Union had the bomb. With this announcement came worldwide fear that tensions between the two nations could escalate into a catastrophic event, and the international community scrambled to regulate and control first atomic, then hydrogen-based thermonuclear weaponry. The nuclear arms race between the Soviet Union and the United States would be the primary concern of international affairs for the next several decades.

Defining Moment

The United States unleashed the greatest destructive weapon ever known when it dropped two atomic bombs, known as Little Boy and Fat Man, on the Japanese cities of Hiroshima and Nagasaki in 1945. These were developed by a team of scientists in the United States through a program dubbed the Manhattan Project. The United States and the Soviet Union were uneasy allies during World War II, but opposing ideologies and deep-seated mistrust ensured that the alliance would be strained further after the US nuclear advantage was revealed. Indeed, some scholars have theorized that the bombs dropped on Japan were as much a reminder to the Soviet Union of US dominance as a strategic way to end the war.

The United States was well aware that the Soviet Union was in pursuit of the technology needed to produce a nuclear weapon, but intelligence reports estimated in 1946 that the Soviets were four to seven years away. In fact, the Soviet Union had access to German scientists who had been involved in the Nazi atomic program, and a complex network of Soviet spies involved in the Manhattan Project had been providing vital information for years. Scientists had a variety of motivations for spying—some were Communist sympathizers; others believed that the only way to control this deadly technology was to have it shared by opposing powers in order to have a balance of power. During the war, some scientists believed that the Soviets would use it to destroy Nazi Germany. The Soviet weapons program began in earnest in 1943 and leapt forward in June 1945. Detailed information about the Fat Man atomic bomb, then untested, was leaked by German-born Klaus Fuchs, a physicist who was instrumental in designing the US nuclear program.

The Soviet Union's single greatest hurdle was its lack of uranium. After the fall of Germany, some uranium was captured. After 1945, uranium was obtained from Poland, Bulgaria, and Czechoslovakia, and eventually in the Soviet Union itself. Secret cities were set up, in which nuclear development, including uranium enrichment, and testing could take place in secret. There were at least four such cities at the time of the first test in 1949. Plutonium for the first Soviet atomic bomb was produced at one of these cities, Chelyabinsk.

First Lightning was detonated at 7 a.m. on August 29, 1949, in the remote steppes of northeastern Kazakhstan. Engineers had designed an entire city, including buildings, bridges, even a mock subway, and had filled the area with caged animals to study the effects of an atomic blast. The blast was later found to be eighty kilotons, much more powerful than its originators had expected and initially reported. The mock city was entirely destroyed, and the test animals incinerated. A specially equipped US plane picked up radiation readings off the coast of Siberia on September 3; the United States tracked the nuclear fallout and determined that an atomic test had taken place. On September 23, President Truman announced to the world that the Soviet Union had the bomb, marking the most significant development to that time in the new Cold War. Truman's secretary of state, Dean Acheson, soon called for an evaluation of foreign policy by the National Security Council, which resulted in massively increased military spending and the accelerated push to develop ever more powerful weaponry.

Author Biography

Harry S. Truman was born in Lamar, Missouri, in 1884, the oldest of three children. His father, a farmer and livestock dealer, was well connected to the local Democratic Party, and Truman served as a page in the 1900 Democratic National Convention. After graduating from high school, Truman worked as a railroad timekeeper and a bank clerk. Truman served in the Missouri National Guard during World War I, despite very poor eyesight, and was elected captain by his troops. After the war, Truman opened a haberdasher shop in Independence, Missouri. The shop failed, but Truman was elected a county court judge in 1922 and served in a variety of public offices until he was elected to the United States Senate in 1934. While in the Senate, Truman became known for investigating claims of graft and corruption in military industries. He was nominated to be Franklin D. Roosevelt's vice president in 1944 and became president of the United States on April 12, 1945, upon Roosevelt's death. Truman learned about the development of the atomic bomb after he became president, and he made the decision to drop two of them on two cities in Japan in August 1945. Truman oversaw the end of the war, the establishment of the United Nations, and the implementation of the Marshall Plan to rebuild Europe. He supported a policy of containment to control the spread of Communism. Truman won a narrow victory in 1948 for a full term as president, but did not seek reelection in 1952. Truman retired to Missouri and died in 1972.

HISTORICAL DOCUMENT

I believe the American people to the fullest extent consistent with the national security are entitled to be informed of all developments in the field of atomic energy. That is my reason for making public the following information.

We have evidence that within recent weeks an atomic explosion occurred in the U.S.S.R.

Ever since atomic energy was first released by man, the eventual development of this new force by other nations was to be expected.

This probability has always been taken into account by us.

Nearly four years ago I pointed out that "scientific opinion appears to be practically unanimous that the essential theoretical knowledge upon which the discovery is based is already widely known. There is also substantial agreement that foreign research can come abreast of our present theoretical knowledge in time." And, in the three-nation declaration of the President of the United States and the Prime Ministers of the United Kingdom and of Canada, dated November 15, 1945. It was emphasized that no single nation could, in fact, have a monopoly of atomic weapons.

This recent development emphasizes once again, if indeed such emphasis were needed, the necessity for that truly effective and enforceable international control of atomic energy which this Government and the large majority of the members of the United Nations support.

Document Analysis

By its brevity, President Truman's statement emphasizes the serious nature of the news he is reporting. He opens with the reason he is making the announcement. The American people have a right to know about developments in atomic weaponry, as long as the information does not compromise national security. This announcement was not just intended for the American people, of course, but would inform the world of this frightening new development, and Truman's speech was carried across the globe. Truman does not explain how the United States got the information, but says that "we have evidence" that there had been a recent explosion in the Soviet Union. This statement was made plainly and without embellishment, underscoring its gravity.

Truman argues that this was not an unexpected development, however. Since "man" (by which he meant the Americans) had unleashed this new power, it had been anticipated that another nation would acquire it. In fact, Truman uses this as an opportunity to argue that the leaders of the United States, Great Britain, and Canada had agreed as far back as 1945 that nuclear capability could not be held by only one country and that he had known even then that the technology needed to produce an atomic weapon was so similar to that already widely available, that "foreign" research would catch up in time. Truman thus portrays the discovery of the Soviet atomic test as a serious development, but also an anticipated one, downplaying the surprise that they had developed this technology so quickly. Yet despite Truman's downplaying of the atomic test, it threw the United States into a panic, as the nation was forced to accept that it no longer had a monopoly on atomic weapons.

Truman's tone at the close of this statement is not belligerent, however. He returns the attention of the world to the need for "truly effective and enforceable international control of atomic energy." This would prove difficult, and mistrust and conflicting ideologies prevented the United States and the Soviet Union from reaching agreements that would control their nuclear arsenal. Both nations, instead, raced to outgun each other, producing more dangerous weapons and stationing them throughout the world.

Essential Themes

The primary theme of this speech is the impact on the world of the Soviet atomic test. The tone is somber, but not belligerent, and a hopeful note is struck at the end that the world will develop and respect controls on this dangerous weapon. The speech takes as a foregone conclusion that the Soviet Union would develop the bomb. In fact, the verification of a successful atomic detonation was very shocking news indeed, as the United States and other Western nations had assumed that the Soviets were several years away from acquiring this technology and, for this reason, hoped to be well ahead in weapons development by then or have worked with the United Nations to ensure that atomic energy could only be used for peaceful purposes. The news of the First Lightning detonation was a turning point in US-Soviet relations and would result in an increasingly hostile arms race between the two superpowers.

—*Bethany Groff, MA*

Bibliography and Additional Reading

Craig, Campbell, and Sergey Radchenko. *The Atomic Bomb and the Origins of the Cold War*. New Haven: Yale UP, 2008. Print.

Gaddis, John Lewis. *The Cold War: A New History*. New York: Penguin, 2005. Print.

Toropov, Brandon. *Encyclopedia of Cold War Politics*. New York: Facts on File, 2000. Print.

■ International Control of Atomic Energy

Date: October 25, 1949
Authors: Representatives of Canada, China, France, the United Kingdom, and the United States
Genre: government document

Summary Overview

The enormous destructive power of atomic weaponry was made clear when the United States bombed the cities of Hiroshima and Nagasaki, Japan, in August 1945, at the end of World War II. Top scientists from across the world had worked in secret on the Manhattan Project, the US-led effort to develop atomic technology. In the years following World War II, the Soviet Union set up Communist governments in most central and Eastern European states, and tensions between the Soviet Union and the United States, former Allies, were high. At the same time, the Soviet Union had an extensive spy network within the Manhattan Project and had itself been working to develop atomic weapons. In August 1949, the Soviet Union detonated an atomic bomb in Kazakhstan, and the world was faced with two powerful opposing nations with nuclear capability. Both the United States and the Soviet Union were members of the United Nations, which had set up an Atomic Energy Commission in 1946 to study the best way to control nuclear technology. In the fall of 1949, the Soviet Union was not interested in giving up the weapon it had worked so hard to develop, however, and talks about control and disarmament were at an impasse. The other members of the Atomic Energy Commission submitted this report to the United Nations, describing the obstacles to an agreement with the Soviet Union.

Defining Moment

The United States unleashed the greatest destructive weapon ever known when it dropped two atomic bombs, known as Little Boy and Fat Man, on the Japanese cities of Hiroshima and Nagasaki in 1945. The United States and the Soviet Union were uneasy allies during World War II, but opposing ideologies and deep-seated mistrust ensured that the alliance would be strained further after the superiority of US weaponry was revealed. Indeed, some scholars have theorized that the bombs dropped on Japan were as much

a reminder to the Soviet Union of US dominance as a strategic way to end the war.

Attempts to control this destructive technology began as soon as the bombs were dropped. The United States was aware that the Soviet Union was working on a nuclear weapon and believed that it would be eight to fifteen years before it had a workable device. Still, the urgency was clear. The United Nations, formally established within months of the bombing of Japan, passed its first resolution on January 24, 1946, establishing the United Nations Atomic Energy Commission (UNAEC) "to deal with the problems raised by the discovery of atomic energy." UNAEC had six permanent members (the United States, Britain, France, the Soviet Union, China, and Canada), and within days of the establishment of the organization, the United States had set up a group, whose members included Undersecretary of State Dean Acheson and the chairman of the Tennessee Valley Authority David E. Lilienthal, to study the problem of nuclear weapons; Bernard Baruch was chosen to present the group's report to UNAEC. Baruch altered the Acheson-Lilienthal report slightly, presenting a plan to establish the Atomic Development Authority, an international body both assigned to manage any facility capable of producing atomic weapons and in charge of inspecting any nuclear research facility pursuing peaceful uses for atomic energy.

The Baruch Plan also made possession of an atomic bomb illegal and imposed sanctions on nations who failed inspections. The Atomic Development Authority could impose sanctions on nations who were not in compliance and had the ability to override the veto of any members of the United Nations who disagreed with its ruling. Once the plan was fully operational, Baruch promised that the United States would begin to destroy its nuclear weapons. The Soviet Union rejected this plan, insisting that existing weapons be destroyed before the plan took effect, arguing against international control of its domestic facilities, and stating that it would not release its veto on the UN Security Council. In December 1946, the Baruch Plan was defeated 10–2 with the Soviet Union and Poland (a temporary member) abstaining. These differences—the insistence by the Soviet Union that the United States' weapons be destroyed, its unwillingness to give up its veto, and its refusal to allow international control of domestic facilities—continued through a series of reports, proposals, and counterproposals over the next three years, with no resolution.

Relations between the United States and the Soviet Union continued to deteriorate over the following years. Tension over the fate of Germany remained high, culminating in the Soviet Union's blockade of Berlin. The Soviet Union initially refused to relinquish territory in Iran in 1946, causing a flurry of activity in the United Nations. As central and Eastern European nations adopted Communist governments, some by force, the United States grew increasingly worried about aggressive Soviet expansion. In April 1949, the United States and eleven other former Allies formed the North Atlantic Treaty Organization. In November 1948, the United Nations General Assembly sent the six permanent members of UNAEC back into consultation, charging them with finding common ground in the control of atomic weapons. This group finally met on August 9, 1949. On August 29, the Soviet Union secretly detonated its first atomic weapon, an event that President Harry S. Truman announced to the American public on September 23. In October, the other five nations sent this report to the United Nations General Assembly, detailing the ongoing negotiations and enumerating the points of contention. The failure to reach agreement, as reported in this document, spelled the beginning of the nuclear arms race and the Cold War.

HISTORICAL DOCUMENT

Statement by the Representatives of Canada, China, France, the United Kingdom, and the United States, October 25, 1949

On 24 October 1949, the representatives of Canada, China, France, the Union of Soviet Socialist Republics, the United Kingdom and the United States of America agreed to send to the Secretary-General of the United Nations, for transmission to the General Assembly, the following interim report on the consultations of the six permanent members of the Atomic Energy Commission:

"In paragraph 3 of General Assembly resolution 191 (III) of 4 November 1948, the representatives of the Sponsoring Powers, who are the Permanent Members of the Atomic Energy Commission, namely, Canada, China, France, the Union of Soviet Socialist Republics, the United Kingdom of Great Britain and Northern Ireland and the United States of America, were requested to hold consultations 'in order to determine if there exist a basis for agreement on the international control of atomic energy to ensure its use only for peaceful purposes, and for the elimination from national armaments of atomic weapons.'"

"The first meeting took place on 9 August 1949. The consultations have not yet been concluded and are continuing but, in order to inform the General Assembly of the position which has so far been reached, the six Sponsoring Powers have decided to transmit to it the summary records of the first ten meetings."

It was agreed by the group that any of the representatives of the Governments taking part in these consultations retained the right to submit to the Assembly their observations on the course of the consultations so far. The representatives of Canada, China, France, the United Kingdom and the United States accordingly submit to the General Assembly this statement, which represents their joint views, in the hope that it may assist the Assembly in its consideration of this problem.

BASIS OF DISCUSSION

It was found desirable to approach these consultations from the viewpoint of general principles rather than specific proposals which had been the basis of most of the discussion in the United Nations Atomic Energy Commission. To this end, the representative of the United Kingdom offered a list of topics as a basis for discussion. Included in this paper was a Statement of

Principles relating to each topic. It was pointed out that the United Kingdom Statement of Principles was based on the plan approved by the General Assembly, but at the same time covered the essential topics with which any plan for the prohibition of atomic weapons and the control of atomic energy would have to deal. The list of topics was then adopted as the basis for discussion. The representatives of Canada, China, France, the United Kingdom and the United States made it clear that their Governments accepted the Statement of Principles set forth in this paper and considered them essential to any plan of effective prohibition of atomic weapons and effective control of atomic energy for peaceful purposes. They expressed the readiness of their Governments to consider any alternative proposals which might be put forward, but emphasized that they would continue to support the plan approved by the General Assembly unless and until proposals were made which would provide equally or more effective and workable means of control and prohibition.

PROHIBITION OF ATOMIC WEAPONS

At the request of the Soviet representative, the question of the prohibition of atomic weapons was taken up first. The texts which served as a basis for the discussion were point four of the Statement of Principles, and a Soviet amendment submitted to replace that text. In the course of the discussion, the Soviet representative declared that the representatives of all six Sponsoring Powers were in agreement in recognizing that atomic weapons should be prohibited, and he therefore drew the conclusion that his amendment should be accepted. The other representatives pointed out that it had always been agreed that the production, possession or use of atomic weapons by all nations must be prohibited. But it was also agreed that prohibition could only be enforced by means of an effective system of control. This was recognized even in the Soviet amendment, but the remainder of the amendment contained a repetition of the earlier Soviet proposals for control which were deemed inadequate.

The Soviet representative insisted that two separate conventions, one on prohibition and the other on control, should be put into effect simultaneously. The other representatives maintained that the important point to be resolved was what constitutes effective control, and that this control had to embrace all uses of atomic materials in dangerous quantities. In their view the Soviet proposals would not only fail to provide the security required but they would be so inadequate as to be dangerous. They would delude the peoples of the world into thinking that atomic energy was being controlled when in fact it was not. On the other hand, under the approved plan, the prohibition of the use of atomic weapons would rest not only on the pledge of each nation, but no nation would be permitted to possess the materials with which weapons could be made. Furthermore, the Soviet Government took an impracticable stand as regards the question of timing or stages by which prohibition and control would be brought into effect.

STAGES FOR PUTTING INTO EFFECT PROHIBITION AND CONTROL

On this topic, the Soviet representative maintained that the entire system of prohibition and control must be put into effect simultaneously over the entire nuclear industry.

The representatives of the other Powers pointed out that this would be physically impossible. The development of atomic energy is the world's newest industry, and already is one of the most complicated. It would not be reasonable to assume that any effective system of control could be introduced and enforced overnight. Control and prohibition must, therefore, go into effect over a period of time and by a series of stages.

The plan approved by the General Assembly on 4 November 194n (sic.) does not attempt to define what the stages should be, the order i8 (sic.) which they should be put into effect, or the time which the whole process of transition would take. The reason for this is that no detailed provisions on stages could be drawn up until agreement is, reached on what the control system should be, and the provisions, would also depend on the state of development of atomic energy in the various countries at the time agreement is reached. Until then, detailed study of the question of stages would be unrealistic.

Meanwhile, the approved plan covers the question of stages in so, far as it can usefully be carried at present.

The plan provides that the schedule of stages of application of control and prohibition over all the many phases of the entire nuclear industry is to be written into the treaty, with the United Nations Atomic Energy Commission as the body to supervise their orderly implementation. No other commitment or position on this question is contained in the approved plan.

CONTROL

(a) Means of Control

The Soviet representative insisted, as in the past, that any plan of control, to be acceptable to the Soviet Union, must be based on the Soviet proposals for control, originally put forward in June 1947 (Document AEC/24, 11 June 1947), which provide for periodic inspection of nationally owned plants producing or using atomic materials, when declared to an international control organ by the Governments concerned.

The representatives of Canada, China, France, the United Kingdom and the United States recalled that the nuclear fuels produced or used in such plants are the very nuclear explosives used in the manufacture of weapons. A new situation therefore was created in the field of armaments where the conversion of a peaceful industry into a war industry could take place rapidly and without warning.

In dealing with such materials a system of control depending merely on inspection would be ineffective. For ordinary chemical or mineral substances and their processing inspection might provide adequate guarantees, but atomic development presented special problems which could not be solved in this way. Materials used in the development of atomic energy were highly radioactive and could not, therefore, be handled except by remote control. The process of measuring atomic fuels was extremely intricate and, at the present stage of our knowledge, subject to appreciable error. It would be impracticable to rely on the inspection of plants and impossible to check the actual amounts of atomic materials inside piles or reactors against the amounts shown in the records.

A system of inspection alone would not prevent the clandestine diversion of atomic materials to war purposes from plants designed for peaceful use and would provide no guarantee that, in spite of any treaty, a nation which was determined to continue the secret manufacture of atomic weapons would be prevented from doing so. A plan based on periodic inspection, on which the Soviet Union insists, would be even less adequate than one based on continuous inspection.

The Soviet representative dismissed these arguments as exaggerated or non-existent.

Since there was evidence that an atomic explosion had been produced in the Soviet Union, the Soviet representative was asked whether he had any new evidence derived from Soviet experience to support his contention that periodic inspection would be sufficient to assure control. No answer has yet been received to this question.

The five Powers remain convinced that any system of inspection alone would be inadequate and that in order to provide security the International Control Agency must itself operate and manage dangerous facilities and must hold dangerous atomic materials and facilities for making or using dangerous quantities of such materials in trust for Member States.

(b) Ownership

During the consultations, the question of ownership, which has often been represented as the real obstacle to agreement on control, was the subject of an extended exchange of views.

The Soviet representative argued that international management and operation were equivalent to international ownership; and that neither international ownership nor international management and operation was essential to control. He stated that his Government would not accept either.

The representatives of the other Sponsoring Powers refuted the interpretation put by the Soviet representative on ownership, management and operation. For the reasons given they believed that the management and operation of dangerous facilities must be entrusted to the International Agency. Management and operation were clearly among the more important rights conferred by ownership. Since effective control would be impossible unless these rights were exercised by the Agency, the nations on whose territories such facilities were situated would have to renounce important rights normally conferred by ownership. This did not necessarily mean the complete devolution of the rights of ownership to the Agency; for example, the Agency would not have the right arbitrarily to close atomic power plants; it would have to conform to national legislation as regards public health and working conditions; it could not construct plants at will but only in agreement with the nation concerned. Moreover, the Agency would not be free to determine the production policy for nuclear fuel since this would follow provisions to be laid down in advance in the treaty. The treaty would also determine the quotas for production and consumption of atomic fuel. Finally, the Agency would hold materials and facilities in trust and would not therefore be able to manage or dispose of them arbitrarily or for its own profit but only for the benefit of Member States.

There might well be other rights which would normally be conferred by ownership and which were not specifically mentioned in the approved plan. Their disposition would follow a simple principle. If there were rights, the exercise of which could impair the effectiveness of control, individual nations would be required to renounce them. Otherwise they might retain them.

If individual nations agreed to renounce national ownership of dangerous atomic materials and the right of managing and operating plants making or using them, in favor of an International Agency acting for the international community, such agreement would be on the basic principle, and there would be no need to quarrel over terminology.

(c) Sovereignty

A further argument put forward by the Soviet representative was that to confer on any international agency the powers suggested in the Statement of Principles would constitute a gross infringement of national sovereignty and would permit the International Agency to interfere in the internal economy of individual nations.

In answer to this argument it was pointed out that any plan for international prohibition and control must involve some surrender of sovereignty. The representatives of the other Powers argued that it was indefensible to reject a plan for the international control of atomic energy on the purely negative ground that it would infringe national sovereignty. The ideal of international co-operation and, indeed, the whole concept on which the United Nations was based would be meaningless if

States insisted on the rigid maintenance of all their sovereign rights. The question was not one of encroachment on sovereignty, but of assuring the security of the world, which could only be attained by the voluntary association of nations in the exercise of certain rights of sovereignty in an open and co-operating world community.

The Soviet representative remarked that, while some representatives had stated that their Governments were prepared to waive sovereignty provided that the majority plan was accepted, the Government of the U. S. S. R. would not agree to do so.

BASIC OBSTACLES IN THE WAY OF AGREEMENT

It appears from these consultations that, as in the past, the Soviet Union will not negotiate except on the basis of the principles set forth in the Soviet proposals of June 1947.

The essential points in the Soviet control proposals, and the reasons for their rejection by the other five Powers, as brought out in the consultations, are as follows:

The Soviet Union proposes that nations should continue to own explosive atomic materials.

The other five Powers feel that under such conditions there would be no effective protection against the sudden use of these materials as atomic weapons.

The Soviet Union proposes that nations continue, as at present, to own, operate and manage facilities making or using dangerous quantities of such materials.

The other Five powers believe that, under such conditions, it would be impossible to detect or prevent the diversion of such materials for use in atomic weapons.

The Soviet Union proposes a system of control depending on periodic inspection of facilities the existence of which the national Government concerned reports to the international agency, supplemented by special investigations on suspicion of treaty violations.

The other five Powers believe that periodic inspection would not prevent the diversion of dangerous materials and that the special investigations envisaged would be wholly insufficient to prevent clandestine activities.

Other points of difference, including Soviet insistence on the right to veto the recommendations of the International Control Agency, have not yet been discussed in the consultations.

Conclusions

These consultations have not yet succeeded in bringing about agreement between the U. S. S. R. and the other five Powers, but they have served to clarify some of the points on which there is disagreement.

It is apparent that there is a fundamental difference not only on methods but also on aims. All of the Sponsoring Powers other than the U. S. S. R. put world security first and are prepared to accept innovations in traditional concepts of international co-operation, national sovereignty and economic organization where these are necessary for security. The Government of the U. S. S. R. put its sovereignty first and is unwilling to accept measures which may impinge upon or interfere with its rigid exercise of unimpeded state sovereignty.

If this fundamental difference could be overcome, other differences which have hitherto appeared insurmountable could be seen in true perspective, and reasonable ground might be found for their adjustment.

ANNEX I

List of Topics and Statement of Principles Prepared by the Representative of the United Kingdom of Great Britain and Northern Ireland

1. International system of control:

(a) There should be a strong and comprehensive international system for the control of atomic energy and the prohibition of atomic weapons, aimed at attaining the objectives set forth in the resolution of the General Assembly of 24 January 1946. Such an international system should be established, and its scope and functions defined by an enforceable multilateral treaty in which all nations should participate on fair and equitable terms.

(b) Policies concerning the production and use of atomic energy which substantially affect world security should be governed by principles established in the treaty. Production and other dangerous facilities should be distributed in accordance with quotas and provisions laid down in the treaty.

2. International Control Agency:

(a) There should be established, within the framework of the Security Council, an international control agency, deriving its powers and status from the treaty under which it is established. The Agency should possess powers and be charged with responsibility necessary and appropriate for the prompt and effective discharge of the duties imposed upon it by the terms of the treaty. Its powers should be sufficiently broad and flexible to enable it to deal with new developments that may hereafter arise in the field of atomic energy.

(b) The personnel of the Agency should be recruited on an international basis.

(c) The duly accredited representatives of the Agency should be afforded unimpeded rights of ingress, egress and access for the performance of their inspections and other duties into, from and within the territory of every participating nation, unhindered by national or local authorities.

3. Exchange of information:

(a) The Agency and the participating nations should be guided by the general principle that there should be no secrecy concerning scientific and technical information on atomic energy.

(b) The Agency should promote among all nations the exchange of basic scientific information on atomic energy for peaceful ends.

4. Prohibition of atomic weapons:

(a) International agreement to outlaw the national production and use of atomic weapons is an essential part of this international system of control.

(b) The manufacture, possession and use of atomic weapons by all nations and by all persons under their jurisdiction should be forbidden.

(c) Any existing stocks of atomic weapons should be disposed of, and proper use should be made of nuclear fuel for peaceful purposes.

5. Development of atomic energy:

(a) The development and use of atomic energy even for peaceful purposes are not exclusively matters of domestic concern of individual nations, but rather have predominantly international implications and repercussions. The development of atomic energy must be made an international co-operative enterprise in all its phases.

(b) The Agency should have positive research and developmental responsibilities in order to remain in the forefront of atomic knowledge so as to render itself more effective in promoting the beneficial uses of atomic energy and in eliminating the destructive ones.

(c) The Agency should obtain and maintain information as complete and accurate as possible concerning world supplies of source material.

6. Control over atomic materials and facilities:

(a) The Agency should hold all atomic source materials, nuclear fuels and dangerous facilities in trust for the participating nations and be responsible for ensuring that the provisions of the treaty in regard to their disposition are executed.

(b) The Agency should have the exclusive right to operate and manage all dangerous atomic facilities.

(c) In any matters affecting security, nations cannot have any proprietary right or rights of decision arising therefrom over atomic source materials, nuclear fuels or dangerous facilities located within their territories.

(d) The Agency must be given indisputable control of the source materials promptly after their separation from their natural deposits, and on taking possession should give fair and equitable compensation determined by agreement with the nation concerned.

(e) Activities related to atomic energy, which are nondangerous to security, such as mining and milling of source material, and research, may be operated by nations or persons under license from the Agency.

7. Means of detecting and preventing clandestine activities:

The Agency should have the duty of seeking out any clandestine activities or facilities involving source material or nuclear fuel; to this end it should have the power to require reports on relevant matters, to verify these reports and obtain such other information as it deems necessary by direct inspection or other means, all subject to appropriate limitations.

8. Stages:

The treaty should embrace the entire programme for putting the international system of control into effect, and should provide a schedule for the completion of the transitional process over a period of time, step by step, in an orderly and agreed sequence leading to the full and effective establishment of international control of atomic energy and prohibition of atomic weapons.

ANNEX II

Amendments Submitted by the Representative of the Union of Soviet Socialist Republics to Point 4 of the List of Topics Prepared by the Representative of the United Kingdom of Great Britain and Northern Ireland

4. Prohibition of atomic weapons:

(a) An international convention outlawing the production, use and possession of atomic weapons is an essential part of any system of international control of atomic energy. In order to be effective such a convention should be supplemented by the establishment of a universal system of international control, including inspection to ensure that the provisions of the convention are carried out and "to protect States observing the convention from possible violations and evasions."

(b) The Atomic Energy Commission should forthwith proceed to prepare a draft convention for the prohibition of atomic weapons and a draft convention on control of atomic energy, on the understanding that both conventions should be concluded and brought into effect simultaneously.

(c) Atomic weapons should not be used in any circumstances. The production, possession and use of atomic weapons by any State, agency or person whatsoever should be prohibited.

(d) All existing stocks of finished and unfinished atomic weapons should be destroyed within three months of the date of entry into force of the convention for the prohibition of atomic weapons. Nuclear fuel contained in the said atomic weapons should be used for peaceful purposes.

GLOSSARY

clandestine: characterized by, done in, or executed with secrecy or concealment; private

egress: opposite of ingress; the act or an instance of going; an exit; a going out

envisaged: to contemplate; visualize

gross: flagrant and extreme; unqualified; complete

impinge: to make an impression; have an effect or impact; to encroach; infinge

ingress: the act of going in or entering; entryway

Document Analysis

This report begins with a summary of its purpose: the six permanent members had been sent into consultation by the United Nations General Assembly. Other attempts at negotiation had broken down. The group was asked to meet in November 1948, but nine months passed before it met. In the interim, NATO had been formed, and the Soviet Union was on the cusp of possessing an atomic weapon. Between the meeting and this report, the Soviet Union had detonated an atomic weapon. After ten meetings, negotiations broke down in October 1949, and the other five members of UN-AEC sent this report to the assembly.

Discussions began with an agreement by representatives of the five countries on the basic principles set forth by the United Kingdom, based on UN agreements. These were accepted as fundamental to "any plan of effective prohibition of atomic weapons and effective control of atomic energy for peaceful purposes." The Soviet Union is silent in this record, though the principals are "adopted as the basis for discussion." The heart of the disagreement comes in the first broad category for discussion, the "prohibition of atomic weapons." Though the Soviet representative is in agreement that "atomic weapons should be prohibited," the Soviet proposal includes controls that the other members feel are "inadequate." The Soviet position is that weapons should be outlawed and regulations put in place simultaneously. The key issue becomes trust: the Soviet plan relied on the "pledge of each nation" rather than international controls. However, the other five nations assert that, if implemented, the Soviet plan would present a danger in that it would "delude the peoples of the world into thinking that atomic energy was being controlled when in fact it was not."

Most of the remainder of this report is devoted to disagreements on the matter of control between the Soviet Union and the other five countries. The Soviet Union wants self-regulation and prohibition, effective immediately. The other members view this as impossible and inadequate. The Soviet Union wants periodic inspection of facilities rather than international control of them. The Soviet Union is unwilling to negotiate what it sees as a violation of national sovereignty on this issue, stating that "international management and operation were equivalent to international ownership."

The report concludes that negotiations are at a standstill, as the Soviet Union will not accept any proposals other than its own. A list of Soviet proposals, and the reasons that the other members cannot accept them, is provided at the conclusion of this document. Indeed, the impasse proved insurmountable, and the UNAEC was officially disbanded in 1952.

Essential Themes

This report provides an excellent example of the tensions between the Soviet Union and the United States after World War II. The United States' monopoly on atomic weapons ended, and the Soviet Union was firm in its unwillingness to relinquish control of its nuclear facilities. UNAEC conducted its work against a backdrop of mounting international tension, and this report provided detailed proof of the mistrust between the Soviet Union and the rest of the group. The controls proposed by the Soviets depended on trust; however, other nations (particularly the United States) that stood to lose their weapons, but might be unable to prevent the Soviet Union from keeping its weapons, were not willing to agree to a system based on trust and self-reporting. For its part, the Soviet Union was unwilling to have what it deemed international ownership of its facilities, viewing such as a violation of its sovereignty.

—*Bethany Groff, MA*

Bibliography and Additional Reading

Craig, Campbell, & Sergey Radchenko. *The Atomic Bomb and the Origins of the Cold War.* New Haven: Yale UP, 2008. Print.

Gaddis, John Lewis. *The Cold War: A New History.* New York: Penguin, 2005. Print.

Kaplan, Lawrence S. *NATO 1948: The Birth of the Transatlantic Alliance.* Lanham, MD: Rowman & Littlefield, 2007. Print.

Luard, Evan. *A History of the United Nations: The Years of Western Domination, 1945–1955.* New York: Macmillian, 1982. Print.

THE RED SCARE

After the first so-called Red Scare in 1919-1920, when persons suspected of communist ties were persecuted by U.S. officials, yet before the rise of Senator Joseph McCarthy and his infamous anticommunist activities in the early 1950s, there was the House Un-American Activities Committee (HUAC), which hunted out "reds" and reached its peak in the late 1940s. Revelations of Soviet espionage, particularly in the case of Alger Hiss, a State Department official, made headlines and brought attention to HUAC. Indeed, the Truman administration as a whole was accused by critics of being "soft on communism," despite some explicit anticommunist undertakings (the Marshall Plan; NATO; the Berlin airlift) in Europe and elsewhere. HUAC investigated many artists and entertainers, particularly those associated with Hollywood. Its actions resulted in the blacklisting of many who refused to answer its questions along with several contempt-of-Congress convictions. Later on, HUAC was criticized for violating First Amendment rights and other abuses. Still, a number of political careers were made or assisted by membership in or collaboration with HUAC, notably the careers of Richard M. Nixon and Ronald Reagan.

■ Executive Order 9835

Date: March 21, 1947
Author: Harry S. Truman
Genre: government document

Summary Overview

At the end of World War II, tensions ran high between the United States and its former ally, the Soviet Union. The two powers disagreed on plans for the future of Europe, and the United States' possession of atomic weapons and refusal to share this technology drove a further wedge between them. As US fears of Communism grew and the Soviet Union pursued its own development of an atomic weapon, some in the US government warned of the threat posed by spies and traitors whose ideological ties to the Soviet Union could lead them to leak sensitive or dangerous information.

President Harry Truman's Executive Order 9835 was designed to root out this alleged subversive element in the federal government. This order required that all federal employees be screened for loyalty as a matter of national security. The effort to expose Communists prompted the widespread influence of the Attorney General's List of Subversive Organizations (AGLOSO), which identified groups whose members could allegedly be suspected of anti-American sympathies. These measures led to a precipitous decline in civil liberties as ever more aggressive investigations sought to uncover Communist plots.

Defining Moment

Even before the end of World War II, the US government had begun attempts to screen its employees for loyalty by banning individuals with ties to Fascist, Communist, or other political groups seen as antidemocratic. The Hatch Act of 1939 led to the creation of a committee to investigate the possibility of subversive activities, as well as a secret version of the AGLOSO that identified groups whose members posed a potential threat. After the war, tensions with the Soviet Union quickly began to rise. Dramatically opposed ideologies between the two nations, an imbalance of power (the Soviet Union had not yet developed nuclear weapons), and economic trouble within the United States led to a highly charged atmosphere of suspicion and distrust.

As the Soviet Union became directly opposed to US foreign policy, rumors circulated that there were extensive Communist spy networks in the United States, including within the government. The House Un-American Activities Committee (HUAC), created in 1938 and made permanent in 1945, was in charge of anti-Communist investigations. The Soviet Union's increasingly hard line views and the discovery of several actual spies in the United States further fueled an obsession in the United States with internal subversion. Some political and cultural leaders, particularly religious and political conservatives, saw this "Red Scare" as a political opportunity, and the Republican Party adopted the threat of Communism and the perceived weakness of the Democrats under Harry Truman as a major issue in the congressional elections of 1946.

In 1946, the HUAC investigated several alleged Communist groups, and concluded that the security of the country was threatened by the employment of anyone with questionable loyalty. Boosted by the argument that Democrats were soft on Communism, the Republican Party gained control of both houses of Congress and demanded action to identify and eliminate subversives in any federal position. According to most accounts, the Truman administration did not view Communist subversion as a major problem, but it felt the political pressure to provide some response to the issue. In November 1946, President Truman established the President's Temporary Commission on Employee Loyalty (TCEL) to study how to best determine the loyalty of federal employees.

The TCEL investigation was based on testimony from various government agencies and officials. Attorney General Tom Clark and the Federal Bureau of Investigation (FBI) under director J. Edgar Hoover helped push the TCEL's final report to recommend the creation of a strict federal loyalty program. Truman followed this recommendation by signing Executive Order 9835 on March 21, 1947, which mandated that all current federal employees as well as all applicants for federal jobs be investigated to determine their loyalty.

Author Biography

Harry S. Truman was born in Lamar, Missouri, in 1884. He served in the National Guard during World War I, aiding in the formation of his regiment and eventually becoming a captain. Thanks to his political connections, Truman was appointed or elected to a series of minor public offices before being elected to the United States Senate in 1934. Truman's strong reputation in the Senate led President Franklin D. Roosevelt to se-

lect him as a running mate in the 1944 presidential election, and Truman won the vice presidency.

When Roosevelt died on April 12, 1945, Truman became the president of the United States. He oversaw Germany's surrender and made the decision to drop two atomic bombs on Japan. After World War II, Truman helped establish the United Nations and the Marshall Plan to rebuild Europe, and was narrowly reelected in 1948. His later initiatives included the Fair Deal domestic policy program and the containment of Communism, including the Korean War. Truman did not seek reelection in 1952, and retired from politics. He died in 1972.

HISTORICAL DOCUMENT

Whereas each employee of the Government of the United States is endowed with a measure of trusteeship over the democratic processes which are the heart and sinew of the United States; and

Whereas it is of vital importance that persons employed in the Federal service be of complete and unswerving loyalty to the United States; and

Whereas, although the loyalty of by far the overwhelming majority of all Government employees is beyond question, the presence within the Government service of any disloyal or subversive person constitutes a threat to our democratic processes; and

Whereas maximum protection must be afforded the United States against infiltration of disloyal persons into the ranks of its employees, and equal protection from unfounded accusations of disloyalty must be afforded the loyal employees of the Government:

Now, Therefore, by virtue of the authority vested in me by the Constitution and statutes of the United States, including the Civil Service Act of 1883 (22 Stat. 403), as amended, and section 9A of the act approved August 2, 1939 (18 U.S.C. 61i), and as President and Chief Executive of the United

States, it is hereby, in the interest of the internal management of the Government, ordered as follows:

PART I—INVESTIGATION OF APPLICANTS

1. There shall be a loyalty investigation of every person entering the civilian employment of any department or agency of the executive branch of the Federal Government.

2. Investigations of persons entering the competitive service shall be conducted by the Civil Service Commission, except in such cases as are covered by a special agreement between the Commission and any given department or agency.

3. Investigations of persons other than those entering the competitive service shall be conducted by the employing department or agency. Departments and agencies without investigative organizations shall utilize the investigative facilities of the Civil Service Commission.

4. The investigations of persons entering the employ of the executive branch may be conducted after any such person enters upon actual employment therein, but in any such case the appointment of such person shall be

conditioned upon a favorable determination with respect to his loyalty.

5. Investigations of persons entering the competitive service shall be conducted as expeditiously as possible; provided, however, that if any such investigation is not completed within 18 months from the date on which a person enters actual employment, the condition that his employment is subject to investigation shall expire, except in a case in which the Civil Service Commission has made an initial adjudication of disloyalty and the case continues to be active by reason of an appeal, and it shall then be the responsibility of the employing department or agency to conclude such investigation and make a final determination concerning the loyalty of such person.

6. An investigation shall be made of all applicants at all available pertinent sources of information and shall include reference to:

7. Federal Bureau of Investigation files.

8. Civil Service Commission files.

9. Military and naval intelligence files.

10. The files of any other appropriate government investigative or intelligence agency.

11. House Committee on un-American Activities files.

12. Local law-enforcement files at the place of residence and employment of the applicant, including municipal, county, and State law-enforcement files.

13. Schools and colleges attended by applicant.

14. Former employers of applicant.

15. References given by applicant.

16. Any other appropriate source.

17. Whenever derogatory information with respect to loyalty of an applicant is revealed a full investigation shall be conducted. A full field investigation shall also be conducted of those applicants, or of applicants for particular positions, as may be designated by the head of the employing department or agency, such designations to be based on the determination by any such head of the best interests of national security.

PART II—INVESTIGATION OF EMPLOYEES

1. The head of each department and agency in the executive branch of the Government shall be personally responsible for an effective program to assure that disloyal civilian officers or employees are not retained in employment in his department or agency.

2. He shall be responsible for prescribing and supervising the loyalty determination procedures of his department or agency, in accordance with the provisions of this order, which shall be considered as providing minimum requirements.

3. The head of a department or agency which does not have an investigative organization shall utilize the investigative facilities of the Civil Service Commission.

4. The head of each department and agency shall appoint one or more loyalty boards, each composed of not less than three representatives of the department or agency concerned, for the purpose of hearing loyalty cases arising within such department or agency and making recommendations with respect to the removal of any officer or employee of such department or agency on grounds relating to loyalty, and he shall prescribe regulations for the conduct of the proceedings before such boards.

5. An officer or employee who is charged with being disloyal shall have a right to an administrative hearing before a loyalty board in the employing department or agency. He may appear before such board personally, accompanied by counsel or representative of his own choosing, and present evidence on his own behalf, through witnesses or by affidavit.

6. The officer or employee shall be served with a written notice of such hearing in sufficient time, and shall be informed therein of the nature of the charges against him in sufficient detail, so that he will be enabled to prepare his defense. The charges shall be stated as specifically and completely as, in the discretion of the employing department or agency, security considerations permit, and the officer or employee shall be informed in the notice (1) of his right to reply to such charges in writing within a specified reasonable period of time, (2) of his right to an administrative hearing on such charges before a loyalty board, and (3) of his right to appear before such board personally, to be accompanied by counsel or representative of his own choosing, and to present evidence on his behalf, through witness or by affidavit.

7. A recommendation of removal by a loyalty board shall be subject to appeal by the officer or employee affected, prior to his removal, to the head of the employing department or agency or to such person or persons as may be designated by such head, under such regulations as may be prescribed by him, and the decision of the department or agency concerned shall be subject to appeal to the Civil Service Commission's Loyalty Review Board, hereinafter provided for, for an advisory recommendation.

8. The rights of hearing, notice thereof, and appeal therefrom shall be accorded to every officer or employee prior to his removal on grounds of disloyalty, irrespective of tenure, or of manner, method, or nature of appointment, but the head of the employing department or agency may suspend any officer or employee at any time pending a determination with respect to loyalty.

9. The loyalty boards of the various departments and agencies shall furnish to the Loyalty Review Board, hereinafter provided for, such reports as may be requested concerning the operation of the loyalty program in any such department or agency.

PART III—RESPONSIBILITIES OF CIVIL SERVICE COMMISSION

1. There shall be established in the Civil Service Commission a Loyalty Review Board of not less than three impartial persons, the members of which shall be officers or employees of the Commission.

2. The Board shall have authority to review cases involving persons recommended for dismissal on grounds relating to loyalty by the loyalty board of any department or agency and to make advisory recommendations thereon to the head of the employing department or agency. Such cases may be referred to the Board either by the employing department or agency, or by the officer or employee concerned.

3. The Board shall make rules and regulations, not inconsistent with the provisions of this order, deemed necessary to implement statutes and Executive orders relating to employee loyalty.

4. The Loyalty Review Board shall also:

(1) Advise all departments and agencies on all problems relating to employee loyalty.

(2) Disseminate information pertinent to employee loyalty programs.

(3) Coordinate the employee loyalty policies and procedures of the several departments and agencies.

(4) Make reports and submit recommendations to the Civil Service Commission for transmission to the President from time to time as may be necessary to the maintenance of the employee loyalty program.

5. There shall also be established and maintained in the Civil Service Commission a central master index covering all persons on whom loyalty investigations have been made by any department or agency since September 1, 1939. Such master index shall contain the name of each person investigated, adequate identifying information concerning each such person, and a reference to each department and agency which has conducted a loyalty investigation concerning the person involved.

6. All executive departments and agencies are

directed to furnish to the Civil Service Commission all information appropriate for the establishment and maintenance of the central master index.

7. The reports and other investigative material and information developed by the investigating department or agency shall be retained by such department or agency in each case.

8. The Loyalty Review Board shall currently be furnished by the Department of Justice the name of each foreign or domestic organization, association, movement, group or combination of persons which the Attorney General, after appropriate investigation and determination, designates as totalitarian, fascist, communist or subversive, or as having adopted a policy of advocating or approving the commission of acts of force or violence to deny others their rights under the Constitution of the United States, or as seeking to alter the form of government of the United States by unconstitutional means.

9. The Loyalty Review Board shall disseminate such information to all departments and agencies.

PART IV—SECURITY MEASURES IN INVESTIGATIONS

1. At the request of the head of any department or agency of the executive branch an investigative agency shall make available to such head, personally, all investigative material and information collected by the investigative agency concerning any employee or prospective employee of the requesting department or agency, or shall make such material and information available to any officer or officers designated by such head and approved by the investigative agency.

2. Notwithstanding the foregoing requirement, however, the investigative agency may refuse to disclose the names of confidential informants, provided it furnishes sufficient information about such informants on the basis of which the requesting department or agency can make an adequate evaluation of the information furnished by them, and provided it advises the requesting department or agency in writing that it is essential to the protection of the informants or to the investigation of other cases that the identity of the informants not be revealed. Investigative agencies shall not use this discretion to decline to reveal sources of information where such action is not essential.

3. Each department and agency of the executive branch should develop and maintain, for the collection and analysis of information relating to the loyalty of its employees and prospective employees, a staff specially trained in security techniques, and an effective security control system for protecting such information generally and for protecting confidential sources of such information particularly.

PART V—STANDARDS

1. The standard for the refusal of employment or the removal from employment in an executive department or agency on grounds relating to loyalty shall be that, on all the evidence, reasonable grounds exist for belief that the person involved is disloyal to the Government of the United States.

2. Activities and associations of an applicant or employee which may be considered in connection with the determination of disloyalty may include one or more of the following:

3. Sabotage, espionage, or attempts or preparations therefor, or knowingly associating with spies or saboteurs;

4. Treason or sedition or advocacy thereof;

5. Advocacy of revolution or force or violence to alter the constitutional form of government of the United States;

6. Intentional, unauthorized disclosure to any person, under circumstances which may indicate disloyalty to the United States, of documents or information of a confidential or non-public character obtained by the person making the disclosure as a result of his employment by the Government of the United States;

7. Performing or attempting to perform his duties, or otherwise acting, so as to serve the interests of another government in preference to the interests of the United States.

8. Membership in, affiliation with or sympathetic association with any foreign or domestic organization, association, movement, group or combination of persons, designated by the Attorney General as totalitarian, fascist, communist, or subversive, or as having adopted a policy of advocating or approving the commission of acts of force or violence to deny other persons their rights under the Constitution of the United States, or as seeking to alter the form of government of the United States by unconstitutional means.

PART VI—MISCELLANEOUS

1. Each department and agency of the executive branch, to the extent that it has not already done so, shall submit, to the Federal Bureau of Investigation of the Department of Justice, either directly or through the Civil Service Commission, the names (and such other necessary identifying material as the Federal Bureau of Investigation may require) of all of its incumbent employees.

2. The Federal Bureau of Investigation shall check such names against its records of persons concerning whom there is substantial evidence of being within the purview of paragraph 2 of Part V hereof, and shall notify each department and agency of such information.

3. Upon receipt of the above-mentioned information from the Federal Bureau of Investigation, each department and agency shall make, or cause to be made by the Civil Service Commission, such investigation of those employees as the head of the department or agency shall deem advisable.

4. The Security Advisory Board of the State-War-Navy Coordinating Committee shall draft rules applicable to the handling and transmission of confidential documents and other documents and information which should not be publicly disclosed, and upon approval by the President such rules shall constitute the minimum standards for the handling and transmission of such documents and information, and shall be applicable to all departments and agencies of the executive branch.

5. The provisions of this order shall not be applicable to persons summarily removed under the provisions of section 3 of the act of December 17, 1942, 56 Stat. 1053, of the act of July 5, 1946, 60 Stat. 453, or of any other statute conferring the power of summary removal.

6. The Secretary of War and the Secretary of the Navy, and the Secretary of the Treasury with respect to the Coast Guard, are hereby directed to continue to enforce and maintain the highest standards of loyalty within the armed services, pursuant to the applicable statutes, the Articles of War, and the Articles for the Government of the Navy.

7. This order shall be effective immediately, but compliance with such of its provisions as require the expenditure of funds shall be deferred pending the appropriation of such funds.

8. Executive Order No. 9300 of February 5, 1943, is hereby revoked.

Harry S. Truman

The White House,
March 21, 1947.

GLOSSARY

adjudication: the act of a court in making an order, judgment, or decree

derogatory: tending to lessen the merit or reputation of a person or thing; disparaging

endowed: to furnish, as with some talent, money, faculty or quality; equip

Document Analysis

Executive Order 9835 begins by laying out the premise for testing the loyalty of all federal employees. It acknowledges that though most—in fact, "by far the overwhelming majority"—of employees are loyal, the possibility of any "disloyal or subversive" people anywhere in public service constitutes a threat to the entire nation. Since the United States needs protection against any possibility of infiltration, it is necessary to investigate all current and potential employees. Truman also states that these investigations will also protect employees against false accusations.

The body of the order lays out the structure for performing these investigations. New applicants for positions will be screened thoroughly by the Civil Service Commission (CSC), and multiple aspects of their lives, including schooling, former employers, and any other records deemed relevant, will be examined. Any indication of disloyalty will be followed by a full investigation. Current employees are to be examined according to a system set up by their department heads, who are held responsible for removing any disloyal individuals serving beneath them. Departments are required to set up loyalty boards, which are to investigate employees to the standards set by the order. If employees are found to be disloyal, they have the right to defend themselves in a hearing. The accused will be given adequate time to prepare their defense, but only as "security conditions permit," and the identities of any informants against them will not be revealed. When a loyalty board recommends the removal of an employee after a hearing, the decision may be appealed by the employee in question.

Truman declares that an overarching Loyalty Review Board is to be established in the CSC to hear appeals and coordinate information sharing between the loyalty boards of individual departments. It will also run the internal management and dissemination of the list of subversive foreign or domestic organizations to be provided by the attorney general or the Department of Justice. The basic standard for disloyalty is laid out; in addition to spying and espionage, reasons for dismissal include membership, affiliation, or "sympathetic association" with any of the organizations on the attorney general's list. All employees' names are given to the FBI for checks against its own records. The heads of the armed forces are given the task of ensuring that they will "continue to enforce and maintain the highest standards of loyalty within the armed services." All information gathered in the federal investigations will be kept in a master index.

Essential Themes

Executive Order 9835 demonstrates the willingness of the Truman administration to take drastic measures in the name of national security in the highly charged postwar atmosphere. The establishment of a federal loyalty program sparked the postwar erosion of civil liberties that marked the Red Scare. Shortly after Truman signed the order, the AGLOSO was published and gained widespread public attention, eventually being used as a blacklist by many private groups as well as government organizations. The frenzy of anti-Communist activity culminated in the egregious persecution led by Senator Joseph McCarthy and the HUAC in the 1950s, which gave rise to the term "McCarthyism" for unsubstantiated accusations of subversion made for political gain. Many of those accused suffered significant professional and personal damages due to the negative impact of being associated with Communism, regardless of their actual level of involvement or political beliefs, and McCarthyism had a deep impact on the social and political landscape of the United States.

Truman's Executive Order 9835 did receive criticism, especially from civil liberties advocates concerned about the lack of effective protection against false accusations. The order itself was eventually revoked by President Dwight D. Eisenhower's Executive Order 10450 in 1953, though the debate over the surrounding issues lived on. The later order took away the powers of the Loyalty Review Board, though it did not reinstate any federal employees who had been previously dismissed for disloyalty. The controversial subject of citizens' rights versus national security would remain for years to come.

—*Bethany Groff, MA*

Bibliography and Additional Reading

Gaddis, John Lewis. *The Cold War: A New History.* New York: Penguin, 2007. Print.

Goldstein, Robert Justin. "Prelude to McCarthyism: The Making of a Blacklist." *Prologue Magazine* 38.3 (2006). Web. 20 Feb. 2015.

Storrs, Landon R. Y. *The Second Red Scare and the Unmaking of the New Deal Left.* Princeton: Princeton UP, 2013. Print.

■ Testimony of J. Edgar Hoover before the House Un-American Activities Committee

Date: March 26, 1947
Author: J. Edgar Hoover
Genre: speech; report

Summary Overview

Whereas the most famous hearings held by the House Un-American Activities Committee (HUAC) were interviews with movie stars, artists, or intellectuals, conducted in order to ferret out Communists within US society—especially in Hollywood—the HUAC's interview with Federal Bureau of Investigation (FBI) director J. Edgar Hoover was of a different sort. Hoover's testimony acted both to provide the HUAC with ideological cover and to demonstrate that various federal organizations were all on the same page regarding the threat posed by Communism and what to do about it. Hoover's authority as FBI director, his almost folk-hero status due to his successes fighting gangsters such as John Dillinger during the 1920s and 1930s, and his long track record of fighting Communism and radicalism beginning in 1919 made his HUAC testimony compelling and gave Hoover a platform to speak to the American people.

Defining Moment

During the years after the end of World War II, the US government turned its focus from defeating fascism in Nazi Germany, Italy, and Japan to defeating Communism in the Soviet Union, Eastern Europe, and especially within the United States itself. Though Communist political ideologies had gained some traction in the United States during the Great Depression of the 1930s, with the country's emergence as a world superpower after World War II, such ideologies were increasingly unwelcome in the context of the threat posed by the other superpower, the Soviet Union. Many Americans feared that American Communists were preparing an overthrow of the government as had occurred in the Soviet Union, and the US government began taking steps to root out the influence of Communism in the United States.

To that end, the House Un-American Activities Committee, which had been formed in 1938 to investigate Americans who potentially had ties to Fascism and Nazism, emerged from World War II to focus almost exclusively on the threat posed by Communism in US society. With the onset of the Cold War, the American people were exceedingly fearful of Communism and the threat it posed to democracy and capitalism within the United States, and thus many eagerly supported the HUAC's investigation of the influence of Communism in Hollywood during 1947.

In 1947, the HUAC began to hold hearings in Hollywood that sought to uncover subversive Communist messages that were allegedly introduced into motion pictures by left-leaning producers, directors, writers, and actors. Though many Americans supported the aims of the HUAC hearings, many also were wary of the tactics used to gain information, such as potentially abusing the power of the subpoena, demanding that witnesses publicly name those they suspected of being Communists even if there was no evidence, and encouraging the firing of those who were seen as possibly having Communist sympathies.

Though the HUAC had been successful in rooting out those it considered to have Communist sympathies within federal arts organizations, such as the Federal Theatre Project, its members felt they needed both the support of FBI director J. Edgar Hoover and the investigative power of the FBI in order to truly make a difference in Hollywood. To that end, HUAC chair J. Parnell Thomas invited Hoover to testify on March 26, 1947. Only two weeks before Hoover testified in front of the HUAC, President Harry S. Truman articulated the Truman Doctrine of containing Communism and authoritarianism, squarely placing the US federal government against those whom they suspected of subverting either US allies or the US government itself.

Further, only four days before Hoover's testimony, Truman issued Executive Order 9835, which instituted a loyalty program to ensure that federal employees posed no threat to the US government.

Hoover was happy to help the HUAC's efforts. After all, he had been fighting Communism for nearly thirty years when he stepped before the committee. His view of the threat's gravity, as well as the appropriate actions to combat it, were in line with the committee's and demonstrated unity within various organizations of the federal government.

Author Biography

J. Edgar Hoover was born on January 1, 1895, and joined the US Department of Justice in 1917. Within his first two years of federal employment, he made a name for himself as an anti-Communist by heading the General Intelligence Division of the Department of Justice, which staged raids against suspected anarchists and Communists at the direction of US Attorney General A. Mitchell Palmer and became part of the Bureau of Investigation in 1921. After becoming director of the Bureau of Investigation in 1924 (which became the Federal Bureau of Investigation in 1935), Hoover made a name for himself by capturing notorious gangsters, but he remained especially vigilant against those whom he considered to have radical political perspectives, carrying out spying operations, often without reporting them to the attorney general or the president. By the beginning of the Cold War in the 1940s, Hoover was seen as one of the greatest anti-Communists of the day and the FBI as an essential tool against Communist subversion. Hoover remained director of the FBI until his death on May 2, 1972.

HISTORICAL DOCUMENT

My feelings concerning the Communist Party of the United States are well known. I have not hesitated over the years to express my concern and apprehension. As a consequence its professional smear brigades have conducted a relentless assault against the FBI. You who have been members of this committee also know the fury with which the party, its sympathizers and fellow travelers can launch an assault. I do not mind such attacks. What has been disillusioning is the manner in which they have been able to enlist support often from apparently well-meaning but thoroughly duped persons....

The communist movement in the United States began to manifest itself in 1919. Since then it has changed its name and its party line whenever expedient and tactical. But always it comes back to fundamentals and bills itself as the party of Marxism-Leninism. As such, it stands for the destruction of our American form of government; it stands for the destruction of American democracy; it stands for the destruction of free enterprise; and it stands for the creation of a "Soviet of the United States" and ultimate world revolution....

The communist, once he is fully trained and indoctrinated, realizes that he can create his order in the United States only by "bloody revolution." Their chief textbook, "The History of the Communist Party of the Soviet Union," is used as a basis for planning their revolution. Their tactics require that to be successful they must have:

1. The will and sympathy of the people.

2. Military aid and assistance.

3. Plenty of guns and ammunition.

4. A program for extermination of the police as they are the most important enemy and are termed "trained fascists."

5. Seizure of all communications, buses, railroads, radio stations, and other forms of communications and transportation....

One thing is certain. The American progress which all good citizens seek, such as old-age security, houses for veterans, child assistance, and a host of others, is being adopted as window dressing by the communists to conceal their true aims and entrap gullible followers....

The mad march of Red fascism is a cause for concern in America. But the deceit, the trickery, and the lies of the American communists are catching up with them. Whenever the spotlight of truth is focused upon them they cry, "Red-baiting." Now that their aims and objectives are being exposed, they are creating a Committee for the Constitutional Rights of Communists, and are feverishly working to build up what they term a quarter-million-dollar defense fund to place ads in papers, to publish pamphlets, to buy radio time. They know that their backs will soon be to the wall....

What is important is the claim of the communists themselves that for every party member there are 10 others ready, willing and able to do the party's work. Herein lies the greatest menace of communism. For these are the people who infiltrate and corrupt various spheres of American life. So rather than the size of the Communist Party, the way to weigh its true importance is by testing its influence, its ability to infiltrate....

The communists have developed one of the greatest propaganda machines the world has ever known. They have been able to penetrate and infiltrate many respectable public opinion mediums. They capitalize upon ill-founded charges associating known honest progressive liberals with left-wing causes. I have always entertained the view that there are few appellations more degrading than "communist" and hence it should be reserved for those justly deserving the degradation.

The communist propaganda technique is designed to promote emotional response with the hope that the victim will be attracted by what he is told the communist way of life holds in store for him. The objective, of course, is to develop discontent and hasten the day when the communists can gather sufficient support and following to overthrow the American way of life....

Communists and their followers are prolific letter writers, and some of the more energetic ones follow the practice of directing numerous letters of protest to editors but signing a different name to each. Members of Congress are well aware of communists starting their pressure campaigns by an avalanche of mail which follows the party line....

The American communists launched a furtive attack on Hollywood in 1935 by the issuance of a directive calling for a concentration in Hollywood. The orders called for action on two fronts: One, an effort to infiltrate the labor unions; two, infiltrate the so-called intellectual and creative fields.

In movie circles, communists developed an effective defense a few years ago in meeting criticism. They would counter with the question "After all, what is the matter with communism?" It was effective because many per-

sons did not possess adequate knowledge of the subject to give an intelligent answer....

I feel that this committee could render a great service to the nation through its power of exposure in quickly spotlighting existing front organizations and those which will be created in the future. There are easy tests to establish the real character of such organizations:

1. Does the group espouse the cause of Americanism or the cause of Soviet Russia?

2. Does the organization feature as speakers at its meeting known communists, sympathizers, or fellow travelers?

3. Does the organization shift when the party line shifts?

4. Does the organization sponsor causes, campaigns, literature, petitions, or other activities sponsored by the party or other front organizations?

5. Is the organization used as a sounding board by or is it endorsed by communist-controlled labor unions?

6. Does its literature follow the communist line or is it printed by the communist press?

7. Does the organization receive consistent favorable mention in the communist publications?

8. Does the organization present itself to be nonpartisan yet engage in political activities and consistently advocate causes favored by the communists?

9. Does the organization denounce American and British foreign policy while always lauding Soviet policy?

10. Does the organization utilize communist "double-talk" by referring to Soviet dominated countries as democracies, complaining that the United States is imperialistic and constantly denouncing monopoly-capital?

11. Have outstanding leaders in public life openly renounced affiliation with the organization?

12. Does the organization, if espousing liberal progressive causes, attract well-known honest patriotic liberals or does it denounce well-known liberals?

13. Does the organization have a consistent record of supporting the American viewpoint over the years?

14. Does the organization consider matters now directly related to its avowed purposes and objectives?

The Communist Party of the United States is a fifth column if there ever was one. It is far better organized than were the Nazis in occupied countries prior to their capitulation. They are seeking to weaken America just as they did in their era of obstruction when they were aligned with the Nazis. Their goal is the overthrow of our government. There is no doubt as to where a real communist's loyalty rests. Their allegiance is to Russia, not the United States....

What can we do? And what should be our course of action? The best antidote to communism is vigorous, intelligent, old-fashioned Americanism, with eternal vigilance. I do not favor any course of action which would give the communists cause to portray and pity themselves as martyrs. I do favor unrelenting prosecution wherever they are found to be violating our country's laws.

As Americans, our most effective defense is a workable democracy that guarantees and preserves our cherished freedoms.

I would have no fears if more Americans possessed the zeal, the fervor, the persistence and the industry to learn about this menace of Red fascism. I do fear for the liberal and progressive who has been hoodwinked and duped into joining hands with the communists. I confess to a real apprehension so long as communists are able to secure ministers of the gospel to promote their evil work and espouse a cause that is alien to the religion of Christ and Judaism. I do fear so long as school boards and parents tolerate conditions whereby communists and fellow travelers, under the guise of academic freedom, can teach our youth a way of life that eventually will destroy the sanctity of the home, that undermines faith in God, that causes them to scorn respect for constituted authority and sabotage our revered Constitution.

I do fear so long as American labor groups are infiltrated, dominated or saturated with the virus of communism. I do fear the palliation and weasel-worded gestures against communism indulged in by some of our labor leaders who should know better, but who have become pawns in the hands of sinister but astute manipulations for the communist cause.

I fear for ignorance on the part of all our people who may take the poisonous pills of communist propaganda.

GLOSSARY

fifth column: a group of people who act traitorously and subversively out of a secret sympathy with an enemy of their country

indoctrinated: to instruct in a doctrine, principle, or ideology, especially to imbue with a specific biased belief or view point; to teach or inculcate

palliation: to relieve or lessen without curing; mitigate; alleviate

Document Analysis

When the House Committee on Un-American Activities invited FBI director J. Edgar Hoover to testify on March 26, 1947, it was ostensibly to discuss the possibility of outlawing the Communist Party of the United States (CPUSA). However, Hoover spoke much more broadly about the threat posed by Communism and the various things that could and should be done to combat its influence. Hoover argued that Communism stood for nothing short of "the destruction of our American form of government" and "the destruction of free enterprise." He asserted that the "the communist, once he is fully trained and indoctrinated, realizes that he can create his order in the United States only by 'bloody revolution.'" Hoover's views on Communism were well known to both the committee and the public, and he acknowledged that he had never hesitated to speak of his "concern and apprehension" about Communism. His testimony that day was less about outlawing the CPUSA and more about forging an alliance between the HUAC and the FBI to fight Communism together moving forward.

To Hoover, the activities of the HUAC worked hand-in-hand with those carried out by the FBI. The FBI could investigate potential Communists, but the HUAC could best publicly disseminate the FBI's findings through its hearings. To Hoover, there were true Americans who aided the Communists in spreading their message, but many who had done so were "apparently well-meaning but thoroughly duped persons." By informing the American people of the dangers of Communist infiltration, the HUAC was performing a public service by creating a well-informed populace. The function of the FBI within the United States throughout the Cold War, on the other hand, was completely different. The FBI could investigate those suspected of Communist sympathies in order to find any violations of the law or any potential threats in terms of espionage or sabotage.

At the time of Hoover's testimony, HUAC's target was the producers, directors, writers, and actors in Hollywood, whom committee members felt were imbuing American movies with subtle Communist messages. Hoover backed the HUAC agenda, noting efforts by Communists to infiltrate labor unions that organized workers on film productions as well as those who actually wrote, directed, and acted in the movies. Again, Hoover's answer is to educate the public on the perils of Communism and the tactics he said Communists used. His greatest fears were that those who might influence public opinion, particularly Hollywood filmmakers, liberal and progressive politicians and activists, left-leaning members of the clergy, and academics who favor academic freedom, would "teach our youth a way of life that eventually will destroy the sanctity of the home, that undermines faith in God, that causes them to scorn respect for constituted authority and sabotage our revered Constitution." To Hoover, these were the real threats that the FBI should investigate and the HUAC should expose.

Essential Themes

Even before Hoover's testimony before the HUAC, the FBI had been involved in working to help shape public opinion about the evils of Communism, arguing that Communists in the United States were, in fact, working at the behest of the United States' Cold War foe, the Soviet Union. The FBI began to play an increasing role in the investigation of Communism within the federal government and within American society as a whole. However, the tide of public opinion about the zealous anti-Communist tactics used by both the FBI and the HUAC began to change during the 1950s, when Republican Senator Joseph R. McCarthy of Wisconsin took the HUAC's tactics to their extreme, even going so far as to televise his hearings, in which he mercilessly harangued those he suspected of hav-

ing Communist sympathies. When McCarthy's tactics became too much for the American public to stomach, the HUAC and FBI also suffered a loss in standing in the public mind.

However, Hoover's zeal never wavered, and in the 1960s he oversaw an expansion of the FBI's Counter Intelligence Program (COINTELPRO), which involved covert espionage, often illegal investigations without probable cause, of individuals the FBI thought might be subversives. Since the HUAC was no longer an effective means to expose Communist sympathizers to public scrutiny, Hoover believed he and the FBI could use covert means to smear those he considered sympathetic to Communism.

Though anti-Communism continued to be a theme in American life throughout the Cold War era, explicit hearings, such as those held by HUAC and McCarthy, ended by the mid-1950s, and operations, such as COINTELPRO, came under public scrutiny when they were exposed in 1971, forcing Hoover to abandon one of the main strategies the FBI used to investigate suspected American Communists. By that time, however, the tenor of the Cold War had changed with the onset of the period of détente and the de-escalation of tensions with Communist nations.

—*Steven L. Danver, PhD*

Bibliography and Additional Reading

Bentley, Eric, ed. *Thirty Years of Treason: Excerpts from Hearings before the House Committee on Un-American Activities, 1938–1968*. New York: Thunder's Mouth, 2002. Print.

Hoover, J. Edgar. *Masters of Deceit: The Story of Communism in America and How to Fight It*. New York: Holt, 1958. Print.

Litvak, Joseph. *The Un-Americans: Jews, the Blacklist, and Stoolpigeon Culture*. Durham: Duke UP, 2009. Print.

May, Lary, ed. *Recasting America: Culture and Politics in the Age of Cold War*. Chicago: U of Chicago P, 1989. Print.

O'Reilly, Kenneth. *Hoover and the Un-Americans: The FBI, HUAC, and the Red Menace*. Philadelphia: Temple UP, 1983. Print.

Sbardellati, John. *J. Edgar Hoover Goes to the Movies: The FBI and the Origins of Hollywood's Cold War*. Ithaca: Cornell UP, 2012. Print.

Ronald Reagan's Testimony before the House Un-American Activities Committee

Date: October 23, 1947
Author: Ronald Reagan
Genre: speech; report

Summary Overview

In October 1947, motion picture actor and future US president Ronald Reagan gave testimony before the House Un-American Activities Committee (HUAC) regarding the influence of Communism within the Screen Actors Guild (SAG), of which Reagan was president. Though the HUAC had been in existence since 1938, its activities had increased dramatically after the conclusion of World War II, as the perceived threat posed by the Soviet Union and Communism within the United States became more widespread. The HUAC had the power to subpoena anyone and exerted pressure on its witnesses to provide the names of people they suspected of being Communists. Refusing to name names could result in the witness being held in contempt of Congress and was likely to lead some members to the conclusion that the person him- or herself was a Communist. Though Reagan was staunchly anti-Communist, with a long track record of opposing the influence of Marxist ideologies, he also expressed reservations about the activities of HUAC.

Defining Moment

The fear of Communism in the United States was nothing new in the late 1940s. As early as 1919—only two years after the Soviet Union came into being—US attorney general A. Mitchell Palmer staged a series of raids on suspected Communists that set the tone for what would become known as the First Red Scare. By 1938, when the House Un-American Activities Committee (HUAC) was formed to investigate domestic disloyalty and subversion, its focus was primarily on Fascism, as the preeminent threats came from Nazi Germany and Japan. However, in the context of the Great Depression, Communists and Communist organizations also came under scrutiny. Whatever the motives for its founding, the HUAC was often used for

political ends, mainly to discredit liberal supporters of President Franklin D. Roosevelt's New Deal domestic policy program.

After the end of World War II, the attention of the HUAC quickly turned fully toward the threat posed by Communism. In 1946, William R. Wilkerson, the publisher of the *Hollywood Reporter*, began to publish a series of articles in which he named actors, directors, and others in the motion picture industry that he claimed were Communists. Usually naming people with either dubious proof or none at all, this first "blacklist" caught the attention of the HUAC, which then began to subpoena those they thought might be in a position to know of any Communist activity in Hollywood.

What the HUAC may not have known was that Reagan and others had already been recruited by the Federal Bureau of Investigation (FBI) to help ferret out Communists in a number of different Hollywood organizations. FBI officials had disclosed their belief that Communists were trying to gain influence in Hollywood in order to use motion pictures to spread their message and that numerous film writers and actors were either Communist Party members or Communist sympathizers. Reagan agreed to work with the FBI. Reagan was briefly involved with two groups, the American Veterans Committee and the Hollywood Independent Citizens Committee of the Arts, Sciences, and Professions, which the FBI considered to be Communist-front organizations. Reagan had left both groups because of his views against Communism, but at the same time had stated to the FBI that he distrusted the motives of the HUAC and worried about its apparent attempts to quell free speech.

Along with animator Walt Disney, Reagan was one of the prominent names subpoenaed by the HUAC in October 1947. As president of the SAG, Reagan was in a unique position to know a wide array of Hollywood stars and to assess whether they were Communists intent on subverting industry groups, or, even more importantly, subtly inserting pro-Communist propaganda into Hollywood movies.

Author Biography

Ronald Reagan was born on February 6, 1911, and came of age during the Great Depression. Like many others of his generation, he initially supported Franklin D. Roosevelt's Democratic Party rather than the Republicans, whom many blamed for the Depression. He became a Hollywood actor in 1937 and joined the SAG, quickly becoming involved in the union's management. Reagan produced military training films during World War II before becoming president of the SAG in 1947. As his acting career wound down in the early 1950s, he became increasingly involved in politics, and his views shifted from liberal to conservative. Reagan was elected governor of California as a Republican in 1966 and, in 1980, was elected to the US presidency. He led a resurgence of conservative ideology in both domestic and foreign affairs and was reelected in 1984. After his retirement, Reagan battled Alzheimer's disease and died on June 5, 2004.

HISTORICAL DOCUMENT

The Committee met at 10:30 A.M. [October 23, 1947], the Honorable J. Parnell Thomas (Chairman) presiding.

THE CHAIRMAN: The record will show that Mr. McDowell, Mr. Vail, Mr. Nixon, and Mr. Thomas are present. A Subcommittee is sitting.

Staff members present: Mr. Robert E. Stripling, Chief Investigator; Messrs. Louis J. Russell, H. A. Smith, and Robert B. Gatson, Investigators; and Mr. Benjamin Mandel, Director of Research.

MR. STRIPLING: When and where were you born, Mr. Reagan?

MR. REAGAN: Tampico, Illinois, February 6, 1911.

MR. STRIPLING: What is your present occupation?

MR. REAGAN: Motion-picture actor.

MR. STRIPLING: How long have you been engaged in that profession?

MR. REAGAN: Since June 1937, with a brief interlude of three and a half years—that at the time didn't seem very brief.

MR. STRIPLING: What period was that?

MR. REAGAN: That was during the late war.

MR. STRIPLING: What branch of the service were you in?

MR. REAGAN: Well, sir, I had been for several years in the Reserve as an officer in the United States Calvary, but I was assigned to the Air Corp.

MR. STRIPLING: Are you the president of the guild at the present time?

MR. REAGAN: Yes, sir. . . .

MR. STRIPLING: As a member of the board of directors, as president of the Screen Actors Guild, and as an active member, have you at any time observed or noted within the organization a clique of either Communists or Fascists who were attempting to exert influence or pressure on the guild?

MR. REAGAN: Well, sir, my testimony must be very similar to that of Mr. [George] Murphy and Mr. [Robert] Montgomery. There has been a small group within the Screen Actors Guild which has consistently opposed the policy of the guild board and officers of the guild, as evidenced by the vote on various issues. That small clique referred to has been suspected of more or less following the tactics that we associated with the Communist Party.

MR. STRIPLING: Would you refer to them as a disruptive influence within the guild?

MR. REAGAN: I would say that at times they have attempted to be a disruptive influence.

MR. STRIPLING: You have no knowledge yourself as to whether or not any of them are members of the Communist Party?

MR. REAGAN: No, sir, I have no investigative force, or anything, and I do not know.

MR. STRIPLING: Has it ever been reported to you that certain members of the guild were Communists?

MR. REAGAN: Yes, sir, I have heard different discussions and some of them tagged as Communists.

MR. STRIPLING: Would you say that this clique has attempted to dominate the guild?

MR. REAGAN: Well, sir, by attempting to put over their own particular views on various issues. . . .

MR. STRIPLING: Mr. Reagan, there has been testimony to the effect here that numerous Communist-front organizations have been set up in Hollywood. Have you ever been solicited to join any of those organizations or any organization which you consider to be a Communist-front organization?

MR. REAGAN: Well, sir, I have received literature from an organization called the Committee for a Far-Eastern Democratic Policy. I don't know whether it is Communist or not. I only know that I didn't like their views and as a result I didn't want to have anything to do with them. . . .

MR. STRIPLING: Would you say from your observation that this is typical of the tactics or strategy of the Communists, to solicit and use the names of prominent people to either raise money or gain support.

MR. REAGAN: I think it is in keeping with their tactics, yes, sir.

MR. STRIPLING: Do you think there is anything democratic about those tactics?

MR. REAGAN: I do not, sir.

MR. STRIPLING: Mr. Reagan, what is your feeling about what steps should be taken to rid the motion-picture industry of any Communist influences?

MR. REAGAN: Well, sir, ninety-nine percent of us are pretty well aware of what is going on, and I think, within the bounds of our democratic rights and never once stepping over the rights given us by democracy, we have done a pretty good job in our business of keeping those people's activities curtailed. After all, we must recognize them at present as a political party. On that basis we have exposed their lies when we came across them, we have opposed their propaganda, and I can certainly testify that in the case of the Screen Actors Guild we have been eminently successful in preventing them from, with their usual tactics, trying to run a majority of an organization with a well-organized minority. In opposing those people, the best thing to do is make democracy work. . . .

Sir, I detest, I abhor their philosophy, but I detest more than that their tactics, which are those of the fifth column, and are dishonest, but at the same time I never as a citizen want to see our country become urged, by either fear or resentment of this group that we ever compromise with any of our democratic principles through that fear or resentment. I still think that democracy can do it.

Document Analysis

In this congressional transcript, Reagan answers question posed by the HUAC chief investigator Robert E. Stripling regarding his background and his knowledge of Communist activity in the motion picture industry. Reagan claims he is aware of some attempts to influence the SAG by individuals he thinks may be Communists or Communist sympathizers, but says they are a small minority. He asserts his own anti-Communist views as well as his belief that promoting democracy is the best way to counteract Communism.

Stripling begins the questioning by going over the

basic facts—where Reagan was born, his occupation, and his wartime military service. Then Reagan is directly asked if he has seen within the SAG "a clique of either Communists or Fascists who were attempting to exert influence or pressure on the guild." Reagan's answer is both nonspecific and noncommittal. He states that, as others had testified, there are some within SAG that he has suspects are Communists, but that he has no direct information about their affiliation. However, he does deem their ideas disruptive and their tactics as those that he would associate with members of the Communist Party.

Reagan states that he has heard that some members of the SAG were thought to be Communists, but is hesitant to cite such hearsay evidence. He agrees that the suspicious faction could be considered to be attempting to dominate the SAG and impose its own ideology on the group. Stripling then asks Reagan if he has been recruited by any Communist-front organizations. Reagan describes receiving literature from a group called the Committee for a Far-Eastern Democratic Policy, claiming that he disregarded it, as he did not like the group's views, but he qualifies that he does not know whether the group is in fact Communist. Stripling then asks if the group's recruitment tactics are typical of Communist organizations, and Reagan agrees that they are and that such methods are undemocratic. Reagan does not mention his involvement in two other groups considered Communist-front organizations, or his work as an informant for the FBI on those groups.

In his conclusion, Reagan is asked what he thinks should be done to purge Hollywood of Communist subversion. He responds by asserting that most people in the motion picture industry are aware of any Communist efforts and that the majority has been largely successful in preventing Communism from having any real impact on the industry. He obliquely critiques the HUAC investigation by claiming that anti-Communist efforts must remain "within the bounds of our democratic rights" and that the best method is to let democracy run its course. Reagan reasserts his opposition to Communist beliefs and tactics, but cautions against allowing fear and resentment to dictate the US response to Communism.

Essential Themes

The key themes of Reagan's testimony are the atmosphere of anti-Communist suspicion fostered by the HUAC, its impact on the motion picture industry, and the conflicting views on how to deal with the perceived Communist threat. Central to the issue is the balance between addressing potential matters of national security and preserving the right to free speech. Reagan illustrates the divisive nature of the subject, as he was strongly opposed to Communism and cooperated with the HUAC, but also understood the risk the investigations posed to democratic values.

The HUAC investigations into Hollywood have been viewed by historians as a major violation of free speech. Investigations often ruined careers, as studios kept blacklists of actors, writers, and directors that were suspected of having Communist sympathies. The HUAC grilled the people they subpoenaed about their personal political beliefs and then asked for the names of any other people who might have also participated in subversive activities. Those who refused to cooperate could be held in contempt of Congress and imprisoned. Those who invoked their Fifth Amendment rights were branded Communists and often blacklisted.

Soon after Reagan testified, ten writers, producers, and directors refused to cooperate with the HUAC investigations and were held in contempt of Congress. The so-called Hollywood Ten were all sentenced to prison and blacklisted by the studios. However, their saga also became a *cause célèbre* among those who thought, as Reagan had alluded, that the right to freedom of speech and thought was of greater importance than whether or not one was or ever had been associated with Communism.

Reagan's call to allow democracy to naturally resist Communist influence went unheeded. The Second Red Scare grew into the 1950s, culminating with Senator Joseph McCarthy's extreme accusations of subversion for his own political gain; such unfounded accusations and persecution became known as "McCarthyism." The Hollywood blacklist lasted into the 1960s, and many careers were damaged beyond repair. The era of fear and paranoia would have a lasting effect on US politics and culture.

—*Steven L. Danver, PhD*

Bibliography and Additional Reading

Bentley, Eric, ed. *Thirty Years of Treason: Excerpts from Hearings before the House Committee on Un-American Activities, 1938–1968.* New York: Thunder's Mouth, 2002. Print.

Litvak, Joseph. *The Un-Americans: Jews, the Blacklist, and Stoolpigeon Culture*. Durham: Duke UP, 2009. Print.

May, Lary, ed. *Recasting America: Culture and Politics in the Age of Cold War*. Chicago: U of Chicago P, 1989. Print.

Vaughan, Stephen. *Ronald Reagan in Hollywood: Movies and Politics*. New York: Cambridge UP, 1994. Print.

■ Testimony Regarding Communist Investigations

Date: October 27, 1947
Author: Eric Allen Johnston
Genre: court testimony

Summary Overview

In October 1947, the House Committee on Un-American Activities (popularized as House Un-American Activities Committee, or HUAC) held a series of investigations into a suspected Communist infiltration of the film industry. Among those summoned to testify was Motion Picture Association of America president Eric A. Johnston, a moderate Republican businessman whose position made him responsible for overseeing Hollywood studios' interests as a whole. While acknowledging the diversity of political viewpoints and the likely presence of at least a few affirmed Communists in Hollywood, Johnston sharply criticized the House committee for its headstrong approach to rooting out subversion. He both strongly contested the implications that Hollywood permitted Communist ideology to inform its films and complained that the scandal stirred by the committee's efforts infringed on free speech and carried the possibility of economic devastation for the film industry. He argued that it was better and more American to resolve the underlying social problems that led people to support Communist ideals.

Defining Moment

Although the political and economic ideology known as Communism developed during the 1800s, it did not become a major force into world politics until the Russian Revolution of 1917 installed the Soviet Communist regime in place of Russia's imperial government. The radical and bloody nature of the Russian Revolution shocked the world and caused many Americans to fear that a similar radical movement could transform into an actively revolutionary one in the United States. The First Red Scare that followed World War I reflected these concerns, and during this time, the American government rooted out both real and perceived threats from the left. Although this fervor soon faded, Americans remained deeply uneasy about Communism.

With the rise of the Nazi government in Germany, however, US leaders such as President Franklin D. Roosevelt began to see the Soviet Union as a useful ally against German aggression. Supported in part by US aid, Soviet leader Joseph Stalin and the Soviet army weakened Nazi troops along the Eastern Front; after the German surrender, the Soviets helped pressure the Japanese to surrender in the Pacific theater. However, the resolution of World War II brought the US-Soviet partnership to an end. Immense wartime damage left traditional European powers such as Great Britain, Germany, and France unusually weakened. The ascendance of the United States ensured its role as the leading geopolitical power of the Western world; despite its own heavy wartime losses, the Soviet Union quickly proved its main challenger. As the Allies sought to remake a tattered Europe, Stalin pressed for greater Soviet influence in Eastern Europe. US leaders saw the existence of Communism as a threat to democratic values and, therefore, strongly opposed its expansion. The theory of containment, which argued that limiting Soviet expansion would ultimately destroy Communism, underpinned the postwar Truman Doctrine, which pledged US assistance to any people resisting Communism. The Cold War had begun.

As it had during the First Red Scare, domestic concern over the threat of Communism skyrocketed during the late 1940s, sparking a Second Red Scare. Two congressional entities came to exemplify the Red Scare of the post–World War II era: the House Un-American Activities Committee, first formed in the late 1930s to investigate subversive activity, and, from 1950 on, the inquiries headed by Senator Joseph McCarthy. Even as President Harry S. Truman issued executive orders requiring government employees to swear loyalty oaths, HUAC held hearings seeking evidence or simple accusations of subversive support for Communist ideals among the nation's people. Among its high-profile and best-known investigations were those into government official Alger Hiss and into entertainers ranging from folk singer Pete Seeger to numerous Hollywood directors, actors, and screenwriters. In 1947, notable figures, including Screen Actors Guild head Ronald Reagan and famed animator Walt Disney, appeared before the committee to discuss the issue of possible Communist influence in Hollywood.

Author Biography

In 1945, Eric Allen Johnston succeeded long-standing Motion Picture Association of America (MPAA) head Will H. Hays as the studio organization's president. In this role, Johnston was primarily responsible for enforcing the studios' self-imposed censorship rules, commonly known as the Hays Code. Before becoming head of the MPAA, Johnston had already built a career in the business world. He worked as a traveling vacuum salesman after World War I, and by the early 1930s, he was at the head of a thriving business in household appliance manufacturing and distribution located in the Pacific Northwest. As his interests expanded, Johnston became active in the Chamber of Commerce. In 1942, members elected him as the organization's president in something of an upset: Johnston held more liberal, pro-labor views than his forebears in that role. Although a Republican, he developed a relationship with the Roosevelt administration and represented the US entrepreneurial spirit abroad throughout the 1940s and 1950s.

HISTORICAL DOCUMENT

I'm not here to try to whitewash Hollywood, and I'm not here to help sling a tar brush at it, either.

I want to stick to the facts as I see them.

There are several points I'd like to make to this committee.

The first one is this: A damaging impression of Hollywood has spread all over the country as a result of last week's hearings. You have a lot of sensational testimony about Hollywood. From some of it the public will get the idea that Hollywood is running over with Communists and communism.

I believe the impression which has gone out is the sort of scare-head stuff which is grossly unfair to a great American industry. It must be a great satisfaction to the Communist leadership in this country to have people believe that Hollywood Communists are astronomical in number and almost irresistible in power.

Now, what are the facts? Not everybody in Hollywood is a Communist. I have said before that undoubtedly there are Communists in Hollywood, but in my opinion the percentage is extremely small.

I have had a number of close looks at Hollywood in the last 2 years, and I have looked at it through the eyes of an average businessman. I recognize that as the world's capital of show business, there is bound to be a lot of show business in Hollywood. There is no business, Mr. Chairman, like show business. But underneath there is the solid foundation of patriotic, hardworking, decent citizens. Making motion pictures is hard work. You just don't dash off a motion picture between social engagements. . . .

I wind up my first point with a request of this committee. The damaging impression about Hollywood should be corrected. I urge your committee to do so in these public hearings.

There is another damaging impression which should be corrected. The report of the subcommittee said that some of the most flagrant Communist propaganda films were produced as the result of White House pressure. This charge has been completely refuted by the testimony before you.

My second point includes another request of the committee.

The report of your subcommittee stated that you had a list of all pictures produced in Hollywood in the last 8 years which contained Communist propaganda. Your committee has not made this list public. Until the list is made public the industry stands condemned by unsupported generalizations, and we are denied the opportunity to refute these charges publicly.

Again, I remind the committee that we have offered to put on a special showing of any or all of the pictures which stand accused so that you can see for yourselves what's in them. The contents of the pictures constitute the only proof.

Unless this evidence is presented and we are given the chance to refute it in these public hearings, it is the obligation of the committee to absolve the industry from the charges against it.

Now, I come to my third point—a vitally important one to every American and to the system under which we live.

It is free speech. . . .

When I talk about freedom of speech in connection with this hearing, I mean just this: You don't need to pass a law to choke off free speech or seriously curtail it. Intimidation or coercion will do it just as well. You can't make good and honest motion pictures in an atmosphere of fear.

I intend to use every influence at my command to keep the screen free. I don't propose that Government shall tell the motion-picture industry, directly or by coercion, what kind of pictures it ought to make. I am as whole-souledly against that as I would be against dictating to the press or the radio, to the book publishers or to the magazines. . . .

To sum up this point: We insist on our rights to decide what will or will not go in our pictures. We are deeply conscious of the responsibility this freedom involves, but we have no intention to violate this trust by permitting subversive propaganda in our films.

Now, my next point is this:

When I was before this committee last March, I said that I wanted to see Communists exposed. I still do. I'm heart and soul for it. An exposed Communist is an unarmed Communist. Expose them, but expose them in the traditional American manner.

But I believe that when this committee or any other agency undertakes to expose communism it must be scrupulous to avoid tying a red tag on innocent people by indiscriminate labeling.

It seems to me it is getting dangerously easy to call a man a Communist without proof or even reasonable suspicion. When a distinguished leader of the Republican Party in the United States Senate is accused of following the Communist Party line for introducing a housing bill, it is time, gentlemen, to give a little serious thought to the dangers of thoughtless smearing by gossip and hearsay.

Senator Robert Taft isn't going to worry about being called a Communist. But not every American is a Senator Taft who can properly ignore such an accusation. Most of us in America are just little people, and loose charges can hurt little people. They take away everything a man has—his livelihood, his reputation, and his personal dignity.

When just one man is falsely damned as a Communist in an hour like this when the Red issue is at white heat, no one of us is safe.

Gentlemen, I maintain that preservation of the rights of the individual is a proper duty for this Committee on Un-American Activities. This country's entire tradition is based on the principle that the individual is a higher power than the state; that the state owes its authority to the individual, and must treat him accordingly.

Expose communism, but don't put any American who isn't a Communist in a concentration camp of suspicion. We are not willing to give up our freedoms to save our freedoms.

I now come to my final point:

What are we going to do positively and constructively about combating communism? It isn't enough to be anti-Communist any more than it is to be antismallpox. You can still die from smallpox if you haven't used a serum against it. A positive program is the best antitoxin of the plague of communism.

Communism must have breeding grounds. Men and women who have a reasonable measure of opportunity aren't taken in by the prattle of Communists. Revolutions plotted by frustrated intellectuals at cocktail parties won't get anywhere if we wipe out the potential causes of communism. The most effective way is to make democracy work for greater opportunity, for greater participation, for greater security for all our people.

The real breeding ground of communism is in the slums. It is everywhere where people haven't enough to eat or enough to wear through no fault of their own. Communism hunts misery, feeds on misery, and profits by it.

Freedoms walk hand-in-hand with abundance. That has been the history of America. It has been the American story. It turned the eyes of the world to America, because America gave reality to freedom, plus abundance when it was still an idle daydream in the rest of the world.

We have been the greatest exporter of freedom, and the world is hungry for it. Today it needs our wheat and our fuel to stave off hunger and fight off cold, but hungry and cold as they may be, men always hunger for freedom.

We want to continue to practice and to export freedom.

If we fortify our democracy to lick want, we will lick communism—here and abroad. Communists can hang all the iron curtains they like, but they'll never be able to shut out the story of a land where freemen walk without fear and live with abundance.

[Applause.]

(The chairman pounding gavel.) . . .

Document Analysis

Speaking to HUAC, Johnston asserts four key points in his defense of Hollywood studios and their role in US society. He uses strong, forthright language to present his positions to the committee, showing neither a great willingness nor a complete refusal to assist in its investigations. This stance of avowed anti-Communism combined with strong support for independent expression and social welfare meant that Johnston could not himself be accused to subversive opinions even as he admonishes the committee for what he saw as its rabid excesses.

Johnston works systematically through four key points. The first of these rests on the claim that HUAC's actions have given the American people the impression that Hollywood—one of the nation's cultural centers—is rife with Communist influence, a suggestion he say is "grossly unfair" to the film industry and to the "patriotic, hardworking, decent citizens," who kept the movies humming. To that end, Johnston asks that the committee back away from its attack on the studios—a goal well in keeping with his role in protecting studios interests.

Johnston also requests that the committee give up some of the secrecy surrounding its suggestions that Hollywood films contain subversive elements by naming the offending films. "Unless this evidence is presented and we are given the chance to refute it in these public hearings, it is the obligation of the committee to absolve the industry from the charges against it," he argues. Later in his testimony, Johnston further argues that accusations based on the slightest perception of leftism threatened individual liberties and could unfairly ruin lives. Indeed, this type of unsupported attack was common of the anti-Communist craze of the era,

and ultimately proved to be its undoing.

Finally, Johnston moves on to two ideological points that applied to society at large. He argues that political intimidation—like that taking place, it is implied, by HUAC—is a threat to free speech, one of the bedrock American ideals. Private individuals have the right to dictate their own content, but also the responsibility to ensure that it is not a danger to liberty. In the same way, he asserts that government has the responsibility to fight Communism through positive measures, such as economic and social support for the poorest and least privileged members of society, as those with the greatest need were the most likely to seek refuge in political radicalism.

Essential Themes

Johnston offered a resounding condemnation of the accusations leveled by HUAC and the accompanying anti-Communist fervor of the Second Red Scare. However, despite his assertions that Hollywood was largely free of Communist influence, he did go on to support an internal measure shortly after his testimony in which Hollywood studios refused to give work to Communists; this also came to include those people who would not deny membership in the Community Party, who would not cooperate with HUAC's inquisition, or who were simply believed to have Communist sympathies or affiliations. The most famous of these blacklisted professionals were the "Hollywood Ten," a group of ten leftist directors and screenwriters who challenged HUAC's tactics and were ruled in contempt of Congress for their protest. Hollywood's blacklist of political radicals endured into the 1960s. Hollywood executives by these actions agreed that protecting the image of the movie industry, which Johnston noted risked being tarnished by HUAC's inquiries, outweighed protecting the free speech or political association rights of its individual employees.

Nevertheless, Johnston's complaints about the baseless nature of many of the accusations leveled at the Hollywood film industry resounded with those offered by critics of the Red Scare across political parties and ideologies. During the 1950s, HUAC's investigations gave way to those of Senator McCarthy, who accused numerous people of Communist involvement without cause or evidence. Fear of domestic subversion reached a fever pitch. Eventually, however, the histrionic and fruitless nature of McCarthy's investigations turned the American public against the anti-Communist witch hunts of the era.

Tensions between film and political free speech remain in the twenty-first century. In 2014, for example, Sony pulled the politically charged comedy The Interview from its scheduled wide release after hackers believed to represent North Korea, whose leader was trivialized in the film, interfered with studio operations and made threats against movie theaters that planned to show the picture. After drawing condemnations from the press, the public, and President Barack Obama, Sony reversed its position and released the film to independent theaters and digital services. Thus, the struggle among corporate interests, political appearances, and artistic expression continues.

—*Vanessa E. Vaughn, MA*

Bibliography and Additional Reading

Ceplair, Larry, & Steven Englund. *The Inquisition in Hollywood: Politics in the Film Community, 1930–1960.* Berkeley: U of California P, 1979. Print.

Dick, Bernard K. *Radical Innocence: A Critical Study of the Hollywood Ten.* Lexington: UP of Kentucky, 1983. Print.

"Eric Johnston Dies; Aided 3 Presidents." *New York Times* 23 Aug. 1963: 1. Print.

Gladchuck, John Joseph. *Hollywood and Anticommunism: HUAC and the Evolution of the Red Menace, 1935–1950.* 2006. Hoboken: Taylor, 2013. Digital file.

DOMESTIC AFFAIRS

The ongoing battle between labor and capital was renewed in the 1940s, albeit in less strident terms than had occurred in the 1920s and 30s. One key piece of legislation was the Taft-Hartley Act (1947), which sought to roll back some of the pro-labor measures of the previous decade, such as the National Labor Relations Act (Wagner Act) of 1937. Unions continued to grow in the 1940s, and strikes continued to occur—at least in the postwar period. There was increased pressure on the Truman administration to keep unions in check, particularly in light of allegations that many of them were corrupt and/or filled with communists.

The Taft-Hartley Act outlawed jurisdictional strikes (i.e., strikes over conflicts in representation among the unions), secondary boycotts (boycotts of those who do business with the target of a boycott), and closed shops (shops in which persons are required to join a particular union), among other things. It also required that unions limit their political contributions and supply annual financial reports to their members and to government regulators. It required that union leaders swear that they were not communists. Although President Truman felt that Taft-Hartley went too far and acted to veto it, the legislation ultimately passed over Truman's veto.

■ Reason Must Be Substituted for Force

Date: October 5, 1945
Author: Charles E. Wilson
Genre: speech

Summary Overview

To defeat the Axis powers in World War II, the United States needed the full cooperation of all its citizens. To bring people together in this way, the federal government established programs that curtailed the traditionally free market and instead imposed regulations on manufacturing industries that produced goods vital to the war effort.

Meanwhile, the organized labor movement, which had seen a decline in popularity from the early twentieth century, boomed during the war. The increased need for manufactured goods and raw materials meant more factory jobs and more opportunities for unions to grow their influence. Union leaders saw a great potential for power and opportunity to define the climate of postwar industry, but corporate leaders had different ideas. In 1945, Charles E. Wilson, president of the automobile manufacturer General Motors, gave a speech, scant weeks after the end of World War II, in which he encouraged industry leaders to reject the alleged aggression, coercion, and Communist influences of unions.

Defining Moment

The US organized labor movement grew significantly during the early part of the twentieth century, but declined in the early 1930s. By 1933, union membership numbered around three million, down from five million about ten years prior. Unions initially struggled to organize workers in rapidly growing mass production industries such as steel, textiles, mining, and automobile manufacturing. But the New Deal and pro-union policies of President Franklin D. Roosevelt's administration paved the way for a resurgence of labor organization. The National Industrial Recovery Act of 1933 authorized collective bargaining, and the National Labor Relations Act of 1935 (or Wagner Act) required employers to bargain in good faith with unions supported by the majority of their employees.

Around the same time, two of the biggest unions in the United States—the American Federation of Labor (AFL) and the Congress of Industrial Organizations (CIO)—aggressively expanded their membership and influence across the country. The CIO in particular largely focused on organizing unskilled workers and factories in modern industries.

World War II brought significant growth in manufacturing jobs, and a corresponding growth in union membership: by the end of the war, about 14.5 million workers—about 35 percent of the nation's employees—belonged to a union. However, the postwar climate proved to be difficult for the manufacturing industry. The decreased need for goods and raw materials related to the war effort brought significant layoffs, which led to walkouts and strikes across the country in 1945 and 1946. Fearing the power unions held to bring their facilities to a halt, many companies initially gave in to union demands.

On October 5, 1945, Charles E. Wilson, president of General Motors (GM), gave a speech during a luncheon of the Chicago Executives' Club. His speech discussed the direction the United States should take with respect to free markets following the end of World War II. Wilson and GM had a significant stake in how the people, the government, and the labor unions addressed this issue in both the near and long terms. Many of GM's suppliers had been shut down due to union strikes, and at the time of Wilson's speech, a strike vote was about to take place that had the potential to close GM's plants as well. Wilson noted that GM had finally returned to making cars after the government-imposed hiatus to produce goods for the war and its operations were already threatened by union action. America, he said, must decide whether to continue the government control established during the war and pursue a path of socialism, or to return to a free capitalist society.

Author Biography

Charles Erwin Wilson was born in Minerva, Ohio, on July 18, 1890. He graduated from the Carnegie Institute of Technology in 1909 as an electrical engineer and went to work for the Westinghouse Electric and Manufacturing Company. In April 1919, Wilson became chief engineer of the Remy Electric Company, a subsidiary of GM. He was promoted through the ranks of management, and in 1929 was named assistant to the president of GM. By May 1929, Wilson was made a vice president; in 1939, he became the executive vice president.

Wilson was appointed acting president of GM on June 18, 1940, and officially elected as the company's tenth president on January 6, 1941. He managed GM throughout the United States' involvement World War II and oversaw operations as the company shifted from manufacturing automobiles to manufacturing aircraft on orders from the federal government, and back again.

Wilson resigned his presidency at GM to become the US secretary of defense under President Dwight D. Eisenhower in January 1953. He served in that position until October 1957, when he resigned from office and rejoined GM as a director. Wilson remained an active associate of GM and its subsidiaries until his death on September 26, 1961.

HISTORICAL DOCUMENT

Mr. Stone, Members of the Chicago Executive's Club and guests: It is a pleasure to be here today. Of course, there are some representatives of Chicago over in Detroit today, and I wouldn't have minded too much seeing them perform. Since I promised to come over here, I thought I might try to call a few balls and strikes myself today. I have really taken a rather ambitious subject to talk to you men about—"America Arrives at the Fork in the Road."

The worst war in history has been over for a few weeks. Our fighting men have crushed our enemies with the huge quantities of weapons produced by American industry. A peace-loving and freedom-loving nation has successfully met the challenge of all-out war. But that is behind us. The aftermath of the war is now our problem.

War is terribly wasteful in blood and treasure. This one was especially so. It was not prosperity, even though to some it may have seemed to be and the immediate aftermath of such a war cannot be prosperity either. The clean up, the mopping up, the reconversion to peacetime activities still require hard work, patience, understanding and some sacrifice on the part of all of us.

About a year and one-half ago six Swedes, prominent in business and Government, made a special visit to this country. They came to Detroit and visited with us as part of their trip. Swedes have a long history as a democratic people—about 500 years—although their traditions and procedures are somewhat different than those of Anglo-Saxons. It was a most interesting visit. They could all speak English, although with a Minneapolis accent, and we seemed to understand each other quite well.

They were interested not only in the course of the war but in the degree of inflation that existed in our country, in the wage-price level, and in the post-war situation that was likely to exist.

I asked them about their country and the degree of inflation—how they had handled prices and wages. They said, "We have agreements with our unions that wages will go up half as fast as the cost of living." I said, "How did you happen to work that out?" They said, "We knew that we could not arm Sweden to defend itself and pay for all the extra costs of being a neutral while the world was on fin and at the same time raise our standard of living." I said, "Of course, that was very true, but how did you persuade the workmen that it was so?" They said, "Oh! Because they are Swedes first, and unionists second."

During the conversation with these same Swedish gentlemen, I happened to say that there is a danger of foreign: people not understanding Americans. Americans have almost dual personalities. At one time we all seemed to be idealists, at another time we seemed to be hard-headed realists—almost to the point where we would sell wooden nutmegs. Unless foreigners understand this, they may think we are inconsistent and unreliable. One of the Swedes said, "Oh, yes, we understand. That is what makes Americans so interesting and fascinating. That is really why we are here."

The Need of Sound Policies

The truth is, of course, that most Americans realize that important decisions, important policies must be morally and ethically sound, must respect the rights of individuals, but at the same time that they must be economically sound and practical and must be for the good of all the people.

If it had been considered politically expedient to do so, we could have paid for the full cost of the war as it progressed. We did not stock pile materials and munitions before the war. No one outside our country supplied us with the materials of war. We lived on what we had left over after the war effort, but the fact that we financed less than one-half of the cost of the war by taxation and more than half by the sale of Government bonds has created the problem of inflation.

As a result, the war to some has looked like prosperity. Perhaps for them it has been. But if that it so, they should realize that they got the breaks as compared to millions of other Americans. Even such synthetic and artificial prosperity could not have continued if the war had lasted much longer. And now, American industry and business cannot follow the example of Government and spend twice what it takes in. For industry and producers generally, money does not grow on trees, nor does it come from printing presses. Their money comes from customers; and to be healthy and even to continue to exist, a business must take in more than it spends. We cannot solve this postwar problem by juggling with the value of money. Only hard work, jobs, and efficient production and distribution will solve it. The current and wartime spending and the longer hours and work at higher wages during the war have created a postwar problem. During the last few days a tune has been running through my mind which came out of World War I—I am not going to attempt to sing it to you—but it goes like this, "How're You Going to Keep 'Em Down on the Farm After They've Seen Paree?"

Which Road to Travel?

We face an even bigger problem as a result of the war. During the war we accepted the draft, the hard work, the high taxes, restriction of business and of job opportunities, the rationing, all of the regimentation, the dictatorship, if I may call it that, required to focus the whole nation's effort on the single objective of winning the war. Now we face the reorganization of all our activities for peacetime living. The big question is which road will we take? Are we going back to a free system, regulated by competition,—to our American conception of the State being the servant of the people? Or are we going to try, or are we going to accept, a big change in our institutions? Are we going to go in for Government planning and an American version of collectivism somewhere between communism and fascism? Are we going to continue and increase the power of the Federal Government? Are we, the people, going to be servants of the State instead of the State the servant of the people?

If I thought the people of our country would be happier, if I thought they would be more prosperous, if I thought they would make more progress as human beings, in some form of socialistic state, then I would be a socialist—but I am sure they would not.

When I was a boy I lived in Ohio near a communist settlement called Zoar. It was about three miles from where I lived. It had been started by some Germans in 1817. The community had everything in common. To a great degree they substituted their communism for religion. For a time they seemed to prosper, but their leader (the so-called King of Zoar) passed on. The zeal of the founders was not inherited by the second and third generation. They tried to operate the society with a committee. There was constant bickering and the more ambitious tried to leave and take their share of the property, but they were not allowed to. Incidentally, it is much easier to get into a fascist or communist state than it is to get out. I understand that the World's Fair in Chicago in 1893 was indirectly responsible for the final dissolution of their society. Their committee of three came to the World's Fair. The others said, "Why didn't we all go—you must have spent our money." They tried to explain they had made the trip in the interests of all the members but they didn't get away with it. They then put the problem up to the Supreme Court of the United States which ruled that if all of the members agreed to dissolve then the property could be divided among the members. After several more years of bickering that is what was finally done. My father explained to me why communism would not work in our country. I could see some of the reasons why it would not even as a boy, so I never went through the stage that some young men do where in their impatience to make progress in a competitive society they develop socialistic ideas. Recently along with the rest of you I have seen state socialism developed on a tremendous and terrible scale. We have witnessed the tragic end of such a socialistic state as it developed into a monstrous Frankenstein that destroyed the wealth, debased the spirit of a great nation, and finally devoured its own masters.

Political Trends

It would be well for all of us to look at the matter squarely and to realize that any form of collectivism or state socialism must lead inevitably to dictatorship and the loss of individual liberty.

History and reason clearly prove that there is no way to operate a socialistic society or an economy based on socialism without dictatorship.

In such a society the negative incentives of fear and coercion replace the positive incentives of hope and ambition

The necessary regimentation of collectivism ultimately stifles the spiritual and material progress of the individual as well as the people as a whole.

Contrary to the American system where competition, free speech, and the free press forced the correction of mistakes made by individuals and groups, the collective system does not have within it the power to automatically correct its own mistakes. This is a very important point. But the dictators make you suffer with their mistakes and like it.

Collectivism—A Step Backward

The idea of collectivism or state socialism is thousands of years old but it was given a new impetus by Marx and others about one hundred years ago. Marxism, with its materialistic concepts, was and is directly opposed to the new liberal philosophy of the western world. In direct contrast to Marxism, our philosophy of government is based on the concepts of individual rights, and freedom from political tyranny and all other forms of arbitrary

interference with personal conduct. This liberal western philosophy is derived from the fundamental doctrines of Christianity. That is why, as collectivism develops, religious liberty is progressively curtailed. That has been the history all over the world. This is so importantly true, that in my opinion, a republic or a representative democracy will ultimately fail, unless a majority of its citizens truly believe in and practice the Christian principles of respect for the rights of others, self-discipline and moral restraint.

Any step toward adopting collectivism or state socialism is a great step backward, not merely to the horse and buggy days, but I fear to the elephants of the Hannibals and the chariots of the Caesars.

So I am still not a socialist. But I do recognize that our American system can be improved; that the problems created by this age of machines, by our big urban populations, by the great dependence we have on each other for the necessities of our daily lives must be dealt with realistically. The solutions for them, however, can and should be found within the principles of our Western civilization and not by the adoption of reactionary ideas coming from East of the Rhine.

Labor Unions too face a fork in the road. There is a provision in the Constitution of the United States that guarantees the right of citizens to petition the Government for the redress of grievances. This basic human right was recognized and expanded by Congress when it passed the National Labor Relations Act to promote industrial peace and guarantee workmen the right to present their grievances, and collectively bargain regarding them. Unfortunately, Congress did not spell out the obligations and responsibility that go with this right and power.

Demands Rule of Reason

The monopolistic power of Unions is now being used as a tool of aggression to promote industrial strife, rather than to safeguard the rights and equities of workmen. The public interest is being completely overlooked. The idea that a few thousand truck drivers can shut off the gasoline supply of the people; that a few thousand elevator operators can keep hundreds of thousands of New Yorkers from getting to their work; that the stockholders and management of a big utility company and their employees, could engage in economic warfare and shut off the power and light of one of our big cities certainly cannot be tolerated in our modern society. The rule of reason must be substituted for the rule of force, especially when the public interest is at stake. Sound procedures for solving such problems must be worked out without jeopardizing the fundamental rights and responsibilities of all parties involved.

So, unions too must now decide which way they are going to go. Will they continue to try to substitute force and coercion for the rule of reason and respect for the rights of others? Or will they take a constructive position in our free competitive society?

Producing Ability Questioned

Incidentally our automobile plants are about ready to go. We would like to have been better prepared for peace but the war requirements for men and material did not make this possible. We made a few cars of each of our makes this week, but the plants of many of our important suppliers are closed by strikes. We will soon run out of necessary parts.

The threat has been made that following the strike vote, which is to be taken October 24th, all General Motors plants will be closed and General Motors and its employees made a victim of the union's new labor blockade policy. Our current problems are not only how much will cars cost and then what they will sell for but whether we will be able to produce any cars at all for many months.

Critical Situation Ahead

And so today America arrives at the fork in the road. Perhaps we would have faced this same fork sometime in the future even though there had been no war. As I have said, the ideologies of our Western civilization and those of collectivism or state socialism are in important conflict. The necessary regimentation of the war effort has brought us to that fork now.

Three generations ago our forefathers decided we could not continue as a nation half slave and half free. We now face another critical situation—this generation will have to decide which way we are to go. We will find that we cannot continue as a nation half collectivist and half free.

Document Analysis

Charles E. Wilson states that World War II ended several weeks prior, but the cleanup of its aftermath has just begun. This effort will require "hard work, patience, understanding and some sacrifice" on everyone's part, and the nation has reached a "fork in the road" where the future must be decided. He observes that during the war, Americans accepted a great deal of government intervention, including higher taxes, the draft, regulation of jobs and manufacturing, rations, and even the "dictatorship" of focusing the entire nation's efforts on winning the war. But as society reorganizes itself for peacetime life, Americans must decide which direction they will pursue. In particular, he asks whether the United States will return to a free market system regulated by competition, or continue to accept increased federal government regulation of business and life.

Wilson concludes that Americans will not be happy as "servants of the State." Instead, he argues, the government should be the servant of the people. He recalls his childhood experience growing up in Ohio near a Communist settlement called Zoar and describes how that society unraveled after its original leader died and its second-generation leaders could not agree on how to share the community's wealth. Wilson cites this as an example of why Communism cannot work in the United States. He then draws parallels to the recent war, explaining that it was an example of socialism's failure on the national scale.

Based on his experiences, Wilson states that "any form of collectivism or state socialism must lead inevitably to dictatorship and the loss of individual liberty." He asserts his support for a "liberal western philosophy" based on political freedom, individual rights, and no interference with personal conduct, concepts he sees as in direct opposition to Marxism. Wilson claims the Western system of government is derived from the principles of Christianity, while collectivism curtails religious freedom.

Finally, Wilson directly discusses labor unions, claiming that they are being used "as a tool of aggression to promote industrial strife, rather than to safeguard the rights and equities of workmen." He asserts that strikes are an unfair form of coercion and go against the public interest, with the potential to disrupt the lives of millions of people through economic warfare. Wilson admits that society can find ways to improve in the face of increased industrialization, but argues that such advances should be achieved with reason rather than force. Unions, too, must decide how to proceed for the future: continue their coercive ways or "take a constructive position in our free competitive society."

Essential Themes

The tone of Wilson's speech reflects the concerns of business executives during the post-World War II period, particularly those in the manufacturing sector. Fearful of the significant power labor unions possessed to cause a complete business shutdown, many executives sought ways to turn public opinion against organized labor. Union opponents equated labor unions with socialism, drawing on the villainous image of German National Socialism and fear of the rising power of Communism in the Soviet Union. After the defeat of the Nazis in World War II, Communists quickly became the main enemy of the United States, and the conflict between capitalism and Communism (and, by association, socialism) was a defining feature of the postwar era, leading directly to the Cold War.

Wilson's anti-Communist and anti-union position is unsurprising, given that GM stood to lose money if labor unions gained influence. Walkouts and strikes were taking place all over the country, and GM could be next to face the pressure of collective bargaining under threat of strike. Wilson's speech was delivered to a group of fellow business executives in similar positions. The theme of business owners in conflict with employees over wages, rights, and regulation has always been at the core of the labor movement.

By 1947, public opinion had largely turned against unions once again, due in part to rhetoric such as Wilson's speech. Organized labor also lost federal government support; the Taft-Hartley Act, enacted over presidential veto in June 1947, amended the pro-labor Wagner Act of 1935 in a way that severely restricted union activity. Employers became increasingly hostile toward union organizers, and there were reports of employees being threatened, intimidated, and beaten for communicating with union representatives.

As the public and government took increasingly anti-union stances, the unions themselves turned against one another. The Taft-Hartley Act contained provisions requiring union leaders to sign anti-Communist affidavits, and each union used these provisions to challenge rival unions whose leaders refused to sign the pledges. Larger unions, such as the CIO and AFL, even engaged in "red baiting" within their own ranks, expelling member unions believed to have strong ties to Communists. Combined with the shift of American workers from manufacturing to office jobs, these factors led to downturns in union membership and influence during the postwar years.

—*Tracey M. DiLascio, JD*

Bibliography and Additional Reading

Dubofsky, Melvyn, & Foster Rhea Dulles. *Labor in America: A History.* 8th ed. Wheeling: Harlan, 2010. Print.

"Generations of GM History: Wilson, Charles E." *GM Heritage Center.* General Motors, 2014. Web. 21 Jan 2015.

Herman, Arthur. *Freedom's Forge: How American Business Produced Victory in World War II.* New York: Random, 2012. Print.

"Labor Unions during the New Depression and New Deal." *Library of Congress.* Lib. of Congress, 2014. Web. 21 Jan 2015.

Wall, Wendy. "Anti-Communism in the 1950s." *Gilder Lehrman Institute of American History.* Gilder Lehrman Inst. of American History, 2015. Web. 21 Jan 2015.

■ Twenty-Second Amendment

Date: March 21, 1947
Author: US Congress
Genre: government document

Summary Overview

Passed in 1947 and ratified about four years later, the Twenty-Second Amendment to the US Constitution established an official term limit for the nation's presidents. Prior to this amendment's ratification, most US chief executives had adhered to the precedent set by first president George Washington of serving no more than two terms in office. The Constitution lacked any formal guidance on this issue, however, and President Franklin D. Roosevelt had successfully stood for election to four consecutive terms during the 1930s and early 1940s. Although Roosevelt had been fairly elected in each instance and no serious accusations emerged that his long tenure in office had contributed to abuse of power, a federal commission recommended the addition of an amendment establishing the two-term limit as part of a series of suggestions aimed at streamlining government operations. The states ratified the amendment with little fanfare, and it has remained largely uncontroversial.

Defining Moment

The Framers of the US Constitution did not all agree on the best length of time for any given person to serve as the nation's president. Many early American leaders were wary of granting too much power to any one person, fearful that the liberty won by the American Revolution would be endangered by allowing an American monarch to come to power. The nation's first plan for government, the Articles of Confederation, had not allowed for an executive branch at all, assigning the office of "president" to the head of the national Congress. However, by the time of the writing of the Constitution, the weaknesses of the central government had become clear, and the Framers decided to create an office (the presidency) to oversee the implementation of government laws and policies.

As debates over ratification raged in the state legislatures and the press, Federalists and Anti-Federalists clashed over the nature and power of the proposed chief executive. Anti-Federalists argued that a president—especially one not subject to any form of term limits—was akin to the British king. Federalists rejected this claim, and the Constitution was ratified with the office of the presidency intact.

Washington—the first president to serve under the Constitution—declined to run for a third term. This decision set a precedent for a two-term presidency that was strongly endorsed by the nation's third president, Thomas Jefferson, who also refused to seek a third term, but did so on grounds more directly related to political philosophy. Only a few outliers challenged the two-term precedent. For example, Theodore Roosevelt became president upon the assassination of William McKinley in 1901 and served nearly all of McKinley's elected term before winning election in his own right in 1904. After leaving office in 1909, he became frustrated with the policies of his successor William Howard Taft and mounted an unsuccessful campaign at the top of the ticket for the Progressive Party in 1912.

Therefore, not until 1940 did a president successfully attain a third term. During the waning years of his second term in the late 1930s, President Roosevelt kept quiet about his intentions for the election of 1940. Roosevelt may have wished to avoid weakening his position in dealing with Congress to address the economic problems of the Great Depression; he may also have wanted to show strength in the face of the rising Axis threat in Europe. Although historians disagree on Roosevelt's motivations in accepting a nomination for a third term in 1940, voters resoundingly returned Roosevelt to the office at the polls. They did so again in 1944, when Roosevelt ran for a fourth term despite his declining health.

Author Biography

First established in 1947, the Commission on Orga-

195

nization of the Executive Branch of the Government was a nonpartisan committee headed by former Republican president Herbert Hoover, a long-time civil servant who believed in the efficacy of small government. Commonly known as the Hoover Commission, the body studied ways to reduce bureaucracy, increase efficiency, and generally improve the operations of the executive branch to meet the needs of the post–World War II United States. Between 1947 and 1949, the commission made dozens of recommendations to then president Harry S. Truman, another proponent of administrative efficiency. Among the first of these recommendations was the introduction of term limits for the presidency. This idea found favor with the Republican Congress that had been elected in 1946, and the federal legislature sent the amendments to the states for ratification short weeks after its members took office. Ratification was completed in February 1951.

HISTORICAL DOCUMENT

AMENDMENT XXII

SECTION 1.

No person shall be elected to the office of the President more than twice, and no person who has held the office of President, or acted as President, for more than two years of a term to which some other person was elected President shall be elected to the office of the President more than once. But this article shall not apply to any person holding the office of President when this article was proposed by the Congress, and shall not prevent any person who may be holding the office of President, or acting as President, during the term within which this article becomes operative from holding the office of President or acting as President during the remainder of such term.

SECTION 2.

This article shall be inoperative unless it shall have been ratified as an amendment to the Constitution by the legislatures of three-fourths of the several states within seven years from the date of its submission to the states by the Congress.

GLOSSARY

inoperative: not operative; not in operation; without effect

ratified: to confirm by expressing consent, approval or formal sanction

Document Analysis

Using clear and simple language, the Twenty-Second Amendment firmly formalizes the traditional two-term cap on the period during which any single person can serve as US president. The heart of the amendment lies in the opening statement of section 1, which stipulates that no one "shall be elected to the office of the President more than twice." Further, section 1 seeks to prevent the creation of loopholes in the amendment's application by establishing a procedure for the relatively uncommon instances in which a vice president ascends to the presidency in the event of the death, resignation, or incapacitation of the elected chief executive. The amendment asserts that "no person who has held the office of President, or acted as President, for more than two years of a term" to which someone else was actually elected can run for office twice, implying that a person who rose to the presidency at the midpoint of an unexpired term could stand for election in his or her own right for a total term in office of ten years. Because vice presidents often act briefly in the capacity of president when the elected chief is unable—for example, during a surgical procedure—this limit allows for needed flexibility in conducting governmental operations, while maintaining the intent of the amendment. The amendment also provides an exemption for the person who was president or acting as president at the time of its proposal and during the presidential term that the amendment becomes effective.

Section 2 establishes a time limit for full ratification of the amendment. Because the Constitution places no set time limit on the period between which an amendment can be sent for ratification and final approval, the time lapse can be quite significant; the Twenty-Seventh Amendment, for example, was approved by Congress in 1789, but did not garner enough support from the states for ratification until 1992. The Eighteenth, Twentieth, and Twenty-First Amendments contain similar language.

Essential Themes

Likely because of the long-standing US presidential tradition of declining to seek election to any term beyond the second, the Twenty-Second Amendment has been generally accepted by the US electorate and office holders without a great deal of protest. Occasionally, representatives or senators of both political parties have called on the US Congress to introduce a measure repealing the amendment. These efforts, however, have never proceeded to a point of serious consideration. Objections to the amendment rest mostly on its limitation of absolute democracy—voters may not always reelect a popular president whom they otherwise would have—and on its creation of so-called "lame duck" presidents, who find it difficult to garner political support for policies in their second terms. Because such presidents cannot constitutionally stand for reelection, political jockeying within a sitting chief executive's own party to receive support for a presidential nomination in the following election can serve as a distraction from the work of governing.

As of 2014, only a handful of individuals have been directly affected by the amendment's provisions: Dwight D. Eisenhower, the first president elected after ratification; Richard M. Nixon, who resigned in disgrace partway through his second elective term; Ronald Reagan, who served two terms in the 1980s; Bill Clinton, a two-term president who served the following decade; and two twenty-first century presidents, Republican George W. Bush and Democrat Barack Obama.

Under the terms of the amendment, incumbent chief executive Truman was exempt from the two-term limit because he was in office when the amendment was proposed as well as when it was enacted. Though Truman had the right to run for a third term in 1952, even after having served most of Roosevelt's elected fourth term and retaining the office in the 1948 election, he declined to run after suffering an early primary defeat. Lyndon B. Johnson would also have been eligible to stand for reelection in 1968 after advancing from the vice presidency to serve part of assassinated president John F. Kennedy's unexpired term in 1963 and winning election in his own right the following year because his total term in office would have remained within the ten-year cap, but Johnson opted not to run in 1968.

The Twenty-Second Amendment has additionally established a constitutional precedent for the usage of term limits that has led to calls for a similar measure to be created for other elected federal officials, particularly US representatives and senators. During the mid-1990s, polls suggested that between two-thirds and three-quarters of Americans would support the passage of a similar amendment placing term limits on members of Congress. Roughly equivalent majorities expressed support for such a measure nearly two decades later. Political gridlock and acrimony, analysts concluded, contributed to the popular belief that term limits helped the government work more effectively—an opinion with which the Hoover Commission would likely have agreed.

—*Vanessa E. Vaughn, MA*

Bibliography and Additional Reading

"Americans Call for Term Limits, End to Electoral College." *Gallup.com*. Gallup, Inc., 18 Jan. 2013. Web. 12 Dec. 2014.

Caress, Stanley M., & Todd T. Kunioka. *Term Limits and Their Consequences: The Aftermath of Legislative Reform*. Albany: State U of New York P, 2012. Print.

Korzi, Michael J. *Presidential Term Limits in American History: Power, Principles, and Politics*. College Station: Texas A&M U Press, 2013. Print.

■ Taft-Hartley Act

Date: June 23, 1947
Author: US Congress
Genre: government document

Summary Overview

Although the US economy roared to life after the Great Depression during World War II, the immediate postwar period was marked by short-term economic decline, labor unrest, and a wave of highly publicized strikes. US support for labor interests weakened, and anti-labor politicians sought to formally limit labor power. Passed by the Republican-controlled US Congress over the veto of President Harry S. Truman, the Labor-Management Relations Act, commonly called the Taft-Hartley Act, modified portions of the 1935 National Labor Relations Act in order to limit the power of labor unions. Among the act's most significant provisions were the elimination of the closed shop (a type of labor agreement that required employers to hire only union members) and the placement of new limitations on unions' rights to strike. Called the "slave labor act" by Truman and other opponents, the act succeeded in dampening some of labor's influence, but also gave Truman a political rallying point that helped shape his Fair Deal domestic agenda.

Defining Moment

The organized labor movement began in the United States with the rise of industrialization in the 1800s. Early labor leaders sought to secure the rights for workers to organize and to bargain collectively, often to achieve aims such as fair wages, reduced working hours, or improved workplace safety. Disputes between labor and management occurred frequently, and workers' strikes and demonstrations sometimes turned violent as tensions rose. During an era when the federal government supported a policy of laissez-faire economics, it avoiding passing legislation that helped the labor cause and even intervened to break up strikes. World War I and the strength of the 1920s economy temporarily halted the rise of labor, and union membership dropped during the 1920s.

By the New Deal era, however, the federal government's interest in supporting labor-management relations had grown. As part of its overall program to boost the slumping US economy during the Depression, the administration of President Franklin D. Roosevelt supported the passage of the National Labor Relations Act—commonly known as the Wagner Act—in 1935. This legislation gave federal protection to the rights of workers to organize into unions and established the National Labor Relations Board (NLRB) as a final mediator in disputes between management and labor. The passage of the Wagner Act gave labor unions unprecedented power in US workplaces, and the percentage of unionized workers nationwide leapt from about 7 percent in the mid-1930s to over 20 percent by the mid-1940s. Labor also became an important ally of the Democratic Party as part of Roosevelt's New Deal coalition.

During World War II, the federal government restricted labor rights because of wartime needs, implementing wage freezes, limitations on striking, and increased working hours. The production focus on war needs resulted in shortages of consumer goods and price hikes, but overall, increased production and employment helped the nation shake off the doldrums of the Depression. When the war ended, however, the economic boom ended. Industrial production declined, just as millions of soldiers demobilized and returned home. Americans feared this combination would lead to widespread unemployment and economic turmoil.

These worries proved largely unfounded. However, labor leaders sought to reassert their influence to attain concessions such as pay raises that they believed were now overdue to workers. Waves of peaceful but large-scale strikes spread across the nation. At the same time, rising tensions with the Soviet Union generated fears of Communist subversion at home. Anti-labor sentiment grew among the American populace amid popular opposition to the postwar strikes and worry that labor leaders sympathized with Communist or socialist principles. In 1946, voters ended the longtime Democratic control of the US Congress and voted in Republican candidates who campaigned against the big-government and prolabor policies of the past. The stage was set for new legislative action limiting the perceived excesses of labor power.

Author Biography

The Taft-Hartley Act was sponsored by two Republicans, US Senator Robert Taft of Ohio and Representative Fred A. Hartley, Jr. of New Jersey. The son of Progressive-era president William Howard Taft, the younger Taft won election to the US Congress in 1938 and soon established himself as a leading conservative voice widely seen as a contender for the presidency. After Republicans gained control of Congress in the 1946 midterm elections, Taft became chair of the Senate's Labor and Public Welfare Committee and soon moved to introduce a bill amending the Wagner Act. At the same time, Hartley assumed leadership of the House's Education and Labor Committee and took action on his own bill to limit labor influence. He was a congressional veteran, having first won election to the House in 1928, and it was perhaps this political experience that spurred him to draft a bill harsher than Taft's; Hartley later claimed he did so in order to make the resulting compromise bill seem less drastic.

HISTORICAL DOCUMENT

LABOR MANAGEMENT RELATIONS ACT

Also cited LMRA; 29 U.S.C. Sec. Sec. 141-197
[Title 29, Chapter 7, United States Code]
short title and declaration of policy

Section 1. [Sec. 141.] (a) This Act [chapter] may be cited as the "Labor Management Relations Act, 1947." [Also known as the "Taft-Hartley Act."]

(b) Industrial strife which interferes with the normal flow of commerce and with the full production of articles and commodities for commerce, can be avoided or substantially minimized if employers, employees, and labor organizations each recognize under law one another's legitimate rights in their relations with each other, and above all recognize under law that neither party has any right in its relations with any other to engage in acts or practices which jeopardize

the public health, safety, or interest.

It is the purpose and policy of this Act [chapter], in order to promote the full flow of commerce, to prescribe the legitimate rights of both employees and employers in their relations affecting commerce, to provide orderly and peaceful procedures for preventing the interference by either with the legitimate rights of the other, to protect the rights of individual employees in their relations with labor organizations whose activities affect commerce, to define and proscribe practices on the part of

labor and management which affect commerce and are inimical to the general welfare, and to protect the rights of the public in connection with labor disputes affecting commerce.

TITLE I, Amendments to
NATIONAL LABOR RELATIONS ACT
29 U.S.C. Sec. Sec. 151–169 (printed above)

TITLE II

[Title 29, Chapter 7, Subchapter III, United States Code]

Conciliation of Labor Disputes in Industries Affecting Commerce; National Emergencies

Sec. 201. [Sec. 171. Declaration of purpose and policy] It is the policy of the United States that—

(a) sound and stable industrial peace and the advancement of the general welfare, health, and safety of the Nation and of the best interest of employers and employees can most satisfactorily be secured by the settlement of issues between employers and employees through the processes of conference and collective bargaining between employers and the representatives of their employees;

(b) the settlement of issues between employers and employees through collective bargaining may by advanced by making available full and adequate governmental facilities for conciliation, mediation, and volun tary arbitration to aid and encourage employers and the representatives of their employees to reach and maintain agreements concerning rates of pay, hours, and working conditions, and to make all reasonable efforts to settle their differences by mutual agreement reached through conferences and collective bargaining or by such methods as may be provided for in any applicable agreement for the settlement of disputes; and

(c) certain controversies which arise between parties to collective-bargaining agreements may be avoided or minimized by making available full and adequate governmental facilities for furnishing assistance to employers and the representatives of their employees in formulating for inclusion within such agreements provision for adequate notice of any proposed changes in the terms of such agreements, for the final adjustment of grievances or questions regarding the application or interpretation of such agreements, and other provisions designed to prevent the subsequent arising of such controversies.

Sec. 202. [Sec. 172. Federal Mediation and Conciliation Service]

(a) [Creation; appointment of Director] There is created an independent agency to be known as the Federal Mediation and Conciliation Service (herein referred to as the "Service," except that for sixty days after June 23, 1947, such term shall refer to the Conciliation Service of the Department of Labor). The Service shall be under the direction of a Federal Mediation and Conciliation Director (hereinafter referred to as the "Director"), who shall be appointed by the President by and with the advice and consent of the Senate. The Director shall not engage in any other business, vocation, or employment.

(b) [Appointment of officers and employees; expenditures for supplies, facilities, and services] The Director is authorized, subject to the civil service laws, to appoint such clerical and other personnel as may be necessary for the execution of the functions of the Service, and shall fix their compensation in accordance with sections 5101 to 5115 and sections 5331 to 5338 of title 5, United States Code [chapter 51 and subchapter III of chapter 53 of title 5], and may, without regard to the provisions of the civil service laws, appoint such conciliators and mediators as may be necessary to carry out the functions of the Service. The Director is authorized to make such expenditures for supplies, facilities, and ser-

vices as he deems necessary. Such expenditures shall be allowed and paid upon presentation of itemized vouchers therefor approved by the Director or by any employee designated by him for that purpose.

(c) [Principal and regional offices; delegation of authority by Director; annual report to Congress] The principal office of the Service shall be in the District of Columbia, but the Director may establish regional offices convenient to localities in which labor controversies are likely to arise. The Director may by order, subject to revocation at any time, delegate any authority and discretion conferred upon him by this Act [chapter] to any regional director, or other officer or employee of the Service. The Director may establish suitable procedures for cooperation with State and local mediation agencies. The Director shall make an annual report in writing to Congress at the end of the fiscal year.

(d) [Transfer of all mediation and conciliation services to Service; effective date; pending proceedings unaffected] All mediation and conciliation functions of the Secretary of Labor or the United States Conciliation Service under section 51 [repealed] of title 29, United States Code [this title], and all functions of the United States Conciliation Service under any other law are transferred to the Federal Mediation and Conciliation Service, together with the personnel and records of the United States Conciliation Service. Such transfer shall take effect upon the sixtieth day after June 23, 1947. Such transfer shall not affect any proceedings pending before the United States Conciliation Service or any certification, order, rule, or regulation theretofore made by it or by the Secretary of Labor. The Director and the Service shall not be subject in any way to the jurisdiction or authority of the Secretary of Labor or any official or division of the Department of Labor.

Functions of the Service

Sec. 203. [Sec. 173. Functions of Service] (a) [Settlement of disputes through conciliation and mediation] It shall be the duty of the Service, in order to prevent or minimize interruptions of the free flow of commerce growing out of labor disputes, to assist parties to labor disputes in industries affecting commerce to settle such disputes through conciliation and mediation.

(b) [Intervention on motion of Service or request of parties; avoidance of mediation of minor disputes] The Service may proffer its services in any labor dispute in any industry affecting commerce, either upon its own motion or upon the request of one or more of the parties to the dispute, whenever in its judgment such dispute threatens to cause a substantial interruption of commerce. The Director and the Service are directed to avoid attempting to mediate disputes which would have only a minor effect on interstate commerce if State or other conciliation services are available to the parties. Whenever the Service does proffer its services in any dispute, it shall be the duty of the Service promptly to put itself in communication with the parties and to use its best efforts, by mediation and conciliation, to bring them to agreement.

(c) [Settlement of disputes by other means upon failure of conciliation] If the Director is not able to bring the parties to agreement by conciliation within a reasonable time, he shall seek to induce the parties voluntarily to seek other means of settling the dispute without resort to strike, lockout, or other coercion, including submission to the employees in the bargaining unit of the employer's last offer of settlement for approval or rejection in a secret ballot. The failure or refusal of either party to agree to any procedure suggested by the Director shall not be deemed a violation of any duty or obligation imposed by this Act [chapter].

(d) [Use of conciliation and mediation services as last resort] Final adjustment by a method agreed upon by the parties is declared to be the desirable method for settlement of grievance disputes arising over the application or interpretation of an existing collective-bargaining agreement. The Service is directed to make its conciliation and mediation services available in the settlement of such grievance disputes only as a last resort and in exceptional cases.

(e) [Encouragement and support of establishment and operation of joint labor management activities conducted by committees] The Service is authorized and directed to encourage and support the establishment and operation of joint labor management activities conducted by plant, area, and industrywide committees designed to improve labor management relationships, job security and organizational effectiveness, in accor-

dance with the provisions of section 205A [section 175a of this title].

[Pub. L. 95–524, Sec. 6(c)(1), Oct. 27, 1978, 92 Stat. 2020, added subsec. (e).]

(f) [Use of alternative means of dispute resolution procedures; assignment of neutrals and arbitrators] The Service may make its services available to Federal agencies to aid in the resolution of disputes under the provisions of subchapter IV of chapter 5 of title 5. Functions performed by the Service may include assisting parties to disputes related to administrative programs, training persons in skills and procedures employed in alternative means of dispute resolution, and furnishing officers and employees of the Service to act as neutrals. Only officers and employees who are qualified in accordance with section 573 of title 5 may be assigned to act as neutrals. The Service shall consult with the Administrative Conference of the United States and other agencies in maintaining rosters of neutrals and arbitrators, and to adopt such procedures and rules as are necessary to carry out the services authorized in this subsection.

[As amended Nov. 15, 1990, Pub. L. 101–552, Sec. 7, 104 Stat. 2746; Aug. 26, 1992, Pub. L. 102–354, Sec. 5(b)(5), 106 Stat. 946.]

[It appears that Sec. 173(f) terminated on October 1, 1995, pursuant to a sunset provision. As of the date of this publication, it does not appear that it was reenacted. Persons having an interest in the application of Sec. 173(f) to proceedings commencing after October 1, 1995, should check to see whether the provision was renewed.]

Sec. 204. [Sec. 174. Co-equal obligations of employees, their representatives, and management to minimize labor disputes] (a) In order to prevent or minimize interruptions of the free flow of commerce growing out of labor disputes, employers and employees and their representatives, in any industry affecting commerce, shall—

(1) exert every reasonable effort to make and maintain agreements concerning rates of pay, hours, and working conditions, including provision for adequate notice of any proposed change in the terms of such agreements;

(2) whenever a dispute arises over the terms or application of a collective-bargaining agreement and a conference is requested by a party or prospective party thereto, arrange promptly for such a conference to be held and endeavor in such conference to settle such dispute expeditiously; and

(3) in case such dispute is not settled by conference, participate fully and promptly in such meetings as may be undertaken by the Service under this Act [chapter] for the purpose of aiding in a settlement of the dispute.

Sec. 205. [Sec. 175. National Labor-Management Panel; creation and composition; appointment, tenure, and compensation; duties] (a) There is created a National Labor-Management Panel which shall be composed of twelve members appointed by the President, six of whom shall be elected from among persons outstanding in the field of management and six of whom shall be selected from among persons outstanding in the field of labor. Each member shall hold office for a term of three years, except that any member appointed to fill a vacancy occurring prior to the expiration of the term for which his predecessor was appointed shall be appointed for the remainder of such term, and the terms of office of the members first taking office shall expire, as designated by the President at the time of appointment, four at the end of the first year, four at the end of the second year, and four at the end of the third year after the date of appointment. Members of the panel, when serving on business of the panel, shall be paid compensation at the rate of $25 per day, and shall also be entitled to receive an allowance for actual and necessary travel and subsistence expenses while so serving away from their places of residence.

(b) It shall be the duty of the panel, at the request of the Director, to advise in the avoidance of industrial controversies and the manner in which mediation and voluntary adjustment shall be administered, particularly with reference to controversies affecting the general welfare of the country.

Sec. 205A. [Sec. 175a. Assistance to plant, area, and industrywide labor management committees]

(a) [Establishment and operation of plant, area, and industrywide committees] (1) The Service is authorized and directed to provide assistance in the establishment and operation of plant, area and industrywide labor management committees which—

(A) have been organized jointly by employers and labor organizations representing employees in that plant, area, or industry; and

(B) are established for the purpose of improving labor management relationships, job security, organizational effectiveness, enhancing economic development or involving workers in decisions affecting their jobs including improving communication with respect to subjects of mutual interest and concern.

(2) The Service is authorized and directed to enter into contracts and to make grants, where necessary or appropriate, to fulfill its responsibilities under this section.

(b) [Restrictions on grants, contracts, or other assistance] (1) No grant may be made, no contract may be entered into and no other assistance may be provided under the provisions of this section to a plant labor management committee unless the employees in that plant are represented by a labor organization and there is in effect at that plant a collective bargaining agreement.

(2) No grant may be made, no contract may be entered into and no other assistance may be provided under the provisions of this section to an area or industrywide labor management committee unless its participants include any labor organizations certified or recognized as the representative of the employees of an employer participating in such committee. Nothing in this clause shall prohibit participation in an area or industrywide committee by an employer whose employees are not represented by a labor organization.

(3) No grant may be made under the provisions of this section to any labor management committee which the Service finds to have as one of its purposes the discouragement of the exercise of rights contained in section 7 of the National Labor Relations Act (29 U.S.C. Sec. 157) [section 157 of this title], or the interference with collective bargaining in any plant, or industry.

(c) [Establishment of office] The Service shall carry out the provisions of this section through an office established for that purpose.

(d) [Authorization of appropriations] There are authorized to be appropriated to carry out the provisions of this section $10,000,000 for the fiscal year 1979, and such sums as may be necessary thereafter.

[Pub. L. 9–524, Sec. 6(c)(2), Oct. 27, 1978, 92 Stat. 2020, added Sec. 205A.]

National Emergencies

Sec. 206. [Sec. 176. Appointment of board of inquiry by President; report; contents; filing with Service] Whenever in the opinion of the President of the United States, a threatened or actual strike or lockout affecting an entire industry or a substantial part thereof engaged in trade, commerce, transportation, transmission, or communication among the several States or with foreign nations, or engaged in the production of goods for commerce, will, if permitted to occur or to continue, imperil

the national health or safety, he may appoint a board of inquiry to inquire into the issues involved in the dispute and to make a written report to him within such time as he shall prescribe. Such report shall include a statement of the facts with respect to the dispute, including each party's statement of its position but shall not contain any recommendations. The President shall file a copy of such report with the Service and shall make its contents available to the public.

Sec. 207. [Sec. 177. Board of inquiry]

(a) [Composition] A board of inquiry shall be composed of a chairman and such other members as the President shall determine, and shall have power to sit and act in any place within the United States and to conduct such hearings either in public or in private, as it may deem necessary or proper, to ascertain the facts with respect to the causes and circumstances of the dispute.

(b) [Compensation] Members of a board of inquiry shall receive compensation at the rate of $50 for each day actually spent by them in the work of the board, together with necessary travel and subsistence expenses.

(c) [Powers of discovery] For the purpose of any hearing or inquiry conducted by any board appointed under this title [29 U.S.C.S. Sec. Sec. 171–183], the provisions of sections 9 and 10 (relating to the attendance of witnesses and the production of books, papers, and documents) of the Federal Trade Commission Act of September 16 [26], 1914, as amended (U.S.C. [19], title 15, secs. 49 and 50, as amended), are hereby made applicable to the powers and duties of such board. (June

23, 1947, ch 120 Title II, Sec. 61 Stat. 155.)

Sec. 208. [Sec. 178. Injunctions during national emergency]

(a) [Petition to district court by Attorney General on direction of President] Upon receiving a report from a board of inquiry the President may direct the Attorney General to petition any district court of the United States having jurisdiction of the parties to enjoin such strike or lockout or the continuing thereof, and if the court finds that such threatened or actual strike or lockout—

(i) affects an entire industry or a substantial part thereof engaged in trade, commerce, transportation, transmission, or communication among the several States or with foreign nations, or engaged in the production of goods for commerce; and

(ii) if permitted to occur or to continue, will imperil the national health or safety, it shall have jurisdiction to enjoin any such strike or lockout, or the continuing thereof, and to make such other orders

as may be appropriate.

(b) [Inapplicability of chapter 6] In any case, the provisions of sections 101 to 115 of title 29, United States Code [chapter 6 of this title] [known as the "Norris-LaGuardia Act"] shall not be applicable.

(c) [Review of orders] The order or orders of the court shall be subject to review by the appropriate circuit court of appeals [court of appeals] and by the Supreme Court upon writ of certiorari or certification as provided in sections 239 and 240 of the Judicial Code, as amended (U.S.C., title 29, secs. 346 and 347). (June 23, 1947, ch 120, Title II Sec. 208, 61 Stat. 155.)

Sec. 209. [Sec. 179. Injunctions during national emergency; adjustment efforts by parties during injunction period]

(a) [Assistance of Service; acceptance of Service's proposed settlement] Whenever a district court has issued an order under section 208 [section 178 of this title] enjoining acts or practices which imperil or threaten to imperil the national health or safety, it shall be the duty of the parties to the labor dispute giving rise to such order to make every effort to adjust and settle their differences, with the assistance of the Service created by this Act [chapter]. Neither party shall be under any duty to accept, in whole or in part, any proposal of settlement made by the Service.

(b) [Reconvening of board of inquiry; report by board; contents; secret ballot of employees by National Labor Relations Board; certification of results to Attorney General] Upon the issuance of such order, the President shall reconvene the board of inquiry which has previously reported with respect to the dispute. At the end of a sixty-day period (unless the dispute has been settled by that time), the board of inquiry shall report to the President the current position of the parties and the efforts which have been made for settlement, and shall include a statement by each party of its position and a statement of the employer's last offer of settlement. The President shall make such report available to the public. The National Labor Relations Board, within the succeeding fifteen days, shall take a secret ballot of the employees of each employer involved in the dispute on the question of whether they wish to accept the final offer of settlement made by their employer, as stated by him, and shall certify the results thereof to the Attorney General within five days thereafter.

Sec. 210. [Sec. 180. Discharge of injunction upon certification of results of election or settlement; report to Congress] Upon the certification of the results of such ballot or upon a settlement being reached, whichever happens sooner, the Attorney General shall move the court to discharge the injunction, which motion shall then be granted, and the injunction discharged. When such motion is granted, the President shall submit to the Congress a full and comprehensive report of the proceedings, including the findings of the board of inquiry and the ballot taken by the National Labor Relations Board, together with such recommendations as he may see fit to make for consideration and appropriate action.

Compilation of Collective-Bargaining Agreements, etc.

Sec. 211. [Sec. 181.] (a) For the guidance and information of interested representatives of employers, employees, and the general public, the Bureau of Labor Statistics of the Department of Labor shall maintain a file of copies of all available collective-bargaining agreements and other available agreements and actions thereunder settling or adjusting labor disputes. Such file shall be open to inspection under appropriate conditions prescribed by the Secretary of Labor, except that no specific

information submitted in confidence shall be disclosed.

(b) The Bureau of Labor Statistics in the Department of Labor is authorized to furnish upon request of the Service, or employers, employees, or their representatives, all available data and factual information which may aid in the settlement of any labor dispute, except that no specific information submitted in confidence shall be disclosed.

Exemption of Railway Labor Act

Sec. 212. [Sec. 182.] The provisions of this title [subchapter] shall not be applicable with respect to any matter which is subject to the provisions of the Railway Labor Act [45 U.S.C. Sec. 151 et seq.], as amended from time to time.

Conciliation of Labor Disputes in the Health Care Industry

Sec. 213. [Sec. 183.] (a) [Establishment of Boards of Inquiry; membership] If, in the opinion of the Director of the Federal Mediation and Conciliation Service, a threatened or actual strike or lockout affecting a health care institution will, if permitted to occur or to continue, substantially interrupt the delivery of health care in the locality concerned, the Director may further assist in the resolution of the impasse by establishing within thirty days after the notice to the Federal Mediation and Conciliation Service under clause (A) of the last sentence of section 8(d) [section 158(d) of this title] (which is required by clause (3) of such section 8(d) [section 158(d) of this title]), or within ten days after the notice under clause (B), an impartial Board of Inquiry to investigate the issues involved in the dispute and to make a written report thereon to the parties within fifteen (15) days after the establishment of such a Board. The written report shall contain the findings of fact together with the Board's recommendations for settling the dispute, with the objective of achieving a prompt, peaceful and just settlement of the dispute. Each such Board shall be composed of such number of individuals as the Director may deem desirable. No member appointed under this section shall have any interest or involvement in the health care institutions or the employee organizations involved in the dispute.

(b) [Compensation of members of Boards of Inquiry] (1) Members of any board established under this section who are otherwise employed by the Federal Government shall serve without compensation but shall be reimbursed for travel, subsistence, and other necessary expenses incurred by them in carrying out its duties under this section.

(2) Members of any board established under this section who are not subject to paragraph (1) shall receive compensation at a rate prescribed by the Director but not to exceed the daily rate prescribed for GS-18 of the General Schedule under section 5332 of title 5, United States Code [section 5332 of title 5], including travel for each day they are engaged in the performance of their duties under this section and shall be entitled to reimbursement for travel, subsistence, and other necessary expenses incurred by them in carrying out their duties under this section.

(c) [Maintenance of status quo] After the establishment of a board under subsection (a) of this section and for fifteen days after any such board has issued its report, no change in the status quo in effect prior to the expiration of the contract in the case of negotiations for a contract renewal, or in effect prior to the time of the impasse in the case of an initial bargaining negotiation, except by agreement, shall be made by the parties to the controversy.

(d) [Authorization of appropriations] There are authorized to be appropriated such sums as may be necessary to carry out the provisions of this section.

TITLE III

[Title 29, Chapter 7, Subchapter IV, United States Code]

Suits by and against Labor Organizations

Sec. 301. [Sec. 185.] (a) [Venue, amount, and citizenship] Suits for violation of contracts between an employer and a labor organization representing employees in an industry affecting commerce as defined in this Act [chapter], or between any such labor organization, may be brought in any district court of the United States having jurisdiction of the parties, without respect to the amount in controversy or without regard to the citizenship of the parties.

(b) [Responsibility for acts of agent; entity for purposes of suit; enforcement of money judgments] Any labor organization which represents employees in an industry affecting commerce as defined in this Act [chapter] and any employer whose activities affect commerce as defined in this Act [chapter] shall be bound by the acts of its agents. Any such labor organization may sue or be sued as an entity and in behalf of the employees whom it represents in the courts of the United States. Any money judgment against a labor organization in a district court of the United States shall be enforceable only against the organization as an entity and against its assets, and shall not be enforceable against any individual member or his assets.

(c) [Jurisdiction] For the purposes of actions and proceedings by or against labor organizations in the district courts of the United States, district courts shall be deemed to have jurisdiction of a labor organization (1) in the district in which such organization maintains its principal offices, or (2) in any district in which its duly authorized officers or agents are engaged in representing or acting for employee members.

(d) [Service of process] The service of summons, subpoena, or other legal process of any court of the United States upon an officer or agent of a labor organization, in his capacity as such, shall constitute service upon the labor organization.

(e) [Determination of question of agency] For the purposes of this section, in determining whether any person is acting as an "agent" of another person so as to make such other person responsible for his acts, the question of whether the specific acts performed were actually authorized or subsequently ratified shall not be controlling.

Restrictions on Payments to Employee Representatives

Sec. 302. [Sec. 186.] (a) [Payment or lending, etc., of money by employer or agent to employees, representatives, or labor organizations] It shall be unlawful for any employer or association of employers or any person who acts as a labor relations expert, adviser, or consultant to an employer or who acts in the interest of an employer to pay, lend, or deliver, or agree to pay, lend, or deliver, any money or other thing of value—

(1) to any representative of any of his employees who are employed in an industry affecting commerce; or

(2) to any labor organization, or any officer or employee thereof, which represents, seeks to represent, or would admit to membership, any of the employees of such employer who are employed in an industry affecting commerce;

(3) to any employee or group or committee of employees of such employer employed in an industry affecting commerce in excess of their normal compensation for the purpose of causing such employee or group or committee directly or indirectly to influence any other employees in the exercise of the right to organize and bargain collectively through representatives of their own choosing; or

(4) to any officer or employee of a labor organization engaged in an industry affecting commerce with intent to influence him in respect to any of his actions, decisions, or duties as a representative of employees or as such officer or employee of such labor organization.

(b) [Request, demand, etc., for money or other thing of value]

(1) It shall be unlawful for any person to request, demand, receive, or accept, or agree to receive or accept, any payment, loan, or delivery of any money or other thing of value prohibited by subsection (a) of this section.

(2) It shall be unlawful for any labor organization, or for any person acting as an officer, agent, representative, or employee of such labor organization, to demand or accept from the operator of any motor vehicle (as defined in section 13102 of title 49) employed in the transportation of property in commerce, or the employer of any such operator, any money or other thing of value payable to such organization or to an officer, agent, representative or employee thereof as a fee or charge for the unloading, or in connection with the unloading, of the cargo of such vehicle: Provided, That nothing in this paragraph shall be construed to make unlawful any payment by an employer to any of his employees as compensation for their services as employees.

(c) [Exceptions]   The provisions of this section shall not be applicable (1) in respect to any money or other thing of value payable by an employer to any of his employees whose established duties include acting openly for such employer in matters of labor relations or personnel administration or to any representative of his employees, or to any officer or employee of a labor organization, who is also an employee or former employee of such employer, as compensation for, or by reason of, his service as an employee of such employer; (2) with respect to the payment or delivery of any money or other thing of value in satisfaction of a judgment of any court or a decision or award of an arbitrator or impartial chairman or in compromise, adjustment, settlement, or release of any claim, complaint, grievance, or dispute in the absence of fraud or duress; (3) with respect to the sale or purchase of an article or commodity at the prevailing market price in the regular course of business; (4) with respect to money deducted from the wages of employees in payment of membership dues in a labor organization: Provided, That the employer has received from each employee, on whose account such deductions are made, a written assignment which shall not be irrevocable for a period of more than one year, or beyond the termination date of the applicable collective agreement, whichever occurs sooner; (5) with respect to money or other thing of value paid to a trust fund established by such representative, for the sole and exclusive benefit of the employees of such employer, and their families and dependents (or of such employees, families, and dependents jointly with the employees of other employers making similar payments, and their families and dependents): Provided, That (A) such payments are held in trust for the purpose of paying, either from principal or income or both, for the benefit of employees, their families and dependents, for medical or hospital care, pensions on retirement or death of employees, compensation for injuries or illness resulting from occupational activity or insurance to provide any of the foregoing, or unemployment benefits or life insurance, disability and sickness insurance, or accident insurance; (B) the detailed basis on which such payments are to be made is specified in a written agreement with the employer, and employees and employers are equally represented in the administration of such fund, together with such neutral persons as the representatives of the employers and the representatives of employees may agree upon and in the event the employer and employee groups deadlock on the administration of such fund and there are no neutral persons empowered to break such deadlock, such agreement provides that the two groups shall agree on an impartial umpire to decide such dispute, or in event of their failure to agree within a reasonable length of time, an impartial umpire to decide such dispute shall, on petition of either group, be appointed by the district court of the United States for the district where the trust fund has its principal office, and shall also contain provisions for an annual audit of the trust fund, a statement of the results of which shall be available for inspection by interested persons at the principal office of the trust fund and at such other places as may be designated in such written agreement; and (C) such payments as are intended to be used for the purpose of providing pensions or annuities for employees are made to a separate trust which provides that the funds held therein cannot be used for any purpose other than paying such pensions or annuities; (6) with respect to money or other thing of value paid by any employer to a trust fund established by such representative for the purpose of pooled vacation, holiday, severance or similar benefits, or defraying costs of apprenticeship or other training programs: Provided, That the requirements of clause (B) of the proviso to clause (5) of this subsection shall apply to such trust funds; (7) with respect to money or other thing of value paid by any employer to a pooled or individual trust fund established by such representative for the purpose of (A) scholarships for the benefit of employees, their families, and dependents for study at educational institutions, (B) child care centers for preschool and school age dependents of employees, or (C) financial assistance for employee housing: Provided, That no labor organization or employer shall be required to bargain on the establishment of any such trust fund, and refusal to do so shall not constitute an unfair labor practice: Provided further, That the requirements of clause (B) of the proviso to clause (5) of this subsection shall apply to such trust funds; (8) with respect to money or any other thing of value paid by any employer to a trust fund established by such representative for the purpose of defraying the costs of legal services for employees, their families, and dependents for counsel or plan of their choice: Provided, That the requirements of clause (B) of the proviso to clause (5) of this subsection shall apply to such trust funds: Provided further, That no such legal services shall be furnished: (A) to initiate any proceeding directed (i) against any such employer or its officers or agents except in workman's compensation cases, or (ii) against such labor organization, or its parent or subordinate bodies, or their officers or agents, or (iii) against any other employer or labor organization, or their officers or agents, in any matter arising under subchapter II of this chapter or this chapter; and (B) in any proceeding where a labor organization would be prohibited from defraying the costs of legal services by the provisions of the Labor-Management Reporting and Disclosure Act of 1959 [29 U.S.C.A. Sec. 401 et seq.]; or (9) with respect to money or other things of value paid by an employer to a plant, area or industrywide labor management committee established for one or more of the purposes set forth in section 5(b) of the Labor Management Cooperation Act of 1978.

[Sec. 302(c)(7) was added by Pub. L. 91-86, Oct. 14, 1969, 83 Stat. 133; Sec. 302(c)(8) by Pub. L. 93-95, Aug. 15, 1973, 87 Stat. 314; Sec. 302(c)(9) by Pub. L. 95–524, Oct. 27, 1978, 92 Stat. 2021; and Sec. 302(c) (7) was amended by Pub. L. 101–273, Apr. 18, 1990, 104 Stat. 138.]

(d) [Penalty for violations]
(1) Any person who participates in a transaction involving a payment, loan, or delivery of money or other thing of value to a labor organization in payment of membership dues or to a joint labor- management trust fund as defined by clause (B) of the proviso to clause (5) of subsection (c) of this section or to a plant, area, or industrywide labor-management committee that is received and used by such labor organization, trust fund, or committee, which transaction does not satisfy all the applicable requirements of subsections (c)(4) through (c)(9) of this section, and willfully and with intent to benefit himself or to benefit other persons he knows are not permitted to receive a payment, loan, money, or other thing of value under subsections (c)(4) through (c)(9) violates this subsection, shall, upon conviction thereof, be guilty of a felony and be subject to a fine of not more than $15,000, or imprisoned for not more than five years,

or both; but if the value of the amount of money or thing of value involved in any violation of the provisions of this section does not exceed $1,000, such person shall be guilty of a misdemeanor and be subject to a fine of not more than $10,000, or imprisoned for not more than one year, or both.

(2) Except for violations involving transactions covered by subsection

(d)(1) of this section, any person who willfully violates this section shall, upon conviction thereof, be guilty of a felony and be subject to a fine of not more than $15,000, or imprisoned for not more than five years, or both; but if the value of the amount of money or thing of value involved in any violation of the provisions of this section does not exceed $1,000, such person shall be guilty of a misdemeanor and be subject to a fine of not more than $10,000, or imprisoned for not more than one year, or both.

[As amended Oct. 27, 1978, Pub. L. 95-524, Sec. 6(d), 92 Stat. 2021; Oct. 12, 1984, Pub. L. 98–473, Title II, Sec. 801, 98 Stat. 2131; Apr. 18, 1990, Pub. L. 101–273, Sec. 1, 104 Stat. 138.]

(e) [Jurisdiction of courts] The district courts of the United States and the United States courts of the Territories and possessions shall have jurisdiction, for cause shown, and subject to the provisions of rule 65 of the Federal Rules of Civil Procedure [section 381 (repealed) of title 28] (relating to notice to opposite party) to restrain violations of this section, without regard to the provisions of section 7 of title 15 and section 52 of title 29, United States Code [of this title] [known as the "Clayton Act"], and the provisions of sections 101 to 115 of title 29, United States Code [chapter 6 of this title] [known as the "Norris-LaGuardia Act"].

(f) [Effective date of provisions] This section shall not apply to any contract in force on June 23, 1947, until the expiration of such contract, or until July 1, 1948, whichever first occurs.

(g) [Contributions to trust funds] Compliance with the restrictions contained in subsection (c)(5)(B) [of this section] upon contributions to trust funds, otherwise lawful, shall not be applicable to contributions to such trust funds established by collective agreement prior to January 1, 1946, nor shall subsection (c)(5)(A) [of this section] be construed as prohibiting contributions to such trust funds if prior to January 1, 1947, such funds contained provisions for pooled vacation benefits.

Boycotts and other Unlawful Combinations

Sec. 303. [Sec. 187.] (a) It shall be unlawful, for the purpose of this section only, in an industry or activity affecting commerce, for any labor organization to engage in any activity or conduct defined as an unfair labor practice in section 8(b)(4) of the National Labor Relations Act [section 158(b)(4) of this title].

(b) Whoever shall be injured in his business or property by reason of any violation of subsection (a) [of this section] may sue therefor in any district court of the United States subject to the limitation and provisions of section 301 hereof [section 185 of this title] without respect to the amount in controversy, or in any other court having jurisdiction of the parties, and shall recover the damages by him sustained and the cost of the suit.

Restriction on Political Contributions

Sec. 304. Repealed.
[See sec. 316 of the Federal Election Campaign Act of 1972, 2 U.S.C. Sec. 441b.]
Sec. 305. [Sec. 188.] Strikes by Government employees. Repealed.
[See 5 U.S.C. Sec. 7311 and 18 U.S.C. Sec. 1918.]

TITLE IV

[Title 29, Chapter 7, Subchapter V, United States Code]
Creation of Joint Committee to Study and Report on Basic Problems Affecting Friendly Labor Relations and Productivity
Secs. 401–407. [Sec. Sec. 191–197.] Omitted.

TITLE V

[Title 29, Chapter 7, Subchapter I, United States Code]
Definitions

Sec. 501. [Sec. 142.] When used in this Act [chapter]—

(1) The term "industry affecting commerce" means any industry or activity in commerce or in which a labor dispute would burden or obstruct commerce or tend to burden or obstruct commerce or the free flow of commerce.

(2) The term "strike" includes any strike or other concerted stoppage of work by employees (including a stoppage by reason of the expiration of a collective-bargaining agreement) and any concerted slowdown or other concerted interruption of operations by employees.

(3) The terms "commerce," "labor disputes," "employer," "employee," "labor organization," "representative," "person," and "supervisor" shall have the same meaning as when used in the National Labor Relations Act as amended by this Act [in subchapter II of this chapter].

Saving Provision

Sec. 502. [Sec. 143.] [Abnormally dangerous conditions] Nothing in this Act [chapter] shall be construed to require an individual employee to render labor or service without his consent, nor shall anything in this Act [chapter] be construed to make the quitting of his labor by an individual employee an illegal act; nor shall any court issue any process to compel the performance by an individual employee of such labor or service, without his consent; nor shall the quitting of labor by an employee or employees in good faith because of abnormally dangerous conditions for work at the place of employment of such employee or employees be deemed a strike under this Act [chapter].

Separability

Sec. 503. [Sec. 144.] If any provision of this Act [chapter], or the application of such provision to any person or circumstance, shall be held invalid, the remainder of this Act [chapter], or the application of such provision to persons or circumstances other than those as to which it is held invalid, shall not be affected thereby.

GLOSSARY

expeditiously: characterized by promptness; quick

inimical: adverse in tendency or effect; harmful

proviso: a clause in a statute, contract, or something similar, by which a condition is introduced; a stipulation or condition

Document Analysis

Intended "to prescribe the legitimate rights of both employees and employers," the Taft-Hartley Act modified and responded to practices established by the Wagner Act, which had greatly expanded the rights of labor. The Taft-Hartley Act also placed new limitations on unions and their leaders. The law protected the role of the federal government as a key mediator in labor relations, but asserted the rights of both the federal and state governments to check the power of unions. The legislation contained several significant provisions to meet these aims. Without exception, these provisions served the interests of management at the expense of those of labor.

On the government side, the act reconfigured the National Labor Relations Board into two separate bodies (the board itself and the General Counsel), allowed states to enact "right-to-work" laws, and gave the federal government the right to issue temporary injunctions against strikes in industries in which stoppages were deemed likely to "imperil the national health or safety." Of these, the most damaging to labor was the allowance of right-to-work laws, which prohibit labor-management agreements that require union membership or the payment of union dues; this weakens the influence of unions where they exist, as workers more favorable to management may be brought in. Possible union influence in elections was limited by a ban on direct contributions to certain types of campaigns; this stricture was later amended.

Much of the remainder of the law details how unions may or may not operate in the workplace. Under the Taft-Hartley Act, new employees of union shops must be given thirty days in which to decide whether to become dues-paying members of the union, and non-unionized employees must be given a voice in workplace operations even if the union oversees these. Furthermore, employers were no longer necessarily required to collect union dues on behalf of the shop's organization. Other provisions dampened the ability of labor to protest workplace conditions. For example, unions were required to provide management with considerable notice of their intention of strike, which weakened the power of this action by allowing employers ample time to plan ways to mitigate the effects of a work stoppage. Certain types of strikes particularly damaging to management, such as sit-down strikes in which workers refuse to leave their work areas and so prevent the continuation of work by temporary "scab" employees, were barred altogether as being unfair labor practices. Such limitations were designed to counterweight the listing of unfair management practices that had been included in the prolabor Wagner Act.

Essential Themes

Despite a general climate opposing labor at the time of its passage, the Taft-Hartley law was controversial. Although not a traditional ally of labor, President Truman firmly denounced the law as counter to the interests of all workers and vetoed it. However, Republicans in Congress were able to drum up enough Democratic support, mostly from conservative Southern politicians, to override Truman's veto and move the bill into law. The Democratic president's unsuccessful stand against the Republican Congress presaged an ongoing battle of political wills between the two branches, and Truman vetoed numerous measures sent to him over the next few years.

Much of the Taft-Hartley Act, however, has remained in force into the twenty-first century. Labor leaders have consistently opposed the act since its passage and, at times, have advocated, albeit unsuccess-

fully, for its repeal. Truman's veto of the act helped cement the political alliance of the Democratic Party and labor interests, but even in times of large Democratic majorities, insufficient political will has existed to substantially weaken or withdraw the act's main provisions. About half of the states have enacted right-to-work laws over time, and the issue remains one still considered by state legislatures; Republican-controlled legislatures in five states began plans to introduce right-to-work laws after a series of sweeping victories in 2014. A handful of changes have nevertheless expanded labor rights limited in the act. Federal legislation allowed labor unions to contribute to political action committees (PACs) that in turn could engage in specific kinds of campaign advertising, for example. The US Supreme Court decision in *Citizens United v. Federal Election Commission (2010)* later wiped out all limits placed on campaign contributions by labor unions and other groups (such as large corporations) under the principle of free speech.

In spite of the regulations that Taft-Hartley placed on labor, union membership continued to grow for some time after its passage, approaching 30 percent in the 1950s. As late as the early 1980s, some 20 percent of all workers were unionized. However, the shifting basis of the US economy away from industry, the traditional center of the labor movement, along with other factors, led to an overall decline in union membership from that time onward, particularly in the private sector. In 2014, the Bureau of Labor Statistics reported that union membership in the United States stood at around 11 percent.

—*Vanessa E. Vaughn, MA*

Bibliography and Additional Reading

Arnesan, Eric, ed. "Taft-Hartley Act." *Encyclopedia of US Labor and Working-Class History.* London: Routledge, 2007. Print.

"1947 Taft-Hartley Substantive Provisions." *National Labor Relations Board.* NLRB, n.d. Web. 3 Feb. 2015.

Weir, Robert E. "Taft-Hartley Act." *Workers in America: A Historical Encyclopedia.* Santa Barbara: ABC-CLIO, 2013. Print.

■ Practical Peacetime Applications

Date: October 17, 1945
Author: Larry E. Gubb
Genre: speech

Summary Overview

During World War II, scientists and engineers in Allied countries made significant technological advances in electronics, radar, and communication technology to gain the upper hand on the battlefield. In this speech, Larry E. Gubb of the Philco Corporation describes some potential peacetime applications of these advancements. For example, he said, electronics developments could improve manufacturing safety; radar developments could improve safety for railroad, air, and sea transportation; and wireless communication developments could improve the geographic reach of broadcasting, bring cultures together, and foster peace. However, Gubb believed that television was one of the most promising and exciting developments: when combined, these breakthroughs would facilitate better television transmission and reception, which in turn could provide entertainment, educational value, and commercial potential to the American public.

Defining Moment

The early twentieth century saw many impressive technological developments, particularly in transportation and communication technology. The first airplanes flew in the early 1900s, and World War I motivated the development of airplane manufacturing shortly thereafter. But these early models had one major limitation: pilots had to navigate using visual cues. As a result, flying at night was difficult, and flying in adverse weather conditions, such as fog or rain, was impossible. Pilots also had to watch the sky for other aircraft to avoid collisions. This limited military use and slowed the expansion of peacetime applications, such as airmail and commercial flight. Radar technology existed as early as the late nineteenth century, but it did not mature enough to be a useful technology until World War II.

Telephone and telegraph also existed during the late nineteenth century, but their use grew dramatically in the early twentieth century. In 1900, the first major

telephone system (the American Bell Telephone Company) had almost 600,000 phones. By 1910, that number reached 5.8 million. The number expanded further when the transcontinental telephone line began operating in 1915. However, telephone and telegraph connections were limited to locations that could be hard wired to each other or to a central system.

Likewise, radio technology existed in the late nineteenth century. Some of its early applications included wireless telegraph communication between ships at sea and voice transmissions from airplanes and emergency vehicles. By 1910, AM radio was broadcast to American homes for entertainment purposes, and in 1920, KDKA in Wilkinsburg, Pennsylvania, became the first commercial radio station in the United States. Radio proved immensely popular for both news and entertainment, but a limited number of bandwidths existed within the AM frequencies. By the 1940s, all of the available AM frequencies were occupied. New interests sought to broadcast over the air, but capacity could not be expanded using the existing technology. Regulatory and market hurdles also blocked expansion into the FM frequencies during the first half of the twentieth century.

In order to gain a strategic advantage during World War I, scientists and engineers in Allied nations undertook enormous research and development efforts. These efforts led to enormous gains in electronics, radar, and wireless broadcasting technology, many of which had enormous potential for peacetime applications. In his speech to the Cornell Club of Michigan on October 17, 1945, Larry E. Gubb discussed some of these technologies. As the chairman of the board of the Philco Corporation, Gubb was closely tied to the world of radio, television, and communication technology. His company saw significant opportunity for peacetime application of these new technologies—particularly the television—and hoped to spread enthusiasm and to create a market for these ideas.

Author Biography

In 1906, the Philadelphia Storage Battery Company emerged from prior efforts of brothers Thomas and Frank Spencer and their business associates to establish an electronics manufacturing company. By 1919, the company sought to grow its business through a national advertising campaign that branded the company with a new, easier-to-remember name: Philco.

After World War I, Philco expanded its product line and developed new technologies to make battery-powered radios more convenient for home use. The company eventually began to manufacture receivers, and business expanded rapidly. By the end of 1929, Philco was the third-largest radio manufacturer in the industry. Meanwhile, engineers busily researched television broadcast and reception technology.

In 1932, Philco split into two subsidiary companies because of legal issues. Larry E. Gubb became the president of the subsidiary Philco Radio & Television Corporation. In 1939, Gubb became the president of the parent company, still known as the Philadelphia Storage Battery Company. In 1941, he was appointed chairman of the board, and he became the name and face publically associated with Philco and its products throughout the 1940s.

HISTORICAL DOCUMENT

Radar and the atomic bomb were unquestionably the two outstanding scientific developments of World War II. The atomic bomb came in the last few days before Japan's capitulation, but radar and its many developments had already made a tremendous contribution to winning the German war and had brought the Japanese phase very near to a victorious conclusion.

Atomic energy seems certain radically to change our technology, our industry—in fact our whole economic life. But in its practical peacetime applications, I doubt if we are to see any great transformations take place in the near future.

Radar and electronics, on the other hand, because of the years of fundamental research in television, and the tremendous impetus resulting from the war in applying this fundamental research, will begin immediately in the postwar period to have peacetime applications never before dreamed of.

The greatest secrecy has surrounded these radar and electronic developments during the war. Their contributions both to the offense and defense were so great that only recently have the Government authorities allowed much of the story to be told.

Practically every key radar project had a code name that kept from revealing its true function. For a long time to come you will hear and read about the "George," the "Dog," the "Loran," and "Rebecca," and most spectacular of all—the "Mickey."

Submarine Menace

Let us go back to the early months of 1942 for a moment The thin thread of trans-Atlantic shipping that tied the United States to Britain was menaced by U-boat wolf packs. Not only the ships on which Britain's very life depended but also American coastal vessels were being sunk within sight of our own cities all along the Atlantic seaboard. At that time, with the U-boat the major German weapon against the United States, a counter weapon had to be developed quickly, . . . and airborne radar was the answer to guide the planes quickly to the surfaced submarines and make them an easy target.

The first American search radar could spot a surfaced submarine no farther than eight nautical miles. Then came the GEORGE. This was the first aircraft radar to present a complete map on its picture tube. From this circular radar picture, it was easy to tell not only the distance of a target but also its exact direction in degrees. Using the GEORGE a plane could spot a surfaced submarine 25 nautical miles away, or three times the range of the earlier equipment. For a long time, the Germans did not know how our planes were so quickly and surely finding their submarines. They did not suspect that it was micro-wave radar!

Gradually the Allies got the upper hand; great numbers of the U-boats were destroyed, and our cargo ships and transports began to move more freely across the Atlantic.

Then the German scientists got busy. They designed

new types of submarines that were far harder to locate. You will remember the scare we had in the early months of 1945 when the Germans put to sea in U-boats that were reported to stay under water for 30 days with only a breathing tube, nicknamed the Schnorkel, above the surface of the water.

By this time, millions of our boys were in England and on the continent, and they had to be constantly supplied with ammunition and food, and this Schnorkel submarine, for a time, offered one of the greatest threats to the Allies winning the war.

Now it was our scientists' turn to produce a counter-weapon, and out of our laboratories came new supersensitive radar equipment which had the power and range to pick up even the tiny portion of the Schnorkel tube sticking above the water.

If the war had not ended when it did, the NEW radar would have revealed and helped to destroy every Schnorkel submarine on the high seas.

Beyond any question, this victory of radar science over the submarines was one of the most thrilling in the entire history of the war!

Radar Bombing

Another scientific triumph was the precision bombing by our Air Forces in all kinds of weather—day or night.

You have read the testimony of Field Marshal Goering as to the devastating effects of precision bombing on Nazi production and communication lines. It was Radar, also, which made this possible.

The development of the "Mickey" Radar Bombsight was what the Army Air Forces and Navy called a crash assignment. They needed it in a desperate hurry. It came at a time when the Eighth Air Force was just beginning to build into a formidable striking force with hundreds of heavy bombers available in England. This huge fleet of bombers, however, was grounded and useless day after day because of bad weather conditions so prevalent in Western Europe.

A new type of Radar Equipment for pin-point bombing regardless of weather was critically needed if our air attack was not to fail. It was designed and produced with such great speed that as early as November 1943 the "Mickey", as the new equipment was nicknamed,

enabled the 8th Air Force Bombers to destroy the U-boat pens at Wilhelmshaven through heavy clouds. And in February 1944 the "Mickey" dealt a death blow to Hitler's Luftwaffe by bombing German ball-bearing and aircraft factories.

It was "Mickey" Radar, again, that made it possible for allied bombers to pulverize Nazi coastal defenses just 30 minutes before the invasion of Normandy, which saved many thousands of American lives.

This bombing attack was so devastating that General H. H. Arnold is reported to have called the Radar Bombsight the most important piece of equipment used by the Army Air Forces in the invasion of France.

Navigation

Another piece of Radar—the Loran—is credited with being the most revolutionary instrument of navigation since the invention of the first compass.

The Loran enables the navigator of a plane to find his exact position at any instant . . . accurately and rapidly. In the plane, signals are picked up from pairs of "Master" and "Slave" beacon stations on the ground. These beacons may be 1500 miles away. Beacon signals appear on an aircraft Loran indicator tube similar to a television picture tube and give the distance of the plane from the beacon stations. Then the navigator consults a simple chart and knows exactly where his plane is at that instant.

So an airplane or ship equipped with this new instrument can travel any predetermined course, day or night, regardless of weather, without depending on celestial navigation.

It was planes equipped with the Loran that carried bombs, explosives . . . incendiaries . . . even the atomic bomb to the homeland of Japan and crushed them without the need of invasion. And Loran helped them to return safely to their tiny island bases in the vastness of the Pacific.

In the peacetime world, this radar system of aerial navigation will help to make worldwide air travel safer and more rapid than ever before.

Proximity Fuse

Another piece of hitherto secret electronic equipment is the Proximity Fuse, containing a tiny radio transmitter and receiver no bigger than a pint milk bottle . .

. with five miniature vacuum tubes placed in the nose of shells, bombs and rockets. After the projectile is fired, this tiny radio sends out radio beams and in return receives a reflected signal. When the projectile is 60–70 feet from the target it is detonated by the fuse, thereby making its explosive force many, many times greater than if it were exploded on contact.

This Proximity Fuse made anti-aircraft fire many times more effective because it was not necessary to hit the target to destroy it. It was a leading factor in curtailing the Buzzbomb attacks on London, at a most critical time, and it saved thousands and thousands of tons of shipping and American lives by neutralizing the Japanese suicide bomber attacks.

War Windup

These are only four of the great electronic developments during World War II. But they may give you some idea of the advances that have taken place in the whole field of electronics in the short space of 48 months.

In his biennial report, General George C. Marshall, Chief of Staff of the United States Army, states that the radar equipment developed by the U. S. and Britain was superior to the electronic devices of either Germany or Japan.

I could spend hours telling you of other wartime developments, but I feel that you are most interested in how this greatly expanded knowledge of electronics may be applied to our peacetime future.

Electronics Peacetime Future

Thanks to the development of Radar, air travel will be far safer than ever before. Planes equipped with radar instruments should never crash into mountains in darkness or bad weather. Nor should there be collisions between planes. Passenger planes will be guided with unerring accuracy to tiny island bases in every sea and ocean.

Installed in ships, Radar will enable even the largest vessels to come into harbors in dense fog. Collision between ships at sea will be avoided; and even icebergs—the ever present dread of mariners—can be detected and avoided by Radar.

Industrial Uses of Electronics

Industrial uses of electronics which were already important before the war have received a tremendous impetus . . . and new industrial uses will continue to be found as the years go by.

Tiny vacuum tubes, some of them no larger than your little finger, are opening up new fields in the way of electronic controls that make manufacturing safer, more precise and more automatic than ever.

We have electronic enumerators that count passing articles far faster than the eye can see.

Electronic sorters that discard oversize and undersize, off color or defective articles . . . with amazing speed.

Electronic devices inspect the inside of things where the eye cannot see.

Other electronic instruments regulate temperature, eliminate smoke and automatically control entire batteries of operating machines.

Great new opportunities for expansion lie ahead in this field of industrial electronics to make factory life easier, better, and safer.

Communications

Tremendous new developments are taking place in the whole field of communications. We are now at work on a technique whereby you may have a telephone in your automobile. Soon you may be able to pick up the telephone in your car and call your home . . . your office . . . while driving along the highway.

You may soon be able to write a letter or a telegram . . . drop it in a slot, and have it reproduced instantly—thousands of miles away . . . by television . . . with the speed of light, and for less than it now costs to send an air-mail letter.

Link System

The day may not be far distant when all our telephone and telegraph wires may be obsolete—replaced by wireless link systems. You will see the beginning of this development in the rebuilding of Europe.

It is inconceivable that the thousands and thousands of miles of wired communications which have been destroyed in Europe will be replaced—when these signals can be beamed through the air by the use of radio links which can be installed so much more cheaply and with such a low cost of maintenance.

And it's inconceivable that this radio link development will not come into widespread use in this country.

For instance, our railroads which depend on wired communications to direct the operation of their trains and to assure the safety of their passengers, have a tremendous problem of maintenance in keeping these wires open in bad winter weather. A series of automatic radio link stations along a railroad's right of way—with uninterrupted service because the signals are carried through the air—would be a tremendous improvement. Several major railroads are already experimenting with such a system.

China

One of the greatest futures for radio relay link systems is in carrying both broadcasting and television signals, as well as other forms of communication, into mountainous and undeveloped areas . . . where cost and maintenance are basic considerations.

We, in America, take for granted and enjoy nationwide network radio programs, which are put on at a central source and carried to the various broadcasting stations by wire. But only a small part of the world has these advantages, and means must be developed for better communication.

Take China, for instance. The Chinese speak a great many different dialects. One province can't even understand the language of another. The Central Government is thinking of establishing broadcast stations in the principal populated areas—connected by radio links—because in that mountainous country the cost of wire installation and maintenance would be prohibitive. The Government then hopes to begin gradually to teach the people a single language and thus help to unite the nation.

Knowledge builds understanding, and there is a tremendous opportunity to educate millions of people in the world through the use of radio broadcasting. It may have a great effect in the future on world peace.

India

There is a similar problem in India with its caste system and many languages. And here again, the Indian government is thinking in terms of a network broadcasting system which will bring their people closer together.

The impact of a centralized communications system upon the lives, customs, and habits of these tremendous populations could be very far reaching.

There are two outstanding immediate developments in the radio industry in which you will participate in the near future. One of them is the development of a new FM broadcasting system, which will be nationwide. The other is Television.

The entire radio industry is on the eve of great revolutionary developments.

For the past 25 years we have had sound radio broadcasting—and while there have been constant advances and improvements—there have been no fundamental changes.

While we had FM in a limited way before the war, tremendous improvements have been made in this radio system during the war . . . for FM radio was one of the principal means of military communications—particularly between tanks.

FM will do two things that have hitherto been impossible.

First of all, it will give us a high degree of freedom from noise and static. It will also make it possible, if the public so desires, to provide improved "high-fidelity" reproduction of musical programs.

How many times, particularly during the summer months, have you wanted to listen to your favorite radio program, only to have it so badly marred by static that you finally had to give it up?

With FM you will be able to listen without interference even during heavy thunderstorms.

In the second place, consider, if you will what it may mean to the public and the radio industry to have hundreds and perhaps thousands of new broadcasters go on the air. We have long since reached the limit in the number of possible AM stations.

Lots of people with the money and a desire to broadcast have not had a chance to do so. There just are not enough AM channels to go around,

FM uses another part of the spectrum and thousands of new stations can go on the air. In Detroit, for example, you have 5 AM stations now in operation. With FM, you may be able to have as many as 25.

Since FM makes it possible for new groups and new

interests to enter broadcasting, it will probably result in greater competition for the attention of the radio audience. You may very well hear new and more varied types of programs on the air.

This development, too, should benefit the listening audience.

I predict that within the next five years, close to $2 billion will be invested in new FM stations and in receiving sets that will allow the public to listen to FM programs.

Television

By far the most important development from which the public will derive the greatest benefit as a result of the electronic advances in World War II, will be Television for the home.

I predict it will not be many years before practically every family in the United States will have a television receiver in their home just as they have a radio set today.

With television, you will be able to sit in your own living room and see the great events of the world pass before your eyes.

Can you imagine the tremendous interest of having television give you a front row seat at the inauguration of the next President of the United States!

Can you imagine watching the finest football games—and see them, play by play—in your own living room in Detroit—even though the game may be in Los Angeles!

Can you imagine the interest your wife will have in viewing fashion's latest creations when she sees them by television right in her own home!

You have been promised for about 10 years that television was just around the corner. We can now tell you definitely that it is here. Probably never before has the product of a great new industry reached such an advanced stage before it was offered to the public.

The radio industry had already invested about $25,000,000 in television research and development before the war. And on top of all the research carried on in this field by the pioneering companies before the war . . . is now added the great store of new knowledge and new experience resulting from the war effort.

It was peacetime television research that made radar the outstanding weapon that it was, and the development of radar in turn greatly advanced the whole television art.

Just a few months ago, the FCC after a thorough study of the entire problem, gave television the "green light" and assigned it definite, permanent frequency allocations in the spectrum.

Broadcasters, set manufacturers and the public can all proceed now with confidence, to get the television industry going on a substantial basis, and I believe you will be surprised at the great speed with which it grows.

It is my opinion that the Commission is to be greatly commended on the vigorous stand it took in clearing the way for television.

In my opinion the Commission has adopted the policy best suited to the public interest—and one that will give the American public television at the earliest possible date. And they held to this position in the face of a great deal of opposition by certain broadcasting groups who wanted television delayed.

They have provided the means for the American public to get the benefit of television in the frequencies we are now using with a black and white picture. And that picture will be highly acceptable, entertaining and exciting to the American people.

The Commission has further provided for a continuation of research in the higher frequencies and in color which will assure that the television art will be continually and steadily advanced.

The problem of launching television is not an easy one—nor is it an inexpensive one. In the advance of television a great deal of programming research and high cost program production is necessary to make it available to the American public. And this must be done in anticipation of later recovering what has been spent—because, of course, there is no television audience of any size at the present time.

But the FCC, by clearing the way for receivers to be made and broadcast programs to be put on the air in the frequencies where our experience lies has assured the American public of television reception in many of our important cities within a matter of months.

Further, I believe that it will take a number of years before satisfactory programs in the high frequencies—and color—on an every-day basis can be given to the American public.

So, in effect, as the industry grows and develops, the American public can and will be enjoying television in black and white and in the lower frequencies.

Eventually, we will have color in the higher frequencies that will give an even finer picture.

I doubt, however, if anyone in this audience would have foregone the pleasure of his automobile as a means of transportation—or the pleasure of motoring—for many years to wait for the development of 1945.

It is my feeling that television, like any other industry, will develop faster and better when put to use, rather than if it were to be restricted to the laboratory.

And television, in my opinion, is far too big an industry and too important to the American people to be held up for nebulous future developments when the present picture is as good as it is today and can give the American public so much in the way of pleasure and entertainment immediately.

Projection Television

As to television receivers, the better ones will probably be of the projection type, where the image, reflected on a screen is large enough and clear enough so that you and your family will be able to see it anywhere in the average size room.

In the latest design of projected television, you will be able to look at the picture in daylight or with the lights on, so that the idea of sitting in total darkness for a television show will soon be a thing of the past.

The lower priced sets will probably be of the present type—where the picture is seen on the end of a cathode-ray tube like that used in radar. The size and detail of this picture will be reflected in its price.

And my prediction is—you will shortly have good television sets from $150 up—and maybe even lower.

Link Development

One of the greatest problems of television is that of establishing network programs.

Network television broadcasts are necessary to good tele* vision. We all have been educated to expensive, elaborate radio network programs—and we will not be satisfied in television with anything less than a network system of programming. Also the economics of television broadcasting indicate the desirability of network programs. This forces on us the need of linking local television stations together into a network.

Sometime previous to the war, the coaxial cable was considered the only satisfactory means of transmitting a television signal from city to city.

But, during the last five years—especially during the war —tremendous advances have been made in radio links, and it now looks as if television will have two choices in building networks:

(1) Coaxial cable

(2) Radio links

Using the coaxial cable to link television broadcast stations together is well known. The problem is the cost of the cable itself—and also the expense of installing it.

Since the war our knowledge of microwave radio relays has progressed tremendously, so that these two systems will undoubtedly be competing with each other as to initial cost, maintenance and technical advantages to determine which is the best method of linking television broadcast stations together.

Philco has pioneered in the development of these radio relay links by carrying television signals from Washington, D. C. to Philadelphia over a series of four intermediate booster stations on April 17, 1945 and our initial experiments were highly satisfactory.

These radio links are so located that there is "line-of-sight" transmission, thus assuring dependable operation in all kinds of weather.

There is no reason why this experimental technique cannot be greatly expanded; so that we look forward in a reasonable length of time to the development of television relay Stations from the Atlantic seaboard to the Pacific Coast, that is, a nationwide television network which permits the same centralized creation of programs in television that we have in radio.

When this is accomplished—can you imagine the advantage to a motor car company in being able to show pictures of—and demonstrate its new models . . . perhaps with a good looking girl at the wheel . . . to thousands and thousands of customers sitting in the living rooms of American homes!

Some of the leading department stores in the East are already tying in with television broadcasting to demonstrate their latest fashions to the ladies. Think what it would mean to a retailer to demonstrate his newest products to the housewife right in her own home!

Think of the educational possibilities when television

programs may be thrown on the screen in schools all over America!

If radio has been a vital factor in affecting public opinion in this country—and you all have a good idea of how much it has contributed—imagine the increased influence of television when sight is added to sound.

Conclusion

So I can see nothing ahead but a great expansion in the entire field of electronics . . . developments in communications . . . in industrial applications of electronics; and in television which will, I believe, forge ahead rapidly.

It has been predicted that the capital expenditures and the production of durable consumer goods in the communications field alone will exceed $5 billions in the next five years.

This means the creation of great employment . . . new wealth . . . new opportunities . . . and a contribution to a higher national standard of living.

The history of the electronics industry in the past 30 years, marked by the introduction of such great new things as the transcontinental telephone and radio, is only a preview of the tremendous developments just ahead of us.

Document Analysis

In this speech, Larry E. Gubb discusses technological advances in radar and electronics developed during World War II and their potential applications in peacetime. With respect to radar, he describes how improvements in American search radar systems allowed the Allies to spot German U-boats in the Atlantic Ocean from a distance of twenty-five nautical miles—a dramatic improvement from earlier systems with a maximum distance of eight nautical miles. Radar bombsight allowed pilots to target bombing raids with great precision and carry out raids even in poor weather conditions. Navigation radar allowed airplanes and ships to navigate using radar beacons rather than visual cues, which revolutionized flight and shipping. A vessel could travel "any predetermined course, day or night, regardless of weather, without depending on celestial navigation."

Gubb explains how these developments can improve transportation safety even during peacetime. Planes equipped with radar systems no longer need to rely on visual cues to navigate. Instead, they can be guided to avoid obstacles and land on target safely even in darkness or bad weather. Radar systems also allow ships to safely enter harbors in fog and avoid obstacles at sea, including icebergs and other ships.

Other general electronics developments likewise have substantial peacetime applications. For example, tiny vacuum tubes used in electronic controls can improve the safety of manufacturing equipment by helping to "regulate temperature, eliminate smoke and

automatically control entire batteries of operating machines."

Wartime research also brought advancements in communication technology. Gubb discusses the wireless link system that could replace damaged telephone and telegraph wires across Europe, as well as allow US railroads to operate uninterrupted service during bad weather. He highlights the usefulness of wireless broadcasting in mountainous and undeveloped areas, where cost and maintenance might make wired connections impractical or impossible. In particular, FM radio—one of the principal means of military communication—has higher fidelity than AM radio, is less likely to be marred by static during poor weather conditions, and provides additional bandwidths to new broadcasters.

Finally, Gubb discusses how these advancements led to significant developments in television transmission and reception technology, and he predicts that color television will soon be available. He believes that television sets will eventually be in every household in the United States and sees television's enormous potential for entertainment and commercial applications. He says that advancements in wireless communication will facilitate the formation of national television networks—similar to those already existing for radio—particularly in areas where physical linkages using coaxial cables are inconvenient or impossible.

Essential Themes

The US government kept many of the most dramatic and impressive research efforts in electronics, radar, and broadcast technology closely guarded secrets during World War II because of their strategic importance. But once the war ended, the American public finally had an opportunity to see the results of these secret projects and experience the changes they could bring to life, culture, and society.

Like many others, Gubb believed that wireless communication technology could help unite the world and promote peace. He specifically mentioned China and India, large countries with geographical features that made a wired national communication system impractical or impossible. Both countries also had many regional subcultures that could not effectively communicate with one another because of differences in language and lifestyle. The government of these nations hoped that wireless broadcasting could facilitate a centralized communication system to educate people and encourage the development of a single national language and a uniform culture.

Developments in FM radio allowed for the establishment of additional commercial and public radio stations. Gubb believed this would "result in greater competition for the attention of the radio audience" and lead to "new and more varied types of programs on the air."

But above all else, Gubb and his fellow researchers were thrilled by the prospect of television. In his speech, he hailed the excitement of having a "front row seat at the inauguration of the next President of the United States," or "watching the finest football games" taking place in Los Angeles from your living room in Detroit. He also believed that placing television sets in schools could provide new educational opportunities. Commercial opportunities abounded, since companies could advertise their goods directly in visually compelling ways "to the housewife right in her own home."

At the time of Gubb's speech, technology existed for black-and-white projection and cathode-ray tube television sets; color television sets were still under development. The Federal Communications Commission (FCC) had recently assigned definite, permanent frequencies for television broadcast, which further paved the way for television to become as ubiquitous as Gubb and his associates dreamed.

—*Tracey M. DiLascio, JD*

Bibliography and Additional Reading

"The Aerial Age Begins." *Smithsonian National Air and Space Museum*. Natl. Air and Space Museum, 2014. Web. 2 Jan 2015.

Brown, Louis. *A Radar History of World War II: Technical and Military Imperatives*. New York: Taylor, 1999. Print.

"The Development of Radio." *American Experience*. PBS, n.d. Web. 2 Jan 2015.

Edgerton, Gary. *The Columbia History of American Television*. New York: Columbia UP, 2007. Print.

"A Short History of Radio." *Federal Trade Commission*. Federal Trade Commission, Winter 2003–4. Web. 2 Jan 2015.

Ramirez, Ron. "The History of Philco." *Philco Radio*, 17 May 2013. Web. 2 Jan 2015.

■ Truman's State of the Union Speech

Date: January 5, 1949
Author: Harry S. Truman
Genre: speech

Summary Overview

At the end of the 1940s, life in the United States was finally returning to normal after World War II. However, the country faced several issues as it entered this peaceful period. Millions of returning soldiers needed civilian jobs. Industrial and agricultural production was high, but still insufficient to meet consumer demand. Economic inflation raised the price of goods. Ongoing struggles between private businesses and labor unions threatened to result in strikes and walkouts. Additionally, social issues that had been obscured by the war returned to light, including unaffordable health care, underperforming schools, and discrimination in employment and educational opportunities.

In his 1949 State of the Union address, President Harry S. Truman offered specific recommendations for issues such as the ongoing labor disputes. For other concerns, such as the need to increase production and employment opportunities, he offered general encouragement for private businesses to cooperate with the federal government to implement effective solutions.

Defining Moment

As the 1940s ended, American life was settling back to normal after the disruptions of World War II. The United States did not suffer severe infrastructure damage, but faced its own postwar issues nonetheless. Millions of soldiers returned from war needing civilian jobs, but companies slowed production due to decreased need for wartime goods. Many feared a repeat of the recession of the early 1920s, when the large influx of returning soldiers from World War I combined with a similar decrease in demand to create widespread unemployment, poverty, starvation, and housing crises.

To avoid a similar economic catastrophe, the federal government created the Employment Act of 1946. The act stated that the federal government would use "all its resources to promote maximum employment, production, and purchasing power" in a manner consistent with the spirit of free and competitive enterprise and general welfare. It did not contain any specific provisions; instead, it left the implementation of its ideals to the administration.

An important part of maintaining purchasing power required combating postwar inflation. Inflation occurs when prices in a market show a marked upward trend over time, decreasing purchasing power as the consumer is able to purchase fewer goods with the same amount of money. After the war, Americans had money to spend, but fewer options for where to spend it. Many manufacturers of consumer goods, such as automobiles, had retooled to produce wartime goods, such as fighter planes. New goods were in short supply while these factories shifted back to normal production, which drove up the prices for the limited items that were available. Some inflation can indicate a healthy growing economy, but too much long-term inflation leads to consumers spending their savings trying to afford basic items, such as food and housing.

Struggles between business owners and labor unions also affected the US economy following the war. The pro-union Wagner Act, passed in 1935 as part of President Franklin D. Roosevelt's New Deal, gave employees the right to unionize and obligated employers to bargain collectively with the employees' unions. But by 1947, high-profile labor strikes had turned both public opinion and the federal legislature against labor unions. Passed over presidential veto in June 1947, the Taft-Hartley Act amended the Wagner Act to restrict unions' organizing and bargaining powers. The federal government and the National Labor Relations Board struggled to find a solution that protected workers from unfair labor practices while allowing for a free market.

The return to normalcy after World War II also revealed shortcomings elsewhere in the American social structure. Social security benefits were insufficient to support citizens in their retirement years, many Americans could not afford health care, public schools were underperforming, and discrimination in education and employment persisted. In his 1949 State of the Union speech, President Harry S. Truman addressed these issues and proposed several specific solutions and guiding principles to encourage Congress, private businesses, and the American people to work together toward a resolution.

Author Biography

Harry S. Truman was born in Lamar, Missouri, on May 8, 1884. He was a member of the Missouri National Guard from 1905 to 1911, and when the United States entered World War I in 1917, he helped to put together the 2nd Regiment of Missouri Field Artillery, which was called to duty and sent to fight in France. A few years after his return, Truman was elected a Jackson County Court judge in Missouri, becoming presiding judge in 1926. In 1934, Truman was elected to the US Senate and reelected in 1940. During his terms, he notably championed the Civil Aeronautics Act of 1938 and the Transportation Act of 1940. In 1945, Truman was sworn in as vice president under Roosevelt. When Roosevelt died unexpectedly less than three months later, Truman became the thirty-third president. After serving two terms, he retired from the presidency in 1953 and died on December 26, 1972.

HISTORICAL DOCUMENT

I am happy to report to this 81st Congress that the state of the Union is good. Our Nation is better able than ever before to meet the needs of the American people, and to give them their fair chance in the pursuit of happiness. This great Republic is foremost among the nations of the world in the search for peace.

During the last 16 years, our people have been creating a society which offers new opportunities for every man to enjoy his share of the good things of life.

In this society, we are conservative about the values and principles which we cherish; but we are forward-looking in protecting those values and principles and in extending their benefits. We have rejected the discredited theory that the fortunes of the Nation should be in the hands of a privileged few. We have abandoned the "trickledown" concept of national prosperity. Instead, we believe that our economic system should rest on a democratic foundation and that wealth should be created for the benefit of all.

The recent election shows that the people of the United States are in favor of this kind of society and want to go on improving it.

The American people have decided that poverty is just as wasteful and just as unnecessary as preventable disease. We have pledged our common resources to help one another in the hazards and struggles of individual life. We believe that no unfair prejudice or artificial distinction should bar any citizen of the United States of America from an education, or from good health, or from a job that he is capable of performing.

The attainment of this kind of society demands the best efforts of every citizen in every walk of life, and it imposes increasing responsibilities on the Government.

The Government must work with industry, labor, and the farmers in keeping our economy running at full speed. The Government must see that every American has a chance to obtain his fair share of our increasing abundance. These responsibilities go hand in hand.

We cannot maintain prosperity unless we have a fair distribution of opportunity and a widespread consumption of the products of our factories and farms.

Our Government has undertaken to meet these responsibilities.

We have made tremendous public investments in highways, hydroelectric power projects, soil conservation, and reclamation. We have established a system of social security. We have enacted laws protecting the rights and the welfare of our working people and the income of our farmers. These Federal policies have paid for themselves many times over. They have strengthened the material foundations of our democratic ideals. Without them, our present prosperity would be impossible.

Reinforced by these policies, our private enterprise system has reached new heights of production. Since the boom year of 1929, while our population has increased by only 20 percent, our agricultural production has increased by 45 percent, and our industrial production has increased by 75 percent. We are turning out far more goods and more wealth per worker than we have ever done before.

This progress has confounded the gloomy prophets—at home and abroad who predicted the downfall of American capitalism. The people of the United States, going their own way, confident in their own powers, have achieved the greatest prosperity the world has even seen.

But, great as our progress has been, we still have a long way to go.

As we look around the country, many of our shortcomings stand out in bold relief.

We are suffering from excessively high prices.

Our production is still not large enough to satisfy our demands.

Our minimum wages are far too low.

Small business is losing ground to growing monopoly.

Our farmers still face an uncertain future. And too many of them lack the benefits of our modern civilization.

Some of our natural resources are still being wasted.

We are acutely short of electric power, although the means for developing such power are abundant.

Five million families are still living in slums and firetraps. Three million families share their homes with others.

Our health is far behind the progress of medical science. Proper medical care is so expensive that it is out of the reach of the great majority of our citizens.

Our schools, in many localities, are utterly inadequate.

Our democratic ideals are often thwarted by prejudice and intolerance.

Each of these shortcomings is also an opportunity— an opportunity for the Congress and the President to work for the good of the people.

Our first great opportunity is to protect our economy against the evils of "boom and bust."

This objective cannot be attained by government alone. Indeed, the greater part of the task must be performed by individual efforts under our system of free enterprise. We can keep our present prosperity, and increase it, only if free enterprise and free government work together to that end.

We cannot afford to float along ceaselessly on a postwar boom until it collapses. It is not enough merely to prepare to weather a recession if it comes. Instead, government and business must work together constantly to achieve more and more jobs and more and more production—which mean more and more prosperity for all the people.

The business cycle is man-made; and men of good will, working together, can smooth it out.

So far as business is concerned, it should plan for steady, vigorous expansion-seeking always to increase its output, lower its prices, and avoid the vices of monopoly and restriction. So long as business does this, it will be contributing to continued prosperity, and it will have the help and encouragement of the Government.

The Employment Act of 1946 pledges the Government to use all its resources to promote maximum employment, production, and purchasing power. This means that the Government is firmly committed to protect business and the people against the dangers of recession and against the evils of inflation. This means that the Government must adapt its plans and policies to meet changing circumstances.

At the present time, our prosperity is threatened by inflationary pressures at a number of critical points in our economy. And the Government must be in a position to take effective action at these danger spots. To that end, I recommend that the Congress enact legislation for the following purposes:

First, to continue the power to control consumer credit and enlarge the power to control bank credit.

Second, to grant authority to regulate speculation on the commodity exchanges.

Third, to continue export control authority and to provide adequate machinery for its enforcement.

Fourth, to continue the priorities and allocation authority in the field of transportation.

Fifth, to authorize priorities and allocations for key materials in short supply.

Sixth, to extend and strengthen rent control.

Seventh, to provide standby authority to impose price ceilings for scarce commodities which basically affect essential industrial production or the cost of living, and to limit unjustified wage adjustments which would force a break in an established price ceiling.

Eighth, to authorize an immediate study of the adequacy of production facilities for materials in critically short supply, such as steel; and, if found necessary, to authorize Government loans for the expansion of production facilities to relieve such shortages, and to authorize the construction of such facilities directly, if action by private industry fails to meet our needs.

The Economic Report, which I shall submit to the Congress shortly, will discuss in detail the economic background for these recommendations.

One of the most important factors in maintaining prosperity is the Government's fiscal policy. At this time, it is essential not only that the Federal budget be balanced, but also that there be a substantial surplus to reduce inflationary pressures, and to permit a sizable reduction in the national debt, which now stands at $252 billion. I recommend, therefore, that the Congress enact new tax legislation to bring in an additional $4 billion of Government revenue. This should come principally from additional corporate taxes. A portion should come from revised estate and gift taxes. Consideration should be given to raising personal income rates in the middle and upper brackets.

If we want to keep our economy running in high gear, we must be sure that every group has the incentive to make its full contribution to the national welfare. At present, the working men and women of the Nation are unfairly discriminated against by a statute that abridges their rights, curtails their constructive efforts, and hampers our system of free collective bargaining. That statute is the Labor-Management Relations Act of 1947, sometimes called the Taft-Hartley Act.

That act should be repealed!

The Wagner Act should be reenacted. However, certain improvements, which I recommended to the Congress 2 years ago, are needed. Jurisdictional strikes and unjustified secondary boycotts should be prohibited. The use of economic force to decide issues arising out of the interpretation of existing contracts should be prevented. Without endangering our democratic freedoms, means should be provided for setting up machinery for preventing strikes in vital industries which affect the public interest.

The Department of Labor should be rebuilt and strengthened and those units properly belonging within that department should be placed in it.

The health of our economy and its maintenance at high levels further require that the minimum wage fixed by law should be raised to at least 75 cents an hour.

If our free enterprise economy is to be strong and healthy, we must reinvigorate the forces of competition. We must assure small business the freedom and opportunity to grow and prosper. To this purpose, we should strengthen our antitrust laws by closing those loopholes that permit monopolistic mergers and consolidations.

Our national farm program should be improved—not only in the interest of the farmers, but for the lasting prosperity of the whole Nation. Our goals should be abundant farm production and parity income for agriculture. Standards of living on the farm should be just as good as anywhere else in the country.

Farm price supports are an essential part of our program to achieve these ends. Price supports should be used to prevent farm price declines which are out of line with general price levels, to facilitate adjustments in production to consumer demands, and to promote good land use. Our price support legislation must be adapted to these objectives. The authority of the Commodity Credit Corporation to provide adequate storage space for crops should be restored.

Our program for farm prosperity should also seek to expand the domestic market for agricultural products, particularly among low-income groups, and to increase and stabilize foreign markets.

We should give special attention to extending modern conveniences and services to our farms. Rural electrification should be pushed forward. And in considering legislation relating to housing, education, health, and social security, special attention should be given to rural problems.

Our growing population and the expansion of our economy depend upon the wise management of our land, water, forest, and mineral wealth. In our present dynamic economy, the task of conservation is not to lockup our resources but to develop and improve them. Failure, today, to make the investments which are necessary to support our progress in the future would be false economy.

We must push forward the development of our rivers for power, irrigation, navigation, and flood control. We should apply the lessons of our Tennessee Valley experience to our other great river basins.

I again recommend action be taken by the Congress to approve the St. Lawrence Seaway and Power project. This is about the fifth time I have recommended it.

We must adopt a program for the planned use of the petroleum reserves under the sea, which are–and must remain—vested in the Federal Government. We must extend our programs of soil conservation. We must place our forests on a sustained yield basis, and encourage the development of new sources of vital minerals.

In all this we must make sure that the benefits of these public undertakings are directly available to the people. Public power should be carried to consuming areas by public transmission lines where necessary to provide electricity at the lowest possible rates. Irrigation waters should serve family farms and not land speculators.

The Government has still other opportunities—to help raise the standard of living of our citizens. These opportunities lie in the fields of social security, health, education, housing, and civil rights.

The present coverage of the social security laws is altogether inadequate; the benefit payments are too low. One-third of our workers are not covered. Those who receive old-age and survivors insurance benefits receive an average payment of only $25 a month. Many others who cannot work because they are physically disabled are left to the mercy of charity. We should expand our social security program, both as to the size of the benefits and the extent of coverage, against the economic hazards due to unemployment, old age, sickness, and disability.

We must spare no effort to raise the general level of health in this country. In a nation as rich as ours, it is a shocking fact that tens of millions lack adequate medical care. We are short of doctors, hospitals, nurses. We must remedy these shortages. Moreover, we need—and we must have without further delay—a system of prepaid medical insurance which will enable every American to afford good medical care.

It is equally shocking that millions of our children are not receiving a good education. Millions of them are in overcrowded, obsolete buildings. We are short of teachers, because teachers' salaries are too low to attract new teachers, or to hold the ones we have. All these school problems will become much more acute as a result of the tremendous increase in the enrollment in our elementary schools in the next few years. I cannot repeat too strongly my desire for prompt Federal financial aid to the States to help them operate and maintain their school systems.

The governmental agency which now administers the programs of health, education, and social security should be given full departmental status.

The housing shortage continues to be acute. As an immediate step, the Congress should enact the provisions for low-rent public housing, slum clearance, farm housing, and housing research which I have repeatedly recommended. The number of low-rent public housing units provided for in the legislation should be increased to 1 million units in the next 7 years. Even this number of units will not begin to meet our need for new housing.

Most of the houses we need will have to be built by private enterprise, without public subsidy. By producing too few rental units and too large a proportion of high-priced houses, the building industry is rapidly pricing itself out of the market. Building costs must be lowered.

The Government is now engaged in a campaign to induce all segments of the building industry to concentrate on the production of lower priced housing. Additional legislation to encourage such housing will be submitted.

The authority which I have requested, to allocate materials in short supply and to impose price ceilings on such materials, could be used, if found necessary, to channel more materials into homes large enough for family life at prices which wage earners can afford.

The driving force behind our progress is our faith in our democratic institutions. That faith is embodied in the promise of equal rights and equal opportunities which the founders of our Republic proclaimed to their countrymen and to the whole world.

The fulfillment of this promise is among the highest purposes of government. The civil rights proposals I made to the 80th Congress, I now repeat to the 81st Congress. They should be enacted in order that the Federal Government may assume the leadership and discharge the obligations dearly placed upon it by the Constitution.

I stand squarely behind those proposals.

Our domestic programs are the foundation of our foreign policy. The world today looks to us for leadership because we have so largely realized, within our borders, those benefits of democratic government for which most of the peoples of the world are yearning.

We are following a foreign policy which is the outward expression of the democratic faith we profess. We are doing what we can to encourage free states and free peoples throughout the world, to aid the suffering and afflicted in foreign lands, and to strengthen democratic nations against aggression.

The heart of our foreign policy is peace. We are supporting a world organization to keep peace and a world economic policy to create prosperity for mankind. Our guiding star is the principle of international cooperation. To this concept we have made a national commitment as profound as anything in history.

To it we have pledged our resources and our honor.

Until a system of world security is established upon which we can safely rely, we cannot escape the burden of creating and maintaining armed forces sufficient to deter aggression. We have made great progress in the last year in the effective organization of our Armed Forces, but further improvements in our national security legislation are necessary. Universal training is essential to the security of the United States.

During the course of this session I shall have occasion to ask the Congress to consider several measures in the field of foreign policy. At this time, I recommend that we restore the Reciprocal Trade Agreements Act to full effectiveness, and extend it for 3 years. We should also open our doors to displaced persons without unfair discrimination.

It should be clear by now to all citizens that we are not seeking to freeze the status quo. We have no intention of preserving the injustices of the past. We welcome the constructive efforts being made by many nations to achieve a better life for their citizens. In the European recovery program, in our good-neighbor policy and in the United Nations, we have begun to batter down those national walls which block the economic growth and the social advancement of the peoples of the world.

We believe that if we hold resolutely to this course, the principle of international cooperation will eventually command the approval even of those nations which are now seeking to weaken or subvert it.

We stand at the opening of an era which can mean either great achievement or terrible catastrophe for ourselves and for all mankind.

The strength of our Nation must continue to be used in the interest of all our people rather than a privileged few. It must continue to be used unselfishly in the struggle for world peace and the betterment of mankind the world over.

This is the task before us.

It is not an easy one. It has many complications, and there will be strong opposition from selfish interests.

I hope for cooperation from farmers, from labor, and from business. Every segment of our population and every individual has a right to expect from our Government a fair deal.

In 1945, when I came down before the Congress for the first time on April 16, I quoted to you King Solomon's prayer that he wanted wisdom and the ability to govern his people as they should be governed. I explained to you at that time that the task before me was one of the greatest in the history of the world, and that it was necessary to have the complete cooperation of the Congress and the people of the United States.

Well now, we are taking a new start with the same situation. It is absolutely essential that your President have the complete cooperation of the Congress to carry out the great work that must be done to keep the peace in this world, and to keep this country prosperous.

The people of this great country have a right to expect that the Congress and the President will work in closest cooperation with one objective—the welfare of the people of this Nation as a whole.

In the months ahead I know that I shall be able to cooperate with this Congress.

Now, I am confident that the Divine Power which has guided us to this time of fateful responsibility and glorious opportunity will not desert us now.

With that help from Almighty God which we have humbly acknowledged at every turning point in our national life, we shall be able to perform the great tasks which He now sets before us.

Document Analysis

President Harry S. Truman begins his State of the Union address by enumerating the positive qualities of Americans. These include the desire to eradicate poverty and injustice, and the belief that prejudice should not bar a US citizen from obtaining an education or job for which he is qualified. He praises the strength of the US economy, adding that the federal government must cooperate with industry, labor, and farmers to keep it running smoothly.

Truman cites public investments in highways, hydroelectric power, soil conservation, and the Social Security system to illustrate how the federal government has been providing for the future needs of Americans. He emphasizes that these federal initiatives helped to improve productivity in the private sector, including a 45 percent increase in agricultural production and a 75 percent increase in industrial production.

However, Truman also calls attention to problems facing the United States. Prices for goods are high, and production of consumer goods is insufficient to meet demand. Minimum wages are low, and small businesses are suffering as large corporate monopolies grow. Poor families continue to live in unsafe environments, medical care is sometimes unaffordable even for those who are employed, and too many schools provide children with inadequate education.

Truman stresses that the federal government cannot solve these problems alone. An effective long-term solution requires the cooperation of private businesses, who must continue to create jobs and increase production. He observes that business should take the long view and work to avoid the cycles of boom and bust, planning for slow, steady expansion. The Employment Act of 1946 was passed to help curb inflation, and he outlines several recommendations to further this goal. In part, he recommends repealing the Taft-Hartley Act and reenacting the Wagner Act, increasing the federal minimum wage, establishing additional price supports for farmers, and expanding modern conveniences, such as electrical service in rural areas.

Truman also emphasizes the need to wisely manage land, water, forests, and other natural resources, proposing that conservation not "lock up" resources, but instead invest in future progress. He recommends developing rivers for power, irrigation, navigation, and flood control, as well as exploring undersea petroleum reserves.

In addition to economic concerns, Truman mentions matters related to Americans' standard of living. He highlights Social Security, health, education, housing, and civil rights and observes that there is much room for improvement in these areas. He believes that the Employment Act of 1946 will motivate private businesses to help solve these problems by, for example, providing financial incentives to construct affordable housing and encouraging further cooperation.

Truman concludes by noting that the "driving force behind our progress is our faith in our democratic institutions." The world looks to the United States for leadership, he states, because of the way it has successfully enacted the principles of democratic government to the benefit of its people.

Essential Themes

The Truman administration faced a variety of economic challenges during the postwar period. The United States assumed a significant role in rebuilding Europe, partly for humanitarian reasons and partly to stem the Soviet Union's influence and prevent Communism's expansion across Europe. The United States authorized billions of dollars in aid to European countries as part of the Truman Doctrine and the Marshall Plan—an unprecedented amount for peacetime spending on foreign affairs—in hopes of helping maintain Europe's democratic governments.

At home, the postwar economic shift sparked potentially crippling inflation, which the federal government sought to reduce. In his address, Truman made several specific recommendations to Congress in accordance with the Employment Act of 1946, including tightening control over consumer and bank credit; regulating speculation on the commodity exchanges; establishing priorities and allocations for transportation spending; reinforcing rent control; imposing price ceilings for scarce commodities; and intervening to improve production quantities for materials in critically short supply.

While some believed that resolving these issues efficiently and effectively required federal intervention, others resented the government's interference in the free market. International concern also ran high about the spread of Communism, and the United States had invested much money to ensure that Europe avoided Communist control as it rebuilt, making Americans suspicious of government control over business affairs. Truman's challenge was to encourage Congress to create and fund social and economic programs using government money—and to gain the support of American citizens and businesses for these programs—by equating government support with effective democracy.

The recommendations proposed by Truman in this address served as the foundation for his extension of Roosevelt's New Deal, which became known as the Fair Deal program. However, unlike his predecessor, Truman was not as successful in overcoming the political resistance to such changes. Though he only succeeded in passing legislation regarding three aspects—Social Security, minimum wage, and housing—these improvements proved significant and reflected on the merit of the issues discussed in his speech.

—*Tracey M. DiLascio, JD*

Bibliography and Additional Reading

Anslover, Nicole L. *Harry S. Truman: The Coming of the Cold War*. New York: Routledge, 2014. Print.

De Luna, Phyliss Komarek. *Public versus Private Power during the Truman Administration: A Story of Fair Deal Liberalism*. New York: Peter Lang, 1997. Print.

Donovan, Robert J. *Tumultuous Years: The Presidency of Harry S. Truman, 1949–1953*. New York: Norton, 1982. Print.

Steelman, Aaron. "Employment Act of 1946." *Federal Reserve System*. Federal Reserve Bank of Richmond, 22 Nov. 2013. Web. 23 Feb. 2015.

THE RISE OF CIVIL RIGHTS

For over 50 years after its 1896 ruling in *Plessy v. Ferguson*, the US Supreme Court upheld the doctrine of "separate but equal"—meaning that African Americans could be discriminated against in public facilities as long as access to separate and nominally equal facilities were made available. In fact, most such facilities in southern states with Jim Crow laws on the books were clearly unequal and often absent. Schools, buses, restrooms, shops, movie houses and a host of other institutions and facilities gave preferential treatment to whites while relegating blacks to secondary status.

Following both World War I and World War II, waves of African Americans migrated from the rural South to urban centers in the Northeast and Midwest. The great migration of blacks brought attention to discriminatory practices and made civil rights an emerging concern on the national front. Still, conservative forces ensured that patterns of segregation and discrimination yielded only slowly. A few Supreme Court rulings in the postwar 1940s began to chip away at the segregationist monolith. It would not be until the 1950s, however, that civil rights efforts would take off and form the beginnings of a movement.

■ *Mendez et al. v. Westminster School District of Orange County et al.*

Date: February 18, 1946
Author: Paul John McCormick
Genre: court case

Summary Overview

Gonzalo Méndez, a Mexican native, became a naturalized citizen of the United States in 1943. Méndez was a successful vegetable farmer and had three children who were fluent in both Spanish and English. When the Méndez family registered their children for school in their primarily Anglo-American school district in California's Orange County, however, they were told that they would need to attend the Hoover School in another district. This school's pupils were all of Mexican descent. Méndez argued for his children to attend the school in their district, but made no headway with the school administration, the local school board, or the county school board. In the course of pursuing his cause, Méndez and his lawyer discovered that other school districts were also segregating their Mexican and Latin American students. In March 1945, Méndez and four other plaintiffs filed suit in a United States district court against four Orange County school districts and their superintendents and school boards. They argued that segregating children of Mexican or Latin American ancestry was a violation of the Fourteenth Amendment promise of equal protection of law. Méndez and his fellow plaintiffs won the case, and on February 18, 1946, the segregation of Mexican American students was declared a violation of the Fourteenth Amendment.

Defining Moment

Mexican Americans were considered second-class citizens in California as early as 1848, when the territory that became the state was won from Mexico by the United States. Racial theories were applied to non-Anglo-American populations, including Mexican Americans and other Latino citizens in the United States. Specific laws excluded African American and Asian American citizens from access to equal education on the basis of race, but Mexican Americans, who were considered white, if culturally inferior, were left out of overt legal discrimination. As farming boomed in the early twentieth century, however, the need for labor led to increased immigration, particularly from Mexico, and the Mexican American population in California exploded. Immigration from Mexico was not restricted until a country-of-origin quota system was implemented in the early 1920s, and hundreds of thousands of Mexicans flooded into California during and after the Mexican Revolution (1910–20). Californian communities responded with growing discrimination against these immigrants and their families, limiting access to employment and education. As Mexican American students were segregated, the quality of the education available to them declined. Teachers in these schools were paid less, the facilities were often in poor repair and overcrowded, and little effort was made to prepare these children for higher education. Aptitude and intelligence tests were administered irregularly or not at all.

Mexican Americans fought with distinction during World War II, and like many other underprivileged groups in the United States, they expected that their service would result in greater opportunities at home. The Méndez family moved into a predominantly Anglo-American school district in Orange County in 1945 and expected to be able to register their three children for public school. When they were denied admission, Gonzalo Méndez appealed to the local and county school boards. When this had no effect, Méndez and four other families filed a class action lawsuit on behalf of the five thousand Mexican Americans living in four Orange County school districts.

The *Mendez v. Westminster* suit was tricky, however. In *Plessy v. Ferguson* in 1896, racial discrimination in education had been supported by law. The *Mendez v. Westminster* case argued that Mexican American students were not racially separate from other students, but were discriminated against based on their national origin. The schools argued that the language barrier necessitated that Spanish-speaking students attend separate schools until they had mastered English. This, of course, would not have applied to the Méndez children, who spoke proficient English, and the lawyers for the plaintiff argued that no reliable language test was given, and the only real basis for segregation was national origin. On February 18, 1946, US district court judge Paul McCormick agreed with Méndez that segregation based on national origin was unconstitutional, as it violated the equal protection of law provision of the Fourteenth Amendment.

Mendez v. Westminster was the first successful court challenge to the segregation in schools that was widespread in the United States. Within five years, similar segregation was outlawed in Texas and Arizona. It established an important legal pathway for other cases challenging the "separate but equal" doctrine that supported segregation.

Author Biography

Paul John McCormick was born in New York City on April 23, 1879. He attended St. Ignatius College in San Francisco and, after passing the California bar in 1900, went into private practice. He served as deputy district attorney of Los Angeles County beginning in 1905. From 1910 until 1921, he was a judge in the California Superior Court, County of Los Angeles, and then an associate justice of the California Appellate Court until 1924. That year McCormick was appointed to a seat on the United States District Court for the Southern District of California. He became the chief justice of this court in 1948 and held that position until 1951. McCormick died on December 2, 1960.

HISTORICAL DOCUMENT

MENDEZ et al. v. WESTMINISTER SCHOOL DIST. OF ORANGE COUNTY et al.

Civil Action No. 4292.

UNITED STATES DISTRICT COURT FOR THE SOUTHERN DISTRICT OF CALIFORNIA, CENTRAL DIVISION

February 18, 1946

Gonzalo Mendez, William Guzman, Frank Palomino, Thomas Estrada and Lorenzo Ramirez, as citizens of the United States, and on behalf of their minor children, and as they allege in the petition, on behalf of "some 5000" persons similarly affected, all of Mexican or Latin descent, have filed a class suit pursuant to Rule 23 of Federal Rules of Civil Procedure, 28 U.S.C.A. following section 723c, against the Westminister, Garden Grove and El Modeno School Districts, and the Santa Ana City Schools, all of Orange County, California, and the respective trustees and superintendents of said school districts.

The complaint, grounded upon the Fourteenth Amendment to the Constitution of the United States1 and Subdivision 14 of Section 24 of the Judicial Code, Title 28, Section 41, subdivision 14, U.S.C.A.2, alleges a concerted policy and design of class discrimination against 'persons of Mexican or Latin descent or extraction' of elementary school age by the defendant school agencies in the conduct and operation of public schools of said districts, resulting in the denial of the equal protection of the laws to such class of persons among which are the petitioning school children.

Specifically, plaintiffs allege:

"That for several years last past respondents have and do now in furtherance and in execution of their common plan, design and purpose within their respective Systems and Districts, have by their regulation, custom and usage and in execution thereof adopted and declared: That all children or persons of Mexican or Latin descent or extraction, though Citizens of the United States of America, shall be, have been and are now excluded from attending, using, enjoying and receiving the benefits of the education, health and recreation facilities of certain schools within their respective Districts and Systems but that said children are now and have been segregated and required to and must attend and use certain schools in said Districts and Systems reserved for and attended solely and exclusively by children and persons of Mexican and Latin descent, while such other schools are maintained attended and used exclusively by and for persons and children purportedly known as White or Anglo-Saxon children.

"That in execution of said rules and regulations, each, every and all the foregoing children are compelled and required to and must attend and use the schools in said respective Districts reserved for and attended solely and exclusively by children of Mexican and Latin descent and are forbidden, barred and excluded from attending any other school in said District or System solely for the reason that said children or child are of Mexican or Latin descent."

The petitioners demand that the alleged rules, regulations, customs and usages be adjudged void and unconstitutional and that an injunction issue restraining further application by defendant school authorities of such rules, regulations, customs, and usages. It is conceded by all parties that there is no question of race discrimination in this action. It is, however, admitted that segregation per se is practiced in the above-mentioned school districts as the Spanish-speaking children enter school life and as they advance through the grades in the respective school districts. It is also admitted by the defendants that the petitioning children are qualified to attend the public schools in the respective districts of their residences.

In the Westminster, Garden Grove and El Modeno school districts the respective boards of trustees had taken official action, declaring that there be no segregation of pupils on a racial basis but that non-English-speaking children (which group, excepting as to a small number of pupils, was made up entirely of children of Mexican ancestry or descent), be required to attend schools designated by the boards separate and apart from English-speaking pupils; that such group should attend such schools until they had acquired some proficiency in the English language.

The petitioners contend that such official action evinces a covert attempt by the school authorities in such school districts to produce an arbitrary discrimination against school children of Mexican extraction or descent and that such illegal result has been established in such illegal result has been established in such school

districts respectively. The school authorities of the City of Santa Ana have not memorialized any such official action, but petitioners assert that the same custom and usage exists in the schools of the City of Santa Ana under the authority of appropriate school agencies of such city. The concrete acts complained of are those of the various school district officials in directing which schools the petitioning children and others of the same class or group must attend. The segregation exists in the elementary schools to and including the sixth grade in two of the defendant districts, and in the two other defendant districts through the eighth grade. The record before us shows without conflict that the technical facilities and physical conveniences offered in the schools housing entirely the segregated pupils, the efficiency of the teachers therein and the curricula are identical and in some respects superior to those in the other schools in the respective districts.

The ultimate question for decision may be thus stated: Does such official action of defendant district school agencies and the usages and practices pursued by the respective school authorities as shown by the evidence operate to deny or deprive the so-called non-English-speaking school children of Mexican ancestry or descent within such school districts of the equal protection of the laws? The defendants at the outset challenge the jurisdiction of this court under the record as it exists at this time. We have already denied the defendants' motion to dismiss the action upon the "face" of the complaint. No reason has been shown which warrants reconsideration of such decision. While education is a State matter, it is not so absolutely or exclusively. *Cumming v. Board of Education of Richmond County*, 175 U.S. 528, 20 S.Ct. 197, 201, 44 L.Ed. 262. In the Cumming decision the Supreme Court said: "That education of the people in schools maintained by state taxation is a matter belonging to the respective states, and any interference on the part of Federal authority with the management of such schools cannot be justified except in the case of a clear and unmistakable disregard of rights secured by the supreme law of the land." See, also, *Gong Lum v. Rice*, 275 U.S. 78, 48 S.Ct. 91, 72 L.Ed. 172; *Wong Him v. Callahan*, C.C., 119 F. 381; *Ward v. Flood*, 48 Cal. 36, 17

Am.Rep. 405; *Piper et al. v. Big Pine School District*, 193 Cal. 664, 226 P. 926.

Obviously, then, a violation by a State of a personal right or privilege protected by the Fourteenth Amendment in the exercise of the State's duty to provide for the education of its citizens and inhabitants would justify the Federal Court to intervene. State of Missouri ex rel. *Gaines v. Canada*, 305 U.S. 337, 59 S.Ct. 232, 83 L.Ed. 208. The complaint before us in this action, having alleged an invasion by the common school authorities of the defendant districts of the equal opportunity of pupils to acquire knowledge, confers jurisdiction on this court if the actions complained of are deemed those of the State. *Hamilton v. Regents of University of California*, 293 U.S. 245, 55 S.Ct. 197, 79 L.Ed. 343; cf. *Meyer v. Nebraska*, 262 U.S. 390, 43 S.Ct. 625, 67 L.Ed. 1042, 29 A.L.R. 1446.

Are the actions of public school authorities of a rural or city school in the State of California, as alleged and established in this case, to be considered actions of the State within the meaning of the Fourteenth Amendment so as to confer jurisdiction on this court to hear and decide this case under the authority of Section 24, Subdivision 14 of the Judicial Code, supra? We think they are.

[3] In the public school system of the State of California the various local school districts enjoy a considerable degree of autonomy. Fundamentally, however, the people of the State have made the public school system a matter of State supervision. Such system is not committed to the exclusive control of local governments. Article IX, Constitution of California, *Butterworth v. Boyd*, 12 Cal.2d 140, 82 P.2d 434, 126 A.L.R. 838. It is a matter of general concern, and not a municipal affair. *Esberg v. Badaracco*, 202 Cal. 110, 259 P. 730; *Becker v. Council of City of Albany*, 47 Cal.App.2d 702, 118 P.2d 924.

[4] The Education Code of California provides for the requirements of teachers' qualifications, the admission and exclusion of pupils, the courses of study and the enforcement of them, the duties of superintendents of schools and of the school trustees of elementary schools in the State of California. The appropriate agencies of the State of California allocate to counties all the State school money exclusively for the payment of teachers' salaries in the public schools and such funds are apportioned to the respective school districts within the counties. While, as previously observed, local school boards and trustees are vested by State legislation with considerable latitude in the administration of their districts, nevertheless, despite the decentralization of the educational system in California, the rules of the local school district are required to follow the general pattern laid down by the legislature, and their practices must be consistent with law and with the rules prescribed by the State Board of Education. See Section 2204, Education Code of California. When the basis and composition of the public school system is considered, there can be no doubt of the oneness of the system in the State of California, or of the restricted powers of the elementary school authorities in the political subdivisions of the State. See *Kennedy v. Miller*, 97 Cal. 429, 32 P. 558; *Bruch v. Colombet*, 104 Cal. 347, 38 P. 45; *Ward v. San Diego School District*, 203 Cal. 712, 265 P. 821. In *Hamilton v. Regents of University of California*, supra, and *West Virginia State Board of Education v. Barnette*, 319 U.S. 624, 63 S.Ct. 1178, 1185, 87 L.Ed. 1628, 147 A.L.R. 674, the acts of university regents and of a board of education were held acts of the State. In the recent Barnette decision the court stated: "The Fourteenth Amendment, as now applied to the States, protects the citizen against the State itself and all of its creatures—Boards of Education not excepted." Although these cases dealt with State rather than local Boards, both are agencies and parts of the State educational system, as is indicated by the Supreme Court in the Barnette case, wherein it stated: "Such Boards are numerous and their territorial jurisdiction often small. But small and local authority may feel less sense of responsibility to the Constitution, and agencies of publicity may be less vigilant in calling it to account." Upon an appraisal of the factual situation before this court as illumined by the laws of the State of California relating to the public school system, it is clear that the respondents should be classified as representatives of the State to such an extent and in such a sense that the great restraints of the Constitution set limits to their action. *Screws v. United States*, 325 U.S. 91, 65 S.Ct. 1051; *Smith v. Allwright*, 321 U.S. 649, 64 S.Ct. 757, 88 L.Ed. 987, 151 A.L.R. 1110; *Hague v. Commit-*

tee for Industrial Organization, 307 U.S. 496, 59 S.Ct. 954, 83 L.Ed. 1423; *Home Tel. & Tel. Co. v. Los Angeles*, 227 U.S. 278, 33 S.Ct. 312, 57 L.Ed. 510.

[5] We therefore turn to consider whether under the record before us the school boards and administrative authorities in the respective defendant districts have by their segregation policies and practices transgressed applicable law and Constitutional safeguards and limitations and thus have invaded the personal right which every public school pupil has to the equal protection provision of the Fourteenth Amendment to obtain the means of education. We think the pattern of public education promulgated in the Constitution of California and effectuated by provisions of the Education Code of the State prohibits segregation of the pupils of Mexican ancestry in the elementary schools from the rest of the school children.

Section 1 of Article IX of the Constitution of California directs the legislature to 'encourage by all suitable means the promotion of intellectual, scientific, moral, and agricultural improvement' of the people. Pursuant to this basic directive by the people of the State many laws stem authorizing special instruction in the public schools for handicapped children. See Division 8 of the Education Code. Such legislation, however, is general in its aspects. It includes all those who fall within the described classification requiring the special consideration provided by the statutes regardless of their ancestry or extraction. The common segregation attitudes and practices of the school authorities in the defendant school districts in Orange County pertain solely to children of Mexican ancestry and parentage. They are singled out as a class for segregation. Not only is such method of public school administration contrary to the general requirements of the school laws of the State, but we think it indicates an official school policy that is antagonistic in principle to Sections 16004 and 16005 of the Education Code of the State.

Obviously, the children referred to in these laws are those of Mexican ancestry. And it is noteworthy that the educational advantages of their commingling with other pupils is regarded as being so important to the school system of the State that it is provided for even regardless of the citizenship of the parents. We perceive in the laws relating to the public educational system in the State of California a clear purpose to avoid and forbid distinctions among pupils based upon race or ancestry4 except in specific situations5 not pertinent to this action. Distinctions of that kind have recently been declared by the highest judicial authority of the United States "by their very nature odious to a free people whose institutions are founded upon the doctrine of equality." They are said to be 'utterly inconsistent with American traditions and ideals.' *Kiyoshi Hirabayashi v. United States*, 320 U.S. 81, 63 S.Ct. 1375, 1385, 87 L.Ed. 1774.

Our conclusions in this action, however, do not rest solely upon what we conceive to be the utter irreconcilability of the segregation practices in the defendant school districts with the public educational system authorized and sanctioned by the laws of the State of California. We think such practices clearly and unmistakably disregard rights secured by the supreme law of the land. *Cumming v. Board of Education of Richmond County*, supra. [6, 7] "The equal protection of the laws" pertaining to the public school system in California is not provided by furnishing in separate schools the same technical facilities, text books and courses of instruction to children of Mexican ancestry that are available to the other public school children regardless of their ancestry. A paramount requisite in the American system of public education is social equality. It must be open to all children by unified school association regardless of lineage. We think that under the record before us the only tenable ground upon which segregation practices in the defendant school districts can be defended lies in the English language deficiencies of some of the children of Mexican ancestry as they enter elementary public school life as beginners. But even such situations do not justify the general and continuous segregation in separate schools of the children of Mexican ancestry from the rest of the elementary school population as has been shown to be the practice in the defendant school districts—in all of them to the sixth grade, and in two of them through the eighth grade.

The evidence clearly shows that Spanish-speaking children are retarded in learning English by lack of exposure to its use because of segregation, and that commingling of the entire student body instills and develops a common cultural attitude among the school children which is imperative for the perpetuation of American institutions and ideals.6 It is also established by the record that the methods of segregation prevalent in the defendant school districts foster antagonisms in the children and suggest inferiority among them where none exists. One of the flagrant examples of the discriminatory results of segregation in two of the schools involved in this case is shown by the record. In the district under consideration there are two schools, the Lincoln and the Roosevelt, located approximately 120 yards apart on the same school grounds, hours of opening and closing, as well as recess periods, are not uniform. No credible language test is given to the children of Mexican ancestry upon entering the first grade in Lincoln School. This school has an enrollment of 249 so-called Spanish-speaking pupils, and no so-called English-speaking pupils; while the Roosevelt, (the other) school, has 83 so-called English-speaking pupils and 25 so-called Spanish-speaking pupils. Standardized tests as to mental ability are given to the respective classes in the two schools and the same curricula are pursued in both schools and, of course, in the English language as required by State law. Section 8251, Education Code. In the last school year the students in the seventh grade of the Lincoln were superior scholarly to the same grade in the Roosevelt School and to any group in the seventh grade in either of the schools in the past. It further appears that not only did the class as a group have such mental superiority but that certain pupils in the group were also outstanding in the class itself.

Not withstanding this showing, the pupils of such excellence were kept in the Lincoln School. It is true that there is no evidence in the record before us that shows that any of the members of this exemplary class requested transfer to the other so-called intermingled school, but the record does show without contradiction that another class had protested against the segregation policies and practices in the schools of this El Modeno district without avail. While the pattern or ideal of segregating the school children of Mexican ancestry from the rest of the school attendance permeates and is practiced in all of the four defendant districts, there are procedural deviations among the school administrative agencies in effectuating the general plan. In Garden Grove Elementary School District the segregation extends only through the fifth grade. Beyond, all pupils in such district, regardless of their ancestry or linguistic proficiency, are housed, instructed and associate in the same school facility. This arrangement conclusively refutes the reasonableness or advisability of any segregation of children of Mexican ancestry beyond the fifth grade in any of the defendant school districts in view of the standardized and uniform curricular requirements in the elementary schools of Orange County. But the admitted practice and long established custom in this school district whereby all elementary public school children of Mexican descent are required to attend one specified school (the Hoover) until they attain the sixth grade, while all other pupils of the same grade are permitted to and do attend two other elementary schools of this district, notwithstanding that some of such pupils live within the Hoover School division of the district, clearly establishes an unfair and arbitrary class distinction in the system of public education operative in the Garden Grove Elementary School District. The long-standing discriminatory custom prevalent in this district is aggravated by the fact shown by the record that although there are approximately 25 children of Mexican descent living in the vicinity of the Lincoln School, none of them attend that school, but all are peremptorily assigned by the school authorities to the Hoover School, although the evidence shows that there are no school zones territorially established in the district.

The record before us shows a paradoxical situation concerning the segregation attitude of the school authorities in the Westminister School District. There are two elementary schools in this undivided area. Instruction is given pupils in each school from kindergarten to the eighth grade, inclusive. Westminister School has 642 pupils, of which 628 are so-called English-speaking children, and 14 so-called Spanish-speaking pupils. The Hoover School is attended solely by 152 children of Mexican descent. Segregation of these from the rest of the school population precipitated such vigorous protests by residents of the district that the school board in January, 1944, recognizing the discriminatory results of segregation, resolved to unite the two schools and thus abolish the objectionable practices which had been operative in the schools of the district for a considerable period. A bond issue was submitted to the electors to raise funds to defray the cost of contemplated expenditures in the school consolidation. The bonds were not voted and the record before us in this action reflects no execution or carrying out of the official action of the board of trustees taken on or about the 16th of January, 1944. It thus appears that there has been no abolishment of the traditional segregation practices in this district pertaining to pupils of Mexican ancestry through the gamut of elementary school life. We have adverted to the unfair consequences of such practices in the similarly situated El Modeno School District.

Before considering the specific factual situation in the Santa Ana City Schools it should be noted that the omnibus segregation of children of Mexican ancestry from the rest of the student body in the elementary grades in the schools involved in this case because of language handicaps is not warranted by the record before us. The tests applied to the beginners are shown to have been generally hasty, superficial and not reliable.

In some instances separate classification was determined largely by the Latinized or Mexican name of the child. Such methods of evaluating language knowledge are illusory and are not conducive to the inculcation and enjoyment of civil rights which are of primary importance in the public school system of education in the United States.

It has been held that public school authorities may differentiate in the exercise of their reasonable discretion as to the pedagogical methods of instruction to be pursued with different pupils.7 And foreign language handicaps may be to such a degree in the pupils in elementary schools as to require special treatment in separate classrooms. Such separate allocations, however, can be lawfully made only after credible examination by the appropriate school authority of each child whose capacity to learn is under consideration and the determination of such segregation must be based wholly upon indiscriminate foreign language impediments in the individual child, regardless of his ethnic traits or ancestry.

[9–11] The defendant Santa Ana School District maintains fourteen elementary schools which furnish instruction from kindergarten to the sixth grade, inclusive.

About the year 1920 the Board of Education, for the purpose of allocating pupils to the several schools of the district in proportion to the facilities available at such schools, divided the district into fourteen zones and assigned to the school established in each zone all pupils residing within such zone. There is no evidence that any discriminatory or other objectionable motive or purpose actuated the School Board in locating or defining such zones. Subsequently the influx of people of Mexican ancestry in large numbers and their voluntary settlement in certain of the fourteen zones resulted in three of the zones becoming occupied almost entirely by such group of people.

Two zones, that in which the Fremont School is located, and another contiguous area in which the Franklin School is situated, present the only flagrant discriminatory situation shown by the evidence in this case in the Santa Ana City Schools. The Fremont School has 325 so-called Spanish-speaking pupils and no so-called English-speaking pupils. The Franklin School has 237 pupils of which 161 are so-called English-speaking children, and 76 so-called Spanish-speaking children.

The evidence shows that approximately 26 pupils of Mexican descent who reside within the Fremont zone are permitted by the School Board to attend the Franklin School because their families had always gone there. It also appears that there are approximately 35 other pupils not of Mexican descent who live within the Fremont zone who are not required to attend the Fremont School but who are also permitted by the Board of Education to attend the Franklin School. Sometime in the fall of the year 1944 there arose dissatisfaction by the parents of some of the so-called Spanish-speaking pupils in the Fremont School zone who were not granted the privilege that approximately 26 children also of Mexican descent, enjoyed in attending the Franklin School. Protest was made en masse by such dissatisfied group of parents, which resulted in the Board of Education directing its secretary to send a letter to the parents of all of the so-called Spanish-speaking pupils living in the Fremont zone and attending the Franklin School that beginning September, 1945, the permit to attend Franklin School would be withdrawn and the children would be required to attend the school of the zone in which they were living, viz., the Fremont School.

There could have been no arbitrary discrimination claimed by plaintiffs by the action of the school authorities if the same official course had been applied to the 35 other so-called English-speaking pupils exactly situated as were the approximate 26 children of Mexican lineage, but the record is clear that the requirement of the Board of Education was intended for and directed exclusively to the specified pupils of Mexican ancestry and if carried out becomes operative solely against such group of children.

It should be stated in fairness to the Superintendent of the Santa Ana City Schools that he testified he would recommend to the Board of Education that the children of those who protested the action requiring transfer from the Franklin School be allowed to remain there because of long attendance and family tradition.

However, there was no official recantation shown of the action of the Board of Education reflected by the letters of the Secretary and sent only to the parents of the children of Mexican ancestry. The natural operation and effect of the Board's official action manifests a clear purpose to arbitrarily discriminate against the pupils of Mexican ancestry and to deny to them the equal protection of the laws.

The court may not exercise legislative or administrative functions in this case to save such discriminatory act from inoperativeness. Cf. *Yu Cong Eng v. Trinidad*, 271 U.S. 500, 46 S.Ct. 70 L.Ed. 1059. There are other discriminatory customs, shown by the evidence, existing in the defendant school districts as to pupils of Mexican descent and extraction, but we deem it unnecessary to discuss them in this memorandum.

We conclude by holding that the allegations of the complaint (petition) have been established sufficiently to justify injunctive relief against all defendants, restrain-

ing further discriminatory practices against the pupils of Mexican descent in the public schools of defendant school districts. See *Morris v. Williams*, 8 Cir., 149 F.2d 703. Findings of fact, conclusions of law, and decree of injunction are accordingly ordered pursuant to Rule 52, F.R.C.P. Attorney for plaintiffs will within ten days from date hereof prepare and present same under local Rule 7 of this court.

Footnotes

1. "Section 1. All persons born or naturalized in the United States, and subject to the jurisdiction thereof, are citizens of the United States and of the State wherein they reside. No State shall make or enforce any law which shall abridge the privileges or immunities of citizens of the United States; nor shall any State deprive any person of life, liberty, or property, without due process of law; nor deny to any person within its jurisdiction the equal protection of the laws."

2. "The district courts shall have original jurisdiction as follows: * * * " Sec. 41, subd. (14) "Suits to redress deprivation of civil rights. Fourteenth. Of all suits at law or in equity authorized by law to be brought by any person to redress the deprivation, under color of any law, statute, ordinance, regulation, custom, or usage, of any State, of any right, privilege, or immunity, secured by the Constitution of the United States, or of any right secured by any law of the United States providing for equal rights of citizens of the United States, or of all persons within the jurisdiction of the United States."

3. "Sec. 16004. Any person, otherwise eligible for admission to any class or school of a school district of this State, whose parents are or are not citizens of the United States and whose actual and legal residence is in a foreign country adjacent to this State may be admitted to the class or school of the district by the governing board of the district."

"Sec. 16005. The governing board of the district may, as a condition precedent to the admission of any person, under Section 16004, require the parent or guardian of such person to pay to the district an amount not more than sufficient to reimburse the district for the total cost, exclusive of capital outlays, of educating the person and providing him with transportation to and from school. The cost of transportation shall not exceed ten dollars

($10) per month. Tuition payments shall be made in advance for each month or semester during the period of attendance. If the amount paid is more or less than the total cost of education and transportation, adjustment shall be made for the following semester or school year. The attendance of the pupils shall not be included in computing the average daily attendance of the class or school for the purpose of obtaining apportionment of State funds."

4. Sec. 8501, Education Code. "Children between six and 21 years of age. The day elementary school of each school district shall be open for the admission of all children between six and 21 years of age residing within the boundaries of the district."

Sec. 8002. "Maintenance of elementary day schools and day high schools with equal rights and privileges. The governing board of any school district shall maintain all of the elementary day schools established by it, and all of the day high schools established by it with equal rights and privileges as far as possible."

5. Sec. 8003. "Schools for Indian children, and children of Chinese, Japanese, or Mongolian parentage: Establishment. The governing board of any school district may establish separate schools for Indian children, excepting children of Indians who are wards of the United States Government and children of all other Indians who are descendants of the original American Indians of the United States, and for children of Chinese, Japanese, or Mongolian parentage."

Sec. 8004. "Same: Admission of children into other schools. When separate schools are established for Indian children or children of Chinese, Japanese, or Mongolian parentage, the Indian children or children of Chinese, Japanese, or Mongolian parentage shall not be admitted into any other school."

6. The study of American institutions and ideals in all schools located within the State of California is required by Section 10051, Education Code. 7. See *Plessy v. Ferguson*, 163 U.S. 537, 16 S.Ct. 1138, 41 L.Ed. 256.

GLOSSARY

Effectuated/effectuating: to make done; effect

evinces: to show clearly; make evident or manifest; prove

gamut: the entire scale or range

inculcation: the act of inculcating or teaching or influencing persistently and repeatedly in order to implant an idea or attitude

peremptorily: leaving no opportunity for denial or refusal; imperious

promulgated: to make known by open declaration; publish

redress: the setting right of what is wrong; relief from wrong or injury

thereof: from or out of that origin or cause; of that

Document Analysis

This court ruling begins with a summary of the case. The five families involved, "all of Mexican or Latin descent," filed a suit against four school systems, all in Orange County, California, arguing that the segregation of "persons of Mexican or Latin descent or extraction" in elementary schools denied these children equal protection of the law guaranteed by the Fourteenth Amendment.

In particular, for an unspecified period, children of Mexican and Latin American descent had been barred from attending certain schools in their districts, which had been restricted to "children purportedly known as White or Anglo-Saxon children," and were forced to attend schools with only Mexican or Latin American students. Though this document does not specifically address this, part of the impetus for this case was the fact that Gonzalo Méndez's nieces, Alice and Virginia Vidaurri, were allowed to register in the school system, as they had a last name that was not identifiable as Mexican, and they were light-skinned. This led to a very subjective, selective enforcement of this segregation, based on skin tone, name, and appearance rather than an objective language or aptitude test that would have identified the kind of special educational needs of students for whom English was a new language. In fact, since the Méndez children were no more Mexican than their cousins and spoke fluent English, the argument made by the schools that the language barrier necessitated separate schools was patently false. The plaintiffs demanded that segregated schools be ended at once.

The court ruling was subject to the criticism that such educational decisions were at the discretion of the local and county school boards and the state, so the court took great pains to establish its jurisdiction over the case. In answer to the charge that educational segregation was a local issue and, therefore, should be subject to state courts, the court argued that since the state set the standards for education and oversaw local boards, education was a state, rather than local, issue. While the court agreed that education was a state issue, "it is not so absolutely or exclusively." If the rights of the citizens, guaranteed to all by the "supreme law of the land," were violated in any state, federal courts has a right to intervene. Certainly, the court argued, an alleged violation of the Constitution qualified. The court ruling first laid out the ways that segregation based on national origin was a violation of California's own constitution, stating, "We perceive in the laws relating to the public educational system in the State of California a clear purpose to avoid and forbid distinctions among pupils."

The court decision picked apart the argument that a language barrier was a compelling reason to segregate students. Some of the schools named in the suit segregated children through the fifth grade, others as far as eighth grade. If the language barrier was so great, the court argued, why the inconsistency? The segregation of Spanish-speaking students also made the acquisition of English more difficult, further affecting the quality of their education. The court declared that providing equal, or in some cases superior, facilities for students of Mexican and Latin American descent was not a compelling reason to deny these students "social equality." Schools must be open to all children, regardless of ancestry.

Essential Themes

This court decision, which was upheld by the Ninth Circuit Court of Appeals, spelled the end of school segregation based on national origin and paved the way for challenges to segregation based on race, which was widespread in the American South. This decision set an important precedent, declaring that "social equality" was protected by the equal protection clause in the Fourteenth Amendment of the Constitution. The primary theme of this document is the court's decision that there was no compelling reason to educate children of Mexican and Latin American descent separately from their peers, even if a language barrier was present. Indeed, the best way to overcome the language barrier was to integrate students and let them learn from each other. This decision led to the end of nationality-based segregation in Texas (1948) and Arizona (1951), and set a precedent used to end race-based segregation in the 1954 ***Brown v. Board of Education*** decision.

—*Bethany Groff, MA*

Bibliography and Additional Reading

Aguirre, Fredrick P. "*Mendez v. Westminster School District*: How It Affected *Brown v. Board of Education*." *Journal of Hispanic Higher Education* 4.4 (2005): 321–32. Print.

"*Mendez v. Westminster* Background." *United States Courts.* Administrative Office of the US Courts, Federal Judiciary, n.d. Web. 16 Feb. 2015.

Strum, Phillipa. *Mendez v. Westminster: School Desegregation and Mexican-American Rights.* Lawrence: U of Kansas P, 2010. Print.

■ *Morgan v. Virginia (1946)*

Date: June 3, 1946
Author: US Supreme Court, Justice Stanley Reed
Genre: court opinion

Summary Overview

A decade before Rosa Parks famously refused to give up her seat on a segregated city bus, African American passenger Irene Morgan sparked a US Supreme Court ruling barring segregation on interstate buses when she rejected a request to give up her seat on a Greyhound bus traveling from Virginia to Maryland to a white passenger as Virginia state law dictated. Morgan was ejected from the bus and arrested for her refusal. The National Association for the Advancement of Colored People (NAACP) took up her case, arguing that the driver's attempt to enforce Virginia segregation laws on an interstate bus violated the Constitution's commerce clause. The US Supreme Court agreed, issuing an opinion that enforcing segregationist laws on interstate buses was not constitutionally valid because the patchwork of state laws placed on undue burden on the companies forced to apply different policies depending on the specific states through which each route traveled.

Defining Moment

Although the 1863 Emancipation Proclamation and following 1865 federal victory in the Civil War made the nationwide abolition of slavery inevitable, centuries of institutionalized racism and discrimination proved impossible to wipe away with a constitutional amendment. Federal agents and military governors attempted to install integrated governments in the former Confederacy that would pass laws supporting the civil rights of freedmen and their descendants. Despite their best efforts, powerful former Confederates, planters, and conservative white Democrats managed to steadily regain control of the region's legislatures.

After President Rutherford B. Hayes ended direct federal intervention in the South after taking office in 1877, the situation of Southern African Americans steadily worsened. Abusive economic structures such as sharecropping and tenant farming kept African Americans desperately poor. Racist organizations and

lynch mobs terrorized individuals and communities. New state laws made it increasingly difficult or impossible for Southern African Americans to exercise the right to vote. In 1896, the US Supreme Court decision in *Plessy v. Ferguson* legitimized the separate-but-equal doctrine and thus the discriminatory Jim Crow laws that instituted segregation in public places as constitutional. Even prominent black leader Booker T. Washington argued that Southern African Americans should accept segregation and discrimination as a way of life.

With the turn of the century came a rising civil rights movement. The NAACP formed in 1909 and began fighting for civil rights through lobbying and court cases. Activists generally believed that reform was most likely to come from federal laws or policies rather than from state legislatures entrenched in centuries of racism.

By the 1940s the United States had a patchwork of Jim Crow laws and discriminatory practices. Most of these laws were centered in the states of the Old South that had made up the long-ago Confederacy; however, some crossed into border states and even into regions well outside of the South. Interracial marriage was banned in much of the West as well as across the South, for example. Maryland required segregation on railroads, streetcars, and steamboats, but not on buses.

When Irene Morgan was riding a Greyhound bus from Gloucester County, Virginia, to Baltimore, Maryland, in July 1944, therefore, she refused a driver's directive that she move from her current seat to a vacant one in the back of the bus. Greyhound policy permitted drivers to seat passengers wherever they deemed appropriate, and when Morgan resisted, she was forced to leave the bus and arrested. A Virginia county court fined her for violating the state's segregation laws; she refused to pay. The NAACP agreed to take up her case and followed it through to the US Supreme Court, where it was heard in March of 1946.

Author Biography

The majority opinion in *Morgan v. Virginia* was penned by Kentucky-born associate justice Stanley Reed, a lawyer who had served in the federal governments under the Herbert Hoover and the Franklin D. Roosevelt administrations. Before Roosevelt named him to the US Supreme Court in 1938, Reed had acted as solicitor general and argued several cases before the court. Although Reed tended to have a conservative stance on social issues, he was a consistent supporter of decisions favoring the expansion of civil rights for African Ameri-

cans. He wrote the majority opinion declaring the practice of whites-only primary elections unconstitutional in *Smith v. Allwright (1944)* and sided with the majority on pivotal decisions, including the unanimous 1954 *Brown v. Board of Education* ruling that ended segregation in public schools. After retiring from the US Supreme Court in 1957, Reed was appointed head of the Eisenhower administration's Commission on Civil Rights for a short time before withdrawing due to the possibility of perceived judicial partiality.

HISTORICAL DOCUMENT

MR. JUSTICE REED delivered the opinion of the Court.

This appeal brings to this Court the question of the constitutionality of an act of Virginia, which requires all passenger motor vehicle carriers, both interstate and intrastate, to separate without discrimination the white and colored passengers in their motor buses so that contiguous seats will not be occupied by persons of different races at the same time. A violation of the requirement of separation by the carrier is a misdemeanor. The driver or other person in charge is directed and required to increase or decrease the space allotted to the respective races as may be necessary or proper and may require passengers to change their seats to comply with the allocation. The operator's failure to enforce the provisions is made a misdemeanor.

These regulations were applied to an interstate passenger, this appellant, on a motor vehicle then making an interstate run or trip. According to the statement of fact by the Supreme Court of Appeals of Virginia, appellant, who is a Negro, was traveling on a motor common carrier, operating under the above-mentioned statute, from Gloucester County, Virginia, through the District of Columbia, to Baltimore, Maryland, the destination of the bus. There were other passengers, both white and colored. On her refusal to accede to a request of the driver to move to a back seat, which was partly occupied by other colored passengers, so as to permit the seat that she vacated to be used by white passengers, a warrant was

obtained and appellant was arrested, tried and convicted of a violation of § 4097dd of the Virginia Code. On a writ of error the conviction was affirmed by the Supreme Court of Appeals of Virginia. 184 Va. 24. The Court of Appeals interpreted the Virginia statute as applicable to appellant since the statute "embraces all motor vehicles and all passengers, both interstate and intrastate." The Court of Appeals refused to accept appellant's contention that the statute applied was invalid as a delegation of legislative power to the carrier by a concurrent holding "that no power is delegated to the carrier to legislate . . . . The statute itself condemns the defendant's conduct as a violation of law and not the rule of the carrier." Id., at 38. No complaint is made as to these interpretations of the Virginia statute by the Virginia court.

[1]
The errors of the Court of Appeals that are assigned and relied upon by appellant are in form only two. The first is that the decision is repugnant to Clause 3, § 8, Article I of the Constitution of the United States, n9 and the second the holding that powers reserved to the states by the Tenth Amendment include the power to require an interstate motor passenger to occupy a seat restricted for the use of his race. Actually, the first question alone needs consideration for, if the statute unlawfully burdens interstate commerce, the reserved powers of the state will not validate it.

[2]
We think, as the Court of Appeals apparently did, that

the appellant is a proper person to challenge the validity of this statute as a burden on commerce. If it is an invalid burden, the conviction under it would fail. The statute affects appellant as well as the transportation company. Constitutional protection against burdens on commerce is for her benefit on a criminal trial for violation of the challenged statute. *Hatch v. Reardon*, 204 U.S. 152, 160; *Federation of Labor v. McAdory*, 325 U.S. 450, 463.

This Court frequently must determine the validity of state statutes that are attacked as unconstitutional interferences with the national power over interstate commerce. This appeal presents that question as to a statute that compels racial segregation of interstate passengers in vehicles moving interstate.

[3]
The precise degree of a permissible restriction on state power cannot be fixed generally or indeed not even for one kind of state legislation, such as taxation or health or safety. There is a recognized abstract principle, however, that may be taken as a postulate for testing whether particular state legislation in the absence of action by Congress is beyond state power. This is that the state legislation is invalid if it unduly burdens that commerce in matters where uniformity is necessary—necessary in the constitutional sense of useful in accomplishing a permitted purpose. Where uniformity is essential for the functioning of commerce, a state may not interpose its local regulation. Too true it is that the principle lacks in precision. Although the quality of such a principle is abstract, its application to the facts of a situation created by the attempted enforcement of a statute brings about a specific determination as to whether or not the statute in question is a burden on commerce. Within the broad limits of the principle, the cases turn on their own facts.

[...]
[7]
In the field of transportation, there has been a series of decisions which hold that where Congress has not acted and although the state statute affects interstate commerce, a state may validly enact legislation which has predominantly only a local influence on the course of commerce. It is equally well settled that, even where Congress has not acted, state legislation or a final court order is invalid which materially affects interstate commerce. Because the Constitution puts the ultimate power to regulate commerce in Congress, rather than the states, the degree of state legislation's interference with that commerce may be weighed by federal courts to determine whether the burden makes the statute unconstitutional. The courts could not invalidate federal legislation for the same reason because Congress, within the limits of the Fifth Amendment, has authority to burden commerce if that seems to it a desirable means of accomplishing a permitted end.

[...]
[9]
This statute is attacked on the ground that it imposes undue burdens on interstate commerce. It is said by the Court of Appeals to have been passed in the exercise of the state's police power to avoid friction between the races. But this Court pointed out years ago "that a State cannot avoid the operation of this rule by simply invoking the convenient apologetics of the police power." Burdens upon commerce are those actions of a state which directly "impair the usefulness of its facilities for such traffic." That impairment, we think, may arise from other causes than costs or long delays. A burden may arise from a state statute which requires interstate passengers to order their movements on the vehicle in accordance with local rather than national requirements.

[10]
On appellant's journey, this statute required that she sit in designated seats in Virginia. Changes in seat designation might be made "at any time" during the journey when "necessary or proper for the comfort and convenience of passengers." This occurred in this instance. Upon such change of designation, the statute authorizes the operator of the vehicle to require, as he did here, "any passenger to change his or her seat as it may be necessary or proper." An interstate passenger must if necessary repeatedly shift seats while moving in Virginia to meet the seating requirements of the changing passenger group. On arrival at the District of Columbia line, the appellant would have had freedom to occupy any avail-

able seat and so to the end of her journey.

Interstate passengers traveling via motor buses between the north and south or the east and west may pass through Virginia on through lines in the day or in the night. The large buses approach the comfort of pullmans and have seats convenient for rest. On such interstate journeys the enforcement of the requirements for reseating would be disturbing.

Appellant's argument, properly we think, includes facts bearing on interstate motor transportation beyond those immediately involved in this journey under the Virginia statutory regulations. To appraise the weight of the burden of the Virginia statute on interstate commerce, related statutes of other states are important to show whether there are cumulative effects which may make local regulation impracticable. Eighteen states, it appears, prohibit racial separation on public carriers. Ten require separation on motor carriers. Of these, Alabama applies specifically to interstate passengers with an exception for interstate passengers with through tickets from states without laws on separation of passengers. The language of the other acts, like this Virginia statute before the Court of Appeals' decision in this case, may be said to be susceptible to an interpretation that they do or do not apply to interstate passengers.

In states where separation of races is required in motor vehicles, a method of identification as white or colored must be employed. This may be done by definition. Any ascertainable Negro blood identifies a person as colored for purposes of separation in some states. In the other states which require the separation of the races in motor carriers, apparently no definition generally applicable or made for the purposes of the statute is given. Court definition or further legislative enactments would be required to clarify the line between the races. Obviously there may be changes by legislation in the definition.

The interferences to interstate commerce which arise from state regulation of racial association on interstate vehicles has long been recognized. Such regulation hampers freedom of choice in selecting accommodations. The recent changes in transportation brought about

by the coming of automobiles does not seem of great significance in the problem. People of all races travel today more extensively than in 1878 when this Court first passed upon state regulation of racial segregation in commerce. The factual situation set out in preceding paragraphs emphasizes the soundness of this Court's early conclusion in *Hall v. DeCuir*, 95 U.S. 485.

The DeCuir case arose under a statute of Louisiana interpreted by the courts of that state and this Court to require public carriers "to give all persons traveling in that State, upon the public conveyances employed in such business, equal rights and privileges in all parts of the conveyance, without distinction or discrimination on account of race or color." Page 487. Damages were awarded against Hall, the representative of the operator of a Mississippi river steamboat that traversed that river interstate from New Orleans to Vicksburg, for excluding in Louisiana the defendant in error, a colored person, from a cabin reserved for whites. This Court reversed for reasons well stated in the words of Mr. Chief Justice Waite. As our previous discussion demonstrates, the transportation difficulties arising from a statute that requires commingling of the races, as in the DeCuir case, are increased by one that requires separation, as here. Other federal courts have looked upon racial separation statutes as applied to interstate passengers as burdens upon commerce.

In weighing the factors that enter into our conclusion as to whether this statute so burdens interstate commerce or so infringes the requirements of national uniformity as to be invalid, we are mindful of the fact that conditions vary between northern or western states such as Maine or Montana, with practically no colored population; industrial states such as Illinois, Ohio, New Jersey and Pennsylvania with a small, although appreciable, percentage of colored citizens; and the states of the deep south with percentages of from twenty-five to nearly fifty per cent colored, all with varying densities of the white and colored races in certain localities. Local efforts to promote amicable relations in difficult areas by legislative segregation in interstate transportation emerge from the latter racial distribution. As no state law can reach beyond its own border nor bar transportation of passengers across its boundaries, diverse seating requirements for the races in interstate journeys result. As there is no federal act dealing with the separation of races in interstate transportation, we must decide the validity of this Virginia statute on the challenge that it interferes with commerce, as a matter of balance between the exercise of the local police power and the need for national uniformity in the regulations for interstate travel. It seems clear to us that seating arrangements for the different races in interstate motor travel require a single, uniform rule to promote and protect national travel. Consequently, we hold the Virginia statute in controversy invalid.

Reversed.

MR. JUSTICE RUTLEDGE concurs in the result.

MR. JUSTICE JACKSON took no part in the consideration or decision of this case.

CONCUR BY: BLACK; FRANKFURTER

CONCUR: MR. JUSTICE BLACK, concurring.

The Commerce Clause of the Constitution provides that "Congress shall have power . . . to regulate commerce . . . among the several States." I have believed, and still believe, that this provision means that Congress can regulate commerce and that the courts cannot. But in a series of cases decided in recent years this Court over my protest has held that the Commerce Clause justifies this Court in nullifying state legislation which this Court concludes imposes an "undue burden" on interstate commerce. I think that whether state legislation imposes an "undue burden" on interstate commerce raises pure questions of policy, which the Constitution intended should be resolved by the Congress.

Very recently a majority of this Court reasserted its power to invalidate state laws on the ground that such legislation put an undue burden on commerce. *Nippert v. Richmond*, supra; *Southern Pacific Co. v. Arizona*, supra. I thought then, and still believe, that in these cases the Court was assuming the role of a "super-legislature" in determining matters of governmental policy.

Id., at 788, n. 4.

But the Court, at least for the present, seems committed to this interpretation of the Commerce Clause. In the Southern Pacific Company case, the Court, as I understand its opinion, found an "undue burden" because a State's requirement for shorter trains increased the cost of railroad operations and thereby delayed interstate commerce and impaired its efficiency. In the Nippert case a small tax imposed on a sales solicitor employed by concerns located outside of Virginia was found to be an "undue burden" even though a solicitor for Virginia concerns engaged in the same business would have been required to pay the same tax.

So long as the Court remains committed to the "undue burden on commerce formula," I must make decisions under it. The "burden on commerce" imposed by the Virginia law here under consideration seems to me to be of a far more serious nature than those of the Nippert or Southern Pacific Company cases. The Southern Pacific Company opinion, moreover, relied in part on the rule announced in *Hall v. DeCuir*, 95 U.S. 485, which case held that the Commerce Clause prohibits a state from passing laws which require that "on one side of a State line . . . passengers, both white and colored, must be permitted to occupy the same cabin, and on the other be kept separate." The Court further said that "uniformity in the regulations by which . . . [a carrier] is to be governed from one end to the other of his route is a necessity in his business" and that it was the responsibility of Congress, not the states, to determine "what such regulations shall be." The "undue burden on commerce formula" consequently requires the majority's decision. In view of the Court's present disposition to apply that formula, I acquiesce.

MR. JUSTICE FRANKFURTER, concurring.

My brother Burton has stated with great force reasons for not invalidating the Virginia statute. But for me *Hall v. DeCuir*, 95 U.S. 485, is controlling. Since it was decided nearly seventy years ago, that case on several occasions has been approvingly cited and has never been questioned. Chiefly for this reason I concur in the opinion of the Court.

The imposition upon national systems of transportation of a crazy-quilt of State laws would operate to burden commerce unreasonably, whether such contradictory and confusing State laws concern racial commingling or racial segregation. This does not imply the necessity for a nationally uniform regulation of arrangements for passengers on interstate carriers. Unlike other powers of Congress (see Art. I, § 8, cl. 1, concerning "Duties, Imposts and Excises"; Art. I, § 8, cl. 4, concerning "Naturalization"; Art. I, § 8, cl. 4, concerning "Bankruptcies"), the power to regulate commerce does not require geographic uniformity. Congress may devise a national policy with due regard to varying interests of different regions. E. g., 37 Stat. 699, 27 U. S. C. § 122; *Clark Distilling Co. v. Western Maryland R. Co.*, 242 U.S. 311; 45 Stat. 1084, 49 U. S. C. § 60; *Whitfield v. Ohio,* 297 U.S. 431. The States cannot impose diversity of treatment when such diverse treatment would result in unreasonable burdens on commerce. But Congress may effectively exercise its power under the Commerce Clause without the necessity of a blanket rule for the country.

DISSENT BY: BURTON

DISSENT: MR. JUSTICE BURTON, dissenting.

On the application of the interstate commerce clause of the Federal Constitution to this case, I find myself obliged to differ from the majority of the Court. I would sustain the Virginia statute against that clause. The issue is neither the desirability of the statute nor the constitutionality of racial segregation as such. The opinion of the Court does not claim that the Virginia statute, regulating seating arrangements for interstate passengers in motor vehicles, violates the Fourteenth Amendment or is in conflict with a federal statute. The Court holds this statute unconstitutional for but one reason. It holds that the burden imposed by the statute upon the nation's interest in interstate commerce so greatly outweighs the contribution made by the statute to the State's interest in its public welfare as to make it unconstitutional.

The undue burden upon interstate commerce thus relied upon by the Court is not complained of by the Federal Government, by any state, or by any carrier. This statute has been in effect since 1930. The carrier concerned is operating under regulations of its own which conform to the statute. The statute conforms to the policy adopted by Virginia as to steamboats (1900), electric or street cars and railroads (1902–1904). Its validity has been unanimously upheld by the Supreme Court of Appeals of Virginia. The argument relied upon by the majority of this Court to establish the undue burden of this statute on interstate commerce is the lack of uniformity between its provisions and those of the laws of other states on the subject of the racial separation of interstate passengers on motor vehicles.

If the mere diversity between the Virginia statute and comparable statutes of other states is so serious as to render the Virginia statute invalid, it probably means that the comparable statutes of those other states, being diverse from it and from each other, are equally invalid. This is especially true under that assumption of the majority which disregards sectional interstate travel between neighboring states having similar laws, to hold "that seating arrangements for the different races in interstate motor travel require a single, uniform rule to promote and protect national travel." More specifically, the opinion of the Court indicates that the laws of the 10 contiguous states of Virginia, North Carolina, South Carolina, Georgia, Alabama, Mississippi, Louisiana, Arkansas, Texas and Oklahoma require racial separation of passengers on motor carriers, while those of 18 other states prohibit racial separation of passengers on public carriers. On the precedent of this case, the laws of the 10 states requiring racial separation apparently can be invalidated because of their sharp diversity from the laws in the rest of the Union, or, in a lesser degree, because of their diversity from one another. Such invalidation, on the ground of lack of nation-wide uniformity, may lead to questioning the validity of the laws of the 18 states now prohibiting racial separation of passengers, for those laws likewise differ sharply from laws on the same subject in other parts of the Union and, in a lesser degree, from one another. In the absence of federal law, this may eliminate state regulation of racial separation in the seating of interstate passengers on motor vehicles and leave the regulation of the subject to the respective carriers.

The present decision will lead to the questioning of the validity of statutory regulation of the seating of intrastate passengers in the same motor vehicles with interstate passengers. The decision may also result in increased lack of uniformity between regulations as to seating arrangements on motor vehicles limited to intrastate passengers in a given state and those on motor vehicles engaged in interstate business in the same state or on connecting routes.

The basic weakness in the appellant's case is the lack of facts and findings essential to demonstrate the existence of such a serious and major burden upon the national interest in interstate commerce as to outweigh whatever state or local benefits are attributable to the statute and which would be lost by its invalidation. The Court recognizes that it serves as "the final arbiter of the competing demands of state and national interests" n2 and that it must fairly determine, in the absence of congressional action, whether the state statute actually imposes such an undue burden upon interstate commerce as to invalidate that statute. In weighing these competing demands, if this Court is to justify the invalidation of this statute, it must, first of all, be satisfied that the many years of experience of the state and the carrier that are reflected in this state law should be set aside. It represents the tested public policy of Virginia regularly enacted, long maintained and currently observed. The officially declared state interests, even when affecting interstate commerce, should not be laid aside summarily by this Court in the absence of congressional action. It is only Congress that can supply affirmative national uniformity of action.

In *Southern Pacific Co. v. Arizona*, 325 U.S. 761, 768-769, 770, this Court speaking through the late Chief Justice said:

"In the application of these principles some enactments may be found to be plainly within and others plainly without state power. But between these extremes lies the infinite variety of cases, in which regulation of local matters may also operate as a regulation of commerce, in which reconciliation of the conflicting claims of state and national power is to be attained only by some appraisal and accommodation of the competing demands of the state and national interests involved. . . . .

"But in general Congress has left it to the courts to formulate the rules thus interpreting the commerce clause in its application, doubtless because it has appreciated the destructive consequences to the commerce of the nation if their [i. e. the courts'] protection were withdrawn, . . . and has been aware that in their application state laws will not be invalidated without the support of relevant factual material which will 'afford a sure basis' for an informed judgment. . . Meanwhile, Congress has accommodated its legislation, as have the states, to these rules as an established feature of our constitutional system. There has thus been left to the states wide scope for the regulation of matters of local state concern, even though it in some measure affects the commerce, provided it does not materially restrict the free flow of commerce across state lines, or interfere with it in matters with respect to which uniformity of regulation is of predominant national concern."

The above-quoted requirement of a factual establishment of "a sure basis" for an informed judgment by this Court calls for a firm and demonstrable basis of action on the part of this Court. In the record of this case there are no findings of fact that demonstrate adequately the excessiveness of the burden, if any, which the Virginia statute has imposed upon interstate commerce, during the many years since its enactment, in comparison with the resulting effect in Virginia of the invalidation of this statute. The Court relies largely upon the recital of a nation-wide diversity among state statutes on this subject without a demonstration of the factual situation in those states, and especially in Virginia. The Court therefore is not able in this case to make that necessary "appraisal and accommodation of the competing demands of the state and national interests involved" which should be the foundation for passing upon the validity of a state statute of long standing and of important local significance in the exercise of the state police power.

The Court makes its own further assumption that the question of racial separation of interstate passengers in motor vehicle carriers requires national uniformity of treatment rather than diversity of treatment at this time. The inaction of Congress is an important indication that, in the opinion of Congress, this issue is better met without nationally uniform affirmative regulation than with it. Legislation raising the issue long has been, and is now, pending before Congress but has not reached the floor of either House. The fact that 18 states have prohibited in some degree racial separation in public carriers is important progress in the direction of uniformity. The fact, however, that 10 contiguous states in some degree require, by state law, some racial separation of passengers on motor carriers indicates a different appraisal by them of the needs and conditions in those areas than in others. The remaining 20 states have not gone equally far in either direction. This recital of existing legislative diversity is evidence against the validity of the assumption by this Court that there exists today a requirement of a single uniform national rule on the subject.

It is a fundamental concept of our Constitution that where conditions are diverse the solution of problems arising out of them may well come through the application of diversified treatment matching the diversified needs as determined by our local governments. Uniformity of treatment is appropriate where a substantial uniformity of conditions exists.

GLOSSARY

appellant: a party that appeals (as to a higher tribunal or court)

contiguous: touching; in contact

postulate: to ask, demand, or claim; to assume without proof; take for granted

pullmans: a railroad sleeping car or parlor car

repugnant: distasteful; making opposition; averse; opposed or contrary

Document Analysis

The US Supreme Court majority opinion investigates a series of issues related to state-level segregation laws and their implementation in determining that such laws are not constitutional when applied to interstate travel. The main issue at stake in the court's determination is the consideration of whether "the state legislation . . . unduly burdens that commerce in matters where uniformity is necessary—necessary in the constitutional sense of useful in accomplishing a permitted purpose." In other words, the court argues, maintaining racial segregation of passengers on interstate transport across states with varying segregation laws is permissible if doing so consistently eases the business of the transportation carriers. Otherwise, requiring carriers to apply these laws on a state-to-state basis violates the Constitution's protections of commerce, and the federal practice of not requiring segregation prevails.

Reed's opinion rests on the circumstances of Morgan's particular journey, the patchwork nature of state segregation laws, and the precedents set by the court in cases testing interstate transportation in the past. In this case, because commercial interstate journeys took place in vehicles designed for long-term comfort, the continual pressure to reconfigure passengers to accommodate state segregation laws weakened the value of the carrier's product; equally, the challenges of managing seating across state lines were deemed excessive. Significant, too, was the court's ruling in the 1878 case *Hall v. Decuir.* That case had tested the applicability of segregation laws on interstate steamboat travel between New Orleans, Louisiana, and Vicksburg, Mississippi, when an African American female passenger was denied a place in a cabin reserved for white female riders, finding that enforcing the provision had violated the interstate commerce clause. Ultimately, Reed concludes, "seating arrangements for the different races in interstate motor travel require a single, uniform rule to promote and protect national travel."

Other justices also issued opinions either concurring or dissenting from the majority opinion. Justices Hugo Black and Felix Frankfurter, although siding with the majority, pointed more firmly to the precedents set by the court, and registered beliefs that the US Congress, rather than the judiciary, should be responsible for enacting changes of this nature. The sole dissenter, Justice Harold Burton, argued that the mere existence of a patchwork of laws did not justify striking down the Virginia law; in the absence of federal law, Burton asserted, the state laws took precedence. Furthermore, he did not believe that implementing the laws truly presented "undue burdens" for transportation carriers as policies already existed to do just that.

Essential Themes

In the short-term, the ruling against segregation in *Morgan v. Virginia* had little practical effect. The US Supreme Court opinion had little effect on private company policies, and weeks after the decision Greyhound established a policy requiring drivers—who retained the right to seat passengers anywhere on the vehicle at their discretion—to seat African American riders in the rear of the bus and place white passengers in the front when traveling through states with segregation laws. Greyhound justified this policy as adhering to local customs and so protecting the comfort and safety of all of its riders. Because most African Americans in the South were leery of risking their personal safety to challenge segregation, people continued to follow these policies in spite of the knowledge that they were not legally supported. The year following the ruling, a group of civil rights activists set out on what was called the "journey to reconciliation," a series of bus travels through parts of the segregated South intended to test whether the order to desegregate was being applied. They had mixed experiences. On some rides, the integrated passengers were accepted with little comment; on travels through Virginia and North Carolina, however, resistance to segregation was still met with violence or arrest.

Despite these continuing challenges to integration, *Morgan v. Virginia* helped set the stage for the widespread civil rights movement of the 1950s and 1960s. Supreme Court decisions and new federal policies enacted during this time period outlawed segregation on interstate passenger and dining cars and integrated related services at shelters and depots. Historians widely acknowledge Irene Morgan as a precursor to Rosa Parks, an African American civil rights activist whose refusal to give up her seat on a Montgomery, Alabama, city bus sparked a citywide bus boycott and its own set of court cases testing segregation laws. In equal measure, the journey of reconciliation presaged the Freedom Rides of the early 1960s. Although full integration lagged behind the law due to lingering social and cultural mores, *Morgan v. Virginia* remains a hallmark of the end of Jim Crow laws as an accepted feature of the public sphere.

—*Vanessa E. Vaughn, MA*

Bibliography and Additional Reading

Catsam, Derek C. *Freedom's Main Line: The Journey of Reconciliation and the Freedom Rides.* Lexington: UP of Kentucky, 2009. Print.

_____ & Brendan Wolfe. "Morgan v. Virginia (1946)." *Encyclopedia Virginia.* Virginia Foundation for the Humanities, 20 Oct. 2014. Web. 5 Jan. 2015.

Klarman, Michael L. *From Jim Crow to Civil Rights: The Supreme Court and the Struggle for Racial Equality.* New York: Oxford UP, 2004. Print.

■ Report of the President's Committee on Civil Rights

Date: October 29, 1947
Author: The President's Committee on Civil Rights
Genre: report

Summary Overview

Though civil rights activism had been ongoing since the end of the Civil War, as World War II drew to an end, many African Americans saw an opportunity for renewed progress. Many black soldiers, fighting in segregated units, served in World War II and returned home with a feeling that they had earned the right to be treated as equals. However, the response they received—especially, but not exclusively, in the Southern states—was that they were still viewed as inferior by white American society. On December 5, 1946, President Harry S. Truman signed Executive Order 9808, forming the President's Committee on Civil Rights and charging it with examining the status of civil rights in the United States and reporting back to the president with recommendations as to how to strengthen and protect those rights. Almost one year later, the fifteen-member committee produced a 178-page report, entitled *To Secure These Rights: The Report of The President's Committee on Civil Rights.*

Defining Moment

As World War II came to an end, some things in the United States had changed—President Franklin D. Roosevelt had died in the last months of the war, with Truman succeeding him; Nazi Germany had been defeated and America's wartime ally, the Soviet Union, was increasingly seen as a threat; and the development of atomic weapons changed the very nature of warfare. Some things, however, remained much the same—racism and segregation were still just as pervasive, despite the fact that so many African Americans had fought and died alongside other Americans from every other racial and ethnic background during the war.

When Truman became president in April 1945, he was primarily concerned with the final stages of the war and the construction of the postwar world, where, increasingly, concern was focused on the perils of Communism both in the Soviet Union and at home. How-

ever, Truman also demonstrated a concern about civil rights that many did not expect. He was born into a family that had supported segregation, and he had even been accused of affiliations with the Ku Klux Klan early in his political career, though he had long since repudiated the Klan and its beliefs. When he became president, the Executive Office Building, adjacent to the White House—as well as all other federal buildings—was completely segregated. Many states had laws specifying public segregation of the races.

This was not only the United States of which Truman became president; it was the country to which the 880,000 African American World War II veterans had just returned. When they did insist upon their rights being respected or spoke out against segregation, groups like the Klan met them with violence. On September 19, 1946, a meeting between Truman and civil rights leaders took place, and Truman was informed about the deterioration of race relations, especially in the South, where even returning soldiers still in uniform were subjected to racial violence at the hands of whites. The day following the meeting, Truman consulted with his attorney general about what could be done to stop the violence, suggesting the appointment of a commission to examine civil rights in the country and to make recommendations. On December 5, 1946, Truman signed Executive Order 9808, officially forming the President's Committee on Civil Rights. The committee had the right to subpoena testimony from whomever it wished, including people with a significant amount of influence in political, business, and civil rights circles.

On June 29, 1947, Truman spoke in front of the Lincoln Memorial to members of the National Association for the Advancement of Colored People (NAACP). He committed the federal government to the advancement of civil rights for the first time, alienating both Republicans and his fellow Democrats, many of whom were from Southern states and had no intention of dismantling segregation. However, the report of the committee four months later would present the nation's first blueprint for doing so.

Author Biography

In December 1946, President Harry S. Truman established the fifteen-member Committee on Civil Rights, whose charge was to make recommendations as to legislation that could be passed by Congress to protect people from racial discrimination. In Executive Order 9808, Truman instructed the committee to scrutinize the state of civil rights in the United States and offer suggestions for legislation and other means of improving upon the defense of those rights in written form. The committee was made up of people from politics, business, and civil rights organizations, including its chairperson, General Electric CEO Charles E. Wilson, African American attorney Sadie T. Alexander, American Civil Liberties Union cofounder Morris L. Ernst, Catholic bishop Francis J. Haas, Charles Luckman, and Franklin D. Roosevelt Jr., the son of Truman's presidential predecessor. The committee's report to President Truman was published in October 1947 and the group disbanded in December of that year.

HISTORICAL DOCUMENT

The Committee's Recommendations

I. *To strengthen the machinery for the protection of civil rights, the President's Committee recommends:*

1. The reorganization of the Civil Rights Section of the Department of Justice to provide for:
The establishment of regional offices;
A substantial increase in its appropriation and staff to enable it to engage in more extensive research and to act more effectively to prevent civil rights violations;
An increase in investigative action in the absence of complaints;
The greater use of civil sanctions;
Its elevation to the status of a full division in the Department of Justice.
The creation of regional offices would enable the Civil Rights Section to provide more complete protection of civil rights in all sections of the country. It would lessen its present complete dependence upon United States Attorneys and local FBI agents for its work in the field. Such regional offices should be established in eight or nine key cities throughout the country, and be staged with skilled personnel drawn from the local areas. These offices should serve as receiving points for complaints arising in the areas, and as local centers of research, investigation, and preventive action. Close cooperation should be maintained between these offices, local FBI agents, and the United States Attorneys.
The Department of justice has suggested that heads of these regional offices should have the status of Assistant United States Attorneys, thereby preserving the centralization of federal criminal law enforcement. The President's Committee is fearful that under this plan the goal of effective, courageous, and nonpolitical civil rights protection in the field will not be reached unless satisfactory measures are taken to prevent these assistants from becoming mere political subordinates within the offices of the United States Attorneys.
Additional funds and personnel for research and preventive work would free the Civil Rights Section from its present narrow status as a prosecutive agency. Through the use of properly developed techniques and by the maintenance of continuous checks on racial and other group tensions, much could be done by the Section to reduce the number of lynchings, race riots, election irregularities, and other civil rights violations. Troublesome areas, and the activities of organizations and individuals who foment race tensions could be kept under constant scrutiny.
A larger staff and field-office facilities would also make it possible for the Section to undertake investigations of suspected civil rights violations, without waiting for the receipt of complaints. There are many problems, such as the possible infringement of civil rights resulting from practices used in committing persons to mental institutions, which might be so studied. These investigations in the absence of complaints could also be combined with educational and mediation efforts to check chronic incidents of police brutality or persistent interferences with the right to vote.

The difficulty of winning convictions in many types of criminal civil rights cases is often great. The Committee believes that the Civil Rights Section should be granted increased authority, by Congress if necessary, to make appropriate use of civil sanctions, such as suits for damages or injunctive relief, suits under the Declaratory Judgment Act, and the right of intervention by means of briefs amicus curiae in private litigation where important issues of civil rights law are being determined.

Finally, the Committee urges congressional action raising the Civil Rights Section to full divisional status in the Department of Justice under the supervision of an Assistant Attorney General. We believe this step would give the federal civil rights enforcement program prestige, power, and efficiency that it now lacks. Moreover, acceptance of the above recommendations looking toward increased activity by the Civil Rights Section and the passage by Congress of additional civil rights legislation would give this change added meaning and necessity.

2. The establishment within the FBI of a special unit of investigators trained in civil rights work.

The creation of such a unit of skilled investigators would enable the FBI to render more effective service in the civil rights field than is now possible. At the present time, its investigators are concerned with enforcement of all federal criminal statutes. In some instances, its agents have seemingly lacked the special skills and knowledge necessary to effective handling of civil rights cases, or have not been readily available for work in this area. These special agents should work in close harmony with the Civil Rights Section and its regional offices.

3. The establishment by the state governments of law enforcement agencies comparable to the federal Civil Rights Section.

There are large areas where, because of constitutional restrictions, the jurisdiction of the federal government as a protector of civil rights is either limited or denied. There are civil rights problems, unique to certain regions and localities, that can best be treated and solved by the individual states. Furthermore, our review of the work of the Civil Rights Section has persuaded us of the cardinal importance of developing specialized units for the enforcement of civil rights laws. We believe that this is true at the state level too. States which have, or will have, civil rights laws of their own, should buttress them with specially designed enforcement units. These would have the further effect of bringing the whole program closer to the people. They would also facilitate systematic local cooperation with the federal Civil Rights Section, and they would be able to act in the areas where it has no authority.

Here and elsewhere the Committee is making recommendations calling for remedial action by the states. The President's Executive Order invited us to consider civil rights problems falling within state as well as federal jurisdiction. We respectfully request the President to call these recommendations to the attention of the states and to invite their favorable consideration.

4. The establishment of a permanent Commission on Civil Rights in the Executive Office of the President, preferably by Act of Congress;

And the simultaneous creation of a joint Standing Committee on Civil Rights in Congress.

In a democratic society, the systematic, critical review of social needs and public policy is a fundamental necessity. This is especially true of a field like civil rights, where the problems are enduring, and range widely. From our own effort, we have learned that a temporary, sporadic approach can never finally solve these problems.

Nowhere in the federal government is there an agency charged with the continuous appraisal of the status of civil rights, and the efficiency of the machinery with which we hope to improve that status. There are huge gaps in the available information about the field. A permanent Commission could perform an invaluable function by collecting data. It could also carry on technical research to improve the fact-gathering methods now in use. Ultimately, this would make possible a periodic audit of the extent to which our civil rights are secure. If it did this and served as a clearing house and focus of coordination for the many private, state, and local agencies working in the civil rights field, it would be invaluable to them and to the federal government.

A permanent Commission on Civil Rights should point all of its work towards regular reports which would include recommendations for action in the ensuing periods. It should lay plans for dealing with broad civil rights problems, such as those arising from the technological displacement and probable migration of southern Negroes to cities throughout the land. It should also investigate and make recommendations with respect to special civil rights problems, such as the status of Indians and their relationship to the federal government.

The Commission should have effective authority to call upon any agency of the executive branch for assistance. Its members should be appointed by the President with the approval of the Senate. They should hold a specified number of regular meetings. A full-time director should be provided with an adequate appropriation and staff.

Congress, too, can be aided in its difficult task of providing the legislative ground work for fuller civil rights. A standing committee, established jointly by the House and the Senate, would provide a central place for the consideration of proposed legislation. It would enable Congress to maintain continuous liaison with the permanent Commission. A group of men in each chamber would be able to give prolonged study to this complex area and would become expert in its legislative needs.

5. The establishment by the states of permanent commissions on civil rights to parallel the work of the federal Commission at the state level.

The states should create permanent civil rights commissions to make continuing studies of prejudice, group tensions, and other local civil rights problems; to publish educational material of a civil rights nature; to evaluate existing legislation; and to recommend new laws. Such commissions, with their fingers on their communities' pulses, would complement at the state level the activities of a permanent federal Commission on Civil Rights.

6. The increased professionalization of state and local police forces.

The Committee believes that there is a great need at the state and local level for the improvement of civil rights protection by more aggressive and efficient enforcement techniques. Police training programs, patterned after the FBI agents' school and the Chicago Park District Program, should be instituted. They should be oriented so as to indoctrinate officers with an awareness of civil rights problems. Proper treatment by the police of those who are arrested and incarcerated in local jails should be stressed. Supplemented by salaries that will attract and hold competent personnel, this sort of training should do much to make police forces genuinely professional.

II. *To strengthen the right to safety and security of the person, the President's Committee recommends*:

1. The enactment by Congress of new legislation to supplement Section 51 of Title 18 of the United States Code which would impose the same liability on one person as is now imposed by that statute on two or more conspirators.

The Committee believes that Section 51 has in the past been a useful law to protect federal rights against encroachment by both private individuals and public officers. It believes the Act has great potential usefulness today. Greater efforts should be made through court tests to extend and make more complete the list of rights safeguarded by this law.

2. The amendment of Section 51 to remove the penalty provision which disqualifies persons convicted under the Act from holding public office.

There is general agreement that this particular penalty creates an unnecessary obstacle to the obtaining of convictions under the Act and that it should be dropped.

3. The amendment of Section 52 to increase the maximum penalties that may be imposed under it from a $1,000 fine and a one-year prison term to a $5,000 fine and a ten-year prison term, thus bringing its penalty provisions into line with those in Section 51.

At the present time the Act's penalties are so light that it is technically a misdemeanor law. In view of the extremely serious offenses that have been and are being successfully prosecuted under Section 52, it seems clear that the penalties should be increased.

4. The enactment by Congress of a new statute, to supplement Section 52, specifically directed against police brutality and related crimes.

This Act should enumerate such rights as the right not to be deprived of property by a public officer except by due process of law; the right to be free from personal injury inflicted by a public officer; the right to engage in a lawful activity without interference by a public officer; and the right to be free from discriminatory law enforcement resulting from either active or passive conduct by a public officer.

This statute would meet in part the handicap in the use of Section 52 imposed by the Supreme Court in *Screws v. United States*. This was the case in which the Court required prosecutors to establish that defendants had willfully deprived victims of a "specific constitutional right." In later prosecutions, the Civil Rights Section has found it very difficult to prove that the accused acted in a "willful" manner. By spelling out some of the federal rights which run against public officers, the supplementary statute would relieve the Civil Rights Section of this extraordinary requirement.

The Committee considered and rejected a proposal to recommend the enactment of a supplementary statute in which an attempt would be made to include a specific enumeration of all federal rights running against public officers. Such an enumeration would inevitably prove incomplete with the passage of time and might prejudice the protection of omitted rights. However, the committee believes that a new statute, such as the one here recommended, enumerating the rights for the protection of which Section 52 is now most commonly employed, is desirable.

5. The enactment by Congress of an anti-lynching act.

The Committee believes that to be effective such a law must contain four essential elements. First, it should define lynching broadly. Second, the federal offense ought to cover .participation of public officers in a lynching, or failure by them to use proper measures to protect a person accused of a crime against mob violence. The failure or refusal of public officers to make proper efforts to arrest members of lynch mobs and to bring them to justice should also be specified as an offense.

Action by private persons taking the law into their own hands to mete out summary punishment and private vengeance upon an accused person; action by either public officers or private persons meting out summary punishment and private vengeance upon a person because of his race, color, creed or religion—these too must be made crimes.

Third, the statute should authorize immediate federal investigation in lynching cases to discover whether a federal offense has been committed. Fourth, adequate and flexible penalties ranging up to a $10,000 fine and a 20 year prison term should be provided.

The constitutionality of some parts of such a statute, particularly those providing for the prosecution of private persons, has been questioned. The Committee believes that there are several constitutional bases upon which such a law might be passed and that these are sufficiently

strong to justify prompt action by Congress.

6. The enactment by Congress of a new criminal statute on involuntary servitude, supplementing Sections 443 and 444 of Title 18 of the United States Code.

This statute should make full exercise of congressional power under the Thirteenth Amendment by defining slavery and involuntary servitude broadly. This would provide a basis for federal prosecutions in cases where individuals are deliberately deprived of their freedom by public officers without due process of law or are held in bondage by private persons. Prosecution under existing laws is limited to the narrow, technical offense of peonage or must be based upon the archaic "slave kidnaping" law, Section 443.

7. A review of our wartime evacuation and detention experience looking toward the development of a policy which will prevent the abridgment of civil rights of any person or groups because of race or ancestry.

We believe it is fallacious to assume that there is a correlation between loyalty and race or national origin. The military must be allowed considerable discretionary power to protect national security in time of war. But we believe it is possible to establish safeguards against the evacuation and detention of whole groups because of their descent without endangering national security. The proposed permanent Commission on Civil Rights and the Joint Congressional Committee might well study this problem.

8. Enactment by Congress of legislation establishing a procedure by which claims of evacuees for specific property and business losses resulting from the wartime evacuation can be promptly considered and settled.

The government has acknowledged that many Japanese American evacuees suffered considerable losses through its actions and through no fault of their own. We cannot erase all the scars of evacuation; we can reimburse those who present valid claims for material losses.

III. *To strengthen the right to citizenship and its privileges, the President's Committee recommends:*

1. Action by the states or Congress to end poll taxes as a voting prerequisite.

Considerable debate has arisen as to the constitutionality of a federal statute abolishing the poll tax. In four times passing an anti-poll tax bill, the House of Representatives has indicated its view that there is a reasonable chance that it will survive a court attack on constitutional grounds. We are convinced that the elimination of this obstacle to the right of suffrage must not be further delayed. It would be appropriate and encouraging for the remaining poll tax states voluntarily to take this step. Failing such prompt state action, we believe that the nation, either by act of Congress, or by constitutional amendment, should remove this final barrier to universal suffrage.

2. The enactment by Congress of a statute protecting the right of qualified persons to participate in federal primaries and elections against interference by public officers and private persons.

This statute would apply only to federal elections. There is no doubt that such a law can be applied to primaries which are an integral part of the federal electoral process or which affect or determine the result of a federal election. It can also protect participation in federal election campaigns and discussions of matters relating to national political issues. This statute should authorize the Department of Justice to use both civil and criminal sanctions. Civil remedies should be used wherever possible to test the legality of threatened interferences with the suffrage before voting rights have been lost.

3. The enactment by Congress of a statute protecting the right to qualify for, or participate in, federal or state primaries or elections against discriminatory action by state officers based on race or color, or depending on any other unreasonable classification of persons for voting purposes.

This statute would apply to both federal and state elections, but it would be limited to the protection of the right to vote against discriminatory interferences based on race, color, or other unreasonable classification. Its constitutionality is clearly indicated by the Fourteenth and Fifteenth Amendments. Like the legislation suggested under (2) it should authorize the use of civil and criminal sanctions by the Department of Justice.

4. The enactment by Congress of legislation establishing local self government for the District of Columbia; and the amendment of the Constitution to extend suffrage in presidential elections, and representation in Congress to District residents.

The American tradition of democracy requires that the District of Columbia be given the same measure of self-government in local affairs that is possessed by other communities throughout the country. The lack of congressional representation and suffrage in local and national elections in the District deprives a substantial number of permanent Washington residents of a voice in public affairs.

5. The granting of suffrage by the States of New Mexico and Arizona to their Indian citizens.

These states have constitutional provisions which have been used to disfranchise Indians. In New Mexico, the constitution should be amended to remove the bar against voting by "Indians not taxed." This may not be necessary in Arizona where the constitution excludes from the ballot "persons under guardianship." Reinterpretation might hold that this clause no longer applies to Indians. If this is not possible, the Arizona constitution should be amended to remove it.

6. The modification of the federal naturalization laws to permit the granting of citizenship without regard to the race, color, or national origin of applicants.

It is inconsistent with our whole tradition to deny on a basis of ancestry the right to become citizens to people who qualify in every other way.

7. The repeal by the states of laws discriminating against aliens who are ineligible for citizenship because of race, color, or national origin.

These laws include the alien land laws and the prohibition against commercial fishing in California. The removal of race as a qualification for naturalization would remove the structure upon which this discriminatory legislation is based. But if federal action on Recommendation 6 is delayed, state action would be eminently desirable.

8. The enactment by Congress of legislation granting citizenship to the people of Guam and American Samoa.

This legislation should also provide these islands with organic acts containing guarantees of civil rights, and transfer them from naval administration to civilian control. Such legislation for Guam and American Samoa has been introduced in the present Congress.

9. The enactment by Congress of legislation, followed by appropriate administrative action, to end immediately all discrimination and segregation based on race, color, creed, or national origin, in the organization and activities of all branches of the Armed Services.

The injustice of calling men to fight for freedom while subjecting them to humiliating discrimination within the fighting forces is at once apparent. Furthermore, by preventing entire groups from making their maximum contribution to the national defense, we weaken our defense to that extent and impose heavier burdens on the remainder of the population.

Legislation and regulations should expressly ban discrimination and segregation in the recruitment, assignment, and training of all personnel in all types of military duty. Mess halls, quarters, recreational facilities and post exchanges should be non-segregated. Commissions and promotions should be awarded on considerations of merit only.

Selection of students for the Military, Naval, and Coast Guard academies and all other service schools should be governed by standards from which considerations of race, color, creed, or national origin are conspicuously absent. The National Guard, reserve units, and any universal military training program should all be administered in accordance with these same standards.

The Committee believes that the recent unification of the armed forces provides a timely opportunity for the revision of present policy and practice. A strong enunciation of future policy should be made condemning discrimination and segregation within the armed services.

10. The enactment by Congress of legislation providing that no member of the armed forces shall be subject to discrimination of any kind by any public authority or place of public accommodation, recreation, transportation, or other service or business.

The government of a nation has an obligation to protect the dignity of the uniform of its armed services. The esteem of the government itself is impaired when affronts to its armed forces are tolerated. The government also has a responsibility for the well-being of those who surrender some of the privileges of citizenship to serve in the defense establishments.

IV. To strengthen the right to freedom of conscience and expression the President's Committee recommends:

1. The enactment by Congress and the state legislatures of legislation requiring all groups, which attempt to influence public opinion, to disclose the pertinent facts about themselves through systematic registration procedures.

Such registration should include a statement of the names of officers, sources of financial contributions, disbursements, and the purposes of the organization. There is no question about the power of the states to do this. Congress may use its taxing and postal powers to require such disclosure. The revenue laws should be changed so that tax returns of organizations claiming tax exemption show the suggested information. These returns should then be made available to the public.

The revenue laws ought also to be amended to require the same information from groups and organizations which claim to operate on a non-profit basis but which do not request tax exemption. The Committee also recommends further study by appropriate governmental agencies looking toward the application of the disclosure principle to profit-making organizations which are active in the market place of public opinion.

Congress ought also to amend the postal laws to require those who use the first-class mail for large-scale mailings to file disclosure statements similar to those now made annually by those who use the second-class mail: The same requirement should be adopted for applicants for metered mail permits. Postal regulations ought also to require that no mail be carried by the Post Office which does not bear the name and address of the sender.

2. Action by Congress and the executive branch clarifying the loyalty obligations of federal employees, and establishing standards and procedures by which the civil rights of public workers may be scrupulously maintained.

The Committee recognizes the authority and the duty of the government to dismiss disloyal workers from the government service. At the same time the Committee is equally concerned with the protection of the civil rights of federal workers. We believe that there should be a public enunciation by responsible federal officials of clear, specific standards by which to measure the loyalty of government workers.

It is also important that the procedure by which the loyalty of an accused federal worker is determined be a fair, consistently applied, stated "due process." Specific rules of evidence should be laid down. Each employee should have the right to a bill of particular accusations, representation by counsel at all examinations or hearings, the right to subpoena witnesses and documents, a stenographic report of proceedings, a written decision, and time to prepare a written brief for an appeal. Competent and judicious people should have the responsibility for administering the program.

The Attorney General has stated to the Committee in a letter, "It is my firm purpose, insofar as my office has control over this program, to require substantial observance of the safeguards recommended by the President's Committee."

V. *To strengthen the right to equality of opportunity, the President's Committee recommends*:

1. In general:

The elimination of segregation, based on race, color, creed, or national origin, from American life.

The separate but equal doctrine has failed in three important respects. First, it is inconsistent with the fundamental equalitarianism of the American way of life in that it marks groups with the brand of inferior status. Secondly, where it has been followed, the results have been separate and unequal facilities for minority peoples. Finally, it has kept people apart despite incontrovertible evidence that an environment favorable to civil rights is fostered whenever groups are permitted to live and work together. There is no adequate defense of segregation.

The conditioning by Congress of all federal grants-in-aid and other forms of federal assistance to public or private agencies for any purpose on the absence of discrimination and segregation based on race, color, creed, or national origin.

We believe that federal funds, supplied by taxpayers all over the nation, must not be used to support or perpetuate the pattern of segregation in education, public housing, public health services, or other public services and facilities generally. We recognize that these services are indispensable to individuals in modern society and to further social progress. It would be regrettable if federal aid, conditioned on non-segregated services, should be

rejected by sections most in need of such aid. The Committee believes that a reasonable interval of time may be allowed for adjustment to such a policy. But in the end it believes that segregation is wrong morally and practically and must not receive financial support by the whole people.

A minority of the Committee favors the elimination of segregation as an ultimate goal but opposes the imposition of a federal sanction. It believes that federal aid to the states for education, health, research and other public benefits should be granted provided that the states do not discriminate in the distribution of the funds. It dissents, however, from the majority's recommendation that the abolition of segregation be made a requirement, until the people of the states involved have themselves abolished the provisions in their state constitutions and laws which now require segregation. Some members are against the non-segregation requirement in educational grants on the ground that it represents federal control over education. They feel, moreover, that the best way ultimately to end segregation is to raise the educational level of the people in the states affected; and to inculcate both the teachings of religion regarding human brotherhood and the ideals of our democracy regarding freedom and equality as a more solid basis for genuine and lasting acceptance by the peoples of the states.

2. For employment:

The enactment of a federal Fair Employment Practice Act prohibiting all forms of discrimination in private employment, based on race, color, creed, or national origin.

A federal Fair Employment Practice Act prohibiting discrimination in private employment should provide both educational machinery and legal sanctions for enforcement purposes. The administration of the act should be placed in the hands of a commission with power to receive complaints, hold hearings, issue cease-and-desist orders and seek court aid in enforcing these orders. The Act should contain definite fines for the violation of its procedural provisions. In order to allow time for voluntary adjustment of employment practices to the new law, and to permit the establishment of effective enforcement machinery, it is recommended that the sanction provisions of the law not become operative until one year after the enactment of the law.

The federal act should apply to labor unions and trade and professional associations, as well as to employers, insofar as the policies and practices of these organizations affect the employment status of workers.

The enactment by the states of similar laws;

A federal fair employment practice statute will not reach activities which do not affect interstate commerce. To make fair employment a uniform national policy, state action will be needed. The successful experiences of some states warrant similar action by all of the others.

The issuance by the President of a mandate against discrimination in government employment and the creation of adequate machinery to enforce this mandate.

The Civil Service Commission and the personnel offices of all federal agencies should establish on-the-job training programs and other necessary machinery to enforce the nondiscrimination policy in government employment. It may well be desirable to establish a government fair employment practice commission, either as a part of the Civil Service Commission, or on an independent basis with authority to implement and enforce the Presidential mandate.

3. For education:

Enactment by the state legislatures of fair educational practice laws for public and private educational institutions, prohibiting discrimination in the admission and treatment of students based on race, color, creed, or national origin.

These laws should be enforced by independent administrative commissions. These commissions should consider complaints and hold hearings to review them. Where they are found to be valid, direct negotiation with the offending institution should be undertaken to secure compliance with the law. Wide publicity for the commission's findings would influence many schools and colleges sensitive to public opinion to abandon discrimination. The final sanction for such a body would be the cease-and-desist order enforceable by court action. The Committee believes that educational institutions supported by churches and definitely identified as denominational should be exempted.

There is a substantial division within the Committee on this recommendation. A majority favors it.

4. For housing: The enactment by the states of laws

outlawing restrictive covenants;

Renewed court attack, with intervention by the Department of justice, upon restrictive covenants.

The effectiveness of restrictive covenants depends in the last analysis on court orders enforcing the private agreement. The power of the state is thus utilized to bolster discriminatory practices. The Committee believes that every effort must be made to prevent this abuse. We would hold this belief under any circumstances; under present conditions, when severe housing shortages are already causing hardship for many people of the country, we are especially emphatic in recommending measures to alleviate the situation.

5. For health services:

The enactment by the states of fair health practice statutes forbidding discrimination and segregation based on race, creed, color, or national origin, in the operation of public or private health facilities.

Fair health practice statutes, following the pattern of fair employment practice laws, seem desirable to the Committee. They should cover such matters as the training of doctors and nurses, the admission of patients to clinics, hospitals and other similar institutions, and the right of doctors and nurses to practice in hospitals. The administration of these statutes should be placed in the hands of commissions, with authority to receive complaints, hold hearings, issue cease-and-desist orders and engage in educational efforts to promote the policy of these laws.

6. For public services:

The enactment by Congress of a law stating that discrimination and segregation, based on race, color, creed, or national origin, in the rendering of all public services by the national government is contrary to public policy;

The enactment by the states of similar laws;

The elimination of discrimination and segregation depends largely on the leadership of the federal and state governments. They can make a great contribution toward accomplishing this end by affirming in law the principle of equality for all, and declaring that public funds, which belong to the whole people, will be used for the benefit of the entire population.

The establishment by act of Congress or executive order of a unit in the federal Bureau of the Budget to review the execution of all government programs, and the expenditures of all government funds, for compliance with the policy of nondiscrimination;

Continual surveillance is necessary to insure the nondiscriminatory execution of federal programs involving use of government funds. The responsibility for this task should be located in the Bureau of the Budget which has the duty of formulating the executive budget and supervising the execution of appropriation acts. The Bureau already checks the various departments and agencies for compliance with announced policy. Administratively, this additional function is consistent with its present duties and commensurate with its present powers.

The enactment by Congress of a law prohibiting discrimination or segregation, based on race, color, creed, or national origin, in interstate transportation and all the facilities thereof, to apply against both public officers and the employees of private transportation companies;

Legislation is needed to implement and supplement the Supreme Court decision in *Morgan v. Virginia*. There is evidence that some state officers are continuing to enforce segregation laws against interstate passengers. Moreover, carriers are still free to segregate such passengers on their own initiative since the Morgan decision covered only segregation based on law. Congress has complete power under the Constitution to forbid all forms of segregation in interstate commerce. We believe it should make prompt use of it.

The enactment by the states of laws guaranteeing equal access to places of public accommodation, broadly defined, for persons of all races, colors, creeds, and national origins.

Since the Constitution does not guarantee equal access to places of public accommodation, it is left to the states to secure that right. In the 18 states that have already enacted statutes, we hope that enforcement will make practice more compatible with theory. The civil suit for damages and the misdemeanor penalty have proved to be inadequate sanctions to secure the observance of these laws. Additional means, such as the revocation of licenses, and the issuance of cease-and-desist orders by administrative agencies are needed to bring about wider compliance. We think that all of the states should enact such legislation, using the broadest possible definition of public accommodation.

7. For the District of Columbia:

The enactment by Congress of legislation to accomplish the following purposes in the District;

Prohibition of discrimination and segregation, based on race, color, creed, or national origin, in all public or publicly-supported hospitals, parks, recreational facilities, housing projects, welfare agencies, penal institutions, and concessions on public property;

The prohibition of segregation in the public school system of the District of Columbia;

The establishment of a fair educational practice program directed against discrimination, based on race, color, creed, or national origin, in the admission of students to private educational institutions;

The establishment of a fair health practice program forbidding discrimination and segregation by public or private agencies, based on race, color, creed, or national origin, with respect to the training of doctors and nurses, the admission of patients to hospitals, clinics, and similar institutions, and the right of doctors and nurses to practice in hospitals;

The outlawing of restrictive covenants;

Guaranteeing equal access to places of public accommodation, broadly defined, to persons of all races, colors, creeds, and national origins.

In accordance with the Committee's division on anti-discrimination laws with respect to private education, the proposal for a District fair education program was not unanimous.

Congress has complete power to enact the legislation necessary for progress toward full freedom and equality in the District of Columbia. The great majority of these measures has been recommended in this report to Congress and to the states to benefit the nation at large. But they have particular meaning and increased urgency with respect to the District. Our nation's capital, the city of Washington, should serve as a symbol of democracy to the entire world:

8. The enactment by Congress of legislation ending the system of segregation in the Panama Canal Zone.

The federal government has complete jurisdiction over the government of the Panama Canal Zone, and therefore should take steps to eliminate the segregation which prevails there.

VI. *To rally the American people to the support of a con-*

tinuing program to strengthen civil rights, the President's Committee recommends:

A long term campaign of public education to inform the people of the civil rights to which they are entitled and which they owe to one another.
The most important educational task in this field is to give the public living examples of civil rights in operation. This is the purpose of our recommendations which have gone before. But there still remains the job of driving home to the public the nature of our heritage, the justification of civil rights and the need to end prejudice. This is a task which will require the cooperation of the federal, state, and local governments and of private agencies. We believe that the permanent Commission on Civil Rights should take the leadership in serving as the coordinating body. The activities of the permanent Commission in this field should be expressly authorized by Congress and funds specifically appropriated for them.
Aside from the education of the general public, the government has immediate responsibility for an internal civil rights campaign for its more than two million employees. This might well be an indispensable first step in a large campaign. Moreover, in the armed forces, an opportunity exists to educate men while in service. The armed forces should expand efforts, already under way, to develop genuinely democratic attitudes in officers and enlisted men.

As the Committee concludes this Report we would remind ourselves that the future of our nation rests upon the character, the vision, the high principle of our people. Democracy, brotherhood, human rights—these are practical expressions of the eternal worth of every child of God. With His guidance and help we can move forward toward a nobler social order in which there will be equal opportunity for all.

Acknowledgments

The Committee wishes to record its sincere tribute to its Executive Secretary, Robert K. Carr, and to its other staff members, without whose talents and devoted services the Committee's task could not have been completed. The staff is listed below:

Professional
Robert K. Carr, Executive Secretary.
Milton D. Stewart, Director of Research.
Nancy F. Wechsler, Counsel.
Charles J. Durham, Assistant to the Executive Secretary.
Frances Harriett Williams, Assistant to the Executive Secretary.
Robert E. Cushman, Special Consultant.
Rachel R. Sady, Research Analyst.
Herbert Kaufman, Research Aide.
Joseph Murtha, Research Aide.
John L. Vandegrift, Research Aide.
Richard A. Whiting, Research Aide.
Robert L. Bostick, Graphics.

Secretarial
Merle Whitford Huntington, Administrative Officer.
Ellen C. Ardinger.
Idamaye C. Boardley.
Jacqueline Carlisle.
Hannah S. Goldenthal.
Mahala B. Johnson.
Ann E. Sudwarth.
Charles N. Coleman.
Edward W. Jackson.

The Committee wishes also to record its deep sense of appreciation for the generous help given to it by many individuals, private organizations, and government agencies. During the period from January to September 1947, the Committee met ten times. At these meetings it heard some two score witnesses. The Committee had correspondence with nearly 250 private organizations and individuals. It was also assisted by some twenty-five agencies of the federal government and by an extended list of state and local public agencies.

GLOSSARY

abridgment: a shortened or condensed form of a book or speech that still retains the basic contents; reduction or curtailment

amicus curiae: "friend of the court"; someone who is not party to a case but gives information regarding the case without the solicitation of the parties.

briefs: a writ summoning one to answer to any action; a memorandum of points of fact of law for use in conducting a case

commensurate: having the same measure; of equal extent or duration; proportionate; adequate

enunciation: utterance of pronunciation; a formal announcement or statement

fallacious: containing a fallacy; logically unsound; misleading

indoctrinate: to instruct in a doctrine, principle, or ideology, especially to imbue with a particular biased belief of point of view; to teach or inculcate

stenographic: the art of writing in shorthand

suffrage: the right to vote, especially in a political election

Document Analysis

After a year-long process of investigation and thought, the President's Committee on Civil Rights issued its report, *To Secure These Rights: The Report of the President's Committee on Civil Rights.* In this document, the committee makes specific recommendations as to the best ways for the federal government to live up to the basic principles upon which the nation had been founded: freedom of conscience, equality of opportunity, and the right to safety and security for all Americans. In doing so, the committee has harsh words and advises direct action to address the problems of racial segregation and discrimination in American society.

The first section of the fourth chapter of the report gives a set of recommendations for improving the offices of the federal government that would deal with civil rights issues. It proposes the improvement of the Civil Rights Section of the Justice Department, by establishing regional offices able to concentrate on areas where civil rights abuses were more prevalent. It proposes that the office act more proactively, rather than simply responding to complaints, and that the state governments establish similar offices. The section advises the founding of a special group within the Federal Bureau of Investigation with training in civil rights matters. The committee also suggests instituting permanent commissions on civil rights at both the federal and state levels, and increasing professionalization of police forces.

The second section deals with recommended changes to federal law, in order to make it easier to convict those guilty of civil rights violations. It proposes the passage of a federal anti-lynching law—something that, although proposed a number of times, all prior administrations had not supported. Laws against involuntary servitude are sought. Also, in direct response to the internment of Japanese Americans during World War II, laws against unlawful detention of people not charged with a crime and in favor of the resolution of claims of losses by Japanese Americans during the war are advocated.

The third section recommends actions to ensure the rights of minorities, such as the right to vote and run for office. In immigration matters, the report proposes the end of all laws discriminating against people of different national origins. Finally, it deals with the problem of segregation and discrimination in the armed forces, urging laws against these practices. It recommends the registration of groups so that their true motives might be known. Interestingly, the president's committee suggests that the president's own loyalty program be revisited to ensure that it did not trample on the civil rights of federal employees.

The concluding sections of the report deal with "the elimination of segregation, based on race, color, creed, or national origin, from American life," in matters of housing, health care, employment, and public services, as well as the end of segregation in facilities of interstate transportation, such as bus stations. Specific suggestions mention the District of Columbia and federal territories, but overall, the report recommends the complete desegregation and end of discrimination in all aspects of American life.

Essential Themes

The recommendations of the President's Committee on Civil Rights were revolutionary, considering the state of race relations in the United States at the time of its formation. It proposed the dismantling of many state and local laws, especially in the American South, but also in many other regions. Truman called for the implementation of the recommendations, despite the fact that he was seeking reelection in 1948 and would need the votes of many Southern Democrats. He made the recommendations a Cold War imperative, stating that how the United States responded would demonstrate its superiority to the Communist world.

Truman took action on his own in 1948, issuing two executive orders that ended segregation in the armed forces and that instituted nondiscriminatory employment practices in the federal government. Many, noting the difficulty Americans had in accepting Truman's views on civil rights, predicted an easy Republican victory in the year's presidential election. When the so-called Dixiecrats walked out of the Democratic National Convention and supported South Carolina governor Strom Thurmond for president, their predictions seemed to be on the verge of coming true. However, in a surprise result, Truman won a second term and was able to institute more of his civil rights agenda.

A 1951 executive order established the Committee on Government Contract Compliance, which sought to impose federal civil rights laws on all federal contractors. Truman's efforts to eliminate poverty in America's slums by replacing run-down housing with new housing "estates" was not as successful, as not enough housing was built to hold those displaced by having their homes razed, and many African American families ended up living on the streets. However, despite the challenges, Truman's actions in creating the President's Committee on Civil Rights and attempting to follow through on its recommendations were the first positive steps toward greater civil rights to take place since the Civil War, setting the stage for the civil rights movement, which followed over the next two decades.

—*Steven L. Danver, PhD*

Bibliography and Additional Reading

Dudziak, Mary L. *Cold War Civil Rights: Race and the Image of American Democracy.* Princeton: Princeton UP, 2000. Print.

Gardner, Michael R. *Harry Truman and Civil Rights: Moral Courage and Political Risks.* Carbondale: Southern Illinois UP, 2002. Print.

Geselbracht, Raymond H., ed. *The Civil Rights Legacy of Harry S. Truman.* Kirksville: Truman State UP, 2007. Print.

To Secure These Rights: The Report of the President's Committee on Civil Rights. Harry S. Truman Library & Museum. Natl. Archives and Records Administration, n.d. Web. 17 Feb. 2015.

Vaughan, Philip H. *The Truman Administration's Legacy for Black America.* Reseda: Mojave, 1976. Print.

■ *Shelley v. Kraemer (1948)*

Date: May 3, 1948
Author: US Supreme Court, Fred M. Vinson
Genre: court case

Summary Overview

During the era of segregation, neighborhoods across the United States—including in many states outside of areas traditionally associated with "Jim Crow" laws—established rules barring property owners from selling or renting their homes to members of certain racial or ethnic groups. In 1945, an African American family in St. Louis, Missouri, purchased a house located in a subdivision with a racially restrictive covenant of this type from an owner who chose not to enforce it. After the purchase, a resident of the subdivision sued to stop the African American family from moving into their home due to the covenant. After Missouri state courts upheld the limitation, the case went to the US Supreme Court. The Supreme Court's 1948 opinion overturned the Missouri court's support for restrictive covenants on the grounds that legal enforcement of the measure by the state violated the equal protection clause of the Fourteenth Amendment, thereby signaling increased legal support for racial equality and African American civil rights.

Defining Moment

During the late 1800s and early 1900s, US society remained largely segregated in practice, even in places where racial divisions were not enforced by law. As the nation's African American populace began to spread from the Deep South to other regions seeking economic, social, and political opportunities, white society developed new ways to keep the races separate. Like other industrial cities of the Northeast and Midwest, St. Louis saw its African American population rise significantly as a result of the ongoing Great Migration of the early to mid-1900s; the city's black population more than doubled between 1910 and 1930 alone. At the same time, overall urban growth led to the construction of new large housing divisions. Property development companies sought to make their housing divisions more desirable to potential white buyers by shutting out black purchasers, as discriminatory attitudes held that nonwhite residents created an undesirable situation and lowered property values.

St. Louis briefly used race-based zoning laws to enforce this segregationist practice, but such municipally-mandated racial zoning was found to be unconstitutional by the 1917 Supreme Court ruling *Buchanan v. Warley*. Instead, neighborhood developers created private racially restrictive covenants that became part of the contract signed by property buyers; this practice came into use throughout much of the country. The Marcus Avenue Improvement Association of St. Louis had a typical restrictive covenant, which barred property owners from selling their homes to nonwhite—specifically African American or Asian—buyers for a period of fifty years beginning in 1911. As the African American population of St. Louis grew, white-restricted housing divisions came to border on predominantly African American neighborhoods.

J. D. and Ethel Shelley were African Americans from Mississippi who moved with their children to St. Louis in the 1930s. In 1945, they purchased a house in the Marcus Avenue neighborhood using an African American real estate agent. This agent, in turn, set up the real estate transaction using a white straw buyer, ostensibly to obtain better mortgage terms. Completing the sale in this way also allowed the Shelley family to avoid the restrictive covenant attached to the property deed, as the property owner believed he was selling the house to a white buyer. The Shelleys were apparently unaware of the racial restriction, and other houses on the block fell outside of the agreement and were already occupied by African American families. In October 1945, the family moved into their new home; within a short time, fellow Marcus Avenue district property owners Louis and Fern Kraemer sued to have them removed from the house on the grounds that their habitation there violated the neighborhood covenant. A trial court found for the Shelleys, stating that the original covenant was poorly designed and, therefore, unenforceable, but the Missouri Supreme Court overturned that ruling. In 1948, the US Supreme Court heard the Shelleys' case.

Author Biography

The unanimous decision in *Shelley v. Kraemer* was authored by Chief Justice of the United States Fred M. Vinson. A native of Kentucky, Vinson served as a member of Congress for nearly fifteen years as a US representative before becoming a judge of the US Court of Appeals for the DC Circuit in 1938. He was later tapped by President Harry S. Truman to act as secretary of the Treasury in 1945. Truman again selected Vinson for high office when he nominated him to the US Supreme Court. Vinson became chief justice in June 1946, remaining in that office until his death in 1953. During his tenure, Vinson tended to support the authority of the federal government over that of the states or individuals. Landmark decisions of the Vinson court barred segregation in higher education as well as in the enforcement of residential restrictive covenants.

HISTORICAL DOCUMENT

Mr. Chief Justice Vinson delivered the opinion of the Court.

These cases present for our consideration questions relating to the validity of court enforcement of private agreements, generally described as restrictive covenants, which have as their purpose the exclusion of persons of designated race or color from the Basic constitutional issues of obvious importance have been raised.

The first of these cases comes to this Court on certiorari to the Supreme Court of Missouri. On February 16, 1911, thirty out of a total of thirty-nine owners of property fronting both sides of Labadie Avenue between Taylor Avenue and Cora Avenue in the city of St. Louis, signed an agreement, which was subsequently recorded, providing in part:

'... the said property is hereby restricted to the use and occupancy for the term of Fifty (50) years from this date, so that it shall be a condition all the time and whether recited and referred to as (sic) not in subsequent conveyances and shall attach to the land, as a condition precedent to the sale of the same, that hereafter no part of said property or any portion thereof shall be, for said term of Fifty-years, occupied by any person not of the Caucasian race, it being intended hereby to restrict the use of said property for said period of time against the occupancy as owners or tenants of any portion of said property for resident or other purpose by people of the Negro or Mongolian Race.'

The entire district described in the agreement included fifty-seven parcels of land. The thirty owners who signed the agreement held title to forty-seven parcels, including the particular parcel involved in this case. At the time the agreement was signed, five of the parcels in the district were owned by Negroes. One of those had been occupied by Negro families since 1882, nearly thirty years before the restrictive agreement was executed. The trial court found that owners of seven out of nine homes on the south side of Labadi Avenue, within the restricted district and 'in the immediate vicinity' of the premises in question, had failed to sign the restrictive agreement in 1911. At the time this action was brought, four of the premises were occupied by Negroes, and had been so occupied for periods ranging from twenty-three to sixty-three years. A fifth parcel had been occupied by Negroes until a year before this suit was instituted.

On August 11, 1945, pursuant to a contract of sale, petitioners Shelley, who are Negroes, for valuable consideration received from one Fitzgerald a warranty deed to the parcel in question. [1] The trial court found that petitioners had no actual knowledge of the restrictive agreement at the time of the purchase. On October 9, 1945, respondents, as owners of other property subject to the terms of the restrictive covenant, brought suit in Circuit Court of the city of St. Louis parrying that petitioners Shelley be restrained from taking possession of the property and that judgment be entered divesting title out of petitioners Shelley and revesting title in the immediate grantor or in such other person as the court should direct. The trial court denied the requested relief on the ground that the restrictive agreement, upon which respondents based their action, had never become final and complete because it was the intention of the parties to that agreement that it was not to become effective until signed by all property owners in the district, and signatures of all the owners had never been obtained.

The Supreme Court of Missouri sitting en banc reversed and directed the trial court to grant the relief for which respondents had prayed. That court held the agreement effective and concluded that enforcement of its provisions violated no rights guaranteed to petitioners by the Federal Constitution. [2] At the time the court rendered its decision, petitioners were occupying the property in question.

The second of the cases under consideration comes to this Court from the Supreme Court of Michigan. The circumstances presented do not differ materially from the Missouri case. In June, 1934, one Ferguson and his wife, who then owned the property located in the city of Detroit which is involved in this case, executed a contract providing in part:

'This property shall not be used or occupied by any person or persons except those of the Caucasian race. It is further agreed that this restriction shall not be effective unless at least eighty percent of the property fronting on both sides of the street in the block where our land is located is subjected to this or a similar restriction.'

The agreement provided that the restrictions were to remain in effect until January 1, 1960. The contract was subsequently recorded; and similar agreements were executed with respect to eighty percent of the lots in the block in which the property in question is situated.

By deed dated November 30, 1944, petitioners, who were found by the trial court to be Negroes, acquired title to the property and thereupon entered into its occupancy. On January 30, 1945, respondents, as owners of property subject to the terms of the restrictive agreement, brought suit against petitioners in the Circuit Court of Wayne County. After a hearing, the court entered a decree directing petitioners to move from the property within ninety days. Petitioners were further enjoined and restrained from using or occupying the premises in the future. On appeal, the Supreme Court of Michigan affirmed, deciding adversely to petitioners' contentions that they had been denied rights protected by the Fourteenth Amendment. [3]

Petitioners have placed primary reliance on their contentions, first raised in the state courts, that judicial enforcement of the restrictive agreements in these cases has violated rights guaranteed to petitioners by the Fourteenth Amendment of the Federal Constitution and Acts of Congress passed pursuant to that Amendment.[4] Specifically, petitioners urge that they have been denied the equal protection of the laws, deprived of property without due process of law, and have been denied privileges and immunities of citizens of the United States. We pass to a consideration of those issues.

I.

Whether the equal protection clause of the Fourteenth Amendment inhibits judicial enforcement by state courts of restrictive covenants based on race or color is a question which this Court has not heretofore been called upon to consider. Only two cases have been decided by this Court which in any way have involved the enforcement of such agreements. The first of these was the case of *Corrigan v. Buckley*, 1926, 271 U.S. 323. There, suit was brought in the courts of the District of Columbia to enjoin a threatened violation of certain restrictive covenants relating to lands situated in the city of Washington. Relief was granted, and the case was brought here on appeal. It is apparent that that case, which had originated in the federal courts and involved the enforcement of covenants on land located in the District of Columbia, could present no issues under the Fourteenth Amendment; for that Amendment by its terms applies only to the States. Nor was the question of the validity of court enforcement of the restrictive covenants under the Fifth Amendment properly before the Court, as the opinion of this Court specifically recognizes. [5] The only constitutional issue which the appellants had raised in the lower courts, and hence the only constitutional issue before this Court on appeal, was the validity of the covenant agreements as such. This Court concluded that since the inhibitions of the constitutional provisions invoked, apply only to governmental action, as contrasted to action of private individuals, there was no showing that the covenants, which were simply agreements between private property owners, were invalid. Accordingly, the appeal was dismissed for want of a substantial question. Nothing in the opinion of this Court, therefore, may properly be regarded as an adjudication on the merits of the constitutional issues presented by these cases, which raise the question of the validity, not of the private agreements as such, but of the judicial enforcement of those agreements.

The second of the cases involving racial restrictive covenants was *Hansberry v. Lee*, 1940, 311 U.S. 32, 132 A.L.R. 741. In that case, petitioners, white property owners, were enjoined by the state courts from violating the terms of a restrictive agreement. The state Supreme Court had held petitioners bound by an earlier judicial determination, in litigation in which petitioners were not parties, upholding the validity of the restrictive agreement, although, in fact, the agreement had not been signed by the number of owners necessary to make it effective under state law. This Court reversed the judgment of the state Supreme Court upon the ground that petitioners had been denied due process of law in being held stopped to challenge the validity of the agreement on the theory, accepted by the state court, that the earlier litigation, in which petitioners did not participate, was in the nature of a class suit. In arriving at its result, this Court did not reach the issues presented by the cases now under consideration.

It is well, at the outset, to scrutinize the terms of the restrictive agreements involved in these cases. In the Missouri case, the covenant declares that no part of the affected property shall be 'occupied by any person not of the Caucasian race, it being intended hereby to restrict the use of said property… against the occupancy as owners or tenants of any portion of said property for resident or other purpose by people of the Negro or Mongolian Race.' Not only does the restriction seek to proscribe use and occupancy of the affected properties by members of the excluded class, but as construed by the Missouri courts, the agreement requires that title of any person who uses his property in violation of the restriction shall be divested. The restriction of the covenant in the Michigan case seeks to bar occupancy by persons of the excluded class. It provides that 'This property shall not be used or occupied by any person or persons except those of the Caucasian race.'

It should be observed that these covenants do not seek to proscribe any particular use of the affected properties. Use of the properties for residential occupancy, as such, is not forbidden. The restrictions of these agreements, rather, are directed toward a designated class of persons and seek to determine who may and who may not own or make use of the properties for residential purposes. The excluded class is defined wholly in terms of race or color; 'simply that and nothing more.'[6]

It cannot be doubted that among the civil rights intended to be protected from discriminatory state action by the Fourteenth Amendment are the rights to acquire, enjoy, own and dispose of property. Equality in the enjoyment of property rights was regarded by the framers of that Amendment as an essential pre-condition to the realization of other basic civil rights and liberties which the Amendment was intended to guarantee.[7] Thus, 1978 of the Revised Statutes, derived from 1 of the Civil Rights Act of 1866 which was enacted by Congress while the Fourteenth Amendment was also under consideration, [8] provides:

'All citizens of the United States shall have the same right, in every State and Territory, as is enjoyed by white citizens thereof to inherit, purchase, lease, sell, hold, and convey real and personal property.'[9]

This Court has given specific recognition to the same principle. *Buchanan v. Warley*, 1917, 245 U.S. 60, L.R.A. 1918C, 210, Ann.Cas.1918A, 1201.

It is likewise clear that restrictions on the right of occupancy of the sort sought to be created by the private agreements in these cases could not be squared with the requirements of the Fourteenth Amendment if imposed by state statute or local ordinance. We do not understand respondents to urge the contrary. In the case of *Buchanan v. Warley*, supa, a unanimous Court declared unconstitutional the provisions of a city ordinance which denied to colored persons the right to occupy houses in blocks in which the greater number of houses were occupied by white persons, and imposed similar restrictions on white persons with respect to blocks in which the greater number of houses were occupied by colored persons. During the course of the opinion in that case, this Court stated: 'The Fourteenth Amendment and these statutes enacted in furtherance of its purpose operate to qualify and entitle a colored man to acquire property without state legislation discriminating against him solely because of color.' [10]

In *Harmon v. Tyler*, 1927, 273 U.S. 668, a unanimous court, on the authority of *Buchanan v. Warley*, supra, declared invalid an ordinance which forbade any Negro to establish a home on any property in a white community or any white person to establish a home in a Negro community, 'except on the written consent of a majority of the persons of the opposite race inhabiting such community or portion of the City to be affected.'

The precise question before this Court in both the Buchanan and Harmon cases, involved the rights of white sellers to dispose of their properties free from restrictions as to potential purchasers based on considerations of race or color. But that such legislation is also offensive to the rights of those desiring to acquire and occupy property and barred on grounds of race or color, is clear, not only from the language of the opinion in *Buchanan v. Warley*, supra, but from this Court's disposition of the case of *City of Richmond v. Deans*, 1930, 281 U.S. 704 . There, a Negro, barred from the occupancy of certain property by the terms of an ordinance similar to that in the Buchanan case, sought injunctive relief in the federal courts to enjoin the enforcement of the ordinance on the grounds that its provisions violated the terms of the Fourteenth Amendment. Such relief was granted, and this Court affirmed, finding the citation of *Buchanan v. Warley*, supra, and *Harmon v. Tyler*, supra, sufficient to support its judgment. [11]

But the present cases, unlike those just discussed, do not involve action by state legislatures or city councils. Here the particular patterns of discrimination and the areas in which the restrictions are to operate, are determined, in the first instance, by the terms of agreements among private individuals. Participation of the State consists in the enforcement of the restrictions so defined. The crucial issue with which we are here confronted is whether this distinction removes these cases from the operation of the prohibitory provisions of the Fourteenth Amendment.

Since the decision of this Court in the Civil Rights Cases, 1883, 109 U.S. 3, the principle has become firmly embedded in our constitutional law that the action inhibited by the first section of the Fourteenth Amendment is only such action as may fairly be said to be that of the States. That Amendment erects no shield against merely private conduct, however discriminatory or wrongful. [12]

We conclude, therefore, that the restrictive agreements standing alone cannot be regarded as a violation of any rights guaranteed to petitioners by the Fourteenth Amendment. So long as the purposes of those agreements are effectuated by voluntary adherence to their terms, it would appear clear that there has been no action by the State and the provisions of the Amendment have not been violated. *Cf. Corrigan v. Buckley*, supra.

But here there was more. These are cases in which the purposes of the agreements were secured only by judicial enforcement by state courts of the restrictive terms of the agreements. The respondents urge that judicial enforcement of private agreements does not amount to state action; or, in any event, the participation of the State is so attenuated in character as not to amount to state action within the meaning of the Fourteenth Amendment. Finally, it is suggested, even if the States in these cases may be deemed to have acted in the constitutional sense, their action did not deprive petitioners of rights guaranteed by the Fourteenth Amendment. We move to a consideration of these matters.

II.

That the action of state courts and of judicial officers in their official capacities is to be regarded as action of the State within the meaning of the Fourteenth Amendment, is a proposition which has long been established by decisions of this Court. That principle was given expression in the earliest cases involving the construction of the terms of the Fourteenth Amendment. Thus, in Commonwealth of *Virginia v. Rives*, 1880, 100 U.S. 313, 318, this Court stated: 'It is doubtless true that a State may act through different agencies, either by its legislative, its executive, or its judicial authorities; and the prohibitions of the amendment extend to all action of the State denying equal protection of the laws, whether it be action by one of these agencies or by another.' In Ex parte Commonwealth of Virginia, 1880, 100 U.S. 339, 347, the Court observed: 'A State acts by its legislative, its executive, or its judicial authorities. It can act in no other way.' In the Civil Rights Cases, 1883, 109 U.S. 3, 11 , 17, 21, this Court pointed out that the Amendment makes void 'state action of every kind' which is inconsistent with the guaranties therein contained, and extends to manifestations of 'state authority in the shape of laws, customs, or judicial or executive proceedings.' Language to like effect is employed no less than eighteen times during the course of that opinion.[13]

Similar expressions, giving specific recognition to the fact that judicial action is to be regarded as action on the State for the purposes of the Fourteenth Amendment, are to be found in numerous cases which have been more recently decided. In *Twining v. New Jersey*, 1908, 211 U.S. 78, 90, 91, 16, the Court said: 'The judicial act of the highest court of the state, in authoritatively construing and enforcing its laws, is the act of the state.' In *Brinkerhoff-Faris Trust & Savings Co. v. Hill*, 1930, 281 U.S. 673, 680 , 454, the Court, through Mr. Justice Brandeis, stated: 'The federal guaranty of due process extends to state action through its judicial as well as through its legislative, executive, or administrative branch of government.' Further examples of such declarations in the opinions of this Court are not lacking. [14]

One of the earliest applications of the prohibitions contained in the Fourteenth Amendment to action of state judicial officials occurred in cases in which Negroes had been excluded from jury service in criminal prosecutions by reason of their race or color. These cases demonstrate, also, the early recognition by this Court that state action in violation of the Amendment's provisions is equally repugnant to the constitutional commands whether directed by state statute or taken by a judicial official in the absence of statute. Thus, in *Strauder v. West Virginia*, 1880, 100 U.S. 303 , this Court declared invalid a state statute restricting jury service to white persons as amounting to a denial of the equal protection of the laws to the colored defendant in that case. In the notice and opportunity to defend, has, Ex parte Virginia, supra, held that a similar discrimination imposed by the action of a state judge denied rights protected by the Amendment, despite the fact that the language of the state statute relating to jury service contained no such restrictions.

The action of state courts in imposing penalties or depriving parties of other substantive rights without providing adequate notice and opportunity to defend, has, of course, long been regarded as a denial of the due process of law guaranteed by the Fourteenth Amendment. *Brinkerhoff-Faris Trust & Savings Co. v. Hill*, supra. Cf. *Pennoyer v. Neff*, 1878, 95 U.S. 714.[15]

In numerous cases, this Court has reversed criminal convictions in state courts for failure of those courts to provide the essential ingredients of a fair hearing. Thus it has been held that convictions obtained in state courts under the domination of a mob are void. *Moore v. Dempsey*, 1923, 261 U.S. 86. And see *Frank v. Mangum*, 1915, 237 U.S. 309. Convictions obtained by coerced confessions, [16] by the use of perjured testimony known by the prosecution to be such, [17] or without the effective assistance of counsel, [18] have also been held to be exertions of state authority in conflict with the fundamental rights protected by the Fourteenth Amendment.

But the examples of state judicial action which have been held by this Court to violate the Amendment's commands are not restricted to situations in which the judicial proceedings were found in some manner to be procedurally unfair. It has been recognized that the action of state courts in enforcing a substantive common-law rule formulated by those courts, may result in the denial of rights guaranteed by the Fourteenth Amendment, even though the judicial proceedings in such cases may have been in complete accord with the most rigorous conceptions of procedural due process.[19] Thus, in *American Federation of Labor v. Swing*, 1941, 312 U.S. 321 , enforcement by state courts of the common-law policy of the State, which resulted in the restraining of peaceful picketing, was held to be state action of the sort prohibited by the Amendment's guaranties of freedom of discussion.[20] In *Cantwell v. Connecticut*, 1940, 310 U.S. 296 , 128 A.L.R. 1352, a conviction in a state court of the common-law crime of breach of the peace was, under the circumstances of the case, found to be a violation of the Amendment's comments relating to freedom of religion. In *Bridges v. California*, 1941, 314 U.S. 252 , 159 A.L.R. 1346, enforcement of the state's common-law rule relating to contempt by publication was held to be state action inconsistent with the prohibitions of the Fourteenth Amendment.[21] And cf. *Chicago, B. & Q.R. Co. v. Chicago*, 1897, 166 U.S. 226.

The short of the matter is that from the time of the adoption of the Fourteenth Amendment until the present, it has been the consistent ruling of this Court that the action of the States to which the Amendment has reference, includes action of state courts and state judicial officials. Although, in construing the terms of the Fourteenth Amendment, differences have from time to time been expressed as to whether particular types of state action may be said to offend the Amendment's prohibitory provisions, it has never been suggested that state court action is immunized from the operation of those provisions simply because the act is that of the judicial branch of the state government.

III.

Against this background of judicial construction, extending over a period of some three-quarters of a century, we are called upon to consider whether enforcement by state courts of the restrictive agreements in these cases may be deemed to be the acts of those States; and, if so, whether that action has denied these petitioners the equal protection of the laws which the Amendment was intended to insure. We have no doubt that there has been state action in these cases in the full and complete sense of the phrase. The undisputed facts disclose that petitioners were willing purchasers of properties upon which they desired to establish homes. The owners of the properties were willing sellers; and contracts of sale were accordingly consummated. It is clear that but for the active intervention of the state courts, supported by the full panoply of state power, petitioners would have been free to occupy the properties in question without restraint.

These are not cases, as has been suggested, in which the States have merely abstained from action, leaving private individuals free to impose such discriminations as they see fit. Rather, these are cases in which the States have made available to such individuals the full coercive power of government to deny to petitioners, on the grounds of race or color, the enjoyment of property rights in premises which petitioners are willing and financially able to acquire and which the grantors are willing to sell. The difference between judicial enforcement and nonenforcement of the restrictive covenants is the difference to petitioners between being denied rights of property available to other members of the community and being accorded full enjoyment of those rights on an equal footing.

The enforcement of the restrictive agreements by the state courts in these cases was directed pursuant to the common-law policy of the States as formulated by those courts in earlier decisions. [22] In the Missouri case,

enforcement of the covenant was directed in the first instance by the highest court of the State after the trial court had determined the agreement to be invalid for want of the requisite number of signatures. In the Michigan case, the order of enforcement by the trial court was affirmed by the highest state court. [23] The judicial action in each case bears the clear and unmistakable imprimatur of the State. We have noted that previous decisions of this Court have established the proposition that judicial action is not immunized from the operation of the Fourteenth Amendment simply because it is taken pursuant to the state's common-law policy. [24] Nor is the Amendment ineffective simply because the particular pattern of discrimination, which the State has enforced, was defined initially by the terms of a private agreement. State action, as that phrase is understood for the purposes of the Fourteenth Amendment, refers to exertions of state power in all forms. And when the effect of that action is to deny rights subject to the protection of the Fourteenth Amendment, it is the obligation of this Court to enforce the constitutional commands.

We hold that in granting judicial enforcement of the restrictive agreements in these cases, the States have denied petitioners the equal protection of the laws and that, therefore, the action of the state courts cannot stand. We have noted that freedom from discrimination by the States in the enjoyment of property rights was among the basic objectives sought to be effectuated by the framers of the Fourteenth Amendment. That such discrimination has occurred in these cases is clear. Because of the race or color of these petitioners they have been denied rights of ownership or occupancy enjoyed as a matter of course by other citizens of different race or color. [25] The Fourteenth Amendment declares 'that all persons, whether colored or white, shall stand equal before the laws of the States, and, in regard to the colored race, for whose protection the amendment was primarily designed, that no discrimination shall be made against them by law because of their color.' [26] *Strauder v. West Virginia,* supra, 100 U.S. at 307. Only recently this Court has had occasion to declare that a state law which denied equal enjoyment of property rights to a designated class of citizens of specified race and ancestry, was not a legitimate exercise of the state's police power but violated the guaranty of the equal protection of the laws. *Oyama v. California*, 1948, 332 U.S. 633. Nor may the discriminations imposed by the state courts in these cases be justified as proper exertions of state police power. [27] Cf. *Buchanan v. Warley*, supra.

Respondents urge, however, that since the state courts stand ready to enforce restrictive covenants excluding white persons from the ownership or occupancy of property covered by such agreements, enforcement of covenants excluding colored persons may not be deemed a denial of equal protection of the laws to the colored persons who are thereby affected. [28] This contention does not bear scrutiny. The parties have directed our attention to no case in which a court, state or federal, has been called upon to enforce a covenant excluding members of the white majority from ownership or occupancy of real property on grounds of race or color. But there are more fundamental considerations. The rights created by the first section of the Fourteenth Amendment are, by its terms, guaranteed to the individual. The rights established are personal rights.[29] It is, therefore, no answer to these petitioners to say that the courts may also be induced to deny white persons rights of ownership and occupancy on grounds of race or color. Equal protection of the laws is not achieved through indiscriminate imposition of inequalities.

Nor do we find merit in the suggestion that property owners who are parties to these agreements are denied equal protection of the laws if denied access to the courts to enforce the terms of restrictive covenants and to assert property rights which the state courts have held to be created by such agreements. The Constitution confers upon no individual the right to demand action by the State which results in the denial of equal protection of the laws to other individuals. And it would appear beyond question that the power of the State to create and enforce property interests must be exercised within the boundaries defined by the Fourteenth Amendment. Cf. *Marsh v. Alabama*, 1946, 326 U.S. 501.

The problem of defining the scope of the restrictions which the Federal Constitution imposes upon exertions of power by the States has given rise to many of the most persistent and fundamental issues which this Court has been called upon to consider. That problem was foremost in the minds of the framers of the Constitution, and since that early day, has arisen in a multitude of forms.

The task of determining whether the action of a State offends constitutional provisions is one which may not be undertaken lightly. Where, however, it is clear that the action of the State violates the terms of the fundamental charter, it is the obligation of this Court so to declare.

The historical context in which the Fourteenth Amendment became a part of the Constitution should not be forgotten. Whatever else the framers sought to achieve, it is clear that the matter of primary concern was the establishment of equality in the enjoyment of basic civil and political rights and the preservation of those rights from discriminatory action on the part of the States based on considerations of race or color. Seventy-five years ago this Court announced that the provisions of the Amendment are to be construed with this fundamental purpose in mind. [30] Upon full consideration, we have concluded that in these cases the States have acted to deny petitioners the equal protection of the laws guaranteed by the Fourteenth Amendment. Having so decided, we find it unnecessary to consider whether petitioners have also been deprived of property without due process of law or denied privileges and immunities of citizens of the United States.

For the reasons stated, the judgment of the Supreme Court of Missouri and the judgment of the Supreme Court of Michigan must be reversed.

Reversed.

Mr. Justice REED, Mr. Justice JACKSON, and Mr. Justice RUTLEDGE took no part in the consideration or decision of these cases.

Footnotes

[1] The trial court found that title to the property which petitioners Shelley sought to purchase was held by one Bishop, a real estate dealer, who placed the property in the name of Josephine Fitzgerald Bishop, who acted as agent for petitioners in the purchase, concealed the fact of his ownership.

[2] *Kraemer v. Shelley*, 1946, 355 Mo. 814, 198 S.W.2d 679.

[3] *Sipes v. McGhee*, 1947, 316 Mich 614, 25 N.W.2d 638.

[4] The first section of the Fourteenth Amendment provides: 'All persons born or naturalized in the United

States, and subject to the jurisdiction thereof, are citizens of the United States and of the State wherein they reside. No State shall make or enforce any law which shall abridge the privileges or immunities of citizens of the United States; nor shall any State deprive any person of life, liberty, or property, without due process of law; nor deny to any person within its jurisdiction the equal protection of the laws.'

[5] *Corrigan v. Buckley*, 1926, 271 U.S. 323, 330 , 331, 523, 524.

[6] *Buchanan v. Warley*, 1917, 245 U.S. 60, 73 , 18, L.R.A.1918C, 210, Ann.Cas.1918A, 1201.

[7] Slaughter-House Cases, 1873, 16 Wall. 36, 70, 81. See Flack, *The Adoption of the Fourteenth Amendment.*

[8] In *Oyama v. California*, 1948, 332 U.S. 633, 640 , 272, the section of the Civil Rights Act herein considered is described as the federal statute, 'enacted before the Fourteenth Amendment but vindicated by it.' The Civil Rights Act of 1866 was reenacted in 18 of the Act of May 31, 1870, subsequent to the adoption of the Fourteenth Amendment. 16 Stat. 144.

[9] 14 Stat. 27, 8 U.S.C. 42, 8 U.S.C.A. 42.

[10] *Buchanan v. Warley*, 1917, 245 U.S. 60, 79 , L.R.A. 1918C, 210, Ann.Cas.1918A, 1201.

[11] Courts of Georgia, Maryland, North Carolina, Oklahoma, Texas, and Virginia have also declared similar statutes invalid discussed, do not involve action by state Amendment. *Glover v. Atlanta*, 1918, 148 Ga. 285, 96 S.E. 562; *Jackson v. State*, 1918, 132 Md. 311, 103 A. 910; *Clinard v. Winston-Salem*, 1940, 217 N.C. 119, 6 S.E.2d 867, 126 A.L.R. 634; *Allen v. Oklahoma City*, 1936, 175 Okl. 421, 52 P.2d 1054; *Liberty Annex Corp. v. Dallas*, Tex.Civ.App. 1927, 289 S.W. 1067; *Irvine v. Clifton Forge*, 1918, 124 Va. 781, 97 S.E. 310.

[12] And see *United States v. Harris*, 1883, 106 U.S. 629 ; *United States v. Cruikshank*, 1876, 92 U.S. 542 .

[13] Among the phrases appearing in the opinion are the following: 'the operation of state laws, and the action of state officers, executive or judicial'; 'state laws and state proceedings'; 'state law * * * or some state action through its officers or agents'; 'state laws and acts done under state authority'; 'state laws or state action of some kind'; 'such laws as the states may adopt or enforce'; 'such acts and proceedings as the states may commit or take'; 'state legislation or action'; 'state law or state authority.'

[14] *Neal v. Delaware*, 1881, 103 U.S. 370, 397 ; *Scott v. McNeal*, 1894, 154 U.S. 34, 45 , 1112; *Chicago, B. & Q.R. Co. v. Chicago*, 1897, 166 U.S. 226, 233 Ä235, 583, 584; *Hovey v. Elliott*, 1897, 167 U.S. 409, 417 , 418, 844; *Carter v. Texas*, 1900, 177 U.S. 442, 447 , 689; *Martin v. Texas*, 1906, 200 U.S. 316, 319 ; *Raymond v. Chicago Union Traction Co.*, 1907, 207 U.S. 20, 35 , 36, 12, 12 Ann.Cas. 757; *Home Telephone and Telegraph Co. v. Los Angeles*, 1913, 227 U.S. 278, 286 , 287, 314; *Prudential Ins. Co. v. Cheek*, 1922, 259 U.S. 530, 548 , 524, 27 A.L.R. 27; *American Ry. Exp. Co. v. Kentucky*, 1927, 273 U.S. 269, 274 , 355; *Mooney v. Holohan*, 1935, 294 U.S. 103, 112 , 113, 341, 342, 98 A.L.R. 406; *Hansberry v. Lee*, 1940, 311 U.S. 32, 41 , 61 S. Ct. 115, 117, 132 A.L.R. 741.

[15] And see *Standard Oil Co. v. Missouri*, 1912, 224 U.S. 270, 281 , 282, 409, Ann.Cas.1913D, 936; *Hansberry v. Lee*, 1940, 311 U.S. 32 , 132 A.L.R. 741.

[16] *Brown v. Mississippi*, 1936, 297 U.S. 278 ; *Chambers v. Florida*, 1940, 309 U.S. 227 ; *Ashcraft v. Tennessee*, 1944, 322 U.S. 143 ; *Lee v. Mississippi*, 1948, 332 U.S. 742 .

[17] See *Mooney v. Holohan*, 1935, 294 U.S. 103, 98 A.L.R. 406; *Pyle v. Kansas*, 1942, 317 U.S. 213.

[18] *Powell v. Alabama*, 1932, 287 U.S. 45, 84 A.L.R. 527; *Williams v. Kaiser*, 1945, 323 U.S. 471; *Tomkins v. Missouri*, 1945, 323 U.S. 485 ; *DeMeerleer v. Michigan*, 1947 329 U.S. 663 .

[19] In applying the rule of *Erie R. Co. v. Tompkins*, 1938, 304 U.S. 64 , 144 A.L.R. 1487, it is clear that the common- law rules enunciated by state courts in judicial opinions are to be regarded as a part of the law of the State.

[20] And see *Bakery Drivers Local v. Wohl*, 1942, 315 U.S. 769; *Cafeteria Employees Union v. Angelos*, 1943, 320 U.S. 293 .

[21] And see *Pennekamp v. Florida*, 1946, 328 U.S. 331; *Craig v. Harney*, 1947, 331 U.S. 367.

[22] See *Swain v. Maxwell*, 1946, 355 Mo. 448, 196 S.W.2d 780; *Koehler v. Rowland*, 1918, 275 Mo. 573, 205 S.W. 217, 9 A.L.R. 107. See also *Parmalee v. Morris*, 1922, 218 Mich. 625, 188 N.W. 330, 38 A.L.R. 1180. Cf. *Porter v. Barrett*, 1925, 233 Mich. 373, 206 N.W. 532, 42 A.L.R. 1267.

[23] Cf. *Home Telephone and Telegraph Co. v. Los Angeles*, 1913, 227 U.S. 278; *Raymond v. Chicago Union Traction Co.*, 1907, 207 U.S. 20, 12 Ann.Cas. 757.

[24] *Bridges v. California*, 1941, 314 U.S. 252, 159 A.L.R. 1346; *American Federation of Labor v. Swing*, 1941, 312 U.S. 321.

[25] See *Yick Wo v. Hopkins*, 1886, 118 U.S. 356; *Strauder v. West Virginia*, 1880, 100 U.S. 303; *Truax v. Raich*, 1915, 239 U.S. 33, L.R.A.1916D, 545, Ann. Cas.1917B, 283.

[26] Restrictive agreements of the sort involved in these case have been used to exclude other than Negroes from the ownership or occupancy of real property. We are informed that such agreements have been directed against Indians, Jews, Chinese, Japanese, Mexicans, Hawaiians, Puerto Ricans, and Filipinos, among others.

[27] See *Bridges v. California*, 1941, 314 U.S. 252, 261, 193, 159 A.L.R. 1346; *Cantwell v. Connecticut*, 1940, 310 U.S. 296, 307, 308, 905, 128 A.L.R. 1352.

[28] It should be observed that the restrictions relating to residential occupancy contained in ordinances involved in the Buchanan, Harmon and Deans cases, cited supra, and declared by this Court to be inconsistent with the requirements of the Fourteenth Amendment, applied equally to white persons and Negroes.

[29] *McCabe v. Atchison, Topeka & Santa Fe R. Co.*, 1914, 235 U.S. 151, 161 Ä162, 71; *Missouri ex rel. Gaines v. Canada*, 1938, 305 U.S. 337; *Oyama v. California*, 1948, 332 U.S. 633.

[30] Slaughter-House Cases, 1873, 16 Wall 36, 81; *Strauder v. West Virginia*, 1880, 100 U.S. 303. See Flack, The Adoption of the Fourteenth Amendment.

GLOSSARY

adjudication: the act of a court in making an order, judgment, or decree

appellants: a person who appeals; a party that appeals to a higher tribunal

certiorari: a writ issuing from a superior court calling up the record of a proceeding in an inferior court for review

panoply: a wide-ranging and impressive array or display; full ceremonial attire or paraphernalia

Document Analysis

Vinson's conclusion was a clear victory for the Shelley family, but a more mixed success for African Americans seeking civil rights at large. According to Vinson's opinion, the Court's considering of *Shelley v. Kraemer* focused on a few key legal questions. First, the plaintiffs argued that the Missouri Supreme Court's enforcement of the racially restrictive covenants against the Shelleys had violated the Fourteenth Amendment's equal protection clause, which guarantees that all citizens, regardless of race, enjoy the same treatment under the law. The US Supreme Court, therefore, had to decide whether the act of establishing restrictive covenants in and of itself was unconstitutional. In weighing this matter, the Court also asserted that the issue of whether Missouri's actions should be considered within the context of the Fourteenth Amendment was well established under Court precedent. Thus, the remaining key issue was whether the state's enforcement of the private restrictive covenant violated the Shelleys' constitutional rights.

The Court's consideration of the legality of restrictive covenants found them to be permissible. Based on existing precedent, the Court agreed that the covenants could exist because they were "simply agreements between private property owners" to abide by certain guidelines. Although the covenants were unquestionably based on an unequal treatment of individuals based on their race, they were entered into freely by individuals and lacked the binding force of public law.

However, when local or state governments stepped in to enforce those guidelines—in this case, by attempting to evict the Shelleys from their St. Louis property—the action of government crossed over into unconstitutionality by giving the private guidelines the authority of the state in violation of the Fourteenth Amendment. As Vinson noted, "but for the active intervention of the state courts, supported by the full panoply of state power, petitioners would have been free to occupy the properties in question without restraint." Pursuing such legal action violated the personal property rights guaranteed under the US Constitution and federal laws such as the Civil Rights Act of 1866 and was the basis for the rejection of racially-based zoning laws by the Court in *Buchanan v. Warley*. Vinson also points to the historical context of the passage of the Fourteenth Amendment and related statutes to inform the decision, noting that the intention of lawmakers was obviously to secure just these kinds of legal rights for African Americans. It was thus the enforcement of the restrictive covenants, rather than the mere existence of the covenants alone, that served to deny affected individuals their constitutionally-guaranteed rights.

Essential Themes

Shelley v. Kraemer successfully undermined the constitutionality of discriminatory housing policies even as it permitted private segregationist efforts to endure. Decades of segregation and centuries of racial discrimination proved too deeply rooted in US society to be so easily overturned. However, *Shelley v. Kraemer* saw the Court's interpretation of the Fourteenth Amendment continue to lean toward supporting civil rights in a sharp contrast to earlier decades, when the Court had permitted segregation under the doctrine of "separate but equal."

The decision, coupled with other key civil rights opinions issued by the Court in the 1940s, signaled to civil rights activists that the possibility for change from the federal level was real. Civil rights lawyers challenged the constitutionality of segregation and other discriminatory practices over the next several years, most famously in the 1954 *Brown v. Board of Education of Topeka* decision that struck down segregation in public schools. Action by the Court encouraged the civil rights movement and drew increased popular attention to issues of race across the nation. By the mid-1960s,

a combination of Court opinion, new federal laws, and a constitutional amendment strengthening African American voting rights had effected a veritable legal revolution in favor of civil rights.

De facto segregation in residential neighborhoods has remained common in much of the United States into the twenty-first century, however. White homeowners were often reluctant to sell to African American families, and African Americans who moved into white neighborhoods could be subject to harassment. Predominantly black neighborhoods typically fell far short of the "separate but equal" principle envisioned by segregation's supporters. For many years after the decision in *Shelley v. Kraemer*, banks were legally permitted to employ discriminatory lending practices known as redlining, which deemed mostly African American or mixed-race neighborhoods less desirable for writing mortgages. These meant that fewer African Americans were able to purchase homes, and those who did paid higher interest rates or fees. At the same time, a reluctance to lend kept property values in black neighborhoods lower than those in their white counterparts. Federal laws in the 1960s and 1970s barred these practices, but this did not effectively lead to true racial integration across most US neighborhoods.

—*Vanessa E. Vaughn, MA*

Bibliography and Additional Reading

Gordon, Colin. *Mapping Decline: St. Louis and the Fate of the American City*. Philadelphia: U of Pennsylvania P, 2008. Print.

Klarman, Michael L. *From Jim Crow to Civil Rights: The Supreme Court and the Struggle for Racial Equality*. New York: Oxford UP, 2004. Print.

Vose, Clement E. *Caucasians Only: The Supreme Court, the NAACP, and Restrictive Covenant Cases*. Berkeley: U of California P, 1959. Print.

Ware, Leland B. "Invisible Walls: An Examination of the Legal Strategy of the Restrictive Covenant Cases." *Washington University Law Review* 67.3 (1989): 737–72. Print.

■ Executive Order 9981

Date: July 26, 1948
Author: Harry S. Truman
Genre: government document

Summary Overview

African Americans have served their country with distinction in every major national conflict, and World War II was no exception. During the war, African Americans were represented in every branch of the military except the Marine Corps, but they served in segregated divisions and, most often, in support positions. The treatment of African Americans in the military mirrored the discrimination and segregation that still existed in the United States, particularly in the South. On July 26, 1948, President Harry S. Truman signed Executive Order 9981, which ordered equal treatment in the United States military without regard to race, religion, or national background. The order also established the President's Committee on Equality of Treatment and Opportunity in the Armed Services, a distinguished advisory board responsible for advising military leadership on the implementation of the order. Reaction to the order was mixed, with the Army initially refusing to implement it. However, the last segregated units of the Army were eliminated in September 1954.

Defining Moment

African Americans made up about 10 percent of the population when the United States went to war in 1941, but the United States military had fewer than four thousand African Americans in its ranks, and only twelve of these were officers. By the end of the war, over a million African Americans had served in uniform, including thousands of women. Many thousands more worked in industries that supported the war effort. While serving with distinction in uniform, African Americans struggled for basic civil rights at home and fought segregation and discriminatory treatment in the military.

Many African Americans had volunteered for duty in World War I, hoping that their patriotic service would be rewarded with improved conditions when they returned home. Instead, veterans found racial discrimina-

tion and segregation in the Jim Crow South unchanged, and racially motivated killings rose precipitously, as returning veterans were seen as a threat. When President Franklin D. Roosevelt instituted the draft in 1940, many African American men were still resentful about having to serve in the army of a country that preached freedom and democracy, but treated them like second-class citizens. Other black draftees and volunteers had deep patriotic feeling and a desire to serve their country and believed, as had the veterans of the previous war, that their service could result in change at home. Activists took on the segregated draft process, arguing that many too many draftees were being rejected by all-white draft boards. After a pledge from Roosevelt that enough African American men would be drafted to make up the same percentage of the military as they occupied in the rest of society, numbers in all branches of service rose (although the stated goal was never reached).

African Americans also made significant headway in desegregating defense industries. In June 1941, President Roosevelt issued Executive Order 8802, which required that African Americans be given job training at defense plants, forbade racial discrimination by defense contractors, and established the Fair Employment Practices Commission (FEPC). In the military, however, African Americans continued to serve in segregated, mostly noncombat units, providing transportation and supplies to the front. As the war continued and casualties rose, however, more African Americans were sent into combat. Still, in the American South, African American soldiers sometimes stood outside while German prisoners were served in segregated restaurants.

At the end of the war, the Fair Employment Practices Commission was ended. As racial tensions escalated and violence increased, as it had at the end of the previous war, President Truman formed the President's Commission on Civil Rights, which published a report, "To Secure These Rights," in October 1947. Its chief recommendations were laws to end lynching (then on the rise in the South), measures to secure voting rights, and increased authority for the Department of Justice to enforce civil rights. When senators from the South blocked the passage of civil rights legislation, Truman chose to use executive power to act on civil rights issues. On July 26, 1948, Truman issued Executive Order 9981, which effectively abolished segregation in the armed forces. This order also established an advisory committee, the President's Committee on Equality of Treatment and Opportunity in the Armed Forces, to implement desegregation in the military. There was significant resistance to desegregation from top military leadership, with the Army and the Marines proving particularly intransigent, but growing casualties during the Korean War in the early 1950s, along with steady pressure from the White House, ensured that the military was desegregated completely by 1954.

Author Biography

Harry S. Truman was born in Lamar, Missouri, in 1884. His parents declined to give him a middle name, using only the initial "S" to honor several relatives. He was the oldest of three children and did not attend school until he was eight. His father was a farmer and livestock dealer and was well connected to the local Democratic Party, and Truman served as a page boy in the 1900 Democratic convention. After graduating from high school, Truman worked several clerical jobs and worked as a railroad timekeeper. Truman served in the Missouri National Guard during World War I, despite very poor eyesight, and was elected captain by his men. After the war, Truman returned to Independence, Missouri, and opened a haberdasher shop. The shop failed, but Truman was elected as a county court judge in 1922 and served in a variety of public offices until he was elected to the United States Senate in 1934. While in the Senate, Truman became known for investigating claims of graft and corruption in military industries. He was elected to the vice presidency in 1944 and became president of the United States on April 12, 1945, upon the death of President Roosevelt. Truman found out about the development of the atomic bomb after he became president, and he made the decision to drop them on two cities in Japan in August 1945. Truman oversaw the end of the war, the establishment of the United Nations, and the implementation of the Marshall Plan to rebuild Europe. He supported a policy of containment to control the spread of Communism. Truman won a narrow victory in 1948 for a full term as president, but did not seek reelection in 1952. Truman retired to Missouri to write his autobiography and died in 1972. He is buried in Independence.

HISTORICAL DOCUMENT

WHEREAS it is essential that there be maintained in the armed services of the United States the highest standards of democracy, with equality of treatment and opportunity for all those who serve in our country's defense:

NOW THEREFORE, by virtue of the authority vested in me as President of the United States, by the Constitution and the statutes of the United States, and as Commander in Chief of the armed services, it is hereby ordered as follows:

1. It is hereby declared to be the policy of the President that there shall be equality of treatment and opportunity for all persons in the armed services without regard to race, color, religion or national origin. This policy shall be put into effect as rapidly as possible, having due regard to the time required to effectuate any necessary changes without impairing efficiency or morale.

2. There shall be created in the National Military Establishment an advisory committee to be known as the President's Committee on Equality of Treatment and Opportunity in the Armed Services, which shall be composed of seven members to be designated by the President.

3. The Committee is authorized on behalf of the President to examine into the rules, procedures and practices of the armed services in order to determine in

what respect such rules, procedures and practices may be altered or improved with a view to carrying out the policy of this order. The Committee shall confer and advise with the Secretary of Defense, the Secretary of the Army, the Secretary of the Navy, and the Secretary of the Air Force, and shall make such recommendations to the President and to said Secretaries as in the judgment of the Committee will effectuate the policy hereof.

4. All executive departments and agencies of the Federal Government are authorized and directed to cooperate with the Committee in its work, and to furnish the Committee such information or the services of such persons as the Committee may require in the performance of its duties.

5. When requested by the Committee to do so, persons in the armed services or in any of the executive departments and agencies of the Federal Government shall testify before the Committee and shall make available for use of the Committee such documents and other information as the Committee may require.

6. The Committee shall continue to exist until such time as the President shall terminate its existence by Executive order.

Harry Truman
The White House
July 26, 1948

Document Analysis

Executive Order 9981 begins by announcing the establishment of the President's Committee on Equality of Treatment and Opportunity in the Armed Services, the key element in the enforcement of the rest of the order. Truman begins his order with two powerful statements. First of all, the armed services should exemplify the "highest standards of democracy," with "equality of treatment and opportunity for all those who serve." Then, citing the president's authority as commander in chief of the armed forces, Truman declares that "there shall be equality of treatment and opportunity for all persons in the armed services without regard to race, color, religion or national origin" and calls on this policy to be implemented as quickly as reasonably possible. The establishment of the President's Committee on Equality of Treatment and Opportunity in the Armed Services was key to achieving desegregation and ending discrimination, and Truman uses the remainder of the order to describe the committee and to direct all agencies of the federal government and the military to cooperate fully with it.

The committee is given an advisory role within the "National Military Establishment" and expected to make recommendations to the president, the secretary of defense, and the civilian heads of the three branches of the armed forces. The committee is to expect full cooperation from the military, according to this order, and should have access to records. If members of the military are called to testify, they are expected to do so immediately.

Though this order was clear in its mission to eliminate discrimination, it met with resistance from some in the military establishment, who argued that it did not specifically prohibit segregation. Truman replied in a later statement that it was the intent of the order to end segregation in the military, and this was eventually accomplished.

Essential Themes

This document was a watershed moment in US civil rights history. After centuries of segregation, the military was commanded to end its discriminatory practices. The United States was a two-sided nation, seen by the world as the defender of freedom and democracy, while many of its citizens struggled to achieve basic civil rights. In the American South, segregation and Jim Crow laws allowed African Americans to hold subservient positions and use substandard facilities. The military followed this model, in part to placate Southern service members and in part because discrimination was standard throughout the country. Executive Order 9981 was the beginning of the end of formal segregation in the United States.

—*Bethany Groff, MA*

Bibliography and Additional Reading

"Desegregation of the Armed Forces." *Harry S. Truman Library and Museum*. Harry S. Truman Lib. and Museum, n.d. Web. 26 Feb. 2015.

Lanning, Michael Lee. *The African-American Soldier: From Crispus Attucks to Colin Powell*. New York: Kensington, 2003. Print.

Taylor, Jon E. *Freedom to Serve: Truman, Civil Rights, and Executive Order 9981*. New York: Routledge, 2013. Print.

■ Southern Legislators Protest Proposed Anti-lynching Legislation

Date: January 24, 1950
Authors: Charles E. Bennett; Boyd A. Tackett; John E. Rankin; Joseph R. Bryson
Genre: speech

Summary Overview

Spurred by recommendations from President Harry Truman and the Commission on Civil Rights he appointed in 1946, in July 1949 and January 1950 a subcommittee of the Judiciary Committee of the US House of Representatives held hearings on several bills designed to provide protection against lynchings, which for decades had been carried out principally against minorities in the South. Many in Congress and a number of private and civic organizations, including the National Association for the Advancement of Colored People (NAACP), supported passage of anti-lynching legislation. However, senators and representatives from Southern states argued that the legislation was unnecessary, claiming that existing state laws provided adequate protection. Furthermore, they viewed the proposed legislation as unconstitutional because it represented a usurpation by the federal government of powers vested in the individual states.

Defining Moment

Lynching, a form of vigilante justice in which an individual is punished for an alleged crime without benefit of trial, has always been illegal in the United States. Historically, while lynchings occurred in many places outside the South, notably in the American West, the surge in this form of vigilantism rose precipitously in southern states after post–Civil War Reconstruction efforts ended in 1877. Beginning in 1882 officials at Tuskegee Institute in Alabama began collecting data on lynchings. Earliest records show that, before 1890, a greater number of whites were lynched, but by the 1920s, the proportion of African American to white victims was as high as ten to one.

Because lynching was considered a form of murder or attempted murder, responsibility for arresting and prosecuting those accused of lynching fell to the in-

dividual states. Unfortunately, for many years communities in the South did not engage in vigorous pursuit of perpetrators or bring them to trial very often. In the few instances where people were tried, acquittals were common.

Efforts to pass federal laws protecting individuals from lynching began in the late nineteenth century. In 1919, the NAACP initiated a vigorous lobbying campaign to convince members of Congress to pass federal legislation that would curb lynching and bring perpetrators to justice. Most proposals also included stiff penalties (usually financial) for communities that failed to pursue alleged perpetrators of this crime. Several attempts were undertaken, most notably in 1922 and 1935, to pass anti-lynching laws in Congress, but Southern legislators managed to stymie action, largely through Senate filibusters.

Many Southerners saw efforts to create federal laws against lynching as part of a larger scheme to eradicate what they considered a time-honored regional lifestyle, where de jure segregation enabled continued economic and social privilege for white people. For example, during World War II, President Franklin Roosevelt created the Fair Employment Practices Commission to ensure that discrimination was not practiced in awarding jobs related to the war industry and government posts. Although this provision was narrow in scope, southerners feared that President Truman would make similar attempts to expand the powers of the federal government. In fact, President Truman did continue his predecessor's reformist agenda on civil rights; in December 1946 he appointed a President's Commission on Civil Rights to recommend appropriate changes to federal laws in order to guarantee equal protection to all citizens. A year later the committee published its final report, To Secure These Rights; in it they proposed sweeping changes to federal statutes, including legislation to provide federal protections against lynching.

In February 1948, President Truman forwarded proposed legislation to incorporate the commission's recommendations into federal statutes. The president's proposal was sent to the appropriate committees in the Senate and House. In July 1949 and again in January 1950, a House judiciary subcommittee held hearings on twelve separate bills that would have made lynching a federal crime. During these hearings, legislators from southern states presented arguments that lynching should remain a crime punishable under state laws and not be subject to federal jurisdiction.

Author Biography

Four members of the House of Representatives, all Democrats and attorneys, testified against the proposals to make lynching a federal crime. The first, Charles E. Bennett (1910–2003) of Florida, a veteran of World War II, was elected to Congress in 1948 and served until 1993. The second, Boyd Tackett (1911–85) served in the Arkansas House of Representatives before enlisting during World War II. He represented Arkansas in the US House of Representatives from 1949 to 1952. John E. Rankin (1882–1960) of Mississippi, the third to speak against anti-lynching legislation, was known throughout the country as a leading opponent of civil rights legislation. He argued against earlier attempts to pass anti-lynching laws. Rankin served in World War I before being elected to Congress in 1920. The fourth to testify, Joseph R. Bryson (1893–1953), also served in World War I before being elected to the South Carolina state senate. He served in the US House of Representatives from 1939 until 1953.

HISTORICAL DOCUMENT

STATEMENT OF HON. CHARLES E. BENNETT, A REPRESENTATIVE IN CONGRESS FROM THE STATE OF FLORIDA

Mr. Bennett. I oppose the enactment of the proposed so-called antilynching bills for a variety of reasons. First of all, I think that the bills are unconstitutional as a violation of the tenth amendment of the Constitution. The Constitution would probably never have been enacted if it had not been for the inclusion of the tenth amendment which is part of the Bill of Rights. It provides that when governmental powers are not given specifically to the Federal Government, they shall remain with the people or the States into which these people may organize themselves or have organized themselves.

Along that same line, I oppose this type of legislation because I feel that it is projecting still further the Federal Government into local government which trend in government in late years I feel to be a mistake and a very dangerous mistake. When our country was founded, it was founded through experience. The colonists had experienced a remote governmental control and they desired to return to what they had experienced somewhat when they were in Europe which was more of a local control; plus that they desired to add to the grassroots control that they anticipated being able to have in this country. In other words, they rebelled against being controlled remotely from England and they wanted to get even a heartier participation in local government than they found possible in England itself when they were actually living in that country or whatever country they happened to live in in Europe.

No one would come here and take up for lynching, and I say that lynching should be a thing that we should not have. Certainly a person who engages in a lynching mob is a person who should have put upon his or her shoulders the responsibility of meeting a charge of crime and being convicted of it if guilty. The State laws, however, in every State of the Union are adequate to cover the question of lynching, and particularly they are in the South. We have murder laws in every State in the Union, and lynching is murder. A person can be and should be convicted of murder when he participates in a lynch mob.

Mr. KEATING. Is there not a serious question, Mr. Bennett, whether or not those laws are being enforced?

Mr. BENNETT. I will get to that in just a minute, if I may.

The history of lynching is a very interesting one. Many people do not understand the background of what brought about lynchings. Of course, some lynchings occurred prior to the War Between the States. There were many lynchings after the War Between the States when the Federal Government, despite the provisions of the Federal Constitution, saw fit, by fire and sword, to force back into the Union the States which had decided and determined their desire to be out of the Union. When the Federal Government did that, it did not use the kindly hand of Abraham Lincoln, nor the somewhat faltering but kindly hand of Andrew Johnson, but the Senate and the House of Representatives ruled the South with an iron hand. They sent down people to control the government; they allowed and encouraged people to assume high office who were not capable of assuming those offices. They overlooked and countenanced great corruption which led to the demoralization of the Government.

With that picture before them, as heinous and as culpable as taking the life of another man is without a just and due trial, these people, some people in the South, at least, took upon themselves to try to gain some sort of order and some sort of government since the constituted government offered them no protection. Therefore, in the early days, there were reasons why lynchings were indulged in and reasons why many good people at least overlooked them.

As the years have gone on, however, and the South has at last been able to reign through its own government, through its own State governments as provided for in the Constitution in State matters, and has gained control of its courts again, there is now no justification for such mob violence, if there ever was any such justification.

The South deplores lynchings more than any other section of the country. There is nothing that makes a southerner more unhappy and more depressed than the occurrence of a lynching—that is, the average southerner. There are people in our midst—I may say a great many

of them, in my opinion, are not true southerners, either by having lived in the South for long or being consistent with the southern principles—who do engage in mob violence occasionally. . . .

You must also investigate the type of lynchings which were referred to or what is defined as a "lynching," because nowadays if two people shoot somebody else and they happen to be of a different race, they consider it a lynching, which is, of course, quite different from the lynchings that most people read about when they read about the situation in the South. In other words, some lynchings which are called lynchings are truly nothing, completely nothing but ordinary types of murder. There is no mob violence in it. Somebody shoots somebody else and they happen to be of another race.

Now that sort of thing occurs in the North as well as the South. I think in the last few years, as I have tried to read the newspapers on this subject, I have found about as many incidents pointed out in the North as there are in the South on the racial basis, about as many white people killing colored people under circumstances which, in the South would be called lynchings, because that is the popular propaganda way to refer to them when they occur in the South. When they occur in the North, they are "murders." . . .

Now, I feel, therefore, that not only is this law unconstitutional, but I feel furthermore that the incidence of lynching has been so greatly on the decline that presently it is almost like the dodo bird, something entirely out of the practical realm of modern-day activity. And the few cases that do occur, most of them are not what most people think about when they think of lynchings. They are just murder. . . .

The Federal Government now proposes to say that the State governments are not sufficient and the Federal Government should come along and lend a helping hand. The ways in which this tender of assistance is offered is important with regard to the reaction that people will have to this legislation. Southern pride is hurt because the South believes it can take care of its own government. It resents the implication that the South is not able to handle its own affairs. It resents the propaganda which is given out with regard to lynching. I remember when I was overseas in New Guinea I read in Time magazine, I believe it was, that there was about 100 lynchings a year on the average. It came back with an apology in a footnote in a letter to the editor saying that there were only three during the average years to which it had been referring. But that is typical of the sort of propaganda that is issued.

We in Congress have a responsibility to look at the facts. We are here to be statesmen, not politicians. When you approach this question with regard to the South, what you are really interested in is trying to decrease the number of lynchings, I think it is quite probable that the enactment of a law of this kind will not decrease the incidence of lynching—it might increase the incidence of lynching because it will be a slap at a person. Just like a crippled person—if you tell him he has to have somebody to look after him there, he is going to resent it and he is perhaps going to take chances he should not take in driving a car, or something of that kind. In other words, the injury which is coming to the southern pride with regard to lynching is first the fact that it does exist, even though in a small number of cases, and second, that we resent antilynching laws because they imply that we are not able to control our own affairs.

We think we can control our affairs pretty well. We certainly think we handle the matters with regard to race relationships much better than the rest of the country, and if I got into that, I would be here all afternoon; but I would like to quickly point out to you some facts with regard to race relations. The great race riots which occur in the country do not occur in the South. The one in Detroit a few years back saw 25 Negroes killed. It has been years and years and years since 25—I do not think there has been any times when 25 Negroes were killed in a race riot in the South, certainly not for many years. . . .

Mr. BYRNE. Mr. Bennett, have you read the letter that was issued by the Tuskegee Institute dated December 29, 1949, for release December 31, 1949, relative to its findings regarding lynching?

Mr. BENNETT. I have not read the letter.

Mr. BYRNE. I am going to put the letter in the record at this point because it would be pertinent to this type of cross-examination that is going to be made of you, perhaps, by some of the members.
(The letter referred to is as follows:)

TUSKEGEE INSTITUTE,
Tuskegee Institute, Ala., December 29, 1949.

DEAR SIR: I send you the following information concerning lynching for the year 1949.

Number of lynchings: According to records compiled in the department of records and research, Tuskegee Institute, I find that three persons were lynched during the year. This is one more than the number two for 1948; two more than the number one for 1947; three less than the number six for 1946; and two more than the number one for 1945. Thus, for the 5-year period, 1945–49, inclusive, 13 lynchings have been recorded.

One of the victims was Caleb Hill, Jr., 28-year-old Negro chalk-mine worker of Irwinton, Wilkinson County, Ga., charged with creating a disturbance and resisting arrest. Lodged in jail, he was removed by a group of men, beaten and shot to death.

The second victim was Malcolm Wright, 45-year-old Negro tenant farmer of near Houston, Chickasaw County, Miss., who is reported to have "hogged the road" and of not moving his wagon over fast enough to permit a group of white men, riding in a motorcar, to pass. He was beaten to death.

The third victim was Hollis Riles, 53-year-old prosperous Negro landowner of near Bainbridge, Decatur County, Ga., found dead with a number of bullet holes in his body after an argument with a group of white men, who had been fishing in his pond without permission. It was reported that sometime previously Riles' home had been riddled with buckshots fired from an automobile.

The States in which the lynchings occurred and the number in each State are as follows: Georgia, two; Mississippi, one.

Punishment of lynchers: Two men jailed in connection with the lynching of Caleb Hill, Jr., were later freed for lack of sufficient evidence to bring them to trial.

Lynchings prevented: In at least 14 instances; lynchings were prevented—4 in the North and 10 in the South. One person escaped from a group of men bent on lynching him by jumping into a river; in the 13 other instances, officers of the law gave protection. A total of at least 17 persons were thus saved from mob violence. Of these, 6 were white persons and 11 were Negroes.

Although there are three clear-cut cases of lynching reported for 1949 according to criteria now used, attention should be called to other killings which according to all intent and purpose would seem to fall into this category. These include murders reported as being committed by less than three persons; killings by specially deputized posses, who in some instances appear to be composed of irresponsible persons bent not on upholding legal institutions but on vengeance; prisoners meeting violent death in jails after confinement; and other cases of police brutality.

Very truly yours,
F. D. PATTERSON, President. . . .

Mr. KEATING. There are cases that have been brought to Nation-wide attention where in my judgment, at least, local law enforcement officials have not taken the action which might be properly expected of them. You may disagree with that.

Mr. BENNETT. I certainly do.

Mr. KEATING. But I do believe firmly that there are such cases.

Mr. BENNETT. There may be such cases, but every one I have had a chance to look into was written with red ink, written by people who wanted to destroy the South and wanted to create fomentation between the North and the South in this country and wanted to serve the communistic cause. When you get to look at the facts, you find different situations.

Mr. KEATING. I do not believe all the reporters in the South are Communists. . . .

Mr. BENNETT. If the committee got the impression that I meant to imply that all stories which emanate from the South and are critical of the handling of lynchings emanate from Communists, I certainly meant to make no such statement; and if I made a statement that all these reports are written by Communists, I hereby retract it—but I don't think I said it. I did say that I felt that this country has been flooded with propaganda with regard to the South that is so remote from the facts that it is hard to recognize it when you actually are faced with it. And I do say that I feel that these reporters who are getting that information out—and I do not think they are southern reporters because I do not think a southern man would do that even to get the money—I do feel that their activity in painting the South in improper colors is very helpful to the Communist cause. I suspect—I do not have any factual foundation to say that this is true—but I suspect that some of them are actually in the pay of the Russian Government or at least are people who are carried away with their desire to help Russia, like Judith Coplon apparently was, through misguided idealism, if you can call it idealism. They think it is to the best interests of the world, whatever is going to happen hereafter, to destroy America by pitting one side against the other. . . .

STATEMENT OF HON. BOYD TACKETT, A REPRESENTATIVE IN CONGRESS FROM THE STATE OF ARKANSAS

Mr. TACKETT. I wish to appear, Mr. Chairman, in opposition to the antilynching bills. I presume that is the only matter you have under discussion at this time.

I have had considerable experience in the State of Arkansas prosecuting and defending criminal cases, and I can truthfully say and can prove it without any fear of contradiction, that there have been more white people lynched during my life in the State of Arkansas than there have been Negroes. During my life of 38 years, I recall four white people being lynched in my home county and I believe that there has been one Negro lynched in those 38 years in the State of Arkansas.

Mr. FRAZIER. What that in the entire State?

Mr. TACKETT. That was within the entire State. If I am in error about that, it was something that happened back when I was a child and do not recall it. But I do recall that four men, four white men, were lynched in my home county because they killed an old peddler. They were burned in jail. Of course, the northern newspapers did not carry that story. I honestly believe that you call homicide in the North murder. And you call homicide in the South lynching. There are more unsolved homicide cases in any eastern or northern city than there is in the whole of the south United States. . . .

I believe that my record as prosecuting attorney down there in the State of Arkansas should be sufficient to show that I am against discrimination. I do not believe in the white people mistreating the colored people, and it is not going on in my State, and I live just as deep in the South as any person in this Congress. We have made a lot of advancement down there. You will have to remember that the Negroes were slaves approximately 90 years ago. They have come a long way. If the white people will leave them alone, they will do well. If we quit meddling in their affairs and trying to bring dissension between the white people and the colored, they are going to advance in life. But every time this Congress meets up here and uses some of this political demagoguery, to stir up the feeling between the white and the colored people, they are not doing but one thing, and that is holding back the colored people within my section. All in the world that the East and the North has done is given the Negro a change to ride in a streetcar and make him think that he has gained something wonderful. Down in the South, we don't put the Negro in the back seat of the car but feel free to ride with them up and down the streets in the front seat. They are free to come into our homes; have more access to our white homes in the South than they have to white homes in the North. . . .

STATEMENT OF HON. JOHN E. RANKIN, A REPRESENTATIVE IN CONGRESS FROM THE STATE OF MISSISSIPPI

When you stir friction, those Negroes are going to move.

Where are they going—Harlem, New York, Philadelphia, St. Louis, Los Angeles, Chicago, Indianapolis? Then what are you going to do with them?

In the rest of the South—and I am speaking particularly of my district where the relationship is the best I have ever known between the whites and the colored people—you talk about lynchings. There has not been a lynching in my county since I was born, and I am as old as the gentleman from New York, nearly. . . .

So, the relationship is the best I have ever known. You are talking about schools, education. At home, schooling is compulsory. The Negroes have their own schools, and they want their own schools. They get along. Negroes in my town now have a better schoolhouse than the one I went to school in when I was a boy. We have no friction with them. They behave themselves better evidently than they do in New York, because we do not send half as many to the penitentiary. They are enjoying a protection that they do not get anywhere else except in the Southern States. If you do not believe it, you just take the records of any other State in this Union now and check and see how many they have living in those States and how many they have in the penitentiary. You will find that those States that are raising the most howl about the conditions in the South have the largest percentage of their Negroes in the penitentiary. When you disturb the peaceful relations now existing between white man and Negro, one of them is going to move. Which one is it? You know who it is going to be. You have done more harm, just such agitation as this has done the Negroes of the South more harm, deprived more of them of homes, than anything else that has occurred since I have been a Member of Congress. And today, as I said, the time has come when they are not needed as servants. We have three servants to take their place: oil, gasoline, and electricity.

You are not doing them any good. And you do not care a tinker's damn about them. That is the tragedy of it. You don't give a tinker's damn, if you will excuse the expression, about the Negroes in the South. This is done to try to create a political furor for political purposes in the North. I was here when this crazy measure was up during the Harding administration. There is a speech I made on it at that time in which I exposed the ridiculousness of a bill of this kind, the antilynching bill.

Of course, the Senate talked it to death; and you know good and well this bill never will become a law. I came to Congress that year, and the Republicans had a 169 majority in the House. They took this thing up, and we filibustered it and turned the spotlight onto it in the House. The Senate did the same thing. The election came off that year, and it took about 2 weeks to organize the House, they came so near losing the House; and Mr. Cooper, from Wisconsin, ran on an independent ticket and tied the House up for 2 or 3 weeks, if I remember correctly. That is what you are doing now. You are not doing yourselves any good. If you want to know about this, go down there. Do not go down there and ask the chief of police or the sheriff. There [indicating] is what they call the Negro section. Go over there. Go and see how they live and ask them and see how ridiculous they will make you feel before you get away from there. This thing is not for a thing in the world but just to create disturbance in the southern States, where we have done the very best we could. Nowhere else under the shining sun—nowhere—has the Negro ever received the treatment at the hands of the white people where he lived in large numbers as he does now among the white people of the South. But you are injuring the cause of the poor Negro. . . .

STATEMENT OF HON. JOSEPH R. BRYSON, A REPRESENTATIVE IN CONGRESS FROM THE STATE OF SOUTH CAROLINA . . .

Mr. BRYSON. I wish to concur in what has been said by these distinguished Members of Congress who have preceded me, and I observe that most of the gentlemen who sit on this distinguished committee live north of the Mason-Dixon line. I seriously doubt—I do not question the sincerity, but I seriously doubt—whether the average man who annually sponsors and introduces these kind of bills knows what he is doing. . . .

God Almighty in His infinite wisdom made distinct differences between the Negro and the white race. I do not know what His purposes were. But since He endowed the different races with different characteristics, I believe it was His purpose for the races to remain separate and distinct and I think it should be unlawful, both against civil law and divine law, for an intermingling of the races. If the average Members of Congress react as I do to some of the exhibitions we saw here yesterday and today, I do not believe we will ever get legislation like this through. With the necking, the fondling, and the loving, even in the gallery of the House, which was called to my attention by other Members of Congress, it seems to me people of different races have no regard for decency. . . .

I have every seriousness in appearing here. Heretofore we probably have not treated the minority race as we should. But I can easily tell the attitudes in the South are changing as well as elsewhere. I believe every person, whether a Yankee or a Rebel, has an inherent God-given desire to do justice to and for all mankind; and I believe we are making great progress toward that end. But some long-haired men and short-haired women, so highly educated, continue to penetrate into our Southland and try to dictate and force their alleged advanced ideas upon our people. It is retarding the progress that we are making.

Although we are poor, as a rule the colored people per capita are much poorer than the white people and they are more prolific, it seems to me; however, the white people are rather prolific in our country. Perhaps the North would be better off if the native-born people who live there were a little prolific and looked after their home work a little bit better rather than try to lift the restriction of the immigration law so as to import a lot of foreigners. If we had more good, native-born American citizens, we would not need to talk about amending the law. . . .

GLOSSARY

filibuster: the use of irregular or obstructive tactics by a member of a legislative assembly to prevent the adoption of a measure generally favored or to force a decision against the will of the majority.

Posse: a body or group armed with legal authority

tinker: a person skilled in various minor kinds of mechanical work; jack-of-all-trades

Document Analysis

Although the four representatives who spoke against anti-lynching legislation in 1950 did not coordinate responses before testifying, certain issues come up in each one's testimony. Several points of argumentation are similar, if not identical, and language used to categorize race relations in the South and describe the motives of those supporting the legislation is remarkably consistent. Given these similarities, the four presentations reveal much about Southerners' attitudes toward civil rights at this crucial time in American history.

Representative Bennett invokes an argument made consistently by southerners for three decades: this form of civil rights legislation is unconstitutional, as it violates the Tenth Amendment of the US Constitution, which grants to states all powers not specifically granted to the federal government by the Constitution. He appeals to reason in asking that Congress consider the facts and provides some to support his claim that lynching—which he says increased in the late nineteenth century because of the white majority's frustration with corrupt Reconstruction governments—is actually declining. He also points out that what is called "lynching" in the South is merely another form of murder, which occurs in the North as well, and that state laws are adequate for dealing with those who commit this crime. Representatives Tackett and Rankin echo this line of reasoning, providing examples to support claims that race relations in their communities are generally harmonious and that African Americans are prospering under existing laws.

Despite calls for reasonable assessment of the facts, all four representatives rely heavily on emotional appeal to make their cases and resort to name-calling or finger-pointing in one form or another in criticizing supporters of anti-lynching laws. Bennett notes that Northern cities are plagued with race riots, while Southern communities remain calm. Tackett suggests that this form of legislation is simply "meddling" and will do more harm than good for African Americans. Rankin makes this point directly, accusing Northern legislations of not "giv[ing] a tinker's damn" about "the Negroes in the South"; instead, they are creating "political furor for political purposes in the North"—to win votes from minority constituencies. Additionally, he argues that these efforts are doomed to backfire and cause problems for northern legislators at the polls.

Representative Bryson is perhaps the most derogatory. He first appeals to religion to support existing Southern practices of segregation, claiming that "God Almighty in his Infinite Wisdom" created the races differently; the implication is that attempts to alter the status quo go against God's plan. He uses the rhetorical devise of synecdoche, describing supporters of the legislation as "long-haired men and short-haired women" (implying that they are deviants) of trying to "dictate and force their alleged advanced ideas upon our people." All four believe that such efforts are, as Bryson says, "retarding the progress" being made in the South.

Essential Themes

On the surface, arguments over anti-lynching laws focused on the issue of states' rights. Southern legislators believed the federal government was usurping powers reserved to the states by taking jurisdiction for crimes of murder, torture, and abuse, which had since the founding of the nation been handled in state courts. Underlying these stated arguments, however, is a fundamental philosophical difference between many people in the nation over the nature of African Americans. Northern legislators operated from the premise that African Americans should be treated no differently than whites in any part of the country. The arguments presented by the four Southern legislators in the hearings on anti-lynching bills reveal a deep-seated belief that African Americans were inferior both socially and morally. Hence, any law giving them equal protection posed a serious threat to the way of life that had existed in the South since the end of Reconstruction.

The arguments over anti-lynching laws also highlight an important difference of opinion over the nature of the United States Constitution. Southerners based their arguments on language of the Tenth Amendment of the Constitution, which gives states all powers not specifically granted to the federal government by the Constitution. Reformers proposing anti-lynching legislation found their authority in the Fourteenth Amendment, which gave the federal government the right (and responsibility) to protect an individual's civil rights. The struggle over which amendment would take precedence in determining actions of the federal government in the area of civil rights would last for several more decades.

The efforts of the Eighty-First Congress to pass anti-lynching legislation met the same fate as earlier attempts. The Truman administration's initiative died in the Senate, the victim of an organized filibustering effort led by Georgia senator Richard Russell, Jr. It would take more than a decade of civil rights protests and the assassination of a reformist president to generate sufficient public outcry to overcome Southern obstruction and pass the comprehensive Civil Rights Act of 1964.

—*Laurence W. Mazzeno, PhD*

Bibliography and Additional Reading

Dray, Philip. *At the Hands of Persons Unknown: The Lynching of Black America.* New York: Random, 2002. Print.

Finley, Keith M. *Delaying the Dream: Southern Senators and the Fight against Civil Rights, 1938–1965.* Baton Rouge: Louisiana State UP, 2008. Print.

Gardner, Michael R. *Harry Truman and Civil Rights: Moral Courage and Political Risks.* Carbondale: Southern Illinois UP, 2002. Print.

Geselbracht, Raymond, ed. *The Civil Rights Legacy of Harry S. Truman.* Kirksville: Truman State UP, 2007. Print.

Zangrando, Robert. *The NAACP Crusade against Lynching, 1909–1950.* Philadelphia: Temple UP, 1980. Print.

APPENDIXES

Chronological List

1945: Act of Chapultepec 107

1945: Executive Order 9547 1

1945: Preamble of the UN Charter 23

1945: Potsdam Agreement 26

1945: Statement by General MacArthur on the Occupation of Japan 40

1945: Reason Must Be Substituted for Force 189

1945: No Sacrificing of Basic Principles for Expediency 43

1945: Complete Integration of Military Operations 48

1945: Practical Peacetime Applications 211

1945: The World Needs the Tonic of Universal Truth 52

1945: Atomic Energy and International Trade 143

1945: No Country Fears a Strong America 61

1946: Mendez et al. v. Westminster School District of Orange County et al. 231

1946: *Morgan v. Virginia (1946)* 241

1946: Truman Statement on Immigration into Palestine 79

1947: Truman Doctrine Speech 83

1947: Executive Order 9835 163

1947: Twenty-Second Amendment 195

1947: Testimony of J. Edgar Hoover before the House Un-American Activities Committee 171

1947: Speech on the Marshall Plan 89

1947: Taft-Hartley Act 198

1947: "The Sources of Soviet Conduct" 67

1947: Nuremberg Code 4

1947: Inter-American Treaty of Reciprocal Assistance 112

1947: Vyshinsky's Speech to the UN General Assembly 94

1947: Ronald Reagan's Testimony before the House Un-American Activities Committee 176

1947: Testimony Regarding Communist Investigations 181

1947: Report of the President's Committee on Civil Rights 250

1948: Pact of Bogota 120

1948: *Shelley v. Kraemer (1948)* 263

1948: Executive Order 9981 274

1948: Establishment and Proceedings of the Tribunal 7

1948: Convention on the Prevention and Punishment of the Crime of Genocide 15

1949: Truman's State of the Union Speech 220

1949: NATO Treaty 98

1949: Memorandum on Lifting the Soviet Blockade 102

1949: Address by Secretary Acheson, September 19, 1949 132

1949: Atomic Explosion in the USSR 149

1949: International Control of Atomic Energy. 152
1950: Southern Legislators Protest Proposed Anti-lynching Legislation. 278

Web Resources

digitalhistory.uh.edu

Offers an online history textbook, Hypertext History, which chronicles the story of America, along with interactive timelines. This online source also contains handouts, lesson plans, e-lectures, movies, games, biographies, glossaries, maps, music, and much more.

docsouth.unc.edu

A digital publishing project that reflects the southern perspective of American history and culture. It offers a wide collection of titles that students, teachers, and researchers of all levels can utilize.

docsteach.org

Centered on teaching through the use of primary source documents. This online resource provides activities for many different historical eras dating to the American Revolution as well as thousands of primary source documents.

edsitement.neh.gov

An online resource for teachers, students, and parents seeking to further their understanding of the humanities. This site offers lesson plan searches, student resources, and interactive activities.

gilderlehrman.org

Offers many options in relation to the history of America. The History by Era section provides detailed explanations of specific time periods while the primary sources present firsthand accounts from a historical perspective.

gilderlehrman.org/history-by-era/postwar-politics-and-origins-cold-war/essays/postwar-politics-and-cold-war

"Postwar Politics and the Cold War," from the Gilder Lehrman Institute of American History, provides an essay and links to related resources.

havefunwithhistory.com

An online, interactive resource for students, teachers, and anybody who has an interest in American histor

history.com/topics/american-history

Tells the story of America through topics of interest, such as the Declaration of Independence, major wars, and notable Americans. Features videos from The History Channel and other resources.

history.com/topics/cold-war/red-scare

"Red Scare," from the History Channel, provides an article, photos, speeches, and videos on the topic of the perceived communist threat in the United States and various anticommunist measures.

historymatters.gmu.edu

An online resource from George Mason University that provides links, teaching materials, primary documents, and guides for evaluating historical records.

memory.loc.gov/ammem/index.html

Covers the various eras and ages of American history in detail, including resources such as readings, interactive activities, multimedia, and more.

ocp.hul.harvard.edu/immigration/

A Harvard University web-based collection, this site contains a large collection of primary sources on immigration to the United States, including 1,800 books and pamphlets, 13,000 pages from manuscripts and 9,000 photographs. Documents from the 1920s include Emergency Quota Act and the Oriental Exclusion Act.

pbs.org/wgbh/americanexperience

Offers an array of source materials linked to topics featured in the award winning American Experience history series.

pbs.org/wgbh/amex/bomb/

From the PBS series American Experience, "The Race for the Superbomb" offers a teacher's guide, a timeline, and more.

si.edu/encyclopedia_si/nmah/timeline.htm

Details the course of American history chronologically. Important dates and significant events link to other pages within the Smithsonian site that offer more details.

smithsonianeducation.org

An online resource for educators, families, and students offering lesson plans, interactive activities, and more.

teachingamericanhistory.org

Allows visitors to learn more about American history through original source documents detailing the broad spectrum of American history. The site contains document libraries, audio lectures, lesson plans, and more.

teachinghistory.org

A project funded by the US Department of Education that aims to assist teachers of all levels to augment their efforts in teaching American history. It strives to amplify student achievement through improving the knowledge of teachers.

trumanlibrary.org/

The Harry S. Truman library provides a host of educational resources related to the 33rd president of the United States.

ushistory.org/us

Contains an outline that details the entire record of American history. This resource offers historical insight and stories that demonstrate what truly an American truly is from a historical perspective.

wilsoncenter.org/program/cold-war-international-history-project

The Wilson Center's "Cold War International History Project" offers a variety of archival and multimedia sources.

Bibliography

"1947 Taft-Hartley Substantive Provisions." *National Labor Relations Board.* NLRB, n.d. Web. 3 Feb. 2015.   210

"About the OAS." *Organization of American States.* OAS, 2015. Web. 21 Jan. 2015. 131

Acheson, Dean. *Present at the Creation: My Years in the State Department.* 1960. New York: Norton, 1987. Print. 139

Aguirre, Fredrick P. "Mendez v. Westminster School District: How It Affected *Brown v. Board of Education." Journal of Hispanic Higher Education* 4.4 (2005): 321–32. Print. 240

Alger, Chadwick F. *The United Nations System: A Reference Handbook.* Santa Barbara: ABC-CLIO, 2006. Print. 25

"A Life in Brief: Dwight David Eisenhower." *Miller Center.* U of Virginia, n.d. Web. 5 Nov. 2014. 66

"Americans Call for Term Limits, End to Electoral College." *Gallup.com.* Gallup, Inc., 18 Jan. 2013. Web. 12 Dec. 2014. 197

Annas, George J., & Michael A. Grodin. *The Nazi Doctors and the Nuremberg Code: Human Rights in Human Experimentation.* New York: Oxford UP, 1992. Print. 6

Anslover, Nicole L. *Harry S. Truman: The Coming of the Cold War.* New York: Routledge, 2014. Print. 227

Applebaum, Anne. *Iron Curtain: The Crushing of Eastern Europe, 1944–1956.* Toronto: McClelland, 2012. Print. 60

Arnesan, Eric, ed. "Taft-Hartley Act." *Encyclopedia of US Labor and Working-Class History.* London: Routledge, 2007. Print.   210

"A Short History of Radio." *Federal Trade Commission.* Federal Trade Commission, Winter 2003–4. Web. 2 Jan 2015.   219

Atkinson, Rick. "Ike's Dark Days." *US News and World Report* 133.16 (2002): 42. Print. 66

Ball, M. Margaret. *The Problem of Inter-American Organization.* Stanford: Stanford UP, 1944. Print. 131

Bandow, Doug. "A Look behind the Marshall Plan Mythology." *Investor's Business Daily.* Cato Inst., 3 June 1997. Web. 2 Feb. 2015.   97

Behrman, Greg. *The Most Noble Adventure: The Marshall Plan and How America Helped Rebuild Europe.* New York: Free, 2007. Print.   97

Behrman, Greg. *The Most Noble Adventure: The Marshall Plan and the Time When America Saved Europe.* New York: Free, 2007. Print.   93

Beisner, Robert. *Dean Acheson: A Life in the Cold War.* New York: Oxford UP, 2006. Print.   139

Benson, Michael T. *Harry S. Truman and the Founding of Israel.* Westport: Greenwood, 1997. Print. 82

Bentley, Eric, ed. *Thirty Years of Treason: Excerpts from Hearings before the House Committee on Un-American Activities, 1938–1968.* New York: Thunder's Mouth, 2002. Print.   175

Bentley, Eric, ed. *Thirty Years of Treason: Excerpts from Hearings before the House Committee on Un-American Activities, 1938–1968.* New York: Thunder's Mouth, 2002. Print.   179

—Bethany Groff, MA   14

Bostdorff, Denise M. *Proclaiming the Truman Doctrine: The Cold War Call to Arms.* College Station: Texas A&M UP, 2008. Print. 88

Brager, Bruce L. *The Iron Curtain: The Cold War in Europe.* New York: Infobase, 2004. Print. 60

_____ & Brendan Wolfe. "Morgan v. Virginia (1946)." *Encyclopedia Virginia.* Virginia Foundation for the Humanities, 20 Oct. 2014. Web. 5 Jan. 2015. 249

Brown, Louis. *A Radar History of World War II: Technical and Military Imperatives.* New York: Taylor, 1999. Print. 219

Buckley, Roger, ed. *The Post-War Occupation of Japan, 1945–1952: Surrender, 1945.* 10 Vols. Leiden: Global Oriental, 2011. Print.42

Bundy, McGeorge. *Danger and Survival: Choices about the Bomb in the First Fifty Years.* New York: Random House, 1988. xiii

Byrnes, Mark S. *The Truman Years, 1945-1953.* New York: Longman, 2000. xiii

Canyes, Manuel S. "The Inter-American System and the Conference of Chapultepec." *American Journal of International Law* 39.3 (1945): 504–17. Print. 111

Caress, Stanley M., & Todd T. Kunioka. *Term Limits and Their Consequences: The Aftermath of Legislative Reform.* Albany: State U of New York P, 2012. Print. 197

Catsam, Derek C. *Freedom's Main Line: The Journey*

of Reconciliation and the Freedom Rides. Lexington: UP of Kentucky, 2009. Print.   249

Ceplair, Larry, & Steven Englund. *The Inquisition in Hollywood: Politics in the Film Community, 1930–1960.* Berkeley: U of California P, 1979. Print. 185

Clesse, Armand, & Archie C. Epps, eds. *Present at the Creation: The Fortieth Anniversary of the Marshall Plan.* New York: Harper, 1990. Print.   93

Cooper, John. *Raphael Lemkin and the Struggle for the Genocide Convention.* New York: Palgrave Macmillan, 2008. Print.   19

Craig, Campbell, and Sergey Radchenko. *The Atomic Bomb and the Origins of the Cold War.* New Haven: Yale UP, 2008. Print.   151

Craig, Campbell, & Sergey Radchenko. *The Atomic Bomb and the Origins of the Cold War.* New Haven: Yale UP, 2008. Print.   160

Darby, Jean. *Dwight D. Eisenhower.* Minneapolis: Twenty-First Century, 2004. Print.   66

De Luna, Phyliss Komarek. *Public versus Private Power during the Truman Administration: A Story of Fair Deal Liberalism.* New York: Peter Lang, 1997. Print. 227

"Desegregation of the Armed Forces." *Harry S. Truman Library and Museum.* Harry S. Truman Lib. and Museum, n.d. Web. 26 Feb. 2015.   277

Dick, Bernard K. *Radical Innocence: A Critical Study of the Hollywood Ten.* Lexington: UP of Kentucky, 1983. Print.   185

Dobbs, Michael. *Six Months in 1945: FDR, Stalin, Churchill, and Truman—From World War to Cold War.* New York: Vintage, 2013. Print.   39

Donovan, Robert J. *Conflict and Crisis: The Presidency of Harry S. Truman, 1945–1948.* New York: Norton, 1977. Print.   3

Donovan, Robert J. *Tumultuous Years: The Presidency of Harry S. Truman, 1949–1953.* New York: Norton, 1982. Print.   227

Dower, John. *War without Mercy.* New York: Pantheon, 1993. Print.   42

Dray, Philip. *At the Hands of Persons Unknown: The Lynching of Black America.* New York: Random, 2002. Print.   286

Dubofsky, Melvyn, & Foster Rhea Dulles. *Labor in America: A History.* 8th ed. Wheeling: Harlan, 2010. Print. 194

Dudziak, Mary L. *Cold War Civil Rights: Race and the Image of American Democracy.* Princeton: Princeton UP, 2000. Print.   262

Edgerton, Gary. *The Columbia History of American Television.* New York: Columbia UP, 2007. Print. 219

"Eric Johnston Dies; Aided 3 Presidents." *New York Times* 23 Aug. 1963: 1. Print.   185

Ferrell, Robert H., ed. *Off the Record: The Private Papers of Harry S. Truman.* New York: Harper, 1980. Print. 3

"Finding Aid for Arthur H. Vandenberg Papers, 1884–1971." *Bentley Historical Lib.* Bentley Hist. Lib, U of Michigan Digital Lib., n.d. Web. 16 Jan. 2015. 60

Finley, Keith M. *Delaying the Dream: Southern Senators and the Fight against Civil Rights, 1938–1965.* Baton Rouge: Louisiana State UP, 2008. Print. 286

Folly, Martin H. "Truman, Harry S." *Oxford Reference Online.* Oxford UP, 2014. Web. 2 Feb. 2015. 97

"For European Recovery: The Fiftieth Anniversary of the Marshall Plan." *Library of Congress Online Exhibition.* LoC, 2015. Web. 2 Feb. 2015.   97

Freidel, Frank, & Hugh Sidey. "Dwight D. Eisenhower." *White House.* United States Govt., 2006. Web. 5 Nov. 2014.   66

Gaddis, John Lewis. *George F. Kennan: An American Life.* New York: Penguin, 2011. Print.   78

Gaddis, John Lewis. *The Cold War: A New History.* New York: Penguin, 2005. Print.   101

Gaddis, John Lewis. *The Cold War: A New History.* New York: Penguin, 2005. Print.   151

Gaddis, John Lewis. *The Cold War: A New History.* New York: Penguin, 2005. Print.   160

Gaddis, John Lewis. *The Cold War: A New History.* New York: Penguin, 2007. Print.   170

Gardner, Michael R. *Harry Truman and Civil Rights: Moral Courage and Political Risks.* Carbondale: Southern Illinois UP, 2002. Print.   262

Gardner, Michael R. *Harry Truman and Civil Rights: Moral Courage and Political Risks.* Carbondale: Southern Illinois UP, 2002. Print.   286

"Generations of GM History: Wilson, Charles E." *GM Heritage Center.* General Motors, 2014. Web. 21 Jan 2015. 194

_____. *Genocide in International Law: The Crime of Crimes.* Cambridge: Cambridge UP, 2009. Print. 19

Geselbracht, Raymond, ed. *The Civil Rights Legacy of Harry S. Truman.* Kirksville: Truman State UP, 2007.

Print. 286

Geselbracht, Raymond H., ed. The Civil Rights Legacy of Harry S. Truman. Kirksville: Truman State UP, 2007. Print.   262

Giangreco, D. M., and Robert E. Griffin. "Background on Conflict with USSR." Harry S. Truman Lib. and Museum. Natl. Archives and Records Admin., 13 Jan. 2015. Web. 16 Jan. 2015.   60

Gladchuck, John Joseph. Hollywood and Anticommunism: HUAC and the Evolution of the Red Menace, 1935–1950. 2006. Hoboken: Taylor, 2013. Digital file.   185

Goldstein, Robert Justin. "Prelude to McCarthyism: The Making of a Blacklist." Prologue Magazine 38.3 (2006). Web. 20 Feb. 2015.   170

Gordon, Colin. Mapping Decline: St. Louis and the Fate of the American City. Philadelphia: U of Pennsylvania P, 2008. Print. 273

Green, David. The Containment of Latin America: A History of the Myths and Realities of the Good Neighbor Policy. Chicago: Quadrangle, 1971. Print. 111

Green, David. The Containment of Latin America: A History of the Myths and Realities of the Good Neighbor Policy. Chicago: Quadrangle, 1971. Print. 139

Green, David. The Containment of Latin America: A History of the Myths and Realities of the Good Neighbor Policy. Quadrangle, Chicago, 1971. Print. 118

Harrington, Daniel F. Berlin on the Brink: The Blockade, the Airlift, and the Early Cold War. Lexington: UP of Kentucky, 2012. Print.   104

Hearden, Patrick J. Architects of Globalism: Building a New World Order during World War II. Fayetteville: U of Arkansas P, 2002. Print.   25

Herman, Arthur. Freedom's Forge: How American Business Produced Victory in World War II. New York: Random, 2012. Print.   194

"History of the Marshall Plan." George C. Marshall Research Library. George C. Marshall Foundation, 2015. Web. 2 Feb. 2015.   97

Hoopes, Townsend, & Douglas Brinkley. FDR and the Creation of the UN. New Haven: Yale UP, 1997. Print. 25

Hoover, J. Edgar. Masters of Deceit: The Story of Communism in America and How to Fight It. New York: Holt, 1958. Print.   175

Immerman, Richard H. John Foster Dulles: Piety, Prag-

matism, and Power in US Foreign Policy. Wilmington: Scholarly Resources, 1999. Print.   47

"Inter-American Treaty of Reciprocal Assistance (Rio Treaty)." Council on Foreign Relations. CFR, 2014. Web. 16 Jan. 2015.   119

Israelyan, Victor. On the Battlefields of the Cold War: A Soviet Ambassador's Confession. University Park: Pennsylvania State UP, 2003. Print.   97

James, Dorris Clayton. The Years of MacArthur. 3 vols. Boston: Houghton, 1985. Print. 51

"Jewish Population of Europe in 1945." Holocaust Encyclopedia. United States Holocaust Memorial Museum, 20 Jun. 2014. Web. 2 Jan. 2015.   82

Jones, Adam. Genocide: A Comprehensive Introduction. New York: Routledge, 2006. Print.   19

Jones, Howard. "A New Kind of War": America's Global Strategy and the Truman Doctrine in Greece. New York: Oxford UP, 1989. Print.   88

Judis, John B. "Seeds of Doubt: Harry Truman's Concerns about Israel and Palestine Were Prescient—and Forgotten." New Republic. The New Republic, 15 Jan. 2014. Web. 2 Jan. 2015. 82

Kaplan, Lawrence S. NATO 1948: The Birth of the Transatlantic Alliance. Lanham, MD: Rowman & Littlefield, 2007. Print. 101

Kaplan, Lawrence S. NATO 1948: The Birth of the Transatlantic Alliance. Lanham, MD: Rowman & Littlefield, 2007. Print. 160

Kennan, George F. "Containment: 40 Years Later." Foreign Affairs. Council on Foreign Relations, Spring 1987. Web. 25 Feb. 2015.   78

Killick, John. The United States and European Reconstruction, 1945–1960. Chicago: Fitzroy Dearborn, 1997. Print.   93

Klarman, Michael L. From Jim Crow to Civil Rights: The Supreme Court and the Struggle for Racial Equality. New York: Oxford UP, 2004. Print. 249

Klarman, Michael L. From Jim Crow to Civil Rights: The Supreme Court and the Struggle for Racial Equality. New York: Oxford UP, 2004. Print. 273

Kochavi, Arieh J. Prelude to Nuremberg: Allied War Crimes Policy and the Question of Punishment. Chapel Hill: U of North Carolina P, 1998. Print.   3

Korzi, Michael J. Presidential Term Limits in American History: Power, Principles, and Politics. College Station: Texas A&M U Press, 2013. Print.   197

Krasno, Jean E., ed. The United Nations: Confronting

the Challenges of a Global Society. Boulder: Rienner, 2004. Print.   25

"Labor Unions during the New Depression and New Deal." *Library of Congress.* Lib. of Congress, 2014. Web. 21 Jan 2015.   194

Lanning, Michael Lee. *The African-American Soldier: From Crispus Attucks to Colin Powell.* New York: Kensington, 2003. Print.   277

Lemkin, Raphael. *Axis Rule in Occupied Europe: Laws of Occupation, Analysis of Government, Proposals for Redress.* Clark: Lawbook Exchange, 2005. Print. 19

Lingeman, Richard B. *The Noir Forties: The American People from Victory to Cold War.* New York: Nation Books, 2012.   xiii

Litvak, Joseph. *The Un-Americans: Jews, the Blacklist, and Stoolpigeon Culture.* Durham: Duke UP, 2009. Print. 175

Litvak, Joseph. The Un-Americans: Jews, the Blacklist, and Stoolpigeon Culture. Durham: Duke UP, 2009. Print. 180

"London Conference on Palestine Suddenly Adjourns until after U.N. General Assembly." *JTA.* Jewish Telegraphic Agency, 2015. Web. 2 Jan. 2015. 82

Luard, Evan. *A History of the United Nations: The Years of Western Domination, 1945–55.* London: Macmillan, 1982. Print.   119

Luard, Evan. *A History of the United Nations: The Years of Western Domination, 1945–1955.* New York: Macmillan, 1982. Print.   111

Luard, Evan. *A History of the United Nations: The Years of Western Domination, 1945–1955.* New York: Macmillian, 1982. Print.   148

Luard, Evan. *A History of the United Nations: The Years of Western Domination, 1945–1955.* New York: Macmillian, 1982. Print.   160

MacArthur, Douglas. *Reminiscences.* Annapolis: Naval Inst. P, 1964. Print.   51

Madoka Futamura. *War Crimes Tribunals and Transitional Justice: The Tokyo Trial and the Nuremberg Legacy.* New York: Routledge, 2008. Digital file. 14

Maga, Timothy P. *Judgment at Tokyo: The Japanese War Crimes Trials.* Lexington: UP of Kentucky, 2001. Print. 14

Manchester, William. *American Caesar: Douglas MacArthur 1880–1964. 1978.* New York: Little, 2008. Print. 42

Mastny, Vojtech. *The Cold War and Soviet Insecurity: The Stalin Years.* New York: Oxford UP, 1996. Print. 47

Mastny, Vojtech. *The Cold War and Soviet Insecurity: The Stalin Years.* New York: Oxford UP, 1996. Print. 78

Mastny, Vojtech. *The Cold War and Soviet Insecurity: The Stalin Years.* New York: Oxford UP, 1996. Print. 88

Mastny, Vojtech. *The Cold War and Soviet Insecurity: The Stalin Years.* New York: Oxford UP, 1996. Print. 104

Mayers, David. *George Kennan and the Dilemmas of US Foreign Policy.* New York: Oxford UP, 1990. Print. 78

May, Lary, ed. *Recasting America: Culture and Politics in the Age of Cold War.* Chicago: U of Chicago P, 1989. Print.   175

May, Lary, ed. *Recasting America: Culture and Politics in the Age of Cold War.* Chicago: U of Chicago P, 1989. Print.   180

May, Lary, ed. *Recasting America: Culture and Politics in the Age of the Cold War.* Chicago: University of Chicago Press, 1989.   xiii

McCullough, David. *Truman.* New York: Simon, 2003. Print. 82

Meisler, Stanley. *United Nations: A History.* New York: Grove, 2011. Print.   19

"Mendez v. Westminster Background." *United States Courts.* Administrative Office of the US Courts, Federal Judiciary, n.d. Web. 16 Feb. 2015.   240

"Milestones: 1945–1952: Occupation and Reconstruction of Japan, 1945–52." *Office of the Historian.* Office of the Historian, Bureau of Public Affairs, US Dept. of State, n.d. Web. 21 Jan. 2015.   51

Mills, Nicolaus. *Winning the Peace: The Marshall Plan and America's Coming of Age as a Superpower.* Hoboken: Wiley, 2008. Print. 93

Miscamble, Wilson D. *George F. Kennan and the Making of American Foreign Policy, 1947–1950.* Princeton: Princeton UP, 1992. Print. 78

Norton, Richard. "Rivals, Victors: Eisenhower, Patton, Bradley, and the Partnership that Drove the Allied Conquest in Europe." *Naval War College Review,* 65.2 (2012): 178–80. Print.   66

Offner, Arnold A. *Another Such Victory: President Truman and the Cold War, 1945–1953.* Stanford: Stanford UP, 2002. Print.   88

O'Reilly, Kenneth. *Hoover and the Un-Americans: The*

FBI, HUAC, and the Red Menace. Philadelphia: Temple UP, 1983. Print.   175

Pechatnov, Vladimir O. "The Soviet Union and the World, 1944–1953." *The Cambridge History of the Cold War: Origins.* Vol. 1. Ed. Melvyn P. Leffler and Odd Arne Westad. New York: Cambridge UP, 2010. 90–111. Print. 88

Pechatnov, Vladimir O. "The Soviet Union and the World, 1944–1953." *The Cambridge History of the Cold War,* Volume I: Origins. Ed. Melvyn P. Leffler & Odd Arne Westad. New York: Cambridge UP, 2010. 90–111. Print.   78

Piotrowski, Tadeusz, ed. *The Polish Deportees of World War II: Recollections of Removal to the Soviet Union and Dispersal throughout the World.* Jefferson: McFarland, 2004. Print.   39

Plokhy, S. M. *Yalta: The Price of Peace.* New York: Viking, 2010. Print.   39

Pogue, Forrest C. *George C. Marshall: Statesman.* New York: Viking, 1987. Print.   93

Rabe, Stephen G. "Inter⊠American Treaty of Reciprocal Assistance." *The Oxford Companion to American Military History.* Ed. John Whiteclay Chambers II. Oxford: Oxford UP, 2004. 337. Print.   119

Ramirez, Ron. "The History of Philco." *Philco Radio,* 17 May 2013. Web. 2 Jan 2015.   219

Rice, Earl, Jr. *The Nuremberg Trials.* San Diego: Lucent, 1997. Print.   3

Robertson, David. *Sly and Able: A Political Biography of James F. Byrnes.* New York: Norton, 1994. Print. 148

Rock, David, ed. *Latin America in the 1940s: War and Postwar Transitions.* Berkeley: U of California P, 1994. Print.   131

Rose, Lisle A. *The Cold War Comes to Main Street: America in 1950.* Lawrence, KS: University Press of Kansas, 1999. xiii

Sbardellati, John. *J. Edgar Hoover Goes to the Movies: The FBI and the Origins of Hollywood's Cold War.* Ithaca: Cornell UP, 2012. Print. 175

Schabas, William A. "Convention on the Prevention and Punishment of the Crime of Genocide." *United Nations Audiovisual Library of International Law.* Codification Division, Office of Legal Affairs, United Nations, 2013. Web. 6 Jan 2015.   19

Schlesinger, Stephen C. *Act of Creation: The Founding of the United Nations.* Boulder: Westview, 2003. Print. 25

Schlesinger, Stephen C. *Act of Creation: The Found-*

ing of the United Nations. Boulder: Westview, 2005. Print. 119

Schlesinger, Stephen C. *Act of Creation: The Founding of the United Nations.* Cambridge: Perseus, 2004. Print. 111

Schlesinger, Stephen C. *Act of Creation: The Founding of the United Nations.* Cambridge: Perseus, 2004. Print. 148

Shlaim, Avi. *The United States and the Berlin Blockade, 1948–1949: A Study in Crisis Decision-Making.* Berkeley: U of California P, 1983. Print.   104

Spitz, Vivien. *Doctors from Hell: The Horrific Account of Nazi Experiments on Humans.* Boulder: Sentient, 2005. Print.   6

Steelman, Aaron. "Employment Act of 1946." *Federal Reserve System.* Federal Reserve Bank of Richmond, 22 Nov. 2013. Web. 23 Feb. 2015.   227

Stivers, William. "The Incomplete Blockade: Soviet Zone Supply of West Berlin, 1948–49." *Diplomatic History* 21.4 (1997): 569–602. Print.   104

Storrs, Landon R. Y. *The Second Red Scare and the Unmaking of the New Deal Left.* Princeton: Princeton UP, 2013. Print.   170

Strum, Phillipa. *Mendez v. Westminster: School Desegregation and Mexican-American Rights.* Lawrence: U of Kansas P, 2010. Print. 240

Takemae, Eiji. *Allied Occupation of Japan.* London: A&C Black, 2003. Print.   42

Taylor, Jon E. *Freedom to Serve: Truman, Civil Rights, and Executive Order 9981.* New York: Routledge, 2013. Print.   277

"The Aerial Age Begins." *Smithsonian National Air and Space Museum.* Natl. Air and Space Museum, 2014. Web. 2 Jan 2015.   219

"The Development of Radio." *American Experience.* PBS, n.d. Web. 2 Jan 2015.   219

"The Doctors Trial: The Medical Case of the Subsequent Nuremberg Proceedings." *Holocaust Encyclopedia.* United States Holocaust Memorial Museum, 20 June 2014. Web. 27 Feb. 2015.   6

"The Eisenhower Presidency, 1953–1961." *Eisenhower Presidential Library,* Museum, and Boyhood Home. Natl. Archives and Records Administration, n.d. Web. 5 Nov. 2014.   66

"The North Atlantic Treaty." *National Archives Featured Documents.* US National Archives and Records Administration, n.d. Web. 12 Jan. 2015.   101

"The Potsdam Conference, 1945." *Office of the Historian.* United States Dept. of State, n.d. Web. 7 Jan.

2014. 39

"The Recognition of the State of Israel." *Harry S. Truman Library and Museum.* Harry S. Truman Library and Museum, 2014. Web. 2 Jan. 2015. 82

The Tokyo War Crimes Trial: A Digital Exhibition." *University of Virginia School of Law*, n.d. Web. 12 Jan. 2015. 14

Toropov, Brandon. *Encyclopedia of Cold War Politics.* New York: Facts on File, 2000. Print. 151

To Secure These Rights: *The Report of the President's Committee on Civil Rights.* Harry S. Truman Library & Museum. Natl. Archives and Records Administration, n.d. Web. 17 Feb. 2015. 262

Toulouse, Mark G. *The Transformation of John Foster Dulles: From Prophet of Realism to Priest of Nationalism.* Macon: Mercer UP, 1985. Print. 47

Tusa, Ann, & John Tusa. *The Nuremberg Trial.* New York: Skyhorse, 2010. Print 3

United Nations. "Resolutions Adopted by the General Assembly during Its First Session." *UN.org.* United Nations General Assembly, n.d. Web. 6 Jan. 2015. 19

"Vandenberg, Arthur Hendrick, (1884–1951)." *Biographical Directory of the United States Congress.* US Congress, n.d. Web. 16 Jan. 2015. 60

Vaughan, Philip H. *The Truman Administration's Legacy for Black America.* Reseda: Mojave, 1976. Print. 262

Vaughan, Stephen. *Ronald Reagan in Hollywood: Movies and Politics.* New York: Cambridge UP, 1994. Print. 180

Vose, Clement E. *Caucasians Only: The Supreme Court, the NAACP, and Restrictive Covenant Cases.* Berkeley: U of California P, 1959. Print. 273

Wall, Wendy. "Anti-Communism in the 1950s." *Gilder Lehrman Institute of American History.* Gilder Lehrman Inst. of American History, 2015. Web. 21 Jan 2015. 194

Ware, Leland B. "Invisible Walls: An Examination of the Legal Strategy of the Restrictive Covenant Cases." *Washington University Law Review* 67.3 (1989): 737–72. Print. 273

Weir, Robert E. "Taft-Hartley Act." *Workers in America: A Historical Encyclopedia.* Santa Barbara: ABC-CLIO, 2013. Print. 210

"World War, Cold War, 1939–1953." *FBI.* US Dept. of Justice, 2015. Web. 27 Jan. 2015. 131

"World War II Time Line." *National Geographic.* National Geographic Soc., 2001. Web. 5 Nov. 2014. 66

"World War II Timeline." *National Geographic.* National Geographic Soc., 2001. Web. 6 Jan. 2015. 42

Zangrando, Robert. *The NAACP Crusade against Lynching, 1909–1950.* Philadelphia: Temple UP, 1980. Print. 286

Index

A

abjectness 49, 50
abridgment 254, 260
abrogation 18
Acheson, Dean Gooderham 132
Acheson, Edward Campion 132
Acheson, Eleanor Gooderham 132
Acheson-Lilienthal 152
Act of Chapultepec v, 105, 107, 110, 111, 112, 113, 117, 118, 132, 290
Additional Protocol to the General Convention of Inter-American Conciliation, of December 26,1933 128
adjudication 165, 168, 265, 272
Adoption of the Fourteenth Amendment, The 271, 272
adroit 73, 77
AEF 65
Agreement on Control Machinery 28
Agreements on Aid to Greece and Turkey 94
Alexander, Leo 4, 5, 251
Alexander, Sadie T. 251
Allen v. Oklahoma City 271
Allied Commission at Vienna 28
Allied Commission on Reparations 29, 31
Allied Control Commissions 34
Allied Control Council 32
Allied Expeditionary Force 62, 65
Allied Governments 33
Allied Powers 1, 7, 8, 9, 40, 43, 102
Allied troops 31, 35
American Bell Telephone Company 211
American Civil Liberties Union 251
American Economic Mission 84
American Expeditionary Force 62, 90
American Federation of Labor 189, 194, 268, 272
American Federation of Labor v. Swing 268, 272
Americanism 173, 174
American Legion 61, 65, 66
American Revolution 195, 292
American Ry. Exp. Co. v. Kentucky 271
American Treaty on Pacific Settlement 128, 129
American Veterans Committee 176
amicus curiae 252, 261
amorphous 69, 75, 77
Anglo-American Committee of Inquiry 79, 80
annals 49, 50
Anti-Federalists 195
anti-lynching act 254

anti-lynching bills 285
anti-lynching laws 278, 279, 285
anti-lynching legislation 278, 279, 285
anti-Nazi 33, 56
antitrust laws 223
Anti-War Treaty of Non-Aggression and Conciliation, of October 10, 1933 128
appellant 242, 243, 247, 248
appellants 265, 272
arbitral 115, 116, 117, 121, 125, 127, 128, 129, 130
Arbitral Tribunal 125, 126, 127, 130
Ardinger, Ellen C. 260
armament race 144
Arnold, H. H. 213
Articles for the Government of the Navy 168
Articles of Confederation 195
Articles of War 168
Article XXIII of the Charter of the Organization of American States 121
Ashcraft v. Tennessee 271
Atlantic Charter 23, 56, 58
atomic age 55, 145
atomic bomb xii, 26, 40, 52, 55, 65, 141, 145, 148, 149, 150, 152, 212, 213, 275
Atomic Development Authority 152
atomic energy 52, 54, 55, 59, 60, 143, 144, 145, 147, 148, 150, 151, 152, 153, 154, 155, 156, 157, 158, 159
Atomic Energy Commission 148, 152, 153, 155, 158
atomic regulation 143
atomic technology 152
atomic test 150, 151
atomic war 144, 148
atomic weapons 24, 55, 141, 143, 144, 145, 148, 149, 150, 151, 152, 153, 154, 155, 156, 157, 158, 159, 163, 250
Attlee, Clement 26, 38, 39, 52, 148
Attorney General's List of Subversive Organizations 163, 169
Auschwitz 5
Austrian Provisional Government 32
Austro-Hungarian Empire 5
axiom 53, 59
Axis Powers 33, 34

B

Bakery Drivers Local v. Wohl 271
Baruch, Bernard 152, 153

Baruch Plan 152, 153
Bastion 49
Bataan Death March 48
Battle of Okinawa 40
Battle of the Bulge 61
Becker v. Council of City of Albany 234
Bennett, Charles E. 278, 279, 281, 285
Berlin Airlift 102
Berlin blockade 103, 104
Berlin Conference 27
Berlin Constitution 104
Berlin Wall 104
Bernard, Henri 8
Bevin, Ernest 56, 92
Big Three 23, 26, 44, 45, 52
Bill of Rights 279
Bishop, Josephine Fitzgerald 270
BLACK 35, 245
Black, Hugo 249
blacklist 169, 176, 179, 184
bloc 44, 95, 96
Blockade v, 102, 104, 290, 296, 298
Boardley, Idamaye C. 260
Board of Appeals and Review 98
Bohlen, Charles 89
Bolívar, Simón 120
Bolshevik Party 69
boon 56, 59, 63
Bosporus 67, 83, 87
Bostick, Robert L. 260
Bradley, Omar 104
Brandeis, Louis 133
Bridges v. California 268, 272
briefs 252, 261
Brinkerhoff-Faris Trust & Savings Co. v. Hill 268
Brown v. Board of Education 240, 242, 273, 294
Brown v. Mississippi 271
Bryson, Joseph R. 278, 279, 284
Buchanan v. Warley 263, 266, 267, 270, 271, 273
Buchenwalds 63
Buddenbrooks 75
Bureau of Labor Statistics 204, 210
Burton, Harold 249
Bush, George W. 197
Butterworth v. Boyd 234
buttressing 146, 147
Buzzbomb 214
Byrnes, James F. xi, 143, 144, 148, 298

C
Cabinet Committee on Palestine and Related Problems 80
Cafeteria Employees Union v. Angelos 271
Cairo Declaration 7, 8, 14, 37
Cantwell v. Connecticut 268, 272
Carlisle, Jacqueline 260
Carr, Robert K. 260
cartels 29, 147, 148
Carter v. Texas 271
caveat emptor 71, 77
certiorari 203, 264, 272
Chambers v. Florida 271
chancellery 54, 59
Chapultepec v, 105, 107, 110, 111, 112, 113, 117, 118, 132, 290, 294
Charter of the OAS 120, 121, 131
Charter of the Organization of American States 121, 129
Charter of the Tribunal 9
Charter of the United Nations 17, 24, 25, 34, 86, 99, 100, 101, 113, 114, 115, 121, 122, 129, 134
chemical weapons 24
Chicago, B. & Q.R. Co. v. Chicago 268, 271
Chicago Executives' Club 189
Churchill, Winston xi, 3, 15, 23, 26, 38, 39, 52, 59, 60, 89, 104, 295
Citizens United v. Federal Election Commission 210
City of Richmond v. Deans 267
Civil Aeronautics Act of 1938 221
civil liberties 135, 163, 169
Civil Rights Act 266, 271, 273, 286
Civil Rights Cases 267
civil rights movement 241, 249, 262, 273
Civil Rights Section of the Justice Department 261
Civil Service Act of 1883 164
Civil Service Commission 164, 165, 166, 167, 168, 169, 258
Civil War 241, 250, 262, 278
clandestine 155, 156, 158
Clark Distilling Co. v. Western Maryland R. Co. 246
Clark, Tom 163
Clay, Lucius 104
Clayton, Will 89
Clinard v. Winston-Salem 271
Clinton, Bill 197
Club, Cornell 211
coalition forces 49, 51
Coleman, Charles N. 260

collectivism 191, 192, 193
Combined Shipping Adjustment Board 32
commensurate 259, 261
commerce clause 241, 246, 247, 248
Commerce Clause of the Constitution 245
COMMISSION 34, 36, 166
Commission of Investigation and Conciliation 122, 123, 124, 130
Commission on Civil Rights 242, 252, 253, 254, 260, 274, 278
Commission on Organization of the Executive Branch of the Government 195
Committee for a Far-Eastern Democratic Policy 178, 179
Committee for the Constitutional Rights of Communists 172
Committee on Civil Rights vi, 250, 251, 252, 261, 262, 290, 299
Committee on Government Contract Compliance 262
Commodity Credit Corporation 223
Commonwealth of Virginia v. Rives 267
Communism 47, 67, 69, 76, 77, 78, 83, 87, 89, 92, 94, 96, 101, 133, 138, 150, 163, 164, 169, 171, 172, 174, 175, 176, 178, 179, 181, 183, 184, 193, 194, 226, 250, 275, 296, 299
Communist Party 69, 72, 73, 75, 94, 95, 172, 173, 174, 176, 177, 178, 179, 183
concentration camp 4, 5, 6, 183
Concerning the Slogans of the United States of Europe 68
Confederacy 241
Conference of Foreign Ministers 103
Congress of Industrial Organizations 189, 194
Connally 137
Constitution 2, 11, 104, 116, 129, 164, 167, 168, 174, 175, 192, 195, 196, 197, 224, 232, 234, 235, 238, 240, 241, 242, 243, 245, 246, 248, 255, 259, 265, 270, 273, 275, 279, 280, 285
Constitution of California 234, 235
contiguous 237, 242, 246, 248
Control Commissions 34
Control Council 28, 29, 30, 31, 32, 34, 35
Control Council at Berlin 28
Conventional War Crimes 9, 14
Convention on the Prevention and Punishment of the Crime of Genocide v, 15, 19, 290, 298
Convention to Coordinate, Extend and Assure the Fulfillment of the Existing Treaties between the American States, of December 23, 1936 128

Coplon, Judith 282
corollary 18, 55, 59
Corrigan v. Buckley 265, 267, 271
Council of Ministers of Foreign Affairs 34
Council of the Organization of American States 122, 123, 127
counterblockade 102, 103, 104
Counter Intelligence Program 175
Craig v. Harney 271
Cramer, Myron Cady 8
Crimea Conference 28, 32, 33, 34, 56
Crime of Genocide, The 15
crimes against humanity xix, 3, 4, 7, 15
crimes against peace xix, 4, 7, 9, 14, 15
Crow, Jim xiii, 229, 241, 249, 263, 273, 274, 276, 296
Cuban Missile Crisis 118
Cumming v. Board of Education of Richmond County 233, 235
Cushman, Robert E. 260

D

Dardanelles 67, 83, 87
D-Day 23, 61, 62
Declaration by the United Nations 107, 112
Declaration of American Principles 108
Declaration of Lima 109
Declaration of Potsdam 8, 14
Declaration of the United Nations 23
Declaration XV 109
Declaratory Judgment Act 252
Decline and Fall of the Roman Empire, The 69
DeCuir 244, 245
demarcated 109, 110, 115, 116
DeMeerleer v. Michigan 271
demobilization xii, 40, 41, 49, 50
denunciations 17, 134, 138
desegregation 262, 275, 276
Dewey, Thomas E. 43
Dillinger, John 171
Disney, Walt 176, 182
disseminated 144, 145, 147
Division of British Commonwealth Affairs 99
Division of West European Affairs 98
Doctors' Trial 4, 5, 6, 298
Dog 212
domino theory 83
Donnedieu de Vabres, Henri 15
draft 1, 4, 15, 23, 84, 97, 144, 158, 168, 191, 193, 199, 274

Dulles, John Foster 43, 44, 46, 47, 78, 194, 295, 296, 299

Dumbarton Oaks Conference 43, 108

Durham, Charles J. 260

E

East and West Germany 104

East Berlin 104

East Germany 21, 67, 102, 103, 104

Eastland, James O. 67

Economic and Social Council 147

Eighteenth 197

Eighty-First Congress 285

Eisenhower, Dwight D. 47, 61, 62, 65, 66, 78, 169, 190, 197, 242, 294, 295, 297, 298

Emancipation Proclamation 241

Employment Act of 1946 220, 222, 226, 227, 298

equal protection clause 240, 263, 265, 272

equilibrium 135, 138

Erie R. Co. v. Tompkins 271

Esberg v. Badaracco 234

Estrada, Thomas 232

European Advisory Commission 28, 38

European Recovery Program 89, 92, 94, 135

European theater 26, 62

ex aequo et bono 125, 130

Executive Order v, vi, 1, 2, 3, 163, 164, 168, 169, 172, 250, 251, 252, 274, 275, 276, 277, 290, 298

Export-Import Bank 136, 137

expropriated 68, 77

expropriation 69, 77

extempore 11, 13

extradition 16, 17, 18, 19

F

Fair Deal 80, 164, 198, 227, 295

Fair Employment Practice Act 257

Fair Employment Practices Commission 274, 278

fallacious 254, 261

Fascist 33, 60, 163

Fat Man 149, 152

Federal Bureau of Investigation 163, 165, 168, 171, 172, 176, 261

Federal Communications Commission 216, 219

Federalists 195

Federal Theatre Project 171

Federation of Labor v. McAdory 243

Ferris, Woodbridge 53

Fifth Amendment 179, 243, 265

fifth column 173, 174, 178

filibuster 284

first commercial radio station 211

First Inter-American Conference on Indian Life 120

First International Conference of American States 107, 108, 112, 132

First Lightning 149, 151

First Red Scare 176, 181

first World War 8

fiscal 136, 138, 200, 202, 223

Fitzgerald 264, 270

Flack 271, 272

Foreign Affairs 34, 57, 67, 68, 78, 94, 95, 109, 115, 127, 130, 296

Forrestal, James V. 67, 68

Foster, John W. 43

Fourteenth Amendment 231, 232, 234, 235, 238, 239, 240, 246, 255, 263, 265, 266, 267, 268, 269, 270, 271, 272, 273, 285

Fourth Pan American Child Congress 120

FRANKFURTER 245

Frankfurter, Felix 249

Frank v. Mangum 268

Frazier 283

Freedom Rides 249, 295

free enterprise 138, 172, 174, 222, 223

free market 189, 193, 220, 226

free trade 29, 148

free trade unions 29

frictionlessly 49, 50

Fuchs, Klaus 149

G

Gaines v. Canada 234, 272

Gatson, Robert B. 177

General Agreement on Tariffs and Trade 148

General Assembly v, 15, 16, 17, 18, 19, 25, 34, 52, 53, 58, 79, 82, 94, 95, 96, 113, 118, 127, 153, 154, 157, 159, 290, 297, 299

General Convention of Inter-American Conciliation 128

General Electric 251

General Intelligence Division 172

General Motors 189, 193, 194, 295

General Treaty of Inter-American Arbitration and Additional Protocol of Progressive Arbitration 128

General Yamashita 50

Genocide v, 15, 16, 19, 290, 295, 296, 298

Genocide Convention 19, 295

German Federal Republic 104

Gestapo 28

Gettysburg Address 92

ghettos 15

Gibbon, Edward 69

Glover v. Atlanta 271

Goering, Field Marshal 213

Goldenthal, Hannah S. 260

Gong Lum v. Rice 233

Grady, Henry F. 80

Grand Alliance 60

Great Depression 171, 176, 177, 195, 198

Great Migration 263

Great Purge 95

Guadalcanal 40, 61, 64

Gubb, Larry E. 211, 212, 218, 219

Guzman, William 232

H

Haas, Francis J. 251

Hague Convention No. III 10

Hague v. Committee for Industrial Organization 234

Hall v. DeCuir 244, 245

Hamilton v. Regents of University of California 234

Hansberry v. Lee 266, 271

Harmon v. Tyler 266, 267

Harrison, Earl 80, 81

Hatch Act of 1939 163

Hatch v. Reardon 243

Hayes, Rutherford B. 241

Hays Code 182

Hays, Will H. 182

Hickerson, John Dewey 98, 99

Higgins, John Patrick 8

Hill, Caleb, Jr. 281, 282

Hirohito xix, 7, 40, 48, 52, 64

Hiroshima 40, 48, 52, 141, 143, 144, 149, 152

Hiss, Alger xii, 161, 182

History of the Communist Party of the Soviet Union, The 172

Hitler, Adolf xix, 1, 21, 26, 28, 43, 52, 62, 64, 65, 67, 73, 79, 107, 112, 213

H.M.S. Petrel 10

Hollywood Independent Citizens Committee of the Arts, Sciences, and Professions 176

Hollywood Reporter 176

Hollywood Ten 179, 184, 185, 295

Holocaust 6, 79, 81, 82, 296, 298

Home Telephone and Telegraph Co. v. Los Angeles 271, 272

Home Tel. & Tel. Co. v. Los Angeles 235

Hoover Commission 196, 197

Hoover, Herbert 196, 242

Hoover, J. Edgar vi, 163, 171, 172, 174, 175, 290, 298

House Un-American Activities Committee vi, xii, 161, 163, 169, 171, 172, 174, 175, 176, 178, 179, 181, 184, 185, 290, 296, 298

Hovey v. Elliott 271

Hull, Cordell 23, 24, 137, 146

Huntington, Merle Whitford 260

I

Institute of Inter-American Affairs 136

Instrument of Surrender 8, 14

Inter-American Conference for the Maintenance of Continental Peace and Security 112, 113

Inter-American Conference for the Maintenance of Peace 107, 108, 112, 132

Inter-American Conference on Problems of War and Peace 109, 110, 112, 113

Inter-American Indian Institute 120

Inter-American Peace Committee 134

Inter-American Peace System 113

inter-American system 113, 134

Inter-American Treaty of Reciprocal Assistance v, 98, 105, 112, 113, 117, 119, 132, 290, 296

Inter-American Treaty on Good Offices and Mediation 128

Intergovernmental Committee on Refugees 81

International American Institute for the Protection of Childhood 120

International Atomic Energy Agency 148

International Bank and the International Monetary Fund 136

International Conference on Trade and Employment 147

International Court of Justice 17, 19, 120, 121, 124, 125, 126, 127, 129, 130, 131

International Military Tribunal 1, 3, 4, 7, 15, 18

International Trade Organization 147, 148

International Union of American Republics 107, 112, 132

international war crimes trial 14

internment 41, 261

interstate commerce clause 246, 248

intransigence 47, 70, 77, 92

ipso facto 124, 129, 130

iron curtain 52, 53, 54, 55, 56, 57, 58, 59, 60
Irvine v. Clifton Forge 271
isolationism xi, xii, 52
Israel 82, 294, 296, 299
Ivy, Andrew 4
Iwo Jima 40

J
Jackson, Edward W. 260
Jackson v. State 271
Japanese Theatre 10
Jaranilla, Delfin 8
Jefferson, Thomas 195
Jessup, Philip Caryl 102, 103, 104
Johnson, Andrew 280
Johnson, Lyndon B. 197, 260, 280
Johnson, Mahala B. 260
Johnston, Eric A. 181, 182, 184, 185, 295
Joint Boundary Commission 116
Ju-ao, Mei 8

K
Kaufman, Herbert 260
Keenan, Joseph B. 7
Kennan, George F. xi, 67, 68, 77, 78, 83, 89, 133, 295, 296, 297
Kennedy, John F. 197
King, William Lyon Mackenzie 148
Kiyoshi Hirabayashi v. United States 235
Koehler v. Rowland 271
Koenig, General 62
Korean War 25, 49, 51, 164, 275
Kraemer, Louis and Fern 263
Kraemer v. Shelley 270
Kremlin 70, 71, 72, 73, 74, 75, 76
Ku Klux Klan 250

L
labor blockade policy 193
Labor-Management Relations Act of 1947 223
labor movement xii, 189, 194, 198, 210
labor unions 131, 173, 175, 189, 193, 194, 198, 210, 220, 258
Labor v. Swing 268, 272
Language Arbitration Board 12
Lansing-Ishii agreement 58
Lansing, Robert 43, 58
Laski, Harold J. 58
League of Nations xi, 23, 24, 25, 43, 147, 148

Lee v. Mississippi 271
Lemkin, Raphael 15, 19, 295, 297
lend-lease settlements 146
Lenin 68, 69, 72, 74, 75
liberal socialism 69
Liberty Annex Corp. v. Dallas 271
Lilienthal, David E. 152
Lincoln, Abraham 92, 280
Little Boy 149, 152
Long Telegram 67, 68, 77
Loran 212, 213
Loyalty Review Board 166, 167, 169
Luckman, Charles 251
Luftwaffe 62, 213
lynch mobs 241, 254

M
MacArthur, General v, 7, 9, 14, 40, 41, 48, 290
Malik, Jacob 102, 103, 104
Mandel, Benjamin 177
Manhattan Project 141, 143, 149, 152
Mann, Thomas 75
Marcus Avenue Improvement Association 263
Marshall, George C. 67, 89, 93, 94, 97, 102, 214, 296, 298
Marshall Plan v, xi, xii, 21, 67, 78, 88, 89, 92, 93, 94, 95, 96, 97, 150, 161, 164, 226, 275, 290, 294, 295, 296, 297
Marsh v. Alabama 270
Martin v. Texas 271
Marxism 77, 172, 192, 193
Marxism-Leninism 172
Marxist 67, 68, 69, 77, 83, 176
Marxist-Leninist 69
Mason-Dixon line 284
McCabe v. Atchison 272
McCarthyism 169, 170, 179, 296
McCarthy, Joseph xii, 161, 169, 179, 181
McCormick, Paul John 231, 232
McDougall, Edward Stuart 8
McKinley, William 195
Meeting of Consultation of Ministers of Foreign Affairs 127, 130
Meiji Restoration 11
Mendez et al. v. Westminster School District of Orange County et al. 290
Méndez, Gonzalo 231, 232, 240
Mendez v. Westminster 231, 232, 240, 294, 297, 298
Mengele, Josef 5

Mexican Revolution 231
Meyer v. Nebraska 234
Mickey Radar Bombsight 213
Monroe Doctrine xii, 58, 107, 112, 132, 134
Montgomery, Robert 177
Mooney v. Holohan 271
Moore v. Dempsey 268
Morgan, Irene vi, 241, 242, 248, 249, 259, 290, 294
Morgan v. Virginia vi, 241, 242, 249, 259, 290, 294
Morrison plan 80, 81, 82
Morris v. Williams 238
Moscow Conference 1, 7, 9, 14
Moscow Declaration 1, 23, 32
Motion Picture Association of America 181, 182
Murphy, George 177
Murtha, Joseph 260
Mussolini 64

N

Nagasaki 40, 48, 52, 141, 143, 149, 152
Napoleon 73
National Association for the Advancement of Colored
    People xiii, 241, 250, 273, 278, 286, 299
National Commanders of the American Legion 61
National Council of Poland 33
National Industrial Recovery Act 189
nationality-based segregation 240
National Labor Relations Act 187, 189, 192, 198, 202,
    208, 209
National Labor Relations Board 198, 204, 209, 210,
    220, 294
National Security Council 78, 150
National Socialism 194
National Socialist Party 26, 28
Nazi Germany 1, 23, 26, 43, 67, 68, 83, 102, 149, 171,
    176, 250
Nazi Party 26, 29, 38
Nazi-style nationalism 26
Neal v. Delaware 271
neutrality 52
New Deal 144, 170, 176, 189, 194, 198, 220, 227,
    297, 298
New Economic Policy 69
Nippert v. Richmond 245
Nixon, Richard M. 161, 197
Nobel Peace Prize 90, 97
Normandy 61, 62, 213
North Atlantic Treaty xii, 47, 51, 78, 80, 98, 99, 101,
    104, 133, 153, 298

Northcroft, Erima Harvey 8
nuclear arms race 141, 148, 149, 153
nuclear weapons xi, xii, 21, 132, 148, 152, 163
Nuremberg v, xix, 1, 3, 4, 5, 6, 7, 8, 14, 15, 290, 294,
    296, 297, 298, 299
Nuremberg Code v, 4, 5, 6, 290, 294

O

OAS Charter 121
Obama, Barack 185, 197
Occupation of Japan v, 40, 42, 290, 294, 298
occupied Japan 7
Oder-Neisse line 38
Office of Economic Stabilization 144
Office of European Affairs 99
Office of War Mobilization 144
Okinawa 40
one-state solution 82
Operation Torch 62
Oppenheimer, J. Robert 143
Organic Pact of the Inter-American System 116
Organization of American States 107, 112, 120, 121,
    122, 123, 127, 129, 131, 132, 137, 138, 294
Osami, Nagano 7
Oyama v. California 270, 271, 272

P

Pacific Fleet 65
Pacific theaters 65
Pact of Bogota v, 105, 120, 121, 128, 129, 131, 290
Pact of Paris 10
Palestine v, 79, 80, 81, 82, 290, 296, 297
Palestinians 82
Palmer, A. Mitchell 172
Palomino, Frank 232
Pal, Radha Binod 8
Panama Canal 107, 112, 259
Pan American Sanitary Code 120
Pan American Society 132, 133, 138
Pan American Union 107, 112, 115, 116, 117, 118,
    120, 123, 124, 127, 128, 132, 134
panoply 269, 272, 273
Paris Peace Conference 43
Parks, Rosa 241, 249
Parmalee v. Morris 271
partition plan 79
Patrick, William Donald 8
Patton, George S. 61
Peace Treaty 33

Peace Treaty for Italy 33
Pearl Harbor 48, 53, 61, 63, 65
Pella, Vespasian 15
Pennekamp v. Florida 271
Pennoyer v. Neff 268
Peoples of the United Nations 23
Permanent Court of Arbitration of The Hague 125, 126
Permanent Joint Board on Defense 99
Pershing, John 62
Philadelphia Storage Battery Company 212
Philco Radio & Television Corporation 211, 212, 217, 219, 298
Philippine Army 49
physiognomy 68, 77
Piper et al. v. Big Pine School District 234
Plenipotentiaries 116, 117, 128
plenipotentiary 124, 130
Plessy v. Ferguson 229, 231, 239, 241
Polish Provisional Government 33, 35, 39, 56
political action committees 210
Porter v. Barrett 271
potash 30, 37
Potsdam v, xi, 7, 8, 9, 14, 26, 38, 39, 40, 43, 48, 49, 50, 52, 56, 59, 89, 102, 290, 299
Powell v. Alabama 271
Preamble to the United Nations Charter 24
preponderance 136, 138
Presidential Medal of Freedom 133
President's Commission on Civil Rights 274, 278
President's Committee on Civil Rights vi, 250, 261, 262, 290, 299
President's Committee on Equality of Treatment and Opportunity in the Armed Services 274, 275, 276
Prince Saionji 13
Proclamation Defining Terms for Japanese Surrender 36
Progressive Party 195
proletarian 68, 77
proletariat 68, 69, 71, 77
prolix 12, 13
promulgated 11, 13, 235, 239
proscription 108, 110
Proximity Fuse 213, 214
Prudential Ins. Co. v. Cheek 271
Pyle v. Kansas 271

Q
Quixote, Don 77

quorum 115, 117
quota system 231

R
race-based segregation 240
racial integration 273
radar 211, 212, 213, 214, 216, 217, 218
Radar Bombsight 213
Ramirez, Lorenzo 232
Rankin, John E. 278, 279
Raymond v. Chicago Union Traction Co. 271, 272
Reagan, Ronald vi, 161, 176, 177, 178, 179, 180, 182, 197, 290, 299
Reciprocal Trade Agreements Act 147, 225
Reconstruction 51, 93, 278, 285, 296, 297
Red army 58
Red-baiting 172
Red fascism 172, 174
redlining 273
redress 192, 238, 239
Red Scare vi, ix, 161, 163, 169, 170, 176, 179, 181, 184, 185, 292, 298
Red Square 76
Reed, Stanley 241, 242, 248
Reims 1, 26
remuneration 124, 127, 130
res judicata 129, 130
Resolution 96 (I) 15, 18
Resolution 260 (III) 15
Review Board 166, 167, 169
Revised Statutes 266
rhumb line 114, 117
right-to-work laws 209, 210
Riles, Hollis 281
Rio de Janeiro treaty 134
Rio Treaty 98, 112, 118, 119, 132, 138, 139, 296
Röling, Bernard Victor 8
Roosevelt, Franklin D. 1, 16, 23, 26, 40, 52, 79, 80, 84, 90, 96, 103, 120, 144, 150, 164, 176, 177, 181, 189, 195, 198, 220, 242, 250, 251, 274, 278
Roosevelt, Theodore 1, 61, 137, 195, 274, 275
Royall, Kenneth 104
Russell, Louis J. 177
Russell, Richard Jr. 285
Russian Revolution 84, 181

S
Sady, Rachel R. 260
Saionji-Harada Memoirs 13

San Francisco Charter 58
San Francisco Conference 23, 24, 25
Sanitary Conference 120
scab 210
school segregation 240
Scott v. McNeal 271
scourge 16, 18, 24
Screen Actors' Guild 176, 177, 178, 179
Screws v. United States 234, 253
Second International 69
Second Meeting of the Ministers of Foreign Affairs 109
Second Red Scare 170, 179, 181, 184, 298
secret police 70
Security Council of the United Nations 103, 113, 114, 121, 127, 130
Seeger, Pete 182
segregated draft process 274
segregated schools 240
segregationist 229, 241, 263, 273
separate but equal 229, 232, 257, 273
Seventh International Conference of American States 108
Shelley, J. D. and Ethel vi, 263, 264, 270, 272, 273, 290
Shelley v. Kraemer vi, 263, 264, 272, 273, 290
Sipes v. McGhee 270
Slaughter-House Cases 271, 272
Smith, H. A. 177
Smith v. Allwright 234, 242
social equality 235, 240
Socialism 68, 71, 72, 194
Social security 220
Socrates 69
Sources of Soviet Conduct, The v, 67, 68, 77, 290
Southern Pacific Company 245
Southern Pacific Co. v. Arizona 245, 247
Soviet and Western blockade 104
Soviet atomic test 151
Soviet blockade 103
Spanish-American War 40
Special Intelligence Service 120
Spencer, Thomas and Frank 212
Stalin, Joseph 26, 38, 39, 47, 52, 57, 67, 69, 70, 72, 74, 75, 77, 78, 88, 92, 102, 104, 181, 295, 297
Standard Oil Co. v. Missouri 271
Standing Committee on Civil Rights 252
Statement of Principles 153, 154, 156, 157
State of Missouri ex rel. Gaines v. Canada 234
State of the Union vi, 220, 221, 226, 279, 290

stenographic 257, 261
Stettinius, Jr., Edward R. 24
Stewart, Milton D. 260
St. Lawrence Seaway and Power project 224
Strauder v. West Virginia 268, 269, 272
Stripling, Robert E. 177, 178
Sudwarth, Ann E. 260
suffrage 33, 56, 255, 261
Swain v. Maxwell 271

T
Tackett, Boyd A. 278, 279, 282, 283
Taft-Hartley Act vi, xii, 187, 194, 198, 199, 209, 210, 220, 223, 226, 290, 294, 299
Taft, Robert vi, xii, 183, 187, 194, 195, 198, 199, 209, 210, 220, 223, 226, 290, 294, 299
Taft, William Howard 195, 199
Tedder, Sir Arthur 62
Temporary Commission on Employee Loyalty 163
Tennessee Valley 152, 224
Tenth Amendment 242, 285
Teraushi, Field Marshal 50
"The Sources of Soviet Conduct" 67, 68, 290
Thirteenth Amendment 254
Thomas, J. Parnell 171, 177
Thoughts on Soviet Foreign Policy and What to Do about It 47
Three Governments 27, 31, 32, 34, 35
Three Great Allies 8
Three Heads of Government 27
Three Powers 31, 32, 33
Thurmond, Strom 262
Tomkins v. Missouri 271
To Secure These Rights: The Report of The President's Committee on Civil Rights 250
Trade Agreements Act 147, 225
transcontinental telephone line 211
Transportation Act of 1940 221
Treaty of Brussels 98
Treaty of Perpetual Union, League, and Confederation 120
Treaty of Potsdam 89
Treaty of Rio de Janeiro 117
Treaty of Versailles 43
Treaty on the Prevention of Controversies 128
Treaty to Avoid or Prevent Conflicts between the American States 128
Tripartite Shipping Commission 32
Truax v. Raich 272

Truman Doctrine v, xi, 53, 83, 87, 88, 94, 95, 96, 97, 171, 181, 226, 290, 294, 296
Tsarist 68, 69
Twenty-First Amendments 197
Twenty-Second Amendment 195, 196, 197, 290
Twenty-Seventh Amendment 197
two-state solution 82

U

U-boats 212, 213, 218
unfettered 33, 39, 56, 59
UN General Assembly Resolution 96 (I) 18
union shops 210
United Nations Atomic Energy Commission 148, 152, 153, 155
United Nations Charter v, 1, 16, 23, 24, 145, 290
United Nations Conference on International Organization 107
United Nations Declaration 132
United Nations General Assembly v, 15, 18, 19, 25, 52, 53, 79, 94, 95, 96, 153, 159, 290, 299
United Nations Relief and Rehabilitation Administration 53, 54
United Nations Security Council 84, 101, 102, 120, 131
United States v. Cruikshank 271
United States v. Harris 271
Universal Declaration of Human Rights 25
UN Relief and Rehabilitation Administration 52, 53, 54, 59, 60
UN Security Council 25, 153
US Council for War Crimes 5
US Far East campaign 40
US Zone 104

V

Vandegrift, John L. 260
Vandenberg, Arthur H. 52, 53, 59, 60, 92, 138, 295, 299
Versailles 43, 46
Vidaurri, Alice and Virginia 240
Vinson, Fred M. 263, 264, 272, 273
violative 45, 46
viva voce 12, 13

Voorhees, Tracy 104
Vyshinsky, Andrey v, 94, 95, 96, 290

W

Wagner Act 187, 189, 194, 198, 199, 209, 210, 220, 223, 226
Wallace, Henry A. 88
war crimes xix, 1, 2, 3, 4, 6, 7, 8, 14, 15, 29
war criminals 1, 4, 6, 7, 8, 32, 37, 38, 40
Ward v. Flood 233
Washington, Booker T. 241
Washington, George 195
Webb, William Flood 8
Wechsler, Nancy F. 260
Weizmann, Chaim 79
West Berlin 102, 103, 104, 298
Western Union Defence Organization 98
West German 102
West Germany 96, 103, 104
Westinghouse Electric and Manufacturing Company 190
Whitfield v. Ohio 246
Whiting, Richard A. 260
Wilkerson, William R. 176
Williams. Frances Harriett 260
Williams v. Kaiser 271
Wilson, Charles E. 189, 190, 193, 251
Wilson, Woodrow 23, 43, 56, 147
Wong Him v. Callahan 233
Woods, Bretton 23, 136
World's Fair 191
World Trade Organization 148
World War II 279, 294
World Wars I and II 65
Wright, Malcolm 281

Y

Yalta Agreement 83
Yalta Conference 23, 26, 38, 39, 77, 83
Yamashika, Tomoyuki 51
Yick Wo v. Hopkins 272
Yom Kippur 79, 81
Yosuke, Matsuoka 7
Yu Cong Eng v. Trinidad 238

Z

Zaryanov, Ivan Michyevich 8
Zionist 79, 81
Zoar 191, 193
Zoar, King of 191